We (God) are nearer to him than signs to those of real faith, and in Quran. The path of Islam; preache the high mystical theory, repentanc<

man, not from man to God. Some one said to Rabia; a great lady saint of Basra, Iraq. I have committed many sins; if I turn in penitence towards God, will He turn in mercy towards me?" Nay," she replied, but if He shall turn towards thee, thou wilt turn towards Him." **further than is necessary. The 'vision of the heart'** (ru'yat al-qalb) is defined as "the heart's beholding by the light of certainty that which is hidden in the unseen world." This is what `Ali (R. A.), fourth truthful Caliph of Islam; meant when he was asked, "Do you see God?" and replied: "How should we worship One whom we do not see?" The light of intuitive certainty (Yaqin) by which the heart sees God is a beam of God's own light cast therein by Himself; else no vision of Him were possible. Thus aim of every Muslim in earth is to see God and talk to him through remebarance all the time and five times prayer, each day, fasting, Hajj, giving Charity etc. and as such Muslims have no time to make any bomb or kill innocent people.

The Election of Caliph/Khalifah And World Peace

By

Khondakar G. Mowla

According to a mystical interpretation of the famous passage in the Koran where the light of Allah is compared to a candle burning in a lantern of transparent glass, which is placed in a niche in the wall, the niche is the true believer's heart; therefore his speech is light and his works are light and he moves in light. "He who discourses of eternity," said Bayazid, "must have within him the lamp of eternity." Bombs are not only solution for World Peace. And only food, cloth and Medicare are most essentials for the poorest of Asia, Africa, Europe and America. Thus all countries in Indian sub-continent must unite for the poorest people of this World. They must establish poverty free World where we can see smile in the face of our poorest brothers. And we must establish justice every where around this World. Gandhi supported Indian Muslims for their struggle for one Islamic State of Caliphate/Khilafah because that was the only way to control World economy from all kind of present day economic exploitation. One bottle of water is costly in the West then same bottle of gas/oil produced by the heartland of Caliphate. What a funny! What a justice! So this book is just a judgement or a plea against "World War I: Diplomacy and Intrigue" i.e. true International Terrorism; and the victims of the terrorism and that oppression are 1.5 billion World Muslims or World of Islam with the references from truthful non-Muslims and Muslims Authors. You can fool once but not all the time. That conspiracy of terrorism started with the permission of doing business to British nationals in India by Emperor Jahangir and ended with the drama of Clive; known as Clive of Bengal in 1757 and that map man, Lawrence of Arabia in Arab in 1916s; both great World Muslim Powers and both of which were part of Caliphate during Mamluk (European) Sultan Byber of Egypt.

UPUBLISH.COM

1998

ISBN: 1-58112-877-0

UPUBLISH.COM
1998

The sacred Kaba in Makkah. Prophet Ibrahim (AS) was ordered, by Allah in 1885 B.C. to rebuild the Kaba with the help of his son, Hazrat Ismail (AS). The stones were brought from various mountains and hills, including Mount Zion. The Aswad stone is kissed by Pilgrims during Tawaf. The Kaba is circumambulated seven times by pilgrims in the fulfillment of their Islamic obligation. Muslims face the Kaba while praying.

The Holy Prophet Mohammed's (SAW) Mosque in Madinah. Inset (top left): Masjid Al Aqsa - Jerusalem, with its resplendent Golden Dome. The Prophet (SAW) was taken from Madinah to this Masjis where he led prayers for 1,24,000 Ambiya on the night of Meraj. Inset (top right): Inside view of a section of the Holy Prophet's (SAW) Mosque in Madinah.

Remains of the House of Sorrows in Madinah where Maulatena Fatima Zahra (AS) daughter of the Holy Prophet Mohammed (SAW) lived and died.

http://www.compsoc.man.ac.uk/~moawalla/dbhp/gallery1.htm

Verily, this Brotherhood Of yours is a single Brotherhood, And I am your Lord And Cherisher: therefore Serve Me (and no other). 21: 92 And verily this Brotherhood Of yours is a single Brotherhood And I am your Lord And Cherisher: therefore Fear Me (and no other) 23: 52

And hold fast, all together, by the rope which Allah (stretches out for you), and be not divided among yourselves and remember with grati-tude Allah's favor on you for ye were enemies and He joined your hearts in love, so that by his grace Ye became brethren and ye were on the brink of the pit of fire, and He saved you from it. Thus doth Allah make his signs clear to you, that ye may be guided. 3:103 Al-Quran

Prophet Muhammad's (Peace be upon him) Last Sermon on the Nineth day of Dhul Hijjah 10 A. H. (7h March, 632).

All Mankind is from Adam and Eve, an Arab has no superiority over a non-Arab nor a non-Arab has any superiority over an Arab, also a white has no superiority over black nor a black has any superiority over a white except by piety and good action.. Learn that every Muslim is a brother to every Muslim and that the Muslims constitute one brotherhood..... All those who listen to me shall pass on any words to others and those to others and may the last ones understand my words better than those who listen to me directly. Be my witness O Allah, that I have conveyed your message to your people. .... Allah has forbidden you to take usury (interest), therefore all interest obligation shall henceforth be waived. Your capital, hover, is yours to keep. You will neither inflict nor suffer inequity. Allah has judged that there shall be no interest and that all the interest due to Abbas ibn' Abu'al Muttalib shall henceforth be waived."

4

Table of Contents

In the Name of Allah, the Most Merciful, the Most Compassionate

Preface

This is a kind of research Work on Caliphate/Khilafah based on references. Thus any mistakes will be corrected in future addition. Any advice from any one will be welcomed.

The Sovereignty only belong to God and thus we know from the Holy Quran :

54: 55 In an Assembly of Truth, In the Presence of A Sovereign Omnipotent.
59: 23 Allah is He, than whom There is no other god;- The Sovereign, the
59: 23 Holy One, The Source of Peace (and Perfection) The Guardian of
59: 23 Faith, The Preserver of Safety, The Exalted in Might, The
59: 23 Irresistible, the Supreme: Glory to Allah! (High is He) Above the
59: 23 partners They attribute to Him.
62: 1 Whatever is In the heavens and On earth, doth declare The
62: 1 Praises and Glory Of Allah-, the Sovereign The Holy One, the
62: 1 Exalted In Might, the Wise.

THE PROPHET MUHAMMAD'S (peace e upon him) LAST SERMON

(This Sermon was delivered on the Ninth Day of Dhul Hijjah 10 A.H in the Uranah Valley of mount Arafat)

"O People, lend me an attentive ear, for I don't know whether, After this year, I shall ever be amongst you again. Therefore Listen to what I am saying to you carefully and TAKE THIS WORDS TO THOSE WHO COULD NOT BE PRESENT HERE TODAY. O People, just as you regard this month, this day, this city as Sacred, so regard the life and property of every Muslim as a sacred trust. Return the goods entrusted to you to their rightful owners. Hurt no one so that no one may hurt you. Remember that You will indeed meet your LORD, and that HE will indeed reckon your deeds. ALLAH has forbidden you to take usury (Interest), therefore all interest obligation shall henceforth be waived... Beware of Satan, for your safety of your religion. He has lost all hope that he will ever be able to lead you astray in big things, so beware of following him in small things.

O People, it is true that you have certain rights with regard to your women, but they also have right over you. If they abide by your right then to them belongs the right to be fed and clothed in kindness. Do treat your women well and be kind to them for they are your partners and committed helpers. And it is your right that they do not make friends with any one of whom you do not approve, as well as never to commit adultery.

O People, listen to me in earnest, worship ALLAH, say your five daily prayers (Salah), fast during the month of Ramadhan, and give your wealth in Zakat (Charity). Perform Hajj if you can afford to. You know that every Muslim is the brother of another Muslim. YOU ARE ALL EQUAL. NOBODY HAS SUPERIORITY OVER OTHER EXCEPT BY

PIETY AND ACTION.

Remember, one day you will appear before ALLAH and answer for your
deeds. So beware, do not astray from the path of righteousness
after I am gone.

O People, NO PROPHET OR APOSTLE WILL COME AFTER ME AND NO NEW
FAITH WILL BE BORN. Reason well, therefore, O People, and understand my words
which I convey to you. I leave behind me two things, the QUR'AN and my example, the
SUNNAH and if you follow these you will never go astray.

All those who listen to me shall pass on my words to others and
those to others again; and may the last ones understand my words
better than those who listen to me directly. BE MY WITNESS O ALLAH
THAT I HAVE CONVEYED YOUR MESSAGE TO YOUR PEOPLE."

Last paragraph direct us to convey his message to all people of this world.
Because many unknown people irrespective of race, religion may understand his message
better than me or many follower of Islam and this is true for all the time. Many people of
this world accepted Islam as they are understand Islam better than me or many follower of
Islam. Thus Islam is a world religion for all mankind.
.
And what is Islamic Political System? Khilafa/Caliphate is the only Political System in
Islam.
This System lasted for long 1300 years until it was abolished in 1924 by
Mustafa Kemal who was a secret Jew called Doenmeh, whose ancestor came to Turkey
after Spanish inquisition. Muslims are not taught to hate non-Muslims. Because Islam is
the only religion of God, which was preached by all Prophets (Peace be upon them). Anti-
Christ are those who are anti-religion or anti-Christ.
Muslim s are not anti-Christ because they accept him (Peace be upon him) as Prophet of
God And according to last Prophet of God (Peace be upon him), Christ will come to this
world to preach Islam and make peace. The name of Anti-Christ is Dajjal. Dajjal will be
killed by Prophet Jesus (Peace be upon him). So world Muslims are waiting for Christ and
another, whose name will be Imam (leader) Mehdi, a descendent of the last Prophet of
Islam (Peace be upon him). Thus Dajjal is an individual and a System. The System was
already there after abolishing of 1300 years old Caliphate. Dajjal or Antichrist System is
very powerful and none can face that System. And for that reason Christ (PBUH) must
come to defeat that individual and system. So antichrist are those who did not obey him in
part or full during his life time. Particularly when he (Christ) invited all to sacrifice their
wealth and other self interest.. So some people revolted against him and they claim they
sent him to cross. But Muslims believe that Christ (peace be upon him) was taken to
heaven alive and he will descent to earth very soon to re-establish Islam and to defeat
Dajjal the individual and Dajjal the System or his followers. Why he will come soon
because in the past all powerful dynasty was defeated by another power. For example Once
powerful Greek Aryan was vanished, so was Roman empire. Even only powerful in earth
like Ummayed Density was defeated by few who revolted against it. It's last ruling family
vanished in
Damascus except Abdur Rahman, who fled to Spain. So was 500 years old
Abbaside and another 500 years of Osmani Khilafat/Caliphate.

The nation States in the holy lands of Prophets (Peace be upon them) are divided into so
many Nation States, violating The Political System of Islam. No Muslim can accept these
nation States as these division is only contributing wastage of billion dollars of wealth
which could be spent to abolish poverty. We, in the West, talk loudly about Democracy and
freedom. But when that democracy fails in Algeria we are silent here. Why? Why we

protect the Kings, Amirs, Bath Party Chiefs and one parry dictator in the land of Caliphate? Why we supply Army , fighter Planes to protect those Dictators? All these helped those rulers to be more violent and more cruel to their own citizens, who can not speak the truth, who can not express their grievances against the ruling classes. This can not continue unchallenged. This must be changed, because Muslims constitute around one fourth of the World population. And The World can not

expect peace with antagonizing the World Muslim. The World owes to the Islam for education , Science for University System and many good things. If Germany can be united, if India and China can remain as a one State, even if Europe can be united under European Union under one currency and even if United State can remain with one great state with so many culture, language, race, so The 1300 years olds Caliphate, which was abolished in 1924 after the long conspiracy of British Government and partly France, must be reestablished and the West should stop supporting their local Governor and withdraw their support. Each Muslim can be a Abraham Lincoln, who defeated the south to keep this great nation united. I should quote these following few line from Abraham Lincoln and the Second American Revolution: "For Lincoln it was the Union, not the Confederacy, that was the true heir of the Revolution of 1776. That revolution had established a republic, a democratic government of the people by the people. This republic was a fragile experiment in a world of Kings, emperors, tyrants, and theories of aristocracy. If secession were allowed to succeed, it would destroy that experiment. It would set a fatal precedent by which the minority stood for, until the United States fragmented into a dozen pitfall, squabbling countries, the laughing stock of the world. Now though God saved this country from division, the Land of The Caliphate was divided into so many nation States and thus contributing to the misery of the entire Muslim World. This must be changed by any cost. To divide other's land by force is not a terrorist act? If you are a Judge what judgment you will pass from the followings which I am quoting from "The Origins and Evolution of the Arab-Zionist Conflict by Michael Cohen, published by University of California Press; pg. 64:

"The new international agency, the League of Nations, was to allot
"mandates," or international trusteeships, under which the powers were to
prepare peoples liberated from the Turks for independence. .....
But once the United States abdicated any further role in the new European
order after the summer of 1919, it was left to Britain and France to divide
the Middle East between them. " Now What judgment you will pass against those terrorist who divided our land of Caliphate and appointed their local agents as their Governor or Sub-Contractors?

In fact, not only Palestine but entire land of 1300 years of Caliphate was given subcontract to the present Amirs/Governors who were given power under partition plan of Western Governments, even under pretext of League of Nation Plan after the defeat of Osmani Caliphate. Who do not know what role was played by Lawrence of Arabia and the secret Anglo-French agreement. The result is entire world Muslims has become slave in the hand of around 5000 or so associates of those Governors. And not even five million slaves as Thaddeus Stevens asked rhetorically how the United States could be a "true Republic" when "twenty-five million of a privileged class exclude five million from all participation in the rights of government.... Without such consent government is a tyranny, and you exercising it are tyrants." Now how United Nation can claim to be a World Organization maintaining peace in this world when it can rivers it's old position now and should take steps to free more then billion world Muslims who has become slave in the hand of few thousand so called Muslims who have been violating the only one political System of Islam of one Umma/Caliphate. Because the United Nation is also a participant of that crime as it also participated in that division of land of 1300 years old Caliphate when it was known as League of Nation.Why League of Nation participated in that partition of Dictatorial rule violating democracy as no consent was taken from World Muslims

for that partition. Where as 1400 years ago last Prophet of Islam (Peace be upon him) abolished slavery and his companions (God be pleased with them) took a path of democracy to elect first four Caliphs of Islam. Even Second Caliph (God be pleased with him) rehabilitated the Jews of Yathrub/Medina in Syria with honor. maintained peace and harmony in Palestine and Jerusalem. Even when electorate process of electing a Caliph was abolished youngest grandson of the Prophet (God be pleased with him) gave his life to defend democracy and Islam in Karbala. Readers can go through an Article came in New York Times in one August Saturday under the heading

"Karbala Journal- Who Hit the Mosques? Not Us, Baghdad says." If any reader went through that article then he will understand the fate behind Kamal Hussain Majid recently. That is the power of Karbala as one Indian said "Islam get new life after each Karbala and that Karbala brought down the Ummayad Dynasty and may be the Abbasyde dynasty too and that Karbala remind each Muslims in this world that they should continue the struggle to establish a truthful Caliphate and for that whatever sacrifice we are to do because no sacrifice can be equal to Karbala where only most of 72 companions of the youngest grandson of the Holy Prophet (Peace be upon him) including children and relative gave their life one after another for truthfulness and Islamic Democracy and Islamic freedom of which protect everyone's moral character and establish true justice in this world along with true law of God i.e. Koranic Law. Today

we are talking about International Seminar of Terrorism. But who first introduced present modern terrorism in the land of 1300 years old Caliphate? What was aim of Lawrence of Arabia when he landed in land of Caliphate? What was aim of League of Nation and it's

founder when it divided that land after defeating the established Caliphate? Was it not an act of Terrorism? In which court the World Muslims will try all those terrorist? Though Muslims have no power to try the Dajjal or Dajjal System or the System of anti Christ.

But there will be no peace in this world until Imam Mehdi , a descendent of the last Prophet of Islam and Prophet Jesus (peace be upon them) appear in very near future and it will appear when Prophet Jesus (peace be upon him) will descend down to big mosque in

Damascus and the antichrist will be killed along with his army. So Muslim are not worried and they are waiting for that moment and as such they should not be part of any terrorism though true terrorists divided their 1300 years old Caliphate and gave the

subcontract to their Governors to suppress all Muslims, and this is the true face of terrorism. Is it not? How the World can be Democratic, when few million people will try to dominate few billion people of this world, because those few million people got a arsenal of nuclear and
hydrozen bombs?

The following article iwas posted in

http://www.mena.net/panarab/
on August 28, 1998.
Subjec: The hypocrisy of it all By Noam Chomsky from:

http://web.ahram.org.eg/weekly/1998/338/in3.htm

"Bill Clinton's claim that "Human rights" has become "the soul of our foreign policy" is a transparent fraud, obviously designed to restore discipline and obedience after the Vietnam war, and accepted as legitimate, indeed holy, by virtually the entire Western intellectual class.

The lead story in the New York Times, reporting Clinton's recent call for China's leaders to protect human rights, was headlined "President Terms Certain Rights 'Universal'". The qualification 'certain rights' is accurate. The generally accepted human rights standard is the Universal Declaration of Human Rights (UD), considered 'customary international law' in US Courts. But contrary to much rhetoric, the US takes a highly relativist stand concerning the UD: even formally, it upholds only 'certain rights' of those enumerated.

Specifically, the US regards the socio-economic rights of the UD as having no status. They are, in the words of UN Ambassador Jeanne Kirkpatrick, "a letter to Santa Claus": "Neither nature, experience, nor probability informs these lists of 'entitlements', which are subject to no constraints except those of the mind and appetite of their authors."

For similar reasons, the US has rejected the UN Declaration on the Right to Development, which upholds "the right of individuals, groups, and peoples to participate in, contribute to, and enjoy continuous economic, social, cultural and political development, in which all human rights and fundamental freedoms can be fully realised." These are not rights, Washington's ambassador informed the UN Commission on Human Rights: the proposals "seem preposterous" and even "a dangerous incitement." The US alone vetoed the Declaration, thus effectively rescinding Article 25 of the UD, which spells out these rights. And indeed, US practices are sharply inconsistent with the socio-economic provisions of the UD. In
fact, the US officially exempts itself from all provisions of the UD by refusing to sign the enabling conventions designed to implement these provisions. The Convention on the Rights of the Child, for example, has been ratified by all countries apart from the US and Somalia. What is more, the few conventions that have been ratified are deemed inapplicable in the US. That is no small matter: Human Rights organisations have repeatedly pointed out that US criminal justice and penal practices are in violation of international conventions, as are many of its labour practices.

Unlike the case of the socio-economic provisions, the US claims to uphold the civil and political rights enumerated in the UD. But these are subject to certain unilateral qualifications. In the US, the most famous of these provisions is Article 13(2), which states that "Everyone has the right to leave any country, including his own." Before the collapse of the Soviet Union, this principle was invoked every year on Human Rights Day (December 10), with demonstrations and indignant condemnations of the USSR for its refusal to allow Jews to leave. Routinely omitted on these occasions, however, was the phrase which follows: "and to return to his country." The significance of the omitted words was spelled out on 11 December 1948, the day after the UD was ratified, when the General Assembly unanimously passed Resolution 194, which affirms the right of Palestinians to return to their homes or receive compensation if
they choose not to return.

Also omitted was the fact that those exhorting the Soviet tyrants to observe Article 13(2) were its most dedicated opponents. This annual rite symbolises quite accurately elite attitudes towards the universality of human rights: Rights are operative when the powerful so declare, an elementary principle that is concealed with impressive displays of hypocrisy and falsification.

It is to Clinton's credit that he removed the hypocrisy in this particular case. At the December 1993 UN session, the Clinton administration reversed official policy, joining with Israel for the first time in opposing UN 194. As is the norm, there was no report or comment. But at least the inconsistency is behind us: the first half of Article 13(2) has lost its relevance, and Washington now officially rejects its second half.

The US also rejects Article 14 of the UD, which declares that "Everyone has the right to seek and to enjoy in other countries asylum from persecution." Again the rationale of the US stance is easy to see. To mention only one case, for 20 years the US has virtually blockaded Haiti, forcing fleeing refugees back to the hands of brutal torturers and murderers, who were generally backed, openly or tacitly, by Washington.

Within the rich industrial societies themselves, human rights protection is generally high by comparative standards. The more serious violations have to do with behaviour beyond the borders. The most extreme are direct participation in horrendous atrocities, and support for them: for example, Washington's Indochina wars, which left millions dead and three countries in ruins, with thousands still dying every year from unexploded ordnance and the effects of chemical warfare; or the US wars in Central America in the '80s, which left hundreds of thousands of tortured and mutilated victims and millions of refugees, widows, and orphans. In this case, the US dismissed with contempt the ruling of the World Court ordering it to terminate its "unlawful use of force" and pay substantial reparations to the victims. According to Lars Schoultz, the leading academic specialist on the US and human rights in Latin America, US aid "has tended to flow disproportionately to Latin American governments which torture their citizens, [...] to the hemisphere's relatively egregious violators of fundamental human rights." The same pattern continues under Clinton: the leading recipient of US military aid and training is Colombia, where the military and its paramilitary associates are compiling a shocking human rights record, the worst in the hemisphere.

Further afield, the US (along with the UK and others) supported Saddam Hussein with enthusiasm throughout his worst atrocities, only turning against him when he disobeyed orders -- and then supporting him again as he slaughtered rebelling Shi'ites immediately after the Gulf War. In Indonesia, Suharto came to power in 1965 with the massacre of hundreds of thousands of people, mostly landless peasants, a "staggering mass slaughter" in the words of the New York Times, which went on to praise the "moderates" who had brought about this "gleam of light in Asia", thus joining in the applause that resounded across the political spectrum for the worst massacre since the Holocaust.

Suharto proceeded to compile one of the world's worst human rights records, invading and illegally annexing East Timor while killing perhaps a quarter of its population, always with strong Western support. Meanwhile he turned his rich country into a "paradise for investors", who were hindered only by the rampant corruption and robbery of the Suharto family and their associates. The Clinton administration hailed Suharto as "our kind of guy" when he visited Washington. As in the case of Saddam, Mobutu, Ceaucescu, Marcos, Duvalier, Somoza, Trujillo and a long list of other gangsters and killers, Suharto lost favour in Washington only when he no longer performed his assigned role, losing the capacity to control the population.

This is only the tip of the iceberg. It makes good sense for people to demand and struggle for the rights that are officially proclaimed, and typically used by the powerful as a weapon against others. They should do so, however, without illusions about power systems and those who serve them."

So though we can not change the foreign policy of any powerful
Nation as that nation is deaf and dump due to the influence of the
Forces of antichrist or Dajjal; we can take our case to
The court of International tribunal headed by great truth seekers like

Mr. *Noam Chomsky and others. Justice delayed, justice is denied.*
Thus World Muslims are deprived from any justice with honor from
Those forces of deaf and dump antichrist as they are too proud about
Their power. Time is a factor and it is already too late. So real
Civilized World must do something immediately, like an election
For Caliph and Hand over all present power from illegal sub-contractor
To that Elected Caliph other wise this World is doomed to destruction
With all kind of bombs those antichrist forces stockpiled for their
Evil desire of depriving any justice to the majority poor and helpless
People of this World including 1.5 billion World Muslims.
But those who think that killing few innocents people through any kind of
Bombing; can change the policy of forces of Dajjal or antichrist;
Are simply wrong. So let us probably Wait for the acts of God/Allah and
Some holy man and lastly Imam Mehdi and Prophet Jesus (peace be upon them). But if any
saint like holy Muslim can have direct guidance from God/Allah Through Salatul
Estekhara, (a prayer through which one can get guidance), Ilham (through which one can
get direct guidance from God/Allah) or Kasf (through which one can see anything in this
Universe); that is Up to him and God/Allah.

And in which court World Muslims will try those criminals and terrorists Who
divided the 1300 years old Caliphate/Khilafah and created illegal Client/nation States
and violence in the pretext of partition plan, UN Resolution and so many other
terrorists act including creating various brotherly wars and stealing trillion of
Dollars through supplying illegal arms and bombs?

Anti Christ (Dajjal)

There are three aspects of Dajjal (Anti Christ). There is Dajjal the individual. There is Dajjal as a World wide social and cultural phenomenon. There is Dajjal as an unseen force. Many of the Signs of the end of the world are clearly indicated in the Hadith collections, and whoever is awake
And aware of the signs in the self and on the horizon, knows these signs and recognizes them when they appear. All the signs of the end of the world are now apparent, except for the last four major signs and it would appear that even these are now imminent The last four major signs are the appearance of Dajjal the individual; the appearance of the Mahdi, the rightly
guided leader of the Muslims who will fight Dajjal; the re-appearance of the prophet Jesus, on him be peace, who as well as breaking all the crosses, killing all the pigs, marrying and having children and praying with the Muslims, will also kill Dajjal; and the appearance of Juge wa ma Juge, a
tribe of people who will scatter across the world, creating destruction.[1]

We should quote from the basic source of Islam which is Hadith or saying of last Prophet of Islam (PBUH) from:

SAHIH MUSLIM, BOOK 40: Pertaining To Turmoil And Portents Of The Last Hour (Kitab Al-Fitan Wa Ashrat As-Sa'Ah)
Translation of Sahih Muslim, Book 40:
Pertaining To Turmoil And Portents Of The Last Hour (Kitab Al-Fitan Wa Ashrat As-Sa'Ah)

Some quotations on last day from Hadith, which is available in:

http://cwis.usc.edu:80/dept/MSA/fundamentals/hadithsunnah/muslim/040.smt.htm

Book 40, Number 6886:
Narrated Umm Salamah:

Harith ibn AbuRabi'ah and Abdullah ibn Safwan both went to Umm Salamah, Ummul Mu'minin. They asked her about the army which would be sunk in the earth. This was at the time of Abdullah ibn az-Zubayr's rule.

Umm Salamah said: Allah's Apostle (peace_be_upon_him) had said that a seeker of refuge would seek refuge in the Sacred House and an army would be sent to him (in order to kill him) and when it would enter a plain ground, it would be made to sink.

I said: Allah's Apostle (peace_be_upon_him) what about him who would be made to accompany this army willy-nilly ? Thereupon he said: He would be made to sink along with them but he would be raised on the Day of Resurrection on the basis of his intention. AbuJa'far said: This plain ground means the plain ground of Medina.

Book 40, Number 6888:
Narrated Hafsah:

---

[1] Dajjal, The King who has no clothes by AHMAD THOMSON, Published by TA-HA PUBLISHERS LTD., 1 Wynne Road, London SW9 0BD

Hafsah heard Allah's Apostle (peace_be_upon_him) as saying: An army would attack this House in order to fight against the inhabitants of this House and when it would be at the plain ground the ranks in the center of the army would be sunk and the vanguard would call the rear flanks of the army and they would also be sunk and no flank would be left except some people who would go to inform them (their kith and kin).

A person (who had been listening to this hadith from Abdullah ibn Safwan) said: I bear testimony in regard to you that you are not imputing a lie to Hafsah. I bear testimony to the fact that Hafsah is not telling a lie about Allah's Apostle (peace_be_upon_him).

Book 40, Number 6897:
Narrated AbuBakrah:

Allah's Apostle (peace_be_upon_him) said: There will soon be turmoil. Behold! There will be turmoil in which the one who is seated will be better than one who stands and the one who stands will be better than one who runs. Behold! When the turmoil comes or it appears, the one who has a camel should stay with his camel, he who has sheep or goats should stay with his sheep or goats and he who has land should stay on the land.

Someone said: Allah's Apostle (peace_be_upon_him), what is your opinion of one who has neither camel nor sheep nor land? Thereupon he said: He should take hold of his sword, sharpen its edge with the help of a stone and then try to find a way of escape. O Allah, I have conveyed (Thy Message); O Allah, I have conveyed (Thy Message).

Someone said: Allah's Messenger, what is your opinion if I am drawn to a rank in spite of myself, or one of the groups, and made to march, and a man strikes me with his sword or there comes an arrow which kills me? Thereupon he said: He will bear the punishment of his sin and that of yours and he will be one of the denizens of Hell.

Book 40, Number 6904:
Narrated Thawban:

Allah's Apostle (peace_be_upon_him) said: Allah drew the ends of the world together for my sake. I have seen its eastern and western ends. The dominion of my Ummah will reach those ends which have been drawn together near me and I have been granted the red and the white treasures. I begged my Lord that my Ummah should not be destroyed by famine, nor be dominated by a foreign enemy who will take their lives and destroy them root and branch.

My Lord said: Muhammad, whenever I make a decision, there is none to change it. Well, I grant you that your Ummah will not be destroyed by famine, nor will it be dominated by a foreign enemy who will take their lives and destroy them root and branch, even if all the people from the different parts of the world join hands together (for this purpose). However, it will be from amongst them, viz. your Ummah, that some people will kill or imprison the others.

Book 40, Number 6906:
Narrated Sa'd ibn AbuWaqqas:

One day Allah's Apostle (peace_be_upon_him) came from a high land. He passed by the mosque of Banu Mu'awiyah, went in and observed two rak'ahs there and we also observed prayer along with him and he made a long supplication to his Lord.

He then came to us and said: I asked my Lord three things and He has granted me two but has withheld one. I begged my Lord that my Ummah should not be destroyed because of famine and He granted me this. And I begged my Lord that my Ummah should not be destroyed by drowning (by deluge) and He granted me this. And I begged my Lord that there should be no bloodshed among the people of my Ummah, but He did not grant it.

Book 40, Number 6913:
Narrated AbuZayd:

Allah's Apostle (peace_be_upon_him) led us in the dawn prayer and then mounted the pulpit and addressed us until it was (time for the) noon prayer.

He then came down the pulpit and observed prayer and then again mounted the pulpit and again addressed us until it was time for the Asr prayer.

He then again came down and observed the prayer and again mounted the pulpit and addressed us until the sun was set and he informed (about) everything (pertaining to turmoil) that lay hidden in the past and what lies in (the womb of) the future and the most learned amongst us is one who remembers them well amongst us.

Book 40, Number 6922:
Narrated Ubayy ibn Ka'b:

I heard Allah's Apostle (peace_be_upon_him) said: The Euphrates would soon uncover a mountain of gold and when the people would hear of it they would flock towards it but the people who would possess that (treasure) (would say): If we allow these persons to take out of it they would take away the whole of it. So they would fight and ninety-nine out of one hundred would be killed.
AbuKamil in his narration said: I and AbuKa'b stood under the shade of the battlement of Hassan.

Book 40, Number 6923:
Narrated AbuHurayrah:

Allah's Apostle (peace_be_upon_him) said: Iraq would withhold its dirhams and qafiz; Syria would withhold its mudd and dinar and Egypt would withhold its irdab and dinar and you would recoil to that position from where you started and you would recoil to that position from where you started and you would recoil to the position from where you started, the bones and the flesh of AbuHurayrah would bear testimony to it.

Book 40, Number 6925:
Narrated Mustawrid al-Qurashi:

I heard Allah's Apostle (peace_be_upon_him) said: The Last Hour would come (when) the Romans would form a majority amongst people. Amr said to him (Mustawrid al-Qurashi): See what you are saying? He said: I say what I heard from Allah's Apostle (peace_be_upon_him) Thereupon he said: If you say that, it is a fact for they have four qualities. They have the patience to undergo a trial and immediately restore themselves to sanity after trouble and attack again after flight. They (have the quality) of being good to the destitute and the orphans, to the weak and, fifthly, the good quality in them is that they put resistance against the oppression of kings.

Book 40, Number 6927:
Narrated Abdullah ibn Mas'ud:

Once there blew a red storm in Kufah and there came a person who had nothing to say but (these words): Abdullah ibn Mas'ud, the Last Hour has come.

He (Abdullah ibn Mas'ud) was sitting reclining against something, and he said: The Last Hour will not come until the people divide inheritance and rejoice over booty. Then He said pointing towards Syria, with a gesture of his hand like this: The enemy will muster strength against the Muslims and the Muslims will muster strength against them (Syrians). I said: You mean Rome? He said: Yes, and there will be a terrible fight. The Muslims will prepare a detachment (for fighting unto death) which will not return unless victorious. They will fight until darkness intervenes. Both sides will return without being victorious and both will be wiped out. The Muslims will again prepare a detachment for fighting unto death so that they may not return unless victorious.
When it is the fourth day, a new detachment from the remnant of the Muslims will be prepared and Allah will decree that the enemy will be routed. They would fight such a fight the like of which has not been seen, so fierce that even if a bird were to pass their flanks, it would fall down dead before reaching the other end. (There will be such a large scale massacre) that when counting will be done, (only) one out of a hundred men related to one another would be found alive. So what can be the joy at the spoils of such war and what inheritance can be divided?
They will be in this very state when they will hear of a calamity more horrible than this. A cry will reach them: The Dajjal has taken your place among your offspring. They will therefore throw away what is in their hands and go forward, sending ten horsemen as a scouting party. Allah's Apostle (peace_be_upon_him) said: I know their names, the names of their forefathers and the colour of their horses. They will be the best horsemen on the surface of the Earth on that day or among the best horsemen on the surface of the Earth on that day.

Book 40, Number 6930:
Narrated Nafi' ibn Utbah:

We were with Allah's Apostle (peace_be_upon_him) on an expedition when there came to Allah's Apostle (peace_be_upon_him) some people from the west. Dressed in woollen clothes, they stood near a hillock and met Allah's Apostle (peace_be_upon_him) as was sitting.

I said to myself: I had better go to them and stand between him and them so that they may not attack him. Then I thought that perhaps there were secret negotiations going on between them. However, I went to them and stood between them and him and remember four of the words (on that occasion), which I repeat (on the fingers of my hand), that he (Allah's Apostle p.) said: You will attack Arabia and Allah will enable you to conquer it, then you will attack Persia and He will cause you to conquer it. Then you will attack Rome and Allah will enable you to conquer it, then you will attack the Dajjal and Allah will enable you to conquer him. Nafi said: Jabir, we thought that the Dajjal would appear after Rome (Syrian territory) was conquered.

Book 40, Number 6931:
Narrated Hudhayfah ibn Usayd Ghifari:

Allah's Apostle (peace_be_upon_him) came to us all of a sudden as we were (busy in a discussion) He said: What do you discuss about? (the Companions) said: We are discussing about the Last Hour.

Thereupon he said: It will not come until you see ten signs before and (in this connection) he made a mention of the smoke, Dajjal, the beast, the rising of the sun from the west, the descent of Jesus son of Mary (Allah be pleased with him), The Gog and Magog, and

16

landslides in three places, one in the east, one in the west and one in Arabia at the end of which fire would burn forth from the Yemen, and would drive people to the place of their assembly.

Book 40, Number 6936:

Narrated AbuHurayrah:
Allah's Apostle (peace_be_upon_him) said: (The Last Hour would not come) until the habitations of Medina would extend to Ihab or Yahab.

Zubayr said: I said to Suhayl how far these were from Medina. He said: so and so miles.

Book 40, Number 6945:
Narrated Aisha:

I heard Allah's Apostle (peace_be_upon_him) said: The (system) of night and day would not end until the people have taken to the worship of Lat and Uzza.
I said: Allah's Apostle (peace_be_upon_him) I think when Allah has revealed this verse: "He it is Who has sent His Messenger with right guidance, and true religion, so that He may cause it to prevail upon all religions, though the polytheists are averse (to it)" (ix.33), it implies that (this promise) is going to be fulfilled.

Thereupon he (Allah's Apostle (peace_be_upon_him)) said: It would happen as Allah would like. Then Allah would send the sweet fragrant air by which everyone who has even a mustard grain of faith in Him would die and those only would survive who would have no goodness in them. And they would revert to the religion of their forefathers.

Book 40, Number 6949:
Narrated AbuHurayrah:

Allah's Apostle (peace_be_upon_him) said: By Him in Whose Hand is my life, a time would come when the murderer would not know why he has committed the murder, and the victim would not know why he has been killed.

Book 40, Number 6961:
Narrated Jabir ibn Abdullah:

AbuNadrah reported: We were in the accompany of Jabir and he said: It may happen that the people of Iraq may not send their qafiz and dirhams (their measures of food-stuff and their money). We said: Who would be responsible for it? He said: The non-Arabs would prevent them. He again said: There is the possibility that the people of Syria may not send their dinar and mudd. We said: Who would be responsible for it? He said: This prevention would be made by the Romans.
He (Jabir ibn Abdullah) kept quiet for a while and then reported Allah's Apostle (peace_be_upon_him) having said: There would be a caliph in the last (period) of my Ummah who would freely give handfuls of wealth to the people without counting it.
I said to AbuNadrah and AbulAla: Do you mean Umar b. AbdulAziz? They said: No

Book 40, Number 6963:
Narrated AbuSa'id al-Khudri:

Allah's Apostle (peace_be_upon_him) said: There would be amongst your caliphs a caliph who would give handfuls of wealth to the people but would not count it.
Book 40, Number 6964:
Narrated AbuSa'id ; Jabir ibn Abdullah:

17

Allah's Apostle (peace_be_upon_him) said: There would be in the last (phase) of the time a caliph who would distribute wealth but would not count.

Book 40, Number 6979:
Narrated AbuHurayrah:

Allah's Apostle (peace_be_upon_him) said: You have heard of the city, one side of which is inclined and the other is on the coast (Constantinople). They said: Yes, Allah's Apostle (peace_be_upon_him). Thereupon he said: The Last Hour will not come until seventy thousand people from Banu Isra'il attack it. When they land there, they will neither fight with weapons nor shower arrows but will only say: "There is no god but Allah and Allah is the Greatest," and one side of it will fall. Thawr (one of the narrators) said: I think that he said: The area on the coast. Then they will say for the second time: "There is no god but Allah and Allah is the Greatest," and the other side will also fall. They will say: "There is no god but Allah is the Greatest," and the gates will be opened for them and they will enter. They will be collecting spoils of war and distributing them among themselves when a noise will be heard and it will be said: Verily, the Dajjal has come. Thus they will leave everything there and turn to (confront) him.
Book 40, Number 6990:
Narrated Abdullah ibn Mas'ud:

We were along with Allah's Apostle (peace_be_upon_him) that we happened to pass by children amongst whom there was Ibn Sayyad. The children made their way but Ibn Sayyad kept sitting there (and it seemed) as if Allah's Apostle (peace_be_upon_him) did not like it (his sitting with the children) and said to him: May your nose be besmeared with dust, don't you bear testimony to the fact that I am the Messenger of Allah? Thereupon he said: No, but you should bear testimony that I am the messenger of Allah.

Thereupon Umar ibn al-Khattab said: Allah's Apostle (peace_be_upon_him) permit me that I should kill him. Thereupon Allah's Apostle (peace_be_upon_him) said: If he is that person who is in your mind (Dajjal), you will not be able to kill him.

Book 40, Number 6992:
Narrated AbuSa'id al-Khudri:

Allah's Apostle (peace_be_upon_him) met him (Ibn Sayyad) and so did AbuBakr and Umar on some of the roads of Medina. Allah's Apostle (peace_be_upon_him) said: Do you bear testimony to the fact that I am the Messenger of Allah? Thereupon he said: Do you bear testimony to the fact that I am the messenger of Allah?

Thereupon Allah's Apostle (peace_be_upon_him) said: I affirm my faith in Allah and in His Angels and in His Books, and what do you see? He said: I see the throne over water. Thereupon Allah's Apostle (peace_be_upon_him) said: You see the throne of Iblis upon the water, and what else do you see? He said: I see two truthfuls and a liar or two liars and one truthful.

Thereupon Allah's Apostle (peace_be_upon_him) said: Leave him. He has been confounded

Book 40, Number 6993:
Narrated Jabir ibn Abdullah:

Allah's Apostle (peace_be_upon_him) met Ibn Sayyad and there were with him AbuBakr and Umar and Ibn Sayyad was in the company of children. The rest of the hadith is the same (as No 6992).

Book 40, Number 6997
Narrated AbuSa'id al-Khudri:
Allah's Apostle (peace_be_upon_him) asked Ibn Sayyad about the earth of Paradise. Thereupon he said: AbulQasim, it is like a fine white musk, whereupon he (the Prophet) said: You have told the truth.

Book 40, Number 7023:
Narrated Abdullah ibn Amr:

Someone came to him and said: What is this hadith that you narrate that the Last Hour will come at a certain time? Thereupon he said: Hallowed be Allah, there is no god but Allah (or words to the same effect). I have decided that I shall not narrate anything to anyone now. I have only said that you will see after some time an important event: that the (sacred) House (Ka'bah) will be burnt and it definitely happen.
He then reported that Allah's Messenger (peace_be_upon_him) said: The Dajjal will appear in my Ummah and he will stay (in the world) for forty--I cannot say whether he meant forty days, forty months or forty years. Allah will then send Jesus, son of Mary, who will resemble Urwah ibn Mas'ud. He (Jesus Christ) will chase him and kill him. Then people will live for seven years, during which time there will be no rancour between any two persons. After that Allah will send a cold wind from the direction of Syria. None will survive on Earth, having a speck of good in him or faith in him: he will die. Even if some among you were to enter the innermost part of the mountain, this wind would reach that place also and cause your death.
I heard Allah's Apostle (peace_be_upon_him) as saying: Only the wicked people will survive and they will be as careless as birds with the characteristics of beasts. They will never appreciate good nor condemn evil. Then Satan will come to them, in human form, and would say: Don't you respond? They will say: What do you order us to do? He will command them to worship the idols but, in spite of this, they will have an abundance of sustenance and lead comfortable lives. Then the trumpet will be blown and he who hears it will bend his neck to one side and raise it from the other side. The first one to hear that trumpet will be the person who is busy in setting right the cistern meant for supplying water to the camels. He will faint and the other people will also faint. Then Allah will send or He will cause to be sent rain which will be like dew and there will grow out of it the bodies of people.
Then the second trumpet will be blown and they will stand up and begin to look (around). Then it will be said: O people, go to your Lord. They will be made to stand there and they will be questioned. Then it will be said: Bring out a group (of them) for the Hell-Fire. It will be asked: How much? It will be said: Nine hundred and ninety-nine out of one thousand for the Hell-Fire That will be the day that will make the children old because of its terror and that will be the day about which it has been said: "On the day when the shank will be uncovered".

Book 40, Number 7025:
Narrated Abdullah ibn Amr ibn al-'As:

I committed to memory a hadith from Allah's Apostle (peace_be_upon_him) and I did not forget it after I had heard Allah's Apostle (peace_be_upon_him) said: The first sign (out of the signs of the appearance of the Dajjal) would be the appearance of the sun from the west, the appearance of the beast before the people in the forenoon and which of the two happens first, the second one would follow immediately after that.

19

Book 40, Number 7028:
Narrated Fatimah, daughter of Qays and sister of ad-Dahhak ibn Qays:

Amir ibn Sharahil ash-Sha'bi said: Fatimah bint Qays was among the first emigrant women. I asked her to narrate to me a hadith which she had heard directly from Allah's Apostle (peace_be_upon_him) and there was no extra link between them. She said: Very well, if you like, I am prepared to do that. He said to her: Well, do so and narrate it to me. She said: I married the son of Mughirah and he was a chosen young man of Quraysh at that time, but he fell as a martyr in the first Jihad (fighting on the side of Allah's Apostle (peace_be_upon_him)).

When I became a widow, AbdurRahman ibn Awf, one of the group of the companions of Allah's Apostle. sent me a proposal of marriage. Allah's Apostle (peace_be_upon_him) also sent me such a message for his freed slave, Usamah ibn Zayd. It had been conveyed to me that Allah's Apostle (peace_be_upon_him) had said (about Usamah): He who loves me should also love Usamah. When Allah's Apostle (peace_be_upon_him) talked to me (about this matter), I said: My affairs are in your hands. You may marry me to anyone you wish.

He said: You had better move now to the house of Umm Sharik. Umm Sharik was a rich lady from among the Ansar. She spent generously for the cause of Allah and entertained guests very hospitably. I said: Well, I shall do as you wish. He said: Do not do that because Umm Sharik is a woman who is very frequently visited by guests and I do not like your head to be uncovered or removed from your shank and the strangers may catch sight of that which you abhor. You had better move to the house of your cousin, Abdullah ibn Amr ibn Umm Maktum. He was one of the Banu Fihr branch of the Quraysh, and he belonged to that tribe (to which Fatimah) belonged.

So I moved to that house, and when my period of waiting was over, I heard the voice of an announcer making an announcement that the prayer would be observed in the mosque (where) congregational prayer (is observed). So I set out towards the mosque and observed prayer with the Allah's Apostle (peace_be_upon_him) and I was in the row of the women which was near the row of men. When Allah's Apostle (peace_be_upon_him) had finished his prayer, he sat on the pulpit, smiling, and said: Every worshipper should remain sitting in his place. He then said: Do you know why I have asked you to assemble? They said: Allah and His apostle know best.

He said: By Allah, I have not made you assemble for exhortation or for a warning. I have detained you here because Tamim Dari, a Christian who came and accepted Islam, told me something which agrees with what I was telling you about the Dajjal. He narrated to me that he had sailed in a ship with thirty men of Banu Lakhm and Banu Judham and had been tossed by waves in the ocean for a month. Then these (waves) took them (near) the land within the ocean (island) at the time of sunset. They sat in a small rowing-boat and landed on that island. There was a beast with long thick hair (and because of this) they could not distinguish his face from his back. They said: Woe to you, who can you be? Thereupon it said: I am al-Jassasah. They said: What is al-Jassasah? It said: O people, go to this person in the monastery as he is very much eager to know about you. He (the narrator) said: When it named a person for us we were afraid of it lest it should be a Devil.

Then we hurried on till we came to that monastery and found a well-built person there with his hands tied to his neck and iron shackles gripping his legs by the ankles. We said: Woe to you, who are you? He said: You soon come to know about me, but tell me who you are. We said: We are people from Arabia and we embarked upon a boat but the waves had been driving us for one month and they brought us near this island. We took to the rowing-boats and landed on this island. Here a beast with profusely thick hair met us and because of the thickness of his hair his face could not be distinguished from his back. We said: Woe be to thee, who are you? It said: I am al- Jassasah. We said: What is al-Jassasah? It said: You go to this very person in the monastery for he is eagerly waiting for you to know about you. So we came to you in hot haste fearing that that might be the Devil.

He (that chained person) said: Tell me about the date-palm trees of Baysan. We said: In which respect do you seek information about it? He said: I ask you whether these trees bear fruit or not. We said: Yes. Thereupon he said: I think these will not bear fruit. He said: Inform me about the lake of Tabariyyah? We said: What do you want to know about it? He said: Is there water in it? They said: There is an abundance of water in it. Thereupon he said: I think it will soon dry up. He again said: Inform me about the spring of Zughar. They said: What do you want to know about it? He (the chained person) said: Is there water in it and does it irrigate (the land)? We said to him: Yes, there is an abundance of water in it and the inhabitants (of Medina) irrigate (land) with its help.

He said: Inform me about the unlettered Prophet; what has he done? We said: He has left Mecca and has settled in Yathrib (Medina). He said: Do the Arabs fight against him? We said: Yes. He said: How does he deal with him? We informed him that he had overcome those in his neighborhood and they had submitted themselves before him. Thereupon he said to us: Had it actually happened? We said: Yes.

Thereupon he said: If it is so that is better for them that they show obedience to him. I am going to tell you about myself. I am the Dajjal and will be soon permitted to leave. So I shall leave and travel in the land, and shall not spare any town where I shall not stay for forty nights except Mecca and Medina: these two (places) are prohibited (areas) for me and I shall not attempt to enter either of them. An angel with a sword in his hand will confront me and bar my way and there will be angels to guard every road leading to it. Then Allah's apostle (peace_be_upon_him) striking the pulpit with the help of the end of his staff said: This implies Tayba mean ng Medina. Have I not told you an account (of the Dajjal) like this? The people said: Yes, and this account narrated by Tamim Dari was liked by me for it corroborates the account which I gave to you in regard to him (Dajjal) at Medina and Mecca. Behold he (Dajjal) is in the Syrian sea (Mediterranean) or the Yemen sea (Arabian sea). Nay, on the contrary, he is in the east, he is in the east, he is in the east, and he pointed with his hand towards the east. I (Fatimah bint Qays) said: I preserved it in my mind (this narration from Allah's Messenger (peace_be_upon_him).

Book 40, Number 7034:
Narrated Anas ibn Malik:
Allah's Apostle (peace_be_upon_him) said: The Dajjal would be followed by seventy thousand Jews of Isfahan wearing Persian shawls.

Book 40, Number 7035:
Narrated Umm Sharik:

I heard Allah's Apostle (peace_be_upon_him) said: The people would run away from the Dajjal seeking shelter in the mountains She said: Where would be the Arabs then on the day? He said: They would be small in number.

Book 40, Number 7037:
Narrated AbuQatadah:

We used to go to Imran b. Husayn passing in front of Hisham b. Amir. He, one day, said: You pass by me (in order) to go to some persons but (amongst the living persons) none remained in the company of Allah's Apostle (peace_be_upon_him) more than I and none knows more hadiths than I. I heard Allah's Apostle (peace_be_upon_him) said: There would be no creation (creating more trouble) than the Dajjal right from the creation of Adam to the Last Hour.

Book 40, Number 7039:
Narrated AbuHurayrah:

Allah's Apostle (peace_be_upon_him) said: Hasten to do good deeds before six things happen: the rising of the sun from the west, the smoke, the Dajjal, the beast and (the death) of one you or the general turmoil.

What Nostradamus. mentioned bellow about AntiChrist is none but Dajjal as quoted from Ahadith from last prophet of Islam (peace be upon him).

> *"The Antichrist returns for the last time...All*
> *the Christian and infidel nations will tremble... for*
> *the space of twenty-five years. Wars and battles*
> *will be more grievous than ever. Towns, cities,*
> *citadels and all other structues will be*
> *destroyed... So many evils by Satan's prince will*
> *find itself undone and desolated, Before these*
> *events, . many rare birds will cry in the air, 'Now!*
> *Now!' and sometime later will vanish."*

Last prophet of Islam (Peace be upon him) also mentioned about bird, which are as follows:

Book 40, Number 7015:
Narrated An-Nawwas ibn Sam'an

Allah's Apostle (peace_be_upon_him) mentioned of the Dajjal one day in the morning. He sometimes described him as insignificant and sometimes described (his turmoil) as very significant (and we felt) as if he were in the cluster of the date-palm trees. When we went to him (to the Holy Prophet) in the evening and he read (the signs of fear) on our faces, he said: What is the matter with you? We said: Allah's Apostle (peace_be_upon_him) you mentioned the Dajjal this morning (sometimes describing him) as insignificant and sometimes very important, until we began to think he was present in some (nearly) part of the cluster of the date-palm trees.

So he said: I harbour fear in regard to you in so many other things besides the Dajjal. If he comes forth while I am among you, I shall contend with him on your behalf, but if he comes forth while I am not among you, a man must contend on his own behalf and Allah will take care of every Muslim on my behalf (and safeguard him against his evil). He (the Dajjal) will be a young man with twisted, cropped hair, and a blind eye. I compare him with AbdulUzza ibn Qatan. He who among you will survive to see him should recite over him the opening verses of Surah al-Kahf (xviii). He will appear on the way between Syria and Iraq and will spread mischief right and left. O servant of Allah! Adhere (to the path of Truth).

We said: Allah's Apostle (peace_be_upon_him), how long will he stay on Earth? He said: For forty days, one day like a year, one day like a month, one day like a week, and the rest of the days will be like your days. We said: Allah's Apostle (peace_be_upon_him) will one day's prayer suffice for the prayers of the day equal to one year? Thereupon he said: No, but you must make an estimate of the time (and then observe prayer).
We said: Allah's apostle (peace_be_upon_him) how quickly will he walk upon the earth? Thereupon he said: Like cloud driven by the wind. He will come to the people and invite

them (to a wrong religion); they will affirm their faith in him and respond to him. He will then give a command to the sky: there will be rainfall upon the Earth and it will grow crops. Then in the evening, their pasturing animals will come to them with their humps very high, their udders full of milk and their flanks distended. He will then come to another people and invite them. But they will reject him so he will go away from them; they will have a drought and nothing will be left with them in the form of wealth.

He will then walk through the desert and say to it: Bring forth your treasures. The treasures will come out and gather before him like a swarm of bees. He will then call someone in the flush of youth, strike him with the sword, cut him into two pieces and (make these pieces lie at the distance which is generally between the archer and his target.
He will then call (that young man) and he will come forward laughing with his face gleaming (with happiness). It will at this very time that Allah will send Christ, son of Mary. He will descend at the white minaret on the eastern side of Damascus, wearing two garments lightly dyed with saffron and placing his hands on the wings of two Angels. When he lowers his head, there will fall beads of perspiration from his head, and when he raises it up, beads like pearls will scatter from it. Every non-believer who smells the odour of his body will die and his breath will reach as far as he is able to see. He will then search for him (Dajjal) until he catches hold of him at the gate of Ludd and kills him.
Then a people whom Allah had protected will come to Jesus, son of Mary, and he will wipe their faces and inform them of their ranks in Paradise. It will be under such conditions that Allah will reveal to Jesus these words: I have brought forth from among My servants such people against whom none will be able to fight; you take these people safely to Tur, and then Allah will send Gog and Magog and they will swarm down from every slope. The first of them will pass the lake of Tiberias and drink out of it. And when the last of them passes, he will say: There was once water there.

Jesus and his companions will then be besieged here (at Tur, and they will be so hard pressed) that the head of the ox will be dearer to them than one hundred dinars. Allah's Apostle (peace_be_upon_him), Jesus and his companions will supplicate Allah, Who will send to them insects (which will attack their necks) and in the morning they would perish as one single person. Allah's Apostle (peace_be_upon_him), Jesus, and his companions, then come down to Earth and they will not find on Earth as much space as a single span that is not filled with putrefaction and stench. Allah's Apostle (peace_be_upon_him), Jesus, and his companions will then beseech Allah who will send birds whose necks would be like those of Bactrian camels and they will carry them away and throw them where Allah wills.

Then Allah will send rain which no house of mud-bricks or (tent of) camel-hair will keep out and it will wash the Earth until it resembles a mirror. Then the Earth will be told to bring forth its fruit and restore its blessing and, as a result thereof, there will grow (such a big) pomegranate that a group of people will be able to eat it and seek shelter under its skin, a dairy cow will give so much milk that a whole party will be able to drink it. The milking camel will give such (a large quantity of) milk that the whole tribe will be able to drink from it, and the milking-sheep will give so much milk that the whole family will be able to drink from it. At that time Allah will send a pleasant wind which will soothe (people) even under their armpits. He will take the life of every Muslim and only the wicked will survive who will commit adultery like asses and the Last Hour would come to them.

Again Nostradamus mention the following poem with some regards for Arab and the last Prophet of Islam, which many western
people do not notice for their too much Anti-Islamic attitude. Nostradamus had no hate for Arab or Islam and the Eastern man
can not be Arab or Muslim as the following poem tell us.

"In the fortunate country of Arabia will be born

23

one powerful in the laws Mohammed.
He will trouble Spain and conquer Granada
as well as most of the Ligurian nation
from the sea."

"The Eastern man will come forth from his seat
and cross the Apennines to France. He will cross
through the sky, the seas and the snows and he
will strike everyone with his rod.

So Eastern man can not be Arab or Muslim as they have no technology to
fly in sky. In fact the opposite is true.

Book 40, Number 7042:
Narrated Ma'qil ibn Yasar:

Allah's Apostle (peace_be_upon_him) said: Worshipping during the period of widespread
turmoil is like emigration towards me.

Last Prophet of Islam (Peace be upon him) mentioned:
"Even if the entire duration of the world's existence has already been
    exhausted and only one day is left before Doomsday (Day of judgment),
    Allah will expand that day to such a length of time, as to accommodate
    the kingdom of a person out of my Ahlul-Bayt who will be called by my
    name. He will then fill out the earth with peace and justice as it
    will have been full of injustice and tyranny before then."

Sunni Reference: Sahih Tirmidhi, V2, P86, V9, P74-75 (There are many more.)

The context of the above precious tradition informs the golden divine
promises will take place, sooner or later, one way or another, as mentioned
in most of the Shi'ite and Sunnit sources.

For our Muslim brothers, there are six authentic collections
of traditions based on the Sunni standards for verifying the authenticity
of a tradition. These six books are: Sahih al-Bukhari, Sahih Muslim,
Sahih al-Tirmidhi, Sunan Ibn Majah, Sunan Abu Dawud, and Sahih al-Nisa'i.
I just quote few traditions from these six books to prove that a
knowledgeable Sunni brother/sister can NOT deny that:
1. Mahdi is going to come in the last days to make a universal Government,
2. Mahdi is from the Ahlul-Bayt (descendent) of Prophet,
3. Mahdi is from the children of Fatimah (AS), the daughter of Prophet,
4. Mahdi is different than Jesus (the messiah),
5. Jesus will be one of the followers of Imam Mahdi and prays behind him.
The following are only some of the traditions out of many, about Imam
Mahdi, and are ALL traditions that the Sunnis admit to their authenticity
and existence:
    The Prophet (PBUH) said: "Even if the entire duration of the world's
    existence has already been exhausted and only one day is left before
    Doomsday (Day of judgment), Allah will expand that day to such a
    length of time, as to accommodate the kingdom of a person out of my
    Ahlul-Bayt who will be called by my name. He will then fill out the
    earth with peace and justice as it will have been full of injustice
    and tyranny before then."

Sunni References

1. Sahih Tirmidhi, V2, P86, V9, PP 74-75
2. Sanan Abi Dawud, V2, P7
3. Musnad Ahmad Ibn Hanbal, V1, P376 & V3, P63
4. Mustadrak al-Sahihain, by al-Hakim, V4, P557
5. Al-Majma', by Tabarani, P217
6. Tahdhib al-Thabit, by Ibn Hajar al-Asqalani, V9, P144
7. Sawaiq al-Muhraqa, Ibn Hajar al-Haythami, P167
8. Fathul Bari, by Ibn Hajar al-Asqalani, V7, P305
9. al-Tathkirah, by al-Qurtubi, P617
10. al-Hawi, by al-Suyuti, V2, pp165-166
11. Sharh al-Mawahib al-Ladunniyyah, by al-Zurqani, V5, P348
12. Fathul Mughith, by al-Sakhawi, V3, P41
13. al-Hafidh Abul-Hasan Muhammad Ibn al-Husayn al-Sijistani al-Aburi
14. al-Shafi'i (d. 363/974). (who said the above hadith is related by
    numerous authorities and were spread far and wide by many narrators).
    and also in the works of Ibn Habban, Abu Nua'ym, Ibn Asakir, etc.

The Prophet (PBUH) said: "Al-Mahdi is one of us, the members of the
household (Ahlul-Bayt)."
Sunni reference: Sunan Ibn Majah, V2, Tradition #4085

As we see Imam Mahdi is from the Ahlul Bayt of Prophet Muhammad, so he can
not be Jesus (the Messiah al-Maseeh). Mahdi and Messiah are two different
personalities but they come at the same time, Mahdi as Imam and Jesus as
his follower. The following tradition clearly mentions that Imam Mahdi is
one of the children of the daughter of Prophet Muhammad (PBUH&HF):

The Messenger of Allah said: "Al-Mahdi is one of the children of
Fatimah (the Prophet's daughter)."

Sunni reference: Sunan Ibn Majah, V2, Tradition #4086

The Prophet (PBUH) said: "We the children of Abd Al-Mutalib are the
Masters of the inhabitants of Heaven: Myself, Hamza (RA), Ali (AS),
Jafar (RA), Hasan (AS), Hussain (AS), and Al-Mahdi (AS)."
Sunni reference: Sunan Ibn Majah, V2, Tradition #4087

The Prophet (PBUH) said: "The Mahdi will appear in my Ummah. He will
appear for a minimum of 7 or a maximum of 9 years; in that time, my
Ummah will experience a bountiful favor like never before. It shall
have a great abundance of food, of which it need not save anything,
and the wealth at that time is in great quantities, such that if a
man asks the Mahdi to give him some, and the Mahdi (AS) will say:
Here! Take!"
Sunni reference: Sunan Ibn Majah, V2, Tradition #5083

Remark: According to Shi'i sources, the Government of Peace and equality
that Imam Mahdi will establish will last hundreds of years with no rival,
and then the day of Judgment will be set. What is mentioned in the above
tradition as 7 or 9 years is related to the length of time that Imam
Mahdi will fight to conquer the world when he starts his mission.

The Prophet (PBUH) said: "We (I and my family) are members of a
household that Allah (SWT) has chosen for them the life of the

25

Hereafter over the life of this world; and the members of my household (Ahlul-Bayt) shall suffer a great affliction and they shall be forcefully expelled from their homes after my death; then there will come people from the East carrying black flags, and they will ask for some good to be given to them, but they shall be refused service; as such, they will wage war and emerge victorious, and will be offered that which they desired in the first place, but they will refuse to accept it, until a man from my family (Ahlul-Bayt) appears to fill the Earth with justice as it has been filled with corruption. So whoever reachs that (time) aught to come to them even if crowling on the ice/snow."

Sunni ref: Sunan Ibn Majah, V2, Tradition #4082, also in the History Tabari

The Messenger of Allah said: "The world will not perish until a man among the Arabs appears whose name matches my name."

Sunni reference: Sahih Tirmidhi, V9, P7

The Messenger of Allah said: "Mahdi from my family will bring about a revolution and will fill the world with justice and equity beforewhich it was filled up with injustice and inequity."
Sunni references:

1. Musnad Ahmad Ibn Hanbal, V1, P84
2. Jami'us Sagheer, by al-Suyuti, PP 2,160
3. al-Urful Vardi, by al-Suyuti, P2
4. Kanzul Ummal, V7 P186
5. Aqd al-Durar Fi Akhbaar al-Mahdi al-Muntazir, V12, Chapter 1,
6. al-Bayan fi Akhbar Sahib al-Zaman, By Ganji Shafi'i, Chapter 12
7. al-Fusool al-Muhimmah, by Ibn Sabbagh Maliki, Chapter 12
8. Arjahul Matalib, by Ubaidallah Hindi hanafi, P380
9. Muqaddimah, by Ibn Khaldoon, P266

Also Ahmad Ibn Hanbal narrated that:
The Prophet (PBUH) said: "Allah will bring out from concealment Mahdi from my Family and Progent before the Day of Judgement, even if only one day were to remain in the life of the world, and he will spread on this earth justice, and equity and eradicate tyranny and opression."

1. Sunni reference: Musnad Ahmad Ibn Hanbal, v1, p99

Ibn Majah in his Sunan quotes Mohammad Ibn Hanafiyyah and Imam Ali saying that the Holy Prophet (PBUH) said:
"Mahdi is from our Ahlul-Bayt, no doubt Allah will enforce his Amr (appearance) within a night (i.e., his coming is very unpredicted)."
Sunni reference: Sunan Ibn Majah, V2, P269

The more recent fatwa in this issue is given in Mecca by the Muslim World League (Rabitatul `Alamul Islami) on Oct. 11, 1976 (23 Shawwal 1396). This fatwa states that more than twenty companions narrated traditions concerning al-Mahdi, and gives a list of those scholars of Hadith who have transmitted these narrations, and those who have written books on al-Mahdi. The fatwa states:

Why the world Muslims are waiting for Imam Mehdi? The answer is the following::

In 1901 the Jewish banker Mizray Crasow and two other Jewish influential leaders came to visit Abdul Hameed,
they offered to give him:

1)Paying all the debts of the Ottoman state.
2)Building the Navy of the Ottoman state.
3)35 Million Golden Leers without interest to support the prosperity of the Ottoman state.
In Exchange for
1)Allowing Jews to visit Palestine anytime they please, and to stay as long as they want "to visit the holy sites."
2)Allowing the Jews to build settlements where they live, and they wanted them to be located near Jerusalem.
Abdul Hameed refused to even meet them, he sent his answer to them through Tahsin Pasha, and the answer was "Tell those impolite Jews that the debts of the Ottoman state are not a same, France has debts and that does not effect it. **Jerusalem became a part of the Islamic land when Omar Bin Alkhattab took the city and I am not going to carry the historical same of selling the holy lands to the Jews and betraying the responsibility and trust of my people. May the Jews keep their money, the Ottoman's will not hide in castles built with the money of the enemies of Islam.".... The Jews did not give up on Abdul Hameed. later in the same year, 1901, the founder of the zionist movement, Theodor Hertzil, visited Istanbul and tried to meet Abdul Hameed. Abdul Hameed refused to meet him and he told his Head of The Ministers Council "Advise Dr. Herzil not to take any further steps in his project. I can not give away a handful of the soilof this land for it is not my own, it is for all the Islamic Nation. The Islamic Nation that fought Jihad for the sake of this land and they have watered it with their blood. The Jews may keep their money and millions. If the Islamic Khalifa State is one day destroyed then they will be able to take Palestine without price! But while I am alive, I would rather push a sword into my body than see the land of Palestine cut and given away from the Islamic State. This is something that will not be, I will not start cutting own bodies while we are alive." Ater this, the Jews turned to the British to turn their dreams into reality.**
The Western world encouraged the Bay of Tunisia to revolt against the Ottoman state (Khilafat) in 1877 and so he did. In 1881 France occupied Tunisia, in 1882 Britain occupied Egypt. Later the netherland invaded Indonesia, Russia invaded Central Asia, Britain expanded deeper into India and Sudan . and it appeared like the West is about to crush the Islamic world. Finally, on On Tuesday the 27th of April 1909, the 240 members of the Ottoman senate agreed under the pressure of the National Young Turks to remove Abdul Hameed from power. Senator Sheikh Hamdi Afandi Mali wrote the Fatwa for the removalThe Ottoman Senate approve it. Here is the translation of that Fatwa:
"If the Imam (leader) of the Muslims took the important religious issue from the legislative books and collected those books, wasted the money of the state and engaged in agreements that contradicted the Islamic law, killed, arrested, exiled the people for no reason, then promised not to do it again and still did it to harm the conditions of Muslims all around the Islamic world then this leader is to be removed from office. If his removal will bring better conditions than his staying then he has the choice of resigning or being removed from office."
The Sheikh of Islam Mohammad Dia' Aldin Afandi
The Fatwa is very strange and any person can see that the conditions set in it do not fit Abdul Hameed's deeds and action/ Afterwards the Head of The Ministers Council, Tawfiq Pasha was called to tell Abdul Hameed about the decision. He refused to do so. So they sent him a group of four people; Aref Hikmat, AramAfandi (Armenia), As'ad Tobatani and

Emanuel Qrasow (Jesis). As they entered his office, they found him standing calmly., Aref Hikmat read the Fatwa to him, then As'd Tobatani came forward and said "The nation has removed you from your office.", Abdul Hameed became angry and said "The nation has remove me from my office, that is okay ... but why did you bring the Jew to the Quarters of the Khilafa?" and he pointed Qrasow. Obviously that was the point of payback, Abdul Hameed rejected selling Palestine to the Jews, and now they show him that they were a part of his removal. A challenge in the face of Abdul Hameed and the face of Islamic Nation. ....The National Young Turks got power and Mustafa Kemal Ataturk cancelled the Islamic Khilafa in 1924. That was the end of a united leadership for Muslims for 1300 years.[2] The West had succeded fully and Jews paid the price for protecting them and giving them shelter in Islamic world from Morocco to Turkey after Spain's inquisition and other European Atrocities against the Jews.

The Literary Digest, October 14, 1922, p. 50
But alongwith Western powers and Jews there were some secret Jews who were conspiring against the Khilafa.
Kamal Ataturk was one of them. He was not even a Turk.. He was a Doenmeh (secret Jew)...
He achieved the objective of not the Turks but of the Doenmehs who slowly took over the Ottoman State by openly converting to and practicing Islam but secretly practicing their old religion.. . He was not a Turk, let alone 'Father of the Turks'...
He was a Doenmeh who wore first a Muslim mask, then a Turkish mask..
[3]

A Spanish Jew by ancestry, an orthodox Moslem by birth and breeding, trained in a German war college, a patriot, a student of the campaigns of the world's great generals, including Napoleon, Grant and Lee - these are said to be a few outstanding characteristics in the personality of the new "Man on Horseback" who has appeared in the Near East. He is a real dictator, the correspondents testify, a man of the type which is at once the hope and fear of nations torn to pieces by unsuccessful wars. Unity and power have come back to Turkey largely through the will of Mustafa Kemal Pasha.
....
There was the pasha himself, tall, still young, good-looking, narrow-hipped, wide-shouldered, with gray, rather sad eyes that spoke eloquently of his Spanish-Jewish ancestry - for Kemal, like Enver Pasha, tho an orthodox Moslem, is descended from those Spanish-Jewish families that, given by Christianity the tolerant choice between death, conversion and exile, found asylum and happiness in the Sultan's domains - and with strong, high-veined hands, broad and flat across the wrist - the hands of an artist, a dreamer, yet, too, those of a doer, a man who knows how to clout his dreams into facts.[4]

This was the origin of the most important group, numerically and

---

[2] From an article is a paraphrased transcript of a series of four lectures delivered by Gharam Allah Al-Ghamdy to the Muslim Student Association at the University of Southern California between November 1991 and January 1992.

[3] The Literary Digest, October 14, 1922, p. 50

[4]

The Secret Jews, Joachim Prinz, Random House, 1973, p. 118-122

28

historically, of Islamic Marranos. The faithful Mohammedan call these hidden Jews "doenmehs", the renegades. ...... Over the years the 'doenmeh' movement became firmly established in Asia Minor. In the nineteenth century the sect was estimated to have twenty thousand members. Salonika remained its main seat until that city became Greek in 1913.

.... The Secret Jews, Joachim Prinz, Random House, 1973, p. 118-122

The revolt of the Young Turks in 1908 against the authoritarian regime of Sultan Abdul Hamid began among the intellectuals of Salonika. It was from there that the demand for a constitutional regime originated. Among the leaders of the revolution which resulted in a more modern government in Turkey were Djavid Bey and Mustafa Kemal. Both were ardent 'doenmehs'. Djavid Bey became minister of finance; Mustafa Kemal became the leader of the new regime and he adopted the name of Ataturk. His opponents tried to use his 'doenmeh' background to unseat him, but without success. Too many of the Young Turks in the newly formed revolutionary Cabinet prayed to Allah, but had as their real prophet Shabtai Zvi, the Messiah of Smyrna.

Let us ignore the case of those who are secular (essentially, anti-religion). Ignorance of or negligence toward religion on their part is understandable. In different societies there are many types of people who are secular or anti-religion. Even in our Muslim societies, there are so-called "secular Muslims" - that is, essentially "anti-religion Muslims." It is such a ridiculous as well as pathetic situation. But we will deal with this aspect on another occasion.

The reality is that secularism, atheism, agnosticism, nationalism, socialism, or capitalism does not give us such as an effective, balance, comprehensive, and coherent framework of moral and ethical standard that in aggregate is beneficial for us. Some may raise the question, what then is the secret of the dazzling success of the West? Is their ethical foundation and moral values ineffective or useless?

We have to analyze these questions at two levels. At one level we have to deal with those who either are not fanatical against a central role of religion in human life or do not have a strong position on this issue one way or another. They generally have a different perspective about religion. Then there are those who would like to see religion as central to human life, among whom Muslims are supposed to be included. The discussion at the first level is important, but its scope is different. Our focus in this article is the second group of people.

Those who identify themselves as Muslims have a well-defined set of ideals and principles as well as a framework of moral and ethical standard. There is no need for or room of blind faith in Islam. Islam doesn't recognize or dignify blind faith and that is why it educates us in no ambiguous terms that to believe in Islam means that we should embrace Islam based on knowledge and understand and in its totality - that is, its philosophy, vision, values and laws. And if we do accept Islam, we should make a sincere and committed effort to organize our entire life according to Islam.

We may have doubts or vacillation about it. Islam fully recognizes

29

our liberty and invites us to the same effect to work toward removing such doubts or vacillation. If such doubts or vacillation cannot be overcome or resolved, why should we accept Islam? What is really then the need to believe in Islam? What is the reason or benefit of such faith and identity? What is the meaning and value of being a Muslim with such doubt, hesitation or ambivalence? Therefore, we need to be clear and honest to ourselves that those who have such ambivalence about Islam neither they will benefit from Islam, nor will they benefit the Muslims or humanity at large.

Let us now briefly discuss the case of those who sincerely believe in Islam. What is the reason behind the moral breakdown of our society, the majority of which are intimately identified with Islam. What is the explanation of the fragility and decadence of such society? Whatever view we hold about the Western societies and whether we have any interest or not in engaging ourselves in a comparative analysis, there is a clear criteria for us as Muslims to evaluate our problems, and that criteria is Islam.

Let us ask ourselves a few more pertinent questions? Why our society has become so unstable? Is there any solution of this in Islam? As Muslims are we facilitators or hindrance in this context? What is the reason behind widespread poverty, deprivation, exploitation and oppression in our society (please ignore that such problems also exist in other societies)? Is Islam a failure in this case; or, do we have these problems due to Islam; or, is it that it is because of us these problems persist? Why corruption, bribery and violent conflict so rampant in our society? Should we place the blame for these as well on Islam?

Should we ignore our worldly problems and cherish our success in the life hereafter by attributing these problems to destiny? Why the control and authority in our societies in the hands of individuals, parties, or groups that have absolutely no integrity? Is Islam's teaching unambiguous in these regards? Why the precious infants in various parts of the Muslim world have to die prematurely due to malnutrition or diseases? Why do we still bear the curse of illiteracy? In the context of all these, what really is the power and benefit of our Iman (belief), Amal (action), and Taqwa (Allah-consciousness)? Does Islam then teach us to abandon this world in favor the life hereafter? Do we really expect to represent Islam to the humanity while we are humiliated, subjugated, dependent, or problem-ridden on one hand, and a laughing stock of the world as we seek the aid, recognition, and status from the West?

Let us ignore others, but is there really any effective answer from the vast number of pious Muslims - who devoutly perform prayer and fasting - to all these problems? Only Allah knows as to which month of Ramadan will be the last one in our life. Yet, if we are to deal with the problems mentioned above, it is vitally important that we understand Taqwa's triangular connection based on the month of Ramadan, fasting, and the Qur'an as the guidance. This connection should held us understand and motivate better that Taqwa, Ramadan, and the Qur'an are not for a ritual-oriented life, but a value-based, action-oriented life for us, which is also for the betterment of the humanity.

Let us welcome this blessed month of Ramadan with that spirit and
awareness, and channel this Akhirah-bound life to the desired
direction by seeking and enhancing our Taqwa that would help us build
a dynamic Islamic life. [5]

*We all know how that first four Khalifas (Caliphs) (God be pleased with them) were
elected and none of them were any direct descendent
of any one of them. In fact they were elected in a way
of Islamic Democracy, where people had right to
elect their leader in the way of Islam. Here Islamic
way is the supreme. Thus Muslims and their leaders
had no right to cross the boundary of Islam, the law of Islam,
which derive from the Holy Quran and Sunna. Bellow are some
scholarly quotation from <img align=center src="http://www-
personal.umich.edu/~luqman/graphics/bis.gif">:*

Recently ideas like "Islamic democracy" and "Democracy in Islam" have been
floating around, significantly missing, however, was a fundamental or
theoretical exploration of this subject rather than concentrating on
similarities and differences in the respective features of the Islamic
political system and democracy.

   In this article I am examining whether Islam and democracy are compatible
or mutually exclusive. So my specific topic is : "Are Islam and Democracy
compatible?" and as a result :"Can they co-exist or not? Is there a
fundamental difference between them or just superficial differences of
terminology?"

   There is no doubt that similarities exist between Islam and Democracy, as
one brother noted: "I thought that Islam is very close to western democracy
as far as selection of the leader and making the leader answerable to the
Muslims, is concerned." It is equally obvious that there are differences
between them. All democrats agree that the people can allow alcohol
consumption if they chose so, while all muslims agree that they can not.

   What I am examining here is the theoretical compatibility of Islam and
Democracy i.e. granting that there are similarities can they really agree,
co-exist, or co-operate? or despite there differences can there be a
compromise?

   In other words, while things can look quite similar or different
superficially, what really controls their relationship is the uncompatability
of their fundamental concepts and theories.

   Let us define each of them first:

---

[5] Mohammad Omar Farooq
Associate Professor of Economics and Finance
Upper Iowa University

* Islam (in my description of Islam here, I will stick to the general concepts that are agreed upon between Muslims and can not accept difference of opinion) is a total way of life. It claims the right to regulate the whole life of the human beings; all human beings regardless of there religions. As such it includes a belief and systems for both public and private life. The sovereignty, the right to define these systems, in Islam is exclusively for Allah.

Allah says in Quran: "Did you see that who made his opinion (desire) a god, would you be responsible for him? Do you think that most of them hear or comprehend; they are just like animals, they are even worse"(Al Furqan). Ibn Katheer, in his exegsis, comments on this verse: "So whenever he (man) leans towards something it becomes his religion and opinion."

Allah also says: "Hukm (ruling) is only for Allah, He defines right and He is the best arbiter." (Al'an'am) and says: "No, by your Lord they will not believe until they ask for your judgement in whatever happens between them" (Al Nisa3)

These verses are explicit in defining Allah as the Sovereign. The word "Hukm" means in arabic either the exercise of political authority (governance) or giving orders and defining values. It means here giving orders and defining actions as good or bad (since political authority can not be attributed to Allah). So "Hukm" (rule) here means the legislative not the executive power. Executive powers is for the people who appoint a person to exercise it. Rasool Allah (saw) said "Whomever gives allegiance to a ruler (Imam)
should vie to obey him as hard as he can." So it is the people's promise of allegiance to a person that obligates them to follow his orders i.e. they are the source of the rulers executive authority.

* Democracy: is only a system of government. It does not claim or try to be a belief or an economic system for example. It is defined both in linguistic and in political terminology as the RULE of PEOPLE. So in a democratic system of government the people have the sovereignty (legislative) and executive authorities. That is they have the right to define the constitution and laws or what is known philosophically as defining actions as good or bad. They also have the right to appoint the ruler. (While, Islam gives the political authority to the people, it gives the sovereignty SOLELY to Allah.) This is how its founders defined it but they differed on how to apply it. So they divided it into three categories:

1- Direct Democracy: (which is considered the perfect ideal for democracy) where all citizens gather in a public forum to vote on laws, appointments of judges and public officials and to conduct foreign and domestic policy. Rosseau, the French philosopher, considered this the only method to practice people's sovereignty and any other method is not and does not fulfill Democracy. This form was practiced in Athens in the Hellenistic period.

2- Constituent (representative) Democracy: where people elect a number of deputies to form a parliament and conduct government. While this practice does not agree with democracy or its definition since the people are not exercising their legislative or executive powers, democrats considered the parliament as a representative of the people's will and the deputies as those conducting government on behalf of the people. Which is definitely not the same as the ideal they claim to embody (people's rule). Look for example at the problem of incumbency and the controversy arising from it as incumbents lose touch with their constituents and still hold their positions on the strength of their incumbency (connections, money...) There is also, the general common knowledge that secular/democratic politicians are a self-serving elite and the fact of a disproportionate role of companies and rich families and elites on the government in the major democracies of the world (Japan is a flagrant example but the rest are not different, only not that obvious). However, they had to adopt such a flawed process since the practice of direct democracy is impossible. So to paper out over that discrepancy they invented the "power of attorney" theory. Thy said that the attorney/deputy acts on behalf of his constituent and his actions are legally committing for his client. Building on that they said that the people in this system place individuals in both the legislative and executive authorities as attorneys to legislate and govern on their behalf and their actions are representative and binding for the people. This was still a false rational since no body can appoint or claim to be an attorney for somebody in his will regarding things which are yet to happen in the future. "I might agree with you today but nothing guarantee that tomorrow!!" So to claim that you represent my will for a legislative period is a false pretense. In the end and since they were unable to show how the constituent democracy relate to the theoretical ideal of democracy western jurists were inclined to state that the constituent democracy is not the result of logical theories or legal resolutions but it is an empirical system refined through long practice.

3- Indirect democracy: this brand evolved as a result of the above contradictions. Here it was proposed to involve the people in practicing the some of their sovereignty as a step in the direction of the ideal. So it gave the people some rights such as plebiscite, petition, write-in election, recall of a deputy or impeachment of the president. Yet this kind of democracy admits by its own definition to with hold some of the people's rights. Since it gives the people some of the sovereignty but not ALL of it.

From these definitions, and regardless of the contradictions in democracy, it is clear that Islam and democracy are mutually exclusive. While Islam will not give the sovereignty to anybody but Allah, democracy claims (at least in theory) to give it all to the people. This position, on top of being impractical, is a fundamental difference with Islam. As such there can not be a compromise between democracy and Islam. No bridge can be established over this gap. Actually Allah repudiate such a notion as democracy in Quran in no uncertain terms. Allah says: "Rule (Muhammed PBUH) between them according to what we revealed and do not follow there leanings, and beware not to be led astray".

In other words, regardless of the end result of the legislative process, the government system in Islam limit Sovereignty to Allah while Democracy vest it in the people. This is a fundamental and unbridgeable difference. In other words, The contradiction is not that some democracies allow Alcohol consumption, rather it is that democracy gives the people the RIGHT to decide on that. Government system in Islam gives that right SOLELY to Allah. So even if a democracy decides to prohibit alcohol consumption (based on the will of the majority) still the contradiction persists because the power to legislate

33

rests in the wrong place.[6]

Why we have no Khilafat now? Who are responsible for destruction of Khalifat?
Are we true Muslim? Are we following true path of Islam. The followings
are some scholarly answer from Mr. Yussuf:

It is also reported through Abu Ubaidah (R) and Muadh ibn-Jabal
     (R) that Rasulullah (SAW) said:

"This affair (Islam) began as prophethood and mercy. Afterwards it
will become khilafat and mercy, and then tyrannical kingdom and then
there will appear imperialism, rebellion and dissension in the
world...." (Baihaqi)
  Which student of Islamic history can deny the truth of these prophetic
traditions?

    "You (Muslims) shall follow the practices of those who were
    before you, span by span and cubit by cubit, so much so that
    if they entered the hole of a lizard, you will follow them."
    (Ahmad)

And how true was Rasulullah (SAW):

    Abdullah bin Amr bin al-Aas (R) reported Rasulullah (SAW) as
    saying, "My Ummah will undergo and experience all those
    conditions which were suffered by Bani-Israel in a manner of
    resemblance in which a shoe of a pair resembles the other
    shoe." (Tirmidhi)

In Surah Bani-Israel, Allah says:

    "And We decreed for the Children of Israel in the Scripture: Ye
    verily will work corruption in the earth twice, and ye will
    become great tyrants. So when the time for the first of the
    two came, We roused against you slaves of Ours of great might
    who ravaged (your) country, and it was a threat performed.
    Then We gave you once again your turn against them, and We
    aided you with wealth and children and made you more in
    soldiery, (Saying): if ye do good, ye do good for your own
    souls, and if ye do evil, it is for them (in like manner). So
    when the time for the second (of the judgements) came (We
    roused against you others of Our slaves) to ravage you, and
    to enter the Temple even as they entered it the first time,
    and to lay waste all that they conquered with an wasting. It
    may be that your Lord will have mercy on you, but if ye
    repeat (the crime) We shall repeat (the punishment), and We
    have appointed hell a dungeon for the disbeliever."

The first of these great chastisements came with the annexation of the
northern kingdom (Israel) in 722 B.C.E. by the Assyrians. Most of the
Israelites (lost tribes) were exiled. This process of chastisement

---

[6] <img align=center src="http://www-personal.umich.edu/~luqman/graphics/bis.gif">
tmur@tnc.airtouch.com

continued with the annexation of the southern kingdom (Judah) in 586 B.C.E. by the Babylonians, under the leadership of King Nebuchadnezzar. He ravaged the Temple of Solomon and exiled all Jews to Babylon. The first period of chastisement came to an end with the fall of Babylon to Dzul Qarnain (King Cyrus) of Persia in 538 B.C.E, when he permitted Bani-Israel to return home. Dzul Qarnain was indeed a messiah to them. (Ref: Isaiah 45:1, Bible) (Note: Dzul Qarnain was a rightly guided King, a Muslim (in the original sense) who believed in Allah, much in difference to Zoroastrians of the later days. Today's Zoroastrianism has retained little of the original teachings, brought by true prophet(s) of Allah.) The rebuilding of the Solomon's Temple (later came to be known as the Second Temple or the Temple of Zerubbabel) was completed in 516 B.C.E. Bani-Israel remained a strong religious community during the subsequent period and regained political freedom briefly only under the Maccabees.

The second period of their great chastisement came after &Icircsa (AS) was rejected as a prophet of Allah. The Temple was demolished in 70 C.E. and Bani-Israel banned from entering Jerusalem. Since then, until the establishment of the modern state of Israel, they remained the "wandering Jews", persecuted everywhere by the Trinitarians (Note: Modern world Jewry has two essential components: Ashkenazim and Sephardim. The first of these, Ashkenazim, traces its root to the Khazar kingdom, once thriving between the Caspian and Black Seas, to the north of Caucasus mountains. Its people converted to Judaism ca. 740 C.E. Read: Arthur Koestler's "The Thirteenth Tribe"; and Prof. Abraham Polliak's (of Hebrew University, Jerusalem) writings.)

The Ummah of Muhammad (SAW) was also two components - the Arabs and non-Arabs. The Islamic world was initially extended through the Umayyads and the Abbasids, both Arabs. But with the worldly power of Islam increasing at a faster pace, the spiritual part of Islam could not keep up with such a pace, and, instead, declined leading to weakening of the central power structure. As a result of this vacuum in power among the Arabs, non-Arab tribes arose from north-east and penetrated to the center of the Islamic world. These were the Kurds and Seljuk Turks of the eleventh century who revived the Islamic world at a time when the political power of Islam was defeated by the Crusaders. Similarly, the Afghans marched into India.

The Ummah of Muhammad (SAW) has also undergone two periods of chastisement.

The first chastisement of the Muslims came in the late 11th century (1099 C.E.), and continued to the 13th century. First, it was in the hands of the Christian Crusaders (just as Allah had chastised the Israelites before with Kafir Assyrians). More than 70,000 unarmed Muslim civilians, mostly elderly men, women and children, were massacred by the savage Christian crusaders in Jerusalem. (Read: Anthony Nutting's account on christian cruelties in "The Arabs.") This was the time when the Abbasid Caliphate was already in its death-bed. Eventually, the non-Arab leadership of Sultan Salahuddin Ayyubi (RA) rescued the Muslims. Then came the Mongol invasion. The Mongols, after ravaging initially Afghanistan and Iran, and finally the capital city of Baghdad, in 1258 C.E., massacred millions of Muslims. (This was very similar to Nebuchadnezzar's invasion and destruction of Jerusalem in 586 B.C.E.) The heart of the Muslim land was so much devastated that it reminded us of that person among Bani-Israel who while passing through the ruins of Jerusalem remarked: "Who is going to revive this dead city?" At the end, Allah showed His mercy on us.

The Abbasid Caliphate collapsed with the fall of Malik Mu'tassim, the Muslim Caliph. In 1260 C.E. the non-Arab Muslims checked the Tartar invasion of the western Islamic world. Since then the leadership of the Muslim Ummah has been transferred to the non-Arabs, especially to the posterity's of Tartars. One branch of Tartars - the Taimuri Turks took control over India, the other branch - Uthmaniya Turks, took control over the Asia Minor and the northern Africa. This second branch revived the institution of the Caliphate (Khilafat).

With the birth of European Imperialism and colonization of non-European territories, the wings of the vast Muslim empire (to the east and the west) were first lost, while the heart (central) land managed to survive. This process of colonization began the second period of chastisement of the Ummah. First, the feeble Andalusia (Spain) was lost to the Catholics. With the Spanish Inquisition not a single Muslim soul survived in Andalusia. In subsequent centuries Indonesia, the Philippines (Mindanao), Malaysia and India were lost. So were lost the entire North Africa, including Muslim countries of West and East Africa. During this period, although the Uthmaniya Empire managed to keep its central (Turkey and West Asiatic) territories, it became the "Sick Man of Europe", with a total incompetence to protect its once held vast territories. The last days of Uthmaniya Empire were similar to those experienced by the Abbasids nearly eight centuries ago. Muslims were once again without any leader or guide.

One interesting feature of the Islamic Khilafah is about the capital city of the Islamic Empire. During Rasulullah's (SAW) time, it was in Madinah. It was then moved to Kufa during Ali's (R) Caliphate. During the Umayyad period, the capital moved further away to Damascus. It moved to Baghdad during the Abbasid period, and finally to Istanbul during the Uthmaniya period, moving further away from the heartland of Islam - Makkah and Madinah.

After the World War I, a ruthless surgery was done on the body of Muslim Ummah. With the single exception of the Turkish mainland, the entire Middle East was divided among the European marauding invaders. It was the fulfillment of our Prophet, Muhammad's (SAW) saying:
> "There will come a time in which the nations of the world will invite one another to invade you (Muslims) in the same manner as a person who prepares a feast, calls his guests to partake of the slaughtered"

The greatest blow to the Ummah came with the establishment of the state of Israel in Palestine and the capture of Jerusalem by the Zionists at the end of the Six-day war in 1967. This alone resulted in the uprooting of millions of Palestinian Muslims. In this way, the second retribution upon the Muslims (similar to the experience of the Jews, when they were totally displaced from Jerusalem and its neighboring territories after 70 C.E.) was completed.

In the post-colonial period, the entire Muslim world was fragmented into pieces, with artificial boundaries. People, who have for centuries lived as brothers, were, all on a sudden, forced to believe that they were ethnically different Thanks to the Divide and Rule policy of the European Imperialists; Even an ethnic community was divided up among many nation-states. Thanks also to the western education system, and the destruction of Islamic Institutions of learning during the imperialistic rule of our territories. The entire political, economic, social system was replaced with an alien system in direct conflict with previously established institutions within the Islamic world.

European military and economic adventurism left in its wake a trail of blood and human misery. The once powerful Islamic world was reduced to "backward", "poor" countries, always at the mercy of the West for their mere survival. What a tragedy What a price we are paying for the mistakes/blunders of our ancestors. (Read: Prof. Ali Mazrui's (of the University of Michigan, Ann Arbor) books for the dire effects of colonization.)

In the newly emerged nation-states, power was given to those who either had previously collaborated with the imperialistic governments, or to those who were culturally "French-fried" (western, secularized groups of individuals). (I am aware of the fact that in certain cases, Muslims earned their independence through bloody revolution, e.g., Algeria. Yet, the French-Algerian war was, in the end, a battle of will power. I dare say that were the Franks not satisfied with the credentials of the Algerian secular, revolutionaries, they would have prolonged the war.) In a nutshell, power was given to every John Doe except the ones to whom it truly belongs, namely the Islamists. (Read: William Hunter's, and Lord Cromer's reports submitted to the English Crown; Maryam Jameelah's books; Dr. Kaleem Siddiqui's essays.)

As a result of this western imposed political surgery and the artificial implantation of foreign, atheistic, materialistic, bankrupt philosophies in our body of the Ummah, our leaders have tried everything that the West had produced. from western style democracy (parliamentary or Presidential forms) to socialism/communism to military oligarchy, but Islam. The end result has been a dismal performance in all of our nation- states Behind the facade of modernization/westernization/urbanization/ progress we have turned our countries into consumer-markets for the western goods. We have obviously failed to earn true independence for our people. Thanks to our western masters and their psychotic stooges. (Read: Dr. Ali Shariati's and Prof. Mazrui's books.)

With the dismemberment of Pakistan in 1971 (as a result of our failure to live as brothers under western pretext), many amongst our Umma mistakenly thought that the worst was over and there remains only hopes for Islamic revitalization. Their hope was not without justification since according to the law of Providence, when our condition had become so degraded, radical attempts to revive Islam were always initiated. One cannot ignore the struggle of Iranian masses to establish an Islamic government, which culminated in the overthrow of the despotic, playboy ruler in 1979, and the struggle of the Afghan Mujahidins in their desire to live under Islam, and many others. And what a price our people had to pay through the imposed war on our territories by the evil empires and their servants. Millions of our people were killed by the Russians and the Baathists. Several millions were uprooted from their soil creating the largest refugee problem the world has ever known. With the defeat of the Russian savages by Muslim Mujahidin in Afghanistan (which was mostly responsible for the collapse of the Soviet empire) many expected the end of foreign incursion into our territories.

Unfortunately, with the genocide of Muslims in Bosnia, the recent killings of Muslims in India (after the destruction of the Babri Mosque) in the hands of Hindus, the burning of Muslim villagers by Tamil Hindus in Srilanka, the carnage in Kashmir by the Indian Military, the gang rape of tens of thousands of Muslim women in Bosnia and destruction of their homes and properties by the Christian forces, the uprooting of Rohinga Muslims from Miyanmar by the Buddhists, the killings of Muslims in Lebanon and the Occupied territories by the Phalangists and the Zionists in Israel, the destruction of (memorable) Baghdad by non-Muslim armies and their hosts in the Arabian peninsula, the killings of tens of thousands of Azeri Muslims by the Armenian Christians, [and now in 1996 the slaughter of the Chechens in the Caucas] it is crystal clear that our second major chastisement has not yet ended. And much more may be in the coming. May Allah protect us. It is true that most of these sufferings could have been avoided had we genuine leaders in our midst, rather than lackeys of the "East" or the "West", who are sometimes worst than our non-Muslim enemies.

The process of revitalization, therefore, may take a long time.

In the past, the process of revitalization was always aimed at the defense and protection of the Muslim land. The religion of Islam in itself was not much threatened (with the possible exception of our intellectual demise, caused as a result of destruction of Baghdad with its many libraries of higher learning's by the Mongols). During this century alone, what we are witnessing is something new - vicious attacks against our very deen, Islam. (One does not have to be an expert to come to this conclusion. (Shaytan) Rushdie's "Satanic Verses" is one such attempt to mock whatever Islam stands for. Even one can see such attacks by browsing the computer nets, esp. soc.culture.india, where the (cow- worshipping) spiteful, polytheistic Hindus have been displaying their demented lowliness.

These vicious attacks against the very religion of Islam is very saddening for any Muslim. Many have tried to alienate by distancing themselves from Islam, fear of being labeled as "fundamentalists" (a term dragged from deranged Christianity and has nothing to do with Islam). Some are trying to assimilate like the Diaspora Jews of old. This reminds me the attempt of a crow who tried to become a peacock by putting some feathers of it. They forget the lessons of history: those experienced through the Diaspora Jews of Europe for about two millennia, and the more recent one involving the Bosnian Muslims. Read their history and learn from their experiences. (Education is the best

38

medicine for all, esp. those suffering from amnesia. Every possession that you have (including your very self) can be enslaved, except your mind, unless you let it happen. Know that once you allow your mind to be controlled, there is nothing left of you to be controlled. Therefore, let us not allow our mind to be controlled by others.) Assimilation has NEVER worked Pure and simple.

Muhammad (SAW) once remarked:

"A time will come to men when the patient of them in his religion will be like the one who holds burning coal in his hand." (Tirmidhi)

Yes, I am sure that Islam, in recent years, has become like a "burning coal", too difficult to hold onto or nurture. Yet, it is necessary for all Muslims to hold on to it. Because, it is in Islam there lies hopes for Muslims, in particular, and for humanity, in general. The Western society can gain a lot through its contact with Islam. Islam can truly solve many man-made problems haunting the western society. That is why it has become more important than ever before to work towards revitalization of our nation.

We need to form an Islamic society which protects the rights of our people and those of non-Muslims, so that every individual is free to practice their religion in their own ways. Let that society be a safe haven for all who wants to lead a moral life. Let that society be a model for the rest of humanity to copy. No, friend it is no utopia. Our forefathers brought about that society and we can Inshallah do it, too. Don't forget that is what Allah intended for us through the teachings of all the prophets/messengers: establishment of peace and justice. Despite the conspiracy of our enemies, no power can resist what Allah has intended for us. "They scheme and Allah doth scheme, and Allah is the Best of the schemers." Inshallah, tomorrow will be a better day for our children. Rasulullah stated that no matter what the kafirs do, they can NEVER succeed in annihilating us. (This hadith is narrated through Thauban (R) and is compiled by Imam Muslim (RA).) All the current sufferings will, Inshallah, end soon. We have already passed many obstacles (from imperialism) and are going through the last phase of the trouble arising out of dictatorship/dissension, etc. What is left is the establishment of Khilafat (as stated by the hadith, already quoted above). Let us work for it. Inshallah, those days are not far, when we, Muslims, retake control over our own affairs and Khilafa will again be established in the model of Rasulullah (SAW) and his rightly guided companions (R).

Know that kuffar is ever weak. Therefore, we should never give up hope in Allah, Let our goodness surpass the goodness of every other human beings on the face of the earth. Let us command the respect of others through our good deeds. Know that Muhammad (SAW) said, as reported by Abu Umama (R):

"When your good deed pleases you and evil deed grieves you, you are a Muslim (believer)." (Ahmad)

Abu Hurayra (R) reported from Rasulullah (SAW):

"Like for others whatever you like for yourself. You will become a perfect Muslim." (Tirmizi; Ahmad)

Abu Shuraih Khuzai' (R) related: "I asked, 'O Rasulullah (SAW), who is not a true believer?' He (SAW) replied: 'The man whose neighbors are in constant fear of his mischief and machinations." (Bukhari)

May Allah guide us to follow His deen and shun falsehood. May Allah weaken the hands of kuffar and ease our task in carrying out His commands. [7]

---

[7] Syed Yusuf
http://www.uidaho.edu/~yusuf921/
From: yusuf921@goshawk.csrv.uidaho.edu (Syed Yusuf)
Newsgroups: soc.religion.islam
Subject: Bani Isra'il punishment and Muslims' punishment identical
Date: 29 Jan 1996 08:36:57 -0800
Organization: On-and-On-Anon
Lines: 446
Sender: ariel@shellx.best.com
Approved: ariel@best.com
Message-ID: <4eit39$fuk@shellx.best.com>
NNTP-Posting-Host: shellx.best.com
Status: RO Moderator: ariel@best.com (Catherine Hampton)

The Islamic Khilafat (Caliphate)

The following universal acceptable quotations on Caliphate/Khilafah are from Syed Amir Ali; author of two great books at that time when there was no English book in Islam by any Islamic Scholar:

The Khelafat (or Caliphate), it is explained, is the Vicegerency of the Prophet; it is ordained by Divine Law for the perpetuation of Islam and the continued observance of its laws and rules.

For the existence of Islam, therefore, there must always be a Caliph (or Khalipha), an actual and direct representative of the last Prophet of Islam (peace be upon him and his descendent and his true companion).

It should be mentioned here that our Holy Prophet Muhammad (may peace be upon him) told during his Last Hajj Address from the top of the Jabal ul-Arafat (7th March, 632), some which are as follows:

" Ye people! Listen to my words and understand the same. Know that all Muslims are brothers unto one another. Ye are one brotherhood. Nothing which belongs to another is lawful unto his brother, unless freely given out of good-will. Guard yourselves from committing injustice."
"Neither any Arab is superior to any Non-Arab nor any Non-Arab is superior to any Arab; (Similarly) neither any black-man is preferable to any Whitman nor a Whitman is preferable to any black-man, and of course the only standard for ones superiority and nobleness is God-fearing."
"Let him that is present tell it unto him that is absent. Happily he that shall be told may remember better than he who hath heard it."

Who is a Caliph? As Christianity could yield obedience to but one Pope, so the Moslem world must yield obedience and allegation on all political and religion matter to but one lawful Caliph. But as three Popes have often pretended to the triple crown, so have three Ameer ul-Muslimin laid claim to supreme rule. After the down fall of the Ommeyyades in Asia and Africa (There was only and only one Caliph for entire land of the faithful Muslims consisting of Asia and Africa) Abdur Rahman, a member of that house fled to Spain through northern Africa and became head of independent state in Spain, while during Abbaside era the family Fatima (R. A.) established a Caliphate in Egypt and established the city Cairo there, and also the oldest modern university of this world the Al-Azhar university after the title of Fatima in Cairo. But none of the three Caliphs divided the Caliphate permanently but with a hope of unifying it in each one's command. And furthermore all the three families originated from one family, one tribe, the family of Prophet Abraham (A. S.), the family of Ismael (A. S.) lastly known as Koreish, the surnamed of Fihr, a descendant of Ma'add, son of Adnan who was a descendants of Ishmael (A. S.) flourished about the first century before Jesus Christ (A. S.). Adnan married the daughter of the Jurhumite chief, who possessed the title of malik or king of Mecca and the southern parts of Hijaz from the ruler of Yemen. After the Prophet, the Caliph is the Vicar and Lieutenant of the Prophet. He is more than a temporal ruler, he is a spiritual chief as well. The Caliph is thus designated the Imam (leader on religion affairs), his position being similar to that of the leader of the congregation at the public prayers.

These doctrines are enunciated in detail in most works on jurisprudence and scholastic theology. The Khilafat, it is explained, is the Vicegerency of the Prophet; it is ordained by Divine Law for the perpetuation of Islam and the continued observance of its laws and rules. For the existence of Islam, therefore, there must always be a Caliph, an actual and direct representative of the Master. The Immamate is the spiritual leadership; but the two dignities are inseparable; the Vicegerent of the Prophet is the only person entitled to lead the prayers when he can himself be present. No one else can assume his functions unless directly or indirectly "deputed" by him. Between the Imam and the mamun (1 This is the term uses in the Fatwai-Alamgiri. The individual follower is usually called the Muktadi) or congregation, there is a spiritual tie which binds the one to the other in the fealty to the Faith. There is no inconsistency between this dogma and the rule that there is no priesthood in Islam. Each man pleads for himself before his Lord, and each soul holds communion with God without the intermediation of any other human being. The Imam (leader) is the link between the individual worshipper and the evangel of Islam. This mystical element in the religion of Islam forms the foundation of its remarkable solidarity.

The above remarks serve to emphasis the statement in the Durr-ul-Mukhtar that Imamate is of two kinds, the Imamat-al-Kurba and the Imamat-as-Sughra, the supreme Headship and the minor derivative right to officiate at the devotions of the Faithful. The Imam al-Kabir, the supreme Pontiff, is the Caliph of the Sunny world. He combines in his person the spiritual and temporal authority which devolves on him as the vicegerent of the Master. Secular affairs are conducted by him in consultation with councilors as under the first four Caliphs, or as in later times, by delegates, collectively or individually. Similarly with religious and spiritual matters. But in the matter off public prayers, unless physically prostrate, he is bound to conduct the congregational service in person.

Among the Shiahs, even Friday prayers and prayers offered at the well-known festivals, may validly be performed individually and in private. According to the Sunny doctrines congregational prayers, where mosques or other places of public worship are accessible, are obligatory; abstention from attendance without valid reason is a sin, and the defaulters incur even temporal penalties. In Najd, under the rule of the Wahabis, who have been called the Convenanters of Islam, laggards were whipped into the mosque. And may be to-day under the king, his followers who designate themselves Ikhwan, or "Brothers in faith," pursue the same method for enforcing the observance of religious rites. Prayers bi'l jama'at being obligatory (farz'ain) naturally made the presence of the Imam absolutely obligatory. (1 There is absolute consensus on these points among the different Sunny schools. The Jurist Khalil ibn Ishak, the author of the monumental work on Maliki Law, enunciates the rules in the same terms as the Hanafis and the Shafeis). The Sunnis affirm that when stricken by his last illness the Prophet (Sm) deputed Abu Bakr to lead the prayers. On his death, but before he consigned to his grave, the Master's nomination was accepted by the "congregation" and Abu Bakr was installed as his vicegerent by the unanimous suffrage of the Moslems. And this has ever since been the universal practice in all regular lines. Amongst the qualifications necessary for occupying the pontifical seat, the first and most essential is that he must be a Moslem belonging to the Sunny communion, capable of exercising supreme temporal authority, free of all outside control. The Caliph being the spiritual and political head must be able to lead the prayers. The Sunnis do not require that the Imam should be ma`sum, or that he should be "the most excellent of mankind," nor do they insist on his descent from the Prophet. According to them he should be an independent ruler, without any personal defects, a man of good character, possessed of the capacity to conduct the affairs of State, and to lead at prayers. The early doctors, on the authority of a saying of the Prophet(Sm), have included a condition which comes at the end of the passage relating to the qualities necessary for the Imamate- viz., that the Caliph-Imam should be a Koreish by birth. The avowed object of inserting this condition, as is stated both in the Durr-ul-Mukhtar and the Radd-ul-Muhtar, was to nullify the Shiah contention that the Imamate was restricted to the House of Mohammed, the descendants of Ali and Fatima, and to bring in the first three Caliphs, and the Ommeyyade and the Abbaside Caliphs, into the circle of legitimate Imams. The great jurist and historian, Ibn Khaldun, (For many years Malikite Chief Kazi of Cairo) a contemporary of Tamerlane, who died in the year 1406 A. C., long before the House of Othman attained the Caliphate, has dealt at great length with this condition in his Mukaddamat (Prolegomena). He does not dispute the genuineness of the saying on which it is based, but explains that it was a mere recommendation which was due to the circumstances of the times. He points out that when the Islamic Dispensation was given to the world the tribe of Koreish were the most advanced and most powerful in Arabia; and in recommending or desiring that the temporal and spiritual guardianship of the Moslems should be confined to a member of his own tribe, the Prophet(Sm) was thinking of the immediate future rather than of laying down a hard and fast rule of succession. At that time a qualified and capable ruler of Islam could only be found among the Koreish; hence the recommendation that the Caliph and Imam should be chosen from among them This view eloquently expressed by one of the most learned of Sunny Jurisconsult is universally accepted by the modern doctors (the Mutakherin), that subject to the fulfillment of all other conditions the law imposes no tribal or racial restriction in the choice of an Imam. Abu Bakr before his death had nominated Omar his successor in the Vicegerency, and the appointment was accepted by the "universality" of the people, including the House of Mohammed(Sm). Omar died from the effects of a mortal wound inflicted on him by a Christian or Magian fanatic who considered himself aggrieved by the acts of this great Caliph. To avoid all imputation of favoritism Omar had, before his death, appointed an electoral committee consisting of six eminent members of the Moslem congregation to choose - his successor. Their choice fell on Osman, a descendant of Ommeyya, who was installed as Caliph with the suffrage of the people. On Osman's unhappy death, Ali, the son-in-law of the Prophet, who, according to the Shias, was entitled by right to the Imamate in direct succession to the Prophet, was proclaimed Caliph and Imam. The husband of Fatima(Ra) united in his person the hereditary right with that of election. But his endeavor to remedy the evils which had crept into the administration under his aged predecessor raised against him a host of enemies. Muawiyah, an Ommeyyade by descent, who held the governorship of Syria under Osman, raised the standard of revolt. Ali proceeded to crush the rebellion but, after an indecisive battle, was struck down by the hand of an assassin whilst at his devotions in the public Mosque of Kufa in Iraq. With Ali ended what is called by the early Sunny doctors of law and theologians, the Khilafat-al-Kamila, "the Perfect Caliphate," for in each case their title to the rulership of Islam was perfected by the universal suffrage of the Moslem nation. On Ali's death Muawiyah obtained an assignment of the Caliphate from Hasan, the eldest son of Ali, who had been elected to the office by the unanimous voice of the people of Kufa and its dependencies; and received the suffrage of the people of Syria to his assumption of the high office. This happened in 661 A.C. It should be noted here that the Ommeyyades and Hashimides were two offshoots from one common stock, that of Koreish. Bitter rivalry existed between these families which it was the great aim of the Prophet throughout his ministry to remove or reconcile. The Hashimides owe their designation to Hashim, the great grandfather of the Prophet(Sm.). His son Abdul Muttalib had several sons; one of them, Abbas(Ra), was the progenitor of the Abbaside Caliphs, Abu Talib, another son, was the father of Ali(Ra) the Caliph, whilst the youngest, Abdullah, was the Prophet's (Sm) father. Muawiyah was the first Caliph of the House of Ommeyya. On the death of Muawiyah's grandson, another member of the same family belonging to the Hakamite branch, named Merwan, assumed the Caliphate. Under his son Abdul Malik and grandson Walid, the Sunny Caliphate attained its widest expansion; it extended from the Atlantic to the Indian Ocean and from the Tagus to the sands of the Sahara and the confines of Abyssinia. In 749 A.C. Abu'l Abbas, surnamed Saffah, a descendant of Abbas, the uncle of the Prophet(Sm), overthrew the Ommeyyade dynasty and was installed as Caliph, in place of Merwan II, the last Pontiff of that House, in the Cathedral Mosque of Kufa, (part of present Iraq) where he received the Bai'at(The sacramental oath of fealty) of the people. He then ascended the pulpit, recited the public sermon which the Imam or his representative delivers at the public prayers. This notable address, religiously preserved by his successors, is to be found in the pages of the Arab historian Ibn-ul-Athir. It is in effect a long vindication of the rights of the children of Abbas to the Caliphate. Abu'l Abbas was henceforth the legitimate ruler of Sunny world and the rightful spiritual Head of the Sunny Church. His first six successors were men of remarkable ability; those who followed were of varying capacity, but a few possessed uncommon talent and learning. Mansur, the brother of Saffah, who succeeded him in the Caliphate, founded Baghdad, which became their capital and seat of Government, and was usually called the Dar-ul-Khilafat and the Dar-us-salam, "The Abode of the Caliphate or The Abode of Peace." Here the house of Abbas exercised undisputed spiritual and temporal authority for centuries. Their great rivals of Cairo became extinct in Saladin's time; the brilliant Ommeyyade dynasty of Cordova disappeared in the first decade of the eleventh century. The Almohades, the Almoravides, and the many Berber and Arab Dynasties which, on the decline of the Almoravides, followed each other in succession in Morocco, had no valid title to the headship of the Sunny Church. The right of the Abbaside to the Sunny Imamate stood unchallenged from the Atlantic to the Ganges, from the Black Sea and the Jaxartes to the Indian Ocean. In 493 of the Hegira (1099 A.C.) Yusuf bin Tashfin, the Almohade conqueror after the epoch-making battle of az-Zallaka, where the Christian hordes were decisively beaten, obtained from the Abbaside Caliph al-Muktadi, a formal investiture with the tittle of Ameer-al-Muslimin; and this was confirmed to him by the Caliph al-Mustazhir. It should be borne in mind that neither the "Caliphs" of Cordova nor any of the Moslem sovereigns in after ages assumed the dignity of the representative of the Prophet (Khalifat-ar-Rasul) or arrogated the tittle of Ameer-ul-Mominin. For full five centuries Baghdad was the center of all intellectual activity in Islam; and here the rules and regulations appertaining to the Caliphate, as also to other matters, secular and religious, were systematized. And the conception that the Caliph-Imam was the divinely-appointed *Vicegerent of the Prophet* became, as it is to-day, welded into religious life of the people. It will thus be seen that according to the Sunny doctrines the *Caliph is not merely a secular sovereign; he is the religious head of a Church and a commonwealth, the actual representative of Divine government (Ref: Suyuti).* The Abbaside Caliphate lasted for five centuries from its first establishment until the destruction of Baghdad by the Mongols in 1258 of the Christian era. At that time Musta'sim b'Illah was the Caliph, and he, together with his sons and the principal members of his family, perished in the general massacre; only those sections of the House of Abbas escaped the slaughter who were absent from the capital, or succeeded in avoiding detection. *For two years after the murder of Musta'sim b'Illah the Sunny world felt acutely the need of an Imam and Caliph;* both the poignancy of the grief at the absence of a spiritual Head of the faith, and the keenness of the necessity for a representative of the Prophet to bring solace and religious merit to the Faithful, are pathetically voiced by the Arab historian of the Caliphs (Ref: Ibid). The devotions of the living were devoid of that religious efficacy which is imparted to them by the presence in the world of an acknowledged Imam; the prayers for the dead were equally without merit. Sultan Baibars felt with the whole Sunny world the need of a Caliph and Imam. The right to the Caliphate had become vested by five centuries of undisputed acknowledgment in the House of Abbas; and a member of this family, Abu'l Kasim Ahmed, who had succeeded in making his escape from the massacre by the Mongols, was invited to Cairo for installation in the pontifical seat. On his arrival in the environs of Cairo, the Sultan, accompanied by the judges and great officers of State, went forth to greet him. The ceremony of installation is described as imposing and sacred. His descent had to be proved first before the Chief Kazi or Judge. After this was done, he was installed in the chair and acknowledged as Caliph, under the title of al-Mustansir b'Illah, "seeking the help of the Lord." The first to take the oath of Bai'at was the Sultan Baiber himself; next came the Chief Kazi (Judge) Taj-ud-din, the principal sheikhs and the ministers of state, and lastly the nobles, according to their rank. This occurred on May 12th, 1261, and the new Caliph's name was impressed on the coinage and recited in the Khutba. On the following Friday he rode to the mosque in procession, wearing the black mantle of the Abbaside (Black was the color of the Abbasides, white of the Ommeyyades and green of the Fatimides, the descendants of Mohammad (Sm)), and delivered the pontifical sermon. As his installation as the Caliph of the Faithful was now complete, he proceeded to invest the Sultan with the robe and diploma so essential in the eyes of the orthodox for legitimate authority. The Abbaside Caliphate thus established in Cairo lasted for over two centuries and a-half. During this period Egypt was ruled by sovereigns who are designated in history as the time" (*Imam-ul-Wakt*) and he professed to exercise his authority as the lieutenant and delegate of the Pontiff. The appointment of ministers of religion and administrators of justice was subject to the formal sanction of the Caliph. Though shorn of all its temporal powers, the religious prestige of the Caliphate Mamelike Sultans. Each Sultan on his accession to power received his investiture from the Caliph and "Imam of his was so great, and the conviction of its necessity as a factor in the life of the people so deep-rooted in the religious sentiments of the Sunny world, that twice after the fall of Baghdad the Musalman sovereigns of India received their investiture from the Abbaside Caliphs. The account of the reception in 1343 A.C. of the Caliph's envoy by Sultan Mohammed Juna Khan Tughlak, the founder of the gignatic unfinished city of Tughlakabad, gives us an idea of the veneration in which the Pontiffs were held even in Hindustan (India), in those days said to be full six month's journey from Egypt. On the approach of the envoy the King, accompanied by the Syeds and the nobles, went out of the capital to greet him; and when the Pontiff's missive was handed to the Sultan he received it with the greatest reverence. The formal diploma of investiture legitimized the authority of the King. The whole of this incident is celebrated in a poem still extant in India by the poet laureate, the famous Badr-ud-din Chach. *About the end of the fifteenth century the star of Selim I., also surnamed Saffah, of the House of Othman, rose in the horizon. His victories over the enemies of Islam had won for him the title of "Champion of the Faith"; and no other Moslem sovereign- not even his great rival Shah Ismail, the founder of the Sufi dynasty in Persia and the creator of the first orthodox Shiah State,- equalled the Osmani monarch in greatness and power. The closing decades of that century had witnessed a vast change in the condition of Egypt, and the anarchy that had set in under the later Mameluke Sultans reached its climax some years later. Invited by a section of the Egyptian people to restore order and peace in the distracted country, Selim easily overthrew the incompetent Mamelukes, and incorporated Egypt with his already vast dominions. At this period the Caliph who held the Vice-gerency of the Prophet bore the pontifical name of Al-Motawakkil 'ala-Allah ("Contented in the grace of the Lord"). According to the Sunny records, he perceived that the only Moslem sovereign who could combine in his own person the double functions of Caliph and Imam, and restore the Caliphate of Islam in theory and in fact, and discharge effectively the duties attached to that office, was Selim. He accordingly, in 1517, by a formal deed of assignment, transferred the Caliphate to the Ottoman conqueror, and, with his officials and dignitaries, "made the Bai'at on the hand of the Sultan." In the same year Selim received the homage of the Sharif of Mecca, Mohammed Abu'l Barakat, a descendant of Ali, who presented by his son Abu Noumy on a silver salver the keys of the Kaaba (of The Holy Mecca) and took the oath by the same proxy. The combination in Selim of the Abbaside right by assignment and by Bai'at, and the adhesion of the representative of the Prophet's House who held at the time the guardianship of the Holy cities, perfected the Ottoman Sultan's title to the Caliphate, "just as the adhesion of (the Caliph) Ali had completed the title of the first three Caliphs." The solemn prayers with the usual Khutbas (Sermon) offered in Mecca and Medina for the Sultan gave the necessary finality to the right of Selim. Henceforth Constantinople, his seat of government became the Dar-ul-Khilafat, and began to be called "Istanbol," "The City of Islam." Before long envoys arrived in Selim's Court and that of his son, Solyman the Magnificent, from the rulers of the Sunny States to offer their homage;*

*and thus, according to the Sunnis, the Caliphate became the heritage of the **House of Othman, which they have enjoyed for centuries without challenge or dispute.***[8]

Even other sovereign of Muslim States had a recognition from the Caliph.

The title of Sultan (An Arabic word meaning a ruler) was for the first time bestowed by Wasik upon Ashnas, the commandant of the Turkish guards, who was decorated with a jewelled crown and double girdle. It seems virtually to have remained in abeyance until the Buyides rose to power, when it was conferred on those princes. The investure was attended with great pomp and ceremony. The recipient of the title was first dressed in royal robes, a jewelled crown was placed on his head, a collar round his neck, a bracelet on his arm, and a sword was buckled round his waist. Finally, to mark the combination of both civil and military powers, two banners were handed to him by the Caliph personally, "one ornamented with silver, fashioned as is customary among the nobles, and the other with gold in the manner of those given to the successor designate to the Caliph." The diploma was then read out in the presence of the assembled multitude, after which the Sultan kissed the Caliph's hand.

The title of Sultan was not, however, confined to the Buyide princes. It was conferred on mighty conquerors like **Mahmud of Ghazni, Tughril. Alp Arsian, Malik Shah, Saladin, etc. Practically once assumed or conferred it became hereditary in the family, although on each succession, a formal investiture was applied for, and almost as a matter of course granted with the usual robes of honor. Later, another title was created, that of Malik (An arabic word analogous to the Latin Rex), or king, which, sometimes jointly with the designation of Sultan and sometimes separately, but always with a qualifying phrase, was bestowed on ruling princes. The first to obtain this honor was the great Nur ud-din Mahmud, the son of Zangi, who received from the Caliph the title of al-Malik al-aadil, the just king.**[9]

Allah (or God) is the only Sovereign and The Holy Quran declares as below:

54: 55 In an Assembly of Truth, In the Presence of A Sovereign Omnipotent
59: 23 Allah is He, than whom There is no other god;- The Sovereign, the
59: 23 Holy One, The Source of Peace (and Perfection) The Guardian of
59: 23 Faith, The Preserver of Safety, The Exalted in Might, The
59: 23 Irresistible, the Supreme: Glory to Allah! (High is He) Above the
59: 23 partners They attribute to Him.
62: 1 Whatever is In the heavens and On earth, doth declare The
62: 1 Praises and Glory Of Allah-, the Sovereign The Holy One, the
62: 1 Exalted In Might, the Wise.
23: 52 And verily this Brotherhood Of yours is a broherhood
23: 52 And I am your Lord And Cherisher: therefore Fear Me (and no other)
23: 57 Verily those who live In awe for fear of their Lord;
23: 60 And those who dispense Their charity with their hearts Full of
23: 60 fear, because They will return to their Lord ;-

The Caliphate of Islam or the Single Brotherhood and under one Sovereign The Holy One, according to above verses of The Holy Quran continued for more than 600 years under the leadership of Bani-Abrahamites or Bani-Islamites in particular until the descendant of

---

[8] **THE SPIRIT OF ISLAM BY The Right Ho. Syed AMEER ALI, P.C. C.I.E pp. 2, 319 & 320, 124-133**

[9] **HISTORY OF THE SARACENS BY SYED AMIR ALI PG. 411-412**

Mongol or the Turk took it from them, from the abbaside after the fall of Baghdad in the hand of Halaku Khan in 1258 and 1514, 1517 formally , and again the Osmanian or the Turkish Caliphate was abolished in 1924 by Kamal Ataturk after a long conspiracy of western countries, particularly by the British and the French which created divisions among the Turk and the Arabs. But the word of the last Holy Prophet became true which is he told in the last sermon in Mecca from the top of the Jabal ul-Arafat on 7th March, 632; that "all Moslems are brothers unto one another; neither a black is superior over a white nor a white over a black; nor an Arab is superior over a Azmi or non-Arab nor a non-Arab is superior over a Arab".

Again in 1260, Sultan Baiber established the Caliphate by installing Abu'l Kasim Ahmed, a descendent of last Abbaside Caliph Ali Abbas in Cairo in 1261 which continued for another 250 years until in 1517 when that office was transferred to to Ottoman through formal deed..

So the Ishmaelites; who was Arab ruled 600 years from 632 A. H. and 11 A.H. upto 1258 A. C. and the Non-Arabs like the Mameluke, the Mongol or the Osmanian Turks rule over another over 600 years from 1244 A. C. upto 1924 when the Caliphate was abolished violating the teaching of Quran and the Sunna or the sayings of the Prophet, the consequences is tremendous still to-day there are only bloodshed of Muslims, it is in Afganisthan or in Iraq or in Somalia or in Bosnia or in India and in every continent there is muslim bloodshed by the fellow muslims for the sake nation states for different language, culture, color or so on, by the natural calamities like draft in Somalia.
Now before we go further let us have a glimpse of those caliphs who ruled about one third of this world consisting of Asia, Africa and even Europe.

The Patriarch Abraham (Peace be upon him) and his descendent The Ishmaelites from his first son Prophet Ishmael(Peace be upon him)

The Last Prophet Islam (SM)

List of Caliphs from Ishmaeltes
with the dates of their accession
to make the text intelligible

Kholafae Rashedin Era or The Caliph with rightful Path

A. H.   A.C.

1. Hazrat Abu Bakr (R. A. means Allah be pleased with him) 11 = 632
2. Hazrat Omar (R. A.)   13 = 634
3. Hazrat Osman (R. A.)   23 = 644
4. Hazrat Ali   (R. A.)   35 = 656
5. Hazrat Hasan (R. A.)   41 = 661

   The Ishmaelite continued under another branch called Ommeyades
6: 1. Muawiyah (not elected by democracy means so first self declared dictator in Islamic history)   41 = 661

So perhaps he took the revenge what his father Abu Sufian could not. Abu Sufian accepted Islam after the defeat in the last Meccan war, a Muslim by situation not for the love of God or his prophet. Muawiyah's mother Hinda even helped to kill the Prophet's uncle Hazrat Amir Hamza (R. A.) and even she ate the liver of dead uncle of the Prophet. So with cap-

47

ture of power Muawiyah; succeeded what his parent could not. We are to mention these because when fifth Caliph and eldest grandson of the Prophet abdicated for Muawiyah on the condition that after the death of Muawiyah the Caliphate must be restored to youngest grandson of the Prophet Hazrat Imam Hussain (R. A.). But Muawiyah started removing almost all formidable opponent like Imam Hassan (R. A.) who was poisoned and Malek al-Ashtar (R. A.) and many others faced the same fate. So Muawiyah did not hesitate to break the word with the grandson of the Prophet (Peace be upon him) and nominated his son Yezid for the Caliphate) and warned Yezid about few companions of the Prophet who are Imam Hussain the son of Ali(the Caliph), Abdullah the son of Omar(the Caliph), Abdur Rahman the son of Abu Bakr(the Caliph) and Abdullah the son of Zubair.

Muawiyah also proceeded to Medina and Mecca to secure the covenant of the people of Hijaz for the oath to Yezid. Muawiyah already took the oath for Yezid from the people of Iraq, Syria through bribe and other means. His advisor was Mughira, the governor of Basra and Ziad who was an illegitimate son of Abu Sufian, the father of Muawiyah.[10]

A. H. A. C.

		A. H.		A. C.
7: 2.	Yezid	61	=	681
8: 3.	Muawiyah II	64	=	683
9: 4.	Merwan I.	65	=	684
10:5	Abdul Malek	65	=	685
11:6	Walid I.	86	=	705
12:7	Sulaiman	96	=	715
13:8	Omar bin Abdul Aziz	99	=	717

Hazrat Omar bin Abdul Aziz (R. A.,God's mercy be with him) was a very pious and honest Caliph among the Ommeyyade. He maintained a very simple life. He was very respectful with the descendent of the Holy Prophet (Sm.) and even he returned those property which was nationalized by Caliph Abu Bakr with the pretext of a verse of the Holy Quran which says that there is no hereditary of the Prophet. He used to take very simple food and dress. He even reduced the allowance when he thought that his family is getting more allowance than what they deserve after a incident which is mentioned that his wife made some sweet for him by saving some money from their daily allowance. But Ommeyyade family members did not like his honesty and he was killed.

		A. H.		A. C.
14:9	Yezid II.	101	=	720
15:10	Hisham	105	=	724
16:11	Walid II.	125	=	743
17:12	Yezid III.	126	=	744
18:13	Ibrahim	126	=	744
19:14	Merwan II	127	=	745

During those 84 years of Ommeyade Caliphate 14 Caliphs ruled, of **which** last 4 Caliphs ruled one year in average where as First Caliph Muawiyah and fifth Caliph Abdul Malek ruled 20 years each, which are the longest period for Ommeyyad density. The tenth Caliph Hisham also ruled around 2o years.

---

[10] **A SHORT HISTORY OF THE SARACENS, (CHAPTER THE NOMINATION OF YEZID),** BY SYED AMIR ALI, EX MEMBER OF THE JUDICIAL COMMITTEE OF HIS MAJESTY'S PRIVY COUNCIL AND AUTHOR OF 'THE SPIRIT OF ISLAM ETC P. 81,

The Ishmaelites continued under another branch called The ABBASIDE after the name of The Prophet's own uncle Hazrat Abbas (R. A.) i.e. the descendent of Abbas.

A. H.   A. C.

		A. H.		A. C.
20:1	As-Saffah, Abul Abbas (Abdullah)	132	=	750
21:2	Al-Mansur, Abu Jafar	136	=	754
22:3	Al-Mahdi (Mohammad)	158	=	775
23:4	Al-Hadi (Musa)	168	=	785
24:5	Ar-Rashid (Harun)	170	=	786
25:6	Al-Amin (Mohammad)	193	=	809
26:7	Al-Mamun (Abdullah)	198	=	813
27:8	Al-Mutasim b'Illah (Abu Ishak Mohammed)	218	=	833
28:9	Al-Wasik b'Illah (Abu Jafar Harun)	227	=	842
29:10	Al-Mutawakkil 'ala-Illah (Jaafar)	232	=	847
30:11	Al-Muntasir b'Illah (Mohammed)	247	=	861
31:12	Al-Mustain b'llah (Ahmed)	248	=	862
32:13	Al-Mu'tazz b'llah (Mohammed)	252	=	866
33:14	Al-Muhtadi b'Illah (Mohammed Abu Ishak)	255	=	869
34:15	Al-Mu'tamid al-Allah (Ahmed Abul Abbas)	256	=	870
35:16	Al-Mutazid b'illah (Ahmed, Abul Abbas)	279	=	892
36:17	Al-Muktafi b'illah (Ali, Abu Mohammed)	289	=	902
37:18	Al-Muktadir b'illah (Jafar, Abu Fazl)	295	=	908
38:19	Al-Kahir b'illah (Mohammed, Abu Mansur)	320	=	932
39:20	Al-Razi b'illah (Mohammed Abul Abbas)	322	=	934
40:21	Al-Muttaki b'Illah (Ibrahim, Abul Ishak)	329	=	940
41:22	Al-Mustakfi b'Illah(Abdullah, Abul Kasim)	333	=	944
42:23	Al-Muti Ullah (Fazl, Abul Kasim)	334	=	946
43:24	At-Tai b'Illah (Abdul Karim, Abu Bakr)	363	=	974
44:25	Al-Kadir b'Illah (Abdul Karim, Abu Bakr)	381	=	991
45:26	Al-Kaim biamr Illah (Abdullah, Abu Jaafar)	422	=	1031
46:27	Al-Muktadi bi'amr-Illah (Abdullah, Abul Kasim)	467	=	1075
47:28	Al-Mustazhir b'Illah (Ahmmed, Abul Abbas	487	=	1094
48:29	Al-Mustarshid b'Illah (Fazl, Abul Mansur)	512	=	1118
49:30	Ar-Rashid b'Illah (Mansur, Abu Jafar)	529	=	1135
50:31	Al-Muktafi bi'amr-Illah(Mohammad, Abu Abdullah)	530	=	1136
51:32	Al-Mustanjid b'Illah (Yusuf, Abul Muzaffar)	555	=	1160
52:33	Al-Mustazil bi'amr-Illah (Hasan, Abu Mohammad)	566	=	1170
53:34	An-Nasir Li-din-Illah (Ahmed, Abul Abbas)	575	=	1180
54:35	Az-Zahir bi'amr-Illah (Mohammed, Abu Nasr)	622	=	1225
55:36	Al-Mustansir b'Illah (Mansur, Abu Jafar)	623	=	1226
56:37	Al-Musta'sim b'Illah (Abdullah, Abu Ahmed)	640	=	1242

So when the Abbaside Caliphate ended, total only 56 Caliphs ruled upto 1242 A. C. of which, atleast period of 10 Caliphs was around one year each.

During the period of Abbaside 14 Fatimide Caliphs ruled in Egypt from 908 A. C. to 1160 A. C and built the city Cairo and the oldest university of this world Al-Azhar after the name of the daughter of the Holy Prophet (Sm). In Spain the Ommeyyade Caliphate separated from mainland Caliphate in Baghdad, first of which is Abdur Rahman I, who fled to Spain via North Africa and ruled in Spain upto 1027 A. C. during 24th Caliph Hisham III.

Seljuk conquest was in 1078 and ended in 1183.

The Mamluk era was noted for the perfection of the post Abbaside slave military system. Before the Mamluk period slave regiments had been employed in all Middle Eastern armies, but the Mamluks were the first Middle Eastern regime to be based entirely on the

49

slave military machine. The elite personnel of the regime, including Sultan were slaves or former slave. In 1250 the Ayyubid house was overthrown by a rebellion of one of its Mamluk or slave regiments, which killed the last Ayybid ruler of Egypt and named one of its own officers Aybeg, to be new Sultan. Thus they were able to unify Egypt and Syria until the Ottoman conquest in 1517 A.C. This was the longest lived Muslim state in Middle East between the Abbaside and the Ottoman empires.
A second phase began with the succession of Nur-al-Din (1146-77), the son of Zengi.

The Delhi regimes stressed allegiance to the Caliph and support for the judicial establishment of the Ulama. Nur al-Din sent his General Shirkah and Shirkak's nephew Salah al-Din (Saladin) with Muslim forces to take Egypt in 1169. The conquest of Egypt by Saladin in 1171 A.C. opened way for the installation of the Sunny School in Egypt.
Sultan Baybar (1260-77) adopted the policy of appointing a head for each of the four major school of Law. Seljuk conquest 1078 and Seljuq states 1078 - 1183.

Summary of other density after Abbaside.

> Seljuk conquest in 1078.
> Seljuk State period 1078 - 1183.
> Ayyubids - 1169-1250.
> Mamluks 1250-1517.

1501 Ismail once Tabriz and pro Shah of Iran

In many cases Muslim populations have become minority citizens and subjects in societies dominated by non-Muslim peoples.[11]

I. 7+(℞$/ ,3+6

On the death of the Prophet Mohammad (sm) in A.D. 632, in the eleventh year after his Flight (Hijra, 622) from Mecca to Medina, his father-in-law Abu-Bakr was elected head of the Muslims, with the title of Khalifa or Caliph('SUCCESSOR'). Three other Caliphs, Omar, Othman, and Ali (God may be pleased with them), were similarly elected in turn, without dynasties, and these first four successors are known as the Orthodox Caliphs (Al-Khulafa Al-Rashidun). On the murder of Ali (God may be pleased with him) in 661 (A.H. 40), Mo'awiya, a descendant of Omayya of the Prophet's tribe of the Kuraysh, assumed the Caliphate, and founded the dynasty of the Omayyad Caliphs, fourteen in number, whose capital was Damascus. In 750 (132) the dynasty was supplanted.[12]

---

[11] **A HISTORY OF ISLAMIC SOCIETIES by Ira M. Lapidus, Cambridge University press Cambridge ,New York Port Chester,Melbourne, Sydney. pp. 134-135, 170,182, 184-186, 189, 351-355, 358, 441, 557.**

[12] # THE MOHAMMADAN DYNASTIES,
CHRONOLOGICAL AND GENEALOGICAL
TABLES WITH HISTORICAL INTRODUCTIONS by STANLEY LANE-POOLE,FIRST EDITION 1893, REPRINT 1977; PUBLISHED BY MOHAMMAD AHMAD FOR IDARAH-I, ADBIYAT-I DELHI, 2009, QASIMJAN ST., DELHI-6 AND PRINTED AT JAYYED PRESS, BALLIMARAN, DELHI-6, P. 3.

Quotation from **'THE MOHAMMADAN DYNASTIES'**, CHRONOLOGICAL AND GENEALOG
ICAL TABLES WITH HISTORICAL INTRODUCTIONS by STANLEY LANE-POOL, continues as follows:

This signal success secured the Turks from invasion from the north, and the history of the next two centuries is a long record of triumphs. Constantinople fell to Mohammad II in 1453, and the last remnant of the Byzantine Empire was thereby destroyed. The Crimea was annexed (1475), the Aegean islands became Ottoman soil, and the Turkish flag waved even in Italy over the castle of Otranto. In his brief reign of eight years, Selim I, 'the Grim,' defeated the Shah of Persia, and added Kurdistan and DiyarBakr to the Turkish Empire; took Syria, Egypt and Arabia from the Mamluks (1517); and not only became the master of the Holy Cities of Mecca and Medina, **but received from the last 'Abbasid Caliph of Cairo** the relics of the Prophet Mohammad and the right of succession to the Caliphate, in virtue of which the Ottoman Sultans have ever since claimed the homage of the faithful.

In the past there was no division of Muslims like son of the soil and outsiders, and or the higher class i.e. Lord and slave, the ruler could be any one irrespective of his race or originality. The Qurdish people, who is now deprived politically, became famous in history. One of such Qurdish tribe was Saladdin. Muhammed Ali, the Commander of an Albanian regiment who and his few generations ruled Egypt was also outsider, probably a mixture of European race, the Slaves known as Mamluk ('owned slave applied to white slave) in Egypt, even in India the slaves ruled in Delhi known as Sultans of Delhi, which started by Kutb-ud-Din (or Kutb-aldin) who was appointed as viceroy of India (Delhi) by his master (Lord) Muhammad Ghor who conquered north India including Delhi. The following quotations from Lanepole are proofs of the internationalization of the Muslim, where there was no difference between a master and a slave, a white and a black, a Arab or Non-Arab, a Asian or African, a European or a Non-European which started from the Holy Prophet (peace be upon him), which he reminded in his last Sermon in his last Hajj address. Thus Hadrat Bilal (a black or Habsi and also slave) was the first Muazzin, Hazrat Salman Farsi (Iranian belonged to rich family, but who also became a slave for his search of God through a Bishop) was a major adviser, though there was slave trade by the European in America and the black was deprived minimum human right by the European race few years ago in U.S.A.:

pg-74 A.H. 564-648   A.D. 1169-1250
28. AYYUBIDS

Salah-al-Din, or Saladin, the son of Ayyub, was of Kurdish extraction, and served under Nur-al-din (Nouredin) Mahmud b. Zangi, who had lately made himself king of Syria. By him Saladin and his uncle Shirkuh were sent to Egypt, where a civil war invited interference. Friendly assistance developed into annexation, and after the death of Shirkuh Saladin became virtual master of Egypt in 1169 (564 A.H.), though the last Fatimid Caliph did not die till three years later. In the first month of 567 (Sept., 1171). Saladin caused the Khutba(Sermon before congregation Friday and yearly 2 festival prayers) or public prayer to be said at Cairo in the name of the contemporary 'Abbasid Caliph, Mustadi, instead of the Fatimid -'Adid who lay on his death-bed. The change was effected without disturbance, and Egypt became once more Sunnite instead of Shite. The Holy Cities of the Hijaz generally formed part of the dominion of the ruler of Egypt; and in 1173 (569) Saladin sent his brother Turan-Shah to govern the Yeman. Tripoli was taken from the Normans in 1172 (568). The death of his former master Nur-al-Din in the same year laid Syria open to invasion, and in 1174 (570) Saladin entered Damascus and swept over Syria (570-572) up to the Euphrates in spite of the opposition of the Zangids. He did not annex Aleppo until 1183 (579), after the death of Nur-al-Din's son, -Salih. He reduced Masil and made the various princes of Mesopotamia his vassals in 1185-6 (581). He was now master of the country from the Euphrates to the Nile, except where the Crusaders retained their strongholds. The battle of Hittin, 4 July, 1187, destroyed the Christian kingdom of Jerusalem; the Holy City was occupied by Saladin within three months; and hardly a castle, save Tyre, held out against him. The fall of Jerusalem roused Europe to undertake the Third Crusade. Richard I of England and Philip Augustus of France set out for the Holy Land in 1190, and joined in the siege of Acre in 1191. After a year and a half fighting, peace was concluded in 1192 for three years without any advantage having been gained by the Crusaders. In March 1193 (589) Saladin died.

Thus important point is first Saladin defeated the Muslim separatist who worked against the unity of one Umma and then he took the Christian Holy city, as he was sure that for the unity of the Muslims he will succeed his war against the unified Christian Crusaders.

On his death, his brothers, sons, and nephews, divided the various provinces of his wide kingdom, but one amongst them, his brother Sayf-al-din -`Adil, the Saphadin of the Crusader chroniclers, gradually acquired the supreme authority. At first Saladin's sons naturally succeded to their father's crowns in the various divisions of the kingdom:- Afdal at Damascus, Aziz at Cairo, Zahir at Aleppo. But in 1196 (592) Afdal was succeeded by Adil at Damascus; in 1199 (596) Mansur the successor of Aziz was supplanted by Adil at Cairo; and Aleppo alone remained to the direct descendants of Saladin until 1260 (648).
Having sequined the sovereignty of Egypt and most of Syria in 1196-9, and appointed one of his sons to the government of Mesopotamia about 1200 (597), Adil enjoyed the supreme authority in the Ayyubid kingdom till his death in 1218 (615). His descendants carried on his rule in the several countries; and we find separate branches reigning in Egypt, Damascus, and Mesopotamia, all sprung from Adil. Those who reigned at Hamah, Emesa, and in the Yaman, were descended from other members of the Ayybid family.
   In 1250 (648) the Adil Ayyubids of Egypt, the chief branch of the family, who also frequently held Syria, made way for the Bahri Mamluks or Slave Kings. The Damascus branch, after contesting the sovereignty of Syria with the Egyptian and Aleppo branches, was incorporated with Aleppo, and both were swept away in the Tatar avalanche of Chinghiz Khan in 1260 (658). The same fate had overtaken the Mesopotamian successors of Adil in 1245 (643). The Mamluks absorbed Emesa in 1262 (661). The Ayyubids had given place to the Rasulids in Arabia as early as 1228 (625). But at Hamah a branch of the family of Saladin continued to rule with slight intermission until 1341 (748), and numbered in their line the well-known historian Abu-l-Fida.

A. H.		- EGYPT -	A. D.	
564	57.1	Nasir Salah-al-din	1169	
589	58.2	Aziz Imad-al-din Othman		1193
595	59.3	Mansur Mohammad	1198	
596	60.4	Adil Sayf-al-din Abu-Bakr*(Saphadin)		1199
615	61.5	Kamil Mohammad*	1218	
635	62.6	Adil Sayf-al-din aAbu Bakr*		1238
637	63.7	Salih Najm-al-din Ayyub*		1240
647	64.8	Muazzam Turan-Shah*		1249
648	65.9	Ashraf Musa	1250	
-650			-1252	

                    [Mamluks]
        * These Sultans also ruled at Damascus.

EGYPT AND SYRIA

650-922   29. MAMLUK SULTANS   1252-1517

Mamluk means `owned,' and was generally applied to a white slave. The Mamluk Sultans of Egypt were Turkish and Circassian slave, and had their origin in the purchased body-guard of the Ayybid Sultan Salih Ayyub. The first of their line was a women, Queen Shajar-al-durr, widow of -Salih; but a representative of the Ayyubid family (Musa) was accorded the nominal dignity of joint sovereignty for a few years. Then followed a succession of slave kings, divided into two dynasties, the **Bahri (`of the river') and the Burji (`of the Fort')** who ruled Egypt and Syria down to the beginning of the 16th century. In spite of their short reigns and frequent civil wars and assassinations, they maintained as a rule a well-organized government, and Cairo is still full of proofs of their appreciation of art and their love of building. Their warlike qualities were no less conspicuous in their successful resistance to the Crusaders, and to the Tatar hordes that overran Asia and menaced Egypt in the 13th century.

A. H.   - EGYPT -   A. D

648-792   A. **BAHRI MAMLUKS**   1250-1390

1.   648 66.1 Shajar-al-durr   1250
2.   648 67.2 Muizz Izz-al-din Aybak   1250
3.   655 68.3 Mansur Nur-al-din Ali   1257
4.   657 69.4 Muzaffar Sayf-al-din Kutuz   1259
5.   658 70.5 Zahir Ruku-al-din Baybars Bundukdari   1260
6.   676 71.6 Sa'id Nasir-al-din Baraka Khan   1277
7.   678 72.7 Adil Badr-al-din Salamish   1279
8.   678 73.8 Mansur Sayf-al-din Kalaun   1279
9.   689 74.9 Ashraf Salah-al-din Khalil   1290
10. 693 75.10 Nasir Nashir-al-din Mohammad   1293
11. 694 76.11 Adil Zayn-al-din Kitbugha   1294
12. 695 77.12 Mansur Husim-al-din Lajin   1296
10.2 698   Nasir Mohammad (again SL. # 10)   1298
13. 708 78.13 Muzaffar Fuku-al-din Bybars -Jashankir   1308
10.3 709   Nasir Mohammad (third time, SL. # 10 & 10.2 1309
14. 741 79.14 Mansur Sayf-al-din Abu-Bakr   1340
15. 742 80.15 Ashraf Ali-al-din Kujuk   1341
16. 742 81.16 Nasir Shihab-al-din Ahmad   1342
17. 743 82.17 Salih Imad-al-din Ismail   1342
18. 746 83.18 Kamil Sayf-al-din Shaban   1345
19. 747 84.19 Muzaffar Sayf-al-din Hajji   1346
20. 748 85.20 Nasir Nasir-al-din Hasan   1347
21. 752 86.21 Salih Salah-al-din Salih   1351
20.2 755   Nasir Hasan (again SL. # 20)   1354
22. 762 87.22 Mansur Salah-al-din Mohammad   1361
23. 764 88.23 Ashraf Nasir-al-din Shaban   1363
24. 778 89.24 Mansur Ala-al-din Ali   1376
25. 783 90.25 Salih Salah-al-din Hajji   1381
26. 784 91.26 Barkuk (see Burjis)   1382
25.1 791   Hajji again,(SL.# 25) with title of Muzaffar 1389
    -792   -1390
               [Burji Mamluks]

784-922   **B. BURJI MAMLUKS**   **1362-1517**

1.2 784   Zahir Sayf-al-din Barkuk   1382

53

(SL. 26 of Bahri Mamluks)
[Interrupted by Hajji 791-2.]

2.	801	92.2 Nasir Nasir-al-din Faraj	1398
3.	808	93.3 Mansur Izz-al-din `Abd-al-Aziz	1405
2.2	809	Nasir Faraj (again SL. # 2)	1406
4.	815	94.4 Adil Mustain (Abbasid Caliph)	1412
5.	815	95.5 Mu'ayyad Shaykh	1412
6.	824	96.6 Muzaffar Ahmad	1421
7.	824	97.7 Zahir Sayf-al-din Tatar	1421
8.	824	98.8 Salih Nasir-al-din Mohammad	1421
9.	825	99.9 Ashraf Sayf-al-din Bars-bey	1422
10.	842	100.10 Aziz Jamil-al-din Yusuf	1438
11.	842	101.11 Zahir Sayf-al-din-Jakmak	1438
12.	857	102.12 Mansur Fakhr-al-din Othman	1453
13.	857	103.13 Asraf Sayf-al-din In??	1453
14.	865	104.14 Muayyad Shihab-al-din Ahmad	1460
15.	865	105.15 Zahir Sayf-al-din Khushkadam	1461
16.	872	106.16 Zahir Sayf-al-din Bilbey	1467
17.	872	107.17 Zahir	1468
18.	873	108.18 Ashraf Sayf-al-din Kai-Bey	1468
19.	901	109.19 Nasir Ahmed	1495
20.	904	110.20 Zahir Kansuh	1498
21.	905	111.21 Ashraf Janhalat	1499
22.	906	112.22 Ashraf Kansuh Ghuri	1500
23.	922	113.23 Ashraf Tuman-Bey	1516

-1517

[Othaman Sultan]

1220-1311	30. KHEDIVES	1805-1893

After the conquest by Salim I in 1517 (922) Egypt remained for three centuries a Turkish Pashalik, where, however, the authority of the Pasha sent from Constantinople was minimized by a council of Mamluk Beys. The arrival of Napoleon in 1798 put an end to this divided system; but after the victories of England at Abu-kir and Alexandria and the consequent retreat of the French in 1801, the old dissentions revived. In 1805, however, Mohammad Ali, the commander of an Albanian regiment in the Turkish army of Egypt, after massacring a number of the Mamluk chiefs, made himself master of Cairo. A second massacre in 1811 completed the work, and hence-forward Egypt has been governed, in nominal subordination to the Porte, by the dynasty of Mohammad Ali, whose fourth successor, Ismail Pasha, in 1866, adopted the official title of Khedive. Syria was annexed in 1831, but restored to Turkey under pressure of England in 1841. The Sudan was conquered in successive expeditions, down to the time of Ismail, but abandoned after the death of General Gordon in 1885. The southern boundary of Egypt is now drawn near the second cataract of the Nile, and since the suppression of `Arabi's military revolt by English troops in 1883, the administration of Egypt has been conducted under the advice of English officials.

1220 Mohammad Ali	1805	
1264 Ibrahim	1848	
1264 Abbas I	1848	
1270 Sa`id	1854	
1280 Ismail	1863	
1300 Tawik	1882	
1309 Abbas II (regnant)	1892	

699-1311	80. OTHMANLI OR OTTOMAN	1299-1893-1924

The Othmanli or Ottoman Turks were a small clan of the Oghuz tribe, who were driven westward from Khurasan by the Mongol migration, and took refuge in Asia

54

Minor early in the thirteenth century. In recognition of their aid in war, the Seljuk Sultan allowed them to pasture their flocks in the province anciently known as Phrygia Epictetus (henceforward called Sultanooni) on the borders of the Byzantine Bithynia, with the town of Sugut (Thebasion) for their headquarters. Here Othman, the eponymous founder of a dynasty which numbers thirty-five Sultans in direct male line, was born in 1258 (655). Othman pushed the Byzantine frontier further back, and his son Orkhan took Brusa and Nicaea, absorbed the neighbouring State of Karasi, and organized the famous corps of Jenizaries (Yani chari 'new soldiery') who for several centuries were the flower of the conquering armies of the Othmanlis.

SULTANS OF DELHI (HINDUSTAN)

602-962 A.H.- 1206-1554 A.D.

Mohammad Ghori, after conquering northern India to the mouth of the Ganges, either by his own campaigns or by those of his generals, appointed his slave Kutb-aldin Aybak to act as his viceroy at Delhi; and on the death of the master in 1206 (602) the slave proclaimed himself sovereign of Hindustan (India); and founded the first Mohammadan dynasty which ruled exclusively in India; for hitherto Mohammadan India had been but an outlying province of the kingdom of Ghazna. This dynasty, the first of five which preceded the Mogul conquest, is commonly known as the Slave Kings.

A. SLAVE KINGS

A.H.		A.D.	
602 Aybak, Kutb-al-din		1206	
607 Aram Shah		1210	
607 Altamish (Iltutmish), Shams-al-din			1210
633 Firuz Shah I, Rukn-al-din			1235
634 Ridiya	1236		
637 Bahram Shah, Mu'izz-al-din			1239
639 Mas'ud Shah, 'Ala-aldin		1241	
644 Mahmud Shah I, Nasir-al-din			1246
664 Balban, Ghiyath-al-din		1265	
686 Kay-Kubad, Mu'izz-al-din		1287	

B. KHALJIS
689 Firuz Shah II, Jalal-al-din	1290
695 Ibrahim Shah I, Rukun-al-din	1295
715 'Omar Shah, Shihab-al-din	1315
716 'Mubarak Shah I, Kutb-al-din	1316
720 Khusru Shah, Nasir-al-din	1320

C. TAGHLAKIDS
720 Taghlak shah I, Ghiyath-al-din		1320
725 Mohammad II b, Taghlak		1324
752 Firuz Shah III	1351	
790 Taghlak Shah II	1388	
791 Abu-bakr Shah	1388	
792 Mohammad Shah III		1389

795 Sikandar Shah I	1392	
797 Nasrat Shah (interregnum)		1394
802 Mahmud II restored	1399	
815 Dawlat Khan Lodi	1412	

D. SAYYIDS

817 Khidr Khan	1414	
824 Mubarak Shah II, Mu'izz-al-din		1421
837 Mohammad Shah IV		1433
847 'Alim Shah	1443	

E. LODIS

855 Bahlol Lodi	1451	
894 Sikandar II b. Bahlol		1488
923 Ibrahim II b. Sikandar		1517
-930 Invasion of Babar		-1526

F. AFGHANS

946 Shir Shah	1539	
952 Islam Shah	1545	
960 Mohammad v. 'Adil Shah		1552
961 Ibrahim III Sur	1553	
962 Sikandar Shah	1554	
[Mogul Emperors] ...... [13]		

Albania's Independence and the first world war.

Only in the spring of 1913 did the idea of recognizing Albania's full independence from the Porte make any headway at the London Conference. Once Turk's withdrawal from the western part of the Balkan peninsula was established, any territorial relationship between vassal and suzerain became impossible: Austria-Hungary and Italy therefore proposed, at the beginning of May, that Albania should break its link with Turkey. On 29 July 1913 Russia at last gave up its resistance and the Ambassadors Conference recognized Albania's independence, proclaiming it a Sovereign hereditary principality, whose neutrality was guaranteed by the Great Powers.[14]

Ali Ibn al-Husa, Al-Kasim Ibn Muhammad, and Salim Ibn Abdullah.

---

[13] **THE MOHAMMADAN DYNASTIES,**
CHRONOLOGICAL AND GENEALOGICAL
TABLES WITH HISTORICAL INTRODUCTIONS by STANLEY LANE-POOLE,FIRST EDITION 1893, REPRINT 1977; PUBLISHED BY MOHAMMAD AHMAD FOR IDARAH-I, ADBIYAT-I DELHI, 2009, QASIMJAN ST., DELHI-6 AND PRINTED AT JAYYED PRESS, BALLIMARAN, DELHI-6, PP. 74, 295,299,301.

[14] **The history of Albania, Routledge of Kegan Paul, London, Boston and Henly, p. 151.**

Even Islam have been maintaining it's equality in Internationalism since its inception through inter-marriage between various races, which started with marriage of three princes of Iranian Emperor after its during Caliph Omar, and even slave mother with variety of races.

Lists of some caliphs whose mother were Slaves.

Caliph	Mother's nationality
Ibrahim the Imam	Berber
Mansur	Berber
Rashid	Harash
Ibrahim Ibn al-Mahdi	Zanj
Mamun	Persian
Muntasir	Abyssinian-Greek
Mustain	Slav
Muhtadi	Greek
Mukhtadir	Turki
Muktafi	Turki
Mustadi	Armenian
Nasir	Turk

Abu Salamah then Abu Muslim who wished to restore Caliphate to Alids.
al-Din Ibn al-Alkani
Halagu took Baghdad in 656
Al-Mustasin appointed in 640, his vizir a shite named Mu'ayyid-al-in.[15]

1. Antecedents: On the eastern side of Cairo, al-Azhar has stood for nearly a thousand years. ..... Founded in the tenth century by the Shiite Fatimids and converted to Sunnism under the Ayyubids, al-Azhar eventually drew students from as far away as Morocco and Java (Indonesia) just as medieval European universities attracted Catholic students from Poland to Spain and from Scotland to Italy.[16]

Writing of the Ottoman Empire, Glibb and Bowen comment upon 'the paradox' of "a government, generally apathetic unprogressive, and careless of the welfare of its subjects, and often arbitrary and violent in its dealing with them, and a society upon whose institutions and activities such a government had little or no effect. The explanations is to be found in the very lack of a complex, all embracing political organization. ..... We may visualize Moslem society as composed of two co-existing groups, the relations between which were for the most part formal and superficial. One group formed the governing merchants, artisans and cultivators. Each was organized internally on independent lines, and neither group interfered with the organization of the other in normal circumstances. [17]

---

[15] History of Islamic civilization by JURJI ZAYDAN, Translated by D. S. MARGOLIOUTH, D. Lit, Prof. of Arabia in the University of Oxford, p. 211.

[16] Cambridge Middle East Library by Donald Malcolm Reid; Cairo University and the making of modern Egypt; p. 23.

[17] THE NATION-STATE AND VIOLENCE Volume two, A contemporary Critique of Historical Matter, Alerson Anthony p. 52.

From the following Table we can feel that the Caliphate was divided into two periods, one by the Arabs, majority rulers of whom were Quraish or the direct descendants of Hazrat Ismael (Peace be upon him) i.e. 4 Rashida Caliphs, 5th Caliph Hazrath Hasan (Peace be upon him), 14 Ummayad Caliphs and lastly 37 Abbaside Caliphs of around 500 years, total Arab Caliphate period of 667 years from A.D. 632-. From Ayyubbide and Osmani period, the Non-Arab Caliphate started which also lasted for about 625 years, from A.D. 1299-1924.

A. C.

57:1	Osman	1299-1326
58:2	Orkhan	1326-1359
59:3	Murad I	1359-1389
60:4	Bayezid I	1389-1402
61-5	Isa	1402-1403
62-6	Sulaymam I	1403-1410
63:7	Mehmed I	1403-1421
64-8	Musa	1410-1413
65.9	Murad II	1421-1444
66.10	Mehmed II	1444-1446
66.9	Murad II	1446-1451
66.10	Mehmud II	1451-1481
67.11	Bayezid II	1481-1512

We got 113 Caliphs upto Mamluk period except few during Seljuk period.
If we do not like include those period of Seljuk, Ayyubid and Mamluk Caliphs, the we can start the number of Caliph after Abbaside as 57 or if if we accept those period then we can start as following nos, as Selim I also was first Osmani Caliph, who got the Holy places of Mecca and Medina which were in the possesion of those 113 Caliphs or rulers upto last Mamluk. (from first Caliph).

A. C.

114.68.12	Selim I	1512-1520
115.69:13	Suleyman I I the Magnificent	1520-1566
116.70:14	Selim II	1566-1574
117.71.15	Murad III	1574-1595
118.72:16	Mehmed III	1595-1603
119.73:17	Ahmed I	1603-1617
120.74:18	Mustafa I	1617-1618
121.75:19	Osman II	1618-1622
122.76.20	Mustafa I	1622-1623
123.77:21	Murad IV	1623-1640
124.78:22	Ibrahim	1640-1648
125.79:23	Mehmed IV	1648-1687
126.80:24	Suleyman III	1648-1687
127.81:25	Ahmed II	1691-1695
128.82:26	Mustafa II	1695-1703
129.83:28	Ahmed III	1703-1730
130.84:29	Mahmud I	1730-1754
131.85:30	Osman III	1754-1757
132.86:31	Mustafa III	1757-1774
133.87:32	Abdul Hamid I	1774-1789
134.88:33	Selim III	1789-1807
135.89:34	Mustafa IV	1807-1808
136.90:35	Mahmud II	1808-1839
137.91:36	Abd ul-Mejid	1839-1861
138.92:37	Abd ul-Aziz	1861-1876

139.93:38 Murad V	1876
140.94:39 Abdul-Hamid II	1876-1909
141.95:40 Mehmed V	1909-1918
142.96:41 Mehmed VI [18]	1918-1922
143.97.42 Abdul Majid (Caliph only)	1922-1923

So there were only 97 Caliphs and except few Seljuk, we got 143 rulers or Caliph including Ayyubids and Mamluks Sultans during for long 1292 years, from 632 A. H. upto 1924, who were also in possession of the Islamic Holy places. Yet the Abbaside Caliphate lasted for five centuries from its first establishment until the destruction of Baghdad by the Mongols in 1258 of the Christian era. At that time Musta'sim b'Illah was the Caliph, and he, together with his sons and the principal members of his family, perished in the general massacre; only those scions of the House of Abbas escaped the slaughter who were absent from the capital, or succeeded in avoiding detection. *For two years after the murder of Musta'sim b'Illah the Sunny world felt acutely the need of an Imam and Caliph;* both the poignancy of the grief at the absence of a spiritual Head of the faith, and the keenness of the necessity for a representative of the Prophet to bring solace and religious merit to the Faithful, are pathetically voiced by the Arab historian of the Caliphs (Ref: Ibid). The devotions of the living were devoid of that religious efficacy which is imparted to them by the presence in the world of an acknowledged Imam; the prayers for the dead were equally without merit.

Though there were other Dynastics namely Fatimid in Egypt and Umayyads in Spain, but each of them wanted to grab the whole territory and not to obey other as Independent of it's own.

THE FATIMIDE CALIPHS OF EGYPT

	A. H.	A. C.
1. Al-Mahdi, Obaidullahh	296	= 908
2. Al-Kaim bi-amr-Illah	322	= 934
3. Al-Mansur bi-amr-Illah	334	= 945
4. Al-Muizz li-din-Illah	341	= 953

	A. H.	A. C.
5. Al-Aziz b'Illah	365	= 975
6. Al-Hakim bi-amr-Illah	386	= 996
7. Al-Zahir I'-azaz-din-Illah	411	=1021
8. Al-Mustansir b'Illah	427	= 036
9. Al-Musta'li b'Illah	487	=1094
10. Al-Amir bi-Ahkam-Illah	494	=1101
11. Al-Hafiz li-din-Illah	523	= 130
12. Az-zaur bi-amr-Illah	544	=1140
13. Al-Faiz bi-amr-Illah	549	=1154
14. Al-Azid li-din-Illah	555	=1160 [19]

THE OMMEYYADE CALIPHS OF CORDOVA

---

[18] **THE CAMBRIDGE HISTORY OF ISLAM, IB, P. 734.**

[19] **THE SPIRIT OF ISLAM BY AMEER ALI PP. 497-498.**

```
                        A.H.  A.C.
Abdur Rahman I (ad dakhil)        138  = 756
Hisham I (Abu'l Walid)           172  = 788
Hakam I, al-Muntasir             180  = 796
Abdur Rahman II, (al-Ausat)       206  = 822
Mohammed I                   238  = 852
Munzir                  273  = 886
Abdullah                275  = 888
An-Nasir li-Din-Illah, Abdur Rahman III  300  = 912
Al-Mustansir b'Illah, Hakam II      350  = 961
Al-Muwayyid b'Illah, Hisham II      366  = 976
Al-Mahdi, Mohammed II            399  =1009
Al-Musta'in b'Illah, Sulaiman       400  =1009
Mohammed II (again)             400  =1010
Hisham II  (again)           400  =1010
Sulaiman (again)             403  =1013
Ali bin Hammud (An-Nasir the Idriside)  407  =1016
Abdur Rahman IV (al-Murtaza)        408  =1018
Kasim bin Hamud (al-Mamun)         408  =1018
Yahya bin Ali bin Hamud (al-Musta'li)  412  =1021
Kasim bin Hamud (again)         413  =1022
Abdur Rahman V (al-Mustazhir b'Illah)  414  =1023
Mohammed III (al-Mustakfi b'Illah)     414  =1024
Yahya bin Ali bin Hamud (again)     416  =1025
Hisham III (al-Mu'tazz b'Illah)    418  =1027 [20]
```

TABLE VII THE DYNASTY OF MUHAMMAD ALI IN EGYPT

1. Muhammad Ali
2. Ibrahim
3. Abbas Hilmi I
4. Muhammad Said
5. Ismail
6. Muhammad Towfiq
7. Abbas Hilmi II
8. Husayn Kamil
9. Ahmad Fuad I
10. Faruq
11. Ahmad Fuad II [21]

Dynastic lists of The Safavids

Safi al-Din
Sadrs al-Din Musa
Khwaja Ali
Ibrahim
Junayed

1. Ismail I

---

[20] **THE SPIRIT OF ISLAM BY AMEER ALI, PG. 498**

[21] **THE CAMBRIDGE HISTORY OF ISLAM, IB, P. 736.**

2. Tahmasp I
3. Ismail II
4. Muhammad Khudabanda
5. Abbas I
6. Safi
7. Abbas II
8. Sulayman
9. Husayn
10. Tahmasp II
11. Abbas III [22]

The learned men had to leave this world, but some of them left for next generation to start
from which they could not proceed for various back ground, religious, culture and so on.
So it will be very worthy one to quote from non-Muslim, but great learned one in the past
history and perhaps without bias and for this ground I am quoting from "Glimpses of
World History" by JAWAHRLAL NEHRU exactly for the authentically of the fact.

"We have considered the history of many countries and the ups and downs of many
kingdoms and empires. Look at the map. To the west is Egypt; to the north Syria and Iraq,
and a little to the east of this Persia or Iraq; a little farther to the north-west are Asia Minor
and Constantinople. Greece is not far; and India also is just across the sea on the other side.
Except for China and the Far East, Arabia was very centrally situated so far as the old
civilizations were concerned. Great cities rose on the Tigris and Euphrates in Iraq,
Alexandria in Egypt, Damascus in Syria, Antioch in Asia Minor. The Arab was a traveler
and a trader, and he must have gone to these cities frequently enough. But still Arabia plays
no notable part in history. There does not seem to be as high a degree of civilization there
as in neighboring countries. It neither attempted to conquer other countries, nor was it easy
to subdue it. Arabia is a desert country, and deserts and mountains breed hard people who
love their freedom and are not easily subdued. It was not a rich country and there was little
in it to attract foreign conquerors and imperialist. There were just two little towns- Mecca
and Yethrib by the sea. For the rest there were dwellings in the desert and the people of the
country were largely Bedouins or Baddus-the "dwellers of the desert". They were proud and
sensitive, these men of the desert, were quarrelsome. They lived in their clans and theirs
families quarreled with other clans and families. Once a year they made peace with each
other and journeyed to Mecca on pilgrimage to their many gods whose images were kept
there. Above all, they worshipped a huge black stone-the Kaaba. It was a nomadic and
patriarchal life-the kind of life led by the primitive tribes in Central Asia or elsewhere,
before they settled down to city life and civilization. The great empires which rose up round
Arabia often included Arabia in their dominions, but this was more nominal than real. It
was no easy to subdue and govern nomadic desert tribes. Once, a little Arab States rose in
Palmyra in Syria, and it had its brief period of glory in the third century after Christ. But
even this was outside Arabia proper. So the Bedouins lived their desert lives, generation after generation, and Arab ships went out to trade, and Arabia went on with little change.
Some people became Christians and some became Jews but mostly they remained
worshippers of the 360 idols and the Black Stones in Mecca. It is strange that this Arab
race, which for long ages had lived a sleepy existence, apparently cut off from what was
happening elsewhere, should suddenly wake up and show such tremendous energy as to
startly and upset the world. The story of the Arabs, and of how they spread rapidly over
Asia, Europe and Africa, and of the high culture and civilization which they developed, is
one of the wonders of history. Islam was the new force or idea which woke up the Arabs
and filled them with self-condition and energy. This was a religion started by a new
prophet, Mohammad, who was born in Mecca in 570 A. C. He was in no hurry to start this

---

[22] **THE CAMBRIDGE HISTORY OF ISLAM IB P. 735.**

religion. He lived a quite life, liked and trusted by his fellow citizens. Indeed, he was known as "Al-Amin"-the Trusty. But when he started preaching his new religion and especially when he preached against the idols at Mecca, there was a loud outcry against him, and ultimately he was driven out of Mecca, barely escaping with his life. Above all he laid stress on the claim that there was only one God, and that he, Mohammad, was the Prophet of God. Driven away by his own people from Mecca, he sought refuge with some friends and helpers in Yethrib. This flight from Mecca is called the Hijrat in Arabic, and the Muslim calendar begins from this date-622 A. C. This Hegira calendar is a lunar calendar-that is, it is calculated according to the moon. It is therefor five or six days shorter than the solar year which we usually observe, and the Hegira months do not stick to the same seasons of the year. Thus the same month may be in winter this year and in the middle of summer after some year. Within seven years of the flight, Mohammad returned to Mecca as its master. Even before this he sent out from Medina a summons to the kings and rulers of the world to acknowledge the one God and his Prophet. Heraclius, the Constantinople Emperor, got it while he was still engaged in his campaign against the Persians in Syria; the Persian King got it; and it is said that even Tai-Tsung got it in China. They must have wondered, these kings and rulers, who this unknown person was who dared to command them! From the sending of these messages we can form some idea of the supreme confidence in himself and his mission which Mohammad must have had. And this confidence and faith he managed to give to his people, and with this to inspire and console them this desert people of no great consequence managed to conquer half the known world. Confidence and faith in themselves were a great thing. Islam also gave them a message of brotherhood of the equality of all those who were Muslims. A measure of democracy was thus placed before the people. Compared to the corrupt Christianity of the day, this message of brotherhood must have had a great appeal, not only for the Arabs, but also for the inhabitants of many countries where they went. Prophet Muhammad(Peace be upon him) died in 632 A. C.; ten years after the Hijrat. He had succeeded in making a nation out of the many warring tribes of Arabia and in firing them with enthusiasm for a cause. He was succeeded by Abu Bakr, a member of his family, as Khalifa or Caliph or chief. This succession used to be by a kind of informal election at a public meeting. Two years later Abu Bakr died, and was succeeded by Omar, who was Khalifa for ten years. Abu Bakr and Omar were great men who laid the foundation of Arabian and Islamic greatness. As Khalifas they were both religious heads and political chiefs - King and Pope in one. In spite of their high position and the growing power of their State, they stuck to the simplicity of their ways and refused to countenance luxury and pomp. The democracy of Islam was a living thing for them. But their own officers and emirs took to silks and luxury soon enough, and irony stories are told of Abu Bakr and Omar rebuking and punishing these officers, and even weeping at this extravagance. They felt that their strength lay in their simple and hard living, and that if they took to the luxury of the Persian or Constantinople Courts, the Arabs would be corrupted and would fall. Even in these short dozen years, during which Abu Bakr and Omar ruled, the Arabs defeated both the Eastern Roman Empire and the Sassanid King of Persia. The Arabs occupied Jerusalem, the holy city of the Jews and Christians, and the whole of Syria and Iraq and Persia became part of the new Arabian Empire. Like the founders of some other religions, Mohammad was a rebel against many of the existing social customs. The religion he preached, by its simplicity and directness and its flavor of democracy and equality, appealed to the masses in the neighboring countries who had been ground down long enough by autocratic kings and equally autocratic and domineering priests. They were tired of the old order and were ripe for a change. Islam offered them this change, and it was a welcome change, for it bettered them in many ways and put an end to many old abuses. Islam did not bring any great social revolution in its train, which might have put an end to a large extent to the exploitation of the masses. But it did lessen this exploitation so far as the Muslims ere concerned, and made them feel that they belonged to one great brotherhood. So the Arabs marched from conquest to conquest. Often enough they won without fighting. Within twenty-five years of the death of their Prophet, the Arabs conquered the whole of

Persia and Syria and a bit of northern Africa on the west. Egypt had fallen to them with the greatest ease, as Egypt had suffered most from the exploitation of the Roman Empire and from the rivalry of Christian sects. There is a story that the Arabs burnt the famous library of Alexandria, but this is now believed to be false. The Arabs were too fond of books to behave in this barbarous manner. It is probable, however, that the Emperor Theodosius of Constantinople, about whom I have told you something already, was guilty of this destruction, or part of it. A part of the library had been destroyed long before, during a siege at the time of Julius Caesar. **In the west they marched on and on. It is said that their general Okba went right across northern Africa till he reached the Atlantic Ocean, on the western coast of what is now known as Morocco. He was rather disappointed at this obstacle, and he rode as far as he could into the sea and then expressed his sorrow to the Almighty that there was no more land in that direction for him to conquer in His name! From Morocco and Africa, the Arabs crossed the narrow sea into Spain and Europe- the Pillers of Hercules, as the old Greeks called these narrow straits. The Arab general who crossed into Europe landed at Gibralter and this name itself is a reminder of him.** His name was Tariq, and Gibralter is really Jabal-ut-Tariq, the rock of Tariq. Spain was conquered rapidly, and the Arabs then poured into southern France. So in about 100 years from the death of Mohammad (Peace be upon him), the Arab Empire spread from south of France and right across northern Africa to Suez, and across Arabia and Persia and Central Asia to the borders of Mongolia. India was out of it except Sindh (now part of Pakistan). Europe was being attacked by the Arabs from two sides- directly at Constantinople, and in France, via Africa. The Arabs in the south of France were small in numbers and they were very far from their homeland. Thus they could not get much help from Arabs, which as busy then conquering Central Asia. But still these Arabs in France frightened the people of Western Europe, and a great coalition was formed to fight them. Charles Martel was the leader of this coalition and in 732 A. C. he defeated them at the battle of Tours in France. This defeat saved Europe from the Arabs. ``On the plains of Tours,'' a historian has said, ``the Arabs lost the empire of the world when almost in their grasp.'' There can be no doubt that if the Arabs had won at Tours, European history would have been tremendously changed. There was no one else to stop them in Europe and they could have marched right across to Constantinople and put an end to the Eastern Roman Empire and the other States on the way. Instead of Christianity, Islam would then have become the religion of Europe, and all manners of other changes might have taken place. But this is just a flight of imagination. As it happened, the Arabs were stopped in France. For many hundreds of years afterwards, however, they remained and ruled in Spain. From Spain to Mongolia the Arabs triumphed. and these nomads from the deserts became the proud rulers of a mighty empire. Saracens they were called perhaps from Sahra and nashin- the dwellers of the desert. But the dwellers of the desert took soon enough to luxury and city life, and palaces grew up in their cities. **In spite of their triumphs in distant countries, they could not get rid of their old habit of quarrelling amongst themselves. Of course, there was something worth quarrelling about now, for the headship of Arabia meant the control of a great empire. So there were frequent quarrels for the place of the Khalifa. There were petty quarrels, family quarrels, leading to civil war. These quarrels resulted in a big division in Islam and two sects were formed the Sunnis and Shiahs which still exist. Trouble came soon after the regimes of the first two great Khalifas -Abu Bakr and Omar. Ali, the husband of Fatima, who was the daughter of Mohammad, was Khalifa for a short while. But there was continuous conflict. Ali was murdered, and some time later his son Hussain, with his family, were massacred on the plain of Karbala. It is this tragedy of Karbala that is mourned year after year in the month of Moharram by the Muslims, and especially the Shiahs. The Khalifa now becomes an absolute king. There is nothing of democracy or election left about him. He was just like any other absolute monarch of his day. In theory he continued to be the religious head also, the Commander of the Faithful. But some of these rulers actually insulted Islam, of which they were supposed to be the chief protectors. For about 100 years the Khalifas belonged to a branch of Mohammad's family, known as** the **Ommeyades. Damascus was made their capital, and this old city became very beautiful, with its palaces, mosques, fountains and kiosks. The water supply of Damascus was famous. During this period the Arabs developed a special style of architecture which has come to be known as saracenic architecture. There is not much of ornamentation in this. It is simple and imposing and beautiful. The idea behind this architecture was the graceful palm of Arabia and Syria. The arches and the pillars and the minarets and domes remind one of the arching and doming of palm groves.**

The Arabs, especially at the beginning of their awakening, were full of enthusiasm for their faith. Yet they were a tolerant people and there are numerous instances of this toleration in religion. In Jerusalem the Khalifa Omar made a point of it. In Spain there was a large Christian population which had the fullest liberty of conscience. In India the Arabs never ruled except in Sindh, but there were frequent contacts, and the relations were friendly. Indeed, the most notice able thing about this period of history is the contrast between the toleration of the Muslim Arab and the intolerance of the Christian in Europe. And Egypt did likewise, and indeed went so far to reclaim another Caliph. Egypt was near enough to be threatened and forced to submit, and this was done from time to time. But Africa was not interfered with, and as for Spain, it was much too far away for any action. So we see that the Arab Empire split up on the accession of the Abbasides. The Caliph was no longer the head of the whole Muslim world, he was not now the Commander of all the Faithful. Islam was no longer united, and the Arabs in Spain and the Abbasides disliked each other so much that each often welcomed the misfortunes of the other. In spite of all this, the Abbaside Caliphs were great sovereigns and their empire was a great empire, as empires go. The old faith and energy which conquered mountains and spread like a praire fire were no more in evidence. There was no simplicity and little of democracy left, and the Commander of the Faithful was little different from the Persian King of kings, who had been defeated by the earlier Arabs or the Emperor at Constantinople. In the Arabs of the time of Mohammad the prophet, there was a strange life and strength which were very different from the strength of kings, armies. They stood out in the world of their time, and armies and princes crumpled up before their irresistible march. The masses were weary of these princes, and the Arabs seemed to bring them the promise of change for the better and of social revolution. All this was changed now. The men of the desert lived in palaces now and instead of dates had the most gorgeous foods. They were comfortable enough, so why should they bother about change and social revolution? They tried to rival the old empires in splendor and they adopted many an evil custom of theirs. One of these, as I told you, was the seclusion of women. The capital now went from Damascus to Baghdad in Iraq. This change of capital itself was significant, for Baghdad used to be the summer retreat of the Persian kings. And as Baghdad was farther away from Europe than Damascus, henceforth the Abbasides looked more towards Asia than to Europe. There were to be still many attempts to capture Constantinople, and there were many wars with European nations, but most of these wars were defensive. The days of conquest seem to have ended, and the Abbaside Caliphs tried to consolidate such of the empire as was left to them. This was great enough even without Spain and Africa. The merchants carried on a vast trade with the East and West. Crowds of Government officials kept in continuous touch with the distant parts of the Empire, and the government, becoming more and more complicated, was divided up into many departments. An efficient costal system connected all the corners of the Empire to the capital. Hospitals abounded. Visitors came to Baghdad from all over the world, especially learned men and students and artists, for it was known that the Caliph welcomed all who were learned or who were skilful in the arts. The Caliph himself lived in great luxury surrounded by slaves, and his women- folk had taken to the harem. The abbaside Empire was at the height of its outward glory during the reign of Harunal-Rashid from 786 to 809 A.C. Embassies came to Harun from the Emperor of China and Emperor Charlemagne in the West. Baghdad and the Abbaside dominions were far in advance of the Europe of those days, except for Arab Spain, in all the arts of government, in trade, and in the development of learning. The old Turks of Central Asia became Muslims and came and took possession of Baghdad. They are known as the Seljuq Turks. They defeated the Byzantine army of

Constantinople utterly, much to the surprise of Europe. For Europe had thought that the Arabs and Muslims had spent their strength and were getting weaker and weaker. It was true that the Arabs had declined greatly but the Seljuq Turks now came on the scene to uphold the banner of Islam and to challenge Europe with it. This challenge was soon taken up, as we shall see, and the Christian nations of Europe organized crusades to fight the Muslims and raconteur Jerusalem, their holy city. For over 100 years Christianity and Islam fought for mastery in Syria, Palestine and Asia Minor and exhausted each other, and soaked every inch of the soil almost of these countries with human blood. And the flourishing cities of these parts lost their trade and greatness, and the smiling fields were often converted into a wilderness. So they fought each other. But even before their fighting was over, across Asia in Mongolia there arose Chengiz Khan, the Mongol Shaker of the Earth, as he was called, who was indeed going to shake Asia and Europe. He and his descendants finally put an end to Baghdad and its empire. By the time the Mongols had finished with the great and famous city of Baghdad, it was almost of heap of dust and ashes and most of its 2,000,000 inhabitants were dead. This was in 1258 A.C. Baghdad is now again a flourishing city and is the capital of the State of Iraq. But is only a shadow of its former self, for it never recovered from the death and desolation which of Mongols brought."[23]

The Muslim conquest of Spain was invited by the people of Spain for internal conflict and to take revenge against the cruel Gothic rulers, as stated in 'A STUDY OF ISLAMIC HISTORY' by Prof. K. Ali. which are as follows:

'Conquest of Spain. The condition of Spain before the Muslim conquest was a miserable one. The whole country was groaning under the oppression and torture of the Gothic kings. The middle class was reduced to ruin and misery while the noble and privileged classes were totally exempted taxation. The country was divided into many camps and the agriculturists were overburdened with taxation. Serfs or slaves had no freedom of action, even of marriage. There were tortured by their masters in many ways. The Jews who were the progressive and enlightened section of the country were mercilessly persecuted. Their freedom of marriage and faith was curtailed and curbed by the bishops who wielded enormous powers. Thus when the impoverished citizens, the wretched slaves or serfs and the persecuted Jews were all waiting for release from the cruel hands of the Gothic ruler, it was at this very moment that the deliverer came from an unexpected quarter to their rescue. Roderick who occupied the throne by murdering the former king, Witiza, this period governed the kingdom of Spain. Ceuta on the African side, was part of Julian's domain but Roderick captured it. The latter was not a man of good temperament. Besides the capture of Julian's empire, he added fuel to the fire by insulting Florinda, the daughter of Julian. So, Count Jullian, in order to drive the invader out of his kingdom, invited Musa Ibn Nusayr, the Governor of the Mediterranean Coast to invade Spain and to avenge this insult. The Muslims had been waiting for a chance to conquer Spain and hence a long-expected desire came to be fulfilled. Musa with the sanction of the Khalifa, sent a young and enterprising officer named Tarik to Spain for detailed information. Tarik came back with a favorable report. Musa then despatched his ablest lieutenant Tariq with a force of 7,000 men who took possession of the fortress called after him Gibraltar (Jabal-ul-Tariq). Tariq advanced forward and inflicted a crushing defeat on Roderick on the banks of the river Guadalete near Medinia-Sidonia in September, 711 A.D. Roderic in his flight was drowned in the water of the Guadalete. After this, Tariq conquered Sidonia, Carmona and Granada one after another. On the conquest of Cordova, he hastened to Toledo, the capital of Spain. Toledo soon fell into his hands. Thus within a short time Tariq reduced the greater part of

---

[23] **Glimpses of World History, by JAWAHARLAL NEHRU, PUBLISHED BY JAWAHARLAL NEHRU MEMORIAL FUND, OXFORD UNIVERSITY PRESS, NEW DELHI, PP. 141-153.**

Spain to submission. The brilliant success of Tariq attracted the attention of Musa who landed in Spain in June, 712 A. D. and rapidly conquered Seville and other cities. He met Tariq near Toledo. At first they quarreled with each other but after sometime they were reconciled. They marched together and occupied Saragossa.[24]

The Muslim conquest according to Nehru's languages which are follows:

"It was in 711 AC that the Arab general crossed to Spain from Africa. He was Tariq, and he landed at Gibraltar (the Jabal-ul-Tariq, the rock of Tariq). Within two years the Arabs had conquered the whole of Spain, and a little later Portugal was added. They went on and on; marched into France and spread all over the south. Thoroughly frightened at this, the Franks and other tribes joined together under Charles Martel, and made a great effort to stop the Arabs. They succeeded, and at the great battle of Tours near Poitiers in France the Franks defeated the Arabs. It was a great defeat and put and ends to Arab dreams of the conquest of Europe. Many times after that the Arabs and the franks and other Christian people in France fought each other; and sometimes the Arabs won and entered France, and sometimes they were pushed back in Spain. Even Charlemagne attacked them in Spain, but he was defeated. On the whole however, for a long period the balance was kept up, and the Arabs ruled in Spain but went no further. Spain was thus made part of the great Arab Empire, which spread right across Africa to the borders of Mongolia. But not for long. You will remember that there was civil war in Arabia and the Abbasides pushed out the Omme-yyade Caliphs. The Arab Governor in Spain was an Ommeyade, and he refused to recog-nize the new Abbaside Caliph. So Spain cut itself off from the Arab Empire, and the Caliph at Baghdad was too far away and too full of his own troubles to do anything in the matter. But bad blood continued between Spain and Baghdad, and the two Arab States, instead of helping each other in the hour of trial, rather welcomed the difficulties of each other. It was somewhat rash of the Spanish Arabs to break loose from their homeland. They were in a far country amid an alien population, and were surrounded by enemies. They were small in numbers. In the event of danger and difficulty there was no one to help them. But in those days they were full of self-confidence and cared little for these dangers. As a matter of fact they did remarkably well in spite of the continuous pressure of the Christian nations in the north, and single-handed, they maintained their dominion over the greater part of Spain for 500 years. Even after this they managed to hold on to a smaller kingdom in the south of Spain for another 200 years. And so they actually outlasted the great Empire of Baghdad; and the city of Baghdad itself had long been reduced to dust when the Arabs said their last farewell to Spain. These 700 years of Arab rule in parts of Spain are surprising enough. But what is more interesting is the high civilization and culture of the Spanish Arabs, or Moors as they were called.

It was this civil war which weakened the Arab State more than the attacks from outside. At the same time the power of some small Christian States in northern Spain was growing and they were pushing away at the Arabs.

About 1000 AC that is, just at the end of the millennium the kingdom of the Emir extended almost all over Spain. It even included a bit of southern France. But collapse came soon, and, as usual, it was due to internal weakness. The fine fabric of Arab civilization, with its arts and luxury and chivalry, was, after all, a rich man's civilization. The starving poor revolted and there were labor riots. Gradually civil war spread, and the provinces fell away, and the Spanish Empire of the Arabs went to pieces. Still the Arabs continued, split up as they were, and it was not till 1236 AC that Cordoba finally fell to the Christian King of Castile.

The Arabs were driven south, but still they resisted. In the south of Spain they carved out a little kingdom, the kingdom of Granada, and held on there. It was a little affair, this kingdom, so far as size went, but it reproduced Arab civilization in miniature. The famous

---

[24] **A STUDY OF ISLAMIC HISTORY BY PROF. K. ALI PP. 179-181.**

Alhambra still stands in Granada, with its beautiful arches and columns and arabesques, a reminder of those days. It was originally called in Arabic "Al-Hamra", the red palace. Arabesques are the beautiful designs you often see on Arab and other buildings influenced by Islam. Islam did not encourage the painting of figures. So the builders took to making fancy and intricate designs. Often they wrote Arabic verses from the Quran over the arches and elsewhere and made of them a beautiful decoration. The Arabic script is a flowing script, which lends itself easily to such decoration.

The kingdom of Granada lasted for 200 years. It was pressed and harassed by the Christian States of Spain, especially Castile, and sometimes it agreed to pay tribute to Castile. It would probably not have lasted so long if the Christian states had themselves not been divided. But in 1469 AC a marriage took place between the rulers of two of these principal States, Ferdinand and Isabella, and this united Castile, Aragon and Leon. Ferdinand and Isabella put an end to the Arab kingdom of Granada. The Arabs fought bravely for several years till they were surrounded and hemmed in Granada. Starved out, they surrendered in 1492 A.C.

Many of the Saracens or Arabs left Spain and went to Africa. Near Granada, overlooking the city, there is a spot which still bears the name of "El ultimo sospiro del moro", the last sigh of the Moor.

But a large number of Arabs remained in Spain, The treatment of these Arabs is a very dark chapter in the history of Spain. There was cruelty and massacre, and the promises made to them about toleration were forgotten. About this time the Inquisition, that terrible weapon which the Roman Church forged to crush all who did not bow down to it, was established in Spain. Jews, who had prospered under the Saracens, were now forced to change their religion and many were burnt to death. Women and children were not spared. "The infidels" (that is the Saracens), so says a historian, "were ordered to abandon their picturesque costume, and to assume the hat and breeches of their conquerors, to renounce their language, their customs and ceremonies, even their very names, and to speak Spanish, behave Spanishly, and rename themselves Spaniards". Of course there were rising and revolts against these barbarities. But they were mercilessly crushed.

The Spanish Christians seem to have been very much against washing and bathing. Perhaps they objected to these simply because the Spanish Arabs were very fond of them and had erected great public baths all over the place. The Christians even went so far as to issue orders "for the reformation of the Moriscos" or Moors or Arabs, that "Neither themselves, their women, nor any other persons, should be permitted to wash or bathe themselves either at home or elsewhere; and that all their bathing houses should be pulled down and destroyed".

Apart from the sin of washing, another great charge brought against the "Moriscos" was that they were tolerant in religion. It is extraordinary to read of this, and yet this was one of the main charges in an account of the "Archbishop of Valencia in 1602, when he was recommending the expulsion of Saracens from Spain. Referring to this he says, "that they (the Moriscos) commended nothing so much as that liberty of conscience in all matters of religion, which the Turks, and all other Mohammedans, suffer their subjects to enjoy". What a great compliment was thus paid unwittingly to the Saracens in Spain, and how different and intolerant was the outlook of the Spanish Christians! Millions of Saracens were driven out forcibly from Spain, mostly into Africa, some to France. The Arabs had been in Spain for seven hundred years; and during this long period they had become to a large extent merged in the people of Spanish. Probably the Spanish Arabs of later years were quite different form the Arabs of Baghdad. Even to-day the Spanish race has much of Arab blood in its veins.

The Saracens had also spread to the south of France and even to Switzerland, not as rulers, but as settlers. Sometimes even now one comes across an Arab type of face among the Frenchmen from the midi.

Thus ended, not only Saracens rule in Spain, but also Arab civilization. For, even earlier, this civilization had collapsed in Asia, as we shall presently see. It influenced many countries and many cultures, and left many a bright souvenir. But it did not rise again by itself in after-history. After the Saracens left, Spain, under Ferdinand and Isabella, grew power. Soon afterwards, the discovery of America brought vast wealth to it, and for a while it was the most powerful country in Europe, dominating others. But its fall was rapid and it sank into insignificance, and while the other countries of Europe advanced, Spain remained stagnant, dreaming still of the Middle Ages and not realizing that the world had changed since then.

Many of the Saracens or Arab Muslims left Spain and went to Africa. Near Granada, overlooking the city, there is a spot which still bears the of "El ultimo sospiro del moro", the last sigh of the Moor. But many Muslims were killed brutally along with all the Jews and for the cruelty of the so called Christianity of the west there is no trace of those Muslims who ruled there for around 800 long years.[25]

In 710 AC a young boy of seventeen, Mohammad ibn Kasim, commanding an Arab army, conquered the Indus valley up to Multan in western Panjab. This was the full extent of the Arab conquest of India.

Muslim Arabs came and went and built mosques, and sometimes preached their religion, and sometimes even converted people. There seems to have been no objection to this in those days, no trouble or friction between Hinduism and Islam. It is interesting to note this because in later days friction and trouble did arise between the two religions. It was only when in the eleventh century Islam came to India in the guise of a conqueror, sword in hand, that it produced a violent reaction, and the old toleration gave way to hatred and conflict.

This wielder of the sword who came to India with fire and slaughter was Mahmud of Ghazni. **Nominally the Central Asian States were under the Caliph of Baghdad, but after Harunal-Rashid's death the Caliph weakened and a time came when his empire split up into a number of independent States. A Turkish slave named Subuktagin carved a State for himself around Ghazni and Kanadahar about 975 AC He raided India also.** *In those days a man named Jaipal was Raja of Very venturesome, Jaipal marched to the Kabul valley against Subuktagin and got defeated. Mahmud succeeded his father Subuktagin. He was a brilliant general and a fine cavalry leader. Year after year he raided India and sacked and killed and took away with him vast treasure and large numbers of captives. Altogether he made seventeen raids and only one of those-into Kashmir-was a failure. The others were successful, and he became a terror all over the north. He went as far as Pataliputra, Mathura and Somnath. From Thaneshwara he took away, it is said, 200,000 captives and vast wealth. But it was in Somnath that he got the most treasure. For this was one of the great temples, and the offerings of centuries had accumulated there. It is said that thousands of people took refuge in the temple when Mahmud approached, in the hope that a miracle would happen and the god they worshipped would protect them. But miracles seldom occur, except in the imaginations of the faithful, and the temple was broken and looted by Mahmud and 50,000 people perished, waiting for the miracle which did not happen. Mahmud died in 1030 A.C. The whole of the Punjab and Sindh was under his sway at the time. He is looked upon as great leader of Islam who came to spread Islam in India. Most Muslims adore him; most Hindus hate him. As a matter of fact, he was hardly a religious man. He was a Mohammedan, of course, but that was by the way. Above everything he was soldier, and a brilliant soldier.*[26]

---

[25] **GLIMPSES OF WORLD HISTORY ON CORDOVA AND GRANADA BY JAWAHARLAL NEHRU, PP. 188-192.**

[26] **GLIMPSES OF WORLD HISTORY (FROM HARSHA TO MAHMUD IN NORTH INDIA) BY NEHRU, PP. 154-155.**

Important point here is that if Jaipal avoided attacking Afghanistan, it may be that Sultan Mahmud may not come to India. Sultan Mahmud invaded India, may be to punish the Indian Raja and to take revenge of the attack by Jaipal during Sultan Mahmud's father when Hindu Raja of Lahore, Jaipal attacked Afganishtan. The invasion of India by the Arab, which Nehru avoided to mention, instead he has welcomed the Arabic Muslim invasion than that of Non-Arab Turks or Afghan. But the fact is the King of Sindh in India was Dahir Shah who treated the Muslim Arabs harshly or treated with insult the way Muslims are treated in India now like the depriving the Muslims their job, the Muslims are even killed by the Police and other para-military forces, their historical Mosque are destroyed in front of several thousand Indian forces and like many, and thus the then Governor of Kufa Hazzaz bin-Yussuf warned Dahir twice but after he received third complain from some Muslims traders, he, Hazzaz bin-Yussuf sent his son-in-law to punish Dahir and in this process Dahir was defeated and the Sindh and Panzab, in India became the part of Islamic Caliphate. Here we should mention that Hazzaz bin-Yussuf is not accepted in Islam as a great man, but a man of terrible Character and he was famous for his torture towards many Muslim, noble Muslim, as was in Nehru's language Sultan Mahmud. So while Nehru was very much critical of Sultan Mahmud, he avoided about Hazzaz bin-Yussuf that was behind first conquest of Muslim or in Nehru's language Arab invasion, which even Nehru welcomed. The followings are the reference of first Muslim invasion of India:

Conquest of Indo-Pakistan: Like Qutayba in Central Asia, Muhammad bin Qasim, cousin of Hajjaj, took the banner of Islam into the land of India. The cause of this expedition was the harassment of the Arab Governor caused by the pirates of Sind. The king of Sind was Dahir who refused to comply with the demand of the Governor. Several attempts were made to punish the king along with the pirates but all efforts were baffled till Muhammad bin Qasim came to save the prestige and honor of the Arab Governor. He attacked the kingdom of Dahir. Dahir tried his best to save his country from the hands of the foreigners but was ultimately defeated and killed. Then Sind, Multan and a part of the Punzab were annexed to the Muslim empire. The Muslim army also made progress by this time in Armenia and Asia Minor. But all other conquests of his reign faded before the conquests of the West.[27]

Imagine the "holy" Emperor, the head of Christendom, joining hands with the Caliph at Baghdad against a Christian power and an Arab power. You will remember that the Saracens of Spain had refused to recognize the Abbaside Caliphs of Baghdad. They had become independent, and Baghdad had a grievance against them. But they were too far apart for conflict. Between Constantinople and Charlemagne there was also not much love lost. *Here also distance prevented any actual fighting.* None the less the proposal was made for the Christian and the Arab to join together to fight another Christian and another Arab Power. The real motives at the back of kings' minds were those of gaining power and authority and wealth, but religion was often made the cloak for this. Everywhere this has been so. In India we saw Mahmud coming in the name of religion but making a good thing out of it. The cry of religion has paid often enough. But people's ideas change from age to age. And it is very difficult for us to judge of others who lived long ago. We must remember this. Many things that seem obvious to us to day would have been very strange to them, and their habits and ways of thinking would seem strange to us. While people talked of high ideals, and the Holy Empire, and the Viceroy of God, and the Pope who was Vicar

---

[27] **A STUDY OF ISLAMIC HISTORY PROF. K. ALI, PP. 179-181.**

of Christ, conditions in the West were as bad as they could well be. Soon after Charlemagne's reign Italy and Rome were in a disgraceful condition. ... [28]

One famous pilgrim, Peter the Hermit, especially went about; staff in hand, reaching to the people to rescue their holy city Jerusalem from the Muslims. Indignation and enthusiasm grew in Christendom, and, seeing this, the Pope decided to lead the movement.

About this time had come the appeal from Constantinople for help against the infidel. All Christendom, both Roman and Greek now seemed to be ranged against the oncoming Turks? In 1095 a great Church Council decided to proclaim a holy war against the Muslim for the recovery of the Holy City of Jerusalem. Thus began the fight of Christendom against Islam, of the Cross against the Crescent.[29]

The fall and decline of the Muslim or its Caliphate was due to its luxury and personal ambition and according to Nehru:

Originality was absent and so was bold and noble design. The polished graces and arts and luxury continued among the rich and the well to do, but little was done to relive the toil and misery of the people as a whole or to increase production. All these are the signs of the evening of a civilization. When this takes place you may be sure that the life of that civilization is vanishing; for creation is the sign of life, not repetition and imitation.[30]

The coming of the Muslims to India as invaders introduced an element of compulsion in religion. The fight was really a political one between conqueror and conquered, but it was colored by the religious element, and there was, at times, religious persecution. But it would be wrong to imagine that Islam stood for such persecution. There is an interesting report of a speech delivered by a Spanish Muslim when he was driven out of Spain, together with the remaining Arabs, in 1610. He protested against the Inquisition and said: "Did our victorious ancestors ever once attempt to extirpate Christianity out of Spain, when it was in their power? Did they not suffer your forefathers to enjoy the free use of their rites at the same time as they wore their chains? If there may have been some examples of forced conversions, they are so rare as scarce to deserve mentioning, and only attempted by men who had not the fear of God and the Prophet before their eyes, and who in doing so, have acted directly and diametrically contrary to the holy precepts and ordinances of Islam, which cannot, without sacrilege, be violated by any who would be held worthy of the honorable epithet of Musalman (Muslim). You can never produce, among us, any bloodthirsty formal tribunal, on account of different persuasions in points of faith, that any wise approaches your execrable Inquisition Our arms, it is true, are ever open to receive all who are disposed to embrace our religion; but we are not allowed by our sacred Quran to tyrannize over consciences."
So religious toleration and freedom of conscience, which were such marked features of old Indian life, slipped away from us to some extent, while Europe caught up to us and then went ahead in establishing, after many a struggle, these very principles. To day, sometimes, there is communal conflict in India, and Hindus and Muslims fight each other and kill each other. It is true that this happens only occasionally in some

---

[28] GLIMPSES OF WORLD HISTORY (THE COUNTRIES OF EUROPE TAKE SHAPE) BY NEHRU, P. 160.

[29] GLIMPSES OF WORLD HISTORY (END OF FIRST MILLENNIUM AFTER CHRIST) BY NEHRU, PP. 176-179.

[30] GLIMPSES OF WORLD HISTORY (ANOTHER LOOK AT ASIA AND EUROPE) BY NEHRU, PP. 180-181.

places, and that mostly we live in peace and friendship, for our real interests are one. It is a shameful thing for any Hindu or Muslim to fight his brother in the name of religion. We must put an end to it, and we will of course do so. But what is important is to get out of that complex ideology of custom, convention and superstition which, under the guise of religion. enchains us.[31]

Islam brought a new impulse for human progress to India. To some extent it served as a tonic. It shook up India. But it did less good than it might have done because of two reasons. It came in the wrong way, and it came rather late. for hundreds of years before Mahmud of Ghazni raided India, Muslim missionaries had wandered about India and had been welcomed. They came in peace and had some success. There was little, if any, ill feeling against Islam. Then came Mahmud with fire and sword and the manner of his coming as a conqueror and a plunderer and killer injured the reputation of Islam in India more than anything else did He was, of course, just like any other great conqueror, killing and plundering, and caring little for religion. But for a very long time his raids overshadowed Islam in India and made it difficult for people to consider it dispassionately, as they might otherwise have done.

This was one reason. The other was that it came late. It came about 400 years after it began, and during this long period it had exhausted itself somewhat, and lost a great deal of its creative energy. If the Arabs had come to India with Islam in the early days, the rising Arabian culture would have mixed with the old Indian culture and the two would have acted and reacted on each other, with great consequences. It would have been the mixing of two cultured races; and the Arabs were well known for their toleration and rationalism in religion. At one period, indeed, there was a club in Baghdad, under the patronage of the Caliph, were men of all religions and no religion met together to discuss and debate about all matters from the point of view of rationalism alone.

But the Arabs did not come to India proper. They stopped in Sindh, and India was little influenced by them. Islam came to India through the Turks and others who did not have the tolerance or the culture of the Arab, and who were primarily soldiers.

Still, a new impulse came to India for progress and creative effort. How this put some new life in India and then worked itself out, we shall consider later.

But they are just geographical expressions, and the problems that face us are not Asiatic or European problems, but world problems or problems of humanity. And unless we solve them for the whole world, there will continue to be troubling such a solution can only mean the ending of poverty and misery everywhere. This may take a long time, but we must aim at this, and at nothing less than this. Only then can we have real culture and civilization based on equality, where there is no exploitation of any country or class. Such a society will be a creative and regressive society, adapting itself to changing circumstances, and basing itself on the co-operation of its members. And ultimately it must spread all over the world. There will be no danger of such a civilization collapsing or decaying, as the old civilizations did.

So while we struggle for the freedom of India, we must remember that the great aim is human freedom, which includes the freedom of our people as well as other peoples.[32]

The Muslim invasion of Asia, Africa or Europe did not destroy the civilization of conquered land and race, though in some region, the Muslims vanished as in Spain and present day Bosnia. But the European invasion did the opposite, it destroyed the old

[31] GLIMPSES OF WORLD HISTORY, (THE FIGHT AGAINST AUTHORITARIANISM) BY NEHRU, PP. 233-234.

[32] GLIMPSES OF WORLD HISTORY (ANOTHER LOOK AT ASIA AND EUROPE) BY NEHRU, PP. 180-183.

civilization and its original people or race as happened in America and other continent like Australia. Some instances follows:

I have warned you, however, that there was a civilization in America in these early days. Not much is known of this and I certainly know very little indeed. Still, I cannot resist the temptation to tell you something about it here, so that you may not make the common mistake of thinking that America was just a savage country till Columbus and other Europeans reached there.

The Aztecs were a military nation. They had military colonies and garrisons, and a network of military roads. It is even said that they were clever enough to make their dependent States quarrel with each other. It was easier to rule them if they are divided. That has been the old policy of all empires. Rome called it: Divide et impera! divide and rule.

The Aztecs, in spite of their cleverness in other matters, were also priest-ridden, and worse still, their religion was full of human sacrifice. Thousands of human beings were sacrificed in this way in a most horrible manner every year.

A State so built and so carried on could not endure. And so it happened. Early in the sixteenth century (in 1519), when the Aztecs were apparently at the height of their power, the whole empire came down with a crash before a handful of its and adventurers! This is one of the most amazing examples of the collapse of an empire. And a Spaniard, Hernan Cortes, and a small troop brought this about with him. Cortes was a brave man, and daring enough. He had two things, which were of great help to him firearms and horses. Apparently there were no horses in the Mexican Empire, and there were certainly no firearms. But neither Cortes's courage nor his guns and horses would have availed him if the Aztec Empire had not been rotten at heart. It had decayed inside, just keeping the outer form, and even a little kick was enough to bring it down. The empire was based on exploitation and was much resented by the people. So when it was attacked, the people at large welcomed the discomfiture of the imperialists. As usual when this happens, there was a social revolution also. Cortes was once driven away, and he barely escaped with his life.[33]

It may occasion some surprise that Umar- a figure virtually unknown in the West- has been ranked higher than such famous men as Charlemagne may and Julius Caesar may. However, the conquests made by the Arabs under Umar, taking into account both their size and their duration, are substantially more important than those of either Caesar or Charlemagne.

In the year 1066, Duke William of Normandy, with only a few thousand troops behind him, crossed the English Channel in an attempt to become ruler of England.

9 CHRISTOPHER COLUMBUS 1451-1506

Columbus, by attempting to find a westward route from Europe to the Orient, inadvertently discovered the Americans, and thereby had a greater influence on world history than he could possibly have anticipated. His discovery, which inaugurated the age of exploration and colonization in the New World, was one of the critical turning points in history. It opened to the people of Europe two new continents for the settlement of their expanding populations, and provided a source of mineral wealth and raw materials that altered the economy of Europe. **His discovery led to the destruction of the civilizations of the American Indian. In the long run, it also led to the formation of a new set of nations in the Western Hemisphere, vastly different from the Indian nations, which had once inhabited the region, and greatly affecting the nations of the Old World**

---

[33] **GLIMPSES OF WORLD HISTORY (THE MAYA CIVILIZATION OF AMERICA), BY NEHRU, PP. 183-185.**

Augustinee: The vehicle for this progress was, of course, the Church. ("There is no salvation outside the Church.") It therefore followed those emperors, whether pagan or Christian or barbarian, were not as important as the Pope and the Church were.

Adolph Hitler was born in 1889, in Braunau, Austria. As a young man, he was an unsuccessful artist, and sometime during his youth he became an ardent German nationalist. During World War I, he served in the German army, was wounded, and received two medals for bravery.

Germany's defeat left him shocked and angered. In 1919, when he was thirty, he joined a tiny, right wing party in Munich, which soon changed its name to the National Socialist German Workers' Party (the Nazi party for short). Within two years he had become its undisputed leader (in German: Fuehrer). ... During his years in power, Hitler engaged in a policy of genocide without parallel in History. He was a fanatical racist, with a particularly virulent animosity toward the Jews. He made it his specific, publicly stated goal to kill every Jew in the world. During his regime, the Nazis constructed large extermination camps, equipped with massive gas chambers for this purpose. In every territory that came under his control, innocent men, women, and children were rounded up and shipped off in cattle cars to be killed in those chambers. In the space of just a few years, almost 6,000,000 Jews died in this way. .... But his territorial conquests, although very large, were ephemeral, and today even West Germany and East Germany combined have less territory than the German Republic did when Hitler took office. It was Hitler's consuming passion to destroy the Jews; but fifteen years after Hitler took office, an independent Jewish state came into existence for the first time in 2,000 years.[34]

FROM THE WORLD'S HEADLINES, The Western allies engage in mutual recrimination as Bosnia burns

THE TIMES, BRITAIN: "If the result of this drawn-out quarrel is to inoculate the American public against the idea of ever coming to the aid of the Europeans again, the harm Bosnia will have done will be incalculable."

LE MONDE, FRANCE: "Whatever the real reasons for the dissensions between Americans and Europeans, they illustrate the difficulty of managing post--cold war crises."

LOS ANGELES TIMES, UNITED STATES: Walter Russell Mead op-ed article: "Clinton's Bosnia policy will be an albatross around the neck of Democratic candidates in 1994, and he will be at most, a one-term President.'

DIE WELT, GERMANY: "Bill Clinton, who a few days ago looked like a determined and impatient potential warlord in the Bosnia conflict, has turned overnight into a quit and embarrassed man."[35]

THE BALKANS, GUNS AND HATE, For months, Muslim residents of Mostar, the capital of Herzegovina, have been fighting off Serbs intent on seizing the eastern part of the city. Last week Serbs were the least of the Muslims' worries as they found themselves savagely attacked by their erstwhile allies, Herzegovina's ethnic Croats. Street battles flared as the paramilitaries of the Croatian Defense Council (HVO) rained artillery fire on Muslim-held areas; scores were killed and thousands prepared to flee.

Disturbing stories emerged, UN officials reported that 1,500 Muslims were being detained under "atrocious" conditions at a former military base outside Mostar. Many were still in

---

[34] **THE 100, A RANKING OF THE MOST INFLUENTIAL PERSONS IN HISTORY BY Michael H. Hart, published by MEERAA PUBLLICATION, Madras 600 040, India;(51 'UMAR IBN AL-KHATTAB), (WILLIAM THE CONQUEROR) (9 CHRISTOPHER COLUMBUS), pp. 275, 361, 77, 281-282, 35,213.**

[35] **TIME, MAY 24, 1993 No. 21, p. 11.**

the nightgowns and pajamas they were wearing when Croat troops ordered them out of their homes; some reported receiving only four biscuits and a glass of water as their daily ration. Bosnian HVO leaders insisted that the Muslims had been evacuated for their own safety-even though Croats living in the same battered neighborhoods were not forced to leave. "The Bosnian Croats don't want Muslims in their areas- they want them ethnical clean," said a UN analyst in Zagreb, Croatia's capital. According to aid workers in Mostar, Croat forces were ordering Muslims to surrender their weapons and fly whit flags from their windows; those who did not comply were thrown out of their homes. In the town of Ljubuski, 26 km southwest of Mostar, HVO fighters dynamited the local mosque. .... In the end the much-derided Vance-Owen plan looks more and more like the only solution left for Bosnia-Herzegov in an opportunity that ethnic Croats have been embracing by open force of arms.[36]

Yet the following interview is another example as published in the TIME OF MAY 24, 1993.

Q. You would not deny that Hizballah [Lebanon's Iran-backed Party of God] has committed violent acts?

A. TERRORISM: RAFSANJANI: PG. 38-39: Can it be that you do not know how many Mujahedin group [an antigovernment faction]? Who hijacked our planes? Who blew up our government headquarters, assassinated our President and Premier, and bombed the Islamic Republican Party's headquarters, resulting in the deaths of 72 high officials? Yet these same terrorists are close to the White House and enjoy U.S. congressional endorsement. If Iran had shot down an American airliner, as the U.S. shot down an Iranian Airbus in the Persian Gulf, what would the U.S. do? Therefore shouldn't we more appropriately accuse the U.S. of terrorism? Interviewed by Time managing editor James R. Gaines and Time International managing editor Karsten Prager in Tehran.

And the Muslim invader or Caliphate like Spain did not cleanse the Christians or Hindu or any race in Europe, in Asia or in Africa, which the European did in America, and Australia, and doing the same thing in Bosnia. The following historical references from Nehru are enough for the judgement of the learned readers:

It was called the Black Death, and it killed off people by the million. About a third of the population of England died, and in China and elsewhere the death roll was stupendous. It is surprising that it did not come to India.
This awful calamity reduced the population greatly and often there were not enough people to till the land. Owing to the lack of men, the wages of workers tended to rise from their miserable level. But the landlords and property-owners controlled the parliaments and they passed laws to force people to work at the old miserable wage and not to ask for more. Crushed and exploited beyond endurance, the peasants and the poor revolted. All over Western Europe these peasant revolts took place one after the other. In France there was what is called a jacquerie in 1358. In England there was Wat Tyler's rebellion, in which Tyler was killed in front of the English King in 1381. These revolts were put down, often with much cruelty. England and France were almost continually at war with each other. From early in the fourteenth century to the middle of the fifteenth century there was what is called the Hundred Years War between them. To the east of France there was Burgundy. This was a powerful State, nominally vassal to the King of France. But Burgundy was a turbulent and troublesome vassal, and the English intrigued with it, as well as with other Powers, against France. France was for a while hemmed in on all sides. A good part of western France was for long in English possession, and the King of England began to call

---

[36] **TIME, MAY 24, 1993, No. 21, by JAMES L. GRAFF, ZAGREB, PP. 22-26.**

himself King of France also. When France was at the lowest ebb of her fortunes and there seemed no hope for her, hope and victory came in the form of a young peasant girl. You know something of Jeanne d'Arc (or Joan of Arc), the Maid of Orleans. She is a heroine of yours. She gave confidence to her dispirited people and inspired them to great endeavor and under her lead they drove out the English from their country. But for all this the reward she got was a trial and sentence of the Inquisition and the stake. The English got hold of her, and they made the Church condemn her, and then in the market-place of Rouen they burnt her in 1430.

But the proud Eastern Roman Empire of 1000 years was reduced to just this city and practically nothing more. Although the Turk was rapidly swallowing up the Eastern Empire, there appear to have been friendly relations between the Sultan and the Emperors, and they married into each other's families. Ultimately in 1453 Constantinople fell to the Turks. We shall now refer to the Ottoman Turks only. The Seljuqs have dropped out of the picture. The fall of Constantinople, though long expected, was a great event which shook Europe.

The great cathedral of Saint Sophia, which had been built by the Emperor Justinian in the sixth century, was turned into a mosque-Aya Sufiya it was called and there was some plundering of its treasures. Europe was excited about this, but it could do nothing. As a matter of fact, however, the Turkish Sultans were very tolerant of the Orthodox Greek Church, and after the capture of Constantinople, Sultan Mohammad II actually proclaimed himself the protector of the Greek Church. A later Sultan, who is known as Suleiman the Magnificent, considered himself the representative of the Eastern Emperors and took the title of Caesar.

Such is the power of ancient tradition.

Their experience of the Latin Crusaders had been bad. It is said that during the last siege of Constantinople in 1453 a Byzantine nobleman said: "Better the turban of the Prophet than the tiara of the Pope".

The Ottoman Sultans, by taking Constantinople, seem to have inherited many of the evil habits of luxury and corruption from their predecessors, the Byzantine emperors. The whole degraded imperial system of the Byzantine enveloped them and gradually sapped their strength.[37]

Two hundred years later, the Ottoman Turks were in possession of the imperial city of Constantinople and a good bit of south-eastern Europe. **After 800 years of fighting between Muslim and Christian, the great prize, which had lured the Arabs and the Seljuqs, had fallen into the hands of the Ottomans. Not content with this, the Ottoman Sultans looked with hungry eyes to the west, even at Rome itself. They threatened the German (Holy Roman) Empire and Italy. They conquered Hungary and reached the walls of Vienna and the frontiers of Italy. In the east they added Baghdad to their dominions; in the south, Egypt. In the middle of the sixteenth century Sultan Suleman, called the Magnificent, ruled over this great Turkish Empire. Even on the seas his fleets were supreme. How, then, did this change occur? How did Europe get rid of the Mongol menace? How did it survive the Turkish danger? and not only survive it, but become aggressive itself and a menace to others? The Mongols did not threaten Europe for long. They went away of their own accord to elect a new Khan and they did not come back. Western Europe was too far away from their homelands in Mongolia. Perhaps also it did not attract them because it was woody country and they were used to the wide open plains and steppes. The capture of Constantinople by the Turks in 1452 is supposed to be a turning-point in European history. It marks, for the sake of convenience, the passing of the Middle Ages and the coming of the new spirit, the Renaissance, which flowered out in a variety of ways. Thus, curiously, just when**

[37] **GLIMPSES OF WORLD HISTORY (THE PASSING OF THE MIDDLE AGES) BY NEHRU, PP. 235-238.**

Europe was threatened by the Turks, and the Turks seemed to have a good chance of success, Europe found her feet and developed strength. The Turks went on advancing in western Europe for a while; and while they advanced, European explorers were discovering new countries and seas and rounding the globe. Under Suleiman the Magnificent, who reigned from 1520 to 1566, the Turkish Empire spread from Vienna to Baghdad and Cairo. But there was no advance after that. The Turks were succumbing to the old weakening and corrupting traditions of the Constantinople of the Greeks. As Europe increased in power, the Turks lost their old energy and became weaker.

In the far west was the Empire of the Golden Horde-what a fascinating name these people had! The Russian nobles paid tribute to it for nearly 200 years after Kublai's death. At the end of this period (1480) the Empire was weakening a little and the Grand Duke of Moscow, who had managed to become the chief Russian noble, refused to pay tribute. This Grand Duke, is called Ivan the Great. .... The Mongols finally retired from Europe.

We need not trouble ourselves much about the remains of the Golden Horde or the other Mongol empires of Central Asia. But one man claims our attention. This man was Timur, who wanted to be a second Chengiz Khan. He claimed to be descendant from Chengiz, but he was really a Turk. He was lame and is therefore called Timur-i-lang or Timur the Lame or Tamurlane. He succeeded his father and became ruler of Samarqand in 1369. Soon afterwards, he started on his career of conquest and cruelty. He was a great general, but he was a complete savage. The Mongols of central Asia had meanwhile become Muslims and Timur himself was a Muslim. But the fact that he was dealing with Muslims did not soften him in the least. Wherever he went he spread desolation and pestilence and utter misery. His chief pleasure was the erection of enormous pyramids of skulls. From Delhi in the east to Asia Minor in the west he caused to be massacred hundreds of thousands of persons and had their skulls arranged in the form of pyramids ![38]

Let us look at the India of the fourteenth and fifteenth centuries. The Delhi Sultanate shrinks till it vanishes away on Timur's coming. There are a number of large independent States all over India, mostly Muslim; but there is one powerful Hindu State Vijayanagar in the south. Islam is no longer a stranger or a new comer in India. It is well established. The fierceness and cruelty of the early Afghan invaders and the Slave kings have been toned down, and the Muslim kings are as much Indians as the Hindus. They have no outside connections. Wars take place between different States, but they are political and not reli-gious. sometimes a Muslim State employs Hindu troops, and a Hindu State Muslim troops . Muslim kings often marry Hindu women and Hindus are often employed as ministers and high officials by the Muslim kings. There is little of the feeling of conqueror and conquered or ruler and ruled. Indeed, most of the Muslims, including some of the rulers, and Indians converted to Islam. Many of these become converted in the hope of gaining Court favor or economic advantage, and in spite of their change of religion they stick to most of their old customs. Some Muslim rulers adopt forcible methods to bring about conversion, but even this is largely with a political object, as it is thought that the converts would be more loyal subjects. But force does not go far in bringing about conversions. A more effective method is the economic. Non-Muslims are made to pay a poll-tax called the jizya and many of them wishing to escape this, become Muslims. But all this takes place in the cities. The villages are little affected, and the millions of villagers carry on in the old way. It is true that the king's officers interfere more in village life. The powers of the village panchayats ate less now than they used to be, but still the panchayats continue and are the center and backbone of village life. Socially, and in the matter of religion and custom, the village is almost un-changed. India as you know, is still a country of hundreds of thousands of villages. The towns and cities sit on the surface, as it were, but the real India has been and still is, village

[38] **GLIMPSES OF WORLD HISTORY (THE BREAK-UP OF THE MONGOL EMPIRES) PP. 245-247.**

India. This village India was not much changed by Islam. Hinduism was shaken up in two ways by the coming of Islam; and strange to say, these ways were contrary to each other. On the one side it became conservative; it hardened and retired into a shell in an attempt at protecting itself against the attack on it. Caste became stiffer and more exclusive; the purdah and seclusion of women became commoner. On the other hand, there was a kind of internal revolt against caste and too much puja (worship of goddes) and ceremonial. Many efforts were made to reform it.

The old Indian rulers had custom and convention to check their autocracy. The new Muslim rulers did not have even this Although in theory there is far more equality in Islam, and, as we have seen, even a slave could become sultan, still the autocratic and unchecked power of the king increased. What more amazing instance of this can one have than that of the mad Tughlaq who moved the capital from Delhi to Daulatabad ?

The Muslim Court language was Persian. Most educated people learnt Persian if they had anything to do with the courts or government offices. Thus large numbers of Hindus learnt Persian. Gradually a new language developed in the camps and bazaars, called "Urdu", which means camp. In reality this was not a new language. It was Hindi with a slightly different dress on; there were more of Persian words in it, but otherwise it was Hindi. This Hindi-Urdu language, or as it is sometimes called Hindustani, spread all over northern and Central India. It is today spoken, with minor variations, by about 150,000,000 people and understood by a far greater number. Thus it is, from the point of numbers, one of the major languages of the world.[39]

Now let us have a few remarks of some researchers which is as follows with their name and other references:

Dan Stewart Gilliland (1972)
Gilliland, Dean Stewart, 1928-
African Traditional Religion in Transition; The influence of Islam on African
Traditional Religion in North Nigeria
The Hartford Seminar Foundation, Ph. D. 1971
Religion

University Microfilms, A xerox Company, Ann Arbor, Michigan

Ref from pg. 178 of the above book as follows:

B. The Individual Against the Community

Loss of Traditional Center and Religious Change

We have said above that one of Islam's strongest influences for the modern Nigerian in the North is when he becomes disoriented from his primary society. Islam can then become a new center of reference for his life. The forces which combine to shatter the tribe are every where. Religion is not to be discounted as one such force, especially when its by-product are education and a redirection of interests which result from status derived outside of the tribe. Wilfred Cantwell Smith, when speaking of the "university" of Islam and its ability to serve the diverse needs of a changing society, makes the following statement:

---

[39] GLIMPSES OF WORLD HISTORY (INDIA TACKLES A DIFFICULT PROBLEM) BY NEHRU, PP. 250-252.

(Islam provides) communities into which any stranger may enter, and where he can meet on equal grounds with the people of other tribes.... universal religions .... serve a useful social function in giving a faith
to live by in providing against insecurity. They help in employment, sickness and death. While they do disintegrate to some extent, they also seek to re-integrate society and to "destroy and overthrow," to "build and to plant"[40]

Islam is essentially a religion for individuals who have been uprooted from their community or whose community have vanished under their feet.[41]

Again reference from Page 188 of the above book as follows:

The Muslim Urban Presence

That the strength of Islam and the hub of its greatest influence has been in the towns is a matter of Islamic history. It was not the nomadic and disunited tribes of the Arabian desert where Muhammad found a base for his new faith. It was rather their urban based kinsmen, divided as they were in Medina and Mecca, that the religion was established and from which it takes its inspiration and momentum.[42]

Reference from page 189-190 of the above book as follows:

This special urban feature of Islam is one that is recognized and appreciated as integral to it's very life. Means quoted from Syed Abdul Latif in the following word:
(Islam cannot exist in its distinctive form without towns and only towns people can conscientiously follow its principles. The farmer instinctively resists it as a disintegrative factor, on the other hand in the town where life and personal relationships are more secularized, Islam is an integrative factor. Town life and trading involve abandoning the local religion; Islamic law can operate over a wider field of social relations, qadi's courts can function and teachers attract pupils from a wide area. In the townsmen class are the occupational groups, clergy..... men of business such as merchants and traders, craftsmen, shopkeepers, vendors.... and finally artisans and manual laborers. The heterogeneity characteristic of towns, however, derives from differences of ethnic origins rather than from divisions of labor. Islam with its power to call the jami for Friday prayers is the only integrative factor.[43] [44]

---

[40]W. C. Smith, "Islam in the Modern World," Current History, 32 no. 190 (/june, 1957), p. 44

[41]IBID., p. 137.

[42]Watt, Islam and Society, chap. ii, esp. pp. 4-20

[43]Syed Abdul Latif, The Mind al-Quran Build (Agapura; Hyderabad The Academy of Islamic Studies, 1962), p. 6 cited in Means, "The Influence od Islam," p. 99

[44] Dan Stewart Gilliland (1972), Gilliland, Dean Stewart, 1928-
African Traditional Religion in Transition; The influence of Islam on African Traditional Religion in North Nigeria, The Hartford Seminar Foundation, Ph. D. 1971, Religion, University Microfilms, A xerox Company, Ann Arbor, Michigan, (B. The Individual Against the Community), PP. 178, 188-190.

Reference from the following Book on Indonesian Islam:

This is an authorized facsimile and was produced by microfilm-xerography
in 1981 by UNIVERSITY MICROFILMS INTERNATIONAL, Ann Arbor, Michigan,
U. S. A., London, England

THE CRESCENT AND THE RISING SUN
INDONESIAN ISLAM UNDER THE JAPANESE OCCUPATION OF JAVA 1942-45
A Thesis presented to the Faculty of the Graduate School of Cornell University for the
Degree of Doctor of Philosophy

by Harry Jindrich Benda, M. A. june, 1955

Introduction-----pg. 1-3
For just over forty months, from March 1942 to August 1945, the former Netherlands
East Indies lived under Japanese occupation. After the gradual political evolution
during the proceeding three and one-half centuries of Dutch rule, the brief Japanese
interregnum was a hectic episode which yet profoundly affected almost all aspects of
Indonesian life.

Although the removal of the Western colonial ruling group was the most important
single factor in all the occupied areas of Southeast Asia - with the limited exception of
Indo-China -, the effects of the occupation were perhaps more far-reaching in
Indonesia than in Burma or the Philippines, e.g., who had politically matured under
Western rule to a higher degree than the Indies. At any rate, Japan came to Indonesia
with an apparently well planned colonial policy which resulted in lasting changes in
the power-structure of the competing elite-groups.
After many years of partial suppression by the Dutch colonial administration,
including banishment of some of its outstanding leaders, the Western-educated
Indonesian nationalist elite was given recognition, official appointments and prestige,
though, at the outset especially, little actual power. The Japanese, in other words,
revised one important aspect of their predecessors' colonial policy, and in doing so
straight the Indonesian nationalist movement far beyond its pre-occupation potential.
Finally Japan's Islamic policy in Indonesia constituted an equally significant
departure from that of the former colonial government. If it would have been difficult
to forecast the early emergence of an Indonesian Republic when Dutch rule ended in
1942, it would have been almost equally difficult to anticipate that free Indonesia's
perhaps largest and most important political party would be an Islamic organization,
the Masjumi, or that the political stability of the new state would be seriously
endangered by Moslem insurgents.

Chapter 1

THE FOUNDATION OF DUTCH ISLAMIC POLICY

IT IS POSSIBLE TO VIEW THE ISLAMIC PROBLEM IN INDONESIA FROM
THREE ASPECTS, AND TO SEE THE ISLAMIC INFLUENCE OPERATING on
three levels in Indonesian society. The first and most basic level is conditioned by the
fact that the overwhelming majority of Indonesians are Moslems. On this grass-roots
level, Islam, like no other force until the most recent times, has been the great unifier:
The long history of revolt against Christian dominance, especially that preceding our
century, was largely written in terms of Moslem uprisings and war.
On the second level, however, the Islamic problem presents itself a far more complex
position than the basic factor would lead us to believe. While it is true that the most

79

Indonesians are (1)(No recent, exact data are available on this point. The Moslem are usually stated as comprising above ninety percent of the total Indonesian population.[45]) and have been Moslems--- for over five centuries in Sumatra for over four in Java [46]----- the victory of Islam has never been more than partial. It has converted the Indonesians only to be converted itself, as an observer has recently put it[47]

On the third level, finally, we find Islam as a political force within the framework of the Indonesian nationalist movement, in which it has played an increasingly important role.
As is true of most artificial classification and segmentation, this division of the Islamic problem should not be pushed too far. It should not obscure the fact that Indonesian Islam --- whether viewed as a grass-roots problem, as a religious demand for greater adherence to the Mohammedan Law, or as part of the political independence movement - is a living reality which has permeated Indonesian life at almost every level.

Dutch Islamic policy on all the three level was of needs dictated by the situational logic posited by the demands of enlightened Christian rule over Moslem subjects. Such a policy could only be negative it its overall ramifications, consisting of a commingling of half-hearted tolerance, benevolent vigilance and active interference.
Confronted by the hard fact of ruling Moslems, the European colonial rulers could not be expected to grant more than a colorless guaranty of religious freedom to the vast majority of Moslems and to the insignificant minority of Christians alike; they could never expect more than sullen acceptance of their "generosity" in matters religious, nor did they ever seek more than just such acceptance, acquiescence, and public peace.

Reference from page 6 - 8 of the above book as follows:

The enemy against whom the barriers had to be erected in 1910-12 was primarily external; it was the Caliphate and Pan-Islam who, from abroad, were potentially at least capable of attracting the allegiance of Indonesian Moslems. Only one local "political" factor -- the preaching of Holy War against the infidel government --- had to be guarded against, as the most dangerous local expression of pan-Islamic sentiment.
Christian Snouck Hurgronje, the noted Dutch Arabicist, and first Adviser for Native and Arabian Affairs to the Netherlands East Indies' Government[48] admitted that the

---

[45]Cf. Report on Indonesia (New York), V, 14 (May 25, 1954), p. 10

[46]Cf. F. W. Stutterheim, Cultuurgeschiedenis van Indonesia. II De Islam en zijn komst in de Archipel (Growingen/Djakarta: J. B. Wolters, 2nd impr., 1952), pp. 33 ff.

[47]Cf. G. H. Bousquet, "Introduction a l'etude de l'Islam Indonesian,"Revue des Etudes Islamiiques (Paris), 1938, II-III, pp. 135-259, p. 225. See also K. P. Landon, Southeast Asia, Crossroad of Religions (Chicago: University of Chicago Press, 1949),p. 163.

[48]pp. 4 Hurgronje (1857-1936) was Adviser to the Indies' Government between 1889 and 1906. & 6

Ottoman Empire was not using Pan-Islam as an active principle of its foreign policy.[49] Yet he feared its grip on the illiterate peasant masses of Indonesia, "which have absorbed [its] ideas just sufficiently to doubt the continuous legality of the European administration"[50]. It was, however, a serious misreading of the nature of Islam to imply, as Snouck Hurgronje did, that the 'continuous legality' of Christian rule over Moslems would ever by psychologically and ethically acceptable to Moslems left free to enjoy a measure of religious freedom. Indonesian Moslems - as Dutch colonial history only too readily shows - had not only been doubting the legality of European rule, they had bitterly fought against its very establishment and continued existence[51].
[52]

The present day Muslim leaders of all the nation States forgot the political System of Islam and the political center of great Islam. But the western researchers know it well the then the its' leader and the scholar's is continued bellow:

It was, perhaps, a basic failure of Snouck's not to realize that this widespread sentiment was latent in Islam rather than in Pan-Islam, and to search for the political center in Islam exclusively in Constantinople, Cairo, or Mecca[53]. Pan-Islam, in other

---

[49]"Even in Turkey," he wrote in 1910, "... it could almost be said that the political leaders have deposited the pan-Islamic program in the museum of their political antiquities."" "Over Pan-Islamisme," pp. 372-73

[50]Ibid., p.375.

[51] For a brief survey, cf. M. Dimyati, Sedjarah perdjuangan Indonesia (Djakarta: Widjaya, 1951, pp. 8-12. On the last large-scale struggle, the Achin War of 1873-1908, see F. S. de klerck, History of the Netherlands Indies (Rotterdam:W. L. & J. Brusse, 1938),II, ch.XVI, pp. 342 ff.

[52] This is an authorized facsimile and was produced by microfilm-xerography in 1981 by UNIVERSITY MICROFILMS INTERNATIONAL, Ann Arbor, Michigan, U. S. A., London, England, THE CRESCENT AND THE RISING SUN INDONESIAN ISLAM UNDER THE JAPANESE OCCUPATION OF JAVA 1942-45
A Thesis presented to the Faculty of the Graduate School of Cornell University for the Degree of Doctor of Philosophy, by Harry Jindrich Benda, M. A. june, 1955, PP. 1-3,6-8.

[53]"Islam," as a recent writer puts it, "has been a political religion from its inception.... [and] the all-embracing demand of religion has, indeed, remained an essential characteristic of Islam up to the present day." Richard Hartman, "Islam and Naticnalismus,"

words, was a political phantom, while the threat of holy war belonged to gross-roots Indonesian Islamic proper. To seek a dividing line between religion and the anti-Christian sentiment was, at best, a pious hope; at worst, it was political blindness[54]. To Snouck, Islam was, briefly put, a matter of the past as much it was a matter of the common people only. It was a spell-binding superstition for the masses of Indonesian peasants, to be broadly tolerated, if guarded against excesses. But Islam contained, in Snouck' view, no seeds for growth, development and evolution towards a more modern, not to say higher, Western-style civilization. Its Indonesian believers were illiterate and ignorant; its leaders - particularly at the village level -- backward-looking teachers of orthodox, lifeless dogma capable of inciting their flock to rebellion, but incapable of leading it towards an enlightened future. In the light of 19th Century liberalism, such a view was not necessarily vicious. Snouck did not ridicule Islam in order to extol Christianity. To him the alternative lay not between Moslems peas.......[55]

We have shown the comment African country like Nigeria and even distant country Like Indonesia, but another researcher work on how the Islam spread in China which is given below:

This is an authorized facsimile and was produced by microfilm-xerography in 1981 by UNIVERSITY MICROFILMS INTERNATIONAL, Ann Arbor, Michigan, U. S. A., London, England, PILLSBURY, Barbara Linne Kroll, 1942 (74-29, 644) COHESION AND CLEAVAGE IN A CHINESE MUSLIM MINORITY, COLUMBIA UNIVERSITY, Ph. D., 1973, Anthropology Submitted in partial

---

Abhandlungen der deutschen Akademie der Wissenschaften zu Berlin, Philosophisch-historische Klasse, No.5, 1945/46 (Berlin, 1948), p.3

[54]Cf. Charles O. van der Plas, "mededeelingen over de stroomingen in de Moslimsche gemeenschap in Nederlandsch-Indie" en de Nederlandsche Islampolitiek," Indisch Genootschap (The Hague), 1934, pp. 253-72, on p. 269: "All classical authoritative texts, all commentaries, and even the Koran itself contain parts..... which are capable of abuse for purposes of agitation."

[55] This is an authorized facsimile and was produced by microfilm-xerography in 1981 by UNIVERSITY MICROFILMS INTERNATIONAL, Ann Arbor, Michigan, U. S. A., London, England, THE CRESCENT AND THE RISING SUN INDONESIAN ISLAM UNDER THE JAPANESE OCCUPATION OF JAVA 1942-45 A Thesis presented to the Faculty of the Graduate School of Cornell University for the Degree of Doctor of Philosophy, by Harry Jindrich Benda, M. A. june, 1955, P. 8.

fulfillment for requirement for the Degree of Doctor of Philosophy in the faculty of Political Science 1973, in pg. 10-11 as follows:

Historians do not agree on the details of Islam's arrival in China.[56] One tradition tells of a maternal uncle of the Prophet who landed at Canton about 629 A. D. bearing gifts from Muhammad to the emperor of china (Hartmann 1955:889; Broomhall 1910, d'Ollone 1911). Legend claims the first official diplomatic relations between China and the Arabic world to have been established in 651 A. D. when Sa'ad Ibn Abi Waqqas, an emissary of the Muslim Caliph Uthman, was received by the T'ang emperor Yung-wei. The latter, allegedly finding the religion of Muhammad compatible with the teaching of Confucius, is said to have ordered China's first mosque to be constructed in the city of Ch'ang-an (Ch'en Yuan 1928:116-117). As of 1953 the mosque involved in this legend stood in good condition in modern Sian (Ting 1958:344). Accounts also tell of 4000 Muslims mercenaries sent by the Caliph Mansur to assist the Chinese emperor in quelling a Tatar rebellion. They were allegedly rewarded with land and permission to settle in China's chief cities (Needham 1954: 215: Sauvaget 1948, XXXVIII).
With Arab and Persian merchants of those cities, they came to be known as fan-K'e or "barbarian guests". They took Chines wives who bore children called t'u-sheng fan-k's or "China-born barbarian guests".
... The Muslim population was able to increase and spread inland.

Reference from page 12 of the book as follows:

Most distinguished of the Yuan dynasty Muslims was Sayyid Edjell (also known as Shams al-Din, Shammsettn Omar, Sai-dienchr Chan-ssu-tung and many other related variants.) He served as Commander-in-Chief of the Mongolian Expeditionary Forces in Szechuan, then as Governor-General of Kansu-Shensi-Szechuan and later as Governor o Yunnan. Muslims today proudly state that he governed[57][58]

---

[56] Nor do they agree on the origin of the term Hui as the common designation for Chinese Muslims. In Chinese, Hui means, literally, "to return." Some scholars say the term was applied to Muslims who settled in China, since, it was assumed, they would one day return to that place from which they had come. Others say it implies submission or eventual return to Allah. Still others say it derives from Hui-ho, a Central Asian people who became Muslims in approximately the eleventh century. See for example, discussions of the question by Bretschneider (1910: 264-274), Broomhall (1910), Fu (1969), Hu (1963:95-98), d'Ollone (1911), Pai (1944, 1948, 1951) and de Thiersant (1878:1:1-15).

[57].... Without prejudice as to race or religion and without forced conversion of the people to Islam--- on the contrary, he was the first to establish Confucian temples in Yunnan. Many of the cultural patterns of the present day are due to this great governor whose name is still revered by the people of Yunnan. Were it not for his religion, he would long since have been worshiped in the temples(Ting 1958:348.

So Caliph Uthman (R. A.) or even Abbaside Caliph Mansur sent emissaries, even army to far country like China. But the leaders of the present Muslim countries had know constructive role to play in even in their region, the result is there is always some war among themselves in their region, proof of such is nine months old war in 1971 over Bangladesh, long nine years war between Iran and Iraq, occupation of Kuwait by Iraq, the death of hungry people in Somalia and so on.

Under what right they divided the single Caliphate into over 50 states? Under what right they divided the vast God's given wealth into over 50 pieces, resulting some nation state with huge and surplus wealth and others without sufficient food to feed its' people. Why those barrier created by man to keep some without daily necessity a creature need? Why those barrier of passport and visa to visit the region which was a single state for long 1300 years? Who gave that right? Even the birds do not obey their barrier of passport and visa. God created every thing in a balance way so that all creature can be benefited by it. We can not stop the birds from coming to other region, like Indian subcontinent, when the Siberian Birds use to visit during winter and go back to Siberia after winter; then why so called civilized human being will make obstacle human beings to go to the countries they like in search of foods, cloths and shelters. Some people may laugh for the above comment? Our question to them is "can you prove that there was any such instances of barrier like passport and visa a hundred years ago in the present day Islamic countries?
In the past the Muslims went wherever they liked; they settled wherever they liked. But why then those restrictions? You could not stop the ancestor of Indian national leader Moulana Abul Kalam Azad from settling in the Holy Mecca? You were not able to halt his father to settle in Calcutta. Even though Moulana Azad was a born Hezazi or Mecci or Saudi, he was elected leader of the Congress party of Indian subcontinent, though he was a Muslim and not an Indian by birth he was able to lead the Congress party more than once and even he is the youngest President of Indian National Congress ever elected. The people of largest democratic country in the world, India elected their leader who was not born in India, but in present day Saudi Arabia, was not a Hindu which are majority people of India. But it is a great pity and irony of fate that we the Muslims, around the same number of be people which now around 1000 million live in this Indian subcontinent (India, Pakistan and Bangladesh), could not elect a Caliph among themselves i. e. Muslims. More pity is that now ordinary Muslims even forgot that for long 1300 years there was a System of Caliphate or Caliph or the Leader of the faithful or Muslims. But in Christianity there was no such combined system which can unify both political and religion matter together.

In Mr. Jawaharlal Nehru's language "This Holy Roman Empire was not a continuation of the old Western Roman Empire. It was something different. It considered itself the Empire, the Emperor being boss over everybody else in the world-except perhaps the Pope. Compare this emperor with Khalifa or Caliph, who was styled the Commander of the

---

[58] **This is an authorized facsimile and was produced by microfilm-xerography in 1981 by UNIVERSITY MICROFILMS INTERNATIONAL, Ann Arbor, Michigan, U. S. A., London, England, PILLSBURY, Barbara Linne Kroll, 1942 (74-29, 644), COHESION AND CLEAVAGE IN A CHINESE MUSLIM MINORITY, COLUMBIA UNIVERSITY, Ph. D., 1973, Anthropology Submitted in partial fulfillment for requirement for the Degree of Doctor of Philosophy in the faculty of Political Science 1973, pp. 10-12.**

Faithful. The Khalifa was really an emperor and Pope combined, to begin with. Later, as we shall see, he became just a figurehead."[5*]

We talk about universal Human right according to United nation,s charter. But before about 1300 years ago Islam gave a ordinary citizen to take revenge against the ruler of entire Muslim world if any one thought that a injustice was done to him and law was equal for the leader and entire people.

Around 35% to 40% of world total Muslim population live in India-Pakistan-Bangladesh sub-continent of which 120 to 200 million of Muslim or 10% to 15% live in India alone. So what is going in Bosnia by the Serbs and former Yugoslavia could happen in India. But thank to the Indian non-Muslim or Hindu population that at least there was some civilized and intellectual people in India like Mahatma Gandhi and Nehru density that helped to minimize the massacre of Muslims in India. Even Gandhi had to give his life before an assassin for his protest over the massacre of Muslims just after the partition of India which was mentioned by Moulana Abul Kalam Azad in his famous book "India weans freedom" with some criticize by Gandhi of the then Home minister Bollove Bhai Patel for his role in that time. Yet there was some massacre of Muslim and Hindus in greater Panzab (in Pakistan and India) and other part of India

But it is an irony of fate that Indian Muslims were against the British Government for its' conspiracy of abolition of Khilafat during world war. Even Gandhi joined the Muslims for the Khelafat movement.

But what a pity it is that since 1924 no Arab leader talked about that Khelafat that has been initiated and headed by the Arabs for long 900 years of Islamic movement from Khelafat Rasheda, Ummaya, and Abbaside era and even during some split of the Khelaphat (Caliphate) era by Fatimite in Egypt and separation of Spain under Umayat from mainstream Khelaphat under Baghdad

But who has been most benefited by this lost Khelafat of 1300 years longest of any period in world history whose purpose was most serve by this lost of Khelafat during last 74 years is a most important question in modern history.

The question now is that who conspired for the abolition of the Khelafat, who helped that conspiracy to implement is most important question in now a days when on almost every days in three continents Muslims are killed by the fellow Muslims and sometime by some non-Muslim like Bosnia or partly in India. And above all what a wonder is that during glorious and powerful era of Caliphate many Sultan or Kings had direct recognition from established Caliph, one such example is like Sultan Mahmud who invaded India several times, reference are as follows:

The Turkish nobles then places on the throne a son of Muktadir named Abul Abbas Mohammad Mohammed, and called him ar-Razi b'Illah (Satisfied in the Lord). With him vanished the last vestiges of power or dignity that had been left to the Caliphs. .... Suspecting Mustakfi of conspiring against his power, Muizud-Dowla deposed and blinded him in January 946, Abul Kasim al-Fazl, another son of Muktadir, was then installed as Caliph under the title of al-Mutii b'Illah (means Obedient to the Lord). The Buyides held the power for nearly a century almost without a rival to contest their title. The Turkish military element was annihilated, the Hamdanites were driven out of Mosul, and the whole

---

[59]**Glimpses of World History by Nehru, p. 158.**

of Mesopotamia, Irak Arab, and Western Persia became subject to their rule. Some of them were undoubtedly cruel, but on the whole their mayoralty conduced to the prosperity of the people and the cultivation of literature and science. Muiz ud-owla died in 356 A.H., and was succeeded in the office of Ameer ul-Umra by his son Bakhtyar, who received the title of Izz ud-Dowla. Seven years later Mutii (the Caliph), struc with paralysis, abdicated on the requisition of the Buyide prince in favor of his son Abu Bakr abdul Karim, who was installed on the pontifical throne under the title of at-Taii b'Illah. (Obedient to the Lord). .....
Shortly after, Izz ud-Dowla was deposed by his uncle Azud ud-Dowla was deposed by his uncle Azud ud-Dowla, and the impotent Caliph as compelled not only to invest him with the insignia of office, but to allow him regal honors (Such as the beating of the drums at the gate of his palace in the morning, at sunset, and at nightfall), with the title of Taj ul-Millat ("Crown of the Faith"). **Azud ud-Dowla** died in 372 A.H., and was succeeded by his son Samsam ud-Dowla (The Sword of the Empire), who received the title of Shams ul-Mill-at("**Sun of the Faith**"). Samsam ud-Dowla was deposed by his brother Sharf ud-Dowla, who held the office for nearly four years(**Sharf ud-Dowla induced the Caliph to bestow on him the mighty title of Shah in-Shah, King of Kings**). He died in 379 A.H., and was succeeded by his son Abu Nasr, who received the title of **Baha ud-Dowla and Ziya ul-Millat ("Glory of the State" and "Lustre of the Faith").**
Taii was deposed by Baha ud-Dowla, and forced to abdicate in favor of his brother, Abul Abbas Ahmed, who was placed on the throne under the title of al-Kadir b'Illah (Strong in the Lord). Kadir b'Illah is described as a virtuous man, distinguished for his piety and rectitude. He spent most of his nights in devotion, and gave a large portion of his income in charity. .... The Samanides, who had ruled Transoxiana and Khorasan with such brilliant success, disappeared at this epoch, and their place was taken by another dynasty. Their rule had lasted from 874 to 999 A.C. A Turkish soldier who had commenced life as mameluke, had by his merits attained a high position in the service of his sovereign. Incurring the displeasure of the succeeding prince, Alptagin escaped from Bokhara and established himself in the mountainous regions of Afghanistan. His seat of government was Ghazni, and here for sixteen years he defied all endeavors to subjugate him. On his death in 995 AC, his power descended to his son-in-law, Subaktagin, who by his wise and vigorous administration won the love of his subjects and the respect of his neighbors. His power and authority were recognized by the Caliph, which gave to his rule the coveted legitimacy. The title of Nasir ud-Dowla, with the standard and customary robes of honor, was conferred on him from Baghdad, and Subaktagin became the legitimate founder of the Ghaznavide dynasty. He carried his arms across the Hindoo Kush into the Punzab, and founded the cities of Bost and Kusdar. As the faithful ally of Nuh, the samanide prince, he defended Transoxiana against the incursions of the Turkoman hordes. On his death there was a struggle for power between his sons Mahmud and Ismail. Mahmud was willing to share the dominion with his brother, but the latter desired to rule alone. Mahmud was successful in the fight, but treated Ismail with great generosity and kindness. The Samanide power now broke to pieces, and in 1000 A.C. the Ghaznavide sovereign made himself the master of Khorasan. The Caliph sent him the usual diploma of investiture, with the title of Yemin ud-Dowla ("the Right Hand of the Empire"), and Amin ul-Millat ("Custodian of the Faith"). Sultan Mahmud's reign was one of the most brilliant in the history of Asia. He beautified Ghazni, and might have said, like the first emperor of Rome, that he found his capital a town of huts and left it a city of marble palaces. ... Sultan Mahmud entered India several times, but did not make any permanent conquest beyond the confines of the Punzab.[60]

---

[60] **HISTORY OF THE SARACENS BY SYED AMIR ALI, PP. 301-308.**

21: 92 Verily, this Brotherhood Of yours is a single Brotherhood ,
21: 92 And I am your Lord And Cherisher: therefore Serve Me (and no
21: 92 other).
23: 52 And verily this Brotherhood Of yours is a single Brotherhood
23: 52 And I am your Lord And Cherisher: therefore Fear Me (and no other)
33: 6 The Prophet is closer To the Believers than Their own selves,
33: 6 And his wives are Their mothers Blood-relations Among each other
33: 6 have Closer personal ties, In the Decree of Allah Than (the
33: 6 Brotherhood of) Believers and Muhajirs: Nevertheless do ye
33: 6 What is just to your Closest friends: such is The writing in the
33: 6 Decree (Of Allah).
49: 10 The Believers are but A single Brotherhood: So make peace and
49: 10 Reconciliation between your Two (contending) brothers; And fear
49: 10 Allah, that ye May receive Mercy.

(4473) It has been narrated on the authority of Abu Huraira that the Messenger of Allah (may peace be upon him) said: People are subservient to the Quraish: the Muslims among them being subservient to the Muslims among them, and the disbelievers among the people being subservient to the disbelievers among them.

(4474) It has been narrated on the authority of Hammam b. Munabbih who said: This is one of the traditions narrated by Abu Huraira from the Messenger of Allah (may peace be upon him) who said: People are subservient to the Quraish: the Muslims among them being subservient to the Muslims among them and the disbeliveers among them being subservient to the disbelievers them.

(4476) It has been narrated on the authority of 'Abdullah that the Messenger of Allah (may peace be upon him) said: The Caliphate will remain among the Quraish even if only two persons are left (on the earth).

(4477) It has been narrated on the authority of Jabir b. Samura who said: I joined the company of the Holy Prophet (may peace be upon him) with my father and I heard him say: This Caliphate will not end until there have been twelve Caliphs among them. The narrator said: Then he (the Holy Prophet) said something that I could not follow. I said to my father: What did said: All of them will be from the Quraish. (Who knows that what the Holy Prophet said, but could not followed by the narrator is the event which we are facing on Caliphate).

(4568) It has been narrated on the authority of Abu Sa'id al-Khudri that the Messenger of Allah (may peace be upon him) said: *When oath of allegiance has been taken for two caliphs, kill the one for whom the oath was taken later.*[61]

---

[61] SAHIH MUSLIM, BEING TRADITIONS OF THE SAYINGS AND DOINGS OF THE PROPHET MUHAMMAD AS NARRATED BY HIS COMPANIONS AND COMPLIED UNDER THE TITLE AL-JAMI-US-SAHIH BY IMAM MUSLIM, Rendered into English by ABDUL HAMID SIDDIQI VOLUME THREE, With Explanatory Notes, AND Brief Biographical Sketches of Major Narrators, PUBLISHED BY Nusrat Ali Nasri for KITAB BHAVAN, 1214, Kalan Mahal, Darya Ganj, NEW DELHI-110002, Chapter DCCLIV, KITAB AL-IMARA (THE

Under the above Quranic verses on One Brotherhood, we can not divide the one brotherhood or Caliphate into nation States. There are many Hadith on the the One Umma and one Brotherhood. I have also mentioned few Hadiths on Caliphate and from one Hadith #4568) we can say even two Caliphs are not allowed so as two States, though there are more than 50 states in this world. Yet the Muslims scholars on Quran and Hadith from Morocco to Indonesia are silent on Caliphate since 1924, when it was formally abolished. We all people of this world show interest for the election of the President of USA, and almost all the countries of the world irrespective of religion, race and culture. This interest is only for world peace and harmony.

(4472) It has been narrated on the authority of A'isha, wife of the Holy Prophet (may peace be upon him), who said: The Messenger of Allah (may peace be upon him) set out for Badr. When he reached Harrat-ul-Wabara (a place four miles from Medina), a man met him who was known for his valour and courage. The Companions of the Messenger of Allah (may peace be upon him) were pleased to see him. He said: I have come so that I may follow you and get a share from the booty. The Messenger of Allah (may) said to him: Do you believe in Allah and His Apostle? He said: no. The Messenger of Allah (may) said: Go back, I will not seek help from a Mushrik (polytheist). He went on until we reached Shajara, where the men met him again. He asked him the same question again and the man gave him the same answer. He said: Go back, I will not seek help from a Mushrik. The man returned and overtook him at Baida? He asked him as he had asked previously: Do you believe in Allah and His Apostle? The man said: Yes. The Messenger of Allah (may) said to him: Then come along with us.[62]

BOOK ON GOVERNMENT), NO. 4476, P, 1009. Chapter DCCLXVIII, p. 1032. **Explanatory Note ON** # 4568:

This means that it is wrong to overthrow the regime established by the common constant of the people and which is run according to the Islamic laws. If the ruling party is to be deposed that should be done through legal means and not by raising the banner of revolt against it. The Muslim community should show allegiance to one ruler and as long as there is nothing definite against him on account of which he loses the support of a vast majority of the people, he should not be deprived of his authority. If an individual or a group does that by an open rebellion, he commits high treason, for which severe punishment may be awarded.

[62] (2285)This hadith apparently contradicts some of the ahadith in which we learn that the Holy Prophet (may peace be upon him) accepted the help offered by a non-muslim in the military campaign, e.g. Safwan b. Umayya fought on the side of Muslims in the Battle of Hunain. Similarly, Quzman went out along with the Messenger of Allah (may peace be upon him) on the Day of Uhud in spite of the fact that he was a polytheist. These two instances go to prove that the help of a non-Muslim can be accepted when it is essential. Moreover, while seeking help of a non-

(4477) It has been narrated on the authority of Jabir b. Samura who said: I joined the company of the Holy Prophet (may peace be upon him) with my father and I heard him say: This Caliphate will not end until there has been twelve Caliphs among them.

(2335) Abu Dharr reported Allah's Messenger (may peace be upon him) as saying: Verily there would arise from my Ummah after me or soon after me a group (of people) who would recite the Quran, but it would not go beyond their throats, and they would pass clean through their religion just as the arrow passes through the prey, and they would never come back to it. They would be the worst among the creation and the creatures. Ibn Samit (one of the narrators) said: I met Rafi' b `Amr Ghifari, the brother of al-Hakam Ghifari and I said: What is this hadith that I heard from Abu Dharr, i.e. so and so?- and then I narrated that hadith to him and said: I heard it from the Messenger of Allah (may peace be upon him).

The Translation of Meanings of Sahih Al-Bukhari, Arabic-English Vol. VIII by Dr. Muhammad Muhsin Khan, Islamic University- Al-Medina Al-Munauwara, (12) CHAPTER. To inflict the legal punishment on the noble and the weak people (impartially). 778. Narrated Aisha : Usama approached the Prophet (Peace be upon him) on behalf of a woman (who had commited theft). The Prophet said. "The people before you were destroyed because they used to inflict the legal punishments on the poor and forgive the

---

Muslim we should take into consideration the attitude of his mind and the qualities of his head and heart. If a non-Muslim is favourably inclined towards Muslims. and his behaviour is sympathetic and he is honest in his words and deeds and there is no apprehension of any foul play on his part, then his help may be sought for and there is no harm in it. But if the attitude of his mind and his general behaviour are suspicious, then the Muslims should strictly avoid seeking the help of a non-Muslim. It is, however, desirable for the Muslims to dispense with the military servoces of a non-Muslim as far as it is possible. The fact is that a Muslim in exhorted to fight merely for the cause of Allah and thus he is required to observe certain lofty principles in the battlefield. It is for the achievement of the loftiest ends and those too with the help of the honest means that a Muslim takes up arms. He is thus equipped with a special mental make-up and his life is regulated with a moral code of behaviour, which can best be expected of a Muslim. Thus the Muslim should avoid getting his help as far as it is humanly possible. (For details see Imam Shawkani, Nail-ul-Autar, Vol. VII,pp.223-5). SAHIH MUSLIM, BEING TRADITIONS OF THE SAYINGS AND DOINGS OF THE PROPHET MUHAMMAD AS NARRATED BY HIS COMPANIONS AND COMPLIED UNDER THE TITLE AL-JAMI-US-SAHIH BY IMAM MUSLIM, Rendered into English by ABDUL HAMID SIDDIQI VOLUME THREE, With Explanatory Notes, AND Brief Biographical Sketches of Major Narrators, PUBLISHED BY Nusrat Ali Nasri for KITAB BHAVAN, 1214, Kalan Mahal, Darya Ganj, NEW DELHI-110002,note by Abdul Hamiid Sddiqi, p. 1006 (4472).

rich. By Him in Whose Hand my soul is! if Fatima (the daughter of the Prophet (R. A.) did that (i.e.) stole), I would cut off her hand."

The following comment by Nehru is enough for the difference between Muslim and Christians for the tolerance and the reason to proclaim to over all religion, as followers of those religions started to proclaim idolatry and instead of following the true path of Islam and following only almighty Allah or only One God or Ishwar (in Hindu Belief of one God).
In Islam force converse was not allowed, for obvious political reasons. Moslem Turkey and Persia entrust their foreign interests to the charge of their Christian subjects. In Christendom, difference of faith has been a crime; in Islam it is an accident. "To Christians." says Urquhart, a difference of religion was indeed a ground for war, and that not merely in dark times and amongst fanatics. From the massacres, in the name of religion, of the Saxons, the Frisians and other Germanic tribes by Charlemagne; from the burning to death of the thousands of innocent men and women; from the frightful slaughters of the Arians, the Paulicians, the Albigenses and the Huguenots, from the horrors of the sacks of Magedeburg and Rome, from the sanguinary scenes of the Thirty Years War, down to the cruel persecutions of Calvinistic Scotland and Lutheran England, there is an uninterrupted chain of intolerance, bigotry, and fanaticism. Can anything be more heart-rending than the wholesale extermination of the unoffending races of America in the name of Christ ?

Immigrant poured into the country. They were all kinds of people from Europe; Germans, Scandinavians, Irish, Italians, Jews, Poles; many were driven by political terrorism at home, and many in search of better living conditions. Overcrowded Europe poured out its surplus population to America. It was an extraordinary jumble of races, nationalities, languages, religions. In Europe they had all lived apart, each in its own little world, full of hatreds and animosities against the others; here they were thrown together in a new atmosphere where their hates did not seem to count for much. A uniform system of compulsory education soon rubbed off their national corners, and the American type began to grow out of this hotchpotch of races. The old Anglo-Saxon stock still considered itself the aristocrats; they were the social leaders. Next to it, and not far from it, came the races from northern Europe. The people from southern Europe, especially from Italy, were looked down upon by these northern Europeans and called, rather contemptuously, "Dagos". The Negros, of course, were quite apart. They were at the bottom of the scale, and they did not mix with any of the white races. On the western coast there were some Chinese and Japanese and Indians, who had come when the demand for labor there was great. These Asiatic races also kept apart from the others. .. (January 1, 1934)

The Muslims had grown more politically minded, and had joined hands with the Congress largely because of their exasperation at the British fighting Turkey. Because of sympathy for Turkey and a vigorous expression of it, two Muslim leaders, the Maulanas Mohammad Ali and Shaukat Ali, had been interned early in the war. Maulana Abul Kalam Azad was also interned because of his connections with Arab countries, where he was very popular owing to his writings. All this served to irritate and annoy the Muslims, and they turned away from the government more and more. (INDIA DURING WAR-TIME)(1916)

BRITAIN SEIZES AND HOLDS ON TO EGYPT- It was not as if the original Mamlukes formed a hereditary caste or class in Egypt. They were continually adding to their numbers by choosing the best of the free slaves belonging to the white races of the Caucasus. These Caucasian races are Aryans, and so the Mamelukes were Aryans. These alien people did not thrive on Egyptian soil, and their families died out after a few generations. But as fresh Mamelukes were being brought, the numbers, and especially the strength and vitality, of this class were kept up. Thus those people did not form a hereditary class, but none the less they formed an aristocracy and a governing class which lasted for a long time.

The following quotations are from:

The Discovery of India by JAWAHARLAL NEHRU; Dec 29, 1945

Obviously we could not consider any problem, much lass plan, without some definite aim and social objective. That aim was declared to be to ensure an adequate standard of living for the masses, in other words, to get ric of the appalling poverty of the people. The irreducible minimum, in terms of money, had been estimated by economists at figures varying from Rs. 15 to Rs. 25 per capita per month. (These in 1945, are all pre-war figures.) Compared to western standards this was very low, and yet it meant an enormous increase in existing standards in India (cf 1945). An approximate estimate of the average annual income per capita was Rs. 65. This included the rich and the poor, the town-dweller, and the villager. **In view of the great gulf between the rich and the poor and the concentration of wealth in the hands of a few, the average income of the villager was estimated to be far less, probably about Rs. 30 per capita per annum. These figures bring home the terrible poverty of the people and the destitute condition o the masses. There was lack of food, of clothing, of housing and of every other essential requirement of human existence. To remove this lack and ensure an irreducible minimum standard for everybody the national income had to be greatly increased, and in addition to this increased production there had to be a more equitable distribution of wealth. We calculated that a really progressive standard of living would necessitate the increase of the national wealth by 500 or 600 percent. That was, however, too big a jump for us, and we aimed at a 200 to 300 per cent increase within ten years.**

That unity is geographical, historical, and cultural, and all that; but the most powerful factor in its favor is the trend of world events. Many of us are of opinion that India is essentially a nation; Mr. Jinnah has advanced a two-nation theory and has lately added to it and political phraseology by describing some religious groups as sub-nations, whatever these might be. His thought identifies a nation with religion. That is not the usual approach to-day. But Whether India is properly to be described as one nation or two or more really does not matter, for the modern idea of nationality has been almost divorced from statehood. The national state is too a unit to-day and small states can have no independent existence. It is doubtful if even many of the larger national states can have any real independence. The national state is thus giving place to the multi-national state or to large federations. The Soviet Union is typical of this development. The United States of America, though bound together by strong national ties, constitute essentially a multi-national state. Behind Hitlers march across Europe there was something more than the nazi lust for conquest. New forces were working towards the liquidation of the small states system in Europe. ....

532   Inevitably, between these two emotional and imaginative approaches there is no meeting ground. And so 'Pakistan' and 'Akhand Hindustan' (undivided India) are bandied about and hurled at each other.

535 The problems of the moment seem big and engross our attention. And yet, in a longer perspective, they may have no great importance and, under the surface of superficial events, more vital forces may be at work. Forgetting present problems then for a while and looking ahead, India emerges as a strong united state, a federation of free units, intimately connected with her neighbors and playing an important part in world affairs. She is one of the very few countries which have the resources and capacity to stand on their own feet.

To-day probably the only such countries are the United States of America and the Soviet Union. Great Britain can only be reckoned as one of these if the resources of her empire are added to her own, and even then a spread-out and disgruntled empire is a source of weakness. China and India are potentially capable of joining that group. Each of them is compact and homogeneous and full of natural wealth, manpower, and human skill and capacity; indeed India's potential industrial resources are probably even more varied and extensive than China's, and so also her exportable commodities which may be required for the imports she needs. No other country, taken singly, apart from these four, is actually or potentially in such a position.

Recent events all over the world have demonstrated that the notion that nationalism is fading away before the impact of internationalism and proletarian movements has little truth. .. The coming of war swept everybody everywhere into the net of nationalism. ... Those who tell us so seem to imagine that true internationalism would triumph if we agreed to remain as junior partners in the British Empire or Commonwealth of Nations.

Babar's success was probably due not only to the weakness of the Delhi Sultanate but to his possessing a new **and improved type of artillery which was not in use in India then. From this period onwards India seems to lag behind in the developing science of warfare.**

World War I and the fate of the Turkish Khilafat (Caliphate) and the Muslim holy places produced a powerful impression on the Moslems of India and made them intensely anti-British.
This search for cultural roots led Indian Moslems (that is, some of them of the Middle class) to Islamic history, and to the periods when Islam was a conquering and creative force in Baghdad, Spain, Constantinople, central Asia and elsewhere. ..... The Afghan Kings of Delhi, especially Muhammad Tughlaq, had acknowledged the Khalifa (Caliph) at Cairo. .... after the complete collapse of the Mughal power early in the nineteenth century that the name of the Turkish Sultan began to be mentioned in Indian mosques. This practice was confirmed after the Mutiny. .. After the Mutiny the Indian Moslems had hesitated which way to turn. The British Government had deliberately repressed them (the Muslims) to an even greater degree than it had repressed the Hindus, and this repression had especially affected those sections of the Moslems from which the new middle class, the bourgeoie might have been drawn.

For the economic background in the early days of the post-war period, Hindus, Muslims, Sikhs, and others were all equally affected by these conditions, for economic conditions pay little heed to religious cleavages. **But Muslims had been, in addition, greatly shaken up by the war against Turkey and the expectation that the British Government would take possession of the *Jazirat-ul-Arab, the islands of Arabia,*** as they are called, the holy cities of Mecca, Medina, and Jerusalem (for Jerusalem is a holy city for the Jews, Christians and Muslims).[63]

The Lucknow Congress of 1916 was notable for another reunion, a Hindu-Muslim one. **The Congress had always clung to a national basis, but in effect it was predominantly a Hindu organization, because of the overwhelming majority of Hindus in it. Some years before the war the Muslim intelligentsia, egged on to some extent by the government,**

---

[63] GLIMPSES OF WORLD HISTORY ON INDIA FOLLOWS GANDHI BY NEHRU, PG. 713

had organized a separate body for themselves, called the All-India Muslim League. This was meant to keep the Muslims away from the Congress, but soon it drifted towards the Congress, and at Lucknow there was an agreement between the two about the future constitution of India. This was called the Congress-League Scheme, and it laid down, among other things, the proportion of seats to be reserved for the Muslim minorities. This Congress-League Scheme then became the joint program which was accepted as the country's demand. The Muslims had grown politically minded, and had joined hands with the Congress largely because of their exasperation at the British fighting Turkey. Because of sympathy for Turkey and a vigorous expression of it, two Muslim leaders, the Maulanas Mohammad Ali and Shaukat Ali, had been interned early in the war. Maulana Abul Kalam Azad was also interned because of his connections with Arab countries, where he was very popular owing to his writings. All this served to irritate and annoy the Muslims, and they turned away from the goverment more and more.[64]

North of Poland are the Baltic States of Lithuania, Latvia, Estonia, and Finland, all successors of the old successors of the old Tsarist Empire. They are small States, but each is a distinct cultural entity with a separate language. You (Nehru's daughter and ex Prime Minister of India) will be interested to know that the Lithuanians are Aryans (like many others in Europe) and their language bears quite a close resemblance to Sanskrit. This is a remarkable fact, which probably many people in India do not realize, and which brings home to us (Nehru's Indian) the bonds which unite distant people.[65]

In western Asia parts of the old Turkish Empire tempted the western Powers. During the war the British had encouraged an Arab revolt against Turkey by promising to create a united Arab kingdom extending over Arabia, Palestine, and Syria. While this promise was being made to the Arabs, the British were making a secret treaty with France partitioning these very territories. It was not a very creditable thing to do and a British Prime Minister, Ramsay MacDonald, called it a tale of "crude duplicity". But this was ten years ago, when he was not a minister, and so could afford, sometimes, to tell the truth. There was almost a stranger sequel still when the British Government played with the idea of breaking not only its promise to the Arabs, but also its secret treaty with France. Before them rose the dream of a great Middle-Eastern empire, stretching from India to Egypt, an enormous block joining their Indian Empire to their vast African possessions. It was a tempting and tremendous dream. And yet it did not seem then very difficult to realize. At that time, in 1919, British troops held all this vast area- Persia, Iraq, parts of Arabia, Egypt. They were trying to keep out the French from Syria. The city of Constantinople itself was in British possession. The dream vanished as the years of 1920 and 1921 and 1922 unfolded what they had in store. The Soviet backgrond and Kemal Pasha in the foreground put an end to these ambitious schemes of British ministers. But still Britain held on to a great deal in western - Iraq and Palestine- and tried to influence the course of events in Arabia by bribery and other means. Syria fell to the lot of the French.[66]

---

[64] GLIMPSES OF WORLD HISTORY ON INDIA DURING WAR-TIME BY JAWAHARLAL NEHRU, PG. 673-674

[65] GLIMPSES OF WORLD HISTORY ON THE NEW MAP OF EUROPE BY NEHRU, PG. 679

[66] GLIMPSES OF WORLD HISTORY ON THE NEW MAP OF EUROPE BY NEHRU, PG. 680

During in 1930's The Arab countries, with the exception of Arabia itself, were still under foreign control. The demand of the Arabs for unity has not been met. The greater part of Arabia has become independent under sultan Ibn Saud. Iraq is independent on paper, but in effect is within the British sphere of influence and control. The little States of Palestine and Trans-Jordan are British mandates, and Syria a French mandate. There was an extraordinarily gallant rebellion in Syria against the French, and it partly succeeded. Egypt also had insurrections and a long-drawn-out struggle against the British. That struggle continues still, though Egypt is called independent and a king, supported by the British, reigns there. To the far west of northern Africa there was also a gallant struggle for freedom in Morocco under the leadership of Abel Karim. He succeeded in driving out the Spanish, but later the full force of the French crushed him. In India the last fourteen years have been very full ones, and have seen an aggressive and yet a peaceful nationalism. Soon after the war, when expectations of great reforms ran high, we had martial law in the Punzab and the horrible massacre of Jallianwala Bagh. Anger at this and Muslim resentment at the treatment of Turkey and the Caliphate led to the non-co-operation movement of 1920-22 under Gandhi's leadership. [67]

I am quoting the following form KHILAFAT MOVEMENT, A STUDY OF INDIAN MUSLIM LEADERSHIP, 1919-24

    Gail Minault Graham
A DISSERTATION in SOUTH ASIA REGIONAL STUDIES

Presented to the Faculty of the Graduate School of Arts and Sciences of the University of Pennsylvania in Partial Fulfillment of the Requirements for the Degree of Doctor of Philosophy. 1972 and This is an authentic facsimile   and was produced by microfilm-xerography in 1981 by UNIVERSITY MICROFILMS INTERNATIONAL Ann Arbor, Michigan, U.S.A.; London, England

INTRODUCTION
The Caliphate and the Khilafat Movement
The Caliph, successor to the Prophet (sm), commander of the faithful, the shadow of God on earth- these exalted titles convey the symbolic importance of the Caliph to the community of Islam. Theoretically, he was both the spiritual and temporal leader of the Muslim community, insuring the defense and expansion of the rule of divine justice on earth, and in thus furthering God's purpose, helped assure eternal salvation for all Muslims. By the late nineteenth century, however, these theories of Caliphate power were about all that remained of the past glories of Islam. The Ottoman Empire was crumbling and Balkan nationalities and European powers alike coveted pieces of its territory. But Ottoman Turkey was still the bulwark of Islam against Christian aggression and the Sultan, Abdul Hamid II, was regarded with reverence by many Muslims in his capacity as Caliph, symbol of Islamic unity. Shrewdly, Abdul Hamid encouraged the pan-Islamic sentiments of Muslims everywhere in order to bolster his own power against European encroachments, and against political opposition at home. This pan-Islamic movement achieved few practical results in spite of the feelings it generated.[68]

---

[67] GLIMPSES OF WORLD HISTORY ON THE POST-WAR WORLD BY NEHRU, PG. 688-689

[68] Wilfred Cantwell Smith defines pan-Islamic thus:"Pan-Islam is, and always has been, primarily a sentiment of co-hesion. It is not cohesion itself nor any institutional or practical expression of it. The unity of the Muslim world is a unity of sentiment." Islam in Modern History (Mentor Books. New York; New American Library, 1959), pp. 88-89

94

pg-2 Its chief propagandist, Jamal al-Din al-Afghani, died in obscurity, a prisoner of the Caliph he had served, albeit uneasily. The Young Turks deposed 'Abdul Hamid and installed a new Caliph. The Balkan wars wrested most of the remaining European territories from the Ottoman Empire, and when World I broke out and the Caliph declared holy war (jihad)[69] against the Triple Entente, Indian Muslim subjects of Britain nevertheless fought against the Turks, and the Arabs declared their independence from the Ottomans. It was hardly an inspiring record to encourage further Islamic appeals, and after the war, the Turkish nationalists led by Mustafa Kemal repudiated the idea of a universal Islamic empire in favor of a regenerated Turkish homeland. The victorious European powers, in seeking to carve up Ottoman territories among themselves, pg-3 encountered little opposition from the Caliph, who was less concerned by the loss of Arab territories than he was by the rising challenge of Turkish nationalism. Pan-Islam emanating from the Caliph was a thing of the past.

And yet, at the same time as the Arabs were seeking to establish their independence from Turkey, and the Turks themselves were drawing away from their imperial past, the Indian Muslims launched a movement in favor of maintaining the boundaries of the Ottoman Empire as they were in 1914, and continuing unabated the caliph's spiritual and temporal powers over his empire. What prompted this romantic adherence to a theory of the Caliphate no longer practicable, this naïve championship of a pan-Islamic cause already dried up at its source? Several studies of the Khilafat movement have stressed its pan-Islamic content as part of a long history of Indian Muslim extra-territorial loyalty to the Muslim world, and as the expression of a minority community at bay.[70] Others stress the religious motivation of individual Indian Muslim leaders, as well as the psychological support which pan-Islamic militancy offered them in their repudiation of loyalty to British rule and their participation in the predominantly Hindu nationalist movement.[71]

---

[69] Jihad: Though usually defined as holy war, Jihad means objective. This need not always be armed struggle.

[70] see, e.g., Aziz Ahmed, Studies in Islamic culture in the Indian Environment (London: Oxford University Press, 1964), pt. I; Hafeez Malik, Moslem Nationalism in India and Pakistan (Washington, D.C.: Public Affairs Press, 1963). passim, especially chs. VIII-IX.

[71] William J. Watson, "Muhammad Ali and the Khilafat Movement" (unpub, M.A. thesis, McGill University, Institute of Islamic Studies, 1955).
The author's Master's thesis, bases mainly on English_sources, also stresses the pan-Islamic aspect of the Khilafat movement. A study of new sources has led to a re-assessment of that thesis. Gail Minault, "The Khilafat Movement; An example of Pan-Islamic Sympathies Among Indian Muslims" (unpub. M.A. thesis, University of Pennsylvania, 1966).

PG-4 The present study, while not denying the importance of pan-Islamic sentiments in the genesis of the Khilafat movement, contends that the movement can only be understood as a uniquely Indian phenomenon.

pg-5-6   The Caliphate in Theory and Practice

The theory of the Caliphate, like all political theories meant to explain a political institution with a long history, underwent many changes over the centuries. The Caliphate came into existence upon the death of the Prophet Muhammad (sm) when his followers selected his successor (Khalifa) from among their number. **The Caliph was both the religious and temporal leader of the Muslim community, whose preservation he was to insure, and whose unity he was to defend. He was not a religious leader in the sense that Muhammad had been, for   he did not succeed to Muhammad's (sm) prophetic status, nor could he promulgate new religious doctrines or laws. The Caliph's main religious function was to insure the supremacy of the Shari,a, the law of Islam bases on divine revelation.**[72]

The Caliphate underwent a rapid transformation with the expansion of Islam. Within a generation of the Prophet's death, the Caliph had become an absolute monarch reigning from Damascus over an area stretching from the Nile to the Oxus. Justification for the this changed state of affairs was then sought in the revealed word of God, The Quran, and the Hadith (Traditions of the saying of the Prophet, peace be upon him and God bless him). Such passages from the Quran as "It is He who has appointed you viceroys in the earth, and has raised some of you in rank above others" (VI:165), were interpreted to mean that the Caliph's power was divinely ordained. And the verse: "Oh believers, obey God, and obey the messengers and those in authority among you(IV:62), was quoted to support the duty of Muslims to obey their rule.[73]

The only theoretical limit to the power of the Caliph was the overriding supremacy of the Sharia, which he, like all other Muslims, had to obey.[74]

A second civil war in 750 AD unseated the Umayyads and placed the Abbasids on the Caliphal throne. A remnant of the Umayyad dynasty later established a rival Caliphate in Spain, further dividing the Islamic world. The Abbaside reigned in Baghdad from 750 to 1258, but by the eleventh century, independent monarchs ruled over large areas, and in the capital itself, the Caliphs were puppets in the hands of powerful chieftains (Amirs).[75]

---

[72] H. A. R. Gibb, "Some Considerations on the Sunni Theory of Caliphate, "Studies on the Civilization of Islam (London; Routledge and Kegan Paul, 1962), p. 141, hereafter cited as Gibb, Studies; T. W. Arnold, The Caliphate (2nd ed. London: Routledge and Kegan Paul, 1965), pp. 20, 26-27

[73] A. J. Arberry, The Koran interpreted I (New York: Macmillan, 1955), pp. 109, 170

[74] Arnold, op. ed., pp 42-53, E. I. J. Rosenthal, Political thought in Medieval Islam (Cambridge, Cambridge University Press, 1962), pp. 22-23, 26

[75] Arnold op. cit., pp. 55-69

pg-8 Theoretically, however, the Caliph was still the spiritual and temporal leader of the Islamic Community, the guardian of the Sharia, and hence the only authority to which a Muslim could legitimately submit. The Amirs, though in political control of the state, thus could not depose the Caliph, but nominally received their political powers from him by delegation. This practice was followed by other independent Muslim princess, such as Mahmud of Ghazna the conqueror of part of India in the eleventh century, who declared his allegiance to the Caliph and received investiture from him, a mere formality, but one which retained the symbolic unity of the Islamic community and the supremacy of the divine Law.[76]

Shorn of his political power, the Caliph was shown increased respect as Imam, or religious leader of the community. But here too, his position was largely symbolic, since the Muslim jurists or 'ulama acted as the interpreters of religious law. Some justification for this division of political and religious powers had to be found, in order to preserve the unity of the Muslim community under the Sharia. *It was at this point the jurist al-Mawardi (d. 1058) first formulated the theory of the Caliphate.[77] Basing his argument on the Quran (IV-62), al-Mawardi stated that the Caliphate is obligatory by divine revelation. He then drew a distinction between a government based on reason and one bases on revealed law. The formers, embodied in the Amirs, merely guards against strife and anarchy, while the latter, clearly the superior, provides for the enforcement of justice. Even more important, enforcement of the divine law enables man to prepare for the hereafter. He thus defended the superior position of the Caliph as guardian of the Shari'a. while providing a place for the Amirs in his scheme.[78]*

Al-Mawardi then discussed the method of choosing the Caliph. Following the tradition established at the death of the Prophet(sm), he said that the Caliph must be elected from a group of qualified candidates by an electorate representing the community. Qualifications for Caliph included justice. knowledge, courage, physical and mental fitness, and descent from the Quraish, the tribe of the Prophet(sm). But the number of electors may be limited to only one, which amounted to nomination of a successor by his predecessor. Al-Marwardi thus justified the hereditary line of Abbasid Caliphs, even while maintaining the elective principle. The succession had then to be ratified by a ceremony of investiture (bay's), an oath of allegiance taken by those qualified to represent the community. presumably the 'ulama'. In return for this submission by the community, the Caliph was bound to uphold the shari'a. guard the faith and territory of Islam (*dar al-Islam*), *wage* **jihad** against the territories of the infidels (*dar al-harb*), **and see to the just administration of the realm.**

---

[76] Rosenthal. op. cit., pp. 27-28, Gibb, "Al-Mawardi's Theory of the Caliphate", Studies, p. 157

[77] Arnold, op. cit., pp. 66-67, Rosenthal, op. cit., p. 28; Gibb "Sunni Theory", studies, p. 152

[78] Rosenthal, loc. cit. Gibb, "Al-Mawardi, "Studies, pp. 152, 155, Gibb maintains that al-Mawardi was writing as the champion of the Caliph in his attempt to reassert political power vis-a-vis the Amirs.

It is in this last stipulation that al-Marwardi's position as a defender of caliphal prerogative is most clear, though of course all these duties could just as legally be delegated to others.[79] The Caliph could only forfeit his office through heresy, infirmity of mind or body, or loss of liberty. Al-Mawardy thus does not deny the right of subjects to depose the Caliph, but neither does he specify a procedure for doing so. "It appears that while a Caliph may legally be deposed, there is no legal means of deposing him"[80]

By the time of al-Ghazzali(1058-1111), the Caliph had lost all pretense of political authority to the Seljuk Turkish Sultans, and the jurists were forced to modify the theory of the Caliphate to justify the new conditions. The Caliph as Imam was necessary for the preservation of the unity of Islam under the shari'a, but al-Ghazzali recognized that:

An evildoing and barbarous sultan, so long as he is supported by   military force, so that he can only with difficulty be deposed... ... must of necessity be left in possession and obedience must be rendered him... Government in these days is a consequence solely of military power, and whosoever he may be to whom the holder of   military power gives his allegiance, that person is the Caliph...[81]

Election of the Caliph is a sham; he is a symbol, legitimizing government established by force.[82] Al-Ghazzali also dispenses with most of al-Mawardi's qualifications and duties for the Caliph. Why should he possess any special knowledge, or carry out administrative and military functions, when he can rely on a vizier for administration, the 'ulama for interpretation of the law, and the Sultan for military prowers? The Caliph's functions were reduced to setting a good example by leading a pious life.[83]

After al-Ghazzali, it was but a slight modification for Ibn Jama'a (1241-1333) to maintain that:

When the Imamate is assumed by one person by means of force and military supremacy, and thereafter there arises another who overcomes the first by his might and his armies,- then the first is deposed and the second becomes Imam, for the reason of the well-being and unity of the Muslims.[84] pg-13 By legitimizing the use of military force to install or depose the Caliph, the jurists were recognizing in legal theory what had been a fact for some time. In so

[79] Rosenthal, op. cit., pp. 29-36; Gibb, "Al-Marwardi," Studies, pp. 155-58.

[80] Ibid., pp. 159-61.

[81] Al-Ghazzali, Ihya' 'Ulm al-Din, quoted in H. A. R. Gibb and Harold Bowen, Islamic Society and the West I (London: Oxford University Press, 1950), p. 31; cf. Gibb, "Sunni Theory," Studies, pp. 142-43.

[82] Gibb and Bowen, op. cit., I. P. 32.

[83] Rosenthal, op. cit., pp. 38-43.

[84] Ibn Jama'a, Tahrir al-Ahkam fi Tadbir Ahl al-Islam, quoted in Gibb and Bowen, op. cit. I, p. 32; cf. Gibb, "Sunni Theory," Studies, p. 143.

doing, however, they were divorcing the Caliphate from the shari'a which it was supposed to preserve. The principles of divine justice had been sacrificed to the necessity of maintaining order and the unity of the Islamic community.[85]

Ibn Taymiya (1263-1328) tried to remedy the foregoing situation by restoring the Shari'a to authority. To him, the just rule of the community under the guidance of divine law was all-important; any ruler could bring this about, however, Ibn Taymiya does not ask how those possessing power got it. He just states that those in authority must be obeyed, but only if their rule is based on the shari'a. Fearing anarchy, however, he does not advocate rebellion to depose the ruler, but rather appeals to the ruler to uphold justice. In this appeal, he championed an increasingly important role for the 'ulama' the interpreters of the law. Since the shari'a which holds the Islamic community; united can be upheld by any de facto power, Ibn Taymiya dispensed with the necessity of a Caliph. This theoretical change was made easier by the fact that he was writing after the sack of Baghdad by the Mongols in 1258, when the last Abbasid Caliph had been put to death.[86]

The destruction of the Abbasid Caliphate called for another revision of theory. Although the Abbasid dynasty continued to exist in a shadowy form under the aegis of the Mamluk Sultans in Cairo, these faineant Caliphs were so patently powerless that no authoritative jurist of the time recognized them.[87]

At present day the same struggle or Jehad for reestablishment of 1300 years Caliphate going in Egypt amid ruthless suppression of the present Government.

The 'ulama' who now more than ever became the intermediaries between the political authority, however constituted, and the community,[88] had to find a new political theory which would preserve the supremacy of the shari'a. One alternative was the theory that the Caliphate had ceased to exist after the pg-15 first four successors of Muhammad(sm), and that subsequent dynasties had only been kings. This, significantly, was the view adopted by the Hanafi jurists, the official school of law in the Ottoman Empire and in India.[89]

But this theory, as Gibb points out, failed to meet the need of the Sunnis for a present and visible authority or Imam, leaving them with nothing but the wielder of temporal power, a conclusion virtually equal to that of Ibn Jama'a.[90]

A second alternative was that presented in the work of al-Dawwani (1427-1501), an adaptation of the Platonic ideal of the philosopher-king to the Islamic concept of the Imam. Like Ibn Taymiya, al-Dawwani insists on the supremacy of the divinely revealed sharia. Sovereignty is divinely bestowed upon the just ruler who upholds the law. A ruler may be either righteous or unrighteous, but it is only the former who merits the title (and the obedience due to it) Caliph or Imam a military usurper does not. It follows that any just

---

[85] Gibb and Bowen, ioc. cit.; Rosenthal, op. cit., pp. 43-51

[86] Rosenthal, op. cit., pp. 51-61; Arnold, op. cit., p. 81.

[87] Gibb, "Sunni Theory," Studies, p. 143; Arnold, op. cit., pp. 98-102

[88] For an interesting study of the role of the 'ulama' as social and political arbiters during the Mamluk period, see Ira M. Lapidus, Muslim Cities in the Later Middle Ages (Cambridge, Mass.: Harvard University Press, 1967), pp. 79-115, 130-42.

[89] Arnold, op. cit., p. 163.

[90] Gibb, "Sunni Theory, "Studies, pp. 143-44.

ruler may assume the title, which justified the practice, common by al-Dawwani's time, of local Muslim princes styling themselves Caliph. The Ottoman Sultan was a Caliph, but so too could be the Mughal Emperor in India.[91]

Ibn Khaldun (1332-1406) formulated a theory of the state which was significantly different from those of the preceding theorists. Like the others, he upheld the theoretical supremacy of the shari'a, even if its principles had been set aside at times for reasons of power politics. But the originality of his contribution lies in his analysis of the power state as it existed.[92]

To Ibn Khaldun, the state was an inevitable result of human life, which requires association; only within a well-organized society with an effective political system could the higher faculties of man develop. In order to establish an effective political system, the would-be ruler requires political power, which is gained by what Ibn Khaldun called 'asabiya. 'Asabiya is a feeling of group solidarity based on some common interest such as blood relationship, material interest, or religious faith. More than any of the other theorists, Ibn Khaldun saw the practical connection between religion and political power. A common religion, and particularly Islam with its emphasis on community solidarity, is an important contribution to 'asabiya. Asabiya is a feeling of group solidarity based on some common interest such as blood relationship, materiel interest, or religious faith. More than any of the other theorists, Ibn Khaldun saw the practical connection between religion and political power. A common religion, and particularly Islam with its emphasis on community solidarity, is an important contributing factor to 'asabiya. Religion, to him, was the most important force in preventing petty revelries from disrupting political action. In his demonstration of the intimate connection between Islamic religion and politics, Ibn Khaldun foreshadowed a number of Muslim political leaders who will be discussed below.[93]

Applying his theory to the history of the Caliphate, Ibn Khaldun showed that the Quraish, by virtue of common lineage and religious faith, had had a strong feeling of solidarity in the early days of Islam, and hence had merited the Caliphate. They had lost this 'asabiya' and with it, the Caliphate, and a new group was needed to revive the caliphal institution. He did not recognize the Caliphate of the Cairo Abbasids of his time, even though they were descendents of the Quraish.[94]

A new group with sufficient strength to warrant being dubbed Caliphs were the Ottomans. It has been shown, however, that the Ottomans were acknowledged as Caliphs only in the later sense that any just ruler might assume the tittle. The Sultan was not accepted by the 'ulama' as the universal Caliph of Islam, an office which they now said had ceased after the first four Caliphs. In fact, Gibb cites an example in which not the Ottoman Sultan, but the Mughal Emperor Aurangzeb, was styled "Commander of the Faithful," a highly laudatory and much rarer title than Caliph, by the chief Hanafi jurist of Damascus in the seventeenth century.[95]

At the height of its power, the Ottoman Empire guarded the frontiers of Islam against the Christian West, combining political supremacy over vast areas of the Muslim world and

---

[91] Ibid., pp. 144-48; Rosenthan, op. cit., pp. 210-23; Arnold, op. cit., pp. 107-20.

[92] Rosenthal, op. cit., p. 99

[93] Rosenthal, op. cit., pp. 85-87, 96-99, 105-06; Gibb, "The Islamic Background of Ibn Khaldun's Political Theory," Studies, pp. 169-74

[94] Rosenthal, op. cit., pp. 29-30.

[95] Gibb and Bowen, op. cit., pp. 34-35.

parts of Christendom with militant religious spirit and adherence the shari'a so desired by the theorists. The shari'a was the established law of the state, but the caliphal function of upholding and administering it was carried out by a state-appointed hierarchy of jurists headed by the Shaikh al-Islam, while the Sultan-Caliph was chiefly regarded as a military leader.[96]

With the decline of Ottoman power, however, the position of the Caliph as a symbol of Muslim religious unity again assumed importance, as with the Abbasids much earlier. When European powers began to chip away at Ottoman territories, the Sultans again reasserted their prerogatives as Caliph. For example, in the Treaty of Kuchuk Kainarji between Turkey and Russia in 1774, Catherine II claimed to be the patroness of all Orthodox Christians living under Ottoman rule. The Sultan, in turn, took this opportunity to claim the spiritual allegiance of the Tartars of the Crimea, lost to Russia. In the nineteenth century, as the Ottoman Empire shrank still further, an increasing emphasis was placed upon the spiritual role of the Sultan-Caliph, even though this was without precedent in earlier Ottoman history. European diplomacy generally accepted the Caliph as a kind of Islamic pope, and though this was erroneous from the point of view of Islamic theory, the Sultans could use this to their advantage. claiming spiritual- and thus also political - allegiance from Muslims in lost territories. As late as 1909-13, in the treaties terminating the Austrian, Italian, and Balkan wars, the European governments acknowledged the authority of the Sultan's appointee, the Shaikh al_islam, to invest Muslim judges in Bosnia-Herzegovina, Libya, Bulgaria, and Greece. In Christian eyes these 'ulama held strictly religious offices, but in the eyes of the Muslims concerned, the Sultan's temporal authority over them was unimpaired. In this way, the Ottomans maintained considerable political influence, in spite of their reduced realm.[97]

In addition to European misunderstanding of the Caliphate which worked in the Sultan's favor, active propaganda among the Muslims was undertaken to further the Ottoman claim to the universal Caliphate. The 'ulama went back to earlier theory condoning the nomination of a Caliph his predecessor, and maintained that Sultan Selim I, the conqueror of Egypt in 1517, had received the Caliphate by designation from the last Abbasid puppet-Caliph of Cairo. Arnold finds no contemporary documentary evidence of this transfer, tracing the source of the account to d'Ohsson's 1787 work, Tableau General de l'Empire Othoman.[98] But even if it did occur, it seems doubtful that contemporary jurists would have recognized it. This fiction was believed and perpetuated, however, and helped to establish the Ottoman claim to the Caliphate in spite of the fact that they were not descendents of the Quraish.[99] Another point which was advanced to support the Ottoman claim was their guardianship over the holy cities of Mecca and Medina. It was true that Selim I had received the homage of the Sharif of Mecca in Cairo, but Arnold points out that the inclusion of the Holy cities in one's realm had never been an obligatory condition of the Caliphate.[100] Nevertheless,

[96] Bernard Lewis, The Emergence of Modern Turkey (London: Oxford University Press, 1961), pp. 13-14.

[97] Arnold, op. cit., pp. 164-76; T. W. Arnold, "The Supposed Spiritual Authority of the Caliph", Home Dept. (Pol) B, 307, December 1918, IOL; Arnold J. Toynbee, Survey of International Affairs I, 1925 (London; Royal Institute of International Affairs, 1927), pp. 33-36; hereafter cited as Toynbee, Survey.

[98] Arnold, op. cit., pp. 142-46

[99] Sayyiid Amir 'Ali, "The Caliphate: A Historical and Juridical Sketch," Contemporary Review (June, 1915), 681-94.

[100] Arnold, op. cit., pp. 148-53.

since haj, pilgrimage to Mecca, is obligatory for all Muslims, the Sultan's suzerainty over the holy cities undoubtedly increased his prestige in Muslim eyes.

Last well known Caliph, Sultan Abdul Hamid II sent emissaries throughout the Muslim world to emphasize the foregoing points, and also the overwhelmingly important fact that he was the last remaining independent Sunni monarch. The recognition of himself as Caliph, religious and temporal commander of the faithful, and the need for pan-Islamic solidarity against European encroachments was urgent. 'Abdul Hamid's panIslamic propaganda had little success close to home. Among Turkish constitutional reformers, he was regarded with dismay for having undone many of the reform of the Tanzimat era. Among the Arabs, an embryonic cultural nationalist móvement saw in the Sultan's reassertion of his caliphate prerogatives only a means of maintaining Turkish rule over them. But among Indian Muslims considerable feeling was aroused in favor of the Ottoman claim to the Caliphate. Toynbee postulates that this was because they were far enough away not to see the less enlightened aspects of Abdul Hamid's rule, but there were other reasons as well.[101]

Pan-Islam or Pan-Indian Islam?

The Indian Muslim community, so often referred to by politicians and historians as monolithic, is in fact far from united. Spear has called it "a necklace of racial, cultural and political pearls strung on the thread of religion."[102] And in the introduction to his study of Indian Muslims, Mujeeb pointedly asks, "Who are the Indian Muslims?" answering the question, by no means conclusively, by citing innumerable variations based on historic, geographic, tribal, and sectarian differences.[103]

This lack of homogeneity has been an important factor in the community's history from the very earliest Muslim conquest of India, and it governed Indian Islam's relationship with the Caliphate. The Sultans of Delhi offered allegiance to the universal Caliph in Baghdad, **and even to the Cairo Abbasids, in return for letters of investiture.**[104]

This may well have been done because of a strong feeling for the religious unity of all believers, but even more, it was an attempt by a line of slave Sultans to grasp some form of legitimacy under Islamic law and thus maintain their power over squeamish 'ulama and factitious nobles. The Mughals, according to inscriptions on their coins, assumed the tittle of Caliph within India.[105] This may also be interpreted as an attempt to establish the legitimacy of their line, their reputation as just rulers, and to create 'asabiya among the

---

[101] DeLacey O'Leary, Islam at the Crossroads (London: Kegan Paul, 1923), pp. 122-23; Toynbee, Survey, pp. 33, 39-41; Lewis, op. cit., p. 170; Ernest Ramsaur, The Young Turks (Princeeton: Princeton University Press, 1957, p. 11; Sylvia G. Haim, Arab Nationalism: An Anthology (Berkeley and Los Angeles: University of California Press, 1964), pp. 22-23.

[102] Percival Spear, "The Position of the Muslims, Before and After Partition," P. Mason, ed., India and Ceylon: Unity and Diversity (London: Oxford University Press, 1967), p. 30

[103] M. Mujeeb, The Indian Muslims (London: George Allen and Unwin, 1967), pp. 9-25.

[104] Arnold, op. cit., pp. 103-105; A. Ahmad, op. cit., pp. 3-11.

[105] Arnold, op. cit., p. 159, citing S. Lane-Poole, Catalogue of Indian Coins in the British Museum, p. 1 xxiii

heterogeneous ruling elements of their empire.[106] But as Mughal power declined, some Indian Muslim princes seeking to establish hegemony in their own regions turned towards the Ottoman Sultan-Caliph as a source of legitimacy. One example of this was Tipu Sultan of Mysore, who sent an embassy to the Ottoman Sultan in 1785-90. His emissaries secured for him letters of investiture allowing him assume the tittle of independent king.[107] Other princes simply seized their piece of the crumbling Mughal cake.

The Caliphate, as a symbol of Muslim unity and of the supremacy of the shari'a, thus had a special significance in the career of Muslim rule in India. The Caliph was particularly useful in times of political confusion and strife as a source of legitimacy based on the shari'a, and as a source of solidarity among the ruler, the 'ulama, and the nobility. The locus of the Caliphate and the person of the Caliph mattered little; it was the existence of the Caliphate which was essential, as an icon before which homage was rendered, as a banner for Muslim rulers to wave when threatened by conquest or internal dissension.

When Mughal power was finally extinguished in 1857, Indian Muslims turned to the Ottoman Sultan as the only possible remaining candidate for Caliph. He was the symbol, not only of the survival of the rule of Islamic law, but also of past Islamic glory. This new and more widespread acknowledgement of the Ottoman Caliphate was manifested in a number of ways. The Sunni 'ulama began to read the Sultan's name in the <u>Khutba</u> (sermon during the congregational prayer service) on Fridays in some Indian mosques. The average Muslim, who knew nothing of the theory involved, thus began to associate the Ottomans with the Caliphate.

pg-26 The few western-educated Muslims admired the Turkish reforms of the Tanzimat, and the Turkish fez became a popular head gear even at that bastion of loyalty to British rule, Aligarh College. And each time the Ottomans were involved in a war, as the Russo-Turkish war of 1877-78 or the Greco-Turkish war of 1897, Indian Muslims launched fund drives for Turkish relief.[108] This was hardly a pan-Islamic movement of major proportions, but it was evidence, nonetheless, of a sympathy for Turkey which could be exploited in the interests of Muslim solidarity, whether within India or without.[109] The first to exploit this pro-Turkish feeling among Indian Muslims were the British, for their own advantage. Just as the revival of Ottoman caliphal claims was in part based on western misunderstanding of the institution of the Caliphate, so too in India increased Muslim acknowledgement of the Ottoman Sultan as Caliph was partially western-inspired. As early as the late eighteenth century, the British governor-general in India forwarded a letter from the Porte to Tipu Sultan, urging the latter to support the British against the French, who were enemies of Islam. And in 1857, the British obtained a proclamation from the Ottoman Sultan calling on Indian Muslims to remain loyal to the British[110]

---

[106] For a more detailed examination of Mughal religious policies as a source of political solidarity, see Gail Minault Graham, "Akbar and Aurangzeb - Syncretism and Separatism im Mughal India; A Re-Examination," <u>Muslim World</u> LIX, 2 (Apil, 1969), 106-26.

[107] Khwaja 'Abdul Qadir, <u>Waqai-e-Manazil-e-Rum</u> (Diary of a Journey to Constantinople), ed. by Mohibbul Hasan (Bombay: Asia Publishing House, 1968), p. 62.

[108] A. Ahmad, <u>op. cit.</u>, pp. 60, 53.

[109] For short studies of the pan-Islamic movement, see Lothrop Stoddard, <u>The New World of Islam</u> (New York: Scribner's, 1923), ch. II; Valentine Chirol, "Pan-Islamism," <u>Proceedings of the Central Asian Society</u> (London: 1906); H. Taqizadeh, "Le Panislamisme et le Panturkisme," <u>Revue du Monde Musulman</u> XXII (1913), 179-220.

110

We may conclude this section by a contemporary Christian document. It refers to the letter of a Nestorian bishop, addressed to a friend of him, which has been preserved: (cf. Assemani,Bible). Orient III, e, p. XLVI). "These Tayites (i.e.Arabs), to whom god has accorded domination in our days, have also become our masters; yet they do not combat at all the Christian religion; on the contrary they even protect our faith, respect our priests and saints, and make donations to our churches and convents."

At the rise into caliph's power of the 'Abbasides, Spain detached itself from the Muslim Orient. After almost a thousand years of domination, in 1942, the last traces of a Muslim state were submerged there by the Castillian Christians molestation. The Moslems, on the other hand, required from others a simple guarantee of peace and amity, tribute in return for protection or perfect equality, - the possession of equal rights and privileges, on condition of the acceptance of Islam.

The converse was not allowed, for obvious political reasons. Moslem Turkey and Persia entrust their foreign interests to the charge of their Christian subjects. In Christendom, difference of faith has been a crime; in Islam it is an accident. "To Christians." says Urquhart, a difference of religion was indeed a ground for war, and that not merely in dark times and amongst fanatics. ics. From the massacres, in the name of religion, of the Saxons, the Frisians and other Germanic tribes by Charlemagne; from the burning to death of the thousands of innocent men and women; from the frightful slaughters of the Arians, the Paulicians, the Albigenses and the Huguenots, from the horrors of the sacks of

Magedeburg and Rome, from the sanguinary scenes of the Thirty Years War, down to the cruel persecutions of Calvinistic Scotland and Lutheran England, there is an uninterrupted chain of intolerance, bigotry, and fanaticism. Can anything be more heart-rending than the wholesale extermination of the unoffending races of America in the name of Christ ?

Islam had fully established itself in the Peninsula. This latter document has, for the most part, furnished the guiding principle to all Moslem rulers in their mode of dealing with their non-Moslem subjects, and if they have departed from it in any instance the cause is to be found in the character of the particular sovereign. If we separate the political necessity which has often spoken and acted in the name of religion, no faith is more tolerant than Islam to the followers of other creeds.

"Reasons of State" have led a sovereign here and there to display a certain degree of intolerance, or to insist upon a certain uniformity of faith; but the system itself has ever maintained the most complete tolerance. Christians and Jews, as a rule, have never been molested in the exercise of their religion, or constrained to change their faith. If they are required to pay as special tax, it is in lieu of military service, and it is but right that those who enjoy the protection of the State should contribute in some shape to the public burdens.

Towards the idolaters there was greater strictness in theory, but in practice the law was equally liberal. If at any time they were treated with harshness, the cause is to be found in the passions of the ruler or the population. The religious element was used only as a pretext.

And who did not accept Islam as their only religion, and accepted those religions which in initial stage was also the only religion of Islam, but in later times, were changed according to the evil desire of the followers, their ultimate end according to

I should also quote from the Holy Bible; GENESIS 17, 18; CHAPTER 17 WHICH IS:
20 : And as for Ish-mael, I have heard the; Behold, I have blessed him, and

will make him fruitful, and will multiply him exceedingly; twelve
princes shall be beget,? and I will make him a great nation.

24: And Abraham was ninety years old and nine, when he was circumcise in the
flesh of his foreskin.

25: And Ish'-ma-el his son was thirteen years old, when he was circumcised in
the flesh of his foreskin.

26: In the selfsame day was Abraham circumcised, and Ish'-ma-el his son.

I am also quoting from GENESIS 21; CHAPTER 2

14: And Abraham rose up early in the morning, and took bread, and a bottle of
water, and gave it unto Ha'gar, putting it on her shoulder, and the
child, and sent her away; and she departed, and wandered in the wilder
-ness of Be'-er-sheba.

15: And the water was spent in the bottle, and she cast the child under one
of the shrubs.

16: And she went, and sat her down over against him a good way off, as it
were a bowshot; for she said, let me not see the death of the child, And
she sat over against him, and lift up her voice, and wept.

17: And God heard the voice of the lad: and the angel of God called to Ha'-
gar out of heaven, and said unto her, What aileth thee, Ha'-gar? fear
not; for God hath heard the voice of the lad where he is.

18: Arise, lift up the lad, and hold him in thine hand; for I will make him
a great nation.

So if we take both the above verse is true then we can understand that
Prophet Abraham (Peace be upon him) kept relation and personal contact with
Ish'-ma-el when Is-'ma-el was thirteen years old as mentioned in verse 25 and
26 above, so our question to learned Jews and Christian are that which is
and personal contact with both Ismael and his mother.

The document produced by the Office of Non-Christian Affairs at the Vatican
"It would seem pointless to maintain that Allah is not really God, as do
certain people in the West! The conciliar documents have put the above asser-
faith in God than by quoting the following extracts from Lumen Gentium:(Lumen
Gentium is the title of a document produced by the Second Vatican Council
(1962-1965)). 'The Muslims profess the faith of Abraham and worship with us
Cultivated Muslims have praised D. Masson's French translation of the Qur'an
Muslims and Christians worship a single God. The Vatican document points out
The Vatican document then undertakes a critical examination of the other
false judgements made on Islam.

'Islamic fatalism' is a widely-spread prejudice; the document examines this
and quoting the Qur'an for support, it puts in opposition to this the notion
Qur'an that are highly misunderstood in the West.

"There is no compulsion in religion" (sura 2, verse 256).

"(God) has not laid upon you in religion any hardship" (sura 22, verse 78).

The document opposes the widely-spread notion of 'Islam, religion of fear' to
'Islam, religion of love'- love of one's neighbor based on faith in God.

The Prophet Muhammad (peace be upon him, his family members, his descendent, and his
true companions) was born at Mecca on the 12th of Rabiul
Awal, in the year of the Elephant, a little more than fifty days after the
destruction of the Abyssinian army, or the 29th of August 570 A.D. His
birth , they say, was attended with signs from which the
Prophethood ended and the seed of a great Nation as promised in The Holy
Bible; GENESIS 17, 18; CHAPTER 17 and GENESIS 21.

We are quoting a Indian Book; "A History of Sufism in India" by Saiyid Athar

Abbas Rizvi, M. A. Ph. D. D. Litt., F. A. H. (Australia)
by Munshiram Manoharlal publishers Pvt. Ltd.,New Delhi, volume one, Chapter t
(The Chishtis, pg 21-22); some of which are follows:
"The decade following the death of Muhammad on 8 June, 632 saw the Arab
Town dwellers and Bedouins, whom he had united into one community (Umma),
became the masters of Syria, Iraq, Iran, Egypt, Tripoli and part of the
African peninsula. They were now not only exposed to the evils of material
continued to lead lives immersed in poverty as asceticism. Most prominent
And among the Sufis, Hazrat Ali (Allah be pleased with him) was a model for
Sufis in respect to the truths of outward expressions and the subleties of
Ramadan in year 40 A. H. (661 A. D.), he was attacked by poisoned sword of
Ibn Mulgan and expired on 21st of Ramadhan.
A contemporary of Prophet Muhammad (sm) and a great Sufi was the ascetic
Uway al-Qarani. The Prophet (sm) never met him, but forecast that Umar and
Ali would visit him some time. After the Prophet (sm) went out of human
and Yemen desert . They conveyed to him the prophet's greeting. According
And a modern scholar says "Muhammad was a Sufi on his way to becoming a
Prophet.
So the main and important aim of the followers of any religion is to sacrifice
 oneself with the will of their Lord and forget the existence of
by his good luch got a very high and unimaginable love for his Lord God,
except the direct order from his Lord, The Great God. Such a lucky and
advice and pleasure of God and act according to the will of God. Such a
God. One such recorded example is a Muslim saint, one of the holy women is
Rabia Basri; whose prayer (particularly midnight prayer) to God was "O
Allah (or God), if I pray for the fear of hell, you give me hell, if I
don't deprive me from you". There are hundred of such example of Islamic
Saints who gave everything for becoming nearest to God. One such of holy
been a rich magnate. He abandoned the world, gave all his riches to the
disciple of Abu Hanifa. He died in 161 A. H.
It was normal practice for the Prophets in the language of Prophet Jesus
(Peace be upon him) from the Bible which was mentioned in earlier chapter
"When the Spirit of truth comes, he will guide you into all the truth; for
"If you love me, you will keep my commandments. And I will pray the Father,
and he will give you another paraclete."(14,15-16)
What does 'Paraclete' mean? The present text of John's Gospel explains its
"But the paraclete, the Holy Spirit whom the Father will send in my name,
"he will bear witness to me"(15,26)
"it is to your advantage that I go away, for if I do not go away, the
Paraclete will not come to you; but if I go I will send him to you. And
Now for eternal love towards our only Lord, God the great if we want to see
Ascension of Jesus.
Luke, the only evangelist to provide an undisputed text of the Ascension
Episode (24,51): 'he parted from them and was carried up into heaven', The
evangelist places the event at the end of the description of the Resurrec-
description imply that the Ascension took place on the day of the Resurrec-
between the Passion and the Ascension in the following terms:
"When the Spirit of truth comes, he will guide you into all the truth; for
According to the rules of logic therefore, one is brought to see in John's
God will later send a human being to Earth to take up the role defined by
John, i.e. to be a prophet who hears God's word and repeats his message to
attributes to the words their proper meaning.
By Ascension of Jesus (A. S.) We, the Muslims believe that he i.e. Prophet Jesus (A.S.)
was taken to heaven for a long a period, but the last   Prophet of Islam (A.S.) went to the
heaven which is called the miraj (Ascension)   and talked directly to God and our Prophet

(A. S.) told according to his   sayings a faithful Muslim's prayer is a lesser miraj(ascension) who perform at least obligatory five times   a day conversion to God though theoretically without seeing him.

The above fact is on spirituality of Islam. But how we can accept the following acts of The British and other Western Government for the destruction of billion or trillion dollars of wealth which could be used for the poor people of Asia and Africa for their welfare as Those wealth belongs to Caliphate. The quotations are from:
"UNHOLY BABYLON, THE SECRET HISTORY OF SADDAM'S WAR" by ADEL DARWISH AND GREGORY ALEXANDER and published by VICTOR GOLLANCZ LTD., LONDON IN 1991:

Unholy Babylon contains am impressive array of little-known facts which show how the West sleepwalked into helping a monstrous regime hold the world to ransom. The authors, who were researching the book before the invasion, demonstrate that the events of 2nd August 1990 were the logical conclusion.....

This book, however, is concerned with the story of Saddam Hussain and his rise to power, and with the West's role as 'kingmakers': the political assistance afforded him both before, during and after the Gulf War as well as the economic and industrial assistance which enabled him to create the most powerful military machine in the Middle East. in Acknowledgements of the Book.

The arrival of US forces was the manifestation of the nightmare long feared by conservative pro-Western Arab regimes, resulting in a show of sympathy towards Iraq from elements of the Arab populace throughout the Middle East - sympathy which Saddam Hussein was quick to exploit by linking any solution to the Kuwaiti crisis with one for the Palestinian problem. ..... The Americans had continually misread Saddam Hussein's hints and signals and had sent him the wrong messages in return. Moreover, why had American analysts failed to see the 'writing on the wall' to such an extent that the Pentagon had no contingency plans to cope with an Iraqi invasion of any of the Gulf States? One valid question asked by a small number of people in the United States after the invasion was 'What happened to $50 billion worth of advanced weapon systems sold to the Saudis for their self-defense over the past few years?' Prologue

By the end of the eighteenth century, the entire responsibility for policing the Gulf had become Britain's. India was by then a British possession and the Dutch and the French had been largely evicted from the subcontinent. Britain was happy to restrict its interests in the Gulf to protecting its trade routes and subduing piracy. In 1820, it succeeded in negotiating a General Treaty of Martime Peace with the sheikhs of the Trucial Coast. (There was no need to make a separate agreement with the Kuwaitis, who took no part in the piracy that plagued the lower Gulf.)

However, the real wealth came after the death of Sheikh Ahmad from a heart attack in February 1950. He was succeeded by Sheikh Abdallah al-Salem. In the same year King Ibn Sa'ud began to put pressure on ARAMCO, which was paying him twenty-one cents a barrel, while making a net profit of $1.10 a barrel. The old and ailing king was informed that Venezuela had passed a law in 1948 enforcing a fifty per cent share of income from American oil companies. Meanwhile Iran's Prime Minister Mossadeq was demanding a much improved deal from the Anglo-Iranian Oil Company. Alarmed by the possibility of Iran setting a precedent for other states in the region, Washington and London had plotted to overthrow Mossadeq on the pretext that he was too close to the communists. Washington's decision was based on a study in January 1953 by the National Security Council.

A paper was jointly issued by the State Department, the Department of Defense and the Department of the Interior. It concluded that the political and economic existence of Middle Eastern countries depended upon the rate and terms on which oil is produced, since oil was the principal source of wealth amongst those countries. The paper recognized the operation of oil companies and the level of their production as well as the price they paid as 'instruments of our foreign policy toward those countries. The paper went on to explain that the way oil companies carried out their operations 'determined the strength of our ties with the Middle Eastern countries and our ability to resist Soviet expansion and influence in the area,. As the paper did not make any distinction between the interests of oil companies and those of the United States, it concluded that 'no settlement with Iran of the Anglo-Iranian dispute was possible., Britain's Secret Intelligence Service (SIS), together with the CIA, which provided all the finance, set up an operational bureau in Cyprus during 'Operation Ajax', the operation to topple Mossadeq. Radio broadcasts and newspaper articles were carefully arranged to stir public opinion in Iran and the Middle East against Mossadeq. In August 1953 the CIA organized street mobs in major Iranian cities, setting off a coup that ousted Mossadeq and restored the Shah to the throne whilst the bodies of nationalists and communists were hanging from lamp-posts.......

While Britain had dominated Middle East oil resources prior to the Second World War, it was the Americans who exercised post-war control through two avenues which evolved into the 'twin pillar, policy on either side of the Gulf two decades later: firstly, US government assistance in spreading the influence of American companies amongst the Arab sheikhdoms and, secondly, forty percent control of Iranian oil. However, the events in 1953 which saw the return of the Shah also sowed the seeds of hatred for the 'Great Satan'-America-which was to boil over a quarter of a century later in a bloody revolution that threw the Gulf into the eye of the storm and led the West- in its rush to contain the Islamic revolution- to condone the behavior of Saddam Hussein. The foundation of Israel on land 'stolen, from the Palestinians was in the view of many Arab and Muslim countries a crime of which Britain was largely (and legally) guilty. In the eyes of the Arabs, therefore, the United States became an accomplice by its continued support for a Jewish state. The subject of Israel proved to be a major complication and frequently a source of conflict between Arab oil-producing countries and Western powers. Inevitably, oil companies became caught in the political crossfire. However, those Arab oil producers did not possess any real political leverage until 1961, twelve years after Palestine had been 'lost, to the Jews, when they founded the Organization of the Petroleum Exporting Countries (OPEC) and imposed oil embargoes on Israel. Those twelve years were a bonanza for Western oil companies who made gross profits of $22.2 billion from the Middle East. The oil-producing countries received $9.4 billion, whilst the oil companies netted $12.8 billion.

The co-ordinated policy of OPEC gave members then benefits of collective bargaining and gradually increased their share of the wealth drilled from beneath their sands. However, through the presence of radical members like Lydia, Iraq and smaller African countries, OPEC, to the dismay of the West, became an increasingly political organization. During the early 1970s, there were frequent debates on the issues of the ownership of oil and the control of oil wealth. pg-46-47-48

The young king Faisal II, who had succeeded his father, Ghazi, at the age of four, was isolated by his uncle, the Prince Regent Abd al-Illah, and the prime minister. There is no evidence that British diplomats gave Nuri al-Sa'id any advice to change his ways and introduce some form of liberalization. As Tahseen Me'alla, a founder member of the Ba'ath who split with the party in 1970, later commented on ... However, on the night of 13th July 1958, the king and his uncle were due to travel in the morning to Ankara but as first light was beaming a column of Abd al-Salam Arif's troops moved to the Baghdad radio station, which was captured just before six o'clock. While Abd al-Salam Arif was leading another column of armor towards the palace, Qasim, his partner in the conspiracy, was still with his brigade at Ba'quba. Outnumbered by the rebels, the king's troops fought bravely but were overwhelmed in a short and bloody battle. The king and his uncle came out into the palace gardens, possible to listen to the rebel's demands, and were shot on the spot. There was a story later on suggesting that the rebels were planning to spare the life of the king. This seems unlikely, as the rebels would have feared that the king, who was popular, might subsequently lead a liberation movement in exile. ... The women in the palace were shot soon afterwards. ... They were the first to move on to the streets, pulling down the status of King Faisal II and Maude, the British general who had captured Baghdad from the Turks during the First World War. pg-15-18

Ataturk, who abolished Caliphate in 1924 giving greatest blow to
World Muslim was a Secret Jew

What we can expect from secret Jews who are controlling Turkish Army? Ataturk was a
secret Jew, whose ancestors were given shelter by Osmani Caliph after Spanish inquisition.
And those secret Jews gave the price to World Muslims by destroying the Caliphate after
Sultan Abdul Hamid refused to allow Jewish State in Palestine.

Caliphate is a must for this world as there will be no restriction of passport and visa, where
no people can be a hostage within a small border, where a few families will become owner
of billion of dollars wealth, where rule of law will be imposed by those few families for
their personal benefit. So the World must know how human right of billions of people
violated by the treacherous way when 1300 years old Caliphate was abolished in 1924. We
all know about the role played by Lawrence of Arab; but many of us was ignorant about the
following: "the new Turkish State is a state of the people and a state by the people." But
why Ataturk abolished Khilafat, which was the political System of majority people of
Turkey? Ataturk was a Jew, secret Jew and the greatest enemy of Islam .as he abolished the
Caliphate and suppressed the Muslims.

But alongwith Western powers and Jews there were some secret Jews who were conspiring
againts the Khilafa. Kamal Ataturk was one of them.

The following is from The Literary Digest, October 14, 1922, p. 50:

He was not even a Turk.. He was a Doenmeh (secret Jew)... He achieved the objective of
not the Turks but of the Doenmehs who slowly took over the Ottoman State by openly
converting to and practicing Islam but secretly practicing their old religion.. . He was not a
Turk, let alone 'Father of the Turks'... He was a Doenmeh who wore first a Muslim mask,
then a Turkish mask.. A Spanish Jew by ancestry, an orthodox Moslem by birth and
breeding, trained in a German war college, a patriot, a student of the campaigns of the
world's great generals, including Napoleon, Grant and Lee - these are said to be a few
outstanding characteristics in the personality of the new "Man on Horseback" who has
appeared in the Near East. He is a real dictator, the correspondents testify, a man of the type
which is at once the hope and fear of nations torn to pieces by unsuccessful wars. Unity and
power have come back to Turkey largely through the will of Mustafa Kemal Pasha. ......
...... There was the pasha himself, tall, still young, good-looking, narrow-hipped, wide-
shouldered, with gray, rather sad eyes that spoke eloquently of his Spanish-Jewish ancestry
- for Kemal, like Enver Pasha, tho an orthodox Moslem, is descended from those Spanish-
Jewish families that, given by Christianity the tolerant choice between death, conversion
and exile, found asylum and happiness in the Sultan's domains - and with strong, high-
veined hands, broad and flat across the wrist - the hands of an artist, a dreamer, yet, too,
those of a doer, a man who knows how to clout his dreams into facts.

This was the origin of the most important group, numerically and historically, of Islamic
Marranos. The faithful Mohemmedans call these hidden Jews "doenmehs", the renegades.
..... Over the years the 'doenmeh' movement became firmly established in Asia Minor. In
the nineteenth century the sect was estimated to have twenty thousand members. Salonika
remained its main seat until that city became Greek in 1913.

Here is a quotation from Joachim Prinz's 'The Secret Jews'; page 122: I did not make the
story nor any member of World Muslim. From the same book written by a Jew the World
can know how Jew lived under Caliphate, Spain to India and Yemen to Bosnia and how
Jews were placed in high post. But what we know now is that the World Muslims who
protected the Jews from inquisition after inquisition by European Christians; were fooled
and by the same Jews Caliphate were abolished.

The revolt of the Young Turks in 1908 against the authoritarian regime of Sultan Abdul
Hamid began among the intellectuals of Salonika. It was from there that the demand for a
constitutional regime originated. Among the leaders of the revolution which resulted in a
more modern government in Turkey were Djavid Bey and Mustafa Kemal. Both were

ardent 'doenmehs'. Djavid Bey became minister of finance; Mustafa Kemal became the leader of the new regime and he adopted the name of Ataturk. His opponents tried to use his 'doenmeh' background to unseat him, but without success. Too many of the Young Turks in the newly formed revolutionary Cabinet prayed to Allah, but had as their real prophet Shabtai Zvi, the Messiah of Smyrna.

The followings are another quotations on Ataturk:

The fact that he was a despot and dictator cannot be denied. It was his cruelty and sadistic treatment of Muslims that makes him stand out as one of the worst enemies of Allah. The above was only what was reported and recorded by mostly Western observers. The extent of what actually went on in the new Turkey by the direct policy of Kamal, was heinous to say the least. He was an enemy of Allah (swt) to the core.

TIME January 9, 1933 p. 64

Squinting skyward last week, Turks looked for the new moon. When they should see it Ramadan would begin. Ramadan the mystic month in which the Koran was revealed to Prophet Mohammed. This year the first glint of the new moon had a special, dread significance. Turks had been ordered by their stern dictator, Mustafa Kemal Pasha who made them drop the veil and the fez (TIME, Feb. 15, 1926 et seq.), that beginning with Ramadan they must no longer call their god by his Arabic name, Allah.

No godly man, Dictator Kemal considers that there is no reason why Turks should not call Allah by his Turkish name Tanri. There is no reason except centuries of tradition, no reason except that Turkish imams (priests) all know the Koran by heart in Arabic while few if any have memorized it in Turkish. Strict to the point of cruelty last week was Dictator Kemal's decree that muezzins, calling the faithful to prayer from the top of Turkey's minarets, must shout not the hallowed "Allah Akbar!" (Arabic for "God is Great!") but the unfamiliar words "Tanri Uludur!" which mean the same thing in Turkish.

When imams threatened to suspend services in the mosques and hide the prayer rugs, the Government announced that it was holding 400 brand-new prayer rugs in reserve, threatened to produce "newly trained muezzins who know the Koran in Turkish and are ready to jump into the breach." ....

Nearer & nearer crept the moon to crescent. Ramadan was almost upon Turkey when officials of the Department of Culture (which includes religion) screwed up their courage and told Dictator Kemal that he simply could not change the name of Turkey's god - at least not last week. Already several muezzirs had been thrown into jail for announcing that they would continue to shout "Allah Akbar!' The populace was getting ugly, obviously sympathized with the Allah-shouters.

Abruptly Dictator Kemal yielded "Let them pray as they please, temporarily" he growled. Beaming, his Minister rushed off to proclaim the glad respite only a few hours before the new moon appeared. "On account of the general unpreparedness of muezzins and imams," they suavely declared, "prayers may be offered and the Koran recited in Arabic during the present month of Ramadan, but discourse by the imams must be in Turkish."

During Ramadan all Moslems are especially irritable because they eat nothing during the hours of daylight. After the fasting is over Turks will be more tractable, may accept from their Dictator a new name for their God.

TIME February 20, 1933 p. 18

Word for God A hard father to his people, Mustafa Kemal told his Turks last December that they must forget God in the Arabic language (Allah), learn Him in Turkish (Tanri). Admitting the delicacy of renaming a 1300-year-old god, Kemal gave the muezzins a time allowance to learn the Koran in Turkish. Last week in pious Brusa, the "green city," a muezzin halloed "Tanri Uludur" from one of the minarets whence Brusans had heard "Allah Akbar" since the 14th Century. Raging at Kemal Pasha's god, they mobbed the muezzin, mobbed the police who came to save him.

Quick to defend his new word for God, quicker to show new Turkey the fate of the old-fashioned, Kemal the Ghazi, "the Victorious One," pounced on Brusa, had 60 of the faithful arrested, ousted the Mufti (ecclesiastical judge) of the Ouglubjami mosque and decreed that henceforth God was Tanri.

111

TIME February 15, 1926 pp. 15-16
"Turkey presents today the most promising and challenging field on the face of the earth for missionary service." Thus wrote James L. Barton, missionary executive, in last week's issue of 'Christian Work.' But first he summarized the revolutionary changes in Turkey since 1923. The changes: .... For a hundred years Christian missionaries have struggled hopelessly to capture the hearts of the Calif-awed Turks. They had come, said Mr. Barton, to suspect that "the Moslem was outside the sphere of the operation of divine grace."
Turkey Emil Lengyel 1941, pp. 140-141
During the early days of Kemal's career, many of his followers were under the impression that he was a champion of Islam and that they were fighting the Christians. "Ghazi, Destroyer of Christians" was the name they gave him. Had thet been aware of his real intentions, they would have called him "Ghazi, Destroyer of Islam."
Grey Wolf, Mustafa Kemal An Intimate Study of a Dictator H.C. Armstrong, 1934
He was drinking heavily. The drink stimulated him, gave him energy, but increased his irritability. Both in private and public he was sarcastic, brutal and abrupt. He flared up at the least criticism. He cut short all attempts to reason with him. He flew into a passion at the least opposition. He would neither confide in nor co-operate with anyone. When one politician gave him some harmless advice, he roughly told him to get out. When a venerable member of the Cabinet suggested that it was unseemly for Turkish ladies to dance in public, he threw a Koran at him and chased him out of his office with a stick.
p. 241:

"For five hundred years these rules and theories of an Arab sheik," he said, "and the interpretations of generations of lazy, good-for-nothing priests have decided the civil and the criminal law of Turkey."

"They had decided the form of the constitution, the details of the lives of each Turk, his food, his hours of rising and sleeping, the shape of his clothes, the routine of the midwife who produced his children, what he learnt in his schools, his customs, his thoughts, even his most intimate habits.

"Islam, this theology of an immoral Arab, is a dead thing." Possibly it might have suited tribes of nomads in the desert. It was no good for a modern progressive State.
"God's revelation!" There was no God. That was one of the chains by which the priests and bad rulers bound the people down.

"A ruler who needs religion to help him rule is a weakling. No weakling should rule.."
And the priests! How he hated them. The lazy, unproductive priests who ate up the sustenance of the people. He would chase them out of their mosques and monasteries to work like men.
Religion! He would tear religion from Turkey as one might tear the throttling ivy away to save a young tree.
p. 243:
Further, it was public knowledge that he was irreligious, broke all the rules of decency, and scoffed at sacred things. He had chased the Sheik-ul-Islam, the High Priest of Islam, out of his office and thrown the Koran after him. He had forced the women in Angora to unveil. He had encouraged them to dance body close to body with accursed foreign men and Christians.
*****
Turkey Emil Lengyel 1941, p. 134

Kemal cared nothing about Allah; he was interested in himself and in Turkey. He hated Allah and made him responsible for Turkey's misfortune. It was Allah's tyrannical rule that paralyzed the hands of the Turk. But he knew that Allah was real to the Turkish peasant, while nationalism meant nothing to him. He decided, therefore, to draft Allah into his

service as the publicity director of his national cause. Through Allah's aid his people must cease to be Mohammedans and become Turks. Then, after Allah had served Kemal's purpose, he could discard him.
*****
Ataturk, The Rebirth of a Nation Lord Kinross, 1965, p. 437

For Kemal, Islam and civilization were a contradiction in terms. "If only," he once said of the Turks, with a flash of cynical insight. "we could make them Christians!" His was not to be the reformed Islamic state for which the Faithful were waiting: it was to be a strictly lay state, with a centralized Government as strong as the Sultan's, backed by the army and run by his own intellectual bureaucracy.
p. 470:

The cleavage in his musical tastes emerged in Istanbul, where he once had two orchestras, one Turkish and one European, brought to the Park Hotel. He listened with constant interruptions, commanding one to stop and the other to play in turn. Finally, as the raki took effect, he lost patience and rose to leave the restaurant, saying, "Now if you like you can both play together." Another evening, incensed by the sound of the muezzin from a mosque opposite, which clashed with the dance-band, he ordered its minaret to be felled - one of those orders which was countermanded next morning. *****

Ataturk, The Rebirth of a Nation Lord Kinross, 1965 p. 365

Some confusion as to his identity persisted, however, for some years to come. Inspecting some soldiers in Anatolia, Kemal once asked, "Who is God and where does He live?"
The soldier, anxious to please, replied, "God is Mustafa Kemal Pasha. He lives in Angora."
"And where is Angora?" Kemal asked.
"Angora is in Istanbul," was the reply.
Farther down the line he asked another soldier, "Who is Mustafa Kemal?"
The reply was, "Our Sultan."
Ataturk's ancestors, who came from Spain after the fall of Islam; were given shelter under the Caliphate. You can get the above book from Jewish division of New York Public Library.
There must be the Caliphate if possible within few days, few months and in fact we don't bother about those illegal immigrants and it is future Caliph who can decide about them and not London, Paris, Moscow or Washington as World Muslims never intend to interfere about policies in those Capitals.

About the creation of child supported by WHO (World Health Organization) in it's Comment Islam, Procreation and the Law by Zulie Sachedina, Volume 16, Number 3, September 1990; some of which follows:

" The message Muhammad preached to the Arabs came to him through a series of revelations Allah gave him throughout Muhammad's prophet-hood until the end of his. The revelations were collected in a book called the Quran, which is the fundamental authority for Muslims in all matters of religious belief and practice and of the law. The Quran is viewed by Muslims as 'Kalam Allah,' or the very words of God."

"Islam is a comprehensive system that regulates the spiritual as well civic aspects of individual and communal life.

"Marriage is seen as twofold. First, it unites the two elements of humanity; this is reflected in the following verse of the Quran:

Amongst His signs is that He created consorts (in marriage) for you from amongst your-selves, so that you may find tranquility with them, and (He) set love and compassion between you. Verily, in this are signs for those who reflect. (Quran S. 30:21)
The second purpose, also stated in the Quran, is the procreative function:

And God has created for you consorts (in marriage) from amongst yourselves, and through your consorts He created children and grand children for you, and provided you of His bounty. Will they then believe in vain things and be ungrateful to God's favors?! (Quran S. 16:72)

The Quran makes clear reference to the progressive development of the fetus:

O mankind! If you are in doubt as to the Resurrection, [consider] that We have created you of earth; then of semen; then of a blood-like clot; then a lump of flesh, [which is] formed or unformed; so that We may demonstrate to you [our power]; and We establish in the wombs what We will, till a stated term; then We bring you out as infants.... (Quran S. 22:5)"

The last verse (S. 22:5) mentioned above was proved by modern science in term of various development stages of a child in fetus.
The above comments are part of long research on family planning method.

There is also another verse in The Holy Quran which is as follows:

40: 67 It is   He Who has Created you from dust. Then from a sperm-drop,
40: 67 Then from a leech-like clot; Then does He get you Out (into the
40: 67 light) As a child: then lets you (Grow and) reach your age Of
40: 67 full strength; then Lets you become old,- Though of you there
40: 67 are Some who die before;- And lets you reach A Term appointed: In
40: 67 order that ye May learn wisdom.

40: 68 It is He Who gives life and Death; and when He Decides upon an
40: 68 affair, Fe says to it, "Be", And it is.

Recent invention of Saddad's mine in Oman.

In its issue dated February 17, 1992 the NEWSWEEK Magazine carried another scientific article The 'Atlantis of the Sands' (by Jeanne Gordon in Los Angeles and Fiona Gleizes in Paris) some of which follows:

Calling on ancient dreams and modern technology, a team may have found the ancient city of Ubar

The Koran describes how the earth swallowed up a sumptuous but decadent "city of towers" called Iram. A British explorer Bertram Thomas, once was told by an Omany Bedouin: "Look, sahib, the road to Ubar," but he never found the lost city. In 1981, a California dreamer happened on the reference in Thomas's 1932 memoir, "Arabia Felix," Film maker Nicholas Clapp combed the texts, enlisted satellite experts in the search, teamed up with British explorer Sir Ranulph Fiennes and finally embarked on a three month expedition. The team may have cracked the riddle. The first artifacts from the side include Roman, Greek, Chinese, Egyptian and Syrian pottery shards, the latter dating from 2800 B. C. "Eight towers once guarded a complex of store rooms, living areas, an administrative center, and possible the majlis (assembly room) of Shaddad ibn Ad... who built Ubar as an "imitation of paradise'," says Clapp.

Middle East archeologist have turned away from searching historical sources because using the Bible has proved largely fruitless.
And the saga already illustrates how technological advances have opened up new vistas for exploration. In 1984, at Clapp's urging, two NASA   scientists scanned the region with sand-penetrating SIR-B radar mounted on the space shuttle Challenger. They cross-checked the findings with images from U. S. and French satellites. That produced a remarkable map of the Empty Quarter, including ancient caravan routes and aquifers. Fiennes, who once served in the Omani army, then received permission from the Sultan of Oman to lead an expedition- and raised the needed funds from British and Omani firms. Fiennes and Clapp began digging near where the caravan route discovered by Thomas crosses an aquier revealed by satellite. The sultan (Omani sultan), he says, "is very excited."
So is Clapp, who documented the find on film. He says diggers can already see that the city center collapsed-as told in the Koran-because it was built over a lime-stone cavern used to store water. That "would have taken down intact rooms full of stuff," he says. Excavation could take 40 workers five years, but the payoff may be a trove of artifacts on a par with Pompeii.
In the article with the picture it is mentioned "As told in the Koran: The ruins of a stone tower still stand guard over the site in Oman, a classical etching depicting the lost city in its heyday."

Again one such verse on the universe is:

41: 12 So he completed them As seven firmaments In two Days and He
41: 12 Assigned to each heaven Its duty and command. And We adorned The
41: 12 lower heaven With lights, and (provided it) With guard. Such Is
41: 12 the Decree of (Him) The Exalted in Might, Full of Knowledge.

And, it will be remembered that at the height of Islam, between the Eighth and Twelfth centuries AD, i.e. at a time when restrictions on scientific development were in force in the Christian world, a very large number of studies and discoveries were being made at Islamic universities. It was there that the remarkable cultural resources of the time were to be found. The Caliph's library at Cordoba contained 400,000 volumes. Averroe was teaching there, and Greek, Indian and Persian Scholars were taught.[111]

_ [111] The Bible, Quran and Science by Maurice Bucaille pg. 123

This is why scholars from all over Europe went to study at Cordoba, just as today people go to the United States to perfect their studies.[112]

We should quote few sentences from "THE SPIRIT OF ISLAM" by SYED AMIR ALI below:

"The doctrine of the trinity in unity, of the three "Nature" in one, of original sin, of tarn substantiation, all gave rise to a certain intellectual tension. The dogmas of the Church accordingly required some such "solvent" as scholasticism before science and free thought could find their way into Christendom. In Islam the case was otherwise; with the exception of the unity of God- the doctrine of Tauhid, which was the foundation of Mohammed's Church - there was no dogma upon which insistence was placed in any such form as to compel Reason to hold back its acceptance. The doctrine of "origin and return" - mabda and maad, "coming (from God) and returning (to Him)"- and of the moral responsibility of man, was founded on the conception of a Primal Cause- the Originator of all things.
In the Prophet's time, as well as under the Rashidin (Truthful) Caliphs, no doubt, free independent inquiry was naturally, and perhaps rightly, discouraged. But no questioning was avoided, no doubt was silenced by terror of authority, and if the teacher was unable to answer the question, the inability was avowed in all humility.[113]
.. The greatest of the philosophers were al-Kindi, al-Farabi, Ibn-Sina, Ibn-Baja, Ibn-Tufail, and Ibn-Rushd.[114] .. Al-Kindi[115] (Abu Yusuf Yakub ibn Ishak), surnamed the Philosopher par excellence, was a descendant of the illustrious family of Kinda, and counted among his ancestors several of the princes of Arabia.
Abu Nasr Farabi (Abu Nasr Mohammed bin Mohammed Turkhan al-Farabi), so called from his native city of Farab in Transoxiana, was a distinguished physician, mathematician, and philosopher. He enjoyed the patronage of Saif ud-Dowla Ali bin Hamadan, Prince of Aleppo, and died at Damascus in December, 950 A. C.. In the Encyclopedia of Science (Ihsa ul-ulum) he gives a general review of all the sciences. A Latin epitome of this work gives an idea of the range over which it extends, being divided into five parts dealing with the different branches of science, viz. language, logic, mathematics, natural sciences, and political and social economy. Another celebrated work of Farabi, largely utilized by Roger Bacon and Albertus Magnus, was his commentary on Aristotle's Organon. His Tendency of the Philosophies of Plato and Aristotle, his treatise on ethics, entitled as-Sirat ul-Fazila, and another on politics, called as-Siyasat ul-Medineyya, which forms part of a larger and more comprehensive work bearing that name
of Mabadi-ul-Moujudat, show the versatile character of his intellect. Besides philosophy and medicine, Farabi cultivated music, which he elevated into a science. He wrote several

---

[112] **THE BIBLE, THE QUR'AN and Science by Maurice Bucaille pg.123**

[113] The answer was, "God knows best."

[114] Shahristani mentions several others, such as-Yahya al-Nahwy, Abul Faraj al-Mufassir, Abu Sulaiman al-Sajzy, Abu Bakr Sabit bin Kurrab, Abu Sulaiman Mohammed al-Mukaddasi, Abu Tamam Yusuf bin Mohammad Nishapuri, Abu Zaid Ahmed bin Saha al-Balkhi, Abu Muharib al-Hasan bin Sahl bin Muharib al-Kumy, Ahmed bin Tayyeb al-Sarrakhsy, Talha bin Mohammed al-Nafsy, Abu Hamid Ahmed bin Mohammed al-Safzari, Isa bin Ali al-Wazir, Abu Ali Ahmed bin Muskuya, Abu Zakaria Yahya bin Adi al-Zumairi, Abu'l Hasan al-Amri. He does not mention single Spanish philosopher.

[115] 813 to 842 A. C.

treatises both on the theory and the art of music, as well as the manufacture of musical instruments. In one he compared the systems of music among the ancients with that in vogue in his own time. Abul Kasim Kinderski, no mean judge, places Farabi on a level with his great successor, Ibn-Sina.[116] Of Ibn-Sina I have already spoken as physician. As a philosopher he occupies a position hardly inferior to that of the great Stagyrite. .... Ibn-Rushd or Averroes (Abu'l Walid Mohammad ibn Ahmed) was born in 520 A.H. (1126 AC) at Cordoba (Spain), where his family had for a long time occupied a prominent position. His grand-father was the Kazi ul-Kuzat of all Andalusia under the Almoravides. Ibn-Rushd was a juriscounsult of the first rank, but he applied himself mainly to medicine, mathematics, and philosophy..... Chemistry, as a science, is unquestionably the invention of the Moslems. Abu Mus Jabir (the Geber of Christian writers)[117] is the true father of modern chemistry. `His name is memorable in chemistry, since it marks an epoch in that science of equal importance to that of Priestly and Lavoisier' ... They calculated the size of the earth from the measurement of a degree on the shore of the Red Sea- this at a time when Christian Europe was asserting the flatness of the globe. Abul Hasan invented the telescope of which he apeakes as 'a tube to the extremities of which were attached diopters.' These `tubes' were improved and used afterwards in the observatories of Maragha and Cairo with great success" ... The first observatory in Europe was built by the Arabs. The Giralda, or tower of Serville, was erected under the super-intendance of the great mathematician Jabir ibn Afiah in 1190 AC for the observation of the heavens. Its fate was not a little characteristic. After the expulsion of the Moors, it was turned into a belfry, the Spaniards not knowing what else to do with it![118]

The Abbaside period is especially interesting for us because of the new interest in science which it started. Science, as you know is a very big thing in the modern world, and we owe a great deal to it. Science does not simply sit down and pray for things to happen, but seeks to find out why things happen. It experiments and tries again and again, and sometimes fails and sometimes succeeds and so bit by bit it adds to human knowledge. This modern world of ours is very different from the ancient world or the Middle Ages. This great difference is largely due to science, for the modern world has been made by science. Among the ancients we do not find the scientific method in Egypt or China or India. We find just a bit of it in old Greece. In Rome again it was absent. But the Arabs had this scientific spirit of inquiry, and so they may be considered the fathers of modern science. In some subjects, like medicine and mathematics, they learnt much from India. Indian scholars and mathematicians came in large numbers to Baghdad. Many Arab Students went to Takshashila in North India, which was still a great university, specializing in medicine. Sanskrit books on medical and other subjects were especially translated into Arabic. Many things for example, paper-making the Arabs learnt from China. But on the basis of the knowledge gained from others they made their own researches and made several important discoveries. They made the first telescope and the mariner's compass. In medicine, Arab physicians and surgeons were famous all over Europe. Baghdad was, of course, the great

---

[116] See also the`Uyun-ul-Masail (Dieterici's ed. p. 52), where he establishes by deductive reasoning that Creation is the work of a Supreme Intelligence, and that nothing in the universe is fortuitous or accidental.

[117] Abu Musa Jabir ibn Hayyar was a native of Tarsus. Ibn Khallikan says "Jabir complied a work of two thousand pages in which he inserted the problems of his master (the Imam) Jafar as-Sadik which formed five hundred treatises", see also the Tarikh-ul-Hukama.

[118] THE SPIRIT OF ISLAM by SYED AMIR ALI, pp. 424 - 429, 384-385, 374-375, 379.

center of all these intellectual activities. In the West, Cordoba, the capital of Arab Spain, was another center. There were many other university centers in the Arab world, where the life of the intellect flourished there was Cairo or al-Qahira, "the victorious", Basra and Kufa. But over all these famous cities towered Baghdad, "the capital of Islam, the eye of Iraq, the seat of empire, the center of beauty, culture and arts" as an Arab historian describes it. It had a population of over 2,000,000 and thus was far bigger than modern Calcutta or Bombay. .. Thousands and thousands of people have never heard of the Abbaside Khalifas and of their empire, but they know of Baghdad of the Alf Laila wa Laila, the "Thousand and one Nights", the city of mystery and romance, The empire of the imagination is often more real and more lasting than the empire of fact.

The Arabs had friendly relations with the Indian rulers of the south, especially the Rashtrakutas. Many Arabs settled along the west coast of India (like Bombay where Muslims were killed by the supposed protector sate Police recently) and built mosques in their settlements. Arab travelers and traders visited various parts of India. Arab students came in large numbers to the northern University of Takshasila or Taxila, which was especially famous for medicine. It is said that in the days of Harunal-Rashid Indian scholarship had a high place in Baghdad and physicians from India went there to organize hospitals and medical schools. Many Sanskrit books on mathematics and astronomy were translated into Arabic. Thus the Arabs took much from the old Indo-Aryans culture. They took also much from the Aryan culture of Persia, and also something from Hellenic culture. They were almost like a new race, in the prime of their vigor, and they took advantage of all the old cultures they saw around them, and learnt from them; and on this foundation they built something of their very own- the Saracenic culture. This had a comparatively brief life, as culture go, but it was a brilliant life, which shines against the dark background of the Middle Ages in Europe. [119]

A historian, carried away by his enthusiasm a little, has said that:

"The Moors organized that wonderful kingdom of Cordoba, which was the marvel of the Middle Ages, and which, when all Europe was plunged in barbaric ignorance and strife, alone held the torch of learning and civilization bright and shining before the Western world." Kurtuba (Cordoba) was capital of this Kingdom for just 500 years.

Kurtuba was the capital of this kingdom for just 500 years. This is usually called Cordoba in English, sometimes Cordoba. I am afraid I have a way of spelling the same name differently at times. But I shall try to stick to Cordoba. This was a great city of a million inhabitants, a garden city ten miles in length, with twenty-four miles of suburbs. There are said to have been 60,000 palaces and 700 public baths. These figures may be exaggerations, but they give some idea of the city. There were many libraries, the chief of these, the Imperial Library of the Emir, containing 400,000 books. The University of Cordoba was famous all over Europe and even in western Asia. Free elementary schools for the poor abounded. A historian says that:

"In Spain almost everybody knew how to read and write, whilst in Christian Europe, save and except the clergy, even persons belonging to the highest ranks were wholly ignorant. Such was the city of Cordova, competing with the other great Arab city of Baghdad. Its fame spread all over Europe and a German writer of the tenth century called it "the ornament of the world". To its university came students from distant places. The influence of Arab philosophy spread to the other great universities of Europe, Paris, Oxford and the universities of northern Italy. Averroes or Ibn Rushd was a famous philosopher of Cordova

---

___ [119] GLIMPSES OF WORLD HISTORY, (BAGHDAD AND HARUNAL-RASHID) BY NEHRU, PP. 151-154.

in the twelfth century. In his later years he fell out with the Spanish Emir and was banished. He went and settled in Paris.[120]

As in other parts of Europe, there was a kind of feudal system in Spain also. Great and powerful nobles grew up, and between them and the Emir, who was the ruler, there was frequent fighting.

An English historian, Lane Poole, writing of the Saracens in Spain says:

"For centuries Spain had been the center of civilization, the seat of arts and sciences, of learning and every form of refined enlightenment. No other country in Europe had so far approached the cultivated dominion of the Moors. The brief brilliancy of Ferdinand and Isabella, and of the Empire of Charles, could found no such enduring pre-eminence. The Moors were banished; for a while Christian Spain shone, like the moon, with a borrowed light; then came the eclipse, and in that darkness Spain has groveled ever since. The true memorial of the Moors is seen in desolate tracts of utter barrenness, where once the Moors grew luxuriant vines and olives and yellow ears of corn; in a stupid, ignorant stagnation and degradation of a people which has hopelessly fallen in the scale of nations, and has deserved its humiliation.[121]

In central and western Asia we see the remnants of the Abbaside Empire of Baghdad. Baghdad still flourishes, and indeed is increasing in power under a newest of rulers, the Seljuq Turks.But the old empire has slit up into many kingdoms. Islam has ceased to be one empire and has become merely the religion of many countries and peoples. Out of the wreck of the Abbaside Empire has arisen the kingdom of Ghazni, which Mahmud has ruled and from which he has swooped down on India. But though the Empire of Baghdad has broken up, Baghdad itself continues to be a great city, attracting artists and learned men from distances. Many great and famous cities also flourish in central Asia at this time Bokhara, Samarqand, Balkh and others And extensive trade is carried on between them and great caravans carry merchandise from one to the other.[122]

Islam brought a new impulse for human progress to India. To some extent it served as a tonic. ... At one period, indeed, there was a club in Baghdad, under the patronage of the Caliph, were men of all religions and no religion met together to discuss and debate about all matters from the point of view of rationalism alone. ... Still, a new impulse came to India for progress and creative effort. How this put some new life in India and then worked itself out ,we shall consider later.[123]

---

[120] GLIMPSES OF WORLD HISTORY, (CORDOBA AND GRANADA) BY NEHRU, PP. 189-190.

[121] GLIMPSES OF WORLD HISTORY ON CORDOVA AND GRANADA BY JAWAHARLAL NEHRU, PG. 152.

[122] GLIMPSES OF WORLD HISTORY ON "END OF FIRST MILLENNIUM AFTER CHRISR" BY JAWAHARLAL NEHRU, P. 176.

[123] GLIMPSES OF WORLD HISTORY (ANOTHER LOOK AT ASIA AND EUROPE) BY NEHRU, P. 181.

Aim of Islam and other Religion

There are about few verses about religion in the Holy Quran some are
as follows :

2:135 They say: "Become Jews Or Christians if ye would be guided (To
2:135 salvation). " Say thou: "Nay! (I would rather) the Religion Of
2:135 Abraham the True, And he joined not gods with Allah.

2:256 Let there be no compulsion In religion: Truth stands out Clear from
2:256 Error: whoever Rejects Evil and believe In Allah hath grasped The
2:256 most trustworthy Hand-hold, that never breaks.   And Allah heareth.
2:256 And knoweth all things.

3: 24 This because they say: "The Fire shall not touch us But for a few
3: 24 numbered days": For their forgeries deceive them As to their own religion.

3: 73 "And believe no one Unless he follows Your religion." Say: "True
3: 73 guidance Is the guidance of Allah: (Fear ye) lest a revelation Be
3: 73 sent to someone (else) Like unto that which was sent Unto you. Or
3: 73 that those (Receiving such revelation) Should engage you in
3: 73 argument Before your Lord. " Say: "All bounties Are in the hand of
3: 73 Allah: He grateth them To whom He pleaseth: And Allah careth for
3: 73 all, And He knoweth all things. "
3: 95 Say : " Allah speaketh The Truth: follow The religion of Abraham,
3: 95 The sane in faith; he Was not of the Pagans,"

4:125 Who can be better In religion than one Who submits his whole self
4:125 To Allah, does good, And follows the way Of Abraham the true in
4:125 faith? For Allah did take Abraham for a friend.

4:146 Except for those who repent, Mend (their life), hold fast To Allah,
4:146 and purify their religion As in Allah's sight: if so They will be
4:146 (numbered) With the Believers. And soon will Allah Grant to the
4:146 Believers A reward of immense value.

4:171 O People of the Book! Commit no excesses In your religion: nor say
4:171 Of Allah aught but truth. Christ Jesus the son of Mary Was (no
4:171 more than) An apostle of Allah, And His Word, Which He bestowed on
4:171 Mary, And a Spirit proceeding From Him: so believe In Allah and His
4:171 apostles Say not "Trinity": desist: It will be better for you: For
4:171 Allah is One Allah: Glory be to Him: (For Exalted is He) above
4:171 Having a son. To Him Belong all things in the heavens And on earth.
4:171 And enough Is Allah as a Disposer of affairs.

Before we go about the follower of Islam as a religion, we must quote who is Allah (God),
our The only and Great God, so The Holy Quran describe about Allah (i.e. God), some of
which are as follows:

2: 29 It is He Who hath created for you All things that are on earth;
2: 29 Moreover His design comprehended the heavens, For He gave order and
2: 29 perfection To the seven firmaments; And of all things He hath

2: 29 perfect knowledge.

2: 30 Behold, thy Lord said to the angels: "I will create A vicegerent on
2: 30 earth," They said, "Wilt Thou place therein one who will make
2: 30 Mischief therein and shed blood?- Whilst we do celebrate Thy
2: 30 praises And glorify Thy holy (name)?" He said: "I know what ye know
2: 30 not."

2: 32 They said :"Glory to Thee: of knowledge We have none, save what
2: 32 Thou Hast taught us : in truth it is Thou Who art perfect in
2: 32 knowledge and wisdom."

2: 33 He said :"o Adam! tell them Their natures." When he had told them,
2: 33 Allah said: "Did I not tell you that I know the secrets of heavens
2: 33 And earth, and I know what ye reveal And what ye conceal?"

2: 34 And behold, We said to the angels, "Bow down to Adam" ;and they
2: 34 bowed down; Not so Iblis: he refused and was haughty: he was of
2: 34 those who reject faith.
2:255 Allah! There is no god But He,- the Living, The Self-subsisting,
2:255 Eternal. No slumber can seize Him Nor sleep. His are all things In
2:255 the heavens and on earth. Who is there can intercede In His
2:255 presence except As He permitteth? He knoweth What (appeareth to His
2:255 creatures As) Before or After Or behind them. Nor shall they
2:255 compass Aught of His knowledge Except as He willeth. His Throne
2:255 doth extend Over the heavens And the earth, and He feelth No
2:255 fatigue in guarding And preserving them For He is the Most High,
2:255 The Supreme (in glory).

6: 1 Praise be to Allah, Who created the heavens And the earth, And made
6: 1 the Darkness And the Light. Yet those who reject Faith Hold
6: 1 (others) as equal With their Guardian-Lord.
6: 3 And He is Allah In the heavens And on earth. He knoweth what ye
6: 3 Hide, and what ye reveal, And He knoweth The (recompense) which Ye
6: 3 earn (by your deeds).
6: 13 "To Him belongeth all That dwelleth (or lurketh) In the Night and
6: 13 the Day. For He is the One Who heareth and knoweth All things."
6: 15 Say: "I would, if I Disobeyed my Lord, Indeed have fear Of the
6: 15 Penalty Of a Mighty Day.
6: 16 "On that day, if the Penalty Is averted from any, It is due to
6: 16 Allah's Mercy; And that would be (Salvation), The obvious
6: 16 fulfillment Of all desire.
6: 20 Those to whom We have given the Book Know this as they know 850
6: 20 Their own sons. Those who have lost Their own souls Refuse
6: 20 therefore to believe.

10: 5 It is He Who made the sun. To be a shining glory And the moon to
10: 5 be a light (Of beauty), and measured out Stages for her: that ye
10: 5 might Know the number of years And the count(of time). No wise did
10: 5 Allah creare this But in truth and righteousness.(Thus) doth He
10: 5 explain His Signs In detail, for those who understand.
13: 12 It is He Who doth show you The lightning, by way Both of fear
13: 12 and of hope: It is He Who doth raise up The clouds , heavy With
13: 12 (fertilizing) rain!
13: 16 Say:" Who is the Lord and Sustainer Of the heavens and the earth?'

13: 16 Say:"(It is) Allah." Say:"Do ye then take (For worship) protectors
13: 16 other Than Him, such as have Nor power either for good Or for
13: 16 harm to themselves?" Say:"Are the blind equal With those who
13: 16 see? Or the depths of darkness Equal with Light?"Or do they
13: 16 assign to Allah Partners who have created (Anything) as He has
13: 16 created, So that the creation seemed To them similar? Say:"Allah
13: 16 is the Creator Of all things : He is The One, the Supreme and
13: 16 Irresistible."

30: 22 And among His Signs Is the creation of the heavens And the earth,
30: 22 and the variations In your language And your colors: verily In
30: 22 that are Signs For those who know.
30: 24 And among His Signs, He shows you the lightning, By way both of
30: 24 fear And of hope and He sends Down rain from the sky And with it
30: 24 gives life to The earth after it is dead: Verily in that are
30: 24 Signs For those who are wise.
30: 29 Nay, the wrong-doers (merely) Follow their own lusts, Being
30: 29 devoid of knowledge. But who will guide those Whom Allah leaves
30: 29 astray? To them there will be No helpers.
30: 30 So set thou thy face Steadily and truly to the Faith: (Establish)
30: 30 Allah's handiwork according To the pattern on which He has made
30: 30 mankind : No change (let there be) In the work (wrought) By Allah:
30: 30 that is The standard Religion: But most among mankind Understand
30: 30 not .

43: 84 It is He Who is Allah In heaven and Allah on earth; And He is Full
43: 84 Of Wisdom and Knowledge .
43: 85 And blessed is He To Whom belongs the dominion Of the heavens
43: 85 and the earth, And all between them: With Him is the knowledge Of
43: 85 the Hour (of Judgment): And to Him shall ye Be brought back.
43: 86 And those whom they invoke Besides Allah have no power Of
43: 86 intercession;-only he Who bears witness to the Truth, And they
43: 86 know (him).

44: 6 As a Mercy From thy Lord : For He hears and knows (All things);
44: 7 The Lord of the heavens And the earth and all Between them,
44: 7 if ye (but) Have an assured faith.

45: 4 And in the creation Of yourselves and the fact That animals are
45: 4 scattered (Through the earth), are Signs For those of assured
45: 4 Faith.

2:115 To Allah belong the East And the west: whithersever Ye turn, there
2:115 is the Presence Of Allah. For Allah is All-Pervading, All-Knowing.

30: 54 It is Allah Who Created you in a state Of (helpless) weakness,
30: 54 then Gave (you) strength after weakness, Then, after strength,
30: 54 gave (you) Weakness and a hoary head: He creates as He wills
30: 54 And it is He Who has All knowledge and power.

48: 14 To Allah belongs the dominion Of the heavens and the earth:
48: 14 He forgives whom He Wills And He punishes whom He Wills: but
48: 14 Allah is Oft-Forgiving, Most Merciful.

59: 22 Allah is He, than Whom There is no other god;- Who knows (all-

59: 22 things) Both secret and open; He Most Gracious Most Merciful.

59: 23 Allah is He, than whom There is no other god;- The Sovereign, the
59: 23 Holy One, The Source of Peace (and Perfection) The Guardian of
59: 23 Faith, The Preserver of Safety, The Exalted in Might, The
59: 23 Irresistible, the Supreme: Glory to Allah! (High is He) Above the
59: 23 partners They attribute to Him.

64: 4 He knows what is In the heavens And on earth: And He knows what Ye
64: 4 conceal and what Ye reveal: yes, Allah Knows well the (secrets)
64: 4 Of (all) hearts.

65: 8 How many populations That insolently opposed The command of their
65: 8 Lord And of His apostles, Did We not then Call to account,- To
65: 8 severe account?- And We imposed on them An exemplary Punishment.
65: 10 Allah has prepared for them A severe Punishment (In the Hereafter).
65: 10 Therefore fear Allah. O ye men of understanding - Who have
65: 10 believed ! For Allah hath indeed Sent down to you A Message,-

102: 3 But nay, ye soon shall Know (the reality).
102: 4 Again ye soon shall know!
102: 5 Nay were ye to know With certainty of mind, (Ye would beware!)

107: 5 Who are neglectful Of their Prayers ,
108: 2 Therefore to thy Lord Turn in Prayer And Sacrifice
109: 1 Say: O ye That reject Faith!
110: 3 Celebrate the Praises Of thy Lord and pray For His Forgiveness:
110: 3 For He is Oft-Returning (In Grace and Mercy).

Aim of any religion and the religion Islam is to surrender to the will of God and to spread good thing in the society and the world; to desist oneself and others from doing any mischief or bad thing and to serve the humanity in particular and to establish justice to all creation of God that may be any animal and even any plant or hill or ocean. Spiritually aim of any religion should be to sacrifice oneself to God completely with a willpower to forget about oneself and in greater sense if possible to merge with the great Almighty.

Religion is an ideal. One who follows that ideal should have faith in it and accept it as true and act accordingly. Else none can be called to be the believer of that ideal. Hence it is not difficult to understand that no man can claim to be the believer of a religious faith by birth only. Yet it is commonly held that it is enough for a man to be called believer of a religion by the very fact of his birth The people of this type are either blind followers or hypocrites and I believe any person who has clear idea about religion must admit this truth. In our language he may be branded as a self deluded fool or a rogue or may be called a hypocrite.[124]

I am quoting the following observation of Pandit (Pandit means learned) Jawhar Lal Nehru on Religion that he has mentioned in his famous book "Glimpses of World History" :[125]

---

[124] Why I accepted Islam by ABUL HUSSAIN BHATTACHARJEE PG. 12

[125] Glimpses of world History by Nehru, INQILAB ZINDABAD PP. 7, 37.

"For the family sacrifice the individual, for the community the family, for the country the community, and for the Soul the whole world" . What the Soul is few of us can know or tell, and each one of us can interpret it in a different way. But the lesson this Sanskrit verse teaches us is the same lesson of co-operation and sacrifice for the larger good.
What, then is one to do with religion? For some people religion means the other world: heaven, paradise or whatever it may be called. In the hope of going to heaven they are religions or do certain things. This reminds me of the child who behaves in the hope of being rewarded with a jam puff or jalebi (sweet) ! If the child is always thinking of the jam puff or the jalebi, you would not say that it had been properly trained, would you? Much less would you approved of boys and girls who did everything for the sake of jam puffs and the like. What, then, shall we say of grown-up persons who think and act in this way? For, after all, there is no essential difference between the jam puff and the idea of paradise. We are all   more or less selfish. But we try to train up our children
So that they may become as unselfish as possible. At any rate, our ideals should be wholly unselfish, so that we may try to live up to them."

The Religion Islam and it's Prophets (Peace be upon them)

There is a misconception regarding Islam as a religion. The Present day Muslim are not only the follower of Islam, instead the followers of all religion; from Prophet Adam (Peace be upon him) to Prophet Muhammad (Peace be upon him and his family members and his true companion) have been following the Islam. God has sent various Prophets to almost all part of this world and according to Muslim beliefs 1,25,000 or 2,25,000 prophets have been sent to this world. We can also know from the verses of the Holy Quran related to word "Islam" that all religions are Islam.

The following verses of the Holy Quran (translation)are enough to explain about the followers
of Islam:

2:177 It is not righteousness That ye turn your faces Towards East or
2:177 West; But it is righteousness- To believe in Allah And the Last Day
2:177 And the Angels, And the Book, And the Messengers; To spend of your
2:177 substance, Out of love for Him, For your kin, For orphans, For the
2:177 needy, For the wayfarer, For those who ask, And for the ransom of
2:177 slaves; To be steadfast in prayer, And practice regular charity; To
2:177 fulfil the contracts Which ye have made; And to be firm and
2:177 patient, In pain (or suffering) And adversity, And throughout All
2:177 periods of panic. Such are the people Of truth, the God-fearing.

There are around 39 verses related to word "Islam" in the Holy Quran which are as follows:

2:132 And this was the legacy That Abraham left to his sons, And so did
2:132 Jacob: "O my sons! Allah hath chosen The Faith for you; then die
2:132 not Except in the Faith of Islam."

2:133 Were ye witnesses When Death appeared before Jacob? Behold, he said
2:133 to his sons: "What will ye worship after me? They said: "We shall
2:133 worship Thy Allah and the Allah of thy fathers, Of Abraham, Ismail,
2:133 and Isaac ,- The one (True) Allah: To Him we bow (in Islam). "
2:136 Say ye: "We believe In Allah, and the revelation Given to us, and
2:136 to Abraham, Ismail, Isaac, Jacob, And the Tribes, and that given To
2:136 Moses and Jesus and that given To (all) Prophets from their Lord:
2:136 We make no difference Between one and another of them: And we bow
2:136 to Allah (in Islam)."

2:208 O ye who believe! Enter into Islam Whole-heartedly; And follow not   2:208 The footsteps
Of the Evil One; For he is to you An avowed enemy.
3: 19 The Religion before Allah Is Islam (submission to His Will) Nor did
3: 19 the People of the Book. Dissent therefrom except Through envy of   3: 19 each other, After
knowledge had come to them. But if any deny the   3: 19 Signs of Allah, Allah is swift in calling
to account.

3: 67 Abraham was not a Jew Nor yet a christian, But he was true in Fait h
3: 67 And bowed his will to Allah's (Which is Islam), And he joined not
3: 67 gods with Allah.

3: 80 Nor would he instruct you To take angels and prophets For Lords
3: 80 and Patrons. What! would he bid you To unbelief after ye have Bowed
3: 80 your will (To Allah in Islam)?
3: 83 Do they seek For other than the Religion Of Allah ?- while all
3: 83 creatures In the heavens and on earth Have, willing or unwilling,
3: 83 Bowed to His Will (Accepted Islam), And to Him shall they All be
3: 83 brought back.

3: 84 Say: "We believe In Allah, and in what Has been revealed to us And
3: 84 what was revealed To Abraham, Ismail, Isaac, Jacob, and the Tribes,
3: 84 And in (the Books) Given to Moses, Jesus, And the Prophets , From
3: 84 their Lord: We make no distinction Between one and another Among
3: 84 them, and to Allah do Bow our will (in Islam). "

3: 85 If anyone desires A religion other than Islam (submission to
3: 85 Allah). Never will it be accepted Of him; and in the Hereafter He
3: 85 will be in the ranks Of those who have lost (All spiritual good).

3:102 O ye who believe! Fear Allah as He should be Feared, and die not
3:102 Except in a state Of Islam.

5: 4 Forbidden to you (for food) Are: dead meat, blood, The flesh of
5: 4 swine, and that On which hath been invoked The name of other than
5: 4 Allah, That which hath been Killed by strangling, Or by a violent
5: 4 blow, Or by a headlong fall, Or by being gored to death: That which
5: 4 hath been (partly) Eaten by a wild animal; Unless ye are able To
5: 4 'slaughter it (in due form); That which is sacrificed 693 On stone
5: 4 (altars); (Forbidden) also is the division (Of meat) by raffling

5: 4 With arrows: that is impiety. his day have those who Reject Faith
5: 4 given up All hope of your religion Yet fear them not But fear Me.
5: 4 This day have I Perfected your religion For you, completed My
5: 4 favor upon you, And have chosen for you Islam as your religion.
5: 4 But if any is forced By hunger, with no inclination To
5: 4 transgression, Allah is Indeed Oft-Forgiving, Most Merciful.
5: 47 It was We Who revealed The Law (to Moses); therein Was guidance and
5: 47 light. By its standard have been judged The Jews, by the Prophet
5: 47 Who bowed (as in Islam) To Allah's Will, by the Rabbis And the
5: 47 Doctors of Law: For to them was entrusted The protection of Allah's
5: 47 Book, And they were witnesses there to: Therefore fear not men, But
5: 47 fear Me, and sell not My Signs for a miserable price If any do fail
5: 47 to judge By (the light of) what Allah Hath revealed, they are (No
5: 47 better than) Unbelievers.

6: 14 Say: "Shall I take For my protector Any other than Allah, The
6: 14 Maker of the heavens And the earth? And He is that Feedeth but is
6: 14 not fed. " Say :"Nay! but I am Commanded to be the first Of those who
6: 14 bow To Allah (in Islam), And be not thou Of the company of those
6: 14 Who join gods with Allah. "

6:125 Those whom Allah (in His Plan) Willeth to guide ,- He openeth Their
6:125 breast to Islam; Those whom He willeth To leave straying ,- He
6:125 maketh Their breast close and constricted As if they had to climb
6:125 Up to the skies: thus Doth Allah (heap) the penalty On those who
6:125 refuse to believe.

9: 74 They swear by Allah that they Said nothing (evil) but indeed
9: 74 They uttered blasphemy And they did it after accepting Islam; and
9: 74 they meditated 1331 A plot which they were unable To carry out:
9: 74 this revenge Of theirs was (their) only return For the bounty
9: 74 with which Allah and His Apostle hand enriched Them! If they
9: 74 repent It will be best for them ; But if they turn back
9: 74 (To their evil ways), Allah will punish them With a grievous
9: 74 penalty In this life and in the Hereafter: They shall have
9: 74 none on earth To protect or help them.

9:100 The vanguard (of Islam)- The first of those who forsook (Their
9:100 homes) and of those Who gave them aid, and (also) Those who follow
9:100 them In (all) good deeds ,- Well-pleased is Allah with them, As
9:100 are they with Him: For them hath He prepared Gardens under which
9:100 rivers flow, To dwell therein for ever: That is the supreme
9:100 Felicity.

10: 72 " But if ye turn back , (consider): No reward have I asked Of you:
10: 72 my reward is only Due from Allah , and I Have been commanded to be
10: 72 Of those who submit To Allah's will (in Islam). "

10: 90 He took the Children Of Israel across the sea: Pharaoh and his
10: 90 hosts followed them In insolence and spite. At length, when
10: 90 overwhelmed With the flood, he said: "I believe that there is no
10: 90 god Except Him Whom the Children Of Israel believe in: I am of
10: 90 those who submit (To Allah in Islam). "

11: 14 "If then they (your false gods) Answer not your (call), Know ye
11: 14 that this Revelation Is sent down (replete) with the knowledge
11: 14 Of Allah, and that there is No god but He! Will ye Even then
11: 14 submit (to Islam)? "

15: 2 Again and again will those Who disbelieve wish that they Had
15: 2 bowed (to Allah's Will) In Islam.

16: 81 It is Allah Who made, Out of the things He created, Some things
16: 81 to give you shade; Of the hills He made some For your shelter;
16: 81 He made you Garments to protect you From heat, and coats of mail
16: 81 To protect you from your (mutual) violence. Thus does He complete
16: 81 His favors on you, that Ye may bow to His Will (In Islam).

21:108 Say: 'What has come to me By inspiration is that Your God is One
21:108 Allah: Will ye therefore bow To His Will (in Islam)? "

22: 34 To every people did We Appoint rites (of sacrifice), That they
22: 34 might celebrate The name of Allah over The sustenance He gave
22: 34 them From animals (fit for food). But your God is One God:
22: 34 Submit then your wills to Him (In Islam) and give thou The good
22: 34 news to those Who humble themselves ,-

27: 42 So when she arrived, She was asked, "Is this Thy throne?"
27: 42 She said, "It was just like this; And knowledge was bestowed
27: 42 On us in advance of this, And we have submitted To Allah
27: 42 (in Islam). "

27: 44 She was asked to enter That lofty Palace: but When she saw it, she
27: 44 Thought it was a lake Of water, and she (tucked up Her skirts),
27: 44 uncovering her legs. He said :" This is But a palace paved Smooth
27: 44 with slabs of glass. " She said :" O my Lord! I have indeed wronged
27: 44 My soul: I do (now) Submit (in Islam), with Solomon, o the Lord of
27: 44 the Worlds. "

27: 81 Nor canst thou be a guide To the Blind, (to prevent them) From
27: 81 straying; only those Wilt thou get to listen Who believe in Our
27: 81 Signs, And they will bow in Islam.

27: 91 For me, I have been Commanded to serve the Lord Of this City, Him
27: 91 Who has Sanctified it and to Whom (Belong) all things: And I am
27: 91 commanded To be of those who bow In Islam to Allah's Will ,-

29: 46 And dispute ye not With the People of the Book. Except with means
29: 46 better (Than mere disputation), unless It be with those of them
29: 46 Who inflict wrong (and injury): But say, "We believe In the
29: 46 Revelation which has Come down to us and in that Which came down
29: 46 to you; Our Allah and your Allah Is One; and it is to Him We bow
29: 46 (in Islam). "

30: 53 Nor canst thou lead back The blind from their straying: Only
30: 53 those wilt thou make To hear who believe In Our Signs and submit
30: 53 (Their wills in Islam).

40: 66 Say :"I have been forbidden To invoke those whom ye Invoke besides
40: 66 Allah ,- seeing that The Clear Signs have come To me from my Lord;
40: 66 And I have been commanded To bow (in Islam) To the Lord of
40: 66 the Worlds. "

41: 33 Who is better in speech Than one who calls (men) To Allah, works
41: 33 righteousness, And says,"I am of those Who bow in Islam" ?

43: 69 (Being) those who have believed In Our Signs and bowed (Their
43: 69 wills to Ours) in Islam.

46: 15 We have enjoined on man Kindress to his parents: In pain did his
46: 15 mother Bear him, and in pain Did she give him birth. The carrying
46: 15 of the (child) To his weaning is (A period of) thirty months.
46: 15 At length, when he reaches The age of full strength And attains
46: 15 forty years, He says," O my Lord! Grant me that I may be Grateful
46: 15 for Thy favor Which Thou hast bestowed Upon me, and upon
46: 15 both My parents, and that I May work righteousness Such as Thou
46: 15 mayest approve; And be gracious to me In my issue. Truly Have I
46: 15 turned to Thee And truly do I bow (To Thee) in Islam. "

49: 17 They impress on thee As a favor that they Have embraced Islam.
49: 17 Say, "Count not your Islam As a favor upon me: Nay, Allah has
49: 17 conferred A favor upon you That He has guided you To the
49: 17 Faith, if ye Be true and sincere.

61: 7 Who doth greater wrong Than one who invents Falsehood against
61: 7 Allah, Even as he is being invited To Islam? And Allah Guides not
61: 7 those Who do wrong.

And following short and scholarly reference is enough for need of last part of Islam and the circumstances during beginning of Islam:

When Islam came, mankind was divided into religious sects and except in a few cases men were strangers to truth and certainty, quarrelling and excommunicating one another and claiming that in so doing they were holding on to the rope of God. Islam repudiated all that and affirmed unmistakably that the religion of God through all times and by the mouth of all prophets is one. God said ' `Religion with God is Islam and those to whom the Scriptures were given disagreed among themselves through jealousy, only after knowledge had been brought to them.'(Surah 3.19) 'Abraham was not a Jew, nor a Christian, he was a hanif, a muslim, a surrendered one; he was not one of those who take gods for God.' (surah 3.67.).[126]

Islam is more than religion, since it embraces a whole social system composed of Muslims: all those who have submitted to Allah, the one and only God. (Islam, in Arabic, means the state of submission, and Muslim is the one who has submitted.) By putting all believers on an equal footing - of submission to Allah - Islam, which originated in western Arabia during the seventh century, created a confraternity above the traditional bonds of clan and tribe. The faithful were united in their belief in Allah and his precepts, as conveyed through

___[126] The Theology of Unity, by Muhammad Abduh, Translated from the Arabic by Ishaq Musa'ad and Kenneth Cragg, published by BOOKS FOR LIBRARIES, A DIVISION OF ARNO PRESS NEW YORK, 1980, p. 129.

Muhammed (literally, praiseworthy), his messenger. `Islam in the Arab world differs from religion in Western society: it permeates the daily life of the individual with its ritualistic obligations,' states Hudson. `It is an important part of socialization; it affects personal status; it plays a political role. Islam also serves to integrate Arab society by inculcating a sense of the Muslim's special relationship with God and in the brotherhood and mutual obligations of all believers.... It is thus a powerful force for social and cultural stability.' (Ibid., p. 52.)[127]

Islam is the religion of Muhammad's mission, as readily understood by his companions and their contemporaries who heeded it. It was actively followed among them for a period without schism or deviations in interpretation or sectarian tendencies. ... The religion of Islam teaches the unity of God, in His essence and His acts, and His transcendence above all comparison with created beings. It has come with proof of the universe having one creator, whose known attributes of knowledge, power, will and so forth are to be traced in the effects of His handiwork. It insists that He is incomparably other than anything in His creation: the only relation between Him and them consists in that He is their originator, that they belong to Him and unto Him is their returning. `Say: He is God alone.... God the selfsubsistent: who does not beget and is not begotten, and unto whom none is equal.' (Sura 112.1-3).[128]

___ [127] INTRODUCTION, INSIDE THE MIDDLE EAST BY DILIP HIRO, PUBLISHED BY ROUTLEDGE & KEGAN PAUL, 39 STORE STREET, LONDON WCIEE7DD AND BROADWAY HOUSE, NEWTON ROAD,HENLEY-on-Thames, Oxon RG91EN. PP. 3-5.

___ [128]   [128]The Theology of Unity, by Muhammad Abduh, Translated from the Arabic by Ishaq Musa'ad and Kenneth Cragg, published by BOOKS FOR LIBRARIES, A DVISION OF ARNC PRESS NEW YORK, 1980, p. 123.

In detail the following verses are some of the guidelines or the condition for the true follower of Islam:

First, we should see about the Believer and their faith according to The Holy Quran, some of The Verses are follows:

2: 6 As to those who reject Faith, It is the same to them Whether thou
2: 6 warn them Or do not warn them; They will not believe.

2: 7 Allah hath set a seal On their hearts and on their hearing, And on
2: 7 their eyes is a veil; Great is the penalty they (incur).

2: 24 But if ye cannot- And of a surety ye cannot- Then fear the Fire
2: 24 Whose fuel is Men and Stones,- Which is prepared for those Who
2: 24 reject Faith.

2: 28 How can ye reject The faith in Allah?- Seeing that ye were without
2: 28 life, And He gave you life; Then will He cause you to die, And will
2: 28 again bring you to life; And again to Him will ye return.

2:178 O ye who believe! The law of equality Is prescribed to you In cases
2:178 of murder: The free for the free. The slave for the slave, The
2:178 woman for the woman. But if any remission Is made by the brother Of
2:178 the slain, then grant Any reasonable demand, And compensate him
2:178 With handsome gratitude; This is a concession And a Mercy From your
2:178 Lord. After this whoever Exceeds the limits Shall be in great
2:178 penalty.

2:181 If any one changes the bequest After hearing it, The guilt shall be
2:181 on those Who make the change For Allah hears and knows All things.
2:186 When My servants Ask thee concerning Me, I am indeed Close (to
2:186 them): I listen To the prayer of every Suppliant when he calleth on
2:186 Me Let them also, with a will, Listen to My call, And believe in
2:186 Me: That they may walk In the right way.

5: 11 Those who reject faith And deny Our Signs Will be Companions Of
5: 11 Hell-fire.
5: 17 There hath come to you From Allah a (new) light And a perspicuous
5: 17 Book,-
5: 18 Wherewith Allah guideth all Who seek His good pleasure To ways of
5: 18 peace and safety, And leadeth them out Of darkness, by His Will,
5: 18 Unto the light,- guideth them To a Path that is Straight.

6: 30 If thou couldst but see When they are confronted With their Lord!
6: 30 He will say: "Is not this the truth? They will say: "Yea, by our
6: 30 Lord!" He will say: "Taste ye then the Penalty, Because ye rejected
6: 30 Faith."

6: 33 We know indeed the grief Which their words so cause thee: It is
6: 33 not thee they reject: It is the Signs of Allah, Which the wicked
6: 33 contemn.

6: 47 Say : "Think ye, if The punishment of Allah Comes to you, Whether
6: 47 suddenly or openly, Will any be destroyed Except those who do
6: 47 wrong?"

6: 49 But those who reject Our Signs,- them Shall our punishment touch,
6: 49 For that they ceased not From transgressing.

6: 50 Say: " I tell you not That with me Are the Treasures of Allah, Nor
6: 50 do I know What is hidden, Nor do I tell you I am An angel. I but
6: 50 follow What is revealed to me." Say: "Can the blind Be held equal
6: 50 to the seeing?" Will ye then consider not?"

6: 53 thus be (One) of the unjust. Thus did We try Some of them by
6: 53 comparison With others, that they Should say: "Is it these Then
6: 53 that Allah hath Favored from amongst us?" Doth not Allah know best
6: 53 Those who are grateful?

6: 58 Say: "If what ye would see Hastened were in my power, The matter
6: 58 would be settled At once between you and me. But Allah knoweth best
6: 58 Those who do wrong."

6: 59 With Him are the keys Of the Unseen, the treasures That none
6: 59 knoweth but He. He knoweth whatever there is On the earth and in
6: 59 the sea. Not a leaf doth fall But with His knowledge: There is not
6: 59 a grain In the darkness (or depths) Of the earth, nor anything
6: 59 Fresh or dry (green or withered). But is (inscribed) in a Record
6: 59 Clear (to those who can read).

6: 60 It is He who doth take Your souls by night, And hath knowledge
6: 60 of all That ye have done by day. By day doth He raise You up again;
6: 60 that a term Appointed be fulfilled; In the end unto Him Will be
6: 60 your return, Then will He show you The truth of all That ye did.

6: 67 "For every Message Is a limit of time And soon shall ye Know it."
6: 70 Leave alone those Who take their religion To be mere play And
6: 70 amusement, And are deceived By the life of this world. But proclaim
6: 70 (to them) This (truth): that every soul Delivers itself to ruin By
6: 70 its own act: It will find for itself No protector or intercessor
6: 70 Except Allah: if it offered Every ransom (or Reparation), none Will
6: 70 be accepted: such is (The end of) those who Deliver themselves
6: 70 to ruin By their own acts: They will have for drink (Only) boiling
6: 70 water, And for punishment, One most grievous: For they persisted In
6: 70 rejecting Allah.
9: 63 Know they not that for those Who oppose Allah And His Apostle Is
9: 63 the Fire of Hell? - Wherein they shall dwell. That is the
9: 63 supreme disgrace.
9: 64 The Hypocrites are afraid Lest a Sura should be sent down About
9: 64 them showing them what Is (really passing) in their hearts .
9: 64 Say:"Mock ye! But verily Allah will bring to Light all That ye
9: 64 fear (should be revealed)."
9: 66 Make ye no excuses: Ye have rejected Faith After ye had accepted
9: 66 it. If We pardon some of you, We Will punish others amongst you
9: 66 For that they are in sin

9: 68 Allah hath promised the Hypocrites Men and women and the rejecters
9: 68 Of Faith the fire of Hell: There in shall they dwell: Sufficient
9: 68 is it for them: For them is the curse of Allah ; And an enduring
9: 68 punishment,-
9: 71 The Believers men And women are protectors One of another:
9: 71 they enjoin What is just and forbid What is evil: they observe
9: 71 Regular prayers practice Regular charity and obey Allah and His
9: 71 apostle. On them will Allah pour His mercy: for Allah Is Exalted
9: 71 in Power Wise.
30: 44 Those who reject Faith Will suffer from that rejection : And those
30: 44 who work righteousness Will spread their couch (Of repose) for
30: 44 themselves (In heaven):

57: 8 What cause have ye Why ye should not believe In Allah?- And the
57: 8 Apostle Invites you to believe In your Lord, and has Indeed taken
57: 8 your Covenant, If ye are men of faith.

57: 28 O ye that believe! Fear Allah, and believe In His Apostle and He
57: 28 will Bestow on you a double Portion of His Mercy: He will provide
57: 28 for you A Light by which ye Shall walk (straight In your path),
57: 28 and He Will forgive you (your past): For Allah is Oft-Forgiving,
57: 28 Most Merciful:

58: 22 Thou wilt not find Any people who believe In Allah and the Last
58: 22 Day, Loving those who resist Allah and His Apostle Even though they
58: 22 were Their fathers or their sons, Or their brothers, or Their
58: 22 kindred. For such He has written Faith In their hearts and
58: 22 strengthened Them With a spirit From Himself. And He Will admit
58: 22 them to Gardens Beneath which Rivers flow, To dwell therein (for
58: 22 ever). Allah will be well pleased With them, and they With Him They
58: 22 are the Party Of Allah. Truly it is The Party of Allah that Will
58: 22 achieve Felicity.

64: 5 Has not the story Reached you, of those Who rejected Faith
64: 5 aforetime? So they tasted the evil Result of their conduct; And
64: 5 they had A grievous Penalty.

64: 8 Believe, therefore, in Allah And His Apostle, and In the Light
64: 8 which We Have sent down. And Allah Is well acquainted With
64: 8 all that ye do.

64: 10 But those who reject Faith And treat Our Signs As falsehoods, they
64: 10 will be Companions of the Fire, To dwell therein for aye: And evil
64: 10 is that Goal.

How a believer should pray for forgiveness to his Almighty Allah (God) in the following way, some Quranic verses are as follows:

59: 10 And those who came After them say: "Our Lord! Forgive us, and our
59: 10 brethren Who came before us Into the Faith, And leave not, In
59: 10 our hearts, Rancor (or sense of injury) Against those who
59: 10 have believed Our Lord! Thou art Indeed Full of Kindness Most
59: 10 Merciful."

We should believe in Allah and work righteous deeds otherwise we will surely go in astray and according to some verses of The Holy Quran some of which are as follows:

5: 58 Your (real) friends are (No less than) Allah, His Apostle, and the
5: 58 (Fellowship Of) Believers,- those who Establish regular prayers And
5: 58 regular charity, And they bow Down humbly (in worship).

5: 60 O ye who believe! Take not for friends And protectors those Who
5: 60 take your religion For a mockery or sport,- Whether among those Who
5: 60 received the Scripture Before you, or among those Who reject Faith;
5: 60 But fear ye Allah, If ye have Faith (indeed).

5: 61 When ye proclaim Your call to prayer, They take it (but) As mockery
5: 61 and sport; That is because they are A people without understanding.
5: 64 When they come to thee, They say: "We believe": But in fact they
5: 64 enter With a mind against Faith, And they go out With the same: But
5: 64 Allah knoweth fully All that they hide.
5: 70 O Apostle! proclaim The (Message) which hath been Sent to thee from
5: 70 thy Lord. If thou didst not, thou Wouldst not have fulfilled And
5: 70 proclaimed His Mission. And Allah will defend thee From men (who
5: 70 mean mischief). For Allah guideth not Those who reject Faith.
5: 71 Say: "O People of the Book! Ye have no ground To stand upon unless
5: 71 Ye stand fast by the Law, The Gospel, and all the revelation That
5: 71 has come to you from Your Lord." It is the revelation That cometh
5: 71 to thee from Thy Lord, that increaseth in most Of them their
5: 71 obstinate Rebellion and blasphemy. But sorrow thou not Over (these)
5: 71 people without faith .

5: 74 They thought there would be No trial (or punishment); So they
5: 74 became blind and deaf: Yet Allah (in mercy) turned To them: yet
5: 74 again many Of them became blind and deaf. But Allah sees well All
5: 74 that they do.

5: 79 Say : "Will ye worship Besides Allah, something Which hath no power
5: 79 either To harm, or benefit you? But Allah,- He it is That heareth
5: 79 and knoweth All things."

5: 94 Satan's plan is (but) To excite enmity and hatred Between you, with
5: 94 intoxicants And gambling, and hinder you From the remembrance Of
5: 94 Allah, and from prayer: Will ye not then abstain?
5: 95 Obey Allah, and obey the Apostle, And beware (of evil): If ye do
5: 95 turn back, Know ye that it is Our Apostle's duty To proclaim (the
5: 95 Message) In the clearest manner.
5:101 Know ye that Allah Is strict in punishment And that Allah is
5:101 Oft-Forgiving. Most Merciful.

5:109 O ye who believe! When death approaches Any of you, (take)
5:109 witnesses Among yourselves when making Bequests,- two just men Of
5:109 your own (brotherhood) Or others from outside If ye are journeying
5:109 Through the earth, And the chance of death Befalls you (thus). If
5:109 ye doubt (their truth), Detain them both After prayer, and let them
5:109 both Swear by Allah: "We wish not in this For any worldly gain,
5:109 Even though the (beneficiary) Be our near relation: We shall hide
5:109 not The evidence before Allah: If we do, then behold! The sin be

5:109 upon us!"
5:110 But if it gets known That these two were guilty Of the sin (of
5:110 perjury), Let two others stand forth In their places,- nearest In
5:110 kin from among those Who claim a lawful right: Let them swear
5:110 by Allah: "We affirm that our witness is truer than that Of those
5:110 two, and that we Have not trespassed (beyond The truth): if we did,
5:110 Behold! the wrong be Upon us!'

5:112 One day will Allah Gather the apostles together, And ask: "What was
5:112 The response ye received (From men to your teaching)?" They will
5:112 say: "We Have no knowledge: it is Thou Who knowest in full All that
5:112 is hidden."

5:114 "And behold! I inspired The Disciples to have faith In Me and Mine
5:114 Apostle: They said, 'We have faith, And do thou bear witness That
5:114 we bow to Allah As Muslims'."

9: 12 But if they violate their oaths After their covenant And taunt you
9: 12 for your Faith Fight ye the chiefs of Unfaith: For their oaths are
9: 12 nothing to them: That thus they may be restrained.
9: 14 Fight them and Allah will Punish them by your hands Cover them
9: 14 with shame, Help you (to victory) over them, Heal the breasts of
9: 14 Believers,
9: 15 And still the indignation of their hearts. For Allah will turn
9: 15 (in mercy) To whom He will; and Allah Is All-Knowing, All-wise.
9: 16 Or think ye that ye Shall be abandoned, As though Allah did not
9: 16 know Those among you who strive With might and main and take None
9: 16 for friends and protectors Except Allah, His Apostle, And the
9: 16 (community of) Believers? But Allah is well-acquainted With (all)
9: 16 that ye do.
64: 11 No kind of calamity Can occur, except By the leave of Allah: And
64: 11 if anyone believes In Allah, (Allah) guides his Heart (aright):
64: 11 for Allah Knows all things.

2: 26 Allah disdains not to use The similitude of things, lowest as well
2: 26 as highest. Those who believe know That it is truth from their
2: 26 Lord; But those who reject Faith say: "What means Allah by this
2: 26 similitude?" By it He causes many to stray, And many He leads into
2: 26 the right path; But He causes not to stray, Except those who
2: 26 forsake (the path),-

30: 45 That He may reward those Who believe and work righteous Deeds,
30: 45 out of His Bounty: For He loves not those Who reject faith.

30: 56 But those endued with knowledge And faith will say: "Indeed ye
30: 56 did tarry, Within Allah's Decree, To the Day of Resurrection,
30: 56 And this is the Day Of Resurrection: but ye- Ye were not aware!"

30: 60 So patiently persevere for Verily the promise of Allah Is true
30: 60 not let those Shake thy firmness who have (Themselves) no
30: 60 certainty of faith.

And again we must offer regular prayer to Allah (God), and before each prayer we must perform waju or ablutions (washing hands, face and other part of the body by water for physical purification, or if water is not available by soil) according to The Holy Quran some of which are as follows:

5: 7 O ye who believe! When ye prepare For prayer, wash Your faces, and
5: 7 your hands (And arms) to the elbows; Rub your heads (with water);
5: 7 And (wash) your feet To the ankles. If ye are in a state Of
5: 7 ceremonial impurity, Bathe your whole body. But if ye are ill, Or
5: 7 on a journey, Or one of you,cometh From offices of nature, Or ye
5: 7 have been In contact with women, And ye find no water, Then take
5: 7 for yourselves Clean sand or earth, And rub therewith Your faces
5: 7 and hands Allah doth not wish To place you in a difficulty, But to
5: 7 make you clean, And to complete His favor to you, That ye may be
5: 7 grateful.

2: 3 Who believe in the Unseen, Are steadfast in prayer, And spend out
2: 3 of what We Have provided for them;

2: 43 And be steadfast in prayer; Practice regular charity; And bow down
2: 43 your heads With those who bow down (in worship).

2: 45 Nay, seek (Allah's) help With patient perseverance And prayer: It
2: 45 is indeed hard, except To those who bring a lowly spirit,-

2: 13 When it is said to them: "Believe as the others believe," They say:
2: 13 "Shall we believe As the fools believe?"- Nay, of a surety they are
2: 13 the fools, But they do not know.

2: 16 These are they who have bartered Guidance for error: But their   2: 16 traffic is profitless, And they have lost true direction.

2: 17 Their similitude is that of a man Who kindled a fire; When it
2: 17 lighted all around him, Allah took away their light And left them
2: 17 in utter darkness, So they could not see.

2: 18 Deaf, dumb, and blind, They will not return (to the path).
2: 20 The lightning all but snatches away Their light; every time the
2: 20 light (Helps) them,they walk therein, And when the darkness grows
2: 20 on them, They stand still. And if Allah willed, He could take away
2: 20 Their faculty of hearing and seeing; For Allah hath power over all
2: 20 things.

2: 22 Who has made the earth your couch, And the heaven your canopy; And
2: 22 sent down rain from the heavens; And brought forth therewith Fruits
2: 22 for your sustenance; Then set not up rivals unto Allah When ye know
2: 22 (the truth).
5: 8 And call in remembrance The favor of Allah Unto you, and His
5: 8 Covenant, Which He ratified With you, when ye said: "We hear and we
5: 8 obey": And fear Allah, for Allah Knoweth well The secrets of your
5: 8 hearts.

6: 72 "To establish regular prayers And to fear Allah; For it is to Him
6: 72 That we shall be Gathered together."

8: 2 For Believers are those Who, when Allah is mentioned, Feel a tremor
8: 2 in their hearts, And when they hear His Signs rehearsed, find Their
8: 2 faith strengthened, And put (all) their trust In their lord;

8: 3 Who establish regular prayers And spend (freely) out of The gifts
8: 3 We have given Them for sustenance:

9: 11 But (even so), if they repent Establish regular prayers And
9: 11 practice regular charity They are your brethren in Faith: (Thus)
9: 11 do We explain Signs In detail for those who understand .

9: 18 The mosques of Allah Shall be visited and maintained By such be
9: 18 as believe in Allah And the Last day, establish Regular prayers,
9: 18 and practice Regular charity and fear None (at all) except Allah.
9: 18 It is they who are expected To be on true guidance.
29: 45 Recite what is sent Of the Book by inspiration To thee, and
29: 45 establish Regular Prayer: for Prayer Restrains from shameful And
29: 45 unjust deeds; And remembrance of Allah Is the greatest (thing in
29: 45 life) Without doubt. And Allah knows The (deeds) that ye do.
29: 49 Nay, here are Signs Self-evident in the hearts Of those endowed
29: 49 with Knowledge: And none but the unjust Reject Our Signs.

30: 31 Turn ye back in repentance To Him,and fear Him: Establish regular
30: 31 prayers And be not ye among those Who join gods with Allah,-
30: 34 (As if) to show their ingratitude For the(favors) We have Bestowed
30: 34 on them! Then enjoy (Your brief day); but soon Will ye know
30: 34 (your folly).
31: 4 Those who establish regular Prayer And give regular Charity, And
31: 4 have (in their hearts) The assurance of the Hereafter.
31: 6 But there are, among men Those who purchase idle tales, Without
31: 6 knowledge (or meaning) To mislead (men) from the Path Of Allah
31: 6 and throw ridicule (On the Path); for such There will be a
31: 6 humiliating Penalty.

31: 7 When Our Sings are rehearsed To such a one he turns Away in
31: 7 arrogance, as if He heard them not, as if There were deafness
31: 7 in both His ears: announce to him A grievous Penalty.
31: 15 "But if they strive To make thee join In worship with Me Things
31: 15 of which thou hast No knowledge, obey them not; Yet bear
31: 15 them company In this life with justice (And consideration),
31: 15 and follow The way of those who Turn to Me (in love): In the End
31: 15 the return Of you all is to Me. And I will tell you The truth
31: 15 (and meaning) Of all that ye did ."
31: 17 "O my son! establish Regular prayer, enjoin what is Just and forbid
31: 17 what is wrong: And bear with patient constancy Whatever betide
31: 17 thee; for this Is firmness (of purpose) In the (conduct of) affairs
31: 20 Do ye not see That Allah has subjected To your (use) all things
31: 20 In the heavens and on earth, And has made His bounties
31: 20 Flow to you in exceeding Measure (both) seen and unseen? Yet
31: 20 there are among men Those who dispute about Allah, Without
31: 20 knowledge and without Guidance, and without a Book To enlighten
31: 20 them !
31: 21 When they are told to follow The (Revelation) that Allah Has sent

31: 21 down, they say: "Nay we shall follow The ways that we found Our
31: 21 Fathers (following)." What! even if it is Satan beckoning them
31: 21 To the Penalty Of the (Blazing) Fire!
31: 23 But if any reject Faith Let not his rejection Grieve thee: to Us
31: 23 Is their Return and We Shall tell them the truth Of their deeds:
31: 23 for Allah Knows well all that is In (men's) hearts.
31: 34 Verily the knowledge Of the Hour is With Allah (alone). It is He
31: 34 Who sends down Rain, and He Who knows What is in the wombs.
31: 34 Nor does anyone know What it is that he will Earn on the morrow:
31: 34 Nor does anyone know In what land he is To die. Verily with Allah
31: 34 Is full knowledge and He Is acquainted (with all things).
32: 6 Such is He, the Knower Of all things, hidden And open, the Exalted
32: 6 (In Power), the Merciful;-
32: 14 "Taste ye then-for ye Forgot the Meeting Of this Day of yours,
32: 14 And We too will Forget you-taste ye The penalty of Eternity For
32: 14 your (evil) deeds!"
32: 16 Their limbs do forsake Their beds of sleep, the while They call
32: 16 on their Lord, In Fear and Hope: And they spend (in charity) Out
32: 16 of the sustenance which We have bestowed on them.
98: 5 And they have been commanded No more than this; To worship Allah,
98: 5 Offering Him sincere devotion, Being True (in faith): To establish
98: 5 regular Prayer; And to practice regular Charity; And that is the
98: 5 Religion Right and Straight.
98: 7 Those who have faith And do righteous deeds They are the best Of
98: 7 creatures.

62: 9 O ye who believe ! When the call is proclaimed To prayer on
62: 9 Friday (The Day of Assembly), Hasten earnestly to the Remembrance
62: 9 Of Allah, and leave off Business (and traffic): That is best for
62: 9 you If ye but knew!

62: 10 And when the Prayer Is finished, then may ye Disperse through the
62: 10 land, And seek of the Bounty Of Allah: and celebrate The Praises
62: 10 of Allah Often (and without stint): That ye may prosper.
2:153 O ye who believe! seek help With patient perseverance And Prayer:
2:153 for Allah is with those Who patiently persevere.

2:238 Guard strictly Your (habit of) prayers, Especially the Middle
2:238 Prayer, And stand before Allah In a devout (frame of mind).
2:239 If ye fear (an enemy), Pray on foot, or riding (As may be most
2:239 convenient), But when ye are In security, celebrate Allah's praises
2:239 in the manner He has taught you, Which ye knew not (before).

60: 1 O Ye who believe! Take not My enemies And yours as friends
60: 1 (Or protectors), offering them (Your) love, even though They have
60: 1 rejected the Truth That has come to you, and have (on the contrary)
60: 1 Driven out the Prophet And yourselves (from your homes) (Simply)
60: 1 because ye believe In Allah your Lord! If ye have come out To
60: 1 strive in My Way And to seek My Good Pleasure, (Take them not as
60: 1 friends), Holding secret converse Of love (and friendship) With
60: 1 them: for I know Full well all that ye Conceal and all that ye
60: 1 Reveal. And any of you That does this has strayed From the Straight

60: 4 There is for you An excellent example (to follow) In Abraham and

60: 4 those with him, When they said To their people : "we are clear of
60: 4 you And of whatever ye worship Besides Allah: we have rejected
60: 4 You, and there has arisen Between us and you, enmity And
60: 4 hatred for ever,- unless Ye believe in Allah And Him alone": But
60: 4 not when Abraham Said to his father: "I will pray for
60: 4 forgiveness For thee, though I have No power (to get) aught On
60: 4 thy behalf from Allah." (They prayed): "Our Lord! In Thee do
60: 4 we trust And to Thee do we turn In repentance to Thee Is (our)
60: 4 final Goal.

And who did not accept Islam as their only religion, and accepted those religions which in
initial stage was also the only religion of Islam, but in later times, were changed according
to the evil desire of the followers, their ultimate end according to The Holy Quran will be as
follows:

2: 89 And when there comes to them A Book from Allah, confirming What is
2: 89 with them,- although From of old they had prayed For victory
2: 89 against those Without Faith,- when there comes To them that which
2: 89 they (Should) have recognized, They refused to believe in it: But
2: 89 the curse of Allah Is on those without Faith.

2: 90 Miserable is the price For which they have sold Their souls, in
2: 90 that they Deny (the revelation) Which Allah has sent down, In
2: 90 insolent envy that Allah Of His Grace should send it To any of His
2: 90 servants He pleases: Thus have they drawn On themselves Wrath upon
2: 90 Wrath, And humiliating is the punishment Of those who reject Faith.

2: 93 And remember We took Your Covenant and we raised Above you (the
2: 93 towering height) Of Mount (sinai): (Saying): "Hold firmly To what
2: 93 We have given you And hearken (to the Law)": They said: "We hear,
2: 93 And we disobey": And they had to drink Into their hearts (Of the
2: 93 taint) of the Calf Because of their Faithlessness. Say: "Vile
2: 93 indeed Are the behests of your Faith If ye have any faith!"

60: 8 Allah forbids you not, With regard to those who Fight you not for
60: 8 (your) Faith Nor drive you out Of your homes, Form dealing kindly
60: 8 and justly With them: for Allah loveth Those who are just.
60: 9 Allah only forbids you, With regard to those who Fight you for
60: 9 (your) Faith, And drive you out Of your homes, and support
60: 9 (Others) in driving you out, From turning to them (For friendship
60: 9 and protection). It is such as turn to them (In these
60: 9 circumstances), That do wrong.

61: 8 Their intention is To extinguish Allah's Light (By blowing)
61: 8 with their mouths: But Allah will complete (The revelation of) His
61: 8 Light, Even though the Unbelievers May detest (it).
61: 10 O ye who believe! Shall I lead you To a bargain that will Save
61: 10 you from A grievous Penalty?-

62: 7 But never will they Express their desire (For Death), because of
62: 7 The (deeds) their hands Have sent on before them! And Allah knows
62: 7 well Those that do wrong!

62: 8 Say, "The Death from which Ye flee will truly Overtake you: then

139

62: 8 will Ye be sent back To the Knower of things Secret and open :
62: 8 and He Will tell you (the truth Of) the things that ye did!"

2:174 Those who conceal Allah's revelations in the Book, And purchase for
2:174 them A miserable profit,- They swallow into themselves Naught but
2:174 Fire; Allah will not address them On the Day of resurrection, Nor
2:174 purify them; Grievous will be Their Penalty.

57: 7 Believe in Allah And His Apostle, And spend (in charity) Out of
57: 7 the (substance) Whereof He has made you Heirs. For, those of you
57: 7 Who believe and spend (In charity),- for them Is a great Reward.

2: 10 In their hearts is a disease; And Allah has increased their disease
2: 10 And grievous is the penalty they (incur). Because they are false
2: 10 (to themselves).

2: 96 Thou wilt indeed find them, Of all people, most greedy Of life,-
2: 96 even more Than the idolaters; Each one of them wishes He could be
2: 96 given a life Of a thousand years: But the grant of such life Will
2: 96 not save him From (due) punishment. For Allah sees well All that
2: 96 they do.

2: 98 Whoever is an enemy to Allah And His angels and apostles, To
2: 98 Gabriel and Michael,- Lo! Allah is an enemy to those Who reject
2: 98 Faith.

2:100 It is not (the case) that Every time they make a covenant, Some
2:100 party among them Throw it aside?- Nay, Most of them are faithless.

2:101 And when came to them An apostle from Allah, Confirming what was
2:101 with them, A party of the People of the book Threw away the Book of
2:101 Allah Behind their backs, As if (it had been something) They did
2:101 not know!

2:103 If they had kept their Faith And guarded themselves from evil, Far
2:103 better had been The reward from their Lord, if they but knew!
2:103 SECTION 13.

2:104 O ye men of Faith! Say not (to the Apostle) Words of ambiguous
2:104 import, But words of respect; And hearken (to him): To those
2:104 without Faith Is a grievous punishment.

2:105 It is never the wish Of those without Faith Among the people of the
2:105 Book,Nor of the pagans, That any thing good should come down to you
2:105 From your Lord. But Allah will choose For His special Mercy Whom He
2:105 will-_for God is Lord of Grace abounding.

2:106 None of Our revelations Do We abrogate Or cause to be forgotten But
2:106 We substitute Something better or similar: Knowest thou not that
2:106 Allah Hath power over all things?

2:107 Knowest thou not That to Allah belongeth The dominion of the
2:107 heavens And the earth? And besides Him ye have Neither patron nor
2:107 helper.

32: 17 Now no person knows What delights of the eye Are kept hidden
32: 17 (in reserve) For them-as a reward For their (good) Deeds.
32: 20 As to those who are Rebellious and wicked, their abode Will be
32: 20 the Fire: every time They wish to get away Therefrom, they will be
32: 20 forced Thereinto, and it will be said To them:" Taste ye The
32: 20 Penalty of the Fire, The which ye were wont To reject as false."
32: 21 And indeed We will make Them taste of the Penalty Of this (life)
32: 21 prior to The supreme Penalty, in order That they may (repent and)
32: 21 return.
32: 24 And We appointed from among Them Leaders, giving guidance Under
32: 24 Our command so long As they persevered with patience And continued
32: 24 to have faith In Our Signs.
33: 1 O prophet! Fear Allah And hearken not To the Unbelievers And
33: 1 the Hypocrites: Verily Allah is full Of knowledge and wisdom.
33: 5 Call them by (the names) Of their fathers: that is Juster in the
33: 5 sight of Allah But if ye know not Their fathers (names, call Them)
33: 5 your Brothers in faith Or your Maulas. But there is no blame On
33: 5 you if ye make A mistake therein : (What counts is) The intention
33: 5 of your hearts: And Allah is Oft-Returning, Most Merciful.
33: 8 That (Allah) may question The (Custodians) of Truth concerning
33: 8 The Truth they (were charged with): And He has prepared For the
33: 8 Unbelievers A grievous Penalty.

5: 26 But on Allah put your trust If ye have faith."

And again we must perform Pilgrimage (to Holy Mecca) for Hajj or Umra, and it is also for
those Muslims who are capable in term of financial position, so according to The Holy
Quran some of the verses are as follows:

2:196 And complete the Hajj or Umra In the Service of Allah. But if ye
2:196 are prevented (From completing it). Send an offering For sacrifice,
2:196 such as ye may find, And do not shave your heads Until offering
2:196 reaches The place of sacrifice. And if any of you is ill, Or has an
2:196 ailment in his scalp, (Necessitating shaving), (He should) in
2:196 compensation Either fast, or feed the poor, Or offer sacrifice; And
2:196 when ye are In peaceful conditions (again), If anyone wishes To
2:196 continue the 'Umra On to the Hajj, He must make an offering, Such
2:196 as he can afford, But if he cannot afford it, He should fast Three
2:196 days during the Hajj And seven days on his return, Making ten days
2:196 in all. This is for those Whose Household Is not in (the precincts
2:196 Of) the Sacred Mosque. And fear Allah, And know that Allah Is
2:196 strict in punishment.
2:197 For Hajj Are the months well known. If anyone undertakes The duty
2:197 therein, Let there be no obscenity Nor wickedness, Nor wrangling In
2:197 the Hajj, And whatever good Ye do, (be sure) Allah knoweth it. And
2:197 take a provision (With you) for the journey. But the best of
2:197 provisions Is right conduct. So fear Me, O ye that are wise!

2:203 Celebrate the praises of Allah During the Appointed Days, But if
2:203 anyone hastens To leave in two days, There is no blame on him, And
2:203 if anyone stays on, There is no blame on him, If his aims is to do
2:203 right. Then fear Allah, and know That ye will surely Be gathered
2:203 unto Him.

2:209 If ye backslide After the Clear (Signs) Have come to you, Then know
2:209 that Allah Is Exalted in Power, Wise.

2:211 Ask the Children of Israel How many Clear (Signs) We have sent
2:211 them. But if anyone, After Allah's favor Has come to him,
2:211 Substitutes (something else), Allah is strict in punishment.
2:212 The life of this world Is alluring to those Who reject faith, And
2:212 they scoff at those Who believe. But the righteous Will be above
2:212 them On the Day of Resurrection; For Allah bestows His abundance
2:212 Without measure On whom He will.

2:214 Or do ye think That ye shall enter The Garden (of Bliss) Without
2:214 such (trials) As came to those Who passed away Before you? They
2:214 encountered Suffering and adversity, And were so shaken in spirit
2:214 That even the Apostle And those of faith Who were with him Cried:
2:214 "When (will come) The help of Allah?" Ah! verily, the help of
2:214 Allah is (always) near!

We must observe fast in the month of Ramadhan as compulsory and if possible during other time, so according to The Holy Quran some of which are as follows:

7:170 As to those who hold fast By the Book and establish Regular
7:170 Prayer;- never Shall We suffer the reward Of the righteous to
7:170 perish.

66: 5 It may be if he Divorced you (all) That Allah will give him In
66: 5 exchange Consorts Better than you-, Who submit (their wills),
66: 5 Who believe, who are devout, Who turn to Allah in repentance, Who
66: 5 worship (in humility), Who travel (for Faith) and fast-, Previously
66: 5 married or virgins

2:185 Ramadhan is the (month) In which was sent down The Qur-an, as a
2:185 Guide To mankind, also clear (Signs) For guidance and judgement
2:185 (Between right and wrong). So every one of you Who is present (at
2:185 his home) During that month Should spend it in fasting, But if any
2:185 one is ill, Or on a journey, The prescribed period (Should be made
2:185 up) By days later. Allah intends every facility For you, He does
2:185 not want To put you to difficulties (He wants you) to complete The
2:185 prescribed period, And to glorify Him In that He has guided you;
2:185 And perchance ye shall be grateful.

64: 18 Knower of what is hidden And what is open, Exalted in Might, Full
64: 18 of Wisdom.

And again very important part of the teaching of Islam is to spend anything possible to the needy even though sacrificing the interest of oneself and everything which one have beyond his minimum need, and it is not enough to pay certain fix amount to pay as alms or charity, some of the verses of The Holy Quran are as follows:

9: 58 And among them are men Who slander thee in the matter Of
9: 58 (the distribution of) the alms: If they are given part thereof,
9: 58 They are pleased but if not Behold ! they are indignant!

9: 60 Alms are for the poor And the needy, and those Employed to
9: 60 administer the (funds); For those whose hearts Have been
9: 60 (recently) reconciled (To Truth); for those in bondage And in debt
9: 60 in the Cause Of Allah ; and for the wayfarer : (Thus is it)
9: 60 ordained by Allah And Allah is Full of Knowledge And Wisdom.
9:103 Of their goods take alms, That so thou mightest Purify and sanctify
9:103 them: And pray on their behalf. Verily thy prayers are a source Of
9:103 security for them: And Allah is One Who heareth and knoweth.

92: 18 Those who spend their wealth For increase in self-purification .
58: 13 Is it that ye are Afraid of spending sums In charity before your
58: 13 Private consultation (with him)? If, then, ye do not so, And Allah
58: 13 forgives you, Then (at least) establish Regular prayer; practice
58: 13 Regular charity; and obey Allah and His Apostle : And Allah is
58: 13 well-acquainted Will all that ye do.

65: 7 Let the man of means Spend according to His means: and the man
65: 7 Whose resources are restricted, Let him spend according To what
65: 7 Allah has given him. Allah puts no burden On any person beyond
65: 7 What He has given him. After a difficulty, Allah Will soon grant
65: 7 relief.

2:195 And spend of your substance In the cause of Allah, And make not
2:195 your own hands Contribute to (your destruction); But do good; For
2:195 Allah loveth those Who do good.

2:215 They ask thee What they should spend (In charity). Say: Whatever Ye
2:215 spend that is good, Is for parents and kindred And orphans And
2:215 those in want And for wayfarers. And whatever ye do That is good,-
2:215 Allah Knoweth it well.

2:216 Fighting is prescribed For you, and ye dislike it. But it is
2:216 possible That ye dislike a thing Which is good for you And that ye
2:216 love a thing Which is bad for you. But Allah knoweth, And ye
2:216 Know not.

2:217 They ask thee Concerning fighting In the Prohibited Month. Say:
2:217 "Fighting therein Is a grave (offence): But graver is it In the
2:217 sight of Allah To prevent access To the path of Allah, To deny Him,
2:217 To prevent access To the Sacred Mosque, And drive out its members."
2:217 Tumult and oppression Are worse than slaughter Nor will they cease
2:217 Fighting you until They turn you back From your faith If they can.
2:217 And if any of you Turn back from their faith And die in unbelief,
2:217 Their works will bear no fruit In this life And in the Hereafter;
2:217 They will be Companions of the Fire And will abide therein.

2:219 They ask thee Concerning wine gambling, Say: "In them is great sin,
2:219 And some profit, for men; But the sin is grater Than the profit."
2:219 They ask thee how much They are to spend; Say: "What is beyond Your
2:219 needs." Thus doth Allah Make clear to you His Signs: in order that
2:219 Ye may consider-

2:220 (Their bearings) on This life and the Hereafter. They ask thee
2:220 Concerning orphans. Say: " The best thing to do Is what is for

2:220 their good; If ye mix Their affairs with yours, They are your
2:220 brethren; But Allah knows The man who means mischief From the man
2:220 who means good.
2:220 And if Allah had wished, He could have put you Into difficulties:
2:220 He is indeed Exalted in Power, Wise."

2:223 Your wives are As tilth unto you: So approach your tilth When or
2:223 how ye will: But do some good act For your souls beforehand; And
2:223 fear Allah, And Know that ye are To meet Him (in the Hereafter) And
2:223 give (these) good tidings To those who believe.

2:233 The mother shall give suck To their offspring For two whole years,
2:233 If the father desires, To complete the term. But he shall bear the
2:233 cost Of their food and clothing On equitable terms. No soul shall
2:233 have A burden laid on it Greater than it can bear. No mother shall
2:233 be Treated unfairly On account of her child, Nor father On account
2:233 of his child. An heir shall be chargeable In the same way If they
2:233 both decide On weaning, By mutual consent, And after due
2:233 consultation, There is no blame on them. If ye decide On a
2:233 foster-mother For your offspring,There is no blame on you, Provided
2:233 ye pay (the mother) What ye offered, On equitable terms. But fear
2:233 Allah and know That Allah sees well What ye do.

2:244 Then fight in the cause Of Allah, and know that Allah Heareth and
2:244 knoweth all things.

2:264 O ye who believe! Cancel not your charity By reminders of your
2:264 generosity Or by injury,- like those Who spend their substance To
2:264 be seen of men, But believe neither In Allah nor in the Last Day.
2:264 They are in Parable like a hard, Barren rock, on which Is a little
2:264 soil; on it Falls heavy rain, Which leaves it (Just) a bare stone.
2:264 They will be able to do nothing With aught they have earned. And
2:264 Allah guideth not Those who reject faith.

2:265 And the likeness of those Who spend their substance, Seeking to
2:265 pleas Allah And to strengthen their souls, Is as a garden, high And
2:265 fertile: heavy rain Falls on it but makes it yield A double
2:265 increase Of harvest, and if it receives not Heavy rain, light
2:265 moisture Sufficeth it. Allah seeth well Whatever ye do.

2:267 O ye who believe! Give of the good things Which ye have
2:267 (honorably) earned, And of the fruits of the earth Which We have
2:267 produced For you, and do not even aim At getting anything Which
2:267 is bad,in order that Out of it ye may give away Something, when
2:267 ye yourselves Would not receive it Except with closed eyes. And
2:267 know that Allah Is Free of all wants, And Worthy of all praise.

2:268 The Evil One threatens You with poverty And bids you to conduct
2:268 Unseemly. Allah promiseth You His forgiveness And bounties. And
2:268 Allah careth for all And He knoweth all things.

2:270 And whatever ye spend In charity or devotion, Be sure Allah knows
2:270 it all. But the wrong-doers Have no helpers.

2:273 (Charity is) for those In need,who, in Allah's cause, Are
2:273 restricted (from travel), And cannot move about In the land,
2:273 seeking (For trade or work). The gnorant man thinks, Because of
2:273 their modesty, That they are free from want. Thou shalt know them
2:273 By their (unfailing) mark: They beg not importunately From all and
2:273 sundry. And whatever of good Ye give, be assured Allah knoweth it
2:273 well.

2:274 Those who (in charity) Spend of their goods By night and by day, In
2:274 secret and in public, Have their reward With their Lord: On them
2:274 shall be no fear, Nor shall they grieve.

2:277 Those who believe, And do deeds of righteousness, And establish
2:277 regular prayers And regular charity Will have their reward With
2:277 their Lord: On them shall be no fear, Nor shall they grieve.

2:282 O ye who believe! When ye deal with each other, In transactions
2:282 involving Future obligations In a fixed period of time,
2:282 Reduce them to writing. Let a scribe write down Faithfully as
2:282 between The parties: let not the scribe Refuse to write: as Allah
2:282 Has taught him, So let him write Let him who incurs The liability
2:282 dictate, But let him fear His Lord Allah, And not diminish Aught
2:282 of what he owes. If the party liable Is mentally deficient, Or
2:282 weak, or unable Himself to dictate, Let his guardian Dictate
2:282 faithfully. And get two witnesses, Out of your own men, And if
2:282 there are not two men, Then a man and two women, Such as ye choose,
2:282 For witnesses, So that if one of them errs, The other can remind
2:282 her. The witnesses Should not refuse When they are called on (For
2:282 evidence). Disdain not to reduce To writing (your contract) For a
2:282 future period, Whether it be small Or big: it is juster In the
2:282 sight of Allah, More suitable as evidence, And more convenient To
2:282 prevent doubts Among yourselves But if it be a transaction Which
2:282 ye carry out On the spot among yourselves, There is no blame on
2:282 you If ye reduce it not To writing. But take witnesses Whenever ye
2:282 make A commercial contract; And let neither scribe Nor witness
2:282 suffer harm, If ye do (such harm), It would be wickedness In you
2:282 So fear Allah; For it is Allah That teaches you. And Allah is well
2:282 acquainted With all things.

2:283 If ye are on a journey, And cannot find A scribe, a pledge With
2:283 possession (may serve The purpose). And if one of you Deposits a
2:283 thing On trust with another, Let the trustee (Faithfully) discharge
2:283 His trust, and let him Fear his Lord. Conceal not evidence; For
2:283 whoever conceals it,- His heart is tainted With sin. And Allah
2:283 Knoweth all that ye do.

2:284 To Allah belongeth all That is in the heavens And on earth.
2:284 Whether Ye show what is in your minds Or conceal it, Allah Calleth
2:284 you to account for it. He forgiveth whom He pleaseth, And punisheth
2:284 whom He pleaseth. For Allah hath power Over all things.

2:285 The Apostle believeth In what hath been revealed To him from his
2:285 lord, As do the men of faith. Each one (of them) believeth In
2:285 Allah, His angels, His books, and His apostles "We make no

2:285 distinction (they say) Between one and another Of His apostles."
2:285 And they say: "We hear, and we obey: (We seek) Thy forgiveness, Our
2:285 Lord, and to Thee Is the end of all journeys."

2:286 On no soul doth Allah Place a burden greater Than it can bear. It
2:286 gets every good that it earns, And it suffers every ill that it
2:286 earns. (Pray:) "Our Lord! Condemn us not If we forget or fall Into
2:286 error; our Lord! Lay not on us a burden Like that which thou Didst
2:286 Lay on those before us; Our Lord! lay not on us A burden greater
2:286 than we Have strength to bear. Blot out our sins, And grant us
2:286 forgiveness, Have mercy on us. Thou art our Protector; Help us
2:286 against those Who stand against Faith.
63: 10 And spend something (in charity) Out of the substance Which
63: 10 We have bestowed On you, before Death Should come to any of you
63: 10 And he should say, "O my Lord ! Why didst Thou not give me
63: 10 Respite for a little while? I should then have given (Largely)
63: 10 in charity, and I Should have been one Of the doers of good."

6:128 One day will He gather Them all together, (and say): "O ye assembly
6:128 of Jinns! Much (toll) did ye take Of men." Their friends Amongst
6:128 men will say: "Our Lord! we made profit From each other: but
6:128 (alas!) We reached our term- Which Thou didst appoint For us." He
6:128 will say: "The Fire be your dwelling -place You will dwell therein
6:128 for ever, Except as Allah willeth." For thy Lord is full Of wisdom
6:128 and knowledge.

6:161 Say: "Verily, my Lord Hath guided me to A Way that is straight,- A
6:161 religion of right,- The Path (trod) by Abraham The true in faith,
6:161 And he (certainly) Joined not gods with Allah."
6:162 Say: "Truly, my prayer And my service of sacrifice, My life and my
6:162 death, Are (all) for Allah, The Cherisher of the Worlds:
6:165 It is He Who hath made You (His) agents, inheritors Of the earth:
6:165 He hath raised You in ranks, some above Others: that He may try you
6:165 In the gifts He hath given you: For thy Lord is quick In
6:165 punishment: yet He Is indeed Oft-Forgiving, Most Merciful.

7: 4 How many towns have We Destroyed (for their sins)? Our punishment
7: 4 took them On a sudden by night Or while they slept For their
7: 4 afternoon rest.
7: 5 When (thus) Our punishment Took them, no cry Did they utter but
7: 5 this: "Indeed we did wrong."
7: 7 And verily We shall recount Their whole story With knowledge, for
7: 7 We Were never absent (At any time or place).

7: 33 Say: The things that my Lord Hath indeed forbidden are: Shameful
7: 33 deeds, whether open Or secret; sins and trespasses Against truth
7: 33 or reason; assigning Of partners to Allah, for which He hath given
7: 33 no authority; And saying things about Allah Of which ye have no
7: 33 knowledge.

7:100 To those who inherit The earth in succession To its (previous)
7:100 possessors, Is it not a guiding (lesson) That, if We so willed, We
7:100 could punish them (too) For their sins, and seal up Their hearts so
7:100 that they could not hear?

7:101 Such were the towns Whose story We (thus) Relate unto thee: There
7:101 came indeed to them Their apostles with clear (Signs): But they
7:101 would not believe What they had rejected before. Thus doth Allah
7:101 seal up The heart of those Who reject Faith.

7:167 Behold! thy Lord did declare That He would send Against them, to
7:167 the Day of Judgment, those who would Afflict them with grievous
7:167 Penalty. Thy Lord is quick In retribution, but He is also
7:167 Oft-Forgiving, Most Merciful.

7:182 Those who reject Our Signs, We shall gradually visit With
7:182 punishment, in ways They perceive not;
7:187 They ask thee about The (final) Hour- when Will be its appointed
7:187 time? Say: "The knowledge thereof Is with my Lord (alone): None but
7:187 He can reveal As to when it will occur. Heavy were its burden
7:187 through The heavens and the earth. Only, all of a sudden, Will it
7:187 come to you." They ask thee as if thou Wert eager in search
7:187 thereof: Say: "The knowledge thereof Is with Allah (alone), But
7:187 most men know not."
7:188 Say: "I have no power Over any good or harm To myself except as
7:188 Allah Willeth. If I had knowledge Of the unseen, I should have
7:188 Multiplied all good, and no evil Should have touched me, I am but
7:188 a warner. And a bringer of glad tidings To those who have faith."

7:189 It is He Who created You from a single person, And made his mate Of
7:189 like nature, in order That he might dwell with her (In love). When
7:189 they are United, she bears a light Burden and carries it about
7:189 (Unnoticed). When she grows Heavy, they both pray To Allah their
7:189 Lord,(saying): "If Thou givest us A goodly child, We vow we shall
7:189 (Ever) be grateful."

9: 23 O ye who believe! Take not For protectors your fathers And your
9: 23 brothers if they love Infidelity above Faith If any of you do so
9: 23 They do wrong.
9: 24 Say: If it be that your fathers' Your sons your brothers Your mates
9: 24 or your kindred; The wealth that ye have gained The commerce in
9: 24 which ye fear A decline; or the dwellings In which ye delight Are
9: 24 dearer to you than Allah Or His Apostle, or the striving In His
9: 24 cause ; then wait Until Allah brings about His Decision and
9: 24 Allah Guides not the rebellious.

6: 73 It is He Who created The heavens and the earth In true
6: 73 (proportions); The day He saith, "Be," Behold! it is. His word Is
6: 73 the Truth. His will be The dominion the day The trumpet will be
6: 73 blown. He knoweth what ye Keep secret and what ye Make known. For
6: 73 He Is the Wise, well acquainted (With all things).

28: 78 He said:" This has been given To me because of a certain
28: 78 Knowledge which I have." Did he not know that Allah Had destroyed,
28: 78 before him (Whole) generations,- which were Superior to him in
28: 78 strength And greater in the amount (Of riches) they had collected?
28: 78 But the wicked are not Called (immediately) to account For
28: 78 their sins.

28: 80 But those who had been granted (True) knowledge said:" Alas For
28: 80 you ! The reward of Allah (In the Hereafter) is best For those
28: 80 who believe And work righteousness: but this None shall attain
28: 80 save those Who steadfastly persevere (in good).
28: 84 If any does good, the reward To him is better than His deed; but
28: 84 if any Does evil, the doers of evil Are only punished (to the
28: 84 extent) Of their deeds.
28: 85 Verily He Who ordained The Qur-an for thee will bring Thee back
28: 85 to the Place Of Return. Say: "My Lord Knows best who it is That
28: 85 brings true guidance And who is in manifest error."
29: 3 We did test those Before them, and Allah will Certainly know
29: 3 those who are True from those who are false.
29: 5 For those whose hopes are In the meeting with Allah (In the
29: 5 Hereafter, let them strive); For the Term (appointed) By Allah is
29: 5 surely coming: And He hears and knows (All things).
29: 8 We have enjoined on man Kindness to parents: but if They
29: 8 (either of them) strive (To force) thee to join With Me (in
29: 8 worship) Anything of which thou hast No knowledge, 3430 obey
29: 8 them not. Ye have (all) to return To Me, and I will Tell you
29: 8 (the truth) Of all that ye did.
29: 10 Then there are among men Such as say, "We believe In Allah"; but
29: 10 when they suffer Affliction in (the cause of) Allah, They treat
29: 10 men's oppression As if it were the Wrath Of Allah! And if help
29: 10 Comes (to thee) from thy Lord, They are sure to say, "We have
29: 10 (always) been With you! "Does not Allah Know best all that is In
29: 10 the hearts of all Creation?
29: 11 And Allah most certainly knows. Those who believe and as certainly
29: 11 Those who are Hypocrites.
29: 21 "He punishes whom He pleases, And He grants mercy to whom He
29: 21 pleases, and towards Him Are ye turned.
29: 23 Those who reject the Signs Of Allah and The Meeting, With Him
29: 23 (in the Hereafter)- It is they who shall despair Of My mercy:
29: 23 it is they Who will (suffer) A most grievous Penalty.
29: 26 But Lut had faith in Him: He said: "I will leave Home for the
29: 26 sake of My Lord: for He is Exalted in Might, and Wise."
29: 32 He said: "But there is Lut there." They said: "Well do we know who
29: 32 Is there: we will certainly Save him and his following,- Except
29: 32 his wife: she is Of those who lag behind!"
29: 34 "For we are going to Bring down on the people Of this township a
29: 34 Punishment From heaven, because they Have been wickedly rebellious.
29: 42 Verily Allah doth know Of (everything) whatever That they call upon
29: 42 Besides Him: and He is Exalted (in Power), Wise.
29: 43 And such are the Parables We set for mankind. But only those
29: 43 understand them Who have Knowledge.
29: 52 Say:" Enough is Allah For a Witness between me And you: He knows
29: 52 What is in the heavens And on earth." And it is Those who
29: 52 believe in vanities And reject Allah, that Will perish (in the
29: 52 end).
29: 53 They ask thee To hasten on the Punishment (For them): had it not
29: 53 been For a term (of respite) Appointed, the Punishment Would
29: 53 certainly have come To them : and it will Certainly reach them,-
29: 53 Of a sudden, while they Perceive not!
29: 54 They ask thee To hasten on the Punishment But, of a surety, Hell
29: 54 will encompass The rejecters of Faith!

29: 55 On the Day that The Punishment shall cover them From above them
29: 55 and From below them, And (a Voice) shall say:"Taste ye (the fruits)
29: 55 Of your deeds!"
29: 60 How many are the creatures That carry not their own Sustenance?
29: 60 It is Allah Who feeds (both) them and you: For He hears and
29: 60 knows (All things).
29: 62 Allah enlarges the sustenance (Which He gives) to whichever
29: 62 Of his servants He pleases; And He (similarly) grants By
29: 62 (strict) measure, (as He pleases): For Allah has full knowledge
29: 62 Of all things.
29: 66 Disdaining ungratefully Our gifts And giving themselves up To
29: 66 (worldly) enjoyment! But soon Will they know .
29: 68 And who does more wrong Than he who invent A lie against Allah
29: 68 Or rejects the truth When it reaches him! Is there not a home In
29: 68 Hell for those who Reject Faith?
30: 7 They know but the outer (Things) in the life Of this world:
30: 7 but Of the End of things They are heedless.
30: 15 Then those who have believed And worked righteous deeds, Shall
30: 15 be made happy In a Mead of Delight.
30: 16 And those who have rejected Faith and falsely denied Our signs
30: 16 and the meeting Of the Hereafter,- such Shall be brought forth to
30: 16 Punishment.

33: 17 Say:" Who is it that can Screen you from Allah If it be His wish
33: 17 To give you Punishment Or to give you Mercy?" Nor will they find
33: 17 for themselves, Besides Allah any protector Or helper.
33: 18 Verily Allah knows those Among you who keep back (Men) and those
33: 18 who say To their brethren," Come along To us," but come not To
33: 18 the fight except For just a little while,
33: 19 Covetous over you. Then when fear comes, Thou wilt see them
33: 19 looking To thee their eyes revolving, Like (those of) one over
33: 19 whom Hovers death : but when The fear is past They will smite
33: 19 you With sharp tongues covetous Of goods. Such men have No faith
33: 19 and so Allah Has made their deeds Of none effect: and that Is easy
33: 19 for Allah.
33: 22 When the Believers saw The Confederate forces They said: 'This is
33: 22 What Allah and His Apostle Had promised us and Allah And His
33: 22 Apostle told us What was true ." And it Only added to their faith
33: 22 And their zeal in obedience.
33: 24 That Allah may reward The men of Truth for Their Truth and punish
33: 24 The Hypocrites if that be His will or turn to them In Mercy:
33: 24 for Allah is Oft-Forgiving, Most Merciful.
33: 30 O Consorts of the Prophet! If any of you were guilty Of evident
33: 30 unseemly conduct The punishment would be Doubled to her and that
33: 30 21 Is easy for Allah. 30
33: 33 And stay quietly in Your houses and make not A dazzling display,
33: 33 like That of the former Times Of Ignorance; and establish
33: 33 Regular Prayer and give Regular Charity; and obey Allah and His
33: 33 Apostle. And Allah only wishes To remove all abomination From
33: 33 you ye Members Of the Family, and to make You pure and spotless.

33: 43 He it is Who sends Blessings on you as do His angels that He may
33: 43 Bring you out from the depths Of Darkness into Light: And He is
33: 43 Full of Mercy To the Believers.

33: 46 And as one who invites To Allah's (Grace) by His leave And as a
33: 46 Lamp Spreading Light .

66: 8 O ye who believe! Turn to Allah With sincere repentance:
66: 8 In the hope that Your Lord will remove From you your ills And
66: 8 admit you to Gardens Beneath which Rivers flow,- The Day that
66: 8 Allah Will not permit To be humiliated The Prophet and those Who
66: 8 believe with him. Their Light will run Forward before them And by
66: 8 their right hands, While they say," Our Lord! Perfect our Light
66: 8 for us, And grant us Forgiveness; For Thou hast power Over all
66: 8 things."
67: 5 And We have. (From of old), Adorned the lowest heaven With Lamps,
67: 5 and We Have made such (Lamps) (As) missiles to drive Away the
67: 5 Evil Ones, And have prepared for them The Penalty Of the Blazing
67: 5 Fire.
67: 6 For those who reject Their Lord (and Cherisher) Is the Penalty of
67: 6 Hell: And evil is (such) destination.
67: 13 And whether ye hide Your word or publish it, He certainly has
67: 13 (full) Knowledge, Of the secrets of (all) hearts.

34: 39 Say: "Verily my Lord enlarges And restricts the Sustenance To such
34: 39 of His servants As He pleases: and nothing Do ye spend in the
34: 39 least (In His Cause) but He Replaces it: for He is The Best of
34: 39 those who Grant Sustenance.

5: 53 who, For a people whose faith Is assured, can give Better judgment
5: 53 than Allah?

5: 57 O ye who believe! If any from among you Turn back from his Faith,
5: 57 Soon will Allah produce A people whom He will love As they will
5: 57 love Him,- Lowly with the Believers, Mighty against the Rejecters,
5: 57 Fighting in the Way of Allah, And never afraid Of the reproaches Of
5: 57 such as find fault. That is the Grace of Allah, Which He will
5: 57 bestow On whom He pleaseth: And Allah encompasseth all, And He
5: 57 knoweth all things.

The Last Prophet of Islam (peace be upon him)

Through Verse 33: 40 of The Holy Quran, Allah (God) declared to the mankind that Prophet Muhammad (Sm) is the seal of the Prophets and we can know about the last prophet of Islam from following four verses by name :

33: 40 Muhammad is not The father of any Of your men but (he is) The
33: 40 Apostle of Allah, And the e Seal of the Prophets: And Allah has full
33: 40 knowledge Of all things.
47: 2 But those who believe And work deeds of Righteousness, and believe
47: 2 In the (Revelation) sent down To Muhammad-for it is The Truth from
47: 2 their Lord He will remove from them Their ills and improve Their
47: 2 condition .
48: 29 Muhammad is the Apostle Of Allah; and those who are With him are
48: 29 strong Against Unbelievers, (but) Compassionate amongst each
48: 29 other. Thou wilt see them bow And prostrate themselves
48: 29 (In prayer), seeking Grace From Allah and (His) Good Pleasure
48: 29 On their faces are their Markes, (being) the traces Of their
48: 29 prostration. This is their similitude In the Taurat; And
48: 29 their similitude In the Gospel is: Like a seed which sends
48: 29 Forth its blade, then Makes it strong; it then Becomes thick.
48: 29 and it stands On its own stem, (filling) The sowers with wonder And
48: 29 delight. As a result, It fills the Unbelievers With rage at him.
48: 29 Allah has promised those Among them who believe And do righteous
48: 29 deeds Forgiveness, And a great Reward.

61: 6 And remember, Jesus The son of Mary, said: "O Children of Israel!
61: 6 I am the apostle of Allah (Sent) to you confirming The Law
61: 6 (which came) Before me, and giving Glad Tidings of an Apostle To
61: 6 come after me, Whose name shall be Ahmad." But when he came to
61: 6 them With Clear Signs, They said," This is Evident sorcery!"

And according to Holy Quran, last Prophet of Islam (Peace be upon him) was sent to proclaim it over all religion and the related verse is as follows:

48: 28 IT IS HE WHO HAS SENT HIS APOSTLE WITH GUIDANCE AND THE RELIGION OF
48: 28 TRUTH, TO PROCLAIM IT OVER ALL RELIGION: AND ENOUGH IS ALLAH FOR
48: 28 A WITNESS.

We can know about many prophets (Allah bless them) from the Holy Quran, but one thing is very important, which is that with what interval of times a Prophet was sent in this world and under what circumstances. For instance from the following list and remark which is derived from Genesis as mentioned by Mr. Maurice Bucaile's famous book, "THE BIBLE, THE QUR'AN and Science" in page 47.

ABRAHAM'S GENEALOGY

Date of birth after creation	Length of	Date of death after creation

	of Adam	life	of Adam
1. Adam		930	930
Seth	130	912	1042
Enosch	235	905	1140
Kenan	325	910	1235
Mahalaleel	395	895	1290
Jared	460	962	1422
Enoch	622	365	987
Methuselah	687	969	1656
Lamech	874	777	1651
10. Noah	1056	950	2056
Shem	1556	600	2156
Arpachshad	1658	438	2096
Shelah	1693	433	2122
Eber	1723	464	2187
Peleg	1757	239	1996
Reu	1787	239	2026
Serug	1819	230	2049
Nahor	1849	148	1997
Terah	1878	205	2083
20 Abraham	1948	175	2123

All the data used in this table come from the Sacerdotal text of
Genesis, the only Biblical text that provides information of this kind .
It may be deduced, according to the Bible, that abraham was born 1,948 years after Adam.
At present, allowing for a slight of error, the time of Abraham is situated at roughly
eighteen centuries before Jesus. Combined with the information in Genesis on the interval
separating Abraham and Adam, this would place Adam a roughly thirty-eight centuries
before Jesus"
  Now without going to the question of accuracy of the above data we may question that
with what interval in average a prophet was sent in this world and under what
circumstances. So if last prophet of Islam as mentioned in the Holy Quran was not
Muhammad (Sm) than why after 1992 years of Prophet Jesus(Allah bless him) why there is
no trace of Massy or Ahmed as mentioned in the Holy Bible (though omitted in most
Bibleby the intrested quarters) and in the Holy Quran.

I should also quote from the Holy Bible; GENESIS 17, 18; CHAPTER 17 WHICH IS:

20 : And as for Ish-mael, I have heard the; Behold, I have blessed him, and   will make
him fruitful, and will multiply him exceedingly; twelve   princes shall be beget,? and
I will make him a great nation.
24: And Abraham was ninety years old and nine, when he was circumcise in the   flesh of
his foreskin.
25: And Ish'-ma-el his son was thirteen years old, when he was circumcised in   the flesh
of his foreskin.
26: In the selfsame day was Abraham circumcised, and Ish'-ma-el his son.

I am also quoting from GENESIS 21; CHAPTER 2

14: And Abraham rose up early in the morning, and took bread, and a bottle of   water,
and gave it unto Ha'gar, putting it on her shoulder, and the   child, and sent her away;
and she departed, and wandered in the wilder ness of Be'-er-sheba.
15: And the water was spent in the bottle, and she cast the child under one   of the shrubs.

16: And she went, and sat her down over against him a good way off, as it were a bowshot; for she said, let me not see the death of the child, And she sat over against him, and lift up her voice, and wept.
17: And God heard the voice of the lad; and the angel of God called to Ha'- gar out of heaven, and said unto her, What aileth thee, Ha'-gar? fear not; for God hath heard the voice of the lad where he is.
18: Arise, lift up the lad, and hold him in thine hand; for I will make him a great nation.

So if we take both the above verse is true then we can understand that Prophet Abraham (Peace be upon him) kept relation and personal contact with his first son Ish-mael and Ish-mael's mother Hadrath Hazera or Ha'gar, and used to go to them otherwise how it was possible that Abraham circumcised and Ish'-ma-el when Is-'ma-el was thirteen years old as mentioned in verse 25 and 26 above, so our question to learned Jews and Christian are that which is true? We think both the verse is true. So Prophet Abraham kept his relation and personal contact with both Ismael and his mother. Here we should mention another event which is as follows:

"Once an old man(stranger) came to Prophet Ismael's (Peace be upon him) house when he was away from his house. So the old man asked the wife of Ismael(A. S.) 'how their days were passing'; the wife replied that "her life is a very tough one and without proper necessity of the family". When the old man left he asked her to tell her husband that he should change the door of the house and when Ishmael (A.S.) returned home she told everything. Ishmael(A.S.) told her "that the old man is none but his father Abraham and through changing the door means to change the wife". So Ishmael divorced his that particular wife. Again in another day one old man came to Ishmael's house when he was away. The old man asked his wife how their days were passing, she replied that "thank God and that they are passing nice life, her husband used to work very hard and that she is very happy and pleased with nice husband". The old man before his departure asked her to tell her husband that he should take care of the door.
So when Ishmael came home she told everything to Ishmael(A.S.). Ishmael told his wife that the old man was his father Abraham and he asked that he should take care of his wife.

But Chapter 33 of Deuteronomy of the Old Testament opens with "the blessing that Moses the Prophet of God pronounced upon the Israelites before his death" and the pronouncement runs as follows:

"The Lord came from Sinai and shone forth from Seir. He showed himself from Mount Paran and with him were myriads of Holy ones streaming along at his right hand".

The above are exactly the verses from the Holy Bible (Old Testament) which were quoted by Hadrath Abdullah bin Salam, a companion of the Prophet Muhammad (Sm), who was a Biblical Scholar and leader of the Jews of Yathrib (Holy Medina) before he embraced Islam. The verses mean, as Hadrath Abdullah bin Salam explained, that the Lord came from Sinai where Moses (a) conversed with almighty Allah and received the Taorat (Tora) and then would shine forth all over the world.

At the very out set it is necessary to explain the word Jesus, as used in the New Testament, in contrast to the word Eisa as used in Holy Quran to denote the same person. In the original Taorat (Tora written in Hebrew language with Aramaic script the name of Jesus is Eisa. But when the Taurat was turned Greek language the original name of Eisa was misspelt and corrupted into Jesus by changing the "Ei" into "Je" and adding "us" at the end of it. Thus the correct name of Jesus is Eisa.

153

As for the Prophecy made by the Prophet Eisa(a) on the advent of the last Prophet Muhammad(sm) let us look into the following:

(i) Act(of the Apostles)3.22-24 of the New Testament contains:

"The Lord will raise up a Prophet for you from among yourselves as he raised me, you shall listen to everything he says to you, and anyone who refuses to listen to that Prophet must be extirpated from Israel."

These verses should be read along with Deuteronomy 18:18 which runs as follows:

"I will raise up for them a Prophet like you, one of their own race, and I will put my words into his mouth".[129]

And in other word on the conquest of Mecca (Paran in the Bible) by the Muslims under the command of the Prophet Muhammad (sm) in 8 A. H. Hadrath Abdullah bin Salam explained and interpreted the above quoted Biblical Verses as the fulfillment of the Prophecy made by the Prophet Moses (a) in those Verses. The verses mean, as a companion of the last Prophet (may peace be upon him), Hazrat Abdullah (Allah may be pleased with him) explained, that the Lord came from Sinai where Hazrat Moses (a) conversed with Almighty Allah and received the Taorat(Tora) and then would shine forth from Sier where from his fame would radiate and shine forth all over the world. The word Sier was explained by Hazrat Abdullah as to have meant Yathrib or the present Medina which became famous as "Madinatun Nabi" or "City of the Prophet" after the Prophet Muhammad (sm) migrated there. The Prophecy was further explained that the promised Prophet would first show himself from the famous Mount Hira at Paran, which the Biblical language stands for Mecca in Arabic. It is in the cave of Mount Hira near Paran that the last Prophet Muhammad(sm) was taught, for the first time, five verses from the Holy Quran by the Angel Jibraeel (Gabriel) and thus received Nabuwat or Prophethood here. The Prophet (sm) had to migrate from Paran (Mecca) to Sier(Medina) and in the 8th year of his migration or Hijrat he conquered it (Paran) with his companions who numbered exactly ten thousand (one myriad). The Prophecy made by the Prophet Moses in the above quoted verses of the Holy Bible was thus fulfilled.[130]

We also mention here that Hazrat Abdullah bin Salam was the chief of the Jews in Medina and was a learned rabbi and his father was also the chief of Jews in Medina, Abdullah bin Salam knew that the last Prophet of Islam will come and as such as soon as The Prophet (Sm) came to Medina, he became a Muslim.[131]

I should quote an Indian writer, Mr. Abdul Haque Vidyarthe from his book "MOHAMMAD IN WORLD SCRIPTURE" published in Delhi, which is as follows:

After the Prophet Noah, Abraham is regarded to be the Patriarch or the father of nations. It is said that Brahmaji known among the Hindus, as the father of mankind, was none else but the Prophet Abraham. In Mundak Upanishad, one of the authentic Upanishad, it is stated that Brahma was the first of the gods. He taught his son Atharva Brahm-Vidya or the Divine Scripture which is the source of all knowledge (Mindak Upanishad 1 : 1). Brahm Vidya is another name of the Atharva Vida. The Prophet Abraham had two sons, Ishmael

---

[129]The Palestine issue and The Muslim World by Mr. A. M. M. Abdul Jalil, M. A. L.L.B, Sr. Advocate of Bangladesh Supreme Court

[130]"THE PALESTINE ISSUE AND THE MUSLIM WORLD BY Mr. A. M. M. Abdul Jalil, M.A., L. L. B. PG. 85-87

[131] The Life of Muhammad, A Translation of Ishaq's SIRAT RASUL ALLAH, PUBLISHED BY OXFORD UNIVERSITY PRESS, PP.240-241

and Isaac, similarly according to Gopath Brahmana, Brahmaji had two sons, Atharba and Angira. The book of the elder is known as Atharva Veda, and that of the younger one is known as Angiras Veda, which is the second half of the Atharva Veda. Again it is said that Brahma was all alone, without any issue and he desired to have a son like him, so he prayed to God in right earnest (Gopath Brahmana, 1 : 1). Similar is the story of Abraham as recorded in the Bible (Genesis XV 1-4). It is also stated in the Gopath Brahmana that these two sons of Brahmaji were born, one of sweet water and the other of Saltish water. Atharva was born of sweet water and Angira was born of saltish water (Atharva or Ismael's mother, Hagar was a meek, patient and forebearing women and Sarah, the mother of Isaac or Angiras was harsh and sour tempered, this is what meant by their being born of sweet and salt water. Sarah, in the Hindu scriptures is known as Saraswati and Hagar is called Parwat-i). Jesus called his people as the salt of the earth.(Matthew. v:13 Similarly, by sweet water is meant Ishmael and his descendants, the Arabs. `A true believer is always sweet-tempered,' says a tradition of the Prophet(sm.).[132]

The Prophet Ahmad: The words of the Mantra, `the praying one', show that this prophecy is meant for the Prophet ahmad, peace be on him. The Sanskrit word Karu, used in the mantra, has been translated by Professor Griffith as `Singer' and Pandit Raja Ram, of the Lahore D.A.V. College, translates it as `Satota' meaning the praying one or Ahmad, the second name of the Prophet Mohammad, who was the hero of the battle of the Allies. Another attribute of the Prophet given in this mantra, is Brihashmate. This word is derived from the root Brhi which means holy grass that is spread in a temple of worship. The man with the holy grass, thus, metaphorically means,`the worshipper' or the one who adores his Lord.[133]

Christianity had been preached to the Arabs for five hundreds years, yet only a small number of Arab Christians could be seen in scattered communities e.g.] Harith in Nazran, Hanif in Yemen and a few others among Tai and that was all. In short when we make a survey of the religions conditions of Arabia, we find the feeble Christian efforts causing a little ruffling of the surface, while Judaism, at times comes in sight heaving as a violent storm. But it was the cult of idol-worship with the vain beliefs of Ismail that came surging from all sides and touched the walls of the Kaba."[134]

The Ishmaelites

As already said, historians have divided the Arab races into three categories: the ancient races no longer extant as Tasm and Jadis, the pure Arabs who are the descendants of Qahtan, for example the Yemenites and the Ansar; and thirdly the Ishmaelites.

___ [132] MOHAMMAD IN WORLD SCRIPTURES BY ABDUL HAQUE VIDYARTHI,   DEEP & DEEP PUBLICATIONS, D-1/24 Rajouri Garden, New Delhi-110027, pp. 150-151.

___ [133] MOHAMMAD IN WORLD SCRIPTURESBY ABDUL HAQUE VIDYARTHI, DEEP & DEEP PUBLICATIONS, D-1/24 Rajouri Garden, New Delhi-110027, pp. 107-108.

___ [134] William Muir, The life of Muhammad, Preface Vol, I.
___ Referred in page   15, SIRAT-UN-NABI (THE LIFE OF THE PROPHET) BY SHIBLI NU'MANI

When Ishmael took his abode in Mecca, the area round about had been occupied by the of Jurham. Ishmael was married to a girl from this tribe. His progency from this union is known as Naturalized Arabs, The majority of modern Arabs belongs to this ancestry. The Holy Prophet and the history of Islam are connected with this race. The Holy Prophet himself was a descendant of Ishmael and the faith he preached was the same that Abraham had preached long ago. The Holy Quran says: The faith of your father Abraham; He named you Muslims before and so in this 22:78 (He is referred as Abraham but some as God). But biased European historians deny these fact outright.

The old Testament or the Tora (Arabic Taorat) and the New Testament, the Gospels or the Evangel (Arabic Anajeel) are together called the Holy Bible. During the early days of Ecclesiastic Rule the Holy Bible remained under exclusive custody of the Jewish and the Christian Priests and, as such, were beyond the reach of the common people. Those Priests could and actually did, therefore, alter and interpolate those religious scriptures of the heavenly books, "with their own hands in order to traffic with it for a miserable price" as referred to in the Holy Quran (Chapter 2, Verse 79). These Priests, however, altered particularly those portions from the Holy Bible which contained reference to the advent of the last (Promised) Prophet Muhammad (sm). The Priests did so for the reason that they knew that the last Prophet (sm) would show himself from Paran (the Biblical name for Mecca) and, naturally from the descendants of the Prophet's Ibrahim's son Ishmail (a) about whom they fabricated hatred by way of stigmatizing his mother Hajira, the Egyptian Princess before marriage with Prophet Ibrahim, as maid slave. They were also aware that the last Prophet(sm) would be an iconoclast and would come with a fiery law or Shariya whereby traffication of corrupt social practices in the name of Mosaic laws and religion would be put to an end. Let us now look into the Holy Bible (Tora) in the context of the Prophecy made by the Prophet Moses on the advent of the last Prophet Muhammad(sm). Chapter 33 of Deuteronomy of the Old Testament opens with "the blessing that Moses the man of God pronounced upon the Israelites before his death" and the pronouncement runs as follows:
"The Lord came from Sinai and shoneforth from Seir. He showed himself from Mount Paran and with him were myriads of Holy ones streaming along at his right hand"

page 119

Now the question is who is the Sacrificed one?
LET US BEAR IN MIND the following facts:
The Jews claim that Isaac was the Sacrificed One; and accordingly they say that Syria was the Place where this sacrifice was offered.

1. According to the ancient religious law, only the first-born could be sacrificed, were it an animal or a human being. It was for this reason that Abel had sacrificed only the first-born lambs. While laying down this law for Levites, God addressed the following words to Moses: "For all the first born of the children of Israel are mine, both man and beast.[135]

2.The preference given to the first-born could in no way be ignored. In the Torah, it is laid down that if one has two wives, one whom he likes and the other whom he does not like, the First-born child shall have preference, no matter if born of the woman who is in disfavor. The Torah has given the following reason for this: "For he is the first issue of his strength, the right of the first born is his".[136]

___ [135] Numbers, 8:17

___ [136] Deuteronomy, 21:17

3. The off-spring who was dedicated to God did not inherit anything from his father. The Torah says: "At that time the Lord set apart the tribe of Levi to carry the Ark of the covenant of the Lord, to stand before the Lord to minister to him and to bless in his name, to this day. Therefore, Levi has no portion or inheritance with his brothers; the Lord is his inheritance, as the Lord your God promised him".[137]

4. The man who was dedicated to God Would let his hair grow; only when he had reached the holy place of worship could he get himself shaved, just as a Haji (pilgrim) does, after he has removed his "IHRAM" (the pilgrim's robe). In the Torah we find the following verses ".....For lo! you shall conceive and bear a son. No razor shall come upon his head, for the boy shall be a Nazarite unto God from birth; and he shall begin to deliver Israel from the hands of the Philistines.[138]

5. For those who were dedicated to the service of God, the words "BEFORE THE LORD" are used; vide Exodus, Numbers (6: 16-20), Genesis 17, Deut,. 10-8.

6. Abraham was ordered to sacrifice the son whom he loved most and who was the only son.[139]

   The majority of Christians believe that the Gospels were written by direct witness of the life of Jesus and therefore constitute unquestionable evidence concerning the vents high-lighting His life and preaching. one wonders in the presence of such guarantees of authenticity how is possible to discuss the teachings derived from them and how one can cast doubt upon the validity of the church as an institution by applying the general instructions Jesus Himself gave. To days popular editions of the Gospels contain commentaries aimed at propagating these ideas among the general public.

The value the authors of the Gospels have as eyewitnesses is always presented to the faithful as axiomatic. In the middle of the Second century, Saint Justin did after all, call the Gospels the 'Memories of the Apostles'. There are more over so many details proclaimed concerning the authors that it is a wonder that one could ever doubt their accuracy; Matthew was a Well-known character 'a customs officer employed at the tollgate or customs house at Capharnaum'; it is even said that he spoke Aramaic and Greek. Mark is also easily identifiable a peter's colleague; there is no doubt that he too was an eye-witness. Luke is the 'dear physician' of whom Paul talks; information on him is very precise. john is the Apostle who was always near to Jesus, son of Zededee, fisherman on the Sea of Galilee.

Modern studies on the beginnings of Christianity show that this way of presenting things hardly corresponds to reality. We shall see who the author of the Gospels really were. As far as the decades following Jesus's mission are concerned, it must be understood that events did not at all happen in the way they have been said to have taken place and that Peter's arrival in Rome in no way laid the foundations for the church. on the contrary, from

---

[137] Ibid., 10:8,9,

[138] Judges, 13:5

[139] Genesis, 22

the time Jesus left earth to the second half of the Second Century, there was a struggle between two factions. One was what one might call Pauline Christianity and the other Judeo- Christianity. It was only very slowly that the first supplanted the second, and Pauline Christianity triumphed over Judeo-Christianity.

Ascension of Jesus.

Contradictions are present until the very end of the descriptions because neither John nor Matthew refer to Jesus's Ascension. Mark and Luke are the only to speak of it.
For Mark (16,19) Jesus was 'taken up into heaven, and sat down at the right hand of God' without any precise date being given in relation to His Resurrection.It must however be noted that the final passage of Mark containing this sentence is, for Father Roguet, an 'invented' text, although for the Church it is canonic!
There remains Luke, the only evangelist to provide an undisputed text of the Ascension Episode (24,51): 'he parted from them and was carried up into heaven', The evangelist places the event at the end of the description of the Resurrection and appearance to the eleven Apostles: The details of the Gospel description imply that the Ascension took place on the day of the Resurrection. in the Acts of the Apostles, Luke (whom everybody believes to be their author) describes in chapter 1,3 Jesus's appearance to the Apostles between the Passion and the Ascension in the following terms: "To them he presented himself alive after his passion by many proofs, appearing to them during forty days, and speaking of the kingdom of God."[140]

"If you love me, you will keep my commandments. And i will pray the Father, and he will give you another paraclete."(14,15-16)[141]

What does 'Paraclete' mean? The present text of John's Gospel explains its meaning as follows:
"But the paraclete, the Holy Spirit whom the Father will send in my name, he will teach you all things, and bring to your remembrance all that I have said to you"(14,26).
"he will bear witness to me"(15,26)
"it is to your advantage that I go away, for if i do not go away, the Paraclete will not come to you; but if I go I will send him to you. And when he comes, he will convince the world of sin and of righteousness and of judgement..."(16,7-8).
"When the Spirit of truth comes, he will guide you into all the truth; for he will not speak on his own authority, but whatever he hears he will speak, and he will declare to you the things that are to come. He will glorify me..."(16,13-14).
According to the rules of logic therefore, one is brought to see in John's paraclete a human being like Jesus, possessing the faculties of hearing and speech formally implied in John's Greek text. Jesus therefore predicts that God will later send a human being to Earth to take up the role defined by John,i.e. to be a prophet who hears God's word and repeats his message to man. This is the logical interpretation of John's texts arrived at if one attributes to the words their proper meaning.
The document produced by the Office of Non-Christian Affairs at the Vatican stresses this fundamental point in the following terms:
"It would seem pointless to maintain that Allah is not really God, as do certain people in the West! The conciliar documents have put the above assertion in its proper place. There is no better way of illustrating Islamic faith in God than by quoting the following extracts from

---

____ [140] The Gospel, The Bible The Quran and Science pg. 108

____ [141]The Munahhemana (God bless and preserve him) in Syriac is Muhammad; in Greek he is the paraclete. pg 104, The Life of Muhammad, a translation of Ishaq's SIRAT RASUL ALLAH

Lumen Gentium:(Lumen Gentium is the title of a document produced by the Second Vatican Council (1962-1965)). 'The Muslims profess the faith of Abraham and worship with us the sole merciful God, who is the future judge of men on the Day of Reckoning...'."
Cultivated Muslims have praised D. Masson's French translation of the Qur'an for having 'at last' written 'Dieu' (God) instead of 'Allah'.
Muslims and Christians worship a single God. The Vatican document points out the following: "Allah is the only word that Arabic-speaking Christians have for God." Muslims and Christians worship a single God.
The Vatican document then undertakes a critical examination of the other false judgements made on Islam.
'Islamic fatalism' is a widely-spread prejudice; the document examines this and quoting the Qur'an for support, it puts in opposition to this the notion of the responsibility man has, who is to be judged by his actions.
Qur'an that are highly misunderstood in the West.
"There is no compulsion in religion" (sura 2, verse 256).
"(God) has not laid upon you in religion any hardship" (sura 22, verse 78).
The document opposes the widely-spread notion of 'Islam, religion of fear' to 'Islam, religion of love'- love of one's neighbor based on faith in God. It refutes the falsely spread notion that Muslim morality hardly exists and the other notion, shared by so many Jews and Christians, of Islamic fanaticism.[142]

The Prophet Muhammad (peace be upon him, his family members, his descendent, and his true companions) was born at Mecca on the 12th of Rabiul Awal, in the year of the Elephant, a little more than fifty days after the destruction of the Abyssinian army, or the 29th of August 570 AD His birth , they say, was attended with signs and prtents from which the nations of the earth could know that the Deliver had appeared. Thus with his birth who was descendent of Ish-mael (peace be upon him) the door of Prophethood ended and the seed of a great Nation as promised in The Holy Bible; GENESIS 17, 18; CHAPTER 17 and GENESIS 21.

Genesis of the Last Prophet of Islam
1. Adam
2. Shith
3. Yanish
4. Qaynan
5. Mahlil
6. Yard
7. Akhnukh, who is the prophet Idris according to what they allege,[143]   but God knows best(he was the first of the sons of Adam to   whom prophecy and writing with a pen were given).
8. Mattushalakh
9. Lamk
10. Nuh
11. Sam
12. Arfakhshadh
13. Shalikh

---

[142] The Gospel, The Bible, The Quran and Science by Bukhali pg. 110,111,113 and 121

[143] The phrase employed indicates that the writer doubts the statement. There is a saying in Arabic: 'There is a euphemism for everything and the polite way of saying "It's a lie" is "they allege" (za 'amu)'.

14. Aybar
15. Falikh
16. Rau
17. Sarugh
18. Nahur
19. Tarih (who is Azar)
20. Prophet Ibrahim, the friend of the Compassionate (Father of the   Islamic Nation)
21. Ismail
22. Nabit
23. Yashjub
24. Ya'rub
25. Tayrah
26. Nahur
27. Muqawwam
28. Udd (or Udad)
29. Adnan
30 Ma'add
31 Nizar
32. Mudar
33. Ilyas
34. Mudrika (Whose name was Amir)
35. Khuzayma
36. Kinana
37. al-Nadr
38. Malik
39. Fihr
40. Ghalib
41. Lu'ayy
42. Ka'b
43. Murra
44. Kilab
45. Qusayy (whose name was Zayd)
46. Abdu Manaf (whose name was al-Mughira)
47. Hashim (whose name was 'Amr)   Oahab   Abd ush-Shams
                        Ommeya
                        Ommeya Density through Maywia
48. Abdul Muttalib (whose name was Shayba)
                        Amena (The mother of Tha Last Prophet)
49. Abdullah (The father of The Last Prophet)   Abbas
                        Abbaside Density
50. The Last Prophet of Islam, The Prophet Muhammad (Peace be upon him).[144]
The last Prophet of Islam; Muhammad (Peace be upon him, His descendent and his
companion) lost his father before his birth. He was named by his grandfather Muhammad
which means "the Praised One". Muhammad lost his mother when he was only 6 years old.
and was looked after by his old grand father. But his grand father Abdul Muttalib died
about 579 A. C., and then he was brought up by the care of his one of the uncle Abu Talib.
At that time the Meccan people were worshippers of the 360 idols and the Black Stone in
Mecca. The learned men in old scriptures knew that a Prophet will come, particularly in
Yathrub which is previous name of Al-Medina.

---

        [144] THE LIFE OF MUHAMMAD, A TRANSLATION OF ISHAQ'S SIRAT RASUL
ALLAH WITH INTRODUCTION AND NOTES BY A. GUILLAUME, OXFORD
UNIVERSITY PRESS, p. 3.

So when Prophet (Sm) went to Medina some of them embraced Islam but not all, those who embraced Islam in Medina was called Ansars or the helper and who came from outside Medina are called Muhazir or Refugee.

It took some time for Christianity to reach China. But Islam came more swiftly. It came, indeed, a few years before the Nestorians and during the lifetime of it's Prophet. The Chinese Emperor received both the embassies Islamic and Nestorian with courtesy and listened to what they had to say. He appreciated their views and showed favor impartially. The Arabs were permitted to build a mosque in Canton. This mosque still exists, although it is 1300 years old, and is one of the oldest mosques in the world.[145]

---

[145] THE GLIMPSES OF WORLD HISTORY BY PANDIT NEHRU PG. 116

SPIRITUAL POWER OF ISLAM

I must quote the following Hadith from "AN-NAWAWI'S FORTY HADITH TRANSLATED BY EZZEDDIN INRAHIM AND DENYS JOHNSON-DAVIES (ABDUL WADOUD);
(HAS BEEN PRINTED AT THE EXPENSE OF HIS HIGNESS SHEIKH ZAYED BIN SULTAN AL-NAHAYNAN FOR FREE DISTRIBUTION., HADITH 38, printed in the United States by R. R. Donnelley & Sons Company; PG. 118"

On the authority of Abu Huraira (may Allah be pleased with him), who said: the Messenger of Allah (may the blessing and peace of Allah be upon him) said:
Allah the Almighty has said: Whosoever shows enmity to a friend of Mine, I shall be at war with him. My servant does not draw near to Me with
anything more loved by Me than the religious duties I have imposed upon him, and My servant continues to draw near to Me with supererogatory works so that I shall love him. When I love him I am his hearing with which he hears, his seeing with which he sees, his hand with which he strikes, and his foot with which he walks. Were he to ask [something] of Me, I would surely give it to him; and were he to ask Me for refuge, I would surely grant him it.

17: 57 Those whom they call upon Do desire (for themselves) means
17: 57 Of access to their Lord ,- Even those who are nearest: They hope
17: 57 for His Mercy And fear His Wrath: For the Wrath of thy Lord Is
17: 57 something to take heed of.
17:100 Say :"If ye had Control of the Treasures Of the Mercy of my Lord
17:100 Behold , ye would keep them Back, for fear of spending Them:
17 100 for man Is (ever) niggardly! "
XVIII - 65.

So they found one[146] of Our servants, on whom We had bestowed mecry from Ourselves and whom We had taught knowledge from Our own[147] presence.

___ [146] One of Our servants; his name is not mentioned in the Qur-an, but Tradition gives it as Khidr. Round him have gathered a number of picturesque folk tales, with which we are not here concerned. "Khidhr" means "Green"; his knowledge is fresh and green, and drawn out of the living sources of life, for it is drawn from God's own Presence. He is a mysterious being, who has to be sought out. He has the secrets of the paradoxes of Life, which ordinary people do not understand or understand in a wrong sense, as we shall see further on. The nearest equivalent figure in the literature of the People of the Book is Melchizedek or Melchisedek (the Greek form in the New Testament). In Gen. xiv, 18-20, he appears as king of Salem, priest of the Most High God; he blesses Abraham, and Abraham gives him tithes. St. Paul allegorises him in his Epistle to the Hebrews (v. 6-10; vii, 1-10); "he was without father, without mother, without descent, having neither beginning of days nor end of life." That is to say, he appeared mysteriously; neither his parentage nor his pedigree is known, and he seems to live for all time. These qualities are also attributed to Khidr in Muslim tradition.
All Quotations are from THE HOLY QURAN TEXT, TRANSLATION & COMMENTARY BY A. YUSUF ALI AND PUBLISHED BY SH MUHAMMAD ASHRAF,
LAHORE, PAKISTAN VOL II PG. 748

XVIII - 66. Moses said to him: "May I follow thee, On the footing that Thou teach me something of the (Higher) Truth which thou hast been taught?"[148]

XVIII - 67. (The other) said: "Verily Thou wilt not be able to have patience with me![149]

XVIII - 68. "And how canst thou have patience about things about which thy understanding is not complete?"[150]

XVIII - 69. Moses said: "Thou wilt find me, if God so will, (Truly) patient: nor shall I disobey thee in aught."[151]

.....

XVIII - 110. Say : "I am but a man like yourselves, (but) the inspiration has come to me, that your God is One God: **whoever expects to meet his Lord,** let him work righteousness, and, in the worship of his Lord, admit no one as partner.[152]

---

[147] Khidhr had two special gifts from God: (1) Mercy from His own Presence, and (2) Knowledge from His own Presence. The first freed him from the ordinary incidents of daily human life; and the second entitled him to interpret the inner meaning and mystery of events, as we shall see further on. Much could be and has been written about this from the mystic point of view. All Quotations are from THE HOLY QURAN TEXT, TRANSLATION & COMMENTARY BY A. YUSUF ALI AND PUBLISHED BY SH MUHAMMAD ASHRAF, LAHORE, PAKISTAN VOL II PG. 749

[3]9 Moses, not understanding the full import of what he was asking, makes a simple request. He wants to learn something of the special Knowledge which God had bestowed on Khidhr.

40 Khidhr smiles, and says that there will be many things which Moses will see with him, which Moses will not copletely understand and which will make Moses impatient. The highest spiritual knowledge often seems paradoxical to those who have not the key to it.

41 Khidhr does not blame Moses. Each one of us can only follow our own imperfect lights to the best of our judgment, but if we have Faith, we are saved many false steps.

42 Moses has Faith. He adopts the true attitude of the learner to the Teacher, and promises to obey in all things, with the help of God. The Teacher is doubtful, but permits him to follow him on condition that he asks no questions about anything until the Teacher himself mentions it first.

43 (I have omitted other verses of S. XVIII AND VERSE # 110 IS THE LAST ONE; INTERESTED READER MAY READ FROM PG. 728- 759 OF THE ORIGINAL BOOK FOR DETAIL) the Sura Righteousness and true respect for God- which excludes the

Syed Amir Ali through his famous book "SPIRIT OF ISLAM " in page. 457 comments the following:

Al-Ghazzali's influence served greatly to promote the diffusion of ufism among the Eastern Moslems, and idealistic philosophy was embraced by the greatest intellects of the Mohammedan East. Moulana Jalal ud-din of Rum (Turkey), whose Masnavi is venerated by the Sufi; Sanai, whom Jalal ud-din himself has called his superior; Farid ud-din Attar, Shams ud-din Hafiz, Khakani, the moralist Sa'di, the romancer Nizami,_ all belonged to this school.

We are quoting a Indian Book; "A History of Sufism in India" by Saiyid Athar Abbas Rizvi, M. A. Ph. D. D. Litt., F. A. H. (Australia)
by Munshiram Manoharlal publishers Pvt. Ltd., New Delhi, volume one, Chapter two (The Chishtis, pg 21-22); some of early sufism are follows:

"The decade following the death of Muhammad on 8 June, 632 saw the Arab Town dwellers and Bedouins, whom he had united into one community (Umma), became the masters of Syria, Iraq, Iran, Egypt, Tripoli and part of the African peninsula. They were now not only exposed to the evils of material prosperity, but to new ideas of the ancient civilized world. These made varying impacts upon the companions of Muhammad. Some amassed immense fortunes. But members of the group known as Ahl-al-Suffa and a few others continued to lead lives immersed in poverty as asceticism. Most prominent of these was Abu Zar-al-Ghifari (died in 652 or 653). His revolutionary outspokenness led him into court exile during the reign of Usman (644-56); the third Caliph. Abu Darda 'Uwaymar bin Zaid, one of the Ahl-al-Suffa, used to say that one hour' **of reflection was better than forty nights of prayer and that are particles of righteousness, combined with godliness and assured faith, was preferable to unlimited ritual observance.**[153]
And among the Sufis, Hazrat Ali (Allah be pleased with him) was a model for Sufis in respect to the truths of outward expressions and the subleties of inward meaning, the stripping of one's self of all property either of this world or of the next and consideration of divine providence".[154] **And though a Caliph and one of truthful Caliph, while he was leading early morning prayer in the mosque in Kufa (ironically now part of Iraq) on 17th Ramadan in year 40 A. H. (661 A. D.), he was attacked by poisoned sword of Ibn Mulgan and expired on 21st of Ramadhan.**

Ali the Caliph and the Imams of his House are regarded as having possessed in superlative degree the ``Inward Knowledge.'"" Abu Nasr as-Sarraj, in his work al-Luma' on the philosophy of Sufism,[155] **quoting Junaid**[156] **says, that had Ali not been**

---

worship of anything else, whether idols, or deified men, or forces of nature, or faculties of man, or Self-these are the criteria of true worship.

[153]**Margaret Smith, An early mystic of Baghdad, London 1935, p. 63**

[154]**ibid, p. 74**

[155] **Al-Luma' fi-tasawwuf; tassawwuf is the philosophy of Sufism. The Luma' of as-Sarra has been recently (in 1922's) edited with great care and erudition by the learned author of Studies in Islamic Mysticism. According to Nur-ud-din Abdur Rahman Jami (Nafahat-ul-Uns, Calcutta ed. p. 319) as-Sarraj occupies an eminent position among the Sufi saints. He appears also from Jami's account to have been a proficient**

occupied in so many wars, he would have imparted to the world the vast measure of the `Ilm-ul-ladanni with which he was endowed.[157] And in the Tazkirat-ul-Awlia[158] of Farid-ud-din 'Attar[159] the first place in the list of Mystic saints is given to Ja'far as-Sadik, the sixth apostolic Imam. It is worthy of note that in the case of almost every Sufi saint the line of spiritual descent is traced back to Ali and through him to the Prophet. A few only trace it to Abu Bakr.

A contemporary of Prophet Muhammad (sm) and a great Sufi was the ascetic Uway al-Qarani. The Prophet (sm) never met him but forecast that Umar and Ali would visit him some time. After the Prophet (sm) went out of human sight Umar and Ali sought out Uways in Qaran an oasis habitation in Nazd and Yemen desert . They conveyed to him the prophet's greeting. According to Uways safety lay in solitude for the heart of the solitary one was free from thoughts of others.[160] Under no circumstances did he wish for anything from men. As long as the devil had captured a man's heart. True isolation was the only means of achieving intimacy with God and those who managed to attain it were then unaffected by human contact. During last part of his life he also went to Kufa.

And a modern scholar says "Muhammad was a sufi on his way to becoming a Prophet.[161]

So the main and important aim of the followers of any religion is to sacrifice oneself with the will of their Lord and forget the existence of oneself except the existence of the Lord God i.e. in general sense one will not do anything except the will of God, for which he will follow the path of God which God has sent through his various Prophet or through a particular Prophet for a particular religion, but in particular sense a man who by his good luck got a very high and unimaginable love for his Lord God, which by the great mercy of God he posses in his heart; will do nothing except the direct order from his Lord, The Great God. Such a lucky and great man always keep eyes towards the sky, the heaven for the necessary advice and pleasure of God and act according to the will of God. Such a lucky person will not want anything from God for his self interest and what he will want is only the pleasure of God. And again greatest among them are those who will not want anything except nearness or the great meeting with God. One such recorded example is a Muslim

---

mathematician, versed in the abstract science. As-Sarraj died in 378 A.H., nearly 100 years before al-Ghazzali.

[156] Al-Luma, p. 129. Junaid was one of the earliest mystics of Islam; he died A.H. 297 (A.C. 910). He is stated to have declared that "the Sufi system of doctrine is firmly bound with the dogmas of the Faith and the Koran" (Ibn Khallikan).

[157] The Indian poet Dabir calls Ali the "Knower of mysteries of God," ramuzdan-i-Khuda.

[158] Biography of the Saints.

[159] 'Attar was born in 545 A.H.(1150 A.C.) and is believed to have been killed by the Mongols in 627 A.A. (1229-30 A.C.).

[160]ibid

[161]D. B. Macdonald, Development of Muslim theology, jurisprudence and constitutional theory, New York, 1903, p. 227

saint, one of the holy women is Rabia Basri; [162] whose prayer (particularly midnight prayer) to God was "O Allah (or God), if I pray for the fear of hell, you give me hell, if I pray for heaven you deprive me from heaven; but if I pray only for you then don't deprive me from you". There are hundred of such example of Islamic Saints who gave everything for becoming nearest to God. One such of holy man is Abu Is Ishak Ibrahim ibn Adham ibn Mansur is spoken of in the Tazkirat-ul-Awlia as the son of a prince of Balkh. His father appears to have been a rich magnate. He abandoned the world, gave all his riches to the poor and lived a life of piety and devotion. He is said to have been a disciple of Abu Hanifa. He died in 161 A. H.

It was normal practice for the Prophets in the language of Prophet Jesus (Peace be upon him) from the Bible which was mentioned in earlier chapter of 'Ishmaelites', which are as follows:

"When the Spirit of truth comes, he will guide you into all the truth; for he will not speak on his own authority, but whatever he hears he will speak, and he will declare to you the things that are to come. He will glorify me..."(16,13-14).

"If you love me, you will keep my commandments. And I will pray the Father, and he will give you another paraclete."(14,15-16)

What does 'Paraclete' mean? The present text of John's Gospel explains its meaning as follows:

"But the paraclete, the Holy Spirit whom the Father will send in my name, he will teach you all things, and bring to your remembrance all that I have said to you"(14,26).
"he will bear witness to me"(15,26)
"it is to your advantage that I go away, for if I do not go away, the Paraclete will not come to you; but if I go I will send him to you. And when he comes, he will convince the world of sin and of righteousness and of judgement..."(16,7-8).

Now for eternal love towards our only Lord, God the great if we want to see through this earthly eyes? We quote from the Bible again:[163]

Ascension of Jesus.

Luke, the only evangelist to provide an undisputed text of the Ascension Episode (24,51): 'he parted from them and was carried up into heaven', The evangelist places the event at the end of the description of the Resurrection and appearance to the eleven Apostles: The details of the Gospel description imply that the Ascension took place on the day of the Resurrection. in the Acts of the Apostles, Luke (whom everybody believes to be their author) describes in chapter 1,3 Jesus's appearance to the Apostles between the Passion and the Ascension in the following terms:

"When the Spirit of truth comes, he will guide you into all the truth; for he will not speak on his own authority, but whatever he hears he will speak, and he will declare to you the things that are to come. He will glorify me..."(16,13-14).

---

[162] **Rabia died in the year 100 A. H. (Ref from page 461 THE MYSTICAL AND IDEALISTIC SPIRIT, SPIRIT OF ISLAM, by SYED AMIR ALI**

[163] **Quran, Bible and Science by Bukhail**

According to the rules of logic therefore, one is brought to see in John's paraclete a human being like Jesus, possessing the faculties of hearing and speech formally implied in John's Greek text. Jesus therefore predicts that God will later send a human being to Earth to take up the role defined by John, i.e. to be a prophet who hears God's word and repeats his message to man. This is the logical interpretation of John's texts arrived at if one attributes to the words their proper meaning.

By Ascension of Jesus we the present day Muslims believe that Jesus (A. S.) was not crucified but he was taken up in the heaven and will come to this world again during Imam Mehedi and they both will preach Islam. Now the fact is Prophet was taken to heaven for a long a period, but the last Prophet of Islam went to the heaven which is called the miraj (Ascension) and talked directly to God and our Prophet (A. S.) told according to his saying (Hadith) that the prayer of the faithful is miraj (ascension); because a faithful Muslims who perform at least obligatory five times prayer everyday and utter the following verse which is a kind of direct conversion to God though theoretically without seeing him.

1: 1 In the name of Allah, Most Gracious, Most Merciful.
1: 2 Praise be to Allah, The Cherisher and Y of the Words;
1: 3 Most Gracious, Most Merciful;
1: 4 Master of the Day of Judgement
1: 5 Thee do we worship, And thine aid we seek,
1: 6 Show us the straight way,
1: 7 The way of those on whom, Thou hast bestowed The Grace, Those
1: 7 whose (portion) Is not wrath, And who go not astray.

Through the above verse which a Muslim utter at least 32 times during each day prayer a Muslim may expect something from God in term of 1:6 a straight path and according to verse 1:7 God has bestowed The Grace.

Following is another quotation from a scholar on Sufism:

Some say: "The Sufis were only named Sufis because of the purity (Safa) of their hearts and the cleanliness of their acts (athar)." Bishr ibn al-Harith said: "The Sufi is he whose heart is sincere(Safa) towards God." Another great Sufi has said: "The sufi is he whose conduct towards God is sincere, and toward whom God's blessing is sincere."
The unveiling of divine gnosis is entirely dependent on inner purity. As the Prophet said: "Mark, in man there is a lump of flesh. If it is kept whole-some the whole body remains in a healthy condition and if it is corrupted, the whole body is corrupted, mark, it is the heart!" (Bukhari)

page 67
The meaning of tajalli, as we have seen is manifestation or revelation and for this 'form' is imperative. The word tajalla appears in the Qur'an in the following verse 183
"And when the Lord revealed (His) Glory (tajalla) to the mountain, He sent it crashing down. And Moses fell down senseless "184
It is clear that this self-revelation pertained to he same Absolute Being that Moses was unable to behold. At another place it appears that God almighty is manifesting Himself before Moses on Mount Sinai through a tree or in the form of light and fire.
"But when he revealed it, he was called from the right side of the valley in the blessed-field, from the tree: O Moses! Lo! I, even I, am Allah, the Lord of the Worlds."
page 3
And that is why Abu Ali al-Rudhbari has defined a Sufi thus:

"One who wears wool over (his) purity, gives his lusts the taste of tyranny, and having overthrown the world, journeys in the pathway of the chosen one"(i.e. the Prophet).

In the light of these historical facts it is now easy to determine the exact meaning o Sufism. If you cast a glance over the various definitions of Sufism given by the themselves you will find not a few necessary attributes ascribed to them.

It is not necessary to try to state them all here. But the gist of them all is beautifully expressed in a definition formulated by Shaykh-al-Islam Zakariyah Ansari, which is follows:

"Sufism teaches how to purify one's self, improve one's morals, and build up one's inner and outer life in order to attain perpetual bliss. Its subject matter is the purification of the soul and its end or aim is the attainment of eternal felicity and blessedness."[164]

The teaching of the Quran which are often quoted in this respect are the following:

Whosoever knoweth himself knoweth God

God was and there was naught beside him

I was a hidden Treasure and I desired to be known

therefore, I created that I might be known.

pg - 35

Love is a passionate longing for an object. The Sufis inherited this principle from Gnosticism. As the life is full of miseries, they recommend its renunciation and return to the original abode i.e. God.

The orthodoxy of Islam does not believe in the homogeneity of man with God and so it rules out possibility of love between the two. According to it love of God means nothing else than obedience to God,. Al-Ghazali makes love of God as the supreme end of man.[165]

Hazrat Ali was so nearer to God that once he rose the setting sun when a Jew did not return his two sons whom he kept with him in exchange of some money as loan he took to donate to an old man to meet the expenses of his daughter's marriage and with the condition that the money must paid in that very day before sun set. But Ali (R. A.) could not arrange money and after sun set with some miracle he got a gold and went to the Jew. On another occasion when the after-noon prayer was delayed he asked the sun to wait for his prayer. So the case was for Hazrat Omar(R. A.). One Friday noon prayer and during offering the sermon he uttered addressing his general to wait on the hill. The Muslims who heard asked him that what he uttered was not mentioned in the Friday noon prayer sermon, in reply Omar told that during the sermon he saw in his palm that the general was coming down of that hill and if he was not halted on the hill the enemy who were following him could come on the hill and the Muslim army could be defeated. After few months when that particular army came back the Muslims in Holy Media asked that particular General who replied that he heard the command of Omar and thus they were save from the defeat as they waited on the top of the hill.

So with all those spiritual power Muslim went on and went on around three continent of Asia, Africa and Europe which of course a world record for any single invasion.

Though the descendent of The Holy Prophet was deprived of political

---

[164] **THE QURANIC SUFISM" BY DR. MIR VALIUDDIN M. A.; Ph. D. (London), Bar-at-law, Formerly Prof and Head of the Department of Philosophy, Osmania University, by MOTILAL BANARSIDASS Delhi; Vanarasi : Patna, pp. 1,67,3.**

[165] **SUFI THOUGHT BY S. R. SHARDA M. A., Ph. D. pp. 11, 35.**

power by the hypocrite Muslim they the power hungry hypocrite could not deprive them the spiritual power the origin of which Allah alone.

So the descendent of the Holy prophet spread around the world time to time. Though during the Ummayat they had to flee from the oppression of the Ummayat and even during the Abbaside period.

In the spiritual power of Muslim divine and saints the greatest, the best and the noblest, is Sultan-ul-Awlia (king of the saints) Syedana Hazrat Ghous-ul-Azam Shaikh Abu Muhammad Abdul Qader Mohiuddin Ji ani (peace be on him), who is the founder of the Qaderia order of Sufis and the ultimate head of every Wali or Sufi (Saint), whatever order he may belong to. He stands at the peak of Wilayet or Sufism(Saintism). Mr. Justice Syed Mahbub Murshed(A barrister from London), an ex chief Justice of East Pakistan (now Bangladesh) High court has mentioned the followings in his book "GULISTAN-E-QADERI":

"The Hazrat was born in Jilan, a place south of the Caspian Sea, in the first day of the holy month of Ramadan in 470 Hejri (1077-1078 A. D.). On the father's side he was a descendant of Syedana Hazrat Imam Hasan and on the mother's side he descended from Syedana Hazrat Imam Hussain, the Holy Martyr of kerbala (now part of Iraq). He was therefore styled 'Al-Hasani Wal-Hussaini (The Hasani and Hussaini)."

"After the completion of his studies the Hazrat performed superhuman spiritual exercises in contemplation of God. In order to observe the Sunnat (Precedent of the Prophet) he accepted Hazrat Hammad as his Pir or spiritual guide. For years he lived on vegetables only. Every year some body would give him a woolen garment for his wear. He used to walk bare-footed even on thorny fields. He dwelt for a long time in the ruins of Madain. For one year he lived simply on vegetables without even water to drink. Another year he neither ate attributes of God who neither eats nor drinks nor sleeps. The are sustained by spiritual nourishment.
For about twenty-five years he traveled alone in the deserts and ruins of Iraq and for forty years together he spent the live-long nights in prayers.
After the Isha prayers (i.e. after the last obligatory prayers in the night) he would stand on one foot and recite the whole of the holy Quran till about the small hours of the morning. For eleven years he stayed in a tower, which on account of his long stay came to be known as Burji-e-Ajami (i. e. tower where an Ajami or non-Arab-lived).
The Hazrat breathed a new life into the decrepit body of Islam. He revived the dying and decadent religion of the Prophet and was therefore given the appellation of 'Mohiuddin' i. e. 'the Reviver of Religion.'
In the year 521 heejra Hazrat Abu Said Mokharrami made over his Madrasha (i. e. college) to the Hazrat. In obedience to a direction given by the Prophet to the Hazrat in a dream, he began to deliver sermons to the public. Among the audience there used to be saints, doctors, religious lawyers, savants, high officials, Khalifa and people of every rank and profession from the richest to the poorest.
At times about seventy thousand persons used to assemble to hear his sermons. It was an instance of the grace of the Hazrat that persons sitting farthest from him could hear him as distinctly as those sitting nearest to him.
the following are a few extracts from the sermons of the Hazrat:

"Correct and perfect your heart, When the heart is perfect all your conditions become perfect"
"You people, be as obedient to God as the good men of the past had been, so that He may be yours to the same extent as He had been theirs. If you desire that God may be yours, then worship Him and be patient with Him and be satisfied with His sanctions."

"Your desire should be for God, the Great and the Majestic, and the things that are with Him."

"If you remain steadfast when calamities come from God. You are a friend of God. Firmness in poverty and calamity, has been made the sign of love of God and His Prophet. "As long as you love God and act for him and not for others and as long as you fear God and not others you have no power to criticize His doings."

"Do not associate with the hypocrites, the liars and the imposter."

"God is with the patient. Be patient with Him and be on your guard so that you may not be negligent."

"O people! be thankful to God for the good things possessed by you and consider them to have come from Him, because God has said. "The good things with you are from God."

"For the sake of God put of the garment of sin with real and not assumed shame."

"As for evil passions conquer them and do not allow them to conquer you."

"O Servant of God, make piety obligatory on yourself."

"You gentlemen, in your seclusion you are in need of such piety which may save you from sins and you also require such contemplation which will remind you of the merciful look of God.

"A true Momin (or Muslim i. e. believer) does not obey his Nafs(baser self), nor Satan, nor avarice."

"You servant of God, unite this world with the next and bring them together, and making your heart quite empty of these, be solely attached to God."

Such were the sermons of Syedana Hazrat Ghous-ul-Azam.

The leading topics are the necessity of purifying on's heart and soul and forming a genuine and true love of God. So splendid are these sermons that even so prejudiced and so biased a writer like] has been constrained to observe "These sermons breath a spirit of charity and philanthropy. "the preacher would like to close the gates of hell and open those of paradise to all mankind."

The Hazrat devoted himself to public education for thirty three years. In 528 Hejri his madrasa (religious school) was extended by acquisition of adjoining premises. Extensive buildings were built thereon. Student from every part of Iraq and from all over the Islamic world began to come to his Madrasha in search of knowledge. Pious, holy and learned men also assembled there to derive benefit from his society and the salutary examples of his life. The Hazrat would feed the Holy and learned men round him as well the strangers and needy persons who came to his Madrasa. Every day in the morning and in the afternoon, he would teach the commentaries of The Holy quran, traditions, principles of law, syntax(grammar) and other subjects.

In the course of his earthly life the Hazrat performed innumerable miracles to guide the erring, to protect the weak and to succor to the needy. Most of these miracles led to the relief of suffering and distress. I shall only quote three instances for the sake of brevity. (1) Once Abu Ghalib Bin Ismail, a merchant of Baghdad came to the Hazrat and said, "O Hazrat, your ancestor the holy Prophet has enjoined that one should accept an invitation and so." The Hazrat replied that he would accept the invitation if it was the will of God. His Holiness remained silent and mediated for a while and then looked up and said. "Yes, I accept your invitation." When the Hazrat reached the house of the merchant he found that great Sufis and the learned and illustrious men of Baghdad had assembled there. After the Hazrat had taken his seat a table -cloth was spread in which various delicious dishes were placed. Two men then brought a big and heavy basket which was placed at the end of the table-cloth.

The merchant requested the Hazrat to take the food spread before him, but he kept silent and neither he ate himself nor asked any one to do so. His holiness then asked Hazrat Ali Bin Hiti and Hazrat Abul Hasan Ali who had accompanied him to the merchant's house, to open the basket. In it was found the merchant's son, a child who was blind, paralytic and leprous from his birth. The Hazrat addressing the child said, "Rise and be all right". And lo; the child got up and began to run. All his deformities and diseases had vanished. There was an uproar in the company that had gathered there and the Hazrat quietly left the place without eating anything

(ii) One night Caliph Al-Mustanjid Billah, coming to the Madrasa of the Hazrat, presented himself before him. The Caliph respectfully sat down with the object of receiving some sage advice from the Hazrat. He brought with him ten bags filled with gold and silver coins and presented them to the Hazrat for favor of his acceptance. But the Hazrat refused to take them. Pressed by the importunate entreaties of the Caliph, the Hazrat took two of the best bags and pressed them with his holy hand. Blood oozed out the bags. The Hazrat then said to the Caliph, "You extorted the money by oppressing the people and have brought it to me for my acceptance. It really represents the blood of the people and I therefore refused it". At this the Caliph was stricken with awe and fainted.

On the 11th day of the holy month of Rabi-us-Sani, Hazrat Syedana Chous-ul-Azam Shaikh Abdul Qader Jilani was translated from this mortal life to the abode of eternal blessedness. On the night of his translation from this world he performed his prayers and heard a voice saying. "Thou peaceful soul return to thy Lord; thou art pleased with Him and he is pleased with thee. Be thou one of my servants and enter my Paradise."" The angel of death came to the Hazrat in the guise of an Arab and gave him a letter which ran thus; "This letter is from the lover to the beloved. Every person and every creature has to meet death". The last words of the Hazrat were; "I solicit the help of God". The Hazrat then recited the name of Allah three times and then the noble soul ascended the throne of God. It was the 11th of Rabbi II, 561 Hejri (1166) A. D.).

GENEALOGY

TABLE I

Sedan Hazard Muhammad (The Holy prophet)
Seed Hazard Fattier Az-zahra =(m) (1) Syedana Hazrat Ali bin Abi Talib

----

(2) Syedana Hazrat Imam Hasan   Syedana Hazrat Imam Husain
(3) Syedana Hazrat Imam Hasan Al-Musanna
(4) Syedana Hazrat Abdullah Mahaz
(5) Syedana Hazrat Musa Jon
(6) Syedana Abdullah Sani
(7) Syedana Hazrat Musa Sani
(8) Syedana Hazrat Da'Ud
(9) Syedana Hazrat Muhammad
(10) Syedana Hazrat Ehyya Zahad
(11) Syedana Hazrat Abdullah Al-Jili
(12) Syedana Hazrat Abi Saleh Musa =(m) Syeda Hazrat Ummal Khair Fatima Sanni (a descendant of Syedana Hazrat Imam Husain)

(13) Syedana Hazrat Ghous-ul-Azam Shaikh Abi Muhammad Abdul Qader Mohi-Uddin Jilani
(14) Syedana Hazrat Abi Bakr Abdur Razzaque Al-Qaderi

(15) Syedana Hazrat Shamsuddin Abi Saleh Nasr Al-Qaderi
(16) Syedana Hazrat Ahmed Al-qaderi
(17) Syedana Hazrat Shahabuddin Al-Qaderi
(18) Syedana Hazrat Badruddin Al-Qaderi

171

(19) Syedana Hazrat Alauddin Al-Qaderi
(20) Syedana Hazrat Qasem-uddin Al-Qaderi
(21) Syedana Hazrat Ahmed As-Sani Al-Qaderi
(22) Syedana Hazrat Sharfuddin Al-Qaderi
(23) Syedana Hazrat Ebrahim Al-Qaderi
(24) Syedana Hazrat Abdul Jalil Al-Qaderi
(25) Syedana Hazrat Ahmed As Sa'les Al-Qaderi
(26) Syedana Hazrat Hedayt -Ullah Al-qaderi
(27) Syedana Hazrat Mashuq-Ullah Al-Qaderi
(28) Syedana Hazrat Abdul Qader Shah Abdullah Al-Qaderi

(29) Syedana Hazrat Zaker Ali Al-Qaderi Syedana Hazrat Raushan Ali Al-Qaderi
    (Nephew)   (Son)
      | |
(30) Syedana Hazrat Tufail Ali Al-Qaderi
(31) Syedana Hazrat Meher Ali Al-Qaderi
(32) Syedana Hazrat Ali Abdul Qader Shamsul Qaderi Murshed Ali Al-Qaderi
(33) Syedana Hazrat Er'shad Ali Al-Qaderi
(34) Syedana Hazrat Rushaid Ali Al-Qaderi

TABLE II

A genealogical table showing the descendent of Syedana Hazrat Ghous-Ul-Azam (The saint of saints from the holy Prophet on the maternal side.

Syedana Hazrat Muhammad (The Holy prophet)
Syeda Hazrat Fatima Az-zahra =(m) (1) Syedana Hazrat Ali bin Abi Talib
     |
----
(2) Syedana Hazrat Imam Husain
(3) Syedana Hazrat Imam Ali Zain-Ul-Abedin
(4) Syedana Hazrat Imam Muhammad Al-Baqer
(5) Syedana Hazrat Imam Ja'afer As-Sadeque
(6) Syedana Hazrat Imam Musa Al-Kazem
(7) Syedana Hazrat Imam Ali-Ar-Raza
(8) Syedana Hazrat Imam Abi Alauddin Muhammad Al-Jau'wad   (9)
Syedana Hazrat Kamaluddin E'sa
(10) Syedana Hazrat Abul Ata Abdullah
(11) Syedana Hazrat Mahmood
(12) Syedana Hazrat Jamaluddin
(13) Syedana Hazrat Abdullah Sowm'aye
(14) Syeda Hazrat Ummal Khair Fatima Sanni=Syedana Hazrat Abi Saleh Musa
(15) Syedana Hazrat Ghous-ul-Azam Shaikh Abi Muhammad Abdul Qader Mohi-Uddin Jilani

Out of 12 Great Imam (leader) upto sl. no. 7 The shite sect Islam accept them as great Imam who are also highly respectable to Sunnis without any doubt for their purity, nobleness and greatness.

Another reference is given below:

172

FUTUH AL-GHAIB
[THE REVELATION OF THE UNSEEN]
BY
HAZRAT SHAIKH MUHYUDDIN ABDUL QADIR GILANI

Translated by
Maulvi AFTAB-UD-DIN AHMAD
Formerly Imam, The Mosque, Waking Associate   Editor, Islamic
Review published by KITAB BHAVAN NEW DELHI-110002

Introduction-pg-xix-xx
A word more to the non-Muslim readers of this book. It has been suggested by outsiders that Sufism is a borrowed plume and not of the soul of Islam. This is based on cross ignorance. All the affairs that led to the formation of the Islamic society and civilisation were based on the verbal revelation coming to the Holy Prophet in moments of spiritual trance and minor revelation coming to his companions every now and then are indisputable facts of history. Exclusive devotional practices of a whole band of disciples called Ashab Suffa are also among the outstanding facts of the Prophet's time. To say in face of this that Islam was a dogmatic and ritualistic faith in its origin and that *tasawwuf* is the soul of Islam and political Islam its physical manifestation. Of course, much of what posses for Sufism is not. Ideas and practices foreign to Islam and even antagonistic to it have undoubtedly entered the body politic even of this living faith, particularly for the last few centuries, because of the general decadence in the Islamic socio-intellectual order. But disease does not prove the non-existence of health altogether nor decay the non-existence of body.

PARENTAGE

PG -1 Sayyid Abu Muhammad Abdul Qadir was born in Naif in the District of Gilan in Persia(Iran) in the month of Ramadan in the year 470 A.H. corresponding to 1077 of the Christian era or thereabout. His father's name was Abu Salih, a God-fearing man and a direct descendant of Hazrat Imam Hasan, the eldest son of Ali, the Holy Prophet's first cousin, and of Fatima his beloved daughter. His mother was the daughter of a saintly person- Abdullah Sawmai who was a direct descendant of Imam Husain, the younger son of Ali and Fatima. Thus Sayyid Abdul Qadir was both Hasani and Hussaini.

EARLY LIFE

From his early childhood he was quiet and sober, given to contemplation and used to what, for want of a better expression, is called `mystic experiences' in English. When he was about eighteen years old his thirst for knowledge and eagerness for the company of holy men took him to the distant city of Baghdad, at that time the center of learning of all kinds. Later in life he was given the title of `Ghauth al-Azam,' i.e. the greatest of all saints called Ghauth.
In the Sufi terminology a Ghauth is next to a Nabi in spiritual rank and in the dispensation of Divine mercy and favor to mankind. A great authority of our times, however, has ranked him with the *Siddiqun*, as the Qur'an would call such people. During his journey to Baghdad for his truthfulness of eighty goldpieces sewn into his garment by his widowed mother, leader of a gang of robbers burst into tears, fell down on his feet and repented for all past sins. It is reported that he was his first disciple.
    Truthful and charitable to the extreme, he had to endure great hardship during the period of his study at Baghdad. By dint of his natural talents and devotion he became very soon the master of all the different subjects that could be learnt by a scholar in those days. He prove to be the greatest jurist of his time. But his deeper spiritual yearnings were restless to

manifest themselves. Even in his adolescence when he was engaged in his studies he was fond of mujahida or ascetic life to rise above his animal self.[166]

The descendant of Peeran Peer Hazrat Ghous-ul-Azam Syedana O Maulana Mohiuddin Shaikh Abdul Kader Jilani al-Baghdadi Al-Hasani-w'l-Hasani i.e. the Saint of Saints went to various parts of the world including Africa and Asia and enlightened Islam upto present day. Some instance is as follows:

Away, on the borders of Bengal and Orissa, in the town of Midnapore, famous in the legends of old, was born on Friday, the twenty-seventh of Ramadan, A. H. 1268, July the sixteenth, A. D. 1852, a Mighty Child of a Mighty Father. He came of the Illustrious Family of the Greatest Saint of the World, Hazrat Sultan-ul-Aulia, Peeran Peer Hazrat Ghous-ul-Azam Syedana O Maulana Mohiuddin Shaikh Abdul Kader Jilani al-Baghdadi Al-Hasani-w'l-Hasani and His Birth was welcomed by a flood of celestial light. It was the Shabe-Kadr. Fifteenth in descent from Hazrat Ghous-ul-Azam and twenty seventh from Hazrat Resalat Panahi (Peace be on Their Souls), Hazrat Syed Shah Abdul Kader Abdulla Al-Jili Al-Baghdadi Al-Hasani-w'l-Hosaini (Peace be on his Soul) was the first of this most Noble and Sacred Family to set His foot in India. This was in the year 1111 A. H. nd He moved on to Delhi which was yet the capital of India but from there, shortly after, returned to His native place, Baghdad, leaving behind His sons, Hazrat Syed Shah Zaker Ali Al-Kaderi Al-Jili Al-Baghdadi Al-Hasani-w'l-Hossaini and Hazrat Syed Shah Raushan Ali Al-Kaderi Al-Jili Al-Baghdadi Al-Hasani-w'l-Hossaini and a number of disciples of whom the famous Moulana Abdul Haque, Mohaddas-e-Delhi was one. Hazrat Syed Shah Zaker Ali Al-Kaderi came to Bengal and Hazrat Syed Shah Raushan Ali Al-Kaderi wended His way to Tirhoot. Thirty miles away from Murshidabad, in Mangalkote, Hazrat Syed Shah Zaker Ali Al-Kaderi settled at last. It was then a flourishing town; a seat of greatlearning; a centre of commerce and industry; a residence of Amirs and Omaras; the head-querters of the Quazi-ul-Quzzat; and a resting place o notable saints where pilgrims flocked from far and near. And 32 generation and Sajjadanashin i.e. successor of Peeran Peer Hazrat Ghous-ul-Azam (Saint of Saints) Syedana O Maulana Mohiuddin Shaikh Abdul Kader Jilani al-Baghdadi Al-Hasani-w'l-Hasani as mentioned in Table I, Hazrat Ali Abdul Kader Shamsul Kader Hazrat Syed Shah Murshed Ali Al-Kaderi Al_Jili Al-Baghdadi Al-Hasani-w'l-Hosaini sat on the Sajjada (A prayer mat or carpet). Like His Ancestor Hazrat Ghouspak (The Saint of Saints or the greatest Saint at Baghdad), He could, at one and the same time, be seen at many a place. Few of his miracles are as follows:

Moulvi Zeaur Rahman, Zamindar, Shahkulipur, Birbhum (West Bengal, India), says, "Once I wanted to come to Huzur and wrote to Him for permission to do so. But in reply, Huzur wrote to me a strange letter `You should never think of coming to me now', said He 'You have still to live long. Had your last days been approaching I would, surely, have told you of it. For, a Peer (Spiritual guide), is but an imperfect Peer, who doesn't know when His murid will die'. On the receipt of this mysterious and unexpected letter I was exceedingly surprised. I couldn't make out what it meant. But all the same, I gave up the idea of going to Calcutta. A few days after, I fell so ill that even my attendant physician gave me up for lost. I was down for over a month and, at last, when I recovered I could then realise what the letter of Huzur did really mean."

166

FUTUH AL-GHAIB, [THE REVELATION OF THE UNSEEN], BY HAZRAT SHAIKH MUHYUDDIN ABDUL QADIR GILANI, Translated by Maulvi AFTAB-UD-DIN AHMAD, Formerly Imam, The Mosque, Waking Associate Editor, Islamic Review published by KITAB BHAVAN, NEW DELHI-110002, Introduction,pp-xix-xx, 1.

Moulana Syed Shah Abdul Hafiz Saheb of Margram, Subdivision Ramporehat, District Birbhum (India), says, "When young, I was very fond of riding and my father purchased for me a horse which, had a few months before, been bought at Chatar for rupees two hundred and fifty. But on the death of my father, which took place soon after, my brothers sold the horse and divided the money among themselves. I appealed to Huzur and He graciously observed 'Don't you fret, you would get a better one.'

"Time rolled on. I learnt, one day, that Mr. J. D. Sifton, (later, Sir James David Sifton, K.C.I.E. Governor of Bihar and Orissa) who was then our Subdivisional Officer, was under orders of transfer and going to Hazaribagh as an Assistant Settlement Officer. I went to him to pay my respects and bid him farewell. We had a long talk and among other things he asked me if I would keep his horse. `But I have no money Sir', said I, `But why bother about my money at all,' said he, `It's a present to you' and so saying he at once sent for his syce and asked him to take the horse to my house. "The horse was nice and valuable and had been purchased by him for rupees six hundred from a notable firm in Calcutta and the gift of it to me was beyond my dream. But Huzur's prophecy was fulfilled and I bowed down my head in gratitude to Him."

The Late Mr. Khondkar Yusuf Ali, Barrister-at-law, related, "Once, my mother-in-law, a European lady, who had been living with me, left my house without any notice and took away with her my son who was then child. It was late at night when I came to know of it and so upset was I for my son that I could hardly sleep.

"The next morning, Huzur sent for me and as I presented myself before Him he cheered me up, saying (although I had spoken to none about the incident) `Don't you worry about your son Counsili Saheb, tomorrow will he be back with his granny.' And to our great delight they did come back the next morning".

Two very close relations of Mrs. Khondkar, a highly educated European lady, died while she was in England but so intense was her grief that she had no peace and yearned to see them even after their death. For it, she went to many religious heads in Europe and in India and also to reputed theosophists but to no effect. At last, her husband after he had become a disciple of Huzur, asked her to apply to Huzur for it, but as she had no faith in Islam she did it most reluctantly in writing. On receipt of her letter, through Mr. Khondkar, Huzur enquired id she would go through some prayer. `By no means', she sent a reply. For, no prayer can do it but the strong spiritual power of some mighty saint.'

After that, she took Mr. Khondkar to Beneras where she went to the famous Sannyyasi, Vaskarananda Swami and told him of her mission.

"But Maiji", said he "It was possible only during Satyug, but this is Kaliyug and none but my Guruji-the Peer Saheb of your Saheb- can do it now. Go back to Him in Calcutta."

She came back to Calcutta with Mr. Khondkar and solicited Huzur to fulfil her object. Huzur gave her a very short and ordinary prayer to say. But to her great delight, **within only a very few days, there suddenly appeared before her those very dead persons whom she wanted to see. "It is on these very chairs, in front of me," she told Maulana Abu Taher Saheb, "That they sat and talked to me as if they were alive-. A thousand thanks to His Holiness- Huzur for this. Give Him my innumerable salams. But I must still say that it's not the prayer He gave me but His mighty Spiritual Power that has wrought this miracle."**

Thenceforth, she used to be absorbed in it, day and night, sitting and talking with them. But that was but the beginning of her spiritual life.

... Huzur's Vesal (Union with God; Death) took place at His residence in Calcutta, at eleven minutes past two on the morning of Sunday, the twenty-seventh of Shawal, A. H. 1318, February the seventh, A. D. 1901. A few days ahead of it, He had asked Moulvi Syed Shah Abdul Malik Saheb, Deputy Magistrate and Deputy Collector, who was then posted at Balasore, to come on the Sunday following, direct to Midnapore to attend His funeral there where His body would be taken. ...

Multitudes of men flock to His Holy Shrine and invoke His help. Difficulties are overcome, calamities removed, diseases cured and wishes granted- all with great speed.

"Why have you come so far"? came the voice of Hazrat Sultan-ul-Aulia Ghous-ul-Azam Hazrat Peeran Peer Syedana O Maulana Mohiuddin Shaikh Abdul Kader Jilani A-Baghdadi Al-Hasani-w'l-Hosaini, when Maulana (A learned man; a term of respect) Abu Taher Saheb, Professor, St. Xavier's College, Calcutta, presented himself at Baghdad, "Very close to you, in the tomb of your Peer (Spiritual guide) it is I who lie, why have you come so far?"[167]

But there are instances that some of them went by the direct command from the Holy Prophet. One such instance is Khaja Moinuddin Chishty (R. A., God's mercy with him); who is call the Sultanul Hind (king of Hind or India). It is said that while he was visiting The holy mazar(Tomb) of the Prophet Muhammad (peace be upon him); The Prophet asked him to go to India; but he answered that he does not know where is India and the prophet showed him the path to India. So he proceeded to India and came to Ajmir where the then king was Prithiraj. The short story is that the King around Ajmir tried to prevent him from staying there but by spiritual power all the means of that king failed and Khaja Mohiuddin was able to defeat him by his great spiritual power and spread Islam throughout India, Even all the leading Indian leaders used to visit the holy shrine and seek his blessing. He even helped the then Muslim rulers with his spiritual power.

We are quoting a Indian Book; "A History of Sufism in India" by Saiyid Athar Abbas Rizvi M. A. Ph. D. D. Litt., F. A. H. (Australia), by Munshiram Manoharlal publishers Pvt. Ltd., New Delhi, volume one, Chapter two, The Chishtis, pg 114.

The Chisti order of sufis is essentially an Indian one, Other branches emanating from the town of Chisht in modern Afghanistan did not survive for long in the Perso-Islamic world. Chist, written as Khisht in the Persian geographical work, the Hudud al-'Alam, which was compiled in 372/982, is now a small village known as Khwaja Chisht on the river Hari Rud, some hundred kilometers east of Herat.[168]

Reference from pg - 116 of the above book are as follows:

Khwaja Mu'inu'd-Din

Both medieval and modern scholars have showered copious praise on Khwaja Muinuddin Chishti, but no reliable information regarding his early life, before he settled in Ajmir, remains. The only information recorded is the name of the area where he was born, the name of his teacher, and the fact that he had traveled widely. Strangely enough, the voluminous book, Khairul-Majalis, does not mention Khwaja Mu'inuddin in any connection, and the Fawa'idu'l-Fuad refers to him merely in passing.

The earliest works which relate anecdes of the early life of Khwaja Muinuddin Chishti and his encounters with the court of Prithviraj at Ajmir are the apocryphal malfuzats. These tend to indicate that within about a hundred and fifty years of his death, the Khwaja had become a legend in India. The Siyaru'l-Auliya', drawing on this literary source and also on family anecdotes, gives the following account of the Khwaja.

Khwaja Muinuddin Sijzi was the embodiment of Sufi virtues and famous for his outstanding spiritual achievements, which included the performance of miracles. He was the Khalifa

---

[167] **MY HUZUR BY ABDUL GAFFAR, Published in Calcutta in 1930s PP 1,3,16,47,67-68,73,126-130.**

[168]**V. Minorsky, tr., Hudud al'Alam, London, 1937, p. 343**

of Khwaja 'Usman Harwani an eminent Chishti sufi who lived in Nishapur. Khwaja Muinuddin related that after he dad entered the service of Khwaja Usman Harwani and been enrolled as his disciple, he then served his master for twenty years without a moment's rest. Finding him steadfast both in service and the practice of spiritual exercises, The Khwaja passed on to his disciple divine blessings which he himself had acquired.

The Sultanu'l Masha'ikh (Shaikh Nizamud'd-Din Auliya') believed that when Khwaja Mu' Din reached Ajmer, India was ruled by Pithaura Ra'i (Prithviraj) and his capital was Ajmer. Pithaura and his high officials resented the Shaikh's presence in their city, but the latter's eminence and his apparent power to perform miracles, prompted them to refrain from taking action against him. A disciple of the Khwaja's was in the service of Pithaura Ra'i. After the disciple began to receive hostile treatment from the Ra'i, the Khwaja sent a message to Pithaura in favor of the Muslim. Pithaura refused to accept the recommendation, thus indicating his resentment of the Khwaja's alleged claims to understand the secrets of the Unseen. When Khwaja Mu Din (the spiritual king of Islam) heard of this reply he prophesied: We have seized Pithaura alive and handed him over to the army of Islam." About the same time, Sultan Muizzud-Din Muhammad's army arrived from Ghazna, attacked the forces of Pithaura and defeated them. Pithaura was taken alive, and thus the Khwaja's prophesy was Fulfilled.[169]

The Akhbari'l-Akhyar also contains the same account,[170] and a large number of medieval and modern scholars confirm the validity of the story and recount fantastic miracles performed by the Khwaja at Ajmer.[171]

---

[169] Amir Khwurd, Siyaru'l-Auliya, Delhi, 1885, pp 45-7.

[170] AA, pp. 22-23

[171]Some of the anecdotes from the Jawahir-i Faridi written in 1623 are as follows: Twelve years before the Khwaja's arrival at Ajmer, Pithaura's mother, an expert in astronomy and magic, had prophesied the Khwaja's arrival. She drew pictures of the Khwaja and the Ra'i distributed them to his officers to prevent his entry into the kingdom. Every foreigner's face was compared with that picture. When the Khwaja reached Delhi from Lahore, the people of Delhi would run away at the sight of Muslims The Khwaja stayed in Delhi with his forty disciples only because of his spiritual power. The Fawaidu'l-Fu'ad say that seven hundred people, besides Hamidu'd-Din Dihlawi, embraced Islam, although this story is not recorded in the Fawaidu'l-Fuad. From there the Khwaja went to Ajmer. At Samana, Pithaura's officials recognized the Khwaja from his picture and, requested that he stay in the palace. But the Prophet Muhammad had warned the Khwaja, during meditation, against the treachery of officials so he left for Ajmer. Reaching there he decided to sit under a tree, but the camel keepers ordered him away as the area belonged to the Ra'i. The Khwaja and his followers moved to a place near the Anasagar Lake. His servants killed a cow and cooked kebabs for him. Some members of the Khwaja's party went to Anasagar and the others to Pansela Lake for ablutions. There were one thousand temples on the two lakes. The Brahmans stopped the ablutions and the party complained to the Khwaja. He sent his servant to bring water for his awer. As soon as the ewer touched the Pansela Lake, all the lakes, tanks and wells around became dry. The Khwaja went to the Anasagar Lake temple and asked the name of the idol. He was told it was called Sawi Deva. The Khwaja asked whether the idol had talked to them. On receiving a negative reply he made the idol recite kalima and converted it into a human being, naming it Sa'di. This caused a sensation in the town. Prithviraj ordered his prime minister Jaipal who was also a magician, to avert the evil influence of the Khwaja. Jaipal proceeded to fight the Khwaja with 700 magical dragons, 1,500 magical discs and 700 disciples. The Khwaja drew a circle bringing his party within it under his protection, and succeeded in killing all the dragons and disciples. Pithaura

Even in modern India million of Muslims and non-Muslim use to visit the Holy shrine of Hazrat Khaja Mainuddin Chisti in Ajmir, in the State of Rajashtan. During annual Urs of the great Saint Lacks of people irrespective of their religion visit the Holy shrine which is telecasted by Dur Darsan (Indian Television) of India, in one such accession a commentator was telling that so many kings went in (Delhi) India and gone which many do not remember, but this king of the kings still to day is the same as he was in first time (in his life time). This year one visitor (a Hindu) was telling trough Dur Darshan interview that he was visiting another shrine in south India to seek blessing for some skin disease of his child, when some one who was coming to Ajmir and he accompanied him to Ajmir after which his child was cured so he decided to visit Azmir in each so long he will be alive. There were many such interviews through Door Darsan.

Many Caliphs or their sons were also Saint like, one important such Caliph was Hadrath Omar Ibn Abdul-Aziz (R. A.) though he was a member of the Ummayed.

Caliph Harunur Rashid had a son who was born before Harunur Rashid became a Abbaside Caliph. **That particular son of Abbaside Caliph Harunur Rashid was a learned one in various subject besides The Holy Quran. When Harunur Rashid became Caliph he left his parent and went to Basra. Before his departure his mother gave him a ring with one valuable stone with the advice of his Caliph father and he also took one Holy Quran. But that son did not use that ring or valuable stone and instead he worked as daily labor to maintain his minimum daily expenditure. Even he used to take only one dirham and one danek (one sixth of a dinar) not more or less. It also happened with one saint like man named Hazrat Abu Amar (R. A.), whose wall was repaired by him.** And wonderful thing is that on the first day work Hazrat Amar saw that young son of Caliph Harunur Rashid did the work of 10 men and in exchange he wanted to pay him two

---

and Jaipal begged the Khwaja's forgiveness. The Khwaja's prayers restored water to the lakes, tanks and wells. A large number of people accepted Islam. Jaipal decided to compete with the Khwaja in the performance of miracles. Sitting on his deer skin he flew to the heavens. The Khwaja ordered his slippers to bring Jaipal back to earth, which they did. On Jaipal's request to show him some miracles, the Khwaja's spirit flew to the highest heaven, where Jaipal also joined him. Getting nearer to the divine presence, on the Khwaja's orders Jaipal accepted Islam in order to gain the full benefit of that spiritual bliss. When they returned the Khwaja and his party stayed in the town. Pithaura refused to accept Islam and the Khwaja prophesied he would be handed over to the Islamic army, 'Ali Asghar Chishti, Jawahir-i Faridi, Lahore, 1884, pp. 155-60. Abu'l-Fazl relates: Before Sultan Mu'izz'ud-Din Sam came from Ghazni to India, his pir permitted him to leave for India. He settled at Ajmer, where Ra'i Pithaura, the ruler of India, resided'. Akbar Nama, II, Calcutta, 1879, p. 154. In the A'in-i-Akbari he writes:'In the same year that Mu'izzu'd-Din Sam seized Delhi, he(the Khwaja) arrived at that city and, in order to lead a life of seclusion, he withdrew to Ajmer.' A'in,III,p.168. Both latter accounts make the Khwaja's encounter with Prithviraj an impossibility. See also Gulshan-i Ibrahimi, Lucknow, and, maqala, XII,o.377. Muhammad Sadiq Dihlawi says that in the year in which Sultan Mu'izzu'd-Din defeated Raja Pithaura and seized Delhi the Khwaja reached Lahore from Ghazni and from there left for the capital. Kalimatu's-Sadiqin, Mashhad MS., 7879,p.23. So Firishta's account that the Khwaja reached Ajmer after its conquest concurs with Abul-Fazl's. (Khwaja received Khirqa from Shaikh Usman at the age fifty two.) See "A History of Sufism in India" by Saiyid Athar Abbas Rizvi M. A. Ph. D. D. Litt., F. A. H. (Australia), by Munshiram Manoharlal publishers Pvt. Ltd., New Delhi, volume one, Chapter two, The Chishtis, pp. 114, 116.

Dirham but he refused to accept more than promise wage. Next day Hazrat Amar (R. A.) went to search that young, but could not find anywhere and at last he knew from one person that the young only works on Saturday in each week and remaining day of the week he can not be traced in that area. Hazrat Amar wanted to wait another week so that the work could by that young. In next week he was found to recite The Holy Quran in the same place where he was first found. He asked the young for his work and the young gave him two condition for the work as before. When he started the work Hazrat Amar watch the work of the young and he saw the young was keeping the soil on the wall and the Brick automatically going up on the soil. Hazrat Amar became astonish seeing this miracle. With the help of Godly help the work was going with full speed and Hazrat Amar believed that the young boy must be pure Godly one. After the job was finished he gave three Dirham but he kept one Dirham and one Danek and returned the remaining money. **Hazrat Amar waited for another week but could no find him and after thorough search the young was traced in jungle and one man took him there in exchange of some money, he saw the young seek, the young was resting on the soil and his head was on a brick, Hazrat Amar took his head on his person but he took his head away and recited a Arabic poem his meaning is as follows:**

Friend, don't be deceived by the earth
The life of this earth coming to end quickly
When you will go to any graveyard with a dead body for last recital
Then think once also that
One day my dead body also will be taken for such last recital.

Then the young told Hazrat Amar that after his death his old cloth will be used as his Coffin. Hadrath Amar answered that he wants to use new cloth for his Coffin. The young replied that the living people deserve for the new cloth. The first Truthful Caliph Hazrat Abu Bakr (R. A.) also gave the same answer. And above new or old all Coffin will be lost and only good thing one did will remain with him. After few moment the young also told him that the pot and one cloth which he was using should be paid to him who will make his grave. Then the young gave him one Helly Quran and one ring and requested him to give those two items to Caliph Harunur Rashid and to tell Harunur Rashid that one foreign boy asked me to give you this thing and that boy asked you (the Caliph) not to die as a attractive one towards this world and he died at the same time.

The following comment of some western scholar is enough to understand about Islamic spiritual power.

In Ritual and Belief in Morocco, Edward Westermarck asserted that the terms baraka and **wali** may be conveniently translated as **blessing** and **saint.** In offering that particular translation, Westermarck has almost every Islamic scholar and sociologist in agreement with him, from Ignaz Goldziher to Ernest Gellner. Indeed, these translations seem to be so obvious that Westermarck felt able to dismiss the problem of conceptual comparison by stating that 'sociologists may more profitably occupy their time than by continuously quarrelling about the meaning of terms_ . The terms **saint** and **marabout** (under which I shall include **wali, Sufi, agurram and sheikh)** are mirror-image terms precisely because Islam and Christianity are, in crucial respects, opposed forms of religion. Thus, all the criteria which define saintship are reversed in the definition of **marabout.** This conceptual discussion will not only serve to bring out many interesting institutional features of Islam, but also help to remind us that the problem of adequate translation is often the most difficult task facing a sociologist. ... A systematic comparison of Christian saintship and Islamic maraboutism would have to take each of the Islamic terms (wali, Sufi, dervish, etc.) and contrast them with the centralized institution of saintship. ... In principle, as we have seen, Christian saints are orthodox. It is possible, however, to argue that the saints are potentially herodox but become co-opted by the church through the process of canonization...... In Islam, thse crucial connections between centralized control of saint labels and orthodoxy seem to be missing. The orthodox core of Islam is to be found in Koranic monotheism, supplemented by the Holy Law. It is sometimes argued, as a qualification, that Islam is 'orthoprax' not orthodox. W. Cantwell Smith, for example, pointed out that in no Islamic language is there a word.

EDITOR'S NOTE on The Mystics of Islam by *REYNOLD A. NICHOLSON,* Published by ROUTLEDGE AND KEGAN PAUL, LONDON,BOSTON AND HENLEY, Printed in Great Britain by Lawe & Brydone Printers Ltd., Thetford, Norfolk

If Judaism, Christianity and Islam have no little in common in spite of their deep dogmatic differences, *the spiritual content of that common element can best be appreciated in Jewish, Christian and Isiamic mysticism, which bears equal testimony to that ever-deepening experience of the soul when the spiritual worshipper, whether he be follower of Moses (A.S.) or Jesus* (A.S.) or Mohammed (S.A.W.), turns whole-heartedly to God. As the Quest Series has already supplied for the first time those interested in such matters with a simple general introduction TO Jewish mysticism, so it now provides an easy approach to the study of Islamic mysticism on which in English there exists no separate introduction. But not only have we in the following pages all that the general reader requires to be told at first about Sufism; we have also a large amount of material that will be new even to professional Orientalists. Dr. Nicholson sets before us the *results of twenty years' unremitting labor, and that, too, with remarkable simplicity and clarity for such a subject; at the same time he lets the mystics mostly speak for themselves and mainly in his own fine versions from the original Arabic and Persian.*[172]

So we should take some lesson from Muslim scholar and non-Muslim Author like Nicholson as a Muslim and non-Muslim that which is the path of truth and God-fearing? Because as a Muslim how much time each of us have given in my life to sacrifice myself in **fana fi'l-Haqq or a `path' (tariqat) to the goal of union with Reality i.e. with Allah or God.**
   God, who is described in the Koran as "the Light of the heavens and the earth," cannot be seen by the inward sight of the `heart.' In the next chapter we shall return to this spiritual organ, but I am not going to enter into the intricacies of Sufi psychology any further than is necessary. The `vision of the heart' (ru'yat al-qalb) is defined as "the heart's beholding by the light of certainty that which is hidden in the unseen world." This is what `Ali (R. A.) meant when he was asked, ~Do you see God?" and replied: ~How should we worship One whom we do not see?" The light of intuitive certainty (yaqin) by which the heart sees God is a beam of God's own light cast therein by Himself; else no vision of Him were possible.
   ~Tis the sun's self that lets the sun be seen."
 According to a mystical interpretation of the famous passage in the Koran where the light of Allah is compared **to a candle burning in a lantern of transparent glass, which is placed in a niche in the wall, the niche is the true believer's heart; therefore his speech is light and his woks are light and he moves in light. ~He who discourses of eternity," said Bayazid, ~ must have within him the lamp of eternity."**

---

[172] **EDITOR'S NOTE on The Mystics of Islam by *REYNOLD A. NICHOLSON,* Published by ROUTLEDGE AND KEGAN PAUL, LONDON,BOSTON AND HENLEY, Printed in Great Britain by Lawe & Brydone Printers Ltd., Thetford, Norfolk p. 28.**

The light which gleams in the heart of the illuminated mystic endows him with a supernatural power of discernment (firasat). Although the Sufis, like all other Moslems, acknowledge Mohammad (S.A.W) to be the last of the prophets (as, from a different point of view, he is the Logos or first of created beings), they really claim to possess a minor form of inspiration. When Nuri was questioned concerning the origin of mystical *firasat*, he answered by quoting the Koranic verse in which God says that He breathed His spirit into Adam; but the more orthodox Sufis, who strenuously combat the doctrine that the human spirit is uncreated and eternal, affirm that *firasat* is the result of knowledge and insight, metaphorically called `light' or `inspiration,' which God creates and bestows upon His favorites. The Tradition, "Beware of the discernment of the true believer, for he sees by the light of Allah," is exemplified in such anecdotes as these:

Abu Abdallah al-Razi said:

"Ibn al-Anbari presented me with a woolen frock, and seeing on the head of Shibli a bonnet that would just match it, a bonnet that would just match it, I conceived the wish that they were both mine. When Shibli rose to depart, he looked at me, as he was in the habit of doing when he desired me to follow him So I foloowed him to his house, and when we had gone in, he bade me put off the frock and took it from me and folded it and threw his bonnet on the top. Then he called for a fire and burnt both frock and bonnet."[173]

Let us return for a moment to The Koran, that infallible touchstone be which every Mohammedan theory and practice must be proved. Are any germs of mysticism to be found there? The Koran, as I have said, starts with the notion of Allah, the One, Eternal, and Almighty God, far above human feelings and aspirations-the Lord of His slaves, **not the Father of His children; a judge meting out stern justice to sinners, and extending His mercy only to those who avert His wrath by repentance, humility, and unceasing works of devotion; a God of fear rather than of love. This is one side, and certainly the most prominent side, of Mohammad's (S. A. W.) teaching; but while he set an impassable gulf between the world and Allah, his deeper instinct craved a direct revelation from God to the soul. There are no contradictions in the logic of feeling. Mohammad, who had in him something of the mystic, felt God both as far and near, both as transcendent and immanent. In the latter aspect, Allah is the light of the heavens and the earth, a Being who works in the world and in the soul of man. "We (God) are nearer to him than his own neck-vein" (50-16); ~And in the earth are signs to those of real faith, and in yourselves. What! do ye not see?" (51-20-21).**

THE PATH According to the high mystical theory, repentance is purely an act of divine grace, coming from God to man, not from man to God. Some one said to Rabia:

~I have committed many sins; if I turn in penitence towards God, will He turn in mercy towards me?" ~Nay," she replied, ~but f He shall turn towards thee, thou wilt turn towards Him."

The Sufi teachers gradually built up a system of asceticism and moral culture which is founded on the fact that there is in man an element of evil-the lower or appetitive soul. This evil self, the seat of passion and lust, is called nafs; it may be considered broadly equivalent to `the flesh,' and with its allies, the world and the devil, it constitutes the great obstacle to the attainment of union with God. The Prophet said: ~Thy worst enemy is thy nafs, which is between thy two sides." I do not intend to discuss the various opinions as to its nature, but the proof of its materiality is too curious to be omitted. Mohammad ibn `Ulyan, an eminent Sufi, relates that on day something like a young fox came forth from his throat, and God caused him to know that it was his nafs. He trod on it, but it grew bigger at every kick that he gave it. He said:

---

[173] **The Mystics of Islam by *REYNOLD A. NICHOLSON,* Published by ROUTLEDGE AND KEGAN PAUL, LONDON,BOSTON AND HENLEY, Printed in Great Britain by Lawe & Brydone Printers Ltd., Thetford, Norfolk pp. 50-52, under the chapter'ILLUMINATION AND ECSTASY'.**

~Other things are destroye by pain and blows: why dost thou increase?"

~Because I was created perverse," it replied; ~what is pain to other things is pleasure to me, and their pleasure is my plan."

The nafs of Hallaj was seen running behind him in the shape of a dog; and other cases are recorded in which it appeared as a snake or a mouse.

Mortification of the nafs is the chief work of devotion, and leads, directly or indirectly, to the contemplative life. All the Sheykhs are agreed that no disciple who neglects this duty will ever learn the rudiments of Sufism. The principle of mortification is that the nafs should be weaned from those things to which it is accustomed, that it should be encouraged to resist its passions, that its pride should be broken, and that it should be brought through suffering and tribulation to recognize the vileness of its original nature and the impurity of its actions. Concerning the outward methods of mortification, such as fasting, silence, and solitude, a great deal might be written, but we must now pass on to the higher ethical discipline which completes the Path.

The Mohammedan saint is commonly known as *wali* (plural, *awliya*). This word is used in various senses derived from its root-meaning of `nearness'; e.g. next of kin, patron, protector, friend.' It is applied in the Koran to God as the protector of the Faithful, to angels or idols who are supposed to protect their worshippers, and to men who are regarded as being specially under divine protection. Mohammad twits the Jews with professing to be *proteges* of God (*awliya lillah*). Notwithstanding its somewhat equivocal associations, the term was taken over by the Sufis and became the ordinary designation of persons whose holiness brings them near to God, and who receive from Him, as tokens of His peculiar favor, miraculous gifts (*karamat, xapiouta*); they are His friends, on whom ``no fear shall come and they shall not grieve";[174] any injury done to them as an act of hostility against Him.

The inspiration of the Islamic saints, though verbally distinguished from that of the prophets and inferior in degree, is of the same kind. In consequence of their intimate relation to God, the veil shrouding the supernatural, or, as a Moslem would say, the unseen world, from their perceptions is withdrawn at intervals, and in their fits of ecstasy they rise to the prophetic level. Neither deep learning in divinity, nor devotion to good works, nor asceticism, nor moral purity makes the Mohammedan a saint; he may have all or none of these things, but the only indispensable qualification is that ecstasy and rapture which is the outward sign of `passing-away' from the phenomenal self. Any one thus enraptured (*majdhub)* is a *wali*,[175] and when such persons are recognized through their power of working miracles, they are venerated as saints not only after death but also during their lives. Often, however, they live and die in obscurity. Hujwiri tells us that amongst the saints ``there are four thousand who are concealed and do not know one another and are not aware of the excellence of their state, being in all circumstances hidden from themselves and from mankind."

The saints form an invisible hierarchy, on which the order of the world is thought to depend. Its supreme head is entitled the *Qutb* (Axis). He is the most eminent Sufi of his age, and presides over the meetings regularly held by his august parliament, whose members are not hampered in their attendance by the inconvenient fictions of time and space, but come together from all parts of the earth in the twinkling of an eye, traversing seas and mountains and deserts as easily as common mortals step across a road.

~One day Abu `I-Hasan Khurqani clenched his fist and extended the little finger and said, `Here is the *qibla*,[176] if any one desires to become a Sufi.' These words were reported to the

---

[174] **Koran 10.63.**

[175] **Waliyyat, if the saint is a woman.**

[176] **The qibla is the point to which Moslems turn their faces when praying,i.e the Ka`ba.**

Grand Sheykh, who, deeming the co-existence of two qiblas an insult to the divine Unity, exclaimed, `Since a second cibla has appeared, I will cancel the former one.' After that, no pilgrims were able to reach Mecca. Some perished on the way, others fell into the hands of robbers, or were prevented by various causes from accomplishing their journey. Nexr year a certain dervish said to the Grand Sheykh, `What sense is there in keeping the folk away from the House of God?' Thereupon the Grand Sheykh made a sign, and the road became open once more. The dervish asked, `Whose fault is it that all these people have perished?' The Grand Sheykh replied, `When elephants jostle each other, who cares if a few wretched birds are crushed to death?'"

~Some persons who were setting forth on a journey begged Khurqani to teach them a prayer that would keep them safe from the perils of the road. He said, `if any misfortune should befall you, mention my name.' This answer was not agreeable to them; they set off, however, and while travelling were attacked by brigands. One of the party mentioned the saint's name and immediately became invisible, to the great astonishment of the brigands, who could not find either his camel or his bales of merchandise; the others lost all their clothes and goods. On returning home, they asked the Sheykh to explain the mystery. `We all invoked God,' they said, `and without success; but the one man who invoked you vanished from before the eyes of the robbers.' `You invoke God formally,' said the Sheykh, `whereas I invoke Him really. Hence, if you invoke me and I then invoke God on your behalf, your prayers are granted; but it is useless for you to invoke God formally and by rote."'

"One night, while he was praying, he heard a voice cry, `Ha! Abu'l-Hasan! Dost thou wish Me to tell the people what I know of thee, that they may stone thee to death?' `O Lord God,' he replied, `dost Thou wish me to tell the people what I perceive of Thy grace, that none of them may ever again bow to Thee in prayer?' The voice answered, `Keep thy secret, and I will keep Mine."'"

"He said, `O God, do not send to me the Angel of Death, for I will not give up my soul to him. How should I restore it to him, from whom I did not receive it? I received my soul from Thee, and I will not give it up to any one but Thee.'"

``He said, `After I shall have passed away, the Angel of Death will come to one of my descendants and set about taking his soul, and will deal hardly with him. Then will I raise my hands from the tomb and shed the grace of God upon his lips.'".....[177]

In the early part of the tenth century Husayn ibn Mansur, known to fame as al-Hallaj (the wool-carder), was barbarously done to death at Baghdad. His execution seems to have been dictated by political motives, but with these we are not concerned. Amongst the crowd assembled round the scaffold, a few, perhaps, believed him to be what he said he was; the rest witnessed with exultation or stern approval the punishment of a blasphemous heretic. He had uttered in two words a sentence which Islam has, on the whole, forgiven but has never forgotten: ``Ana 'l-Haqq"-``I am God."......[178]

[177] The Mystics of Islam by *REYNOLD A. NICHOLSON*, Published by ROUT-LEDGE AND KEGAN PAUL, LONDON,BOSTON AND HENLEY, Printed in Great Britain by Lawe & Brydone Printers Ltd., Thetford, Norfolk, (Introduction), pp-21-22, 39-40,50-52, 122-124 (SAINTS AND MIRACLES), 134-136.

[178] The Mystics of Islam by *REYNOLD A. NICHOLSON*, Published by ROUT-LEDGE AND KEGAN PAUL, LONDON,BOSTON AND HENLEY, Printed in Great Britain by Lawe & Brydone Printers Ltd., Thetford, Norfolk,(on THE UNITIVE STATE) pp. 149-151,

Nationality in Islam

During initial time of Islam and before conquest of The Holy Mecca, those companion of the Holy Prophet who accepted Islam was due to their love for God and the Prophet, among those were Ali, Abu Bakr, Omar, Osman (R. A.).

They were all from Holy Mecca and some of them were closely related to the Holy Prophet. But among them there were also from distant land with different race and language, which can be known from the followings:

During life time of the Holy Prophet (Sm) his companion was a mixture of all culture and race, not particularly that original people of Mecca and Medina.

The first Moazzin (Moazzin is the person who use to call the faithful from the mosque for obligatory five times prayer in each day) was a black, Hazrat Belal (Allah be pleased with him). Before his acceptance of Islam he was slave. He was slave born, but was a faithful Muslim, pure of heart. His father's name was Ribah and his mother was Hamama. He was freed by Hazrat Abu Bakr. He was tortured by the polytheists during his slave life due to his acceptance of Islam.

One of the closest companion was Hazrat Salman Farshhi, originally he was a Iranian. From his early life how he was in search of God and The Holy Man; and he even left his country and family leaving his all future property and went to Christian Bishop one after another. I am quoting some paragraph from a book which are as follows:

Asim b, 'Umar b. Qatada al-Ansari told me on the authority of Mahmud b. Labid from 'Abdullah b. 'Abbas as follows: Salman said while I listened to his words: 'I am a Persian from Ispahan from a village called Jayy. My father was the principal landowner in his village and I was dearer to him than the whole world. His love for me went to such lengths that he shut me in his house as though I were a slave girl. I was a zealous Magian that I became keeper of the sacred fire, replenishing it and not letting it go out for a moment. Now my father owned a large farm, and one day when he could not attend to his farm he told me to go to it and learn about it, giving me certain instructions. "Do not let yourself be detained," he said, "because you are more important t me than my farm and worrying about you will prevent me about my business." So I started out for the farm, and when I passed by a Christian church I heard the voices of the men praying. I knew nothing about them because my father kept me shut up in his house. When I heard their voices I went to see what they were doing; their prayers pleased me and I felt drawn to their worship and thought that it was better than our religion, and I decided that I would not leave them until sunset. So I did not go to the farm. When I asked them where their religion originated, they said "Syria". I returned to my father who had sent after me because anxiety on my account had interrupted all his work. He asked me where I had been and reproached me for not obeying his instructions. I told him that I had passed by some men who were praying in their church and was so pleased with what I saw of their religion that I stayed with them until sunset. He said, "My son, there is no good in that religion; the religion of your fathers is better than that." :No," I said, "it is better than our religion." My father was afraid of what I would do, so he bound me in fetters and imprisoned me in his house.

'I sent to the Christians and asked them if they would tell me when a caravan of Christian merchants came from Syria. They told me, and I said to them: "When they have finished their business and want to go back to their own country, ask them if they will take me." They id so and I cast off the fetters from my feet and went with them to Syria. Arrived there I asked for the most learned person in their religion and they directed me to the bishop. I went to him and told him tat I liked his religion and should like to be with him and serve him in his church, to learn from him and to pray with him. He invited me to come in and I did so. Now he was a bad man who used to command people to give alms and induced them to do so and when they brought him money he put it in his own coffers and did not give it to the poor. Another Bishop was appointed after his death. Salman considered that

Bishop was very virtuous, more ascetic, more devoted to the next life, and more consistent night and day than the first one. Before his death Salman asked him about his order, and he was asked to go Mausil, where a Bishop follow his path. So Salmon went there, and after his death that man of Mausil asked him to go Nasibin where he lived, after his death he recommended him to go Ammuriya. He went to Ammuriya, where the Bishop told him before his death that a prophet was about to arise who would be sent with religion of Abraham; he would come forth in Arab a and would migrate to a country between two lava belts, between which were palms. And Salman with a Kalbite merchants he went Wadi'lQ-ura, when they sold him to a Jew as a slave.

Salman was freed with three hundred palm-trees and paying forty okes of gold which the Apostle gave him He took part with the Apostle in the battle of the Ditch as a free man and thereafter he was at every other battle.[179] He was one of the closest and dear companion of the Holy Prophet(Sm).

When the Iranian Emperor Yeadjgar was defeated and killed in 21 Hizra his three princess were brought to Medina. The Caliph Omar called a meeting of Majli-e-Shura for a decision of the three Princes. But after long meeting as solution could not be reached The Caliph Omar gave the responsibility of a decision to Hazrat Ali. So Hazrat advised since those princess are helpless and they belong to a great generation and for the il-luck they are under the care of Muslims. So Hazrat proposed that a sum of money should be decided for their freedom which he will deposit to the Baitul-Mal and the they will accept Islam and then they may marry three young of The Medina or they go some other places with their choice. All accepted this proposal and those three Princes became very wonderful and they gladly accepted Islam by Hazrat Ali's hand. The eldest princess cast Caliph's son Abdullah (R. A.); second Princess choice The First Caliph's son Muhammad and youngest princes Shaharb-anu cast Hazrat Hussain as their individual husband. Three great man of Islam was born from these three Princes, namely Hazrat Imam Jainul Abedin son of Imam Hussain, and two other learned man in Fiqah Imam Salem son of Abdullah ibne Omar and Imam Kasem son of Muhammad ibne Abu Bakr.

---

[179] **THE LIFE OF MUHAMMAD, A TRANSLATION OF ISHAQ'S SIRAT RASUL ALLAH WITH INTRODUCTION AND NOTES BY A. GUILLAUME, OXFORD UNIVERSITY pp. 95-98**

Prophet Muhammad's (Peace be upon him) contribution towards Humanity, Freedom of Women and even to Animal

His humanity even extended itself to the lower creation. He forbade the employment of living birds as targets for marksmen (Ibid., i., 273); and remonstrated with those who ill-treated their camels.[180] ....

To the same genuine humanity we may ascribe the one innovation of **Islam which ordinarily receives praise even from its enemies: the abolition of the practice of burying girls alive.**[181]

The seclusion and veiling of women were, as Muir has well observed, a direct consequence of polygamy and facility of divorce. Polygamy is itself an attempt at solving a problem which Indo-Germanic nations solve by harboring prostitution. .... If by the introduction of the veil Muhammed (My peace be upon him) curtailed women's liberty, **he undoubtedly secured for them by laws the rights of inheriting and holding property, which under the older system were precarious.**[182]

Some of his regulations in the matter were humane: the parting of a captive mother from her child was forbidden, and threatened with an appropriate punishment in the next world: .... The parting of brothers when sold was similarly forbidden. (Musnud, i., 98.) On the whole however the Prophet did something to alleviate the existence of captives. [183]

At the Farewell Pilgrimage he is said to have ordered his followers to feed and clothe their slaves as they fed and clothed themselves. A Himyari chief is said to have freed four thousand slaves at the Prophet's request (Ibn Duraid, 308). A system was further encouraged by which slaves might contract for their own manumission, and assistance of such persons with presents was regarded by the code with favor. When a man died without heirs, but leaving a slave, the slave was manumitted by the Prophet(Musnad, i., 221), and received the inheritance. A man who shared one slave with seven brothers, and had cuffed

---

180

MOHAMMED AND THE RISE OF ISLAM BY D.S.MARGOLIOUTH Published VOICE OF INDIA, 2/18, ANSARI ROAD, NEW DELHI-110002, P.458.

181

MOHAMMED AND THE RISE OF ISLAM BY D.S.MARGOLIOUTH Published VOICE OF INDIA, 2/18, ANSARI ROAD, NEW DELHI-110002, P. 459

182

MOHAMMED AND THE RISE OF ISLAM BY D.S.MARGOLIOUTH Published VOICE OF INDIA, 2/18, ANSARI ROAD, NEW DELHI-110002, PP. 460-461

183

MOHAMMED AND THE RISE OF ISLAM BY D.S.MARGOLIOUTH Published VOICE OF INDIA, 2/18, ANSARI ROAD, NEW DELHI-110002, P. 461

the slave, was made to manumit him (Ibid., iii, 447.); and murder or maiming of slaves was to be punished by retaliation (Ibid., v., 18.).[184]

It has been difficult for Western people to understand the violent Muslim reaction to Salman Rushdie's fictional portrait of Muhammad (Sm) in the Satanic verses. It seemed incredible that a novel inspire such murderous hatred, a reaction which was regarded as proof of the incurable into brain of Islam. It was particularly disturbing for people in Britain to learn that the Muslim communities in their own cities lived according to different, apparently alien values and were ready to defend them to death. But there were also uncomfortable reminders of the Western past in this tragic affair. When British people watched the Muslims of Bradford burning the novel, did they relate this to the bonfires of books that had blazed in Christian Europe over the centuries? In 1242, for example, king Louis IX of France, a canonized saint of the Roman Catholic Church, condemned the Jewish Talmud as a vicious attack on the person of Christ. The book was banned and copies were publicly burned in the presence of the King. Louis had no interest in discussing his difference with the Jewish communities of France in a peaceful, rational way. He once claimed that the only way to debate with a Jew was to kill him 'with a good thrust in the belly as far as the sword will go.'[185]

At the very end of the eighteenth century, a telling incident showed the direction in which the new European confidence was tending. In 1798 Napoleon sailed to Egypt, accompanied by scores of Orientalists from his Institute de'Egypte. He intended to use all this new scholarship and understanding to subjugate the Islamic world and challenge the British hegemony of India. As soon as they landed, Napoleon sent the scholars off on what we should call a fact-finding mission, giving his officers strict instructions to follow their advice. The had obviously done their homework well. Napoleon had cynically addressed the Egyptian crowd at Alexandria with the claim: 'Nous sommes les vrais musulmans.' Then he had sixty sheikhs of al-Azhar, the great mosque in Cairo, brought with full military honors into his quarters. He carefully praised the Prophet, discussed with them Voltaires's Mohomet and seems to have held his own with the learned ulema. Nobody took Napoleon very seriously as a Muslim, but his sympathetic understanding of Islam did allay the hostility of the people to a degree. Nepoleans's expedition came to nothing: he was defeated by the British and Turkish armies and sailed back to Europe. The nineteenth century was characterized by the colonial spirit, which was giving Europeans the unhealthy belief that they were superior to other races; it was up to them to redeem the barbarous world of Asia and Africa in a mission civilisatrice. This inevitably affected the Western view of Islam, as the French and the British looked covetously towards the declining Ottoman empire. In the French Christian apologist Francois Rene de Chateaubriand, for example, we find a revival of the Crusading ideal which had been adapted to meet the new conditions. He had been impressed by Napoleon's expedition, seeing him as a Crusader-pilgrim. The Crusaders had tried to bring Christianity to the East, he argued. Of all religions, Christianity was the one 'most favorable to freedom', but in the Crusading venture it had clashed with 'Islam'; 'a cult that was civilization's enemy, systematically favorable to ignorance, to despotism and to

---

[184] MOHAMMED AND THE RISE OF ISLAM BY D.S.MARGOLIOUTH Published VOICE OF INDIA, 2/18, ANSARI ROAD, NEW DELHI-110002, PP. 461-462.

[185] John of Joinville, The life of St. Louis, trans. Rene Hague and ed. Natalis de Wailly, London, 1955 pg. 36 which were quoted in MUHAMMAD, A WESTERN ATTEMPT TO UNDERSTAND ISLAM BY KAREN ARMSTRONG published by VICTOR GOLLANCZ LTD., LONDON; PG. 21

slavery. (note: Quoted in Said, Orientalism, p. 172). In the heady days after the French Revolution, 'Islam' had once again become the opposite of 'us'. During the hierarchically minded Middle Ages, some critics of Islam had blamed Muhammad for giving too much power to menials, like slaves and women. This stereotype had now been reversed, not because people necessarily had a fuller knowledge of Islam but because it suited 'our' needs and was as always a foil against which we could measure our achievements.

In his best seller 'Journey from Paris to Jerusalem and from Jerusalem to Paris (1810-11), Chateaubriand applied his Crusading fantasy to the situation in Palestine. The Arabs, he wrote, 'have the air of soldiers without a leader, citizens without legislators, and family without a father'. They were an example of 'civilized man fallen again into a savage state'. (Ibid) Therefore they were crying out for the control of the West, because it was impossible for them to take charge of their own affairs. In the Quran there was 'neither a principle for civilization nor a mandate that can elevate character'. Unlike Christianity , 'Islam' preaches 'neither hatred of tyranny nor love liberty'. (Ibid., pg 171) pg 41 Even though Western scholars continued to attempt a more objective picture of the Arab and Muslim world, this colonial superiority made many people believe that 'Islam' was beneath serious attention.

certainly this offensive Western attitude has succeeded in alienating the Muslim world. Today anti-Western feeling seems rife in Islam, but that is an entirely new development. The West may have harbored fantasies of Muhammad as its enemy, but in fact most Muslims remained unaware of the West until just over 200 years ago. The Crusades were crucial in the history of Europe and had a formative influence on the Western identity, as I have argued elsewhere.(Holy War; The Crusades and Their Impact on Today's World(London, 1988). But, though they obviously deeply affected the lives of Muslims in the Near East, the Crusades had little impact on the rest of the Islamic world, where they were simply remote border incidents. The heartlands of the Islamic empire in the Iraq and Iran remained entirely unaffected by this medieval Western assault. They had, therefore, no concept of the West as their enemy. When Muslims thought of the Christian world, they did not think of the West but of Byzantium; at that time Western Europe seemed a barbarous, pagan wilderness, which was indeed far behind the rest of the civilized world. [186]

But Europe caught up and the Muslim world, which was occupied with its own concerns, failed to notice what was happening. Napoleon's expedition to Egypt was an eye-opener for many thoughtful people in the Near East, who were much impressed by the easy, confident bearing of the French soldiers in this post-revolutionary army. Muslims had always responded to the ideas of other cultures, and many were drawn to the radical, modernizing ideas of the West. At the turn of this century, nearly every leading intellectual in the Islamic world was a liberal and a Westerniser. These liberals may have hated Western imperialism, but they imagined that liberals in Europe would be on their side and would oppose people like Lord Cromer. They admired the quality of the Western way of life, which seemed to have enshrined many ideals that were central to the Islamic tradition. In the last fifty years, however, we have lost this goodwill. One reason for the alienation of the Muslim world has been its gradual discovery of the hostility and contempt for their Prophet and their religion which is so deeply embedded in Western culture and which they consider still affects its policy towards Muslim countries even in the post-colonial period. As the Syrian writer Kabbani points out in Letter to Christendom:[187]

---

[186] MUHAMMAD, A WESTERN ATTEMPT TO UNDERSTAND ISLAM BY KAREN ARMSTRONG PG. 38-39, 41

[187] MUHAMMAD, A WESTERN ATTEMPT TO UNDERSTAND ISLAM BY KAREN ARMSTRONG published by VICTOR GOLLANCZ LTD., LONDON; PP. 40- 42.

Is the Western conscience not selective? The West feels sympathy for the Afghan Mujahedin, propped up by American intelligence just as the Nicaraguan Contras were, but feels no sympathy for militant Muslims who are not fighting its Cold War battles but have political concerns of their own. As I write, Palestinians are dying every day in the Occupied Territories-nearly 600 dead at the latest count, over 30,000 wounded and 20,000 in detention without trial ....yet Israel remains a democracy in Western eyes, an outpost of Western civilization. What is one to think of such double standards?[188]

Introduction

There are surprisingly few accessible biographics of Muhammad(sm) for the general reader. I have been particularly indebted to the two volumes by W. Montgomery Watt, Muhammad at Mecca and Muhammad at Medina, but these are for students and presuppose a basic knowledge of Muhammad's life that not everybody has; Martin Lings' Muhammad, His life Based on the Earliest Sources gives a wealth of fascinating information from Muhammad's biographers of the eighth, ninth and tenth centuries. But Lings is writing for the converted. An outsider will have many questions to ask of a basic, even of an argumentative nature which Lings does not address perhaps the most attractive of the biographics currently in print is **Maxime rodinson's Mohammad (sm). Rodinson wears his considerable erudition lightly and I have learned a great deal from his book, but he has written as a sceptic and a secularist. Concentrating as he does on the political and military aspects of the Prophet's (sm) life, he does not really help us to understand Muhammad's spiritual vision. My own approach has been rather different. We know more about Muhammad than about the founder of any other major faith so that a study of his life can give us an important insight into the nature of the religious experience. All religions represent a dialogue between an absolute ineffable realities and mundane events. In Muhammad's (sm) Prophetic career we can examine this process more closely than is usually possible. We shall see that Muhammad's (sm) spiritual experience bears an arresting similarity to that of the Prophets of Israel, St. Teres of Alveoli and Dane Gallein of Norwich. I have also used various incidents in the Prophet's life to illustrate the particular emphasis of the Muslim traditions all major religions cover many of the same themes but each has its own particular insight. Thus we shall have to consider why Muslims regard politics as a religious duty. Muhammad achieved an extraordinary political success and Christians tend to see such worldly triumph as of questionable godliness; but is a Christ-like failure the only way to God? I also look at the Prophet (sm) from the point of view of a person with particular preconceptions about Islam. Thus, when we see Muhammad waging a war against the city of Mecca, we shall have to ask whether he really did found a religion of the sword? How could a man of God be prepared to fight and kill? When we consider Muhammad's relationship with his wives and daughters, we must ask whether he really was a chauvinist, who founded a misogynistic religion.** The Gulf War of 1991 showed that, whether we like it or not, we are deeply connected with the Muslim World. Despite temporary alliances, it is clear that the West has largely lost the confidence of people in the Islamic world. A breakdown in communications is never the fault of one party and if the West is to regain the sympathy and respect that it once enjoyed in the Muslim world it must examine its own role in the Middle East and consider its own difficulties vis-a-vis Islam. That is why the first chapter of this book traces the history of Western hatred for the Prophet of Islam (sm). But the picture is not entirely black. From the earliest days, some Europeans were able to achieve a more balanced view. They were always in a minority and they had their failing but this handful of people tried to correct the errors of

---

[188] **Rana Kabbani, Letter to Christendom (London, 1989),p. 54.**

189

their contemporaries and rise above received opinion. It is surely this more tolerant compassionate and courageous tradition that we should seek to encourage now.[189]

It has been difficult for Western people to understand the violent Muslim reaction to Salman Rushdie's fictional portrait of Muhammad in The Satanic Verses. It seemed incredible that a novel could inspire such murderous hatred, a reaction which was regarded as proof of the incurable intolerance of Islam. It was particularly disturbing for people in Britain to learn that the Muslim communities in their own cities lived according to different, apparently alien values and were ready to defend them to death. But there were also uncomfortable reminders of the Western part in this tragic affair. When British people watched the Muslims of Bradford burning the novel, did they relate this to the bonfires of books, that had blazed in Christian Europe over the centuries?
In 1242, for example, King.....

It was Louis who called the first Inquisition to bring Christian heretics to justice and burned not merely their books but hundreds of men and women. He was also a Muslim-hater and led two crusades against the Islamic world. In Louis' day it was not Islam but the Christian West which found it impossible to coexist with others. Indeed the bitter history of Muslim - Western relations can be said to have begun with an attack on Muhammad in Muslim Spain. In 850 a monk called Perfectus went shopping in the souk of Cordova, capital of the Muslim State of al-Andalus. Here he was accosted by a group of Arabs who asked him whether Jesus (peace be upon him) or Muhammad (sm) was the greater prophet. Perfectus understood at once that it was a trick question, because it was a capital offence in the Islamic empire to insult Muhammad (sm), and at first he responded cautiously. But suddenly, he snapped and burst into a passionate stream of abuse, calling the prophet of Islam ....This incident was unusual for Cordova, where Christian-Muslim relations were normally good. **Like the Jews, Christians were allowed full religious liberty within the Islamic empire and most Spaniards were proud to belong to such an advanced culture, light years ahead of the rest of Europe. They were often called "Mozarabs" or "Arabisens".[190]**
This curious incident was uncharacteristic of life in Muslim Spain for the next 600 years, members of the three religions of historical monotheism were able to live together in relative peace and harmony: the Jews, who were being hounded to death in the rest of Europe were able to enjoy a rich cultural renaissance of their own. But the story of the martyrs of Cordova reveals an attitude that would become common in the West. At that time Islam was a great world power while Europe, overrun by barbarian tribes, had become a cultural backwater. **Later the whole world would seem to be Islamic, rather as it seems Western today, and Islam was a continuous challenge to the West until the eighteenth century. Now it seems that the cold war against the Soviet Union is about to be replaced by a Cold War against Islam.**
In 1095 Pope Urban II summoned the Knights of Europe to liberate the tombs of Christ in Jerusalem in the expedition that would become known as the First Crusade.

---

[189] INTRODUCTION IN MUHAMMAD, A WESTERN ATTEMPT TO UNDERSTAND ISLAM BY KAREN ARMSTRONG published by VICTOR GOLLANCZ LTD., LONDON; PG. 14-15

[190] MUHAMMAD, A WESTERN ATTEMPT TO UNDERSTAND ISLAM BY KAREN ARMSTRONG published by VICTOR GOLLANCZ LTD., LONDON; PG. 21-22

Rashidin, the Rightly Guided Caliphs, because they governed in accordance with Muhammad's principles. Ali in particular emphasized that a Muslim ruler must not be tyrannical. He was, under God, on a par with his subjects and must take care to lighten the burden of the poor and destitute. That is the only way for a regime to survive.

So if your subjects complain of burden, of blight, of the cutting of irrigation water, of lack of rain, or of the transformation of the   1q```````````````````earth through its being inundated by a flood or ruined by drought, lighten their burden to the extent you wish your affair to be rectified. And let not anything by which you have lightened their burden weigh heavily against you, for it is a store which they will return to you by bringing about prosperity in your land and establishing your rule. .... Truly the destruction of the earth only results from the destitution of its inhabitants, and its inhabitants become destitute only when rulers concern themselves with amassing wealth, when they have misgivings about the endurance of their own rule and when they protect little from warning example. (Instructions given by Ali to Malik al-Ashtar, when he was appointed governor of Egypt.[191]

[1] (Ibn Ishaq, Sira 1, 017, in Guillaume, trans. and ed., The Life of Muhammad p. 687. and as stated in MUHAMMAD, A WESTERN ATTEMPT TO UNDERSTAND ISLAM BY KAREN ARMSTRONG published by VICTOR GOLLANCZ LTD., LONDON; PG. 258)

[1] MOHAMMED AND THE RISE OF ISLAM BY D.S.MARGOLIOUTH Published by VOICE OF INDIA, 2/18, ANSARI ROAD, NEW DELHI-110002

After he had been elected, Abu Bakr addressed the community, laying down the principles that should henceforth apply to all Muslim rulers:

[1] (Ibn Ishaq, Sira 1, 017, in Guillaume, trans. and ed., The Life of Muhammad p. 687. and as stated in MUHAMMAD, A WESTERN ATTEMPT TO UNDERSTAND ISLAM BY KAREN ARMSTRONG published by VICTOR GOLLANCZ LTD., LONDON; PG. 258)

"I have been given authority over you but I am not the best of you. If I do well, help me, and if I do ill, then put me right. Truth consists in loyalty and falsehood in treachery. The weak among you shall be strong in my eyes until I secure his right if God will; and the strong among you shall be weak in my eyes until I wrest the right from him. If a people refrain from fighting in the way of God, God will smite them with disgrace. Wickedness is never widespread in a people but God brings calamity upon them all. Obey me as long as I obey God and His apostle, and if I disobey them - you owe me no obedience. Arise to prayer, God have mercy on you (Ibn Ishaq, Sira 1, 017, in Guillaume, trans. and ed., The Life of Muhammad p 687.)[192]

Another Jewess, Zainab, the wife of Sallam, son of Mishkam, who figures as a partisan of Mohammed, tried with partial success a plan which others had attempted- to fail entirely. She found out what joint was the Prophet's favorite food, and cooked it for him, richly seasoned with poison. The Prophet's guest, Bishr, son of Al-Bara, took some and swallowed

---

[191] In William C. Chittick (trans and ed.) A shite Anthology (London 1980, p. 75) and as stated in MUHAMMAD, A WESTERN ATTEMPT TO UNDERSTAND ISLAM BY KAREN ARMSTRONG published by VICTOR GOLLANCZ LTD., LONDON; PG. 24-25

[192] (Ibn Ishaq, Sira 1, 017, in Guillaume, trans. and ed., The Life of Muhammad p. 687. and as stated in MUHAMMAD, A WESTERN ATTEMPT TO UNDERSTAND ISLAM BY KAREN ARMSTRONG published by VICTOR GOLLANCZ LTD., LONDON; PG. 258)

it; and presently died in convulsions. The Prophet bethought him in time of the enemies who bring gifts; and spued the morsel before it passed down his throat, and had his shoulder bled at once, as a means of excreting the poison(Isabah,iv., 400.). But when three years after he died of fever, he thought it was Zainab's poison still working within him, and among his other honours could claim that of martyrdom.[193]

[193] **MOHAMMED AND THE RISE OF ISLAM BY D.S.MARGOLIOUTH Published by VOICE OF INDIA, 2/18, ANSARI ROAD, NEW DELHI-110002, P. 361.**

FUNDAMENTALIST

First let us see what the western researchers found about Islam, it's fundamental law and it's political and other democratic role.

The following paragraphs are from **'THE POLITICAL ECONOMY OF THE ISLAMIC STATE, A COMPARATIVE STUDY' BY Ausaf Ali (1934), A Dissertation Presented to the FACULTY OF THE GRADUATE SCHOOL UNIVERSITY OF SOUTHERN CALIFORNIA In partial Fulfillment of the requirements for the degree, DOCTOR OF PHILOSOPHY (Economics), June 1970. PP. 10-13.**

DEMOCRACY :-

A democratic political order is one in which all citizens have or feel they have an equal say in the affairs of the state. This supposed political equality creates and supports the doctrine of one man-one vote and the procedure of majority rule. This makes government responsible and responsive to the people. The important thing to clearly understand about democracy is that it is a flow concept and not a stock concept. Democracy refers to a process and not to an outcome or a fixed position.

Arthur Schlesinger has stated:

Democracy requires unremitting action on many fronts. It is, in other words, a process, not a conclusion. However painful the thought, it must be recognized that its commitments are unending.[194]

Thus conceived, democracy implies or in fact prescribes a procedure or a process to be observed in order to hire and fire governors (or rulers), determine rational policies, and resolve conflicts in the society.

Sharia

By Sharia is meant Islamic Law. Sharia consists of 1) The Quran, i.e., the revealed Book of Islam, and 2) The Sunna, i.e., the traditions of belief and action established by the Prophet and considered to embody the interpretation of the revelation contained in the Quran.

Islamic State

Any state which proclaims and promulgates Sharia as the fundamental law of its land, i.e. the Constitution, is an Islamic state.

.... before an Islamic State can be established, Islam must undergo secularization. In the absence of such a secular development of Islamic thought, any move, policy, or action toward the creation of the Islamic state is unthinkable, unwise, and, in fact, irrational, and may perhaps turn out to be regression to the primitive forms of life. Chances are that such a social policy will, in all probability, fail anyone who hopes to, or promises to, deliver a state based on the Quern and Sunni without a fairly clearly thought out and preplanned blueprint of its Society, Polity, and Economy i.e. either living in a fool's paradise or wants to make political capital out of Islam, or both. The need for formulating the theoretical

---

[194] **Arthur M. Schlesinger, Jr., The Vital Center (Boston: Houghton Mifflin Company, 1962), p. 254.**

systems of the social, political, and economic organization of the Islamic State can therefore hardly be overemphasized.[195]

We should be rational in the sense that in each country where religion policy is the state policy, still the particular state is run by the belief or faith of the majority people and those policy of the particular state is fundamental. Even particular section of that state have separate belief or faith they are bound to obey the fundamental policy of the particular state. And as such many minority communities of a nation state is bound to obey many law against their religious belief in all most in all the so called secular State. For the feeling and understanding of the readers following reference is quoted:

A. For Islamic Caliphate:

Al-Ghazzali (1058-1111) similarly combined allegiance to religious tradition with a pragmatic awareness of political realities. He too wanted to restore the Caliphate to its true function as the protector of the tradition of the Prophet and of Muslim law, to recapture the unity of Muslim peoples, and to restore their military and worldly might. To do this, he realized, it was necessary to assimilate the Turkish military aristocracy, subordinate them to the Caliphate, reform political administration, and above all to use the combined powers of Caliphs and reigning sultans to suppress the enemies of Islam, ... Most important for al-Ghazzali was the need to inculcate in every individual Muslim true belief, true piety, and true practice of Muslim law. Despite the continuing commitment to the Caliphate, there were subtle accommodations to the risk to power of nomadic chieftains and slave warlords. Al-Ghazzali was realistic enough to recognize that military lords often appointed the Caliphs who in turn legitimized their power. His theories conceived of Muslim government as a condominium of the authority of the Caliphs and the effective powers of the Sultans. More important was the ever increasing emphasis upon the necessity of obedience. The sanctions for this lies in The Quran and in Hadiths which stressed the need for obedience to the state. The Hanbali theologian, Ibn Batta (d. 997), condemned armed revolt against an established government. Obedience was required of all subjects, he held, but this obedience was limited, in that the individual should refuse to disobey a command of God. Similarly, al-Ghazzali held that rulers should be obeyed because resistance, even to tyranny, was a worse alternative, for fear of civil war, any government had to be accepted as a matter of necessity.
 In accord with his own political role, Ibn Taymiya held that the "Ulama" were responsible for upholding the law by giving religious advice to rulers, teaching true principles to the community of Muslims, and "commanding the good and forbidding the evil."
 Al-Ghazzali's Book of Counsel for kings also stresses the importance of justice. The ruler should understand that God loves a just Sultan and that God will judge him at the final day. The ruler should see that his officers, servants, and slaves are also disciplined.
 The three genres also agree that the proper social order requires a good ruler be it a philosopher, Caliph, Sultan. Happiness is society is made to depend upon the person of the ruler. In the Sunny theory the ruler is selected by God through election of the communities in order to implement his commands.

---

[195] **This is an authorized microfilm-- in 1981 by UNIVERSITY MICROFILMS INTERNATIONAL by ANN ARBOR, MICHIGAN, U. S. A., LONDON, ENGLAND; THE POLITICAL ECONOMY OF THE ISLAMIC STATE, A COMPARATIVE STUDY BY Ausaf Ali (1934), A Dissertation Presented to the FACULTY OF THE GRADUATE SCHOOL UNIVERSITY OF SOUTHERN CALIFORNIA In partial Fulfillment of the requirements for the degree, DOCTOR OF PHILOSOPHY (Economics), June 1970. PP. 10-13.**

The Caliph is seen in the image of God as the upholder of order and justice. He is mighty, capricious, inscreetable, and deserving of loyalty regardless of his actual deeds. An ordered society is unimaginable without a ruler, just as an ordered universe is unimaginable without God.

'The Muslims have a bible, the Koran, a translation of the holy book of Islam

B. For non-Muslim country:

In many cases Muslim populations have become minority citizens and subjects in societies dominated by non-Muslim peoples.

It seems clean that the teachings of the Nation of Islam precludes fighting for the United States not because of objections to participation in war in any form but rather because of political and racial objections to policies of the United States as interpreted by Elijah Muhammad. .....
It is therefore our conclusion that registrant's claimed objection to participation in war in so far as they are based upon the teachings of the Nation of Islam, rest on grounds which primarily are political and racial.[196]

C And important point is that in U. S. A. and many western coutries, many Muslims are granted all the facilities as a human being, though with some allegations against them. But if some of them return to Egypt, Saudi and other Muslim countries, my be they will be charged linking with many islamic movement, and probably will be hanged with summary trial, the fate faced by Banana and Qutb in the recent past. Yet what happened to Muslim scholars in Muslim country like Egypt, though those Muslim scholars were struggling for the true Islamic principles which are fundamental. And most disgust thing is that the killing of Banana and Qutb happened in the land where when after the destruction of Baghdad and Abbaside caliphate the rulers in Egypt restored the Caliphate by selecting a prince of Abbaside Caliphs as Caliph who was also accepted as Caliph by the then Indian ruler Muhammad bin Toghloque Instances are as following event in Egypt:

Banana and Qutb were killed and the Muslim Brotherhood all but destroyed.

.

He volunteered to obtain a copy of Aligarh's college for Father's colleagues to study presumably Cromer had good political reasons for not wanting the Egyptians to imitate the Indian Universities at Calcutta, Bombay, and Madras.

World War 1 brought Captain Creswell of Royal Flying Corps to Egypt, and for twenty years from 1931, he was the Egyptian University's Professor of Islamic architecture.[197]

---

[196] **The Constitutional Politics of the Black Muslim Movement in America by Olives Jones, Jr; This is an authorized facsimile and was produced by microfilm xerography in 1981 by University MICROFILMS INTERNATIONAL, Ann Arbor, Michigan, USA, London, England, B.S., Savannah State College, 1971; A. M., University of Illinois, 1974; Thesis submitted : P. 82.**

[197] **The Constitutional Politics of the Black Muslim Movement in America by Olives Jones, Jr; This is an authorized facsimile and was produced by microfilm xerography in 1981 by University MICROFILMS INTERNATIONAL, Ann Arbor, Michigan,**

Again now a days in those so called secular state, a very common word is mentioned in the western and in local Radio, Television and News paper; about fundamentalist Islam. Those who use this term; they never use it for the follower of other religion; they never normally use "fundamentalist Jews" or "fundamentalist Christians" or "fundamentalist Buddhist" or "fundamentalist Hindus" or "fundamentalist non-believer" or "fundamentalist Communists" or even "fundamentalist Homo-sexist" or "fundamentalist abortionist" or "fundamentalist kingship" or "fundamentalist Amir-ship" or "fundamentalist Bathism" or "fundamentalist materialism" or "fundamentalist British laws" or "fundamentalist French laws" or "fundamentalist chemist" or "fundamentalist physician" or "fundamental mathematician" or as a whole "fundamentalist scientist" "fundamentalist philosopher" or "fundamentalist Historian" and so on.

But when as a judge of any supreme court, High court or any court of in Muslim countries you do not pass any judgement of the land or according to faith of the people of the Land; but according to British law a law of a distant country; or as a lawyer when you plead before the court in these countries you go through British law, British panel code; so you are a British fundamentalist; a foreign fundamentalist which do not fulfil the people of the land; it's people. The same also apply to former colony of French like north African Muslim countries and some countries in Arab and Muslim world ruled by the British.

Again as a physician you must follow certain fundamental rule, you can not give a medicine for stomach trouble when someone is suffering from fever. You must follow certain fundamental rule otherwise as a doctor you will kill your patient.

So as a follower of any profession you are to go through certain fundamental theory and rule. As a computer programmer you can not go in your own will, but you are to follow certain system for the hardware and software which you are using otherwise your computer will not run and you can not develop your software. You are to proceed the way it is mentioned in the hardware and software manual.

As a pilot of any military or civilian aircraft you are to push the correct bottom otherwise you will face an accident; even a plan crash by which you will be responsible for destruction of the plan and some human life. So you must follow some fundamental system of the particular plan. Here you must be a fundamentalist not a liberal.

So when you claim to be a follower of any particular religion you must follow certain fundamental law prescribed by the Lord of the Universe which he sent to a particular nation of any land through a particular Prophet. This particular religion law may be changed by selfish human beings for their selfish contumacy, for which almighty used to send another prophet another new Law to enforce in this world. This way, time to time God has sent various Prophets through this world when He thought it necessary. As a Muslim we believe Prophet Muhammad (Sm.) came as the last Prophet with the Holy Quern as a last prescribed religious Law. Previously it was a continuous process and at a time during the time of Prophet Noah when all the people went against the Prophet and against the God's prescribed law God thought it necessary to destroy all the human being and to destroy the human beings great flood was necessary and He asked Prophet Noah to create the Boat and asked him to take a pair of each animal and his family members and even God asked him to

---

USA, London, England, B.S., Savannah State College, 1971; A. M., University of Illinois, 1974; Thesis submitted : PP. 41, 82, 99, 149, 151, 195.

abandon one of his son who did not believe him and The God. So after the great flood a new generation of human being came into being with other creatures.

So Prophet Musa (Moses), (peace be upon him) came and this way came Prophet Jesus (peace be upon him), and last came the last Prophet of Islam Prophet Muhammad (Sm.); after which according to the belief of the Muslims no other prophet will come.

The last Prophet left this world leaving the Holy Quran and his Sunna (His sayings) which are the guideline for all the generation to come

So it is fundamental for all the Muslims of this world to follow the Holy Quran and His Sunna for the generation after generation. If some of the Muslims in any part of this world do not believe the verse of The Holy Quran and Sunna as fundamental then he can not be recognized as a citizen of Muslim Umma or in other word he is not a Muslim and even he deserves some punishment for opposing and violation of the Islamic law.

When Islam came, mankind was divided into religious sects and except in a few cases men were strangers to truth and certainty, quarrelling and excommunicating one another and claiming that in so doing they were holding on to the rope of God. Islam repudiated all that and affirmed unmistakably that the religion of God through all times and by the mouth of all prophets is one. God said'' `Religion with God is Islam and those to whom the Scriptures were given disagreed among themselves through jealousy, only after knowledge had been brought to them.'(Surah 3.19) 'Abraham was not a Jew, nor a Christian, he was a hanif, a Muslim, a surrendered one; he was not one of those who take gods for God.' (surah 3.67.).[198]

The light of Islam shone in the lands where its devotees went, and the only factor at work in their relation with the local people was the Word of God heard and apprehended. At times the Muslims were pre-occupied with their own affairs and fell away from the right path. Then Islam halted like a commander whose allies have disappointed him and is about to give ground. `God brings about what He intends.' (Surah 65.3.). The Islamic lands were invaded by the Tartar peoples, led by Cenghiz Khan, pagans who despoiled the Muslims and were bent on total conquest, plunder and rapine. But it was not long before their successors adopted Islam as their religion and propagated it among their kin with the same consequences as elsewhere. They came to conquer the Muslims and they stayed to do them good. The west made a sustained attack the east, involving all the kings and peoples, and continuing more than two hundred years, during which time the west engendered a quite unprecedented zeal and fervor for religion. With military forces and preparations to the utmost of their capacity, they advanced towards the Muslim hearth-lands, fired by religious devotion. They overran many countries of Islamic allegiance. Yet in the end these violent wars closed with their evacuation. Why did they come and why did they return? The religious leaders of the west successfully aroused their peoples to make havoc of the eastern world and to seize the sovereignty over those nations on what they believed to be their prescriptive right to tyrannize over masses of men. They came in great numbers of all sorts of men, estimated in millions, many settling in Muslim territory as residents. There were periods of truce in which the angry fires abated and quieter tempers prevailed, when there was even time to take a look at the surrounding culture, pick up something from the medley of ideas and react to what was to be seen and heard. It became clear that the exaggerations of their idle dreams which had shaped into such grievous efforts had no vestige of truth. And, furthermore, they found freedom in a religion where knowledge, law and art could be

---

[198] The Theology of Unity, by Muhammad Abduh, Translated from the Arabic by Ishaq Musa'ad and Kenneth Cragg, published by BOOKS FOR LIBRARIES, A DIVISION OF ARNO PRESS NEW YORK, 1980, p. 129.

possessed with entire certitude .... Indeed, some of the reforming groups brought their doctrines to a point closely in line with the dogma of Islam, with the exception of belief in the prophetic mission of Muhammad. Their religion was in all but name the religion of Muhammad; it differed only in the shape of worship, not in meaning or anything else. Then it was that the nations of Europe began to throw off their bondage and reform their condition, re-ordering the affairs of their life in a manner akin to the message of Islam, though oblivious of who their real guide and leader was. So were enunciated the fundamental principles of modern civilization in which subsequent generations as compared with the peoples of earlier days have found their pride and glory. All this was like a copious dew falling on the welcoming earth, which stirs and brings forth a glad growth of every kind. Those who had come for strife, stayed to benefit and returned to benefit others in turn. Their rulers thought that in stirring up their peoples they would find an outlet for their rancor and secure their own power. Instead they were shown up for what they were and their authority foundered. What we have shown about the nature of Islam, well enough known to every thoughtful student, is acknowledged by many scholars in western countries and they know its validity and confess that Islam has been the greatest of their mentors in attaining their present position. `God's is the final issue of all things.'(Surah 22.41.).[199]

Islam is the religion of Muhammad's mission, as readily understood by his companions and their contemporaries who heeded it. It was actively followed among them for a period without schism or deviations in interpretation or sectarian tendencies. ... The religion of Islam teaches the unity of God, in His essence and His acts, and His transcendence above all comparison with created beings. It has come with proof of the universe having one creator, whose known attributes of knowledge, power, will and so forth are to be traced in the effects of His handiwork. It insists that He is incomparably other than anything in His creation: the only relation between Him and them consists in that He is their originator, that they belong to Him and unto Him is their returning. `Say: He is God alone.... God the selfsubsistent: who does not beget and is not begotten, and unto whom none is equal.' (Sura 112.1-3).[200]

Although divided into thirteen sovereign states, the eighty-nine million inhabitants of the Arab East are remarkably homogeneous. They share a common language, culture and - excepting parts of Lebanon - religion. They believe in the concept of the Arab Nation (Umma al Arabia), and are proud of the predominance enjoyed by the Arabs in Islam and Islamic history. `The principal dimensions of Arab nationhood appear to be a collective awareness of a common history, a distinctive language and culture (literature, art, folkways), a degree of similarity in appearance - which is not racial since the Arabs are an amalgam of races and do not practice racial exclusivity - and a historic, geographic homeland', states Michael C. Hudson, an American specialist on the Middle East. (1. Michael C. Hudson, Arab Politics: The Search for Legitimacy, Yale University Press, New Haven, Com. and London, 1977, p. 34. Arabic is a major unifying factor; and all those who speak it are regarded as part of the Arab Nation. Spoken Arabic varies widely from area to area, but the literary language is more or less the same throughout the Arab Middle East. `Arabic is the holy language of Islam,

---

[199] The Theology of Unity, by Muhammad Abduh, Translated from the Arabic by Ishaq Musa'ad and Kenneth Cragg, published by BOOKS FOR LIBRARIES, A DVISION OF ARNO PRESS NEW YORK, 1980, p 148-150.

[200] The Theology of Unity, by Muhammad Abduh, Translated from the Arabic by Ishaq Musa'ad and Kenneth Cragg, published by BOOKS FOR LIBRARIES, A DVISION OF ARNO PRESS NEW YORK, 1980, p. 123.

and specifically- in its classical formnguage of the Koran', notes David Holden, a British author and journalist. `Its meaning and symbols are woven into the entire fabric of Arab life, providing, as it were, a common nervous system through a complex inheritance of linguistic and religious cross-references.(David Holdon, Farewell to Arabia, Faber, London, 1966, p. 242). Islam is more than religion, since it embraces a whole social system composed of Muslims: all those who have submitted to Allah, the one and only God. (Islam, in Arabic, means the state of submission, and Muslim is the one who has submitted.) By putting all believers on an equal footing - of submission to Allah - Islam, which originated in western Arabia during the seventh century, created a confraternity above the traditional bonds of clan and tribe. The faithful were united in their belief in Allah and his precepts, as conveyed through Muhammed (literally, praiseworthy), his messenger. `Islam in the Arab world differs from religion in Western society: it permeates the daily life of the individual with its ritualistic obligations,' states Hudson. `It is an important part of socialization; it affects personal status; it plays a political role. Islam also serves to integrate Arab society by inculcating a sense of the Muslim's special relationship with God and in the brotherhood and mutual obligations of all believers.... It is thus a powerful force for social and cultural stability.' (Ibid., p. 52.)[201]

The history of Saudi Arabia goes back to the mid-eighteenth century when Mohammed ibn Abdul Wahhab (1703-87), a militant alem (religious -legal scholar), led a puritanical movement for the abolition of the elaborate Islamic structure which had evolved over the past millennium, and which was being perpetuated by the ruling Ottoman caliph in Constantinople. He called for a return to the simplicity of the Islam of the prophet Mohammed's days, and the strict application of the Sharia, the Islamic law. In 1744 he allied himself with Mohammed ibn Saud, the leader of the Saudi tribe from Najd in central-eastern Arabia; and this gave considerable military muscle to his movement. By the early nineteenth century a coalition of tribes, fired by the tents of Wahhabism and led by Mohammed ibn Saud, had conquered a large part of the Arabian Peninsula. Further advances by these tribes were checked by the British- who controlled the Peninsula's coastline from Bahrain to Aden- and the Ottomans. The latter then went on the offensive, and pushed the leading Saudi tribe into its home territory of Najd. In 1891 the Rashedis, acting as clients of Ottomans, sent the Saudis into exile to Kuwait. It was not until 1902 that Abdul Aziz ibn (Abdul) Abdur Rahman al Saud (1881-1953) ventured out of Kuwait to regain Riyadh, the capital of Najd. Within the next decade he had extended his domain to the rest of Najd as well as the eastern province of Hosa. He prepared to attack the western province of Hejaz (containing the holy cities of Mecca and Medina) then ruled by Sharif Hussain ibn Ali. But his plans were interrupted by the outbreak of the First World War during the course of which Sharif Hussain formed an alliance with the British against the Ottoman Turks.[202]

---

[201] INTRODUCTION, INSIDE THE MIDDLE EAST BY DILIP HIRO, PUBLISHED BY ROUTLEDGE & KEGAN PAUL, 39 STORE STREET, LONDON WCIEE7DD AND BROADWAY HOUSE, NEWTON ROAD,HENLEY-on-Thames, Oxon RG91EN. PP. 3-5.

[202] INSIDE THE MIDDLE EAST (on ARAB MONARCHES) BY DILIP HIRO, PUBLISHED BY ROUTLEDGE & KEGAN PAUL, 39 STORE STREET, LONDON WCIEE7DD AND BROADWAY HOUSE, NEWTON ROAD,HENLEY-on-Thames, Oxon RG91EN. PP. 11-12.

S. Bobrovnikoff of St. Petersburg though at the time that "the strength of Muslims lies in their fanaticism and unity". The position of Muslims in China and Japan was similarly kept under constant review, Marshall Broomhall (Ibid, p. 35) found it remarkable that Islam "which deprecates the translation of the Koran into other languages has prospered so much as it has in China where its tents have not been propagated by the sword or by much political influence, "What was the threat of Islam as seen by this group of missionaries in 20th century?[203]

There were only 92 Caliphs and around 141 Caliphs if we include few Seljuk, Ayyubids and Mamluks Sultans during for long 1292 years, from 632 A. H. upto 1924. Yet the Abbaside Caliphate lasted for five centuries from its first establishment until the destruction of Baghdad by the Mongols in 1258 of the Christian era. At that time Musta'sim b'Illah was the Caliph, and he, together with his sons and the principal members of his family, perished in the general massacre; only those scions of the House of Abbas escaped the slaughter who were absent from the capital, or succeeded in avoiding detection. *For two years after the murder of Musta'sim b'Illah the Sunny world felt acutely the need of an Imam and Caliph;* both the poignancy of the grief at the absence of a spiritual Head of the faith, and the keenness of the necessity for a representative of the Prophet to bring solace and religious merit to the Faithful, are pathetically voiced by the Arab historian of the Caliphs (Ref: Ibid). The devotions of the living were devoid of that religious efficacy which is imparted to them by the presence in the world of an acknowledged Imam; the prayers for the dead were equally without merit. Sultan Baibars felt with the whole Sunny world the need of a Caliph and Imam. The right to the Caliphate had become vested in five centuries of undisputed acknowledgment in the House of Abbas; and a member of this family, Abu'l Kasim Ahmed, who had succeeded in making his escape from the massacre by the Mongols, was invited to Cairo for installation in the pontifical seat. On his arrival in the environs of Cairo, the Sultan, accompanied by the judges and great officers of State, went forth to greet him. The ceremony of installation is described as imposing and sacred. His descent had to be proved first before the Chief Kazi or Judge. After this was done, he was installed in the chair and acknowledged as Caliph, under the title of al-Mustansir b'Illah, "seeking the help of the Lord." The first to take the oath of Bai'at was the Sultan Baiber himself; next came the Chief Kazi (Judge) Taj-ud-din, the principal sheikhs and the ministers of state, and lastly the nobles, according to their rank. This occurred on May 12th, 1261, and the new Caliph's name was impressed on the coinage and recited in the Khutba. On the following Friday he rode to the mosque in procession, wearing the black mantle of the Abbaside (Black was the color of the Abbasides, white of the Ommeyyades and green of the Fatimides, the descendants of Mohammad (Sm)), and delivered the pontifical sermon. As his installation as the Caliph of the Faithful was now complete, he proceeded to invest the Sultan with the robe and diploma so essential in the eyes of the orthodox for legitimate authority. The Abbaside Caliphate thus established in Cairo lasted for over two centuries and a-half. During this period Egypt was ruled by sovereigns who are designated in history as the Mameluke Sultans. Each Sultan on his accession to power received his investiture from the Caliph and "Imam of his time" (*Imam-ul-Wakt*) and he professed to exercise his authority as the lieutenant and delegate of the Pontiff. The appointment of ministers of religion and administrators of justice was subject to the formal sanction of the Caliph. Though shorn of all its temporal powers, the religious prestige of the Caliphate was so great, and the conviction of its necessity as a factor in the life of the people so deep-rooted in the religious sentiments of the Sunny world, that twice after the fall of Baghdad

---

[203] **The Challenge of Islam edited by Altaf Gauhar, Foreword by Salem Azzam, Islamic Council of Europe, Islamic Information Services Limited, Radnor House, 93/97 Regent Street, London W1R7TD, Introduction, pp. XVII-XVIII.**

the Musalman sovereigns of India received their investiture from the Abbaside Caliphs. The account of the reception in 1343 A.C. of the Caliph's envoy by Sultan Mohammed Juna Khan Tughlak, the founder of the gigantic unfinished city of Tughlakabad, gives us an idea of the veneration in which the Pontiffs were held even in Hindustan (India), in those days said to be full six month's journey from Egypt. On the approach of the envoy the King, accompanied by the Syeds and the nobles, went out of the capital to greet him; and when the Pontiff's missive was handed to the Sultan he received it with the greatest reverence. The formal diploma of investiture legitimized the authority of the King. The whole of this incident is celebrated in a poem still extant in India by the poet laureate, the famous Badr-ud-din Chach. *About the end of the fifteenth century the star of Selim I., also surnamed Saffah, of the House of Ottoman, rose in the horizon. His victories over the enemies of Islam had won for him the title of "Champion of the Faith"; and no other Moslem sovereign- not even his great rival Shah Ismail, the founder of the Sufi dynasty in Persia and the creator of the first orthodox Shiah State,- equaled the Osmani monarch in greatness and power. The closing decades of that century had witnessed a vast change in the condition of Egypt, and the anarchy that had set in under the later Mameluke Sultans reached its climax some years later. Invited by a section of the Egyptian people to restore order and peace in the distracted country, Selim easily overthrew the incompetent Mamelukes, and incorporated Egypt with his already vast dominions. At this period the Caliph who held the Vice-gerency of the Prophet bore the pontifical name of Al-Motawakkil 'ala-Allah ("Contented in the grace of the Lord"). According to the Sunny records, he perceived that the only Moslem sovereign who could combine in his own person the double functions of Caliph and Imam, and restore the Caliphate of Islam in theory and in fact, and discharge effectively the duties attached to that office, was Selim. He accordingly, in 1517, by a formal deed of assignment, transferred the Caliphate to the Ottoman conqueror, and, with his officials and dignitaries, "made the Bai'at on the hand of the Sultan." In the same year Selim received the homage of the Sharif of Mecca, Mohammed Abu'l Barakat, a descendant of Ali, who presented by his son Abu Noumy on a silver salver the keys of the Kaaba (of The Holy Mecca, and took the oath by the same proxy. The combination in Selim of the Abbaside right by assignment and by Bai'at, and the adhesion of the representative of the Prophet's House who held at the time the guardianship of the Holy cities, perfected the Ottoman Sultan's title to the Caliphate, "just as the adhesion of (the Caliph) Ali had completed the title of the first three Caliphs." The solemn prayers with the usual Khutbas (Sermon) offered in Mecca and Medina for the Sultan gave the necessary finality to the right of Selim. Henceforth Constantinople, his seat of government, became the Dar-ul-Khilafat, and began to be called "Istanbol," "The City of Islam." Before long envoys arrived in Selim's Court and that of his son, Solyman the Magnificent, from the rulers of the Sunny States to offer their homage; and thus, according to the Sunnis, the Caliphate became the heritage of the House of Othman, which they have enjoyed for centuries without challenge or dispute.*[204]

Even other sovereign of Muslim States had a recognition from the Caliph.

The title of Sultan (An Arabic word meaning a ruler) was for the first time bestowed by Wasik upon Ashnas, the commandant of the Turkish guards, who was decorated with a jewelled crown and double girdle. It seems virtually to have remained in abeyance until the Buyides rose to power, when it was conferred on those princes. The investure was attended with great pomp and ceremony. The recipient of the title was first dressed in royal robes, a jeweled crown was placed on his head. a collar round his neck, a bracelet on his arm, and a sword was buckled round his waist. Finally, to mark the combination of both civil and

---

[204] **THE SPIRIT OF ISLAM BY** The Right Ho. Syed AMEER ALI, P.C. C.I.E pp. 2, 319 & 320, 124-133

military powers, two banners were handed to him by the Caliph personally, "one ornamented with silver, fashioned as is customary among the nobles, and the other with gold in the manner of those given to the successor designate to the Caliph." The diploma was then read out in the presence of the assembled multitude, after which the Sultan kissed the Caliph's hand.

The title of Sultan was not, however, confined to the Buyide princes. It was conferred on mighty conquerors like **Mahmud of Ghazni, Tughril. Alp Arsian, Malik Shah, Saladin, etc. Practically once assumed or conferred it became hereditary in the family, although on each succession, a formal investiture was applied for, and almost as a matter of course granted with the usual robes of honor. Later, another title was created, that of Malik (An Arabic word analogous to the Latin Rex), or king, which, sometimes jointly with the designation of Sultan and sometimes separately, but always with a qualifying phrase, was bestowed on ruling princes. The first to obtain this honor was the great Nur ud-din Mahmud, the son of Zangi, who received from the Caliph the title of al-Malik al-aadil, the just king.**[205]

Following verses are on fundamental:

3: 7 He it is Who has sent down To thee the Book: In it are verses Basic
3: 7 or fundamental (Of established meaning); They are the foundation of
3: 7 the Book: others Are allegorical. But those In whose hearts is per-
3: 7 versity follow The part thereof that is allegorical, Seeking discord
3: 7 and searching For its hidden meanings, But no one knows Its hidden
3: 7 meanings except Allah. And those who are firmly grounded In   3: 7
knowledge
3: 7 ge say: "We believe In the Book; the whole of it Is from our Lord":
3: 7 and none Will grasp the Message Except men of understanding.
11: 1 A. L. R. (This is) a Book, With verses basic or fundamental (Of
11: 1 established meaning), Further explained in detail,- From one Who   11: 1 is Wise
And Well- Acquainted (with all things):

Some of the leader in the Muslim leader say that until the people do not try to change their economy, God will not change that. But the irony is that from the following verse God has hinted that in the past many nations or people went back from religion or from the path of religion law and for which they were destroyed with God's punishment and no body was able to protect them from that punishment.

13: 11 for each (such person)There are (angels)in succession, Before and
13: 11 behind him: They guard him by command Of Allah. Verily never Will
13: 11 Allah change the condition Of a people until they Change it them
13: 11 selves (With their own souls). But when (once) Allah willeth A
13: 11 people's punishment, There can be no Turning it back, nor Will
13: 11 they find, besides Him, Any to protect.
14: 28 Fast thou not turned The vision to those who Have changed the
14: 28 favor of Allah Into blasphemy and caused Their people to descend
14: 28 To the House of perdition?-
14: 48 One day the Earth will be Changed to a different Earth, And so
14: 48 will be the Heavens, And(men) will be marshaled Forth, before
14: 48 Allah the One The Irresistible;
17: 56 Say:"call on those- Besides Him- whom ye fancy: They have
17: 56 neither the power To remove your troubles From you nor to
17: 56 change them"

---

[205] **HISTORY OF THE SARACENS BY SYED AMIR ALI PG. 411-412**

17: 77 (This was Our) way With the apostles We sent Before thee:thou
17: 77 wilt find No change in Our ways.

18: 27 And recite (and teach) What has been revealed To thee of the
18: 27 Book Of thy Lord: none Can change His Words And none wilt thou
18: 27 find As a refuge other than Him,
18: 36 "Nor do I deem That the Hour (of Judgment) Will (ever) come: Even
18: 36 if I am brought back To my Lord I shall Surely find (there)
18: 36 Something better in exchange."

From the following verse we can understand that we must surrender before the will and law
of God otherwise we will not remain dearer to God. Because though Iblis (Satan) was a
member of Zin, he was very dearer to God by virtue of his prayer to God. But when Iblish
did not obey God's command and instead he violated the Command of God for which he
was driven from God's mercy and was cursed. So it is compulsory for us to accept the
command of God or Law of God. And if in any pretext we violate God's Command we are
to face the fate of Iblis (now Satan).

18: 50 Behold! We said To the angels," Bow down To Adam": they bowed down
18: 50 Except Iblis. He was One of the Jinns, and he Broke the
18: 50 Command Of his Lord. Will ye then take him And his progeny as
18: 50 protectors Rather than Me? And they Are enemies to you!Evil
 18: 50 would be the exchange For the wrong-doers!

If we go through the right path, the path shown by God we will be benefited from God.
Now what are those right path?
We should believe in God who has created us; who has created this beautiful earth for us to
leave along with other creature and He has created all the things in proportion. If we do not
misuse those creature none of us will be deprived by those things, which may be foods,
shelter, weather and everything. We should make justice to our relative, neighbors, to the
wayfarer with the help of food, shelter and everything which God has given us; for which
we must have a sacrificing tendency, a mutual sharing mentality, a will to do good to
others, a will to know other's problem and all these will help to create a harmony, to create
a brotherhood relation among the people, among the nation and toward all the creature of
this world. We can do all these things if we have a love for entire mankind, entire creatures
and this universe.

If we go back from the path guided by the Holy Quran and the Holy Prophet (His Sunna or
Sayings) the Muslim will face the consequences as other nations who came before our Holy
Prophet.. The following (English translation) verses of the Holy Quran is the reply for all
The conspiracies against Islam and Caliphate(Khilafah):

God has sent us to create good things, good instances and for which time to time he has also
sent Prophets to earth to propagate good thing and to refrain from doing mischief.

 2: 30 Behold, thy Lord said to the angels:"I will create A vicegerent on
 2: 30 earth," They said, "Wilt Thou place therein one who will make
2: 30 Mischief therein and shed blood?- Whilst we do celebrate Thy
 2: 30 praises And glorify Thy holy (name)?" He said:"I know what ye know
 2: 30 not."

We must do righteous deeds for mutual benefit of us and the entire creatures.

103: 0 In the name of Allah, Most Gracious, Most Merciful.
103: 1 By (the Token of) Time (through the Ages)
103: 2 Verily Man Is in loss,
103: 3 Except such as have Faith And do righteous deeds, And (join
103: 3 together In the mutual teaching Of Truth and of Patience and
103: 3 Constancy.

 3: 16 (Namely),those who say:"Our Lord! we have indeed Believed: forgive
 3: 16 us, then, Our sins, and save us From the agony of the Fire!"-
 4: 16 If two men among you Are guilty of lewdness, Punish them both. If
 4: 16 they repent and amend, Leave them alone; for Allah Is
 4: 16 Oft-Returning, Most Merciful.

 72: 18 "And the places of worship Are for Allah (alone): So invoke not
 72: 18 anyone Along with Allah;

  2: 19 Or (another similitude) Is that of rain-laden cloud From the sky:
 2: 19 in it are zones Of darkness, and thunder and lightning: They press
 2: 19 their fingers in their ears To keep out the stunning thunder-clap,
 2: 19 The while they are in terror of death. But Allah is ever round the
 2: 19 rejecters of Faith !
 2: 20 The lightning all but snatches away Their light; every time the
 2: 20 light (Helps) them,they walk therein, And when the darkness grows
 2: 20 on them, They stand still. And if Allah willed, He could take away
 2: 20 Their faculty of hearing and seeing; For Allah hath power over all
 2: 20 things.
 2: 21 O ye people! Adore your Guardian-Lord, Who created you And those who
 2: 21 came before you, That ye may have the chance To learn righteousness

 68: 32 "It may be that our Lord Will give us in exchange A better
 68: 32 (garden) than this: For we do turn to Him (In repentance)!"
 74: 29 Darkening and changing The color of man!
 96: 0 In the name of Allah, Most Gracious, Most Merciful.
 96: 1 Proclaim! (or Read) In the name Of thy Lord and Cherisher, Who
 96: 1 created-
 96: 2 Created man, out of A (mere) clot Of congealed blood;
 96: 3 Proclaim! And thy Lord Is Most Bountiful,-
 96: 4 He Who taught (The use of) the Pen,-
 96: 5 Taught man that Which he knew not.
 96: 6 Nay, but man doth Transgress all bounds,
 96: 7 In that he looketh Upon himself as self-sufficient.
 96: 8 Verily, to thy Lord Is the return (of all)
 96: 9 Seest thou one Who forbids-
 96: 10 A votary when he (Turns) to pray?
 96: 11 Seest thou if He is on (the road Of) Guidance?-
 96: 12 Or enjoins Righteousness?
 96: 13 Seest thou if he Denies (Truth) and turn away?
 96: 14 Knoweth he not That Allah doth see?
 96: 15 Let him beware! If he Desist not,We will Drag him by the forelock,
 96: 16 A lying, sinful forelock!
 96: 17 Then, let him call (For help) to his council (Of comrades);
 96: 18 We will call On the angels of punishment (To deal with him)!
 96: 19 Nay, heed him not; But bow down in adoration, And bring thyself

96: 19 The closer (to Allah)'

100: 0 In the name of Allah, Most Gracious, Most Merciful.

100: 1 By the (Steeds) That run, with panting (breath)

100: 2 And strike sparks of fire

100: 3 And push home the charge In the morning .

100: 4 And raise the dust In clouds the while

100: 5 And penetrate forthwith Into the midst (of the foe) En masse;-

100: 6 Truly Man is To his Lord Ungrateful;

100: 7 And to that (fact) He bears witness (By his deeds):

100; 8 And violent is he In his love of wealth .

100: 9 Does he not know, When that which is In the graves is Scattered

100: 9 abroad .

100: 10 And that which is (Locked up) in (human) breasts Is made manifest-

100: 11 That their Lord had been Well acquainted with them (Even to) that Day ?

113: 2 From the mischief Of created things ;

113: 3 From the mischief Of Darkness as it overspreads;

113: 4 From the mischief Of those who practice Secret Arts;

113: 5 And from mischief Of the envious one As he practices envy.

114: 0 In the name of Allah Most Gracious, Most Merciful.

114: 1 Say: I seek refuge With the Lord And Cherisher of Mankind

114: 2 The King (or Ruler) Of Mankind,

114: 3 The Allah (or Judge) Of Mankind-

114: 4 From the mischief Of the Whisperer (Of Evil) who withdraws

114: 4 After his whisper)-

114: 5 (The same) who whispers Into the hearts of mankind,-

114: 6 Among Jinns And among Men.

We the Muslims are neglecting the fundamental political System of Islam, which is Caliphate, and only one Caliph, not even two, though at present, there are more than 50 separate Muslim States, even in Arabia proper there are more than 13 States, which is against the basic principle of Islam. And violating this fundamental Principle of Islam we are unable to do good thing in this world in term of charity to the poor, to the Islamic land, to save the massacre of Muslims in Asia, Africa and in Europe, for internal and external conflict. Following the Hadith or saying of our Prophet (Peace be upon him, his descendant and his companions).

(4568) It has been narrated on the authority of Abu Sa'id al-Khudri that the Messenger of Allah (may peace be upon him) said: When oath of allegiance has been taken for two caliphs, kill the one for whom the oath was taken later.[206]

---

[206] **SAHIH MUSLIM, BEING TRADITIONS OF THE SAYINGS AND DOINGS OF THE PROPHET MUHAMMAD AS NARRATED BY HIS COMPANIONS AND COMPLIED UNDER THE TITLE AL-JAMI-US-SAHIH BY IMAM MUSLIM, Rendered into English by ABDUL HAMID SIDDIQI VOLUME THREE, With Explanatory Notes, AND Brief Biographical Sketches of Major Narrators, PUBLISHED BY Nusrat Ali Nasri for KITAB BHAVAN, 1214, Kalan Mahal, Darya Ganj, NEW DELHI-110002,** [206]12 Chapter DCCLXV-III, p. 1032. **Explanatory Note ON # 4568:**

Under the above Hadith or a clause of the Muslim constitution, are the leaders of the Muslim countries are ready to accept the penalty for their misdeeds during last 100 years, accepted money from British Government to help British in the fight against Turkey, which happened in the great World War, and with this defeat of Turkey, Caliphate was abolished in 1924. Not only that from the following clause of our constitution, they are accused of violating another clause by accepting the money from British which helped to abolish the Caliphate.

p 1006 (4472) It has been narrated on the authority of A'isha, wife of the Holy Prophet (may peace be upon him), who said: The Messenger of Allah (may) set out for Badr. When he reached Harrat-ul-Wabara (a place four miles from Medina), a man met him who was known for his valor and courage. The Companions of the Messenger of Allah (may peace be upon him) were pleased to see him. He said: I have come so that I may follow you and get a share from the booty. The Messenger of Allah (may) said to him: Do you believe in Allah and His Apostle? He said: no. The Messenger of Allah (may) said: Go back, I will not seek help from a Mushrik (polytheist). He went on until we reached Shajara, where the men met him again. He asked him the same question again and the man gave him the same answer. He said: Go back, I will not seek help from a Mushrik. The man returned and overtook him at Baida? He asked him as he had asked previously: Do you believe in Allah and His Apostle? The man said: Yes. The Messenger of Allah (may) said to him: Then come along with us.[207]

This means that it is wrong to overthrow the regime established by the common constant of the people and which is run according to the Islamic laws. If the ruling party is to be deposed that should be done through legal means and not by raising the banner of revolt against it. The Muslim community should show allegiance to one ruler and as long as there is nothing definite against him on account of which he loses the support of a vast majority of the people, he should not be deprived of his authority. If an individual or a group does that by an open rebellion, he commits high treason, for which severe punishment may be awarded.

[207] **(2285)This hadith apparently contradicts some of the ahadith in which we learn that the Holy Prophet (may peace be upon him) accepted the help offered by a non-muslim in the military campaign, e.g. Safwan b. Umayya fought on the side of Muslims in the Battle of Hunain. Similarly, Quzman went out along with the Messenger of Allah (may peace be upon him) on the Day of Uhud in spite of the fact that he was a polytheist. These two instances go to prove that the help of a non-Muslim can be accepted when it is essential. Moreover, while seeking help of a non-Muslim we should take into consideration the attitude of his mind and the qualities of his head and heart. If a non-Muslim is favourably inclined towards Muslims, and his behaviour is sympathetic and he is honest in his words and deeds and there is no apprehension of any foul play on his part, then his help may be sought for and there is no harm in it. But if the attitude of his mind and his general behaviour are suspicious, then the Muslims should strictly avoid seeking the help of a non-Muslim. It is, however, desirable for the Muslims to dispense with the military servoces of a non-Muslim as far as it is possible. The fact is that a Muslim in exhorted to fight merely for the cause of Allah and thus he is required to observe certain lofty principles in the battlefield. It is for the achievement of the loftiest ends and those too with the help of the honest means that a Muslim takes up arms. He is thus equipped with a special mental make-up and his life is regulated with a moral code of behaviour, which can best be expected of a Muslim. Thus the Muslim should avoid getting his help as far as it is humanly possible. (For details see Imam Shawkani, Nail-ul-Autar, Vol.**

(4473) It has been narrated on the authority of Abu Huraira that the Messenger of Allah (may peace be upon him) said: People are subservient to the Quraish: the Muslims among them being subservient to the Muslims among them, and the disbelievers among the people being subservient to the disbelievers among them.

(4477) It has been narrated on the authority of Jabir b. Samura who said: I joined the company of the Holy Prophet (m) with my father and I heard him say: This Caliphate will not end until there hae been twelve Caliphs among them.

(2335) Abu Dharr reported Allah's Messenger (may peace be upon him) as saying: Verily there would arise from my Ummah after me or soon after me a group (of people) who would recite the Quran, but it would not go beyond their throats, and they would pass clean through their religion just as the arrow passes through the prey, and they would never come back to it. They would be the worst among the creation and the ceatures. Ibn Samit (one of the narrators) said: I met Rafi' b `Amr Ghifari, the brother of al-Hakam Ghifari and I said: What is this hadith that I heard from Abu Dharr, i.e. so and so?- and then I narrated that hadith to him and said: I heard it from the Messenger of Allah (may peace be upon him).

The Translation of Meanings of Sahih Al-Bukhari, Arabic-English Vol. VIII by Dr. Muhammad Muhsin Khan, Islamic University- Al-Medina Al-Munauwara, (12) CHAPTER. To inflict the legal punishment on the noble and the weak people (impartially). 778. Narrated Aisha : Usama approached the Prophet (Peace be upon him) on behalf of a woman (who had commited theft). The Prophet said. "The people before you were destroyed because they used to inflict the legal punishments on the poor and forgive the rich. By Him in Whose Hand my soul is! if Fatima (the daughter of the Prophet (R. A.) did that (i.e.) stole), I would cut off her hard."

VII,pp.223-5). SAHIH MUSLIM, BEING TRADITIONS OF THE SAYINGS AND DOINGS OF THE PROPHET MUHAMMAD AS NARRATED BY HIS COMPANIONS AND COMPLIED UNDER THE TITLE AL-JAMI-US-SAHIH BY IMAM MUSLIM, Rendered into English by ABDUL HAMID SIDDIQI VOLUME THREE, With Explanatory Notes, AND Brief Biographical Sketches of Major Narrators, PUBLISHED BY Nusrat Ali Nasri for KITAB BHAVAN, 1214, Kalan Mahal, Darya Ganj, NEW DELHI-110002,note by Abdul Hamiid Sddiqi, p. 1006 (4472).

THE SWORD OF ISLAM

Now before I go further I should quat some part of an article published in the TIME by Mr. James Walsh bellow:

The whole world, in fact, is watching and wondering about the impact of this tectonic shift, just as medieval Europe crouched when Islam reached the apogee of its power. With the death of the Soviet empire, some Western policy makers are concerned whether Islamic "fundamentalism-a term rejected by Muslims as a misnomer-may shape up as the next millennial threat to liberal democracy.

But in the same the writer mentioned "They (Muslims) look back to Muhammad's temporal rule in Arabia in the 7th century, and the "Rightly Guided Caliphs," whose regimes ensued, as the perfect model for statecraft today-even though their societies have been uprooted from the agricultural, nomadic, tribal world of the Prophet."

But respectable writer is perhaps ignorant about the democracy process of Islam during it's initial stage; which may be first in The world History at least at that time; by which those four rightly Guided Caliphs were elected when there was no trace of any democracy in Britain or in any European country. I am quoting from "Glimpses of World History" by Pandit (learned) Jawhar Lal Nehru, ex Prime Minister of India which was ruled my Muslims by the same period of long 800 (eight hundred) years as Christian Spain; though in christian Spain Muslims vanished; not a single muslim survived, but in present day India around one eighth of world Muslim live.

King Harsha died in 648 A.C. But even before his death a little cloud appeared on the north-west frontier of India, in Baluchistan - a cloud which was the forerunner of a mighty storm that was breaking in western Asia, Africa and southern Europe. A new prophet had arisen in Arabia, and Muhammad was his name, and he had preached a new religion called Islam. Fired with zeal for their new faith, and full of confidence in themselves, the Arabs dashed across continents, conquering as they went. It was an amazing feat, and we must examine this new force which came into the world and made so much difference to it. But before we consider it, we must pay a visit to South India and try to make out what it was like in those days.[208]

"It is strange that this Arab race, which for long ages had lived a sleepy existence, apparently cut off from what was happening elsewhere, should suddenly wake up and show such tremendous energy as to startly and upset the world. The story of the Arabs, and of how they spread rapidly over Asia, Europe and Africa, and of the high culture and civiliza- tion which they developed, is one of the wonders of history.

Within seven years of the flight, Mohammad returned to Mecca as its master. Even before this he sent out from Medina a summons to the kings and rulers of the world to acknowledge the one God and his Prophet. Heraclius, the Constantinople Emperor, got it while he was still engaged in his campaign against the Persians in Syria; the Persian King got it; and it is said that even Tai-Tsung got it in China. They must have wondered, these kings and rulers, who this unknown person was who dared to command them! From the

---

[208] **GLIMPSES OF WORLD HISTORY (SOUTH INDIA PRODUCES MANY KINGS) BY NEHRU PG. 126**

sending of these messages we can form some idea of the supreme confidence in himself and his mission which Mohammad must have had. And this confidence and faith he managed to give to his people, and with this to inspire and console them this desert people of no great consequence managed to conquer half the known world.

Confidence and faith in themselves were a great thing. Islam also gave them a message of brotherhood of the equality of all those who were Muslims. A measure of democracy was thus placed before the people. Compared to the corrupt Christianity of the day, this message of brotherhood must have had a great appeal, not only for the Arabs, but also for the inhabitants of many countries where they went.

Mohammad died in 632 A.C., ten years after the Hijrat. He had succeeded in making a nation out of the many warring tribes of Arabia and in firing them with enthusiasm for a cause. He was succeeded by Abu Bakr, a member of his family, as Khalifa or Caliph or chief. This succession used to be by a kind of informal election at a public meeting. Two years later Abu Bakr died, and was succeeded by Omar, who was Khalifa for ten years.

Abu Bakr and Omar were great men who laid the foundation of Arabian and Islamic greatness. As Khalifas they were both religious heads and political chiefs - King and Pope in one. In spite of their high position and the growing power of their State, they stuck to the simplicity of their ways and refused to countenance luxury and pomp. The democracy of Islam was a living thing for them. But their own officers and emirs took to silks and luxury soon enough, and irony stories are told of Abu Bakr and Omar rebuking and punishing these officers, and even weeping at this extravagance. They felt that their strength lay in their simple and hard living, and that if they took to the luxury of the Persian or Constantinople Courts, the Arabs would be corrupted and would fall.

Even in these short dozen years, during which Abu Bakr and Omar ruled, the Arabs defeated both the Eastern Roman Empire and the Sassanid King of Persia. Jerusalem, the holy city of the jews and Christians, was occupied by the Arabs, and the whole of Syria and Iraq and Persia became part of the new Arabian Empire.[209]

The religion he preached, by its simplicity and directness and its flavor of democracy and equality, appealed to the masses in the neighboring countries who had been ground down long enough by autocratic kings and equally autocratic and domineering priests. They were tired of the old order and were ripe for a change. Islam offered them this change, and it was a welcome change, for it bettered them in many ways and put an end to many old abuses. Islam did not bring any great social revolution in its train which might have put an end to a large extent to the exploitation of the masses. But it did lessen this exploitation so far as the Muslims ere concerned, and made them feel that they belonged to one great brotherhood. So the Arabs marched from conquest to conquest. Often enough they won without fighting. Within twenty-five years of the death of their Prophet, the Arabs conquered the whole of Persia and Syria and a bit of northern Africa on the west. Egypt had fallen to them with the greatest ease, as egypt had suffered most from the exploitation of the Roman Empire and from the rivalry of Christian sects. There is a story that the Arabs burnt the famous library of Alexandria, but this is now believed to be false. The Arabs were too fond of books to behave in this barbarous manner. It is probable, however, that the Emperor Theodosius of Constantinople, about whom I have told you something already, was guilty of this de-

---

[209] **GLIMPSES OF WORLD HISTORY (THE COMING OF ISLAM) BY NEHRU PG. 142-145**

struction, or part of it. A part of the library had been destroyed long before, during a siege at the time of Julius Caesar.[210]

With the accession of 'Abdul-Malik (685-705),the government was stabilized, and a new wave of conquests began. Morocco, Spain, North of the Indo-Pakistanian continent as Transoxiana were added to the domain of the Muslims. Bordeaux,Narbonne and Touluse (in France) also passed into their hands. The Metropolis moved from Medina to Damascus and religious devotion was weakened in favor of secular activities.Luxury, favoritism and the consequent revolts and upheavals were not lacking. The short reign of "Umar ibn ' Abd al-Aziz (817-20) was particularly brilliant and epoch-making. He, by his piety, brought a renewal of the period of Abu Bakr and 'Umar. He revised the old files of confiscations, in order to return properties to the rightful owners or to their heirs.

He went so far as to order the evacuation of towns-Samarqand, for instance-which were treacherously occupied by Muslim armies. And he had not hesitated to order demolition of part of the grand mosque of the capital, built on an usurped piece of land. The result was astonishing. At the start of this dynasty,the revenues of Iraq, which for instance,amounted to 100 million dirhams, which fell to 18 million under the Caliph preceding 'Umar ibn "Abd al-Aziz. But under him they soared to as much as 120 million. His religious devotion produced a world-wide impression of good, and the rulers of Sindh, Turkistan and other lands embraced Islam. Everyone began to take interest in religious studies, and a whole galaxy of Muslim savants entered the fields of science and greatly extended the frontiers of knowledge through their painstaking investigations.

The ruins or remains of monuments at Damascus and elsewhere including the Dome of the Rock, at Jerusalem, constructed in 691 A.D., bear witness to the great progress of Muslims in architecture. Great development of music is also noted, although the sings of musical notations were not yet invented. The two great sects among Muslims, the Sunnites and Shites, date from the same period. The difference between these two sects is based on a political question, whether the succession to the Prophet was to take place by election or by inheritance among the close relatives of the Prophet? This became a question of dogma to the Shites resulting in a schism which led to civil wars. It is one such uprising which swept away the Umayyad dynasty, and made it yield its place in 750 f to the "Abbasids, but the Shiates did not profit by the change. In our days, there are about ten per cent Shiaites among the Muslims of the world, the rest being almost all Sunnites, not to speak of the infinitesimally small sect of the Kharijites, which also came into existence at the same time.

The "Abbasids" rise to power in 750 A.D., coincides with the division of the Muslim territory first into two, and later into ever-increasing independent states. At Cardova (Spain), a rival caliphate was established, which never reconciled itself till its downfall in 1492, to union with the East, where Baghdad had taken the place of Damascus as the seat of the caliphate.

The history of the "Abbasids does not show any big military conquest.
About a century after their assuming power, the "Abbaside Caliphs began to delegate and even lose their sovereign prerogatives in favor of centrifugal governors;and gradually their sovereignty was limited to their own palace, the rest being controlled by emirs, of whom the most powerful occupied even the metropolis.

---

[210] **GLIMPSES OF WORLD HISTORY (THE ARABS CONQUER FROM SPAIN TO MONGOLIA) BY NEHRU PG. 145**

We see therein a strange contrast with Papacy:The Popes began without any political power, but later acquired it after some centuries particularly with the creation of the Holy Roman Empire. For some time they became even more powerful than emperors, only to lose this authority in course of time.

It was under the "Abbasids that the governor of Tunis of the Aghlabid dynasty was invited to intervene in the civil wars of Sicily.He occupied the island, and also much of the mainland of Italy itself, advancing as far as the walls of Rome. The South of France was annexed as also a considerable part of Switzerland. This wave of expansion was the work of the Aghlabids, who were later replaced by force, evidently by the Fatimids of the Shiite sect who transferred their capital to Cairo, where they established a rival caliphate.

There was no central authority in the Islamic world at that time,but dozens of petty states warring with each other. The Kurds and Turks replaced the Arabs in the struggle against the occident. Saladin not only expelled the Europeans from Syria-Palestine but also swept away the Fatimids of Egypt.

In 921 A.D., the king of 'Bulgar' (i.e. the region of Kazan, on the river Volga, in Russia) solicited a Muslim missionary from Baghdad. Ibn Fadlan was sent. According to the report of his travel, which is extremely interesting, the King of Bulgar embraced Islam, and created, so to say, an Islamic island in the midst of the non-Muslim regions. The Islamization of Caucasus and the neighboring regions continued slowly.

In 1858 the British annexed three-fifth of the country for the British Crown, the rest being divided among indigenous states, some of which were Muslim, which preserved the Indo Muslim cultures until our own times.

With their rise to power in the 11th Century, they subjugated not only Central Asia, but extended their conquests even as far as the farthest ends of Asia Minor, with Konia (Iconium) as their capital. After some generations of brilliant rule, they yielded place to the Ottoman Turks, who crossed the Bosphorus and extended the Islamic dominion to the walls of Vienna. Their capital was first at Brusa (Bursa), then Constantinople (Byzantium, now Istanbul), and is at present Ankara (Angora, ancyre). Their recoil began in the 18th Century, with their evacuating region after region of the European soil, and reached its climax in 1919, when they lost everything in the first World War. Turkey rose again in the form of republic, which was at the outset nationalist and secular, but being democratic by nature, its regime had to conform more and more to the religious sentiments of the people which are profoundly Islamic. In the 16th Century, the Ottoman Turks ruled in Europe as far as Austria, in North Africa as far as Algeria, and in Asia from Georgia to Yemen passing in between through Mesopotamia Arabia and Asia Minor. Some of their former Muslim possessions are now independent states, but others have passed under the Soviet domination.

At the rise into caliphate power of the 'Abbasids, Spain detached itself from the Muslim Orient. After almost a thousand years of domination, in 1242, the last traces of a Muslim state were submerged there by the Castillian Christians.

The Muslims crossed the Pyrenees and entered France, but were checked at Poitiers, hardly 100 miles from Paris. 750-1258 "Abbasid Caliphate."

Even a scholar metioned the following on Muslim rule in America Continent:

In spite of the destruction of historical documents, there is every reason to believe that the Muslims of Black Africa and the Berbers participated in the colonization of America as the name of Brazil suggests, since Birzalah is a well-known Berber tribe, and the collective name of the members of this tribe is precisely Brazil. The island of Palma, in the Atlantic, was formerly called Bene Hoare after the name of the Berber tribe Beni Huwara. The relation of the Muslim West Africa with America continued till the fall of Muslim Spain and the commencement of the European voyages to America.

The Arabs discovered the Azores, and it is surmised that they even penetrated as far as America.[211]

You can go through a Book, "BEFORE COLUMBUS, LINKS BETWEEN THE OLD WORLD AND ANCIENT AMERICA" by CYRUS H. GORDON; PUBLISHED BY Crown Publishers, Inc., New York..
The followings are quotation from the above book: pag-68:
Nearly all the coins are Roman, from the reign of Augustus to the fourth century AD; two of the cooins, however are Arabic of the eighth century AD.... A Moorish ship, perhaps from Spain or North Africa, seems to have crossed the Atlantic around AD 800. The Coimbra Map of AD 1424 shows parts of North America. ......To place the subject in depth, we return to the map of Piri Reis which were rediscovered in 1929 in the old Imperial Palace in Istanbul. The principal map was painted on parchment in 1513 by the Turkish Admiral Piri.....
I got another document in which I knew that in nineteenth century a contact was signed by USA Government with a Red Indian Muslim
Still there are more than 1200 million Muslims in the world today, i.e., about one-fifth of the human race, and wherever they are, they turn their faces every day towards the Kabah to proclaim about "Allah-o-Akbar,"that God alone is great.

It has been said that a warlike spirit was infused into medieval Christianity by aggressive Islam ! The massacres of Justinian and the fearful wars of Christian Clovis in the name of religion, occurred long before the time of Mohammed.

Compare, again, the conduct of the caliph Omar took Jerusalem, A.D. ,637 he rode into the city by the side of the Patriarch Sophronius, conversing with him on its antiquities. At the hour of prayer, he declined to perform his devotions in the Church of the Resurrection, in which he chanced to be, but prayed on the steps of the Church of Constantine; for, said he to the Patriarch, had I done so, the Musulmans in a future age might have infringed the treaty, under color of imitating my example; But in the capture by the Crusaders, the brains of young children were dashed out against the walls; infants were pitched over the battlements; men were roasted at fires; some were ripped up, to see if they had swallowed gold; the Jews were driven into their synagogue, and there burnt; a massacre of nearly 70,000 persons took place; and the pope's legate was seen partaking in the triumph! When Saladin recaptured the city, he released all Christians, gave them money and food, and allowed them to depart with a safe- conduct.2

Islam grasped the sword in self-defence: Christianity grasped it in order to stifle freedom of thought and liberty of belief. With the conversion of Constantine, Christianity had become the dominant religion of the Western world. It had thenceforth nothing to fear from its enemies; but from the moment it obtained the mastery, it developed its true character of isolation and exclusiveness.

---

[211] **HISTORY OF THE SARACENS (COMMERCIAL ACTIVITY) BY SYED AMIR ALI PG. 461**

Wherever Christianity prevailed, no other religion could be followed without molestation. The Moslems, on the other hand ,required from others a simple guarantee of peace and amity, tribute in return for protection, or perfect equality, - the possession of equal rights and privileges, on condition of the acceptance of Islam.

Has any conquering race or Faith given to its subject nationalities a better guarantee than is to be found in the following words of the Prophet? "To [the Christians of] Najran and the neighboring territories, the security of God and the pledge of His Prophet are extended for their lives ,their religion, and their property-to the present as well as the absent and others besides; shall be no interference with [the practice of] their faith or their observances; nor any change in their rights or privileges; no bishop shall be removed from his bishopric; nor any monk from his monastery, nor any priest from his priesthood, and they shall continue to enjoy every thing great and small as heretofore; no image or cross shall be destroyed; they shall not oppress or be oppressed; they shall not practice the rights of blood-vengeance as in the Days of Ignorance; no tithes shall be levied from them nor shall they be required to furnish provisions for the troops.

After the subjugation of Hira, and as soon as the people had taken the oath of allegiance, Khalid bin-Walid issued a proclamation by which he guaranteed the lives, liberty and property of the Christians, and declared that "they shall not be prevented from beating their nakus and taking out their crosses on occasions of festivals." "And this declaration," says Imam Abu-Yousuf, was approved of and sanctioned by the Caliph and his council.

Jesus was a Jew, and the Jews were and are a peculiar and strangely persevering people. After a brief period of glory in the days of David and Solomon they fell on evil days. Even this glory was on a small scale, but it was magnified in their imaginations till it became a kind of Golden Age of the past, which would come again at the appointed time were the Jews would become great and powerful. They spread out all over the Roman Empire and elsewhere, but held together, firm in the belief that their day of glory was coming and that a messiah would usher this in. It is one of the wonders of history how the Jews, without a home or a refuge, harassed and persecuted beyond measure, and often done to death, have preserved their identity and held together for over 2000 years.

The Jews expected a messiah, and perhaps they had hopes of Jesus. But they were soon disappointed. Jesus talked a strange language of revolt against existing conditions and the social order. In particular he was against the rich and the hypocrites who made of religion a matter of certain observances and ceremonial. Instead of promising wealth and glory, he asked people to give up even what they had for a vague and mythical Kingdom of Heaven. He talked in stories and parables, but it s clear that he was a born rebel who could not tolerate existing conditions and was out to change them. This was not what the Jews wanted, and so most of them turned against him and handed him over to the Roman authorities.

The Roman people were not intolerant so far as religions went, for the Empire tolerated and religions, and even if someone chose to blaspheme or curse any of the gods, he was not punished. As one of the emperors, Tiberius, said: "If the gods are insulted, let them see to it themselves." The Roman governor, Portius Pilate, before whom Jesus was produced, could not therefore have worried about the religions aspect of the matter. Jesus was looked upon as a political, and by the Jews as a social, rebel; and as such he was threatened sentenced and crucified at Golgotha. In the hour of his agony even his chosen disciples deserted him and denied him, and by their betrayal made his suffering almost unbearable, so that, before he died, he uttered those strangely moving words: "My God! My God! why hast thou forsaken me ?"
Jesus was quite young, being only a litt e over thirty when he died. We read in the beautiful language of the Gospels the tragic story of his death, and are moved.

But when a person is prepared to die for a cause, and indeed to glory in such a death, it is impossible to suppress him or the cause he represents. And the Roman Empire wholly failed to suppress the Christians. Indeed, it was Christianity that came out triumphant in the conflict, and early in the fourth century after Christ one of the Roman emperors himself became a Christian, and Christianity became the official religion of the Empire. This was Constantine, who founded Constantinople. We shall come to him later.

Similarly, Jesus claimed no divinity. His repeated statements that he was the son of God and the son of man do not necessarily mean any divine or superhuman claim. But human beings like to make gods of their great men, whom, having deified, they refrain from following! Six hundred years later the Prophet Muhammad started another great religion, but profiting perhaps by these instances, he stated clearly and repeatedly that he was human, and not divine.

These internal disputes took place as the Church grew in power. They have continued between various Christian sects till quite recent times in the West.

Christianity came to India long before it want to England or western Europe, and when even in Rome it was a despised and proscribed sect. Within 100 years or so of the death of Jesus, Christian missionaries came to South India by sea. They were received courteously and permitted to preach their new faith. They converted a large number of people, and their descendants have lived there, with varying fortunes, to this day. Most of them belong to old Christian sects which have ceased to exist in Europe. Some of these have their hindquarters now in Asia Minor.

Christianity is politically the dominant religion to-day, because it is the religion of the dominate peoples of Europe. But it is strange to think of the rebel Jesus preaching non-violence and ahimas and a revolt against the social order, and then to compare him with his loud-voiced followers of to-day, with their imperialism and armaments and were and worship of wealth. The Sermon on the Mont and modern European and American Christianity how amazingly dissimilar they are![212]

After Islam began, for many hundred years Musalmans lived in all parts of India in perfect peace with their neighbors. They were welcomed when they came as traders and encouraged to settle down. But I am anticipating. So India welcomed the Zoroastrians, just as a few hundred years before, she had also welcomed many Jews who fled from Rome in the first century after Christ on account of persecution. In the fifteenth century the Muslims finally obtained control, and soon after came the Portuguese and the Spaniards, the Dutch and the English, and last of all the Americans. We find especially the Arabs settling down in South China, near Canton, about 300 AC This was before Islam came - that is, before the birth of the Prophet Muhammad. With the help of these Arabs an overseas trade developed and was carried in Arab as well as Chinese ships.[213]

It took some time for Christianity to reach China. But Islam came more swiftly. It came, indeed, a few years before the Nestorians and during the lifetime of its Prophet. The

---

[212] **GLIMPSES OF WORLD HISTORY (JESUS AND CHRISTIANITY, THE ROMAN EMPIRE) PG. 85-87**

[213] **GLIMPSES OF WORLD HISTORY (PARTHIA AND THE SASSANIDS, SOUTH INDIA COLONIZES, CHINA FLOURISHES UNDER THE TANGS) BY NEHRU PG. 98, 101, 115**

Chinese Emperor received both the embassies Islamic and Nestorian with courtesy and listened to what they had to say. He appreciated their views and showed favor impartially. The Arabs were permitted to build a mosque in Canton. This mosque still exists, although it is 1300 years old, and is one of the oldest mosques in the world.[214]

[214] GLIMPSES OF WORLD HISTORY (CHINA FLOURISHES UNDER THE TANGS) BY NEHRU PG. 116

SPIRITUAL POWER VS SWORD OF ISLAM

The true power of Islam is spiritual, not any kind of sword and that is why during the life time of the Prophet (Sm), Islam spread in the far country like China where one of the oldest mosque exist to-day in Canton. The first invasion of Arab in India was in Punzab and Sind which are now part of Pakistan now also brought many muslim Saints in it's early stage along with the first invasion by Karim bin Kasim. And the fact is that Islam came to India, particularly in South India during the life time of the Holy Prophet (Sm). **But in Spain it vanished because the Umayads who took Islam there only through sword not thorough any Saints, of whom most were from the descendant of the holy Prophet(Sm), because Spain was cut up from mainland Arab Islam after the fall of Umayds by the Iranian General   though the Abbaside took the Caliphate. In whole of India the Muslims exit because many Saints (R. A.), who were direct descendant of the Holy Prophet came to India with their spiritual power and with love to the Indian people and spread all over India, one such example is Ajmir. Though there were some excess by some rulers it is not true for all the rulers even for Babar who was a saint like man.**

Again Islam was not spread by Sword but by the Saint with their high spiritual power. In south-east Asia like Indonesia and Malaysia no soldier went there to conquer those countries but the Muslim Saints and perhaps traders: Following reference from India's Nehru which are follows:

Now a new influence comes on the scene. This is brought by the Arabs. Burma and Siam were not affected by this, but Malay and the islands succumb to it, and soon a Muslim empire grows up. Arab traders had visited these islands and settled there for 1000 years or more. But they were intent on business, and did not otherwise interfere with the governments. In the fourteenth century Arab missionaries came out from Arabia, and they met with success, especially in converting some of the local rulers.

As is usual with imperialists, they were tyrannous, and many people preferred going to the new State of Malacca to remaining under Madjapahit. Siam was also at the time rather aggressive. So Malacca became a place of refuge for many people. There were both Buddhists and Muslims. The rulers were at first Buddhists, but later they adopted Islam.
 The young State of Malacca was menaced by Java on the one side and Siam on the other. It tried to find friends and allies among the other small Muslim State in the islands. It even appealed to China for protection. At that time the Mings, who had displaced the Mongols, ruled in China. It is remarkable how all the little Islamic States in Malaysia turned to China for protection at the same time. This shows that there must have been some immediate threat from powerful enemies.
 So the State of Malacca became the head of the opposition to Madjapahit. Its strength grew and gradually it seized the colonies of Java. In 1478 the city of Madjapahit itself was captured. Islam then became the religion of the Court and of the cities.[215]

The Timurids were Turks, and they had succumbed largely to Persian culture. ....
At the beginning of the sixteenth century Iranian nationalism triumphed, and the Timurids were finally driven out from Persia. A national dynasty, the Safavi or Safavids, came on the

---

[215] **GLIMPSES OF WORLD HISTORY (THE MALAYSIAN EMPIRES) PG. 262-263**

Persian throne. It was the second of this dynasty, Tahmasp I, who gave refuse to I Humayun fleeing from India before Sher Khan. The Safavi period lasted for 220 years from 1502 to 1722. ... The Safavis in Persia were more or less contemporaneous with the Great Moguls in India. Babar, the first of the Indian Moguls, was one of the Timurid princes of Samarqand. As the Persians had gained strength they had driven the Timurids away, and only parts of Transoxiana and Afghanistan remained under various Timurid princes. Babar had to fight from the age of twelve among these petty princes. He succeeded, and made himself ruler of Kabul, and then came to India. The high culture of the Timurids at the time can be judged from Babar, from whose memoirs I gave you (Nehru's daughter Indira Gandhi) some quotation in a previous letter. Shah Abbas, the greatest of the Safavi rulers, was a contemporary of Akbar (Babar's grandson) and Jehangir. Between the two countries all along there must have been the most intimate contact. For long they had a common frontier, Afghanistan being part of the Mogul Indian Empire. [216]

---

[216] **GLIMPSES OF WORLD HISTORY BY NEHRU, PG. 494-495**

Conspiracy for the abolition of Caliphate by European countries particularly by Britain.

A strange patchwork was India during the hundred years following Aurangzeb's death, a kaleidoscope, ever changing, but not very beautiful to look at. Such a period is an ideal one for adventures and those who are bold and unscrupulous enough to seize opportunities without caring for the means or methods adopted. So adventurers rose all over India, adventurers who were native to the soil, and those who came across the north-west frontier, and those, like the English and French, who came across the seas. Each man or group played his or its own hand and was prepared to send all the others to the devil; sometimes two or more combined to crush a third, only, later, to fall out among themselves. There were frantic attempts to carve out kingdoms and to get rich quickly, and to plunder, often undisguised and unashamed, sometimes under a thin disguise of trade. And behind all this was the vanishing Mogul Empire, disappearing like the Cheshire cat, till not even the smile remained, and the so-called Emperor was an unhappy pensioner or prisoner of others. But all this upheaval and turmoil, and turning and twisting, were the outward indications of a revolution going on below the surface. The old economic order was breaking up; feudalism had its day and was collapsing. It was not in keeping with the new conditions in the country. We have seen this process in Europe, and we have seen the merchant classes rise, only to be checked by absolute monarchs. Only in England, and to some extent in Holland, were the monarchs subdued. When Aurangzeb came to the throne, England was under the short-lived republic which followed the execution of Charles I. And it was during Aurangzeb's reign also that the British revolution was completed by the running away of James II and the victory of Parliament in 1688. The fact that England had a semi-popular council like Parliament helped greatly in the struggle. There was something which could be set up against the feudal nobles and later, the king.[217]

The Caliphate System was never a new system, but it started after the last Prophet of Islam went out of human sight. The Pope System started, several hundred years after the Prophet Jesus (peace be upon him) was taken to heaven alive, and not like Muslim Caliphat. Yet Pope was only religious head. The following comment of Nehru is enough about the Caliph:

Compare this emperor(Holy Roman Empire) with the Khalifa or Caliph, who was styled the Commander of the Faithful. The Khalifa was really an emperor and Pope combined, to begin with. Later, as we shall see, he became just a figurehead.[218]

A Mongol army sent to Palestine was defeated by Sultan Baibers of Egypt. This Sultan had an interesting surname -"Bandukdar"- because of a regiment of men armed with banduks or firearms. We now come to the era of the firearms. The Chinese had long known gunpowder. The Mongols probably learnt it from them and it may be that firearms helped

---

[217] GLIMPSES OF WORLD HISTORY BY NEHRU, PP. 317-318.

[218] GLIMPSES OF WORLD HISTORY BY NEHRU, PG. 158

them in their victories. It was through the Mongols that firearms were introduced into Europe.[219]

Recently, we the people of this world are observing various terrorism around the world, and most of these terrorism's are state terrorism. Helplessly we are presiding over all these state terrorism like killing of Muslims in India by the government police and paramilitary forces whose duty is to defend the citizen of the country. Even under the coverage of United Nations we are observing how a community like Muslims, who once was the leader of vast territories of Asia, Africa and Europe, during the time of caliphate upto 1924, has been cleansed in Bosnia. More wonderful event is that those Muslims have not been allowed to defend themselves, they were denied the minimum arms to defend themselves. But the Muslim used to protest those state terrorism they are branded as terrorist. But can you fool the entire humanity?

The Muslim rulers around the world did not misbelieve to any race or the followers of any religion. They even allowed the foreign tourists of many religion to do business in the Muslim held countries, in the Arab Gulf and in India. Though when those outsiders took the chance of correct moment to fight with those ruler who allowed them to stay in their country. And ultimately even those outsiders who were given chance to do business, even ousted those rulers who gave them selters and the facilities. Those outsiders eve did not hesitate to kill those with the whole family member, whenever they got such chance with the help of bribing some local people or some members of the ruling family. This happened with the killing of princes of last Mogul Emperor, Bahadur Shah Jafar. Bahadur Shah Jafar was even expelled to Burma. Before that Nawab Sirajud-Dowla of Bengal was killed. This happened to Tipu Sultan and many rulers in India. And finally this happened in the process of abolition of Caliphate in Arab World. Following references are the proof of my above observation:

As a matter of fact, the first so-called legal title of the East India Company in Bengal was that of revenue-farmer on behalf of the Mogul Emperor. This was the grant of the diwani to the Company in 1765. The Company thus became a kind of diwan of the Moghal Emperor at Delhi. But all this was fiction. After Plassey, in 1757, the British were predominant in Bengal, and the poor Mogul Emperor had little or no power anywhere. The East India Company and its officers were terribly greedy. ... They tried to squeeze Bengal and Bihar and extract the maximum of land revenue. ....The revenue-farmers for some time past had been behaving like landowners. The result was that for the first time India got this new type of middleman, and the cultivators were reduced to the position of mere tenants. The British dealt with these land-holders or zamindars directly, and left them to do what they liked with their tenantry. There was no protection of any kind for the poor tenant from the rapacity of the landlord.

This settlement that Cornwallis made with the zamindars of Bengal and Bihar in 1703 is called the "Permanent Settlement". The word "settlement" means the fixing of the amount of land revenue to be paid by each zamindar to the Government. [220]

Let us see what what God directs us through Holy Quran directs us:

---

[219] GLIMPSES OF WORLD HISTORY BY NEHRU, PP. 222-223.

[220] GLIMPSES OF WORLD HISTORY BY NEHRU, PP. 425-426.

2:120 Never will the Jews Or the Christians be satisfied With thee unless
2:120 thou follow Their form of religion. Say: "The Guidance of Allah ,-
2:120 that Is the (only) Guidance. " Wert thou to follow their desires
2:120 After the knowledge Which hath reached thee, Then wouldst thou find
2:120 Neither Protector nor Helper Against Allah.

The above verse has proved for the Islamic Khelafat a reality, what happened during for past about 100 years not by the story of the muslim writers but by the western researchers, one such recent book is "UNHOLY BABYLON" by ADEL DARWISH AND GREGORY ALEXANDER.

In the above book in page 7 under the caption "LINES IN THE SAND" the authors has mentioned "On the eve of the First World, Britain was conspiring to use the warlike bedouin to protect its interest in the Middle East, either under the leadership of their sheikhs or under British officers - such as T. E. Lawrence - rather than deploying its own soldiers in the desert. To secure the support of Mubarak, Britain agreed to recognize Kuwait as independent of the Ottoman Empire. In exchange, Mubarak was to support Britain against Turkey in the coming war.

Kuwait emerged as an emirate, as it was known in the Ottoman administration, or sheikhdom as the Arabs knew it, during a period when the entire area was suffering from a political vacuum. ottoman rule, which had been established in Iraq in 1550, could not control the tribes of the coast whilst at the same time the new european powers had begun to fight over maritime supply lines to secure a route to India. What is now known as Kuwait was part of Lewa'a Al-Basra. In theory, it came under the control of Vali Al-Basra(the Governor of Basra), but his grip on the upper Gulf had weakened by the early eighteenth century.

In about 1710, a new clan led by Sheikh Sabah bin Jaber arrived, with other clans, on the sea coast in the north-eastern corner of the Arabian Peninsula Some 160 years later, The long-running conflict between the Ottomans and the Persians gave a defacto independence to the emirate which had not existed two decades earlier. By the time Abdullah died in 1815, the tribes of U'tubs dominated Bahrain as well as Kuwait, controlling the entire Arab maritime trade and pearling in the Gulf.

Dutch maps dated 1740 make no mention of Kuwait, but they show the island of Failaks, calling it Peleche. It was there that in 322 BC Nearchus, the admiral who led the fleet of Alexander the Great, built of fortress when Alexander ordered him to return from India to the Euphrates via the Gulf, hoping to secure a maritime link between Babylon, the capital of his eastern Empire, and India.

The name Kuwait first appeared, written next to a tower on the coastal area known as Graen, on a navigation map drawn up by the Dutch East India Company and dated 1765. The word is the plural of Kut, which means a tower or small coastal castle.

But can any muslim leader claim to be a follower of Islam who conspire with non-muslim leader to divide the Islamic world?

2: 86 These are the people who buy The life of this world at the price Of
2: 86 the hereafter: their penalty Shall not be lightened, Nor shall they
2: 86 be helped.

And according to Holy Quran last Prophet of Islam (Peace be upon him) was sent to proclaim it over all religion the verse is as follows:

48 28 IT IS HE WHO HAS SENT HIS APOSTLE WITH GUIDANCE AND THE RELIGION OF
48 28 TRUTH, TO PROCLAIM IT OVER ALL RELIGION: AND ENOUGH IS ALLAH FOR
48 28 A WITNESS.

In page 71 of the above book under heading "IRAQ AND THE WEST", more references from the above book are given bellow:

"On 5th September 1990, in a comment on the Western response to Iraq's invasion of Kuwait, Moroccan writer Abdellatif Laabi wrote in the magazine Zeune

In 1492 A. C. the Arab Muslims had to surrender to the King Ferdinand and Queen Isabella after 800 long years and for the division among the Muslim rulers.
The Muslims could not get any lessons from the event in Spain and the division among them in the name of language and culture effected ultimately the abolition of long 1300 years long Caliphate, and even most Muslims do not remember the past glorious period of Muslims Caliphate during which the whole world enlightened by their high culture when the Muslims introduced science in whole world, even in Spain, when the oldest university like Al-Agar was established in Cairo, though certain university in Cordoba, Spain was destroyed by Christians, in Baghdad by Halaku Khan, but suddenly since 1924 when Caliphate was formally abolished, The Muslim Leaders now pretends in such a way that we forgot the basis of Islamic Political System of Caliphate and we are satisfied with so called OIC or Organization of Islamic Conference, though no benefit was derived from OIC, except fighting among Muslims, between Iraq and Iran, between, Iraq and Kuwait and so many. The result of all these violent among Muslims are due to lost of memory of the past which are as follows:

Jerusalem is sacred to the Jews, the Christians and the Muslims. But when Jerusalem was conquered by the Muslims during the Caliphate of Hadrat Umar, he allowed the freedom of all religion, and even he did not offer Muslim prayer in the Church for which the then Bishop requested him just to honor him. Hadrat Umar (God be pleased with him) knew that if he offered prayer in the church the future Muslims will convert it into a mosque. In return of this true Muslim gesture, after few hundred years, the Christian world imposed an unnecessary war on Muslims which is called 'Crusade Wars which continued from 1096 to 1202 A. C. It should be mentioned here that during the third Crusade all the great Monarchs of the Christian Europe, namely, Frederick Barbarous of Germany, Philip Augustus of France and Richard I of England led a United expedition against the Muslims on Jerusalem, but they were defeated by Ghazi Salahuddin Ayubi and they were forced to retreat after concluding a treaty in November, 1192 A. C. The Crusade War came to an end by the end of Thirteenth Century when the Christians lost their faith in the old ideal of Crusade as "the way of God" and failure brought lassitude to them. Jerusalem finally came under the Muslim occupation and remained in the possession of the Turkish or Osmani Caliphate until December, 1917 A. C. when the British army marched from Egypt and occupied it at the closure of the first World War. It is however, in 1917 that the British General **Allenby standing at the foot of the Citadel in Jerusalem declared, "the crusade wars have finally ended". This declaration thoroughly unmasked the British's true intention of making 'alliance' with the Arabs who were completely disillusioned. Thus Arab Muslims are responsible for the defeat of the Muslims at the hand of Christians because they conspired against the Osmani Caliphate and took the Christians as their friend when Lawrence of Arabia arrived in the Arab land with a mission of dividing the**

Muslims into two group i. e. The Arabs and the Turks, and with the same mission the British's arrived in the soil of almost all Muslim world. They came to India and established it's base in Bengal and other coastal area of India and particularly divided the ruling Muslims with the same dose of assurance of future power to the greedy power hungry Muslim relative of Nawab Sirajjod Dowla and probably used the Hindus against ruling Muslims. They established British government in Bengal after the defeat of Sirajjod Dowla in Bengal and step by step they abolished the Muslim rule in India. But before the British's came to India the majority Hindus and minority Muslim rulers lived together in harmony and in peace. There was no communal riot in India. The Muslims fought bravely against the British and gave their own life and the life of dear one for the defense and sovereignty of India, among them was Tipu Sultan in south India, who when was killed by the Englishman was still holding his sword in his hand. Bahadur Shah Jafar, the last Mogul Emperor of Muslim ruled India was expelled to Rangoon, Burma and his sons were killed along with other freedom fighters in 1857. But still then Rana Ranajit Sing was holding Punjab and his area of authority was extended upto Afghanistan and many of his General was Muslim though he himself was a great Sikh Leader which is enough proof that before British rule there was at least less or negligible communal feeling between different religious groups in India. But it is a irony of fate that when the British handed over power to leaders of India and Pakistan, and when the Governor General of Independent India was Mount Baton who himself was a British national, there was cleansing of Hindus and Sikh in Pakistani part West Punjab and cleansing of Muslims in Indian part East Panzab, although for long 900 years those Muslims, Hindus and Sikhs lived as a closed neighbor sharing their sorrows and pleasure among themselves and even sharing the administration among themselves fighting against the British occupation for independent movement, but the result was that still to-day the Sikhs and Hindus have been shedding their blood among themselves because once People of a particular region become intolerable and love for fellow neighbors vanishes, the trend continues for next generation and that used to continue which are still happening in East Panzab. The same things happened between Arab and Turkey who lived as a single Umma (Nation) for long 1300 years as Muslims, but with the conspiracy of British and other power like French, One single nation was divided first by two The Arab and Turk then again by so many states like Iran and Iraq, Iraq and Kuwait, Saudi Arabia and Iraq, Yemen and Saudi Arabia, Saudi Arabia and Jordan, Egypt and Syria, so around thirteen Arab States under the pretext of so called Arab League with division of people, economy, Army, sometime fighting in the name of Iran and Iraq, Iraq and Kuwait and so many. The power hungry and illegally occupied Leaders of so many Muslim Countries are not True Muslim but hypocrite as those Western leaders who talk about defending democracy and freedom around the world, who installed three members of a particular family, father and two sons in three divided and so called nation States which existed into a single state for long 1300 years. Yes I mean Hejaj where Sharif Hossain was in power and his two sons Abdullah and Faruque were installed in Iraq and Syria. How foolish were those Arab people that they were divided into so many states but power were given to few family like the Gulf States like Kuwait, Bahrain, Abu Dhabi and Saudi Arabia to the members of a single tribe called 'Utub', and Iraq, Syria, Jordan to another family i. e. the family of Sharif Hossain of Mecca, when the seed of division and abolition of Caliphate was created.

Here as mentioned earlier, I should again quote a very recent book namely "UNHOLY BABYLON, THE SECRET HISTORY OF SADDAM'S WAR" by ADEL DARWISH AND GREGORY ALEXANDER and published by VICTOR GOLLANCZ LTD, LONDON IN 1991, some of the important events mentioned in the book and in support of my observation mentioned above are as follows:

The authors, who were researching the book before the invasion, demonstrate that the events of 2nd August 1990 were the logical conclusion to twenty years of diplomatic duplicity, intelligence bungling, greed and corruption, particularly on the part of Britain, the US, France and Germany. The pursuit of short-sighted and relentlessly self-interested foreign policies led them to arm Hussein with a terrifying arsenal capable of mass destruction while overlooking his deplorable record on human rights and the legitimate interests of other states in the area.[221]

During his press conference a few days later, General Qasim said, Kuwait is an inseparable part of Iraq; the Iraqi republic has decided not to recognize the 1899 Anglo-Kuwait agreement signed by the former Sheikh of Kuwait for 15000 Indian rupees from the British Commissioner in Abadan... and the Iraqi republic has decided to protect the people of Kuwait who are the same people of Iraq.' He declared that Kuwait was part of the province of Basra and promised to issue 'a presidential decree appointing the Sheikh of Kuwait an executive administrator to the Muhafadha [country] of Kuwait'. **Thus another Middle Eastern crisis was created, but this claim to Kuwait was not the first; it was merely a chapter in a long-running drama.**
'It is all the fault of the British,' declared the editorials of the Iraqi papers next morning. 'Kuwait is part of Iraq, we are one nation, separated by the criminal knife of British imperialism.' The story was generations old.
By the end of the eighteenth century, the entire responsibility for policing the Gulf had become Britain's. **India was by then a British possession and the Dutch and the French had been largely evicted from the subcontinent. Britain was happy to restrict its interests in the Gulf to protecting its trade routes and subduing piracy. In 1820, it succeeded in negotiating a General Treaty of Maritime Peace with the sheikhs of the Trucial Coast. (There was no need to make a separate agreement with the Kuwaitis, who took no part in the piracy that plagued the lower Gulf.)**
Britain required some for of legal framework as pretext for intervention if needed, as it was worried about the growing presence of Turkish naval power in the waters of the Gulf. The Turks had also been known to encourage Arab piracy against the French and Portuguese.
Britain proceeded to establish posts and naval bases along the trade route to India via the Suez canal, which was opened in 1866, and also signed exclusive agreements with Arab rulers throughout the Gulf. The first was with Bahrain in 1880, prohibiting the sheikhdom from making any treaties or agreements with any state other than Britain or establishing diplomatic relations with other countries without British consent. With a history of living under threats from hostile neighbors, the Kuwaitis also wanted British protection.

When Sheikh Mubarak became ruler in 1896, he was forced to fight off his two brothers. He managed to defeat and kill them both, this bloody episode marking the start of his reign. Such conflict was unusual among the Sabahs and shocked members of the other ruling families were quick to ally themselves with Mubarak before they shared the same fate. A feud within the Sabah clan was thus prevented. Mubarak subsequently built up a 25,000 strong force of loyal tribesmen and used it to defend the emirate, its caravans and other interests from marauding bedouins......
In 1897 the Baghdad Vali-the **Ottoman governor of Baghdad - tried to assert control over Kuwait. Mubarak sought British protection in the form of an alliance, but the British refused his request......**
Lord Curzon, an expert on the Gulf and a pillar of British imperialism, became India's viceroy. He managed to persuade the British government to sign an agreement with Sheikh

---

[221] "UNHOLY BABYLON, THE SECRET HISTORY OF SADDAM'S WAR" by ADEL DARWISH AND GREGORY ALEXANDER and published by VICTOR GOLLANCZ LTD, LONDON IN 1991, Comments.

Mubarak in 1899, ensuring that no territories would be leased, sold or given to any other power without British consent. At the same time, **Britain's growing rival in Europe, imperial Germany, announced that it was to build a railway from Berlin to Baghdad. Mubarak received a letter assuring him of 'the good offices of Her Majesty's Government towards you, your heirs and successors, plus 15,000 rupees.**[222]

So only 15,000 Indian rupees, and surely that was Indian money, the India was also taken from Muslim rulers and money is given to another Muslim with the same mission of destruction of Muslim interest around the world, the Caliphate and the Muslim influence with the help of so called Muslim agents in Bengal, like Mirzafar and in Arab like those who received the money and not British money but Indian money.
In July 1913, the storm clouds of war were gathering over Europe and Britain urgently wished to resolve matters in the Gulf. Mubarak, never one to miss an opportunity, wanted to make the best of the options facing him.
The British and the Ottomans reached an agreement recognizing Kuwait as 'an autonomous district of Ottoman empire'. The agreement defined the frontiers of the emirate, whose population had doubled since 1898, while its pearling and fishing fleet now included more than 800 vessels.
On the eve of the First World War, Britain was conspiring to use the warlike Bedouin to protect its interest in the Middle East, either under the leadership of their sheiks or under British officers- such as T. E. Lawrence-rather than deploying its own soldiers in the desert. To secure the support of Mubarak, Britain agreed to recognize Kuwait as independent of the Ottoman Empire. In exchange, Mubarak was to support Britain against Turkey in the coming war.
Mubarak and his family continued smuggling and trading with all comers and leaving doors open for new deals with many parties. It was war, an ideal situation in which to make money.
Turkey joined Germany and her central European allies, while Mubarak took Britain's side but did not fight. He persuaded Abdul Aziz ibn Sa'ud, the Sultan of Najd-later Saudi Arabia-to join the alliance. Sharif Hussain, the Emir of Mecca, whose son Faisal led the Arab tribes with Lawrence against the Turks, also joined.[223]
The above event as mentioned in the book and mentioned earlier is enough proof how the so called Muslims in Arabia worked as British agent violating The Quranic Law not to believe the Jews and Christians and take them as the friend of Muslims, and thus so called Arab Muslims helped to abolish the 1300 years old Caliphate and thus weakened the Muslim power around the world, a situation now the Muslims are in everywhere in this world. Even the Ummayad leaders like Mawbia or Yazid did not take such treacherous act like accepting the advice of Jews and Christians, so far there was no such historical evidence when they revolted against the elected fourth truthful Caliph of Islam Hazrat Ali(may Allah be pleased with him), or against the great grandsons of the last Prophet of Islam, Hazrat Imam Hassan and Hazrat Imam Hussain(may Allah be pleased with them).

Quotation from the above book are continuing as follows:

Mubarak's son Salem, who masterminded smuggling for the Turks, succeeded his father in 1915 and declared his sympathy for Muslim Turkey. He also permitted the Syrians, who were under naval blockade by the Allies, to use Kuwait as a conduit for trade. **Seven years**

---

[222] "UNHOLY BABYLON, THE SECRET HISTORY OF SADDAM'S WAR" by ADEL DARWISH AND GREGORY ALEXANDER and published by VICTOR GOLLANCZ LTD, LONDON IN 1991, pp.1-6.

[223]pg. 7 of the above book

later, in 1922, Britain punished the Kuwaitis for their treachery when Sir Percy Cox, the British High Commissioner in Iraq, carved away an oil-rich coastal slice of Kuwait land and handed it over to Ibn Sa'ud. However, it continued to honor the 1899 agreement guaranteeing Kuwait's status as a British protectorate.

After the war, Ibn Sa'ud pressed his territorial claims along the border lines agreed by Turkey and Britain. In 1920 he placed and embargo on Kuwait trade which caused great damage to the emirate's economy, whilst his Wahhabi warriors carried out many raids across the border. In October 1920, Sheikh Salem marched with his forces to meet those of Ibn Sa'ud at Al-Jahrah, some thirty miles east of Kuwait City. Unlike 2nd August 1990, **the Kuwaitis managed to halt the advance of their well-armed and battle-hardened adversaries. Despite heavy losses, they** were able to prevent the invaders form occupying Kuwait City until British warships arrived and landed Royal Marines. The Wahhabis withdrew and Sir Percy Cox proposed to resolve the border dispute a year later.

Cox had arrived in what was to become Iraq in October 1920, replacing as High Commissioner Sir arnold Wilson, who had wanted to set up a British protectorate. Wilson's plan had been ill-received in the newly founded country, already in turmoil since General Maude had captured Baghdad from the Turks in March 1917 at a cost to the British of two and a half years of bitter fighting and 98,000 casualties. **Maude proceeded to put into effect the secret Sykes-Picot agreement, drawn up in 1916 between Britain and France, in which the two powers shared out the spoils of their coming victory over the Ottoman Empire, (The Ottoman and last long 1300 years Caliphate.)** Mesopotamia, comprising the two former Ottoman velayets (provinces) of Basra and Baghdad, was given to Britain. The Northern Velayets (provinces) of Basra and Baghdad, was given to Britain. The northern valayet of Mosul was initially given to France, but was the subject of a dispute which was settled in Britain's favor in 1919.
The Kurds were in constant revolt, demanding an independent home land, and found the defeat of the Ottomans and the occupation of Mosul a few days after the Armistice a golden opportunity for pressing their claim for a free state. They were further encouraged by the promises of autonomy that American president Woodrow Wilson appeared to offer in his fourteen-point plan. Initially the British had encouraged the appointment of 'suitable' local Kurdish leaders in the administration of Al-Mosul velayet.

However, Arab state under its control when it was the Sunny minority that gained from the collapse of the Ottoman Empire. A group of Western-educated politicians who wanted an independent, secular Iraqi state or a British-style constitutional monarch, they included Nuri al-Sa'id and the pro-Western nationalist group Ahdal'Iraq, who had been encouraged by the Syrian congress in Damascus which had elected Abdullah as King of Transjordan and Faisal King of Syria. They were the sons of Sharif of Mecca who with Lawrence had led the Arabs to fight Britain's war in the desert.
Sir Percy Cox abolished British military rule and implemented an 'Arab solution' by setting a national council of ministers to draft an electoral law and establish a national assembly. Britain insisted, however, on maintaining control of foreign policy. It was the national council which approved Faisal as constitutional monarch when he arrived for the first time on Iraqi soil in June 1921, after the French had dethroned him as King of Syria. With Faisal's help, Cox proceeded to establish a strong hold on the fledgling country..... Cox and Faisal had feared that the lawlessness on the country's southern border might be a threat to the stability of the nation. In 1922, in order to put an end to the trouble, Cox summoned Ibn Sa'ud to a conference at Uqair, near the seaport of Al-Hasa on the Gulf coast near Bahrain. Cox wanted to define the northern borders of Najd in an attempt to prevent any further incursions by the king's Bedouin followers who cared little for artificial frontiers. Their loyalties were to their own tribal chiefs, not to some distant government or ruler. ....To put an end to

these disagreements, Cox decided to draw the borders himself. The red pencil line denoting the new borders was arbitrary and unfortunately the map he used was inaccurate, so even the exact geographical position of the border was far from certain. However, it marked the division between Saudi Arabia and Iraq, as well as two neutral zones, and thus temporarily settled the disputes. The aggressive Ibn Sa'ud accepted Cox's newly marked border at the time, but trouble simmered endlessly therefore, eventually culminating in the events of 2nd August, 1990.

Knowing that many more deals would be made with Faisal in future, Cox gave Iraq a large slice of the Najd territory it claimed. In order to placate Ibn Sa'ud, he had to exact a price from the Kuwaitis for their co-operation with both the Turks and British during the First World War. He gave the Najd tribes about two thirds of the land that was governed by the Kuwaitis according to a 1913 Anglo-Turkish agreement, now forcibly annulled. Kuwait also lost its right to part of the hinterland south of 1913 agreement lines and this became a neutral zone. Another neutral zone was created between Iraq and Saudi Arabia, and the two zones were the source of endless arguments and feuds for years to come. .... Cox drew his lines after weighing up claims by the conflicting tribes and assessing their real force on the ground. He later explained to Sheikh Ahmad al-Jaber, Kuwait's ruler, that at the time nothing could be done to prevent Ibn Sa'ud from taking this territory by force if he wished to do so. He added, however, that Britain would not stand in the way if Kuwait was to fight to win it back. Compared to Mubarak, who had ambitiously and vigorously defended Kuwait's interest, Ahmed took fewer risks. He based his policies on the fact that Kuwait needed the help of a powerful friend like Britain while keeping good relations with its neighbors in order to preserve independence

After Cox's rearrangement of the borders, which left Iraq virtually landlocked, British officials in the region worked hard to persuade the Arabs to recognize them. When the subject arose again in March 1923, Major Moore, the British political resident (agent) in Kuwait, asked the emir, Sheikh Ahmed Jaber al-Ahmed, to define the borders formally. The latter replied in a letter dated 4th April 1923, referring to Mubarak's letter of 1920 to Cox which stated that 'the borders were the same which Sheikh Salem al-Mubarak defined to the British High Commissioner in Baghdad in a letter dated 17th September 1920 as the green line defined in the Anglo-Ottoman treaty of 1913'. ....

In the summer of 1932, Britain nominated Iraq for membership of the League of Nations, which asked for a copy of the border agreements between Iraq and its neighbors. Iraq's prime minister, Nuri al-Sa'id, wrote on 21st July 1932 to Sir Francis Humphrie, the British High Commissioner in Baghdad, recognizing the borders exactly as outlined in Sheikh al-Mubarak's letter of 1920.

Another border crisis followed five years later. In 1935, a retired British officer, one Colonel Ward, was director-general of the port and navigation works in Basra. At that time, developments in artillery had resulted in considerable increases in the maximum ranges of field guns and howitzers. Consequently, Ward was of the opinion that Basra was too near to the Iranian border-a mere thirteen miles away-which put it in danger in any future conflict. He advised the Baghdad government to build a port in Umm Qasr as an outlet to the sea, instead of at Basra which ships could only reach by sailing up the Shatt al-Arab waterway along the Iranian borders. (Thirty years later the Shah of Iran implemented a similar idea by moving oil export facilities from Abadan on the Shatt al-Arab to Kharg Island.) The Baghdad government showed great interest in the project, which was known as Khor Abdullah (the Abdullah Canal). ......

Iraq's head of state at the time was young King Ghazi, a playboy with a taste for fast cars who had succeeded his father Faisal in 1933. An inexperienced but sincere Arab nationalist, Ghazi denounced France rule in Syria, Zionist claims in Palestine and the British colonialist presence in the Gulf. Annexing Kuwait was also an important item on his nationalist agenda and he made his first move in this respect in 1938. Using propaganda broadcast through the Iraqi press and his own private broadcasting station in his Baghdad palace of Azzohour, Ghazi exploited political unrest in Kuwait. ... Clashes between the Kuwaitis au-

thorities and those citizens gathering to discuss democratic demands gave the Iraqis an opportunity to build up a persuasive propaganda campaign in which they extolled the virtues of their constitutional monarchy whilst putting forward persuasive arguments for a Kuwaiti federation with Iraq. ...King Ghazi massed troops near the borders,...
Britain informed the now-independent Iraq that it would militarily intervene if there was any move into Kuwait. However, the Sabah family again had luck on their side. Late at night on 4th April 1939, King Ghazi drove his sports car at high speed into a lamp-post inside the gardens of the Azzohour palace. His instant death drew the curtain on this chapter of Iraqi attempts to annex Kuwait.[224]

The above events are enough proof how the Caliphate was abolished step by step how the holy land was divided, and divided in such way that in future they will be fighting among themselves, and every time will be calling their British friends to save them from one another, this way there will be no peace and there will no Muslims but few hypocrite who were installed in power, will be protected by the British and other western powers. So those division of the Holy Land by the red pencil line by Mr Cox can never be accepted by any Muslim any where in this world.

As Tahseen Me'alla, a founder member of the Ba'ath who split with the party in 1970, later commented on Britain's involvement with Nuri al-Sa'id, "The British ruling classes wanted democracy and liberty in Britain but not for the peoples they once ruled. They only wanted oil and a slice of the profit given to a ruling oligarchy adopting a British lifestyle and advised by British officials. The oligarchy took all the oil income themselves and, while the local population was being oppressed and deprived of its basic civil rights, Britain looked the other way.'[225]

References from the above book continues as follows:

The Baghdad Pact was a treaty between Iraq and Turkey in which Muslim countries such as Pakistan and Iran were included. Britain also joined, thus giving it the opportunity of negotiating new leases for its military bases in the region. Nasser, however, refused to join. ...
The king (Faisal II) and his uncle were due to travel in the morning to Ankara but as first light was breaking a column of Abd al-Salam Arif's troops moved to the Baghdad radio station, which was captured just before six o'clock. .....
Outnumbered by the rebels, the king's troops fought bravely but were overwhelmed in a short and bloody battle. The King and his uncle came out into the palace gardens, possibly to listen to the rebel's demands, and were shot on the spot. There was a story later on suggesting that the rebels were planning to spare the life of the king. This seems unlikely, as the rebels would have feared that the king, who was popular, might subsequently lead a liberation movement in exile. .....
Britain also deployed troops to the Middle East. At the request of Jordan's King Hussain, who was related to the Iraqi royal family and had seen the pictures of his uncle and cousin's dismembered bodies in Baghdad, the 16th Independent Parachute Brigade Group was flown to Amman to deter any attempts at a coup against the king.

---

[224] "UNHOLY BABYLON, THE SECRET HISTORY OF SADDAM'S WAR" by ADEL DARWISH AND GREGORY ALEXANDER and published by VICTOR GOLLANCZ LTD, LONDON IN 1991,pp. 7-13.

[225] "UNHOLY BABYLON, THE SECRET HISTORY OF SADDAM'S WAR" by ADEL DARWISH AND GREGORY ALEXANDER and published by VICTOR GOLLANCZ LTD, LONDON IN 1991, pp. 16.

In Iraq itself, it was too late to salvage the monarchy. As the conspirators were only a handful of men in the 3rd Division, the majority of its troops were still outside Baghdad. The bulk of the Iraqi army hesitated during the first two days and did not lend its full support to the revolution. General Mirza, chief of staff of the Pakistan army (subsequently president of Pakistan), was later reported as stating that if plans for dealing with such an eventuality had existed amongst the armed forces of the Baghdad Pact a joint British-Muslim force could have succeeded in overthrowing the rebel regime in Iraq within the first twenty-four hours, after which it would have been too late. However, there were no such plans and in any case implementing them would have been a very big gamble.[226]

So now the first question to the Muslims of the world is 'How member of a single family i.e. three sons of Sharif of Mecca can be the head of three separate States of Jordan, Syria and Iraq, which were created after the fall of Caliphate under the leadership Osmani Turkey and under the guidance and advice of British Authority?' Secondly 'If ruler of a particular family can from one family then why the people of three will be kept separate with separate identity like Jordanian, Iraqi, and Syrian.'

The further event as mentioned in above book still continues as follows:

Britain also deployed troops to the Middle East. At the request of Jordan's King Hussein, who was related to the Iraqi royal family and had seen the pictures of his uncle and cousin's dismembered bodies in Baghdad, the 16th Independent parachute Brigade Group was flown to Amman to deter any attempts at a coup against the king.

A number of these attempts were attributed to America's Central Intelligence Agency (CIA) which, in one of the more fanciful accounts, was reported to have sent the Iraqi dictator a poisoned handkerchief as a present. Earlier in 1958,the CIA was also accused by Cairo Radio of plotting to assassinate Nasser. The plan was exposed by Abd al-hamid al-Sarraj, the head of the Deuxieme Bureau in Syria during the Federation, who had been given a large sum of money by king Sa'ud bin abd al-Aziz of Saudi Arabia to assassinate the Egyptian president.

King Fahad of Saudi Arabia, who calls himself Khademul H'aramine on 'the Custodian of the Two Shrines' to give his rule true Muslim authority has always kept the Americans at arm's length, despite his country's heavy reliance on the United States for everything from air-conditioning machines to fighter aircraft. This time he had to bite the bullet and ask the Americans to protect his kingdom, the greatest gamble of his reign. The reason for their alacrity in doing so can be summed up in one magic word - oil.

Fahd was no different from his Arab brothers and from the West, all of whom had appeased Saddam Hussein and looked the other way while he was committing his appalling crimes. As long as the 'Butcher of Baghdad' was keeping the tide of Islamic fundamentalism from their doorsteps, they were happy to contribute arms and finance for his war effort. Even when the conflict with Iran was over, and Saddam Hussein had returned to brutally repressing the Kurdish element of his population whilst building his formidable war machine, the oil-rich states of the Middle East turned a blind eye. Yet, when there was a threat to oil, the knives were unsheathed and the details of his grisly record were put on display, thanks to Saudi Arabian petro-dollar influence on Arab journalists.

---

[226] "UNHOLY BABYLON, THE SECRET HISTORY OF SADDAM'S WAR" by ADEL DARWISH AND GREGORY ALEXANDER and published by VICTOR GOLLANCZ LTD, LONDON IN 1991, pp. 17-19.

The discovery of oil on the Iranian side of the Gulf imposed on the Middle East a strategic importance even greater than that which it had formerly possessed when it had provided a series of military bases on the maritime route to India.

Just as the East India Company and the spices trade led to a revolution in maritime politics and the expansion of empires- interrupted by the inevitable wars - so the new oil trade made it difficult to discern the dividing line between the lopocies of privately owned companies and those of successive governments. It provided a license to run states within states conduct policies, mount coups d'etat and change governments.

Oil was first mentioned in association with the region by the Greed writer Eratosthenes of Cyrene (276-194 B.C.): 'Asphaltus is found in great abundance in Babylonia. The liquid asphaltus, which is called naphtha ...is of singular nature. When it is brought near the fire, it burns with flames...'

Oil had been found in Masjid al-Sulaiman, Persia (now Iran), in 1908. In 1903 the Anglo-Persian Oil Company (APOC), later renamed the Anglo-Iranian Oil Company and subsequently British petroleum, was founded, but it did not commence trading until 1909 when it secured a concession from the Shah. The first oil refinery a Abadan began production in 1912 and by 1914 had exported quarter of a million tons of oil.

When oil was discovered in persia, Britain was dependent on oil from the United states and from the American-controlled Gulf of Mexico. London wanted to explore the new oil fields in the Middle East to reduce the reliance on America, which was monopolizing the supply and emerging as a new superpower with growing overseas interests.

A few days before August 1914, the shares or the Anglo-Persian Oil Company; Britain later gained a large interest in the Turk sh Petroleum Company-which controlled concessions to exploit oil in what would later become Iraq-after Churchill had managed to push the agreement through the House of Commons.

Lord Curzon, the British Foreign Secretary, was quoted at the Lausanne conference in 1923 as telling the italian representative, 'When we have definitely settled the question of Mosul [which we have no intention of relinquishing] we would give them [the Iraqis] a share of the oil.'

In July 1925, the League of Nations Boundary Commission recommended that Mosul should form part of Iraq. There was a condition that Britain's mandatory powers were to be extended for twenty-five years, until Iraq's entry into the League of Nations.

However, those Arab oil producers did not possess any real political leverage until 1961, twelve years after Palestine had been lost to the Jews, when they founded the Organization of the Petroleum Exporting Countries (OPEC) and imposed oil embargoes on Israel. Those twelve year were a bonanza for Western oil companies who made gross profits $22.2 billion from the Middle East. The oil-producing countries received $9.4 billion, whilst the oil companies netted $12.8 billion.
Such support of Iraq, which was encouraged by the United States ultimately backfired. In footing a large proportion of the bill for Western arms supplies for Saddam Hussain, for use in his war against the revolutionary Islamic regime in Iran, the Americans helped to create monster.

After incorrectly interpreting signals from Washington during 1990. Saddam Hussein approached his oil-wealthy neighbors for grants of money to help pay off the massive debts incurred by eight long years a war. had he not saved America's allies from the flames of the Islamic revolution?

'But you know you are not the ones who protected your friends during the war with Iran,'he lectured US ambassador April Glaspie on 25th July 1990. 'As a country, we have the right to prosper. We lost so many opportunities and the others should value the Iraqi role in their protection,' said Saddam as he pointed at the interpreter. 'Even this Iraqi feel bitter like all other Iraqis.'

Saddam Hussein was right when he told the ambassador that there was great resentment in Iraq and in many parts of the Arab world the Kuwaitis and Gulf state Arabs were living in luxury, using their money to gamble in Europe's casinos while the children of those who had given their blood to defend Kuwait went hungry. 'Is this Iraq's reward for its role in securing the stability of the region and for protecting it from an unknown flood.' he asked Mrs Glaspie, only eight days before he sent his tanks to the heart of Kuwait City.

The Ba'ath did not recognize national borders and referred to the former Ottoman empire provinces as Al'Umma al-Arabiyah ('The Arab Nation').

Brussels, Dec 14: In less than three weeks the European Community will reach one of the most important dates in its history - January 1, 1993, the day that is supposed to user in a "Europe without frontier," writes Reuter.

The Palestine background is one very important problem nowadays in the Middle East. The Palestine and other Islamic problems are related to the abolition of Caliphate after a long diplomatic conspiracy by the Anglo Saxon or the present day British Imperialism against 1300 old Caliphate and the Arab Muslims since eighteenth century and particularly during great world war (1914-1918).

The majority of the present day so called artificial Nation States of the Arab world including Mecca, Medina in Hejaj and Jerusalem in Palestine are holiest places of Islam and Najaf, Karbala and Baghdad which are also some of the holiest place of just post Islamic period were under the Osmani Caliphate then based in Turkey. The British Government with a intention of controlling the vast wealth of black gold (Oil) which was just discovered at that time and for this end they were conspiring with certain local tribe leaders of that region. Through making secret conspiracy employing many so called 'Political Officers', of them may be named like Sir Gilbert Clayton and T. E. Lawrence who is also known as the Lawrence of Arabia with a mission of espionage and divide and rule policy against the Central Caliphate based on Turkey at that time and under the following three Machiavellian nature of Treaties:

1. Hussain Mac-Mahon correspondence of 1915-1916 ended in an Anglo-Arab secret Agreement against the Caliphate based on Turkey just to create hatred between Arab and Turkey and thus abolish 1300 years long Caliphate the only acceptable political System of Islam.
On the basis of that agreement the Arab Muslims entered the War under the Command of Sherif Hussain and they fought so well against the Turkish Muslims that their role was highly acclaimed by no less a personality than Captain Lindel Hart, the well known strategist and the chief Military Commentator of the well known strategist and the Chief Military Commentator of the Allies at that time, in the following words:

"It was the Arabs almost entirely who wiped out the fourth (Turkish) army, the still intact force that might have barred the way to final victory".[227]

But the price of the Agreement has been paid by entire Muslim Umma during last 70 years. **What a irony of fact that and what type fool we the Muslims nowadays are that two own brother i.e. two sons of Sharif Hossain became the king of two separate and so called (because a Muslim can not recognize any so called Muslim State as sovereign and true reply of a Muslim against the nation state is in Iqbal's language 'China is ours, India is ours and whole world is ours' because according to a Hadith or saying of the Holy Prophet (SM) 'to God the whole world is like a garden') to sovereign States of Jordan and Iraq the by product of abolition of Caliphate which started 1400 years ago with the coming of last religion Islam in this world. And most wonderful is that there was no protest for this mockery division of the land and it's people who were but only part of Single Islamic Umma or Caliphate from the very inception of Islam since 7th century.**

2. Sykes Picot Secret Agreement of 1916 between Britain and France, thus the price of the Arabs for violation of Quranic injunction not to believe the Christians for their own affairs.

The conspiracy by the British and France to divide the Arab World among themselves after the fall of the Caliphate. Under this agreement Britain agreed to give Syria and Lebanon to France, in exchange France agreed that Britain will get Iraq while the Palestine will be given under an International Administration. All those conspiracy was kept secret to Sharif Hussain, the Leader of Arab nationalist i.e. the Arab Leader abandoned the idea of Single Islamic Umma or Caliphate in exchange of their hunger of power which they expected defeating Osmani Caliph with British help.

3. Anglo Jewish Secret Treaty shaped as 'The Balfour Declaration" of November 2, 1917, thus also paying the price of the good will shown to them by all the ruler in Islam during last 1300 years of Caliphate period.
The European countries had common Policy of colonial settlement in the Afro-Asian and also American and for this propose they brought a new theory of 'Civilizing Mission' which is also a by product of Industrial revolution in Britain, then France and other European countries.
But for this purpose though they succeeded in the American Continent abolishing the old culture and people of that original inhabitant which started by fall of the Muslims in Spain and with rising of Christians power in Spain, they had a rivalry in Arab, Turkey and India because the then Caliph or Muslim Emperor had some firing or Artillery power in hand it was not that much easy to cleanse the local people of Afro-Asian countries where the European power went to conquest and rule. For instance the founder of Mogul Emperor Babar introduced Canon in India which he brought from Central Asia and so was in entire land under Caliphate in Arab. North Africa, and in Turkey. So the British, France, Dutch and other European power got a strong resistance to invade those counties. And that is why they took 'Divide and Rule' policy which they succeeded for some power hungry so called Muslims who simply became the agent of Britain, French and other European powers otherwise they never could enter those counties for the purpose of becoming a ruling class there. **All those conspiracy by the European in general and the British in particular and with the help their local agents around the Islamic World from Morocco to Indonesia; they succeeded to abolish the Caliphate which existed since First Caliph Hazrat Abu Bakr**

---

[227] THE PALESTINE ISSUE AND THE MUSLIM WORLD by Mr. A. M. M. Abdul Jalil, M.A., L.L.B., pp. 1-2.

(R. A.); and what a wonderful event is that no Muslim leader talked or proposed about the reinstallation or recovery of the 1300 old Caliphate since 1924 when formally it was abolished by Kamal Ataturk of Turkey. Perhaps Ataturk was fed up for the hatred of the Arab Muslims which British agent like Sir Gilbert Clayton and T. E. Lawrence created among the faithful Muslims. And as a seret Jew Ataturk formally destroyed 1300 years old Caliphate. Thus mission for a illegal State for illegal immigrants from Europe in Palestine also started through secret Jews in Turkey and elsewhere. Thus the Colonial in interest appears to be the motive behind the creation of the Israel in Palestine although the religious bias has been made a basis thereof. Another claim, as suggested, is that the motive behind the Balfour Declaration was humanitarian because it is intended to solve the problem of Jewish oppression. However, Winston Churchill denied this allegation when he said:

"The Balfour Declaration must.... not be regarded as a promise given from sentimental motives; it was a practical measure taken in the interest of a common cause."

Lloyd George tried to hide the colonialist and political motives behind the Balfour Declaration by presenting it as an award given to the Scientist Weizmann who had invented, during the War, a material necessary for making explosive. Herbert Samuel exposed the real colonialist reasons behind the Balfour Declaration when he passed the following remarks, in his memoirs, on the above claim of Lloyd George:- "...... it was Weizmann....the Diplomat, who is entitled to high credit whenever the story is told..... without derogation to his service in the manufacture of cordits, if acetone had never been heard of, I believe that the Balfour Declaration would have taken precisely the shape that it did and been promulgated just when it was."

Still there was, difference of opinion among the Jews themselves in the matter of the kind of the proposed Israel State whether it would be purely Jewish State as it exists now or a binational Palestine, a common Homeland of both the Palestinian Arabs and the Jews.[228]

In 1903, Britain had offered a part of East Africa, Kenya for Jewish settlement and Theodor Herzi, the founder of the modern political Zionism, had accepted it until the 1905 Zionist Congress, held in Basle, Switzerland, turned down the offer. It was the development of British Imperialistic interest in the Middle East that facilitated the interpretation of a Jewish mythological home land in Palestine and it is an established fact that Cecil Rhodes, the founder of Rhodesia and other Southern colonial settlements, was one of the main architects of Zionist Colonial settlements in Palestine. Coming back to the main discussion, it is Arthur James Balfour, an outstanding British Parliamentarian that served as the Prime Minister of Great Britain from 1902 to 1905 and as her Foreign Secretary from 1916 to 1918, who is best remembered for his political endeavor "The Balfour Declaration"-a heinous product of British Imperialism-in which he expressed official British approval of and co-operation with Zionism. The calamitous Balfour Declaration which was issued on November 2, 1917 is the result of series of secret correspondence between the British Officials and the Zionist leaders. It resulted in the great impetus to the movements that eventually uprooted the Palestine Muslims from their mother land Palestine with the establishment of Zionist (the so called Israeli) State in Palestine (the heart of the Arab World) on May, 1948. The Balfour Declaration was kept strictly secret to France, with whom she divided the Arab lands on the basis of Sykes Picot Agreement of 1916 and to the Arabs (Sherif Hussain) with whom she made arrangement to wipe out the Muslim Turks from the Arab soil on which she had to implement her plan. The time when the Balfour Declaration

---

[228] THE PALESTINE ISSUE AND THE MUSLIM WORLD by Mr. A.M.M.Abdul Jalil, M.A.,L.L.B pp. 1 - 7.

was pronounced it was too late for the Arab Muslims to realize their blunder. They acted against the order of Allah (One God, the Great Lord) by accepting the Christians and the Jews as their friends and by taking them into confidence. For the Muslims have strictly been forbidden against such unholy all ance of package deal. They violated the Holy Quranic injunction that "The believers should not accept the unbelievers, other than the believers, as friends". (Chapter 3 verse 28). This is the calamitous Balfour declaration prepared by six British individuals (Members of the British War Cabinet) who issued in London, thousands of miles away from Palestine, a declaration consisting sixty seven words by which Palestine was allotted to a Foreign people who had never set in it.[229]

What a pity it is that The Last Holy Prophet of Islam tried to make peace with the Jews and Christian population of his State in Medina and made agreement with them with ..... , which is known as Charter of Medina and gave them full security of life, property and everything they needed with the only condition that they the Jews and Christian will not make any conspiracy with the enemy of the State of Islam, which the Jews did and even a Jew invited the Prophet which the Prophet accepted, and that Jew mixed poison with the food for the reaction a companion died, but as a prophet He did not at that time to fulfill his remaining mission but the action of the poison was in his holy body. But for this criminal act of an individual neither any action or revenge was taken against the Jews or Christian Community and the Jews and Christian have been living throughout the Islamic world for long 1400 years without the any major human right violation of modern age which happened in Spain after fall of Muslim rule towards the Muslims who ruled there for long 800 years and also towards the Jews who lived before Muslim went there; what happened in Germany by the Christian Nazi to wards Jews and other part of Europe. But In Muslim Arab Jews and Christians have been living with their fellow Muslim from earliest period of those religion and that is why Mr. Tariq Aziz is a Arab Christian in Iraq holding important position with Saddam; present United Nation's Secretary General Butraz Ghali in Egypt is a Arab Christian; even the founder of the Arab Bath Party which included present day Syria and Iraq is a Christian, and all these prove that the Muslim leader never made any injustice towards it's fellow Jews and Christians from beginning of the history and those religion. **What behavior was done towards Charl's of Great Britain after his defeat at the hand of Muslim Leader Salauddin during the Crusade war. We quote the observation of Jawharlal Nehru in his Glimpses of World History bellow:**

Even the Crusaders who fought Saladin came to appreciate this chivalry of his. There is a story that once Richard was very ill and was suffering from the heat. Saladin, hearing of this, arranged to send him fresh snow and ice from the mountains. Ice could not be made artificially then by freezing water, as we do now. So natural snow and ice from the mountains had to be taken by swift messengers.

There are many stories of the time of the Crusades. Perhaps you have read Walter Scott's talisman.

One batch of Crusaders went to Constantinople and took possession of it. They drove out the Greek Emperor of the Eastern Empire and established a Latin kingdom and the Roman Church. Terrible massacres also took place in Constantinople and the city itself was partly burnt by the Crusaders. But this Latin kingdom did not last long. The Greeks of the Eastern |Empire, weak as they were came back and drove away the Latins after a little over fifty years. The Eastern Empire of Constantinople continued for another 200 years, till 1453, when the Turks finally put an end to it.

---

[229] THE PALESTINE ISSUE AND THE MUSLIM WORLD by Mr. A.M.M.Abdul Jalil, M.A.,L.L.B. pg. 3-4

This capture of Constantinople by the Crusaders brings out the desire of the Roman Church and the Pope to extend their influence there. Although the Greeks of this city had, in a moment of panic, appealed to Rome for help against the Turks, they helped the Crusaders little, and disliked them greatly.[230]

Jerusalem remained in Muslim hands, but the kings and people of Europe were no longer interested in wasting more lives and treasure for its recovery. Since then for nearly 700 years Jerusalem continued to be under the Muslims. It was only recently, during the Great War, in 1981, that it was taken from the Turks by an English general.

One of the later Crusades was interesting and unusual. Indeed, it was hardly a crusade at all in the old sense of the word. The Emperor Frederick II, of the Holy Roman Empire, came and, instead of fighting, had an interview with the then Sultan of Egypt and they came to a friendly understanding !Frederick was an extraordinary person. At a time when most kings were hardly literate, he knew many languages, including Arabic. He was known as the "Wonder to the World". He cared little for the Pope, and the Pope thereupon excommunicated him but this had little effect on him.

The Crusades thus failed to achieve anything. But this continuous fighting weakened the Seljuq Turks. Even more than this, however, feudalism sapped the foundations of the Seljuq Empire. The big feudal lords considered themselves practically independent. They fought each other. Sometimes they even went so far as to ask for Christian help against each other. It was this internal weakness of the Turks that played into the hands of the Crusaders sometimes. When, however, there was a strong ruler like Saladin, they made little progress.

According to the roman Church, after death a soul goes to purgatory, which is a place somewhere between heaven and hell, and there it suffers for the sins committed in this world. Afterwards the soul is supposed to go the heaven. The Pope issued promises to people, for payment, that they would escape purgatory and go straight to heaven. Thus the faith of the simple was exploited by the Church, and even out of crimes and what it considered sins, it made money. This practice of selling "indulgences" grew up some time after the Crusades. It became a great scandal, and was one of the reasons why many people turned against the Church of Rome.

In Islam there is supposed to be no priesthood, and in the past this helped a little in protecting its followers from religious exploitation. But individuals and classes arose, calling themselves specialists in religion, learned men, maulavis and mullas and the like, and they imposed upon the simple Muslims of faith and exploited them. Where a long beard, or a tuft of hair on the crown of the head, or a long mark on the forehead, or a fakir's dress, or a sanyasin's yellow or ochre grab is a passport to holiness, it is not difficult to impose on the public.

If you go to America, most advanced of countries, you will find there also that religion is a big industry living on the exploitation of the people.

---

[230] Glimpses of World History by Nehru pg. 194-195

It will interest you to know that Mahmud of Ghazni, who was the greatest destroyer that northern India had known, and who is said to have been a champion of Islam against the "idolaters", had a Hindu army corps under a Hindu general, named Tilak. He took Tilak and his army to Ghazni and used him to put down rebellious Muslims. So you will see that for Mahmud the object was conquest. In India he was prepared to kill "Idolaters" with the help of his Muslim soldiers; in central Asia he was equally prepared to kill Muslims with the help of his Hindus soldiers.

Yet another wave of conquest and destruction took place in Mangu's time. His Brother Hulagu was Governor in Persia. Annoyed with the Caliph at Baghdad about something, Hulagu sent a message to him chiding him for not keeping his promises, and telling him to behave better in future or else he would lose his empire. The Caliph was not a very wise man, nor could he profit by experience. He sent an offensive reply, and the Mongol envoys were insulted by a mob in Baghdad. Hulagu's Mongol blood was up at this. In a rage he marched on Baghdad, and after forty days siege he took it. That was the end of the city of the Arabian Nights,
and all the treasures that had accumulated there during 500 years of empire. The Caliph and his sons and near relatives were put to death. There was a general massacre for weeks, till the river Tigris was dyed red with blood for miles.
It is said that a million and a half people perished. All the artistic and literary treasures and libraries were destroyed. Baghdad was utterly ruined. Even the ancient irrigation system of western Asia, thousands of years old, was destroyed by Hulagu.

Later they became part of the Ottoman Turkish Empire. During the Great War of 1914-18 there was an Arab rebellion against the Turks, engineered by the English, and since then Arabia has been more or less independent.

There was no Caliph for two years. Then Sultan Baibers of Egypt nominated a relative of the last Abbaside Caliph as Caliph. But he had no political power and was just a spiritual head. Three hundred years later the Turkish Sultan of Constantinople obtained this title of Caliph from the last holder. The Turkish Sultans continued to be Caliph till both Sultan and Caliph were ended a few years ago by Mustafa Kamal Pasha.

Arabia is an enormous country; in size and area it is about two-thirds as big as India. And yet the population of the whole country is about one-seventieth or one-eightieth of the population of India-Pakistan-Bangladesh. It is obvious from this the it is very thinly population of India. It is obvious from this that it is very thinly populated; most of it is indeed a desert, and it was because of this that it escaped the attentions of greedy adventures in the past, and remained a relic of medievalism, without railways or telegraphs or telephones or the like, in the midst of a changing world. It was largely inhabited by wandering nomad tribes the Bedouins they are called and they traveled across the desert sands on their swift camels, the "ships of the desert" and on the backs of their beautiful Arab horses, known the world over. They lived a patriarchal life which had changed little in 1000 years. The World War changed all this as it changed many other things. If you will look at the map you will find that the great Arabian peninsula lies between the Red Sea and the Persian gulf. To the south of it lies the Arabian Sea, to the north lie Palestine and Trans-Jordan and the Syrian desert, and to the north east the green and fertile valleys of Iraq. Along the west coast, bordering the Red Sea, lies the land of Hejaz, which is the cradle of Islam, containing the holy cities Mecca and Medina and the Port, Jeddah, where thousands of pilgrims land every year on their way to Mecca. In the center of Arabia and towards the east up to the Persian Gulf lies Nejd. The Hejaz and Nejd are the two main divisions of Arabia. In the south west lies Yemen, known from the old Roman times as Arabia Felix, Arabia the fortunate, the Happy, because it was fertile and fruitful, in contrast with the rest, which was largely barren and desert. This part is as one would expect, thickly populated. Almost at the south-western tip of Arabia lies Aden, a British possession and a port of call for ships passing between East and West. Before the World war nearly the whole country was under Turkish control or acknowledged Turkish overlordship. But in Nejd the Emir Ibn Saud was gradually emerging as an independent ruler and was spreading out by conquest to the Persian Gulf. This was in the years preceding the war. Ibn Saud was the head of a particular community or sect of Muslims known as Wahabis, which was founded in the eighteenth century by Abdul Wahab. This was really a reform movement in Islam, something like the Puritans in Christianity. The Wahabis were against many ceremonies and the saint-worship that had become so popular with the Muslim masses, in the form of worship of tombs and what were supposed to be the relice of holy men. The Wahabis called this idolatry, just as the Puritans of Europe had called the Roman Catholics, who worshipped the images and relics of saints, idolaters. Thus, even apart from political rivalry, there was a religious feud between the Wahabis and the other Muslim sects in Arabia. During the World War Arabia became a hotbed of British intrigue, and British and Indian money was lavishly spent in subsidizing and bribing the various Arab chiefs. All manner of promises were made to them, and they were encouraged to revolt against Turkey. Sometimes two rival chiefs, who were fighting each other, were both receiving British subsidies! The British succeeded in getting the Sherif Hussein of Mecca to raise the Arab standard of revolt. Hussein's importance consisted in the fact that he was a descendant of the Prophet Mohammad, and was therefore greatly respected. Hussein was promised by the British the kingdom of a united Arabia.

Ibn Saud was cleverer. He got himself recognized as an independent sovereign by the British, accepted a tidy little sum of pound 5000 per month from them, and promised to remain neutral. So while others were fighting, he consolidated his position and strengthened it, to some extent with the help of British gold. The Sherif Hussein was becoming unpopular in Islamic countries, including India, because of his rebellion against the Sultan of Turkey, who was also then the Caliph. Ibn Saud, by quietly remaining neutral, took full advantage of changing conditions and slowly built up a reputation for himself to being the strong man of Islam.

In the south was Yemen. The Imam, or ruler, of Yemen remained loyal to the Turks right through the was. But he was cut off from the scene of operations and could not do much. After Turkey's defeat he became independent. Yemen is still an independent State. The end of the war found England dominating Arabia and trying to use both Hussein and Ibn Saud as her tools. Ibn Saud was too clever to allow himself to be exploited. The Sherif Hussein's family, however, suddenly blossomed out in full glory, backed as it was by British force. Hussein himself became King of the Hejaz; one of his sons, Feisal, became ruler of Syria; and another son, Abdullah, was made by the British the ruler of the small new state Trans-Jordan. The glory was short-lived for as we have seen, Feisal was driven out of Syria by the French, and Hussein 's kingship vanished away before the advancing Wahabis of Ibn saud. Feisal having joined the unemployed again, was provided by the British with the rulership of Iraq, reigning there by the grace of his patrons.

During the brief period of Hussein's kingship of the Hejaz, the Turkish Parliament at angora abolished the Caliphate in 1924. There was no Caliph, and Hussien, greatly daring, jumped on to the empty throne and proclaimed himself the Caliph of Islam. Ibn Saud saw that his time had come, and he appealed both to Arab nationalism and to Muslim internationalism against Hussain. He stood out as the champion of Islam against and ambitious usurper, and with the help of careful propaganda managed to gain the good will of Muslims in other countries. The Khalifat Committee in India sent him their good wishes. Seeing which way the wing was blowing, and realizing that the horse they had so far backed was not likely to win, the British quietly withdrew their support of Hussain. Their subsidies were stopped, and poor Hussain, who had been promised so much, was left almost friendless and helpless before a powerful and advancing enemy. Within a few months, in October 1924, the Wahabis entered Mecca and in accordance with their puritan faith, destroyed some tombs. There was a good deal of consternation in Muslim countries at this destruction; even in India much feeling was aroused. Next year Median and Jeddah fell to Bin Saudi, and Hussein and his family were driven away from the Hedges. Early in 1926 Bin Saud proclaimed himself King of the Hejaz. In order to consolidate his new position and to keep the good will of Muslims abroad, he held an Islamic World Congress at Mecca in June 1926, to which he invited representative Muslims from other countries. Apparently he had no desire to become Caliph, and in any event he was not likely to be accepted as such by large numbers of Muslim because of his Wahabism. King Fuad of Egypt, whose anti-national and despotic record we have already examined, was keen on becoming the Caliph but nobody would have him, not even his own people of Egypt. Hussein, after his defeat, had abdicated from the Caliphate he had assumed. The Islamic congress held at Mecca did not come to any important decision, and it was perhaps not meant to do so. It was a device adopted by Ibn Saud to strengthen his position, especially before foreign Powers. Indian representatives of the Khalifat Committee , and I think Maulana Mohammad Ali was one of them, returned disappointed and angry with Ibn Saud. But this did not make much difference to him. He had exploited the Indian Khilafat Committee when he wanted its help, and now he could well do without its good will. Ibn Saud was soon master of nearly the whole country with the exception of Yemen which continued as an independent State under it's old Imam. But for this corner in the south-west, he was lord of Arabia and he took the title of King of Nejd, thus becoming a double king. King of Hejaz and King of Nejd. Foreign Power recognized his independence, and foreigners were not allowed any special privileges, as they are in Egypt still. Indeed, they could not even take wines and other alcoholic drinks.[231]

After the war, Ibn Sa'ud pressed his territorial claims along the border lines agreed by Turkey and Britain. In 1920 he placed and embargo on Kuwaiti trade which caused great damage to the emirate's economy, whilst his Wahhabi warriors carried out many raids across the border. In October 1920, Sheikh Salem marched with his forces to meet those of Ibn Sa'ud at Al-Jahrah, some thirty miles east of Kuwait City. Unlike 2nd August 1990, they were able to prevent the invaders form occupying Kuwait City until British warships arrived and landed Royal Marines.The Wahhabis withdrew and Sir Percy Cox proposed to resolve the border dispute a year later.

Cox had arrive in what was to become Iraq in October 1920, replacing as High Commissioner Sir arnold Wilson, whc had wanted to set up a British protectorate. Wilson's plan had been ill-received in the newly founded country, already in turmoil since General Maude had captured Baghdad from the Turks in March 1917 at a cost to the British of two and a half years of bitter fighting and 98.000 casualties. Maude proceeded to put into effect the secret Sykes-Picot agreement, drawn up in 1916 between Britain and France, in which the two powers shared out the spoils of their coming victory over the Ottoman Empire. Mesopotamia, comprising the two former Ottoman velayets (provinces) of Basra and Baghdad, was given to Britain. The Northern Velayets (provinces) of Basra and Baghdad,

[231] GLIMPSES OF WORLD HISTORY (ARABIA- A JUMP FROM THE MIDDLE AGES) BY NEHRU PG. 767-771

was given to Britain. The northern valayet of Mosul was initially given to France, but was the subject of a dispute which was settled in Britain's favor in 1919.

However, Arab state under its control when it was the Sunny minority that gained from the collapse of the Ottoman Empire. A group of Western-educated politicians who wanted an independent, secular Iraqi state or a British-style constitutional monarch, they included Nuri al-Sa'id and the pro-Western nationalist group Ahdal'Iraq, who had been encouraged by the Syrian congress in Damascus which had elected Abdullah as King of Transjordan and Faisal King of Syria. They were the sons of Sharif of Mecca who with Lawrence had led the Arabs to fight Britain's war in the desert.

The British policy of 'divide and rule' was applied wherever they went with motive of conquering that country. To many countries like India they went under the guess of trading partner and when the time came with the policy of divide and rule they divided the people of that country or region and became a ruler. As in India they took coastal area as the place operation and started their real desire, say in Bengal they selected the area of present Calcutta and divided the both Hindus and Muslims, they used the Hindu population against the ruling class Muslim, and again some Muslim against the Muslim rulers and then defeated the then Muslim ruler of Bengal, Orissa and Assam; Nowab Sirajjod Dowla and installed one of his relation Mirzafar Ali Khan and in a proper opportunity the British established themselves as ruler and from there step by step they conquered the whole of India which end in 1947 when British became freedom and the State of India and Pakistan came into existence.
The above policy the British applied in the other part of the Islamic world particularly the Islamic Caliphate headed by Ottoman Turks. Here they divided the Muslims into two group The Arab and the ruling class Turks. They used the coastal area of Arab continent from present day Kuwait, Saudi Arab, and the Hejaj. That conspiracy also started in the eighteenth century they captured India from Bengal, Madras and other coastal area of Islamic India.
We should quote few lines from a research book 'THE SECRET HISTORY OF SADAM'S WAR, UNHOLY BABYLON' BY Mr Adel Darwish and Mr. Gregory Alexander below:
In July 1925, the League of Nations Boundary Commission recommended that Mosul should form part of Iraq. There was a condition that Britain's mandatory powers were to be extended for twenty-five years, until Iraq's entry into the League of Nations.

However, those Arab oil producers did not possess any real political leverage until 1961, twelve years after Palestine had been'lost' to the Jews, when they

The authors, who were researching the book before the invasion, Demonstrate that the events of 2nd August 1990 were the logical conclusion to twenty years of diplomatic duplicity, intelligence bungling, greed and corruption, particularly For Britain, the US,France and Germany.
The pursuit of short-sighted and relentlessly self-interested foreign policies led them to arm Hussein with a terrifying arsenal capable o mass destruction while overlooking his deplorable record on human rights and the legitimate interests of other states in the area.

During his press conference a few days later, General Qasim said, Kuwait is an inseparable part of Iraq; the Iraqi republic has decided not to recognize the 1899 Anglo-Kuwait agreement signed by the former Sheikh of Kuwait for 15000 Indian rupees from the British Commissioner in Abadan.

The Petroleum Exporting countries founded the Organization of the Petroleum Exporting Countries (OPEC) and imposed oil embargoes on Israel. Those twelve year were a bonanza

238

for Western oil companies who made gross profits $22.2 billion from the Middle East. The oil-producing countries received $9.4 billion, whilst the oil companies netted $12.8 billion.

In the eighteenth century there was a scramble for colonies in America and Asia. Many European Powers took part in this, but the chief contest ultimately lay between two-England and France. England had got a great lead in the race, both in America and India In 1776 came the famous "Declaration of Independence" of the colonies in America. In 1782 the war ended, and the Peace between the warring countries was signed in 1783. So the thirteen American colonies became an independent republic-the United States of America as they are called. The Declaration of Independence of 1776 stated that "all men are born equal". This is hardly correct statement if analyzed, for some are weak and some are strong. "All men are born equal"- and yet there was the poor Negro, a slave with few rights! What of him? How did he fit in with the constitution He did not fit in and he was not yet fitted in. Many years later there was a bitter civil war between the northern and southern States, and as a result slavery was abolished.

Jerusalem remained in Muslim hands, but the kings and people of Europe were no longer interested in wasting more lives and treasure for its recovery. Since then for nearly 700 years Jerusalem continued to be under the Muslims. It was only recently, during the Great War, in 1918, that it was taken from the Turks by an English general.

One of the later Crusades was interesting and unusual. Indeed, it was hardly a crusade at all in the old sense of the word. The Emperor Frederick II, of the Holy Roman Empire, came and, instead of fighting, had an interview with the then Sultan of Egypt and they came to a friendly understanding !Frederick was an extraordinary person. At a time when most kings were hardly literate, he knew many languages, including Arabic. He was known as the "Wonder to the World". He cared little for the Pope, and the Pope thereupon excommunicated him but this had little effect on him.

The Crusades thus failed to achieve anything. But this continuous fighting weakened the Seljuq Turks. Even more than this, however, feudalism sapped the foundations of the Seljuq Empire. The big feudal lords considered themselves practically independent. They fought each other. Sometimes they even went so far as to ask for Christian help against each other. It was this internal weakness of the Turks that played into the hands of the Crusaders sometimes. When, however, there was a strong ruler like Saladin, they made little progress.

According to the roman Church, after death a should goes to purgatory, which is a place somewhere between heaven and hell, and there it suffers for the sins committed in this world. Afterwards the soul is supposed to go the heaven. The Pope issued promises to people, for payment, that they would escape purgatory and go straight to heaven. Thus the faith of the simple was exploited by the Church,and even out of crimes and what it considered sins, it made money. This practice of selling "indulgences" grew up some time after the Crusades. It became a great scandal, and was one of the reasons why many people turned against the Church of Rome.

In Islam there is supposed to be no priesthood, and in the past this helped a little in protecting its followers from religious exploitation. But individuals and classes arose, calling themselves specialists in religion, learned men, maulavis and mullas and the like, and they imposed upon the simple Muslims of faith and exploited them. Where a long beard, or a tuft of hair on the crown of the head, or a long mark on the forehead, or a fakir's dress, or a sanyasin's yellow or ochre grab is a passport to holiness, it is not difficult to impose on the public.

If you go to America, most advanced of countries, you will find there also that religion is a big industry living on the exploitation of the people.

It will interest you to know that Mahmud of Ghazni, who was the greatest destroyer that northern India had known, and who is said to have been a champion of Islam against the "idolaters", had a Hindu army corps under a Hindu general, named Tilak. He took Tilak and his army to Ghazni and used him to put down rebellious Muslims. So you will see that for Mahmud the object was conquest. In India he was prepared to kill "Idolaters" with the help of his Muslim soldiers; in central Asia he was equally prepared to kill Muslims with the help of his Hindus soldiers.

Yet another wave of conquest and destruction took place in Mangu's time. His Brother Hulagu was Governor in Persia. Annoyed with the Caliph at Baghdad about something, Hulagu sent a message to him chiding him for not keeping his promises, and telling him to behave better in future or else he would lose his empire. The Caliph was not a very wise man, nor could he profit by experience. He sent an offensive reply, and the Mongol envoys were insulted by a mob in Baghdad. Hulagu's Mongol blood was up at this. In a rage he marched on Baghdad, and after forty days siege he took it. That was the end of the city of the Arabian Nights, and all the treasures that had accumulated there during 500 years of empire. The Caliph and his sons and near relatives were put to death. There was a general massacre for weeks, till the river Tigris was dyed red with blood for miles.
It is said that a million and a half people perished. All the artistic and literary treasures and libraries were destroyed. Baghdad was utterly ruined. Even the ancient irrigation system of western Asia, thousands of years old, was destroyed by Hulagu.

Later they became part of the Ottoman Turkish Empire. During the Great War of 1914-18 there was an Arab rebellion against the Turks, engineered by the English, and since then Arabia has been more or less independent.

There was no Caliph for two years. Then Sultan Baibers of Egypt nominated a relative of the last Abbaside Caliph as Caliph. But he had no political power and was just a spiritual head. Three hundred years later the Turkish Sultan of Constantinople obtained this title of Caliph from the last holder. The Turkish Sultans continued to be Caliph till both Sultan and Caliph were ended a few years ago by Mustafa Kamal Pasha.

The coming of the Muslims to India as invaders introduced an element of compulsion in religion. The fight was really a political one between conqueror and conquered, but it was colored by the religious element, and there was, at times, religious persecution. But it would be wrong to imagine that Islam stood for such persecution. There is an interesting report of a speech delivered by a Spanish Muslim when he was driven out of Spain, together with the remaining Arabs, in 1610. He protested against the Inquisition and said: "Did our victorious ancestors ever once attempt to extirpate Christianity out of Spain, when it was in their power? Did they not suffer your forefathers to enjoy the free use of their rites at the same time as they wore their chains? If there may have been some examples of forced conversions, they are so rare as scarce to deserve mentioning, and only attempted by men who had not the fear of God and the Prophet before their eyes, and who in doing so, have acted directly and diametrically contrary to the holy precepts and ordinances of Islam, which cannot, without sacrilege, be violated by any who would be held worthy of the honorable epithet of Musalman. You can never produce, among us, any bloodthirsty formal tribunal, on account of different persuasions in points of faith, that any wise approaches your execrable Inquisition Our arms, it is true, are ever open to receive all who are disposed to embrace our religion; but we are not allowed by our sacred Quran to tyrannize over consciences."

So religious toleration and freedom of conscience, which were such marked features of old Indian life, slipped away from us to some extent, while Europe caught up to us and then went ahead in establishing, after many a struggle, these very principles. To-day, sometimes, there is communal conflict in India, and Hindus and Muslims fight each other and kill each other. It is true that this happens only occasionally in some places, and that mostly we live in peace and friendship, for our real interests are one. It is a shameful thing for any Hindu or Muslim to fight his brother in the name of religion. We must put an end to it, and we will of course do so. But what is important is to get out of that complex ideology of custom, convention and superstition which, under the guise of religion, enchains us.

It is obvious from this the it is very thinly population of India. It is obvious from this that it is very thinly populated; most of it is indeed a desert, and it was because of this that it escaped the attentions of greedy adventures in the past, and remained a relic of medievahsm, without railways or telegraphs or telephones or the like, in the midst of a changing world. It was largely inhabited by wandering nomad tribes the Bedouins they are called and they traveled across the desert sands on their swift camels, the "ships of the desert" and on the backs of their beautiful Arab horses, known the world over. They lived a patriarchal life which had changed little in 1000 years. The World War changed all this as it changed many other things.

If you will look at the map you will find that the great Arabian peninsula lies between the Red Sea and the Persian gulf. To the south of it lies the Arabian Sea, to the north lie Palestine and Trans-Jordan and the Syrian desert, and to the north east the green and fertile valleys of Iraq. Along the west coast, bordering the Red Sea, lies the land of Hejaz, which is the cradle of Islam, containing the holy cities Mecca and Medina and the Port, Jeddah, where thousands of pilgrims land every year on their way to Mecca. In the center of Arabia and towards the east up to the Persian Gulf lies Nejd. The Hejaz and Nejd are the two main divisions of Arabia. In the south west lies Yemen, known from the old Roman times as Arabia Felix, Arabia the fortunate, the Happy, because it was fertile and fruitful, in contrast with the rest, which was largely barren and desert. This part is as one would expect, thickly populated. Almost at the south-western tip of Arabia lies Aden, a British possession and a port of call for ships passing between East and West.

Before the World war nearly the whole country was under Turkish control or acknowledged Turkish overlordship. But in Nejd the Emir Ibn Saud was gradually emerging as an independent ruler and was spreading out by conquest to the Persian Gulf. This was in the years preceding the war. Ibn Saud was the head of a particular community or sect of Muslims known as Wahabis, which was founded in the eighteenth century by Abdul Wahab. This was really a reform movement in Islam, something like the Puritans in Christianity. The Wahabis were against many ceremonies and the saint-worship that had become so popular with the Muslim masses, in the form of worship of tombs and what were supposed to be the relice of holy men. The Wahabis called this idolatry, just as the Puritans of Europe had called the Roman Catholics, who worshipped the images and relics of saints, idolaters. Thus, even apart from political rivalry, there was a religious feud between the Wahabis and the other Muslim sects in Arabia.

During the World War Arabia became a hotbed of British intrigue, and British and Indian money was lavishly spent in subsidizing and bribing the various Arab chiefs. All manner of promises were made to them, and they were encouraged to revolt against Turkey. Sometimes two rival chiefs, who were fighting each other, were both receiving British subsidies! The British succeeded in getting the Sherif Hussein of Mecca to raise the Arab standard of revolt. Hussein's importance consisted in the fact that he was a descendant of the Prophet Mohammad, and was therefore greatly respected. Hussein was promised by the British the kingdom of a united Arabia.

Ibn Saud was cleverer. He got himself recognized as an independent sovereign by the British, accepted a tidy little sum of pound 5000 per month from them, and promised to remain neutral. So while others were fighting, he consolidated his position and strengthened it, to some extent with the help of British gold. The Sheriff Hussein was becoming unpopular in Islamic countries, including India, because of his rebellion against the Sultan of Turkey, who was also then the Caliph. Ibn Saud, by quietly remaining neutral, took full advantage of changing conditions and slowly built up a reputation for himself to being the strong man of Islam.

In the south was Yemen. The Imam, or ruler, of Yemen remained loyal to the Turks right through the was. But he was cut off from the scene of operations and could not do much. After Turkey's defeat he became independent. Yemen is still an independent State. The end of the war found England dominating Arabia and trying to use both Hussein and Ibn Saud as her tools. Ibn Saud was too clever to allow himself to be exploited. The Sherif Hussein's family, however, suddenly blossomed out in full glory, backed as it was by British force. Hussein himself became King of the Hejaz; one of his sons, Feisal, became ruler of Syria; and another son, Abdullah, was made by the British the ruler of the small new state Trans-Jordan. The glory was short-lived for as we have seen, Feisal was driven out of Syria by the French, and Hussein 's kingship vanished away before the advancing Wahabis of Ibn saud. Feisal having joined the unemployed again, was provided by the British with the rulership of Iraq, reigning there by the grace of his patrons. During the brief period of Hussein's kingship of the Hejaz, the Turkish Parliament at angora abolished the Caliphate in 1924. There was no Caliph, and Hussien, greatly daring, jumped on to the empty throne and proclaimed himself the Caliph of Islam. Ibn Saud saw that his time had come, and he appealed both to Arab nationalism and to Muslim internationalism against Hussain. He stood out as the champion of Islam against and ambitious usurper, and with the help of careful propaganda managed to gain the good will of Muslims in other countries. The Khalifat Committee in India sent him their good wishes. Seeing which way the wing was blowing. and realizing that the horse they had so far backed was not likely to win, the British quietly withdrew their support of Hussain. Their subsidies were stopped, and poor Hussain, who had been promised so much, was left almost friendless and helpless before a powerful and advancing enemy.

Within a few months, in October 1924, the Wahabis entered Mecca and in accordance with their puritan faith, destroyed some tombs. There was a good deal of consternation in Muslim countries at this destruction; even in India much feeling was aroused. Next year Medina and Jeddah fell to Ibn Saud, and Hussein and his family were driven away from the Hejaz. Early in 1926 Ibn Saud proclaimed himself King of the Hejaz. In order to consolidate his new position and to keep the good will of Muslims abroad, he held an Islamic World Congress at Mecca in June 1926, to which he invited representative Muslims from other countries. Apparently he had no desire to become Caliph, and in any event he was not likely to be accepted as such by large numbers of Muslims because of his Wahabism. King Fuad of Egypt, whose anti-national and despotic record we have already examined, was keen on becoming the Caliph but nobody would have him, not even his own people of Egypt. Hussein, after his defeat, had abdicated from the Caliphate he had assumed. The Islamic congress held at Mecca did not come to any important decision, and it was perhaps not meant to do so. It was a device adopted by Ibn Saud to strengthen his position, especially before foreign Powers. Indian representatives of the Khalifat Committee , and I think Maulana Mohammad Ali was one of them, returned disappointed and angry with Ibn Saud. But this did not make much difference to him. He had exploited the Indian Khilafat Committee when he wanted its help, and now he could well do without its good will. Ibn Saud was soon master of nearly the whole country with the exception of Yemen which continued as an independent State under it's old Imam. But for this corner in the south-west, he was lord of Arabia and he took the title of King of Nejd, thus becoming a double king. King of Hejaz and King of Nejd. Foreign Power recognized his independence, and foreigners were not allowed any special privileges, as they are in Egypt still. Indeed, they could not even take wines and other alcoholic drinks.

The following quotations are from Nehru's "Glimpses of World History" on Islam and early Caliphate:

It is strange that this Arab race, which for long ages had lived a sleepy existence, apparently cut off from what was happening elsewhere, should suddenly wake up and show such tremendous energy as to startly and upset the world. The story of the Arabs, and of how they spread rapidly over As a, Europe and Africa, and of the high culture and civilization which they developed, is one of the worders of history.

Abu Bakr and Omar were great men who laid the foundation of Arabian and Islamic greatness. As Khalifas they were both religious heads and political chiefs - King and Pope in one. In spite of their high position and the growing power of their State, they stuck to the simplicity of their ways and refused to countenance luxury and pomp. The democracy of Islam was a living thing for them. But their own officers and emirs took to silks and luxury soon enough, and irony stories are told of Abu Bakr and Omar rebuking and punishing these officers, and even weeping at this extravagance. They felt that their strength lay in their simple and hard living, and that if they took to the luxury of the Persian or Constantinople Courts, the Arabs would be corrupted and would fall. Even in these short dozen years, during which Abu Bakr and Omar ruled, the Arabs defeated both the Eastern Roman Empire and the Sassanid King of Persia. Jerusalem, the holy city of the jews and Christians, was occupied by the Arabs, and the whole of Syria and Iraq and Persia became part of the new Arabian Empire. Like the fouer of some other religions, Mohammad (Peace be upon him) was a rebel against many of the existing social customs.
The religion have reached, by its simplicity and directness and its flavor of democracy and equality, appealed to the masses in the neighboring countries who had been ground down long enough by autocratic kings and equally autocratic and domineering priests. They were tired of the old order and were ripe for a change. Islam offered them this change, and it was a welcome change, for it bettered them in many ways and put an end to many old abuses. Islam did not bring any great social revolution in its train which might have put an end to a large extent to the exploitation of the masses. But it did lessen this exploitation so far as the Muslims ere concerned, and made them feel that they belonged to one great brotherhood.

Within twenty-five years of the death of their Prophet, the Arabs conquered the whole of Persia and Syria and a bit of northern Africa on the west. Egypt had fallen to them with the greatest ease, as Egypt had suffered most from the exploitation of the Roman Empire and from the rivalry of Christian sects. There is a story that the Arabs burnt the famous library of Alexandria, but this is now believed to be false. The Arabs were too fond of books to behave in this barbarous manner. It is probable, however, that the Emperor Theodosius of Constantinople, about whom I have told you something already, was guilty of this destruction, or part of it. A part of the library had been destroyed long before, during a siege at the time of Julius Caesar.

About Khalipha or Khelafat I should quote the following letters of 4th elected Khalipha:

letter

To the people of Egypt sent through Malik al-Ashtar when he was made the Governor of that place:

Now, Allah the Glorified, deputed Muhammad (may Allah bless him and his descendants) as a warner for all the worlds and a witness for all the prophets. When the Prophet expired, the Muslims quarreled about power after him. By Allah, it never occurred to me, and I never imagined, that after the Prophet the Arabs would snatch away the caliphate from his Ahlu'l-bayt (the members of his house)' nor that they would take it away from me after him, but I suddenly noticed people surrounding the man to swear him allegiance.[232]
I therefore withheld my hand till I saw that many people were reverting from Islam and trying to destroy the religion of Muhammad (may Allah bless him and his descendants), I then feared that if I did not protect Islam and its people and there occurred in it a breach or destruction, it would mean a greater blow to me than the loss of power over you which was, in any case, to last for a few days of which everything would pass away as the mirage passes away, or as the cloud scuds away. Therefore, in these happenings I rose till wrong was destroyed and disappeared, and religion attained peace and safety.

A part of the same letter

---

[232]. The Prophet's declaration about Amir-al mu'minin (leader of the faithful) that "This is my brother, my vicegerent and my caliph among you", and while returning from his farewell hajj at Ghadir Khum that "For whosoever I am the master, "Ali is his master" had settled the issue of his own replacement and succession after which there was no need at all for any new election, nor could it be imagined that the people of Medina would feel the need for an election. But some power-thirsty individuals so ignored these clear injunctions as if their ears had never been acquainted with them, and considered the election so necessary, that, leaving the burial rites of the Prophet, they assembled in the Saqifah of um Sa'idah and elected Abu Bakr as caliph with a show of democracy. This was a very critical moment for Amir al-mu'minin. On one side some interested persons declared that he should take up arms and on the other hand he noticed that those Arabs who had accepted Islam by dint of its military strength were leaving it and Musaymimah ibn Thumamah al-Hanifa the liar (al-Kadhdhab) and Tulayhah ibn Khuwaylid al-Asadi (the liar) were throwing tribe after tribe into misguidance. In these circumstances, if there had been a civil war and the Muslim had fought against the Muslims, the forces of hearse and hypocrisy would have joined together and swept Islam off the surface of the globe. Therefore, Amir al-mu'minin preferred to keep quit rather than to fight, and, with the purpose of maintaining the solidarity of Islam, confined himself to protesting peacefully rather than taking up arms. this was because formal power was not so dear to him as the good and prosperity of the community. For stopping the machinations of the hypocrites and defeating the aims of the mischief mongers there was no other course but that he should not fan the flames of war by giving up his own claim. This was such a big act for the preservation of Islamic polity that it is acknowledged by all the sects of Islam.

By Allah, if I had encountered them alone and they had been so numerous as to fill the earth to the brim, I would not have worried or become perplexed. I am clear in myself and posses conviction from Allah about their misguidance and my guidance. I am hopeful and expectant that I will meet Allah and get His good reward. But I am worried that silly and wicked people will control the affairs of the entire community, with the result that they will grab the funds of Allah as their own property and make His people slaves,[233] fight with the virtuous, And ally with sinful. Indeed, there is among them he who drank (wine) unlawfully.[234]

---

[233]. This refers to the saying of the Holy Prophet about the children of Umayyah and the children of Abi al-As ibn Umayyah (the grandfather of 'Uthman ibn 'Affan and the dynasty of Marwan's caliphs) as related by Abu Dhar al-Ghifari that the Holy Prophet said:

When the number of ear (children of) Umayyah reaches forty   men they will make Allah's people their slaves, grab Allah's   funds as their own property and make the Book of Allah a   cause of corruption.
(al--Mustadrak, vol. 4, p. 479; Kanz al-ummal, vol.II, p.149)

About the children of Abi al-As it is related by Abu Dharr,   Abu Said al Khudri, Ibn Abbas, Abu Hurayrah and others that the Holy Prophet said:

When the number of heatry (children of) Abi al-As reaches   thirty men, they will grab the funds of Allah as their own property, make Allah's people their slaves and make the religion of Allah a cause of corruption. (al-Musnad, Ahmed ibn Hanbal, vol 3, p.80; al-Mustadrak, al-Hakim, vol.4 p.480; al-Matalib al-aliyah, Ibn Hajar, vol.4, p.332; Majma az-zawa'id, al-Hytami, vol.5, pp.241, 243; Kanz al-ummal, al-Muttaqi vol.II, pp.148,149- ,351,354).

The history of Islam (after the death of the Holy Prophet) has enough evidence to prove this prophecy of the Holy Prophet; and the fear of Amir al-mu'minin for the Muslim community was based on this reason.

[234]. The man who drank wine was al-Walid ibn Uqbah ibn Abi Muayt. He was of the same mother as Caliph Uthman and his Governor of Kufah. al-Walid on an occasion in a state of intoxication led the morning prayers in the Central mosque of Kufah with four units (raka'ah) instead of the usual two as prescribed by the Holy Prophet. The congregation, which consisted of several pious persons like Ibn Mas'ud, was much incensed and still more irritate when , finishing the four units, al-Walid said:

What a pleasant morning! I would like to extend the prayers further if you consent.

Repeated complaints had already been made to the Caliph against al-Walid on account of his debauchery, but as often dismissed. People now reproached Uthman for not listening to their grievances, and favoring such a scoundrel. By chance they succeeded in taking off the signet ring from the hand of the Governor while he lay senseless from the effects of a debauch, and carried it off to Medina. Still the Caliph was slow and hesitated to enforce punishment upon his Governor (of the same mother); giving cause to be himself reproachfully accused of ignoring the law; though at last he was persuaded to have al-Walid scourged with forty strokes. He was consequently deposed from his office. Sa'id ibn al-As, a cousin of Uthman was appointed to take his place, and this was a matter of great reproach against Uthman. (Ansab al-ashraf, al-Baladhuri, vol. 5 pp.33-35; al-Aghani, Abu'l-Faraj al-Isfahani, vol.5 pp.91-92; at-Tabari, vol.1, pp.2843-2850; Ibn al-Athir, vol.3 pp.105-107; Ibn Abi'l-Hadid, vol.17,pp.227-245)

Even Hazrat Imam Hasan (Allah be pleased with him) eldest son of Ali (Allah be pleased with him) was poisoned though he made peace with Muawiyah with the condition that after Muawiyah dies The Caliphate be handed over to elected one and real Leader but Muawiyah did not fulfil that condition instead he nominated the Caliphate to his son Yazid and in this process Hazrat Imam Hussain (Allah be pleased with him) second grandson of Holy Prophet (may peace be upon him) and second son of Hazrat Ali (Allah be pleased with him) did not take the oath to Yazid as it was against the principal of Democratize process which was maintained until now. So Hazrat Imam Hussain (Allah be pleased with him) with most of his family members had to accept martyrdom before a dictator and a force of evil and Hazrat Imam Hussain (Allah be pleased with him) became the first in this world who gave His life and life of his dear ones for the Democracy and divine Law and equal justice for all which we nowadays talk most around this world and that of freedom, the freedom limited with certain limit which was prescribed in the Holy Quran by Almighty God, and also Sunna (whatever our Prophet (may peace be upon him) as messenger of God told was law) not a kind of freedom which violate ones' moral, ones' individual right or abuse a great man.

In the present day world where all the countries are dependent on each other and are willing to cooperate with each other we the Muslims can reestablish a exploitation free society and real Islamic System as per teaching of Holy Quran and our Holy Prophet (may peace be upon him).

Many a time, Abu Huraira (Allah be pleased with him) reports, had the Prophet (may Peace be upon him) to go without a meal. Dates and water frequently formed his only nourishment. Often, for months together, no fire could be lighted in his house from scantiness of means. God, say the Moslem historians, had indeed put before him the key to the treasures of this world, but he refused it!

How much property was left by our Holy Prophet (peace be upon him) who was also the first Head of a Islamic State. Our Holy Prophet (may peace be upon him) used to say "poverty is his proud". So we the Muslims also should be proud to be poor if we want to be companion of our Holy Prophet (may peace be upon him) in the next world.

So under Islamic economy no Muslim or region can hold unlimited wealth and it should be distributed through Zakat (Alms or Charity) other gifts as directed by Holy Quran and our Holy Prophet (may peace be upon him). But we make any obstacle for that we should know our limit, our power. If we close our eyes and imagine we are blind we can feel how much helpless we are. So we should help the helpless the needy even though we are to share, sacrifice our individual wealth.

We are sorry to mention that in a local English daily news paper we saw a report that the richest man in this world is a ruler of a Muslim country with his wealth of 25 billion US dollars; another Muslim leader with 18 billion US dollars and another with 4.5 billion US dollars and a total of the wealth in possession of these three Muslim ruler is 47.5 billion US dollars. So imagine if the report is true (Though the names of the rulers were mentioned in that news paper none of them challenged this statement) then only with this 47.5 billion US dollars we can create a vast fund with which we can establish many production oriented in-dustry which will eliminate poverty not only in the Islamic world but from the entire world; probably with such fund we can establish several organization like Co-operative American Relief Everywhere these are US based organization founded after the World War. These organization have been giving various aid to the poor of about 40 countries, for example Title II of PL 480 of USA.

488. Narrated Zaid bin Wahab: I passed by a place called Ar-Rabadha and by chance I met Abu Dhar and asked him, "What has brought you to this place?" He said, "I was in Sham (Syria) and differed with him on the meaning of the following verses of the Qur'an": "They who hoard up gold and silver and spend them not in the way of Allah" 9:34

They said, "This verse is revealed regarding the people of the scriptures." I said, It was revealed regarding us and also the people of the scriptures." So we had a quarrel and sent a complaint against me to Uthman.
Uthman wrote to me to come to Medina, and I came to Medina. Many people came to me as if they had not seen me before. So I told this to Uthman who said to me, "You may depart and live nearby if you wish." That was the reason for my being here for even If an Ethiopian had been nominated as my ruler, I would have obeyed him.

489. Narrated Al-Ahnaf bin Qais. While I was sitting with some people from Quraish, a man with very rough hair, clothes, and appearance came and stood in front of us, greeted us and said, "inform those who hoard wealth, that a stone will be heated in the Hell-fire and will be put on the nipples of their breasts till it comes out from the bones of their shoulders and then put on the bones of their shoulders till it comes through **the nipples of their breasts the stone will be moving and hitting." After saying that, the person retreated and sat by the side of the pillar, I followed him and sat beside him, and I did not know who he was. I said to him, "I think the people disliked what you had said." He said , "These people do not understand anything, although my friend told me." I asked, "Who is your friend?" He said, "The Prophet (Peace be upon him) said (to me), 'O Abu Dhar! Do you see the mountain of Uhud" And on that I (Abu Dhar) started looking towards the sun to judge how much remained of the day as I thought that Allah's Messenger (Peace be upon him) wanted to send me to do something for him and I said, 'Yes!' He said, 'I don not love to have gold equal to the mountain of Uhud unless I spend it all (in Allah's cause) except three Dinars (pounds). These people do not understand and collect worldly wealth, No, by Allah, Neither I ask them for worldly benefits nor am I in need of their religious advice till I meet Allah, The Honorable, The Majestic.""**

496. Narrated Abu Masuud (Allah be pleased with him): When the verses of Charity were revealed, we used to work as porters. A man came and distributed objects of charity in abundance. And they (the people) said, "He is showing off." And another man came and gave a Sa (a small measure of food grains); they said, "Allah is not in need of this small amount of charity." And then the Divine Inspiration came: "Those who criticize such of the believers who give in charity voluntarily and those who could not find to give in charity except what is available." (9:79)

497. Narrated Abu Masud Al-Ansari (Allah be pleased with him): Whenever Allah's Messenger (Peace be upon him) ordered us to give in charity , we used to go to market and work as porters and get a Mudd (a special measure of grain) and then give it in charity. (Those were the days of poverty) and to-day some of use have one hundred thousand.

498. Narrated Adi bin Hatim (Allah be pleased with him): I heard the Prophet (Peace be upon him) saying: "Save yourself from Hell-fire even by giving half a date-fruit in charity."

499. Narrated Aisha (Allah be please with her): A lady along with her two daughters came to me asking (for some alms), but she found nothing with me except one date which I gave to her and she divided it between her two daughters, and did not eat anything herself, and then she got up and went away. Then the Prophet (Peace be upon him) came in and I informed him about this story. He said, "Whenever is put to put to trial by these daughters and he treats them generously (with benevolence) then these daughters will act as a shield for him from Hell-Fire. (See Hadith No. 24. Vol. 8)

So instead of giving all responsibilities and burden to developed countries we the Islamic countries should share our vast resources to eliminate poverty from this world. We can take the help of Computer to calculate, to plan and distribute all our resources which may be food, technology, industry, manpower and any other resources.

DIFFERENCE OF TOLERANCE BETWEEN MUSLIMS AND OTHER RELIGION LIKE JEWS, CHRISTIANS AND HINDUS

The last Prophet of Islam did not allow his followers to take any revenge against the non-Muslims for any personal grievances accept the punishment a Muslim deserves for any crime.

There were three tribes of the Jews namely tribe Kainufa, Nazir and Banu Kuraiza who lived around Medina. So when the Prophet (Sm) first came to Medina he made a contract for good relation between the Ansars (Muslims of Medina) and Jews, which is called Charter of Medina. There were many clause in that Charter which are around 51 which can be compared with many modern charter including United Nations Charter which were formed after 1300 years of the Medina Charter.[235]

After the fall of Mecca to the Last Prophet (SWS), the new Religion Islam, or Religion of peace, safety and salvation began to make rapid progress in the Arabian Peninsula, and tribe after tribe gave up their old evil ways and adopted Islam. In the sixth year of the Hegira(migration to Medina), the Prophet granted to the monks of the Monastery of St. Catherine, near Mount Sina, and to all Christians, Charter, which is a monument of enlightened tolerance. By it the Prophet secured to the Christians important privileges and immunities, and the Moslems were prohibited under severe penalties from violating and abusing what was therein ordered. In this charter the Prophet undertook himself, and enjoined on his followers, to protect the Christians, to guard them from all injuries, and to defend their churches, and the residences of their priests. They were not to be unfairly taxed; no bishop was to be driven out of his bishopric; no Christian was to be forced to reject his religion; no monk was to be expelled from his monastery; no pilgrim was to be detained from his pilgrimage; nor were the Christian churches to be pulled down for the sake of building mosques or houses for the Moslems. If the Christians should stand in need of assistance for the repair of their churches or monasteries, or any other matter pertaining to their religion, the Moslems were to assist them.[236]

Though the Jews made conspiracy with the non-Muslim community in Mecca against the Muslims the Prophet did not take any action against them at that time.

And after the victory of last war in Mecca the Prophet of Islam (Peace be upon him) granted generous amnesty to the people of Mecca, and even to the greatest enemy like Abu Sufian and he accepted him along with others in his community of Muslim.

Even in later stage the Prophet accepted an invitation from a Jewess, Zainab, wife of Harith, a Jewish Chief. But the Jewess mixed poison with the food which the Prophet ate, but only, as a companion of the prophet, Bishir Ibn Basa died from that poison; that particular Jewess Zainab was given death sentence for that killing. But the Prophet did not take any action on the other Jews for the crime of one Jew. This trend of tolerance continued in the whole Muslim world. Whenever the Muslims conquered any country the majority people was not subject to any torture or injustice. The Muslims did not force the people for conversion into

---

[235] **Letters of Holy Prophet (Sm) by Sultan Ahmed, Noor Publishing, Qureshi House, Farash Khana, Delhi.**

[236] **HISTORY OF THE SARACENS (THE FALL OF MECCA) BY SYED AMIR ALI, PG. 14-15.**

Islam, for which after ruling around 800 years in Spain and India, the Muslims in those two countries were in minority.

Non-Moslems were eligible for the office, although their appointment might not have been viewed with approval by the orthodox. This feeling was not peculiar to the Saracens. The Buyide Azud ud-Dowla's Christian vizier i.e. minister (Nasir bin Harun) wielded great influence. The Fatimides of Egypt had frequently Hebrew and Christian viziers (ministers).[237]

The following comment by Nehru is enough for the difference between Muslim and Christians for the tolerance.

In Islam force converse was not allowed, for obvious political reasons. Moslem Turkey and Persia entrust their foreign interests to the charge of their Christian subjects. In Christendom, difference of faith has been a crime; in Islam it is an accident. "To Christians." says Urquhart, a difference of religion was indeed a ground for war, and that not merely in dark times and amongst fanatics. From the massacres, in the name of religion, of the Saxons, the Frisians and other Germanic tribes by Charlemagne; from the burning to death of the thousands of innocent men and women; from the frightful slaughters of the Arians, the Paulicians, the Albigenses and the Huguenots, from the horrors of the sacks of Magedeburg and Rome, from the sanguinary scenes of the Thirty Years War, down to the cruel persecutions of Calvinistic Scotland and Lutheran England, there is an uninterrupted chain of intolerance, bigotry, and fanaticism. Can anything be more heart-rending than the wholesale extermination of the unoffending races of America in the name of Christ ?

But when a person is prepared to die for a cause, and indeed to glory in such a death, it is impossible to suppress him or the cause he represents. And the Roman Empire wholly failed to suppress the Christians. Indeed, it was Christianity that came out triumphant in the conflict, and early in the fourth century after Christ, one of the Roman emperors himself became a Christian, and Christianity became the official religion of the Empire. This was Constantine, who founded Constantinople. We shall come to him later.

Similarly, Jesus claimed no divinity. His repeated statements that he was the son of God and the son of man do not necessarily mean any divine or superhuman claim. But human beings like to make gods of their great men, whom, having deified, they refrain from following! Six hundred years later the Prophet Mohammad started another great religion, but profiting perhaps by these instances, he stated clearly and repeatedly that he was human, and not divine.
Nehru also mentioned about the **great tolerance of the Islamic faith some of which are follows:**

We may conclude this section by a contemporary Christian document. It refers to the letter of a Nestorian bishop, addressed to a friend of him, which has been preserved: (cf. Assemani,Bible. Orient III, e, p. XLVI). "These Tayites (i.e.Arabs), to whom god has accorded domination in our days, have also become our masters; yet they do not combat at all the Christian religion; on the contrary they even protect our faith, respect our priests and saints, and make donations to our churches and convents."

---

[237] HISTORY OF THE SARACENS BY SYED AMIR ALI PG. 413

At the rise into caliph's power of the 'Abbasids, Spain detached itself from the Muslim Orient. After almost a thousand years of domination, in 1942, the last traces of a Muslim state were submerged there by the Castillian Christians molestation. The Moslems, on the other hand, required from others a simple guarantee of peace and amity, tribute in return for protection, or perfect equality, - the possession of equal rights and privileges, on condition of the acceptance of Islam.

The converse was not allowed, for obvious political reasons. Moslem Turkey and Persia entrust their foreign interests to the charge of their Christian subjects. In Christendom, difference of faith has been a crime; in Islam it is an accident. "To Christians," says Urquhart, a difference of religion was indeed a ground for war, and that not merely in dark times and amongst fanatics. From the massacres, in the name of religion, of the Saxons, the Frisians and other Germanic tribes by Charlemagne; from the burning to death of the thousands of innocent men and women; from the frightful slaughters of the Arians, the Paulicians, the Albigenses and the Huguenots, from the horrors of the sacks of Magedeburg and Rome, from the sanguinary scenes of the Thirty Years War, down to the cruel persecutions of Calvinistic Scotland and Lutheran England, there is an uninterrupted chain of intolerance, bigotry, and fanaticism. Can anything be more heart-rending than the wholesale extermination of the unoffending races of America in the name of Christ ?

Islam had fully established itself in the Peninsula. This latter document has, for the most part, furnished the guiding principle to all Moslem rulers in their mode of dealing with their non-Moslem subjects, and if they have departed from it in any instance the cause is to be found in the character of the particular sovereign. If we separate the political necessity which has often spoken and acted in the name of religion, no faith is more tolerant than Islam to the followers of other creeds.

"Reasons of State" have led a sovereign here and there to display a certain degree of intolerance, or to insist upon a certain uniformity of faith; but the system itself has ever maintained the most complete tolerance Christians and Jews, as a rule, have never been molested in the exercise of their religion, or constrained to change their faith. If they are required to pay as special tax, it is in lieu of military service, and it is but right that those who enjoy the protection of the State should contribute in some shape to the public burdens. Towards the idolaters there was greater strictness in theory, but in practice the law was equally liberal. If at any time they were treated with harshness, the cause is to be found in the passions of the ruler or the population. The religious element was used only as a pretext.

In support of the time-worn thesis that the non-Moslem subjects of Islamic States labor under severe disabilities, reference is made not only to the narrow views of the later colonists and lawyers of Islam, but also to certain verses of the Koran, in order to show that the Prophet did not view non-Moslems with favor, and did not encourage friendly relations between them and his followers.

In dealing with this subject, we must not forget the stress and strain of the lift-and -death struggle in which Islam was involved when those verses were promulgated, and the treacherous means that were often employed by the heathens as well as the Jews and the Christians, to corrupt and seduce the Moslems from the new Faith. At such a time, it was incumbent upon the Teacher to warn his followers against the wiles and insidious designs of hostile creeds. And no student of comparative history can blame him for trying to safeguard his little commonwealth against the treachery of enemies and aliens. But when we come to look at his general treatment of non-Moslem subjects, we find it marked by a large-hearted tolerance and sympathy.

But the irony of fate is that though the Muslims in India survived except some minor incident, in Christian Europe the Muslims were massacred and not a single Muslim was survived after the fall of Muslim rule in Spain. Even in this modern age, lack of Muslims are killed in Bosnia and Bosnian and Kosovo Muslims were driven out from their home, around 40,000 Muslim women were raped, the way it was done in fifteenth century Spain. There is no difference what happened in Spain and what is now happening in Bosnia. Though so many meetings were held under United Nation and European powers on Bosnia, there was no quick action taken during past one year, though quick action was taken after the invasion of Kuwait by Iraq, still all type of blocked has been continuing even though the Iraqi children has been dying for the misdeed of it's leader Saddam Hossain, the so called so many leaders of the Muslim Umma have closed their eyes, perhaps the Muslim leaders have been waiting the completion of cleansing of the entire Muslim population in Bosnia and that is why they even could not arrange any meeting of The OIC (Organization of Islamic Countries), once they even shifted the date for the meeting of the OIC, as if, just to wait to see the cleansing of the Muslims there, and whatever those leaders say that is just to satisfy their own Muslim population, they are not sincere for the sake of humanity or particularly they are not serious about Islam or the followers of Islam or for the massacre of the followers of Islam, they do not bother about the cleansing of the Muslims in Europe or in India as happened in the past in Spain, they forgot about the Jihad, and what they bother is that they should stay in power even though sacrificing all the Muslims, or the all fundamental pillar of Islam.

But still you will not find any Muslim News Paper Reporter killed in Bosnia, because perhaps the Muslims are now afraid of death, so even not interested to know how the Muslims are killed there, though on the other hand the Western Reporters particularly from USA gave their life for the cause of humanity, they have been helping the whole world to know what happened in Bosnia, even in exchange of giving their own life. Without the brave adventure and **sacrifice of the Western Reporter the world could not know what is happening in Bosnia. Still there are every doubt that if there are any conspiracy and silent permission of the Western leaders for the cleansing of the Muslims by the Christian Serbs because when they were quick in action against Saddam's Iraq the central place of 500 years long Abbaside Caliphate, why they are silent and slow to save the life of million Muslims in European Bosnia and at the same time in India, as there are mass killing of Muslims in the city like Bombay by Police who are suppose to save them as a citizen, and there are no great pressure to the Western Leaders to save the Muslims there or to maintain the sovereignty of Muslim Bosnia. Perhaps the Western Reporters, one, day will find out the secret conspiracy of the Western Leaders for the cleansing of the Muslims there, so that not a single Muslim state can be in existence in Europe as TIME Magazine in it's issue of August 24, 1992 mentioned in page 24 that "While the world was recoiling in shock from the visible inhumanity, Western reaction was more rhetorical than real. Under pressure to do something-anything-the U. N. Security Council passed a vague resolution that provided for "all measures necessary" to ensure delivery of relief supplies. Observer could be forgiven if they somehow got the idea that U. N. had authorized the use of force to stop the war and end the barbarities. That was hardly the case. U. S. Deputy Secretary of State Lawrence Eagleburger spelled it out carefully: What we are talking about is the provision of humanitarian assistance. We are not talking about going beyond that.**

...... The ultimate reality may be that the war is virtually over and the Serve has won. "We have everything," declared Serb leader Karadzic last week. "All we need now is a negotiates settlement." The Serb irregulars know how hard it will be for any international body to reclaim what they have taken. And regardless of the political outcome, the war has already done damage that cannot be settled at any peace table. A new chapter of

Resentment and reprisal has already been written that promises to keep the Balkans unstable for decades. People who have been seen their parents slaughtered and their children killed will never forget, let alone forgive.'- reported by James L. Graff/Trnopolje, John Moody/Zagreb and William Mader/London.

The TIME Magazine as mentioned earlier have also mentioned in the same pages some are as follows:

'The Serbs have constructed their own version of reality to justify their aggression. "there is no ethnic cleansing," said Serb leader Radovan Karadzic, "but ethnic shifting. We are doing it to protect people." They have conjured up a phantom Islamic jihad from which they are saving Europe. "This is not a civil war," insists Prejedor police chief Drljaca. "It's a religious war," The operative lie is that Bosnia's Muslim leader, Alija Izetbegovic, is bent on creating a Muslim fundamentalist state. Never mind that Bosnia's Muslims are not fundamentalist, indeed are among the more secular followers of the Prophet Muhammad. Croatian President Franjo Tudjman, who shares the Serb ambition to carve up Bosnia, parrots the charge that "there are tendencies to create an Islamic state." Serbs claim that an "Islamic Declaration" that Izetbegovic wrote in the 1970s is proof of his intention to establish a religious state. "There was nothing in it," says Ivo Banac, a Croat who is a professor of history at Yale University, "that alluded in any sense to Bosnia-Herzegovina." That hardly matters if the threat works. The excuse has allowed Serbs and Croats to turn on the Muslims with such ferocity that many Muslims now conspire in their own flight. So too do international officials, who have been put in the excruciating position of aiding the evacuation of endangered Muslims-and thereby abating ethnic cleansing. The Serbs agreed to safe passage for 300 women and children from Sarajevo last week for humanitarian reasons, for public relations advantage, though relief officials believe their motive was really to depopulate the city. In northern Bosnia, Serbs announced a plan to push 28,000 Muslims from towns in the region, after the U. N aided the expulsion of 7,000 Muslims into Croatia a week before. This time the U. N. has decided to ward off a mass exodus by sending in food and medicine. Said U.N.H.C.R. operations director Tony in Zagreb; "We can't allow ourselves to be drawn into this kind of unwitting collaboration."

Again in it's issue of October, 1992, NEWSWEEK (PG. 25) in the last paragraph, Mr. David H. Hackworth mentioned the followings:

"Hard winter: Still, the Serbs would be fools to launch a full-scale attack. They're wining militarily without wasting a grant. Winter with its freezing conditions is on the way. Those who have survived the high explosive slaughter will turn into a block of ice. There is no winter fuel. Most of the local wood has been burned to heat water and food. The snowfall is five to six meters even in a gentle winter, the forecast for this year is worse. I noticed that the shelling had blown away Sarajevo's fleet of snowplows. Snow, ice and fog will close down the airport and roads. The United Nations will find it far harder to distribute relief. If the siege continues into winter, Sarajevo will be a repeat of Stalingrad in 1942 where Russians and Germans froze to death by the tens of thousands. The answer is simple; the United Nations should tell Belgrade that Sarajevo is a no-fire zone. And the United States, France and Great Britain should back the U.N., stand with the same kind of resolve they applied against Baghdad.
There were many such reports in TIME, NEWSWEEK and other Western magazines since the war for cleansing of Muslims, started in former Yugoslavia. The fact is that the Muslims of former Yugoslavia will be cleansed by next winter as 70% of their land has already been occupied by the Serbs and Croat, and another permanent refugee problem like Palestine, will be created for those who lost their parents and dear one, after cleansing or killing of, may be quarter million Muslims of which around half was already cleaned or killed, and those survived Muslims will be starting to take revenge against the Serbs and others, who are responsible for those killing and forcing the survived one to leave their homeland, where they have been living for several centuries; will ultimately be known to the outside world as terrorist and will face veto power from the Western Big Powers if there is any agenda passed in U. N., in their favor, the organi-

253

zation those survived Bosnian Muslims will form, will be know as a terrorist Organization like the PLO, which is known to the western world after so many sacrifices like PLO Muslims were forced to leave their homeland in Palestine, and this is the Western Justice and human right towards the Muslims around the World, though behind those massacre of Muslims in Yugoslavia, who knows that there is another Sykes-Picot like agreement among the Western leaders and that is why they are ready to send foods to Bosnia for the surviving Muslims who will be survived/spared as a Minority and helpless community and there will be no Muslim State in Europe, may be there is understanding among themselves that the Serb should clean the Muslims in European Bosnia as soon as they can and the Western Leaders will not send any Armed Forces to Bosnia as they sent to Saudi Arabia, Kuwait and other Gulf Countries without delay to force Saddam Hossain out of Kuwait, nor they will allow the Muslim Nation to send any such Army if some of them wanted to do so. The fact behind all this drama will be known by us from the Western Reporters, who are almost in each day, informing the whole World what is happening in Bosnia, sometime sacrificing their valuable life for the truth and with a great mind with sympathy and love towards human being irrespective or their faith.

The above is the story of the past. But that history did not end; it is still continuing in Kosovo against Albanian Muslims. There are now half a million refugees and the World can see more such drama against World Muslims every where until Caliphate is re-established; the sooner the better.

But the 1400 years old history of Islam is not like above which are happening in Europe and at the same time in India now, as happened in Muslim ruled Spain in the past, as the present day, the so called Leaders of illegal Muslim nation state who were installed in power in the Muslim World and in particular in the Arab World by the Western Leaders, particularly ancestors of many like Lord Owen, who conspired to abolish the Caliphate and those division of 1300 years long Islamic Caliphate into many the Kings, Amirs(or Emirs), and other Dictator like in the shape of Bath Party or even Military Dictator, who are now in power, have not been done by the majority Muslims around this world, the general Muslims were ignorant about those conspiracy in the Eighteenth century and during last World Wars. But the condition of the **Islamic Political System was Democracy and due election through Democratic norm the way the First Four** truthful Caliphs were elected, who were not hereditary survivor to one another, and that way Caliph Ali (R. A.) was fourth in term though he was the husband of the **daughter of the** last Prophet of Islam (Sm). **Even after the introduction of hereditary kingship instead of electoral System, the Caliphs were not associated with the conspiracy of becoming any agent of** European Countries, instead the Ummaite advanced their conquer of the region one after another though internally they became Dictator did many misdeeds like killing of Holy Family members (R. A.) of the Last Prophet (Sm.), still they were not any type of agent of any Christian or Jews or any country.
Where as the present day Rulers in that region are busy to protect the interest of the Western Leaders not of Allah (God) or his **religion Islam, because they have been given the umbrella of the Western Military Powers to protect them from Democratic System, generation after Generation during last 100 years.**

So the Reporters, some of those, mentioned above are non-Muslims but we salute them for their truthfulness and above all greatness of mind as and how they commented on the activities of their fellow Christians for their atrocities against the Muslims and we are personally shocked like many in this world, when we see almost in each day, **how the beautiful children are leaving by Bus for unknown places, leaving behind their dead parents and everything,** in the Television reported by the Western Reporter.

How inhuman we have become in the so called civilized era. Even during Muslim holy Jihad or Islamic Holy War, the aim of the war was only God, not to kill anybody except only the cause of God, no self interest or personal hatred or to take any personal or national revenge, one such example is Hadrat Ali (R. A.), who was also 4th truthful Caliph of the Sunni thought and 2nd Imam (Leader) of Shia Thought, who once left a non-Muslim when he (the non-Muslim) threw split in his holy face in the moment he (Hadrat Ali) was almost to kill him. When Hadrat Ali (R. A.) was asked that why he did not kill him, he answered that the moment he was about to kill him, his only and only cause was God i.e. to defend the cause of Islam, but as soon as he (the non-Muslim) threw split around his face, he was afraid that if he killed him after that event, it might be due to personal Gregg or to revenge and might not be the cause of Islam or God. **Once Hadrat Ali (R. A.), when he was Caliph saw his sword in the possession of a Jew, perhaps who stolen it, so Hadrat Ali (R. A.) lodged complain to the Kazi (Judge). The Kazi sought witnesses and Hadrat Ali (R. A.) produced his two sons as witnesses. But the Kazi (Judge) did not accept the witnesses as they were his sons and in such the verdict of the Kazi (Judge) went against the Caliph Ali (R. A.), and for such good judgement, the Jew became astonished and became a Muslim for the justice of Islam. So what** in present day, we the Muslim are doing are not Islamic, in the name of Islam we are doing many misdeeds which are not Islamic, the division of so many Muslim States, the continuation of hereditary dictatorship in the shape of hereditary Kingship, Amirship, one party, Bath party and leadership, spending **huge money with the only aim is that is to stay in power, generation after generation, to deny proper justice and human rights, to deny basic human need in term of food, shelter and other necessity to the common citizens, if those citizens work something against the interest of the man who is in power, the ultimate result is mis-representation of Islam to the outside world that Islamic System is not Democratic and under it there is no human right, where as Islamic System gave human right 1400 years ago to all people irrespective of color or race or even religion, the Charter of Medina is enough proof of that, and even Democracy, the proof is that how the first 4 truthful** Caliphs were elected and there was no difference of the ordinary people and the Caliphs in their way of life as a citizen.

Once Hadrat Ali was coming to join the congregation of the Prayer or Jamat in the Mosque in **Prophet's Mosque in Medina, when he faced an old Jew, who was walking in the same road towards the Mosque, but Hadrat Ali (R. A.) did not cross that old Jew** as the old Jew will be hearted, though Hadrat Ali (R. A.) was afraid that he will miss the Jamat (congregation) as he will be late, still he was walking behind the Jew, and **God was so pleased with Hadrat Ali that God** asked the Prophet (sm) to make the prayer lengthy **so that** Hadrat Ali (R. A.) can join the congregation. The Companion of the Prophet (R. A.) thought that there may be some revelation from God and as such after the prayer they (the Companions) asked about that delay. The Prophet replied that The God was so pleased with Hadrat Ali for **the honor he shown to the old Jew by not crossing him behind that God asked him to make the** prayer longer so that Hazrat Ali can join the prayer. **So those mentioned above are the teaching of Islam that how a Muslim should behave with others even with non-Muslim.**

Has any conquering race or Faith given to its subject nationalities a better guarantee than is to be found in the following words of the Prophet? "To [the Christians of] Najran and the neighboring territories, the security of God and the pledge of His Prophet are extended for their lives, their religion, and their property-to the present as well as the absent and others besides; shall be no interference with [the practice of] their faith or their observances; nor any change in their rights or privileges; no bishop shall be removed from his bishopric; nor any monk from his monastery, nor any priest from his priesthood, and they shall continue to enjoy every thing great and small as heretofore; no image or cross shall be destroyed; they shall not oppress or be oppressed;

255

they shall not practice the rights of blood-vengeance as in the Days of Ignorance; no tithes shall be levied from them nor shall they be required to furnish provisions for the troops.

After the subjugation of Hira, and as soon as the people had taken the oath of allegiance, Khalid bin-Walid issued a proclamation by which he guaranteed the lives, liberty and property of the Christians, and declared that "they shall not be prevented from beating their nakus and taking out their crosses on occasions of festivals." "And this declaration," says Imam Abu-Yousuf, was approved of and sanctioned by the Caliph and his council.

It has been said that a warlike spirit was infused into medieval Christianity by aggressive Islam ! The massacres of Justinian and the fearful wars of Christian Clovis in the name of religion, occurred long before the time of Mohammed. Compare, again, the conduct of the Caliph (or Khalif) Omar took Jerusalem, A.D.,637 he rode into the city by the side of the Patriarch Sophronius, conversing with him on its antiquities. At the hour of prayer, he declined to perform his devotions in the Church of the Resurrection, in which he chanced to be, but prayed on the steps of the Church of Constantine; for, said he to the Patriarch, had done so, the Musulmans in a future age might have infringed the treaty, under color of imitating my example; But in the capture by the Crusaders, the brains of young children were dashed out against the walls; infants were pitched over the battlements; men were roasted at fires; some were ripped up, to see if they had swallowed gold; the Jews were driven into their synagogue, and there burnt; a massacre of nearly 70,000 persons took place; and the pope's legate was seen partaking in the triumph![238] When Saladin recaptured the city, he released all Christians, gave them money and food, and allowed them to depart with a safe- conduct.[239] Islam grasped the sword in self-defence: Christianity grasped it in order to stifle freedom of thought and liberty of belief. With the conversion of Constantine, Christianity had become the dominant religion of the Western world. It had thenceforth nothing to fear from its enemies; but from the moment it obtained the mastery, it developed its true character of isolation and exclusiveness. Wherever Christianity prevailed, no other religion could be followed without molestation. The Moslems, on the other hand, required from others a simple guarantee of peace and amity, tribute in return for protection, or perfect equality, - the possession of equal rights and privileges, on condition of the acceptance of Islam.[240]

An incident which occurred during the Caliphate of **Omar** shows the absolute equality of all men in Islam. Jabala, king of the Ghassanides, having embraced the Faith, had proceeded to **Medina** to pay his homage to the Commander of the Faithful. He had entered the city with great pomp and ceremony, and been received with much consideration. Whilst performing the tawaf or circumambulating of the Kaba (grand Mosque in Holy Mecca), a humble pilgrim engaged in the same sacred duties accidentally dropped a piece of his pilgrim's dress over the royal shoulders. Jabala turned round furiously and struck him a blow which knocked out the poor man's teeth. The rest of this episode must be told in the memorable words of Omar himself to Abu Obaidah, commanding the Moslem troops in Syria. "**the poor man came to me,**" writes the Caliph, "**and prayed for redress; I sent for Jabal, and when he came before me** *I asked him why he had so ill-treated a brother-Moslem. He answered that the man had insulted him, and that were it not for the sanctify of the place he would have killed him on the spot. I answered that his words added to the gravity of his offence, and that unless he obtained the pardon of the injured man he would*

---

[238] Draper, History of the Intellectual Development of Europe, vol. ii. p. 22.

[239] For a full account, see The Short History of the Saracens by Syed Amir Ali pp. 356.

[240] THE SPIRIT OF ISLAM BY SYED AMEER ALI PP. 220-221.

have to submit to the usual penalty of the law. Jabala replied, 'I am a king, and the other is only a common man.' "King or no king, both of you are Musulmans and both of you are equal in the eye of the law.' He asked that the penalty might be delayed until the next day; and, on the consent of the injured, I accorded the delay. In the night Jabala escaped, and has now joined the Christian dog (such was the designation usually given to the Byzantine emperors by the early Moslems). But God will grant thee victory over him and the like of them...." This letter was read by Abu Obaidah at the head of his troops. These communications appear to have been frequent under the early Caliphate. No person in the camp or in the city was a stranger to public affairs. Every Friday after divine service, the Commander of the Faithful mentioned to the assembly the important nominations and events of the day. The prefects in their provinces followed the example. No one was excluded from these general assemblies of the public. It was the reign of democracy in its best form. The Pontiff of Islam, the Commander of the Faithful, was not hedged round by any divinity. He was responsible for the administration of the State to his subjects. The stern devotion of the early Caliphs to the well-being of the people, and the austere simplicity of their lives, were in strict accordance with the example of the Master. They preached and prayed in the mosque like the Prophet; received in their homes the poor and oppressed, and failed not to give a hearing to the meanest. Without cortege, without pomp or ceremony, they ruled the hearts of men by the force of their character. Omar traveled to Syria to receive the capitulation of Jerusalem, accompanied by a single slave. Abu Bakr on his death-bed left only a suit of clothes, a camel, and a slave to his heir. Every Friday, Ali distributed his own allowance from the public treasury among the distressed and suffering; and set an example to the people by his respect for the ordinary tribunals. Whilst the Republic lasted none of the Caliphs could alter, or act contrary to, the judgement of the constituted courts of justice. (The first sentence of a court of justice which was not carried into execution was Muawiya, who pardoned a man found guilty by the judge upon the criminal reciting a poem in praise of the usurper). Naturally, it is difficult for a new government, introduced by force of arms, to conciliate the affection of the people at once. But the early Saracens offered to the conquered nations motives for the greatest confidence and attachment. Headed by chiefs of the moderation and gentleness of Abu Obaidah, who tempered and held in check the ferocity of soldiers like Khalid, they maintained intact the civil rights of their subjects. They accorded to all the conquered nations the completest religious toleration. Their conduct might furnish to many of the civilized governments of modern times the noblest example of civil and religious liberty. They did not condemn innocent females to Siberian mines and the outrages of their guards. They had the sagacity not to interfere with any beneficent civil institution, existing in the conquered countries, which did not militate with their religion.[241]

But in exchange of the above tolerance of the Muslim rulers. the present day any leaderless (one and only one true Caliph) Muslims have become the victim of State terrorism of almost all religion, where they are united for the misery and sufferings of Muslims of all the continents, sometimes with the help of so called leaders of so called Muslim countries. The followings are extract of the International Press and magazines:

The heedlessness of international organizations towards **the Serbs atrocities on Bosnian Muslims has surpassed all limits. The escalation of the deplorable events in Bosnia-Herzegovina is because of the indifference shown by big powers too. Peace and tranquility cannot be established in Croatia as long as war rages in the Muslim**

[241] THE SPIRIT OF ISLAM BY AMEER ALI, PUBLISHED BY B.I. PUBLICATIONS, BOMBAY, CALCUTTA, DELHI, MADRAS, BY ARRRANGEMENT WITH CHATTO & WINDUS, LONDON, PP. 279-281.

republic. The international community is as guilty as the Serbs for the crimes being committed in Bosnia-Herzegovina because it allowed the continuation of the Serbs atrocities through its indifference.

The Security Council on the other hand is considering a resolution to provide UN protection for European Human Rights monitors visiting Bosnian detention camps where Serbs are systematically involved in rapes and massacres. Initiated by France, the draft resolution asks Secretary General Boutrs Boutros Ghali to provide escorts for the European delegation without suggesting any specifics. The European Community at its summit in Edinburgh over the weekend decided to send a delegation headed by Dame Anne Warburton of Britain to investigate the camps following reports of the rapes and other atrocities. A Croatian journalist and novelist Slavenka Drakutic wrote in New York Times recently that women were being raped by Serbian soldiers "in an organized and systematic way as a planned crime to destroy a whole Muslim population". She said Bosnia's Interior ministry estimates that 50,000 women and girls had been raped and many impregnated on purpose. She also published testimony from witnesses who alleged they watched Serbs mutilate women with Knives before raping them, kill those who screamed on the spot and murder their children. This is height of barbarism.

A story of a mental hospital lying perilously close to a front line in war ravaged Bosnia may see two thirds of its 420 patients die before the winter ends. The Pazaric asylum, 30 km west of the besieged capital and only two km from the front is witness to the worst of human. The President of the Human Rights Commission in Bosnia-Herzegovina Dr. Mustafa Sarech declared recently while on a visit to Pakistan that every Muslim country was under obligation to raise voice against the genocide of Muslims in Bosnia. He rightly said that if Caliph Umar (RA) felt answerable for the death of dog due to thirst on the bank of Dajla river, those in authority in Muslim States at present could not obviate this responsibility on any ground. Without mincing works he told a reception. "We are being killed because we want to live as Muslims. They are killing us, our children and even our animals. I was born as Muslim and wanted to die as a Muslim. They say there is no room for Islam in Europe. But I ask them what has Christianity to do with Europe."

I pose a question to the Muslim world. Do you want the valiant Muslims of Bosnia braving all odds to give up? Should they go to the Pope or contact Tel-Aviv? Whenever the Christians in any part of the world were in trouble, the Christian rulers considered their responsibility to come to their help and then the Pope was responsible for every Christian on the globe.

It is a sad commentary on the affluent, Muslim world that the blood of the Muslims was being shed in Kashmir, Burma, Palestine, Lebanon and now in Bosnia. Who is responsible for this? The United Nations for these Muslims is superfluous. It took fifteen days for the UN Secretary General, himself a Christian to convene Security Council meeting to consider OIC demand for lifting in a world of discrimination and certainly this is an issue to feel disheartened. We are now living in a world of hypocrisy, a word of double standards. We have learnt that all talk of humanism, human rights and civil liberties is simply a big farce.

Time is ripe now for the Muslim world to rise to the occasion and do something substantive to save their suffering brethren. They should exert further pressure on the United Nations to act on a war footing to save millions from starvation, massacre and atrocities. There is no misery. Now with the bitter Balkan winter looming, heating is the most pressing problem.

The Secretary General of the Organization of Islamic conference Hamid Al Gabid the other day hailed a call by the United States for the United Nations to reconsider an arms embargo on Bosnia-Herzegovina. Muslim nations have been agitating for an exemption for Bosnia and have hinted that if no action is taken by mid-January, they could begin to supply arms to Muslim forces in the former Yugoslav republic. He desired European support on OIC request for the embargo to be lifted to allow the republic of Bosnia-Herzegovina to exercise its right of self-defense. There should be enforcement of a two month old UN Security Council resolution creating a 'no-fly zone' over Bosnia-Herzegovina, but the US cannot act on its own as stated by the Secretary of State Lawrence Eagelburger. Concern is growing among the western leaders about the danger of spill over of the Bosnian conflict into the Kosovo. So now Kosovo massacre also started.

The situation in Bosnia is deteriorating fast. There is real danger of mass starvation. The Security Council resolution authorizing the use of "all necessary means" to assure delivery of humanitarian supplies must be implemented. In a strong speech in Geneva the US secretary of state denounced Serbian leaders for authorizing attacks on Bosnians Muslims. Eagelburger believed the UN should reconsider an embargo as it affects the Bosnian government forces. The measure at present covers all of the former Yugoslavia. At an international conference of foreign ministers on December 16 Eagellburger called for the men, mainly Serbs to be tried before a Second Nuremberg Court for crimes against humanity. Mere denouncement or proposals to tackle the horrifying situation in Bosnia-Herzegovina cannot improve the situation. These are platitudes and mere consolation. Can one forget the mass massacres of 3000 Muslims near the north eastern town of Breka, terrorizing of 30,000 Muslims in the nationalist Serbian stronghold of Banja Luka. How can the ill-fated and innocent Muslim-victims forget the siege of Bosnian capital Sarajevo since April, where daily shelling has left countless dead. The blockade of humanitarian aid has claimed large number of deaths.

Point depending on the United Nations and waiting for the response. The Islamic member states of the United Nations should implement their own strategy with a mere intimation to the United Nations. Let the Muslim bloc really prove their mettle in tackling the Bosnian issue by liberating it from the clutches of the Serbian hordes and display the sense of Islamic brotherhood and unity in diversity. It is the bounden duty of the Muslim governments and rulers the world over to save their compatriots from annihilation. This is a herculean task indeed, but where there is a will there is a way.[242]

Almost in each issue of Newsweek, Times and other western magazine of each week during last one there are only horrifying news of atrocities of the Christian Serbs on the helpless Muslims of Bosnia with which a big book can be published, one of such recent is as follows from the Newsweek issue of January 11, 1993.

Crimes of War: by Tom Post with ALEXANDRA Stiglmayer in Zenic and Zagreb, Charles Lane in Orasje, Joel Brand in Sarajevo, Margaret Garrard Warner in Washington and Robin Sparkman in New york on A Pattern of Rape in Bosnia Now, on top of documented cases of systematic torture and murder in Bosnia, come charges of a new Serb atrocity- the rape of as many as 50,000 women, mostly Muslims. Testimony from Bosnia refugees tells of girls as young as 6 being subjected to repeated rapes, of schools and in some cases possibly entire villages turned into military bordellos, of gang rapes so brutal their victims die and of deliberate programs to impregnate Muslim women with unwanted Serb babies. A torrent of wrenching first-person testimonies tells of a new Serb atrocity:systematic sexual abuse. About all she has left is her name, which she prefers to keep to herself, and the shocking memories of last July. That's when Serbian troops stormed the northwest

---

[242] Bosnia-- and some questions, the bell tolls by
Sayed Eqbal Rezvi

Bosnian village of Rizvanovici, and S., a 20 year-old Muslim woman with a ponytail, was rounded up with 400 other women in the yard of a neighbor's house. Two soldiers, wearing camouflage uniforms and Serbian crosses around their necks, picked S. and her friend I. out of the crowd. "They brought us to an empty house and there they did what they wanted to do," says S. dully. "First we had to excite them and then we had to satisfy them." Afterward the Serbs traded partners. The girls had been virgins. "They were laughing at us," S. recalls. "They said we were pretty girls and [that] we saved ourselves for them." Her ordeal didn't end there. After being raped and dumped at the yard, one of the soldiers came back to bring S. to his commander. "He told me to take off my clothes and to lie down on the bed," she says. "Then he did the same thing. He started to kiss and to caress me. He saw that I didn't feel anything. I looked into eyes and asked him if he had a wife. He said no. I asked if he had a sister. He said he had one. Then I said, 'How would your sister feel if somebody did the same thing to her that you are doing to me?' Then he jumped up and told me to get dressed and leave." S., who now lives in a refugee center in northern Croatia, is a survivor of what may be the most sadistic violence to haunt Europe since the Nazi campaigns: "ethnic cleansing." Now, on top of documented cases of systematic torture and murder in Bosnia, come charges of a new Serb atrocity-mass rape. No one knows how many victims there are, though estimates range from 30,000 to 50,000 women, most of them Muslim. In the last few months, a torrent of wrenching first-person testimonies from refugees has emerged, suggesting widespread sexual abuse by Serb forces. They tell of repeated rapes of girls as young as 6 and 7; violations by neighbors and strangers alike; gang rapes so brutal their victims die; rape camps where Serbs routinely abused and murdered Muslim and Croat women; rapes of young girls performed in front of fathers, mothers, siblings and children; rapes committed explicitly to impregnate Muslim women and hold them captive until they give birth to unwanted Serbian babies. Many reports are unconfirmed, and some may never be independently corroborated. But as anecdotal evidence pile up, Western media and women's groups are pressuring their governments to take some kind of action. So far it has resulted in little more than intelligence gathering by the United States and the European Community. The U.N. Security Council, citing "massive, organized and systematic detention and rape," voted unanimously on Dec. 18 to condemn "atrocities committed against women, particularly Muslim women, in Bosnia and Herzegovina." In blithe defiance of international outrage, the Serbs continue to attack Bosnia towns. Do the Serbs have a deliberate policy of rape? Have they, as Bosnian Foreign Minister Haris Silajdzic alleges to NEWSWEEK, used rape in the "systematic humiliation and genocide of the Bosnian people"? U.S. government analysts haven't yet uncovered anything as obvious as a speech or direct order by a Serbian leader calling on troops to violate Muslim women. But there does seem to be widespread pattern of on-the-ground commanders encouraging-or even ordering-their men to rape. The testimonies of so many victims and witnesses, and of some captured Serb perpetrators, have a consistency that cannot be accidental. "It's hard to believe that all these Serbian men, no matter how animalistic you think human nature is, would suddenly get it in their heads to find a 7 year-old girl and rape her," says the lead State Department researcher, of eradicating entire areas of their historic Muslim populations through brutal intimidation, expulsion and outright murder. In such Bosnian towns as Brcko, Bejeljina, Kljuc, Sanski Most, Prijedor, Kotor Varos, Zvornik, leading citizens-anyone who owned a business, participated in the Party of Democratic Action, held a university degree- were hunted down and liquidated. The rest of the male population was packed off to prison camps. Rape clearly was the coup de grace delivered to tens of mortally wounded towns, a way of ensuring that women would never want to return to their homes. For 12-year-old Vasvija, the terror began after she was evicted from her village of Jelec in August. During her first night in Partizan Hall, a Serb-run detention camp in the nearby eastern Bosnian town of Foca, two soldiers picked her from among the 70 detainees, all women, children and elderly civilians. "They brought me to a flat, an empty flat," she says, a single tear running down an otherwise passive face. "They raped me." Both soldiers? "Both." Over nine consecutive nights, Vasvija endured the same hideous treatment at the hands of different men. Once she was taken out with her mother and another inmate. They were all raped by the same Serbian soldier. Exchanged on Sept. 17 for Serb prisoners, Vasvija, her siblings and her mother now live in a refugee center near Sarajevo. .... The Serbian forces, after all, still occupy 70 percent of Bosnia. Proving mass rape is difficult. No allegation is so emotionally charged-or so susceptible to exaggeration and propaganda. "It will be years before the full picture of what has transpired emerges," reports a U.S. government specialist. "When we finally can survey the interior of Bosnia, I think we'll find a mass grave associated with each and every camp and village that was ethnically cleansed. And in every one of them will be women who were raped." The attempt to pin down numbers enrages some advocacy groups. "What happens to men is called politics, what happens to women is called culture, " says Gloria Steinem. She has a point: rape has historically been treated as an incidental atrocity of war. Along with groups like the International League for Human Rights and the Center for Reproductive Law & Policy, the Ms. Foundation has labored to place rape in Bosnia at the center of international attention. Many organizations hope to provide psychological support to rape survivors. But a chief aim is to prosecute war criminals. Says Steinem: "These people must be held responsible." But sorting out "these people" won't be easy. In his call for a war-crimes trial, Secretary of State Lawrence Eagleburger lumped together the chief architects of a Greater Serbia-including Serbian President Slobodan Milosevic and Radovan Karadzic and Ratko Mladic, the political and military leaders of the Bosnian Serbs-with low ranking henchmen like Borislav Herak. A 21-year-old Serb laborer from Sarajevo, Herak admits to raping seven Muslim women and to killing two of his victims in addition to the 18 murders to which he has already confessed. "We were ordered to rape so that our morale might be higher," he says from a military prison in the Bosnian capital. "We were told we would fight better if we raped the women." He claims that he and fellow soldiers frequented the Sonja Cafe-one of several alleged "rape camps" outside Sarajevo-which maintained a population of 70 Muslim women and girls; those who were killed were quickly replaced. Entire villages, such as Miljevina in eastern Bosnia, may have been converted to rape camps. About 100 people, "all young Muslim women and girls, were raped," says a 20-year-old named Aida. Her attacker was Dragan J., a Serb policeman and neighbor, who excused his behavior, she says, on the ground that "'It is war, you can't resist, there is no law and order'." Rasema, a 33-year-old mother, offers a similar account. She claims that her assailants raped her in front of her two girls. When she resisted, they threatened, "We will cut out your teeth! Do you want us to slaughter your children, to watch us cutting them into pieces, piece after piece?" In his own defence, one attacker told Rasema, "I have to do it, otherwise they will kill me." He may have been telling the truth. Two young Serb deserters, Slobodan Panic and Cvijetin Maksimovic, now being held in a prison in Orasje, Bosnia, told Newsweek they were ordered to rape and murder for the amusement of their commander in Brcko, in northeastern Bosnia, last May. Panic says he balked when two battered women, each about 18, were brought to him in a room in a ware-house where 500 to 600 civilians were imprisoned. Serb soldiers "said they'd kill me if I didn't" rape them, he recalls, insisting that he "only did a little" to his screaming victims, not consummating the act. Three other women were dragged out for the same humiliating display. During these episodes, Panic says, soldiers stood around in a circle and laughed. Then they hauled two badly beaten Muslim prisoners before Panic and handed him a gun. "I said, 'I can't, they've never done anything to me'," he remembers. "'You have to or else we'll kill you'," Panic says he was told. He shot each man in the chest. Two more male prisoners appeared. A soldier handed Panic a knife. "Butcher them," he commanded. When Panic protested, the soldier replied, "I'll show you how it's done." Then, holding Panic's hand around the knife handle, he seized the man by the hair, jerked back his head and cut his throat. Death, at least, brings an end to suffering. Rape victims who became pregnant relive their horror every day. Sofija, a 30-year-old Muslim, was released from a school turned prison camp in the village of Parzavic in mid-September, after being raped every night for six months by five or six different Serb soldiers. Now she is hiding from her family in a cold Sarajevan hospital, tormented by the thought of the unwanted child growing inside her. "I do not want to see the baby," the mother of two says without emotion. "I will not feed it. I do not want anything to do with it." Her roommate says that Sofija talks in her sleep every night, debating whether to kill the baby when it arrives in mid-January. Somewhere in Sarajevo are 12 other pregnant women and girls from the same village as Sofija who were similarly raped and held until long past the time for a safe abortion. .... Rape is the ultimate act in the Serbs' program of annihilation. They have robbed countless civilians of their possessions, their land, their lives and their dignity. Bosnia will be haunted by hundreds, if not thousands, of Serbian children forced on unwilling Muslim mothers. The Serbs do seem to be winning their ugly war. But their crimes have guaranteed that Greater Serbia will be an international pariah for years to come.

While in the same issue, **Tom Masland with Margaret Garrard Warner in Washington mentioned on Will there be "a Second Nuremberg"?, some of which are follows:**

A second Nuremberge is in store for the practitioners of ethnic cleansing','"declared U.S. Secretary of State Lawrence Eagleburger, naming 10 candidates for prosecution as war criminals, including Serbian President Slobodan Milosevic. The United Nations Security Council, he noted, has created a five-member Commission of Experts to investigate war crimes in the Balkans, the first such body since 1943, when the World War II Allies began assembling evidence against the Nazis. Since October, the five have been poring through a six-foot stack of detailed reports on atrocities in the Balkans-"some of the worst things you can imagine," in the words of one of those experts, De Paul University law professor Cherif Bassiouni. It all sounds deadly serious. But what are the odds that Milsevic or anyone else in the former Yugoslavia will be hauled before a tribunal? .... The laws are clear enough. Any case against Milosevic or the others would rest on'"grave breaches" of international agreements dating to 1907, when the Hague Convention prohibited attacks on undefended civilian targets. That basic principle was elaborated in the Geneva Conventions of 1929 and 1949, which set up strict guidelines for the treatment of prisoners of war and civilians caught in war zones; among its many provisions are prohibitions on the transfer of civilian populations and "outrages against personal dignity." In addition, a separate Genocide Convention, adopted in 1951, bans acts committed "with intent to destroy, in whole or in part, a national, ethnical, racial or religious group, as such" and requires the United Nations to take "appropriate" action to stop it. Reports on "ethnic cleansing" provide a powerful case that violations of all these conventions are rife. But fully investigating a crime is far different from compiling allegations. And what the United Nations has created is the shell of an investigative force-without a staff, budget or any clear authority to do more than shuffle papers. "It's a question of political will," said one member. "I think they're hoping that the crisis will go away." Telford Taylor, one of the chief Nuremberg prosecutors, predicts that "the outcome will depend much more on political developments than on getting out the books on the laws of war." Ultimately, what produced the Nuremberg judgment was an Allied victory in World War II: the victors set up their own tribunal. And in the Balkans, so far it's the Serbs who are winning.

Now it seems that there is a competition of how much Muslims can be killed in around the world, in European Bosnia, in Algeria in the name of fundamentalist Muslims by the so called Muslims who did not even allow the Muslims to take power in a Democratic way which they got, and in Germany Muslims are killed, in Democratic India Muslims are being killed during last two month by the Police, by the Hindus with the help of the Police, some of which are as follows:

Kuldip Nayar writes from New Delhi with the heading "Serving the History of Conflict: Destroying the Ethos of India,(BETWEEN THE LINES).

I returned from Pakistan **a few days ago, head high, because anyone I met had a sneaking admiration for India's secular polity. It was taken for granted that the disputed Babri Masjid (mosque) structure would not be harmed and Hindu fundamentalists, whatever their postures, would disperse from Ayodhya after carrying out cosmetic construction work (kar seva), as the Supreme Court had ordered. Little did I** realize then that I would not be able to face those who had faith in our institutions and claims of having tamed the tiger of communalism. The retaliation in Pakistan and Bangladesh, however mindless, does not lessen our culpability. It is condemnable, but we provoked first. Moreover, we are the ones who have opted for secularism, not they.

The Babri Masjid structure **had come to be a symbol of our belief in a society that did not mix religion with politics and ensured equality to all communities before law. Both the tenets have been defeated. Still bigger damage has been done to our reputation of being a law-abiding nation, particularly when even the Supreme Court has been flouted. Yet some leaders have the cheek to say that their** religious faith has more sanctity than the law of the land.

The Rashtriya Swayamsevak Sangh (RSS) which controls the Bhartiya Janata Party (BJP) and the Vishwa Hindu Parishad (VHP), has never believed in secular principles. It has always stood for the Hindu Rashtriya, to the exclusion of Muslims. Therefore, it was a folly to expect anything else from the BJP leaders, the RSS creatures. Still many liberals put faith in Kalyan Singh, the dismissed Uttar Pradesh chief minister, who talked glibly, and Lal Krishna Advani, who has resigned as the opposition leader after having destroyed the ethos of India or, for that matter, of Hinduism.

They could not have been expected to take the wind out of the sails of extremists because the two were riding a tiger, the mob frenzy, which was bound to go out of control. After collecting half a million people on the promise that the temple would be built on the place where the Babri Masjid structure stood, they could not have disciplined such a large throng, even if the two were not wanting to go to the extent the crowed went.

My thesis is that a core of the RSS, the BJP and the VHP had a plan to demolish the structure from the beginning. Persons like Atal Behari Vajpayee, Jaswant Singh and Sikander Bakht were not a party to the plan.

But then they hardly count. They have stuck to the party for the limelight they enjoy and the positions of the parliament membership they occupy, not for principles.

Even if the whole operation was not according to a game plan, it is difficult to make out why there was only a small police force present between the Babri Masjid structure and the barricade, easy to scale. The policemen have given in writing that they had instructions not to use force. The sequence of events only confirms the suspicion.

The first shovel at the structure is struck at a little after 11 am. Till then Kalyan Singh continues to press the Central government to withdraw its forces which, under the constitution, can be deployed only at the specific request of a state government. Around 1 PM., when one dome of the masjid (mosque) has been pulled down, he gets in touch with Union Home Minister to send him more troops. But, in the meanwhile, Advent eggs on the public to intercept the central forces, then already on the way. It throws scores of burning tyres - how did they appear if they were not piled -up earlier - and stalls the soldiers' entry into the area.

The demolition of the structure spreads over five hours. But there are no policemen, no para-military troops or the authorities in sight to try and stop the destruction even for the appearance sake. There was no contingency plan to protect the structure if the story of the mob going berserk is true. The much-maligned government of Mulayam Singh Yadav at least fired at the intruders and the VP Singh government paid the price of losing in the Lok Sabha after stopping Advani's rath, which was allowed right up to Ayodhya this time.

Narasimha Rao was all words and rhetoric. **Surprisingly, he convenes the Union Cabinet meeting at 6 PM after the damage had been done.** The meeting does not immediately discuss the restoration of the mosque or other steps, which were announced after seeing the ugly mood of the opposition. It heaps the blame on the Kalyan Singh government. **The post cabinet meeting broadcast of Narasimha Rao was so listless and boring that even the two minutes, for which he spoke, sounded a long period. Had he announced the steps, which he did 30 hours later, the communal situation in the country would not have probably deteriorated to the extent it did.**

Significantly, the director of the Intelligence Bureau (IB) was present at the cabinet meeting. Some cabinet ministers tell me that he did not claim to have given prior information about the destruction of the masjid (mosque). However, his department continues to take the credit of informing Narasimha Rao five days before the happening. Who is telling the truth can be verified against President Shankar Dayal Sharma's reported statement to some opposition members that he had warned Narasimha Rao against the possibility of the masjid's destruction on the basis of intelligence reports. His public statement asking prime Minister to 'uphold the rule of law' is a straight condemnation of the Rao government.

I do not accuse Narasimha Rao of conniving at the destruction of the structure. But I believe that he was riding two horses at the same time, not displeasing the BJP on the one hand and making efforts to find a solution on the other. Somehow I cannot get over the compliments which Balasaheb Deoras, the RSS chief, paid to him during my visit to Nagpur last month. He said: "He is a good man who is trying to do his best, at one time attending to one problem and another some other time."

Whether the BJP led Narasimha Rao up garden path or whether he was loathe to take any action against it is difficult to say. There could have been more information on this point forthcoming if Advani had not been silenced through the arrest. It is a foolish act because he has been served the ignominy of explaining his conduct in parliament.

In this context, it is pertinent to know that the central government had decided around November 25 to impose President's rule in UP; even the gazette notification was prepared. But then everything was kept in abeyance. What happened behind the scenes to justify it is not yet clear. One cabinet minister has explained to me that the action had to be dropped because of the Supreme Court's fiat not to construct the temple on the disputed site.

This may well be true. But it only shows that New Delhi never appreciated the seriousness of the situation and treated it as a Congress party feud. The decision to restore the mosque is the minimum that we could have done to a tone for the sins of Hindu fundamentalists. But all our remorse cannot wash off the damage we have done to secularism.

The banning of religious bodies is a futile exercise. This has been done before with no concrete results. A secular name of a party does not guarantee its secular credentials. And what about the people in different parties who hide their fundamentalism behind secular cliches?

What the Congress, the BJP and other political parties should realize is that they have been pandering to religious sentiments of the people for too long. They have been wanting to build their vote banks. But this game has gone for too many times to a point where it has been difficult to retrieve it. What is more intriguing is that they are all united in serving the history of conflicts and confrontations that India has been.

TIME magazine in it's December 21, 1992 issue mentioned the following:

UNHOLY WAR WITH COVER STORIES: After Hindu extremists destroy a Muslim mosque, the subcontinent is shaken and the pillars of the modern Indian state-democracy, secularism and the rule of law-are at risk.

IN A PLUME OF DUST, THE CENTRAL DOME of an ancient mosque in the Indian state of Uttar Pradesh collapsed under the blows of 4,000 Hindu fanatics last week- and shook the subcontinent to its foundations. When the smoke finally clears from angry protest and communal rioting in at least 1,000 villages, towns and districts-not only in India but in Pakistan and Bangladesh, with reverberations in the Persian Gulf states and as far off as the Asian communities in Britain-India is not likely to be same. For like the three domes that crowned the 464-year-old Babri mosque in the small town of Ayodhya, the three pillars of the modern Indian state-democracy, secularism and the rule of law-are at risk from a hostile and potent force: Hindu nationalism. At week's end the site of the site of the devastated mosque was ringed with razor wire and guarded by paramilitary commandos. The thousands of kar sevaks, or Hindu holy workers, who had destroyed-some using their bare hands- the Muslim shrine in the belief that it covered the birthplace of the Hindu god Rama, had been driven off by security forces wielding staves and tear gas. Though sporadic outbreaks continued to flare up, army and police contingents had restored a semblance of order in a dozen major cities across India where Muslim-Hindu rioting left more than 1,100 dead and 4,000 injured. .....
Sectarian violence has often haunted India; somewhere between 500,000 and 1 million people were killed in four months of Hindu-Muslim clashes that followed the partition of British India into India and Pakistan in 1947. Thousands more have since died in confrontations between the two groups as well as in uprising by Assamese, Sikhs, Tamils, Kashmiris and other ethnic groups. The destruction of the Babri mosque is seen by many analysts as the most ominous watershed yet. "It is a violation of Hinduism," argues Romila Thapar, a professor of ancient history at New Delhi's Jawaharlal Nehru University. "It has never been a crusading religion like Christianity or Islam. But now suddenly that perception of tolerance is shattered.
..... The campaign to build the Rama temple was spearheaded by the World Hindu Organization, which is dedicated to renewing Hindu culture. Discredited after a former member assassinated Mahatma Gandhi in 1948, the R.S.S. survived to beget a refurbished political presence in 1980 with the founding of the Bharatiya Janata Party, a relatively moderate group that initially avoided the Muslim baiting practiced by hard-line groups, but maintained links with Hindu radicals. The B.J.P. bears the lion's share of blame for the Ayodhya calamity. Over the past six years, the party and its parliamentary leader, L.K. Advani, have cynically used anti-Muslim feeling among Hindus to advance their political cause-tactics that have increasingly paid off. In the 1984 elections, the B.J.P. garnered only 7.4% of the national vote and two seats in the 542-member Lok Sabha, the lower house of Parliament. Two years later, the party greatly enhanced its public profile by denouncing the government of Prime Minister Rajiv Gandhi for effectively reversing a Supreme Court decision that would have increased settlements granted to Muslim women in divorce cases. Advani accused Gandhi of "pandering to Muslims, playing on the view wide-spread among Hindus that Muslims and other minorities receive special privileges in India; **the fact is that the majority of India's Muslims rank among the poorest of the poor. ..... While the negotiations bore a facade of civility, other Hindu extremists were drumming up support through appeals to racism and violence. Fundamentalist Hindu shock troops were drawn from gangs that included the Shiv Sena (Shiva's Army) and the Bajrang Dal (Brigade of the Monkey God). Despite discussions about building a shrine to Rama on an alternative site, members of these groups never gave up their plan to tear down the mosque. Sadhvi Rithambara, a saffron-robed rabble-rouser for the World Hindu Organization, suggested that the only way to get rid of Muslims was to** "stamp them to death." .... As it turned out, four died in the demolition of the mosque, which took the screaming mob five hours as it attacked with metal rods, axes and bare hands. About 400 policemen under the control of the B.J.P. government of Uttar Pradesh stood by and did

nothing while the mob rampaged. Afterward Vinay Katiyar, the leader of the Bajrang Dal gang, exulted, "We have proved that the feeling of the people are above the law!" Proclaimed Uma Bharati, a B.J.P. Member of Parliament: "For centuries Hindus have waited for this moment." .... Home Minister S.B. Chavan extended the charge of betrayal to include Kalyan Sing, the B.J.P. chief minister of Uttar Pradesh . Singh had promised to use local security forces to prevent an assault; instead, in what Chavan called a "total breach of faith," Sing failed to give the required authorization for the use of 14,000 federal troops who were standing by near Ayodhya in case of trouble.

But who is Ram? What we can know from Nehru's Glimpses of World history is that Ram was not at all a historical fact and Ramayana and Mahabharata were written by outsider Aryans, not by any original Indian, and those two books were like Iliad and Odyssey in Greece, which were also written the same time in India by the Aryans who came to India as invaders and created a caste system by which the original Indian people were exploited by the outsider Aryans, the Muslim invaders or spiritual Saints treated Indians as a equal human being not into any caste, contrary to the Aryans who became Brahmin and ruled over the simple but innocent Indian people. What the Muslims gave to Indians, the Aryans deprived the simple people of India,which are still continuing still to day in the name cast, upper cast and lower or schedule caste. Here are the proofs from Nehru's letter to his daughter former Prime Minister of India, Indira Gandhi:

Undoubtedly people do differ from one another, but they resemble each other also a great deal, and it is well to keep this in mind and not be misled by the colors on the map or by national boundaries.

I have written to you in some of my earlier letters about the ancient civilization of India, about the Dravidians and the coming of the Aryans, because I do not know much about them.

Hinduism, the oldest of the great religious existing to-day, is of course the product of India. So also is its great sister-religion Buddhism, which now spreads all over China and Japan and Burma and Tibet and Ceylon. The religion of the Jews and Christianity are also Asiatic religions, as their origin was in Palestine on the west coast of Asia. Zoroastrianism, the religion of the Parsis began in Persia, and you know that Mohammad, the Prophet of Islam, was born in Mecca in Arabia. Krishna, Buddha, Zoroaster, Christ, Mohammad, and Confucius and Lao-Tse, the great philosophers of China- you could fill pages with the names of the great thinkers of Asia. pg. You could also fill pages with names of the great men of action of Asia. ... How times have changed! But they are changing again even before our eyes. History usually works slowly through the centuries, though sometimes there are periods of rush and burst-ups. To-day, however, it is moving fast in Asia, and the old continent is waking up after her long slumber. The eyes of the world are upon her, for everyone knows that Asia is going to play a great part in the future.

We compared and contrasted Europe and Asia in my letter. Let us have a brief look at old Europe, as it supposed to have been. For a long time, Europe meant the countries round about the Mediterranean Sea. We have no records of the northern countries of Europe in those days. Germany and England and France were supposed by the people of the Mediterranean to be inhabited by wild and barbarous tribes. Indeed, to begin with, civilization is supposed to have been confined to the eastern Mediterranean. As you know, Egypt (which, of course, is in Africa and not in Europe) and Knossos were the first countries to go ahead. Gradually the Aryans poured westwards from Asia, and invaded Greece and the neighboring countries. These were the Aryan Greeks whom we now know and admire as the ancient Greeks. To begin with, I suppose, they were not very different from the Aryans who, perhaps earlier, had descended into India. But changes must have crept in, and gradually the two branches of the Aryan race became more and more different. The Indian Aryans were influenced greatly by the still older civilization of India- that of the Dravidians, and perhaps the remains of the civilization whose ruins we see at Mohen-jo

Daro (in present Pakistan). The Aryans and the Dravidians gave much to each other and took much from each other also, and thus built up a common culture for India. .... In the mainland of Greece famous cities grew up. Athens and Sparta and Thebes and Corinth. The early days of the Greeks, or the Hellenes as they were called, were celebrated in two famous epics, the Iliad and the Odyssey. You know something about these two epics, which in a way correspond to our own epics, the Ramayana and Mahabharata. They are said to have been written by Homer, who was blind.....

In the mainland of Greece famous cities grew up: Athens and Sparta and Thebes and Corinth. The early days of the Greeks, or the Hellenes as they were called, were celebrated in two famous epics, the Iliad and the Odyssey. You know something about these two epics, which in a way correspond to our own epics, the Ramayana and Mahabharata. They are said to have been written by Homer, who was blind. The Iliad tells us how Paris carried away the beautiful Helen to his town of Troy, and how the Greek kings and chiefs then laid siege to Troy to recover her. ....

We have had a glimpse of Greece and the Mediterranean, of Egypt, of Asia Minor and Persia. Let us now come back to our own country. We have one great difficulty in studying the early history of India. The early Aryans here- or the Indo-Aryans as they are called- cared to write no histories. We have seen already in our earlier letters how great they were in many ways. The books they have produced-the Vedas, the Upanishads, the Ramayana, the Mahabharata, and other books- could only have been written by great men. These books and other material help us in studying past history. When the Aryans entered India, India was already civilized. Indeed, it now appears certain from the remains at Mohen-jo-Daro in the north-west (Now part of Pakistan) that a great civilization existed here for a long time before the Aryans came.

Compare these Indo-Aryans to the Aryan Greek. There were many differences, and yet there were many points in common. There was some kind of democracy in both places. But let us always remember that this democracy was more or less confined to the Aryans themselves. Their slaves, or those whom they placed in low castes, had no democracy or freedom. The caste system, with its innumerable divisions, as we know it, did not exist then. In those days there were, among the Indian Aryans, four divisions of society, or four casts. These were the Brahmans or learned men, priests, sages; the Kshattriyas or rulers; Vaishyas or merchants and the men engaged in commerce; and Shudras or the laborers and workers. These divisions were thus based on occupation. It is possible that the caste system was partly based on the desire of the Aryans to keep themselves aloof from the conquered race. The Aryans were sufficiently proud and conceited to look down upon all other races, and they did not want their people to get mixed up with them. The very word for caste in Sanskrit is varna or color. This also shows that the Aryans who came were fairer in complexion than the original inhabitants of India. Thus we have to bear in mind that, on the one side, the Aryans kept down the working class and did not allow it any share in their democracy; on the other, they had a great deal of freedom among themselves. They would not allow their kings or rulers to misbehave; and if any ruler misbehaved, he was removed. The kings were usually Kshattriyas, but sometimes, during wars and times of difficulty, even a Shudra, or a member of the lowest class, could win a throne, if he were able enough. In later days the Aryans degenerated and their caste system became rigid. Too many divisions made the country weak, and it fell, They also forgot their old idea of freedom. For, in the old days it was said that never shall an Aryan be made a slave, and that for him death was preferable to dishonor of the Aryan name. The settlements of the Aryans, the towns and villages, did not grow up in a haphazard way. They were made according to plan; and geometry, you will be interested to know, had a good deal to do with these plans. Indeed, geometrical figures were also used then in Vedic pujas. Even now in many Hindu households some of these figures are used during various pujas. ...... Opposite Anand Bhawan (Nehru's house in Allahabad in Uttar Pradesh) is Bharadwaj Ashram. You know it well. Perhaps you also know that Bharadwaj is supposed to have been a very learned man in the old days of the Ramayana, and Ramachandra is said to have visited him during his exile. It is stated that thousands of pupils and students lived with him. ....Those early days were the great period of the Aryans in India. Unfortunately we have no history of this period, and can only rely on non-historical books for such facts as we know. .... You will remember that the great teacher of the Pandavas in the Mahabharata was Dronacharya, a Brahman, who taught them, among other things, the way to fight.

In India we have just hinted at the old civilization represented now by the ruins at Mohenjo Daro in the Indus valley; and the Dravidian civilization with its trade with foreign countries; and lastly the Aryans. We have referred to some of the famous books which the Aryans produced in those days, the Vedas and Upanishads, and the epics, the Ramayana and the Mahabharata. And we have followed them spreading out over northern India, and even penetrating to the south and, in contact with the old Dravidians, building up a new civilization and culture, which had something of the Dravidian in it and a great deal of the Aryan. Especially have we seen how their village communities grew up on a democratic basis and developed into towns and cities, and forest ashrams became universities. In Mesopotamia and Persia we have only briefly referred to the growth of empire after empire; one of these later empires, that of Darius, extending to the river Indus in India. In Palestine we have had a glimpse of the Hebrews, who, though few in number and living in a tiny corner of the world, have attracted a great deal of attention. Their kings, David and Solomon, are remembered when greater kings have been forgotten, because they find mention in the Bible. In Greece we have seen the new Aryan civilization grow up on the ruins of the older civilization of Knosses. The City-States have grown up and Greek colonies have sprung up on the borders of the Mediterranean. Rome, which was to be great, and Carthage, its bitter rival, are just appearing on the horizon of history.

Those outsider Aryans who are known in India as Brahmin and other upper caste people could not tolerate any other religion. They even destroyed the Buddhist people, though Buddhism was founded in India. Here are the proofs from Nehru's version:

When Buddha was born , the old Vedic religion prevailed in India. But already it had changed and fallen from its high astate. The Brahman priests had introduced all manner of rites and pujas and superstition, for the more there is of puja the more do the priests flourish. Caste was becoming stricter, and the common people were frightened by omens and spells and witchcraft and quackery. The priests got the people under their control by these methods and challenged the power of the Kshattriya rulers. There was thus rivalry between the Kshattriyas and the Brahmans. Buddha came as a great popular reformer, and he attacked this priestly tyranny and all the evils which had crept into the old Vedic religion. He laid stress on people living a good life and performing good deeds, and not performing pujas and the like. He organized the Buddhist Sangha, an association of monks and nuns, who followed his teaching. Buddhism, as a religion, did not spread much in India for some time. Later, we shall see how it spread and how again, in India, it almost ceased to exist as a separate religion. While it triumphed in distant countries from Ceylon to China, the land of its birth, Buddhism was absorbed back into Brahminism or Hinduism. But it exercised a great influence on Brahminism, and rid it of some at least of its superstition and ritual. Buddhism to-day is the religion of the greatest number of people in the world. Other religions which have the largest number of followers are Christianity, Islam and Hinduism. There are, besides, the religions of the Hebrews, of the Sikhs, of the Parsis, and others. Religions and their founders have played a great part in the history of the world, and we cannot ignore them in any survey of history. But I find some difficulty in writing about them. There can be no doubt that the founders of the great religions have been among the greatest and noblest men that the world has produced. But their disciples and the people who have come after them have often been far from great or good. Often in history we see that religion, which was meant to raise us and make us better and nobler, has made people behave like beasts. Instead of bringing enlightenment of them, it has often tried to keep them in the dark; instead to broading their minds, it has frequently made them narrow-minded and intolerant of others. In the name of religion many great and fine deeds have been performed. In the name of religion also thousands and millions have been killed, and every possible crime has been committed.[243]

Quotations from Nehru's "Glimpses of World History" continues:

Christianity is politically the dominant religion to-day, because it is the religion of the dominate peoples of Europe. But it is strange to think of the rebel Jesus preaching non-violence and ahimas and a revolt against the social order, and then to compare him with his loud-voiced followers of to-day, with their imperialism and armaments and were and worship of wealth. The Sermon on the Mont and modern European and American Christianity how amazingly dissimilar they are!

You will find that after Islam began, for many hundred years Musalmans lived in all parts of India in perfect peace with their neighbors. They were welcomed when they came as traders and encouraged to settle down. But I am anticipating. So India welcomed the Zoroastrians, just as a few hundred years before, she had also welcomed many Jews who fled from Rome in the first century after Christ on account of persecution.

In the fifteenth century the Muslims finally obtained control, and soon after came the Portuguese and the Spaniards, the Dutch and the English, and last of all the Americans.

We find especially the Arabs settling down in South China, near Canton, about 300 AC This was before Islam came - that is, before the birth of the Prophet Mohammad. With the help of these Arabs an overseas trade developed and was carried in Arab as well as Chinese ships.

It took some time for Christianity to reach China. But Islam came more swiftly. It came, indeed, a few years before the Nestorians and during the lifetime of its Prophet. The Chinese Emperor received both the embassies Islamic and Nestorian with courtesy and listened to what they had to say. He appreciated their views and showed favor impartially. The Arabs were permitted to build a mosque in Canton. This mosque still exists, although it is 1300 years old, and is one of the oldest mosques in the world.

In spite of their triumphs in distant countries, they could not get rid of their old habit of quarrelling amongst themselves. Of course, there was something worth quarrelling about now , for the headship of Arabia meant the control of a great empire. So there were frequent quarrels for the place of the Khalifa (Caliph). There were petty quarrels, family quarrels, leading to civil war. These quarrels resulted in a big division in Islam and two sects were formed the Sunnis and Shiahs which still exist.

---

[243] Glimpses of World History by Pandit (Learned) JAWAHARLAL NEHRU PP. 4-5, 9, 10, 13, 14, 22, 24-26, 30, 36-37.

Trouble came soon after the regimes of the first two great Khalifas (Caliph)-Abu Bakr and Omar. Ali, the husband of Fatima, who was the daughter of Mohammad, was Khalifa for a short while. But there was continuous conflict. Ali was murdered, and some time later his son Hussain, with his family, were massacred on the plain of Karbala. It is this tragedy of Karbala that is mourned year after year in the month of Moharram by the Muslims, and especially the Shiahs.

The Khalifa now becomes an absolute king. There is nothing of democracy or election left about him. He was just like any other absolute monarch of his day. In theory he continued to be the religious head also, the Commander of the Faithful. But some of these rulers actually insulted Islam, of which they were supposed to be the chief protectors.

The Abbaside period is especially interesting for us because of the new interest in science which it started. Science, as you know, is a very big thing in the modern world, and we owe a great deal to it. Science does not simply sit down and pray for things to happen, but seeks to find out why things happen. It experiments and tries again and again, and sometimes fails and sometimes succeeds and so bit by bit it adds to human knowledge. This modern world of ours is very different from the ancient world or the Middle Ages. This great difference is largely due to science, for the modern world has been made by science. Among the ancients we do not find the scientific method in Egypt or China or India. We find just a bit of it in old Greece. In Rome again it was absent. But the Arabs had this scientific spirit of inquiry, and so they may be considered the fathers of modern science. In some subjects, like medicine and mathematics they learnt much from India. Indian scholars and mathematicians came in large numbers to Baghdad. Many Arab Students went to Takshashila in North India, which was still a great university, specializing in medicine. Sanskrit books on medical and other subjects were especially translated into Arabic. Many things for example, paper-making the Arabs learnt from China. But on the basis of the knowledge gained from others they made their own researches and made several important discoveries. They made the first telescope and the mariner's compass. In medicine, Arab physicians and surgeons were famous all over Europe.

So they fought each other. But even before their fighting was over, across Asia in Mongolia there arose Chengiz Khan, the Mongol Shaker of the Earth, as he was called, who was indeed going to shake Asia and Europe. He and his descendants finally put an end to Baghdad and its empire. By the time the Mongols had finished with the great and famous city of Baghdad, it was almost of heap of dust and ashes and most of its 2,000,000 inhabitants were dead. This was in 1258 AC. Baghdad is now again a flourishing city and is the capital of the State of Iraq. But is only a shadow of its former self, for it never recovered from the death and desolation which of Mongols brought.

Islam brought a new impulse for human progress to India. To some extent it served as a tonic. It shook up India. But it did less good than it might have done because of two reasons. It came in the wrong way, and it came rather late. for hundreds of years before Mahmud of Ghazni raided India, Muslim missionaries had wandered about India and had been welcomed. They came in peace and had some success. There was little, if any, ill-feeling against Islam. Then came Mahmud with fire and sword, and the manner of his coming as a conqueror and a plunderer and killer injured the reputation of Islam in India more than anything else. He was, of course, just like any other great conqueror, killing and plundering, and caring little for religion. But for a very long time his raids overshadowed Islam in India and made it difficult for people to consider it dispassionately, as they might otherwise have done.

This was one reason. The other was that it came late. It came about 400 years after it began, and during this long period it had exhausted itself somewhat, and lost a great deal of its creative energy. If the Arabs had come to India with Islam in the early days, the rising Arabian culture would have mixed with the old Indian culture and the two would have acted and reacted on each other, with great consequences. It would have been the mixing of two cultured races; and the Arabs were well known for their toleration and rationalism in religion. At one period, indeed, there was a club in Baghdad, under the patronage of the Caliph, were men of all religions and no religion met together to discuss and debate about all matters from the point of view of rationalism alone.

But the Arabs did not come to India proper. They stopped in Sindh, and India was little influenced by them. Islam came to India through the Turks and others who did not have the tolerance or the culture of the Arab, and who were primarily soldiers.

Still, a new impulse came to India for progress and creative effort. How this put some new life in India and then worked itself out, we shall consider later.

But they are just geographical expressions, and the problems that face us are not Asiatic or European problems, but world problems or problems of humanity. And unless we solve them for the whole world, there will continue to be trouble Such a solution can only mean the ending of poverty and misery everywhere. This may take a long time, but we must aim at this, and at nothing less than this. Only then can we have real culture and civilization based on equality, where there is no exploitation of any country or class. Such a society will be a creative and regressive society, adapting itself to changing circumstances, and basing itself on the co-operation of its members. And ultimately it must spread all over the world. There will be no danger of such a civilization collapsing or decaying, as the old civilizations did.

In Islam there is supposed to be no priesthood, and in the past this helped a little in protecting its followers from religious exploitation. But individuals and classes arose, calling themselves specialists in religion, learned men, maulavis and mullas and the like, and they imposed upon the simple Muslims of faith and exploited them. Where a long beard, or a tuft of hair on the crown of the head, or a long mark on the forehead, or a fakir's dress, or a sanyasin's yellow or ochre grab is a passport to holiness, it is not difficult to impose on the public.

If you go to America, most advanced of countries, you will find there also that religion is a big industry living on the exploitation of the people.

It will interest you to know that Mahmud of Ghazni, who was the greatest destroyer that northern India had known, and who is said to have been a champion of Islam against the "idolaters", had a Hindu army corps under a Hindu general, named Tilak. He took Tilak and his army to Ghazni and used him to put down rebellious Muslims. So you will see that for Mahmud the object was conquest. In India he was prepared to kill "Idolaters" with the help of his Muslim soldiers; in central Asia he was equally prepared to kill Muslims with the help of his Hindus soldiers.

Yet another wave of conquest and destruction took place in Mangu's time. His Brother Halagu was Governor in Persia. Annoyed with the Caliph at Baghdad about something, Halagu sent a message to him childing him for not keeping his promises, and telling him to behave better in future or else he would lose his empire. The Caliph was not a very wise man, nor could he profit by experience. He sent an offensive reply, and the Mongol envoys were insulted by a mob in Baghdad. Halagu's Mongol blood was up at this. In a rage he marched on Baghdad, and after forty days siege he took it. That was the end of the city of

the Arabian Nights, and all the treasures that had accumulated there during 500 years of empire. The Caliph and his sons and near relatives were put to death. There was a general massacre for weeks, till the river Tigris was dyed red with blood for miles.
It is said that a million and a half people perished. All the artistic and literary treasures and libraries were destroyed. Baghdad was utterly ruined. Even the ancient irrigation system of western Asia, thousands of years old, was destroyed by Halagu.

Later they became part of the Ottoman Turkish Empire. During the Great War of 1914-18 there was an Arab rebellion against the Turks, engineered by the English, and since then Arabia has been more or less independent.

There was no Caliph for two years. Then Sultan Baibers of Egypt nominated a relative of the last Abbaside Caliph as Caliph. But he had no political power and was just a spiritual head. Three hundred years later the Turkish Sultan of Constantinople obtained this title of Caliph from the last holder. The Turkish Sultans continued to be Caliph till both Sultan and Caliph were ended a few years ago by Mustafa Kamal Pasha.

The Ottoman Sultans, by taking Constantinople, seem to have inherited many of the evil habits of luxury and corruption from their predecessors, the Byzantine emperors. The whole degraded imperial system of the Byzantines enveloped them and gradually sapped their strength.

The Mongols of central Asia had meanwhile become Muslims and Timur himself was a Muslim. But the fact that he was dealing with Muslims did not soften him in the least. Wherever he went he spread desolation and pestilence and utter misery. His chief pleasure was the erection of enormous pyramids of skulls. From Delhi in the east to Asia Minor in the west he caused to be massacred hundreds of thousands of persons and had their skulls arranged in the form of pyramids!

Let us look at the India of the fourteenth and fifteenth centuries. The Delhi Sultanate shrinks till it vanishes away on Timur's coming. There are a number of large independent States all over India, mostly Muslim; but there is one powerful Hindu State Vijayanagar in the south. Islam is no longer a stranger or a new comer in India. It is well established. The fierceness and cruelty of the early Afghan invaders and the Slave kings have been toned down, and the Muslim kings are as much Indians as the Hindus. They have no outside connections. Wars take place between different States, but they are political and not religious. sometimes a Muslim State employs Hindu troops, and a Hindu State Muslim troops .
Muslim kings often marry Hindu women and Hindus are often employed as ministers and high officials by the Muslim kings. There is little of the feeling of conqueror and conquered or ruler and ruled. Indeed, most of the Muslims, including some of the rulers, and Indians converted to Islam. Many of these become converted in the hope of gaining Court favor or economic advantage, and in spite of their change of religion they stick to most of their old customs. Some Muslim rulers adopt forcible methods to bring about conversion, but even this is largely with a political object, as it is thought that the converts would be more loyal subjects. But force does not go far in bringing about conversions. A more effective method is the economic. Non-Muslims are made to pay a poll-tax called the jizya and many of them wishing to escape this, become Muslims. But all this takes place in the cities. The villages are little affected, and the millions of villagers carry on in the old way. It is true that the king's officers interfere more in village life. The powers of the village panchayats ate less now than they used to be, but still the panchayats continue and are the center and backbone of village life. Socially, and in the matter of religion and custom, the village is almost unchanged. India as you know, is still a country of hundreds of thousands of villages. The towns and cities sit on the surface, as it were, but the real India has been and still is, village

India. This village India was not much changed by Islam. Hinduism was shaken up in two ways by the coming of Islam; and strange to say, these ways were contrary to each other. On the one side it became conservative; it hardened and retired into a shell in an attempt at protecting itself against the attack on it. Caste became stiffer and more exclusive; the purdah and seclusion of women became commoner. On the other hand, there was a kind of internal revolt against caste and too much puja and ceremonial. Many efforts were made to reform it.

The old Indian rulers had custom and convention to check their autocracy. The new Muslim rulers did not have even this Although in theory there is far more equality in Islam, and, as we have seen, even a slave could become sultan, still the autocratic and unchecked power of the king increased. What more amazing instance of this can one have than that of the mad Tughlaq who moved the capital from Delhi to Daulatabad ?

The Muslim Court language was Persian. Most educated people learnt Persian if they had anything to do with the /courts or government offices. Thus large numbers of Hindus learnt Persian. Gradually a new language developed in the camps and bazaars, called "Urdu", which means camp. In reality this was rot a new language. It was Hindi with a slightly different dress on; there were more of Persian words in it, but otherwise it was Hindi. This Hindi-Urdu language, or as it is sometimes called Hindustani, spread all over northern and Central India. It is today spoken, with minor variations, by about 150,000,000 people and understood by a far greater number. (this number was 60 years ago, so it is more than that though Hindi, Indian national language replaced Urdu in India). Thus it is, from the point of numbers, one of the major languages of the world.

Now a new influence comes on the scene. This is brought by the Arabs. Burma and Siam were not affected by this, but Malay and the islands succumb to it, and soon a Muslim empire grows up. Arab traders had visited these islands and settled there for 1000 years or more. But they were intent on business, and did not otherwise interfere with the governments. In the fourteenth century Arab missionaries came out from Arabia, and they met with success, especially in convert ng some of the local rulers.

As is usual with imperialists, they were tyrannous, and many people preferred going to the new State of Malacca to remaining under Madjapahit. Siam was also at the time rather aggressive. So Malacca became a place of refuge for many people. There were both Buddhists and Muslims. The rulers were at first Buddhists, but later they adopted Islam.

The young State of Malacca was menaced by Java on the one side and Siam on the other. It tried to find friends and allies among the other small Muslim State in the islands. It even appealed to China for protection. At that time the Mings, who had displaced the Mongols, ruled in China. It is remarkable how all the little Islamic States in Malaysia turned to China for protection at the same time. This shows that there must have been some immediate threat from powerful enemies.

So the State of Malacca became the head of the opposition to Madjapahit. Its strength grew and gradually it seized the colonies of Java. In 1478 the city of Madjapahit itself was captured. Islam then became the religion of the Court and of the cities. But in the countryside, ad in India, the old faith and myths and customs continued.
It is obvious from this the it is very thinly population of India. It is obvious from this that it is very thinly populated; most of it is indeed a desert, and it was because of this that it escaped the attentions of greedy adventures in the past, and remained a relic of medievahsm, without railways or telegraphs or telephones or the like, in the midst of a changing world. It was largely inhabited by wandering nomad tribes the Bedouins they are

called and they traveled across the desert sands on their swift camels, the "ships of the desert" and on the backs of their beautiful Arab horses, known the world over. They lived a patriarchal life which had changed little in 1000 years. The World War changed all this as it changed many other things.

Difference oftreatment of slave by Christian dominated Europe vs the followers of Islam

The story of how these Negroes were brought from Africa is a very sad one. The slave trade began early in the seventeenth century, and a regular supply was kept up till 1863. At first, cargo-boats passing the West Africa coast-a part of it is still called the "Slave Coast"- picked up the Africans, whenever they could do so easily, and carried them to America. Among the Africans themselves there was very little slavery; only prisoners of war or debtors were so treated. It was found that this carrying of Africans to America and selling them as slaves was a very profitable business. The slave trade grew, and was subsidized as a business chiefly by the English, the Spanish, and the Portuguese. Special ships- slave-traders- were built with galleries between decks. In these galleries the unhappy Negroes were made to lie down, all chained up, and each couple fettered together. The voyage across the Atlantic lasted many weeks, sometimes months. During all these weeks and months these Negros lay in these narrow galleries, shackled together, and all the space that was allowed to each of them was five and a half feet long by sixteen inches wide! Liverpool became a great city on the foundation of the slave trade. As early as 1713, in the Peace of Utrecht, England extorted from Spain the privilege of carrying slaves between Africa and Spanish America. Even before this England had supplied slaves to the English territories in America. An attempt was thus made in the eighteenth century to make the Africa-America slave trade an English monopoly. In 1730 Liverpool had fifteen ships engaged in this trade. The number went on growing, till in 1792 there were 132 ships employed by Liverpool in the slave trade. ... In 1790 there were 697,000 slaves in the United States; in 1861 the number rose to 4,000,000. Early in the nineteenth century the British Parliament passed stringent laws against slavery. Other countries in Europe and America followed. But even when the slave trade was thus outlawed, Negroes were still carried from Africa to America, with this difference, that the conditions of their journey were far worse. They could not be carried openly, so they were hidden away from sight on loose shelves, one on top of the other. Sometimes , an American writer tells us, "one crowded on to the lap of another, and with legs on legs, like riders on a crowded toboggan!" ...... It is difficult to imagine the full horror of all this. Conditions were so filthy that the slave ships had to be abandoned after four or five voyages. But the profits were huge, and during the height of the trade at the end of the eighteenth and the beginning of the nineteenth centuries as many as 100,000 slaves were carried every year from the African Slave Coast . And remember that the carrying away of this number meant the killing of far greater numbers in the raids to capture the Negroes. ....
A historian of the time says that this was a "period of famine for science and virtue". A Mongol army sent to Palestine was defeated by Sultan Baibers of Egypt. This Sultan had an interesting surname "Bandukdar", because of a regiment of men armed with banduks or firearms. We now come to the era of the firearms. The Chinese had long known gunpowder. The Mongols probably learnt it from them and it may be that firearms helped them in their victories. It was through the Mongols that firearms were introduced into Europe. .....
An extraordinary semi-secret organization, called the "Ku Klux Klan", was formed, and its members went about in masks terrorizing the Negros and preventing them from even voting at the elections. ... Everywhere they are segregated and kept apart from the Whites- in hotels, restaurants, churches, colleges, parks, bathing-beaches,

trams, and even in stores! In railways they have to travel in special carriages called
"Jim-Crow cars". Marriage between the White and the Negro is forbidden by law.
Indeed, there are all manner of strange laws. A law passed by the State of Virginia as
recently as 1926 prohibited white and colored persons from sitting on the same floor!
..... Have you read or heard of Harriet Beecher Stowe's Uncle Tom's Cabin? This book
is about the old slave Negroes in the southern States, and gives their sad story. It came
out ten years before the Civil War, and had great influence in rousing the American
people against slavery.[244]

Islam made the slaves kings in India and Arab world

   After Shahab-ud-din, the Afghan, who defeated Prithwi Raj, there came a succession of
Sultans of Delhi called the Slave Kings The first of them was Qutub-ud-din. He had been a
slave of Shahab-ud-din, but even slaves could rise to high positions, and he managed to
become the first Sultan of Delhi. Some others after him were also originally slaves, and
hence this is called the slave dynasty. . . Among the Sultans there was a women named
Razia. She was the daughter of Iltutmish. ... the slave kings ended in 1290
   Unlike the Greeks, and unlike the Chinese and the Arabs, Indians in the past were not
historians. ......There is really only one old book, Kalhana's 'Rajatarangini', a history of
Kashmir written in the twelfth century A. C., which may be considered as history. For the
rest we have to go to the imagined history of the epics and other books, architectural
remains, to coins, and ......to the many records of foreign travelers who came to India,
notably Greeks, and Chinese, and, during a later period, Arabs.

   Nevertheless the Afghan and Mughal rulers took special care
not to interfere with old customs and connections and no fundamental
changes were introduced and the economic and social structure of Indian
life continued as before. Ghyasud-Din Tughlak issued definite
instructions to his officials to preserve customary law and to keep the
affairs of the state apart from religion, which was a personal matter of
individual preferences.
In the ancient days when Indo-Aryans culture first took shape, religion
had to provide for the needs of man who were as far removed from each
other in civilization and intellectual and spiritual development as it
is possible to conceive.

   Babar died within four year of his coming to India, and much of his time was spent in
fighting and in laying out a splendid capital of Agra, for which he obtained the services of a
famous architect from **Constantinople. Those were the days of Suleiman the
Magnificent in Constantinople, when fine buildings were rising up in that city.** .[245]

[244] GLIMPSES OF WORLD HISTORY BY NEHRU, PP. 563-564, 222-223, 566-567.

[245] GLIMPSES OF WORLD HISTORY BY NEHRU, PP. 212-213, 249-250

Long Conspiracy to abolish the Caliphate System

First we should mention a commentary published in the Time magazine in its June 15, 1992 issue under the caption "THE SWORD OF ISLAM" by JAMES WALSH; some quotation was already mentioned earlier in the same heading in this book and some other from the same below:

At gut level, though the West's nervous response to the Islamic revival springs from the movement's anti-Western rhetoric and impulses. The single greatest catalytic event that supercharged Islam as a mass political jihad, or holy war, was the 1979 Iranian revolution, which was nakedly hostile toward "Great Satan" America and Europe. Today Islamic proselytizers vary widely in tone and emphasis; nonetheless, they tend to pay homage to the cause that toppled the shah and inspired other Muslims to strive for a new cultural ascendancy. Iran's example and in some cases its active aid have re-emerged as potent influences now that alienation from established regimes is deepening in step with economic hardships across the Islamic
belt of Africa, the Middle East, South Asia, even into the Muslim desert reaches of western China.

And yet the Islamizing movement at heart is a reaction sometimes virulent, against simply the ways of modernity exemplified by Western culture. The West's "next confrontation is definitely going to come from the Muslim world," predicts M. J. Akbar, an Indian Muslim author and adviser to his country's Human Resources Minister. "It is in the swept of the Islamic nations from the Maghreb to Pakistan that the struggle for a new world order will begin."

The above article start in the following comment:

Fourteen hundred years ago, a new faith burst out of the Arabian deserts and exploded like forked lightning onto three continents. Under the oasis green banner of the Prophet Muhammad, the warriors of Islam converted whole civilizations to their holy book, their way of life and their world view. To-day a reconstructed idea of Islam is spreading at what often appears to be the same speed over much the same territory. From the north African coast to the steppes of Central Asia, Muhammad's precepts interpreted as a code of earthly behavior are galvanizing Muslim societies with hope for renewal- and fear of upheaval. The whole world, in fact, is watching and wondering about the impact of this tectonic shift, just as medieval Europe crouched when Islam reached the apogee of its power. With the death of the Soviet empire, some Western policy makers are concerned whether Islamic "fundamentalism"-a term rejected by Muslims as a misnomer-may shape up as the next millennial threat to liberal democracy.

The following selected verses of the English translations of The Holy Quran are the answers For all; kindly read and think deeply:

2: 19 Or (another similitude) Is that of rain-laden cloud From the sky:
2: 19 in it are zones Of darkness, and thunder and lightning: They press
2: 19 their fingers in their ears To keep out the stunning thunder-clap,
2: 19 The while they are in terror of death. But Allah is ever round the
2: 19 rejecters of Faith!

2: 55 And remember ye said: "O Moses! We shall never believe in thee
2: 55 Until we see Allah manifestly," But ye were dazed Nith thunder and
2: 55 lighting Even as ye looked on.

2: 86 These are the people who buy The life of this world at the price Of
2: 86 the hereafter: their penalty Shall not be lightened, Nor shall they
2: 86 be helped.

2:162 They will abide therein: Their penalty will not Be lightened, nor
2:162 will Respite be their (lot).

2:257 Allah is the Protector Of those who have faith: From the depths of
2:257 of darkness He will lead them forth Into light. Of those Who reject
2:257 faith the patrons Are the Evil Ones: from light They will lead them
2:257 forth. Into the depths of darkness. They will be Companions Of the
2:257 fire, to dwell therein (For ever).

3: 11 (Their plight will be) No better than that Of the people of Pharaoh
3: 11 And their predecessors: They denied Our Signs, And Allah called
3: 11 them to account For their sins. For Allah is strict In punishment.
3: 76 Nay- Those that keep Their plighted faith And act aright,- verily
3: 76 Allah loves those Who act aright.
3: 77 As for those who sell The faith they owe to Allah And their own
3: 77 plighted word For a small price, They shall have no portion In the
3: 77 Hereafter: Nor will Allah (Deign to) speak to them Or look at them
3: 77 On the Day of Judgement, Nor will He cleanse them (Of sin): they
3: 77 shall have A grievous Penalty.
3: 88 In that will they dwell; Nor will their penalty Be lightened, nor
3: 88 respite Be their (lot):-
3:107 But those whose faces Will be (lit with) white,- They will be in
3:107 (the light Of) Allah's mercy: therein To dwell (for ever).
4: 97 When angels take The souls of those Who die in sin Against their
4: 97 souls They say;"In what (plight) Were ye?" They reply; "Weak and
4: 97 oppressed Were we in the earth." They say;"Was not The earth of
4: 97 Allah Spacious enough for you To move yourselves away (From evil)?"
4: 97 Such men Will find their abode In Hell,- What an evil Refuge!-
4:153 The People of the Book Ask thee to cause A book to descend to them
4:153 From heaven: indeed They asked Moses For an even greater (Miracle)
4:153 for they said: "Show us Allah in public." But they were dazed For
4:153 their presumption, With thunder and lightning. Yet they
4:153 worshipped the calf Even after Clear Signs Had come to them; Even
4:153 so We forgave them; And gave Moses manifest Proofs of authority.
4:174 O mankind! Verily There hath come to you A convincing proof From
4:174 your Lord: For We have sent unto you A light (that is) manifest.

57: 20 Know ye (all) that The life of this world Is but play and
57: 20 amusement, Pomp and mutual boasting And multiplying , (in rivalry)
57: 20 Among yourselves riches And children : Here is a similitude:
57: 20 How rain and the growth Which it brings forth, delight (The hearts
57: 20 of) the tillers; Soon it withers; thou Wilt see it grow yellow;
57: 20 Then it becomes dry And crumbles away. But in the Hereafter
57: 20 Is a Penalty severe (For the devotees of wrong), And Forgiveness
57: 20 from Allah And (His) Good Pleasure (For the devotees of Allah).
57: 20 And what is the life Of this world, but Goods and chattels Of
57: 20 deception?

65: 11 An Apostle, who rehearses To you the Signs of Allah Containing

65: 11 clear explanations, That he may lead forth Those who believe And do
65: 11 righteous deeds From the depths of Darkness Into Light. And those
65: 11 who Believe in Allah and work Righteousness, He will admit To
65: 11 Gardens beneath which rivers Flow, to dwell therein For ever:
65: 11 Allah has indeed Granted for them A most excellent provision.

67: 21 Or who is there That can provide you With sustenance if He
67: 21 Were to withhold His provision? Nay, they obstinately persist
67: 21 In insolent impiety And flight (from the Truth).
68: 34 Verily, for the Righteous Are Gardens of Delight, In the Presence
68: 34 Of their Lord.
69: 5 But the Thamud,- They were destroyed By a terrible Storm Of thunder
69: 5 and lightning!
71: 6 "But my call only Increases (their) flight (From the Right).
71: 16 "And made the moon A light in their midst, And made the sun As a
71: 16 (Glorious) Lamp?
72: 12 But we think that we Can by no means frustrate Allah throughout
72: 12 the earth Nor can we frustrate Him By flight.
74: 40 (They will be) in Gardens (Of Delight): they will Question each
74: 40 other,
76: 11 But Allah will deliver Them from the evil Of that Day and will Shed
76: 11 over them a Light Of Beauty and A (blissful) Joy.
78: 13 And placed (therein) A Light of Splendor?
79: 29 Its night doth He Endow with darkness, And its splendor doth He
79: 29 Bring out (with light).
81: 1 When the sun (With its spacious light) Is folded up;
83: 15 Verily, from (the Light Of) their Lord, that Day Will they be
83: 15 veiled.
91: 8 And its enlightenment As to its wrong And its right;-
92: 1 By the Night as it Conceals (the light),
93: 1 By the Glorious Morning Light ,
101: 8 But he whose Balance (of good deeds) Will be (found) light,-
105: 3 And He sent against them Flights of Birds.

In the same issue in page 26 under the caption "THE CONSEQUENCES OF POWER" by
MICHAEL S. SERRILL mentioned the following:

The sort of rhetoric has led the U. S. and Europe to remain silent during the brutal
suppression of the Islamic revival by many of the Middle East's secular governments. The
latest victim was Algeria's Islamic Salvation Front (F. I. S.), which was repressed by the
ruling military when it became clear that the Front would benefit from low voter turnout to
become the first Islamic party to take power at the ballot box. The coup was applauded by
Algeria's secular majority, and particularly by professional women. "They were little
fascists just waiting for their moment," urban-studies professor Ouardia Ider told the New
York Times. "Believe me, if the army had not acted, there would have been civil war."

In it's February 16th, 1991 edition of "The Economist"; under the heading "Arab hearts,
Arab minds, the writer mentioned the following comments:

When the Iraqi army briefly occupied the Saudi town of Khafji in the second week of the
Gulf war, somebody had the
"Pan-Arabism and hatred of Israel go together. Indeed, hating Israel-sometimes for good
reason, sometimes not-has helped Arab governments keep the spirit of pan-Arabism alive
long after they abandoned serious attempts at unification. **Islam has reinforced their**

278

efforts; like pan-Arabism, it is unfriendly to the idea of the nation-state, preferring to collect all believers in a single umma ruled by Koranic law.

Muslim Conspirators for the abolition of Caliphate

Muslim Conspirators for the abolition of Caliphate who were installed in power by the Western Powers, particularly by the British who became the main Conspirator for the abolition of long 1300 years old Caliphate and to create so many weak Muslim Nation States under the Muslim Conspirators.

If you will look at the map you will find that the great Arabian peninsula lies between the Red Sea and the Persian gulf. To the south of it lies the Arabian Sea, to the north lie Palestine and Trans-Jordan and the Syrian desert, and to the north east the green and fertile valleys of Iraq. Along the west coast, bordering the Red Sea, lies the land of Hejaz, which is the cradle of Islam, containing the holy cities Mecca and Medina and the Port, Jeddah, where thousands of pilgrims land every year on their way to Mecca. In the center of Arabia and towards the east up to the Persian Gulf lies Nejd. The Hejaz and Nejd are the two main divisions of Arabia. In the south west lies Yemen, known from the old Roman times as Arabia Felix, Arabia the fortunate, the Happy, because it was fertile and fruitful, in contrast with the rest, which was largely barren and desert. This part is as one would expect, thickly populated. Almost at the south-western tip of Arabia lies Aden, a British possession and a port of call for ships passing between East and West.

Before the World war nearly the whole country was under Turkish control or acknowledged Turkish overlordship. But in Nejad the Emir Ibn Saud was gradually emerging as an independent ruler and was spreading out by conquest to the Persian Gulf. This was in the years preceding the war. Ibn Saud was the head of a particular community or sect of Muslims known as Wahabis, which was founded in the eighteenth century by Abdul Wahab. This was really a reform movement in Islam, something like the Puritans in Christianity. The Wahabis were against many ceremonies and the saint-worship that had become so popular with the Muslim masses, in the form of worship of tombs and what were supposed to be the relic of holy men. The Wahabis called this idolatry, just as the Puritans of Europe had called the Roman Catholics, who worshipped the images and relics of saints, idolaters. Thus, even apart from political rivalry, there was a religious feud between the Wahabis and the other Muslim sects in Arabia.

During the World War Arabia became a hotbed of British intrigue, and British and Indian money was lavishly spent in subsidizing and bribing the various Arab chiefs. All manner of promises were made to them, and they were encouraged to revolt against Turkey. Sometimes two rival chiefs, who were fighting each other, were both receiving British subsidies! The British succeeded in getting the Sherif Hussein of Mecca to raise the Arab standard of revolt. Hussein's importance consisted in the fact that he was a descendant of the Prophet Mohammad, and was therefore greatly respected. Hussein was promised by the British the kingdom of a united Arabia.

Ibn Saud was cleverer. He got himself recognized as an independent sovereign by the British, accepted a tidy little sum of pound 5000 or about Rs. 70,000 per month from them, and promised to remain neutral. So while others were fighting, he consolidated his position and strengthened it, to some extent with the help of British gold. The Sherif Hussein was becoming unpopular in Islamic countries, including India, because of his rebellion against the Sultan of Turkey, who was also then the Caliph.Ibn Saud, by quietly remaining neutral, took full advantage of changing conditions and slowly built up a reputation for himself to being the strong man of Islam.

In the south was Yemen. The Imam, or ruler, of Yemen remained loyal to the Turks right through the was. But he was cut off from the scene of operations and could not do much. After Turkey's defeat he became independent. Yemen is still an independent State.

The end of the war found England dominating Arabia and trying to use both Hussein and Ibn Saud as her tools. Ibn Saud was too clever to allow himself to be exploited. The Sherif Hussein's family, however, suddenly blossomed out in full glory, backed as it was by British force. Hussein himself became King of the Hejaz; one of his sons, Feisal, became ruler of Syria; and another son, Abdullah, was made by the British the ruler of the small new state Trans-Jordan. The glory was short-lived for as we have seen, Feisal was driven out of Syria by the French, and Hussein 's kingship vanished away before the advancing Wahabis of Ibn saud. Feisa having joined the unemployed again, was provided by the British with the rulership of Iraq, reigning there by the grace of his patrons.

During the brief period of Hussein's kingship of the Hejaz, the Turkish Parliament at angora abolished the Caliphate in 1924. There was no Caliph, and Hussien, greatly daring, jumped on to the empty throne and proclaimed himself the Caliph of Islam. Ibn Saud saw that his time had come, and he appealed both to Arab nationalism and to Muslim internationalism against Hussain. He stood out as the champion of Islam against and ambitious usurper, and with the help of careful propaganda managed to gain the good will of Muslims in other countries. The Khalifat (Caliphate) Committee in India sent him their good wishes. Seeing which way the wing was blowing. and realizing that the horse they had so far backed was not likely to win, the British quietly withdrew their support of Hussain. Their subsidies were stopped, and poor Hussain, who had been promised so much, was left almost friendless and helpless before a powerful and advancing enemy.

Within a few months, in October 1924, the Wahabis entered Mecca and in accordance with their puritan faith, destroyed some tombs. There was a good deal of consternation in Muslim countries at this destruction; even in India much feeling was aroused. Next year Medina and Jeddah fell to Ibn Saud, and Hussein and his family were driven away from the Hejaz. Early in 1926 Ibn Saud proclaimed himself King of the Hejaz. In order to consolidate his new position and to keep the good will of Muslims abroad, he held an Islamic World Congress at Mecca in June 1926, to which he invited representative Muslims from other countries. Apparently he had no desire to become Caliph, and in any event he was not likely to be accepted as such by large numbers of Muslims because of his Wahabism. King Fuad of Egypt, whose antinational and despotic record we have already examined, was keen on becoming the Caliph but nobody would have him, not even his own people of Egypt. Hussein, after his defeat, had abdicated from the Caliphate he had assumed.

The Islamic congress held at Mecca did not come to any important decision, and it was perhaps not meant to do so. It was a device adopted by Ibn Saud to strengthen his position, especially before foreign Powers. Indian representatives of the Khalifat Committee , and I think Maulana Mohammad Ali was one of them, returned disappointed and angry with Ibn Saud. But this id not make much difference to him. He had exploited the Indian Khilafat (Caliphate) Committee when he wanted its help, and now he could well do without its good will.

Ibn Saud was soon master of nearly the whole country with the exception of Yemen which continued as an independent State under it's old Imam. But for this corner in the south-west, he was lord of Arabia and he took the title of King of Nejd, thus becoming a double king. King of Hejaz and King of Nejd. Foreign Power recognized his independence, and foreigners were not allowed any special privileges, as they are in Egypt still. Indeed, they could not even take wines and other alcoholic drinks.

Why we only 55 Islamic States like the states of USA can not be united under a single Caliphate under a common Constitution as described in the Holy Quran and which is our part of faith too. Due to division of so many states some of the Islamic States do not have their own people to accept Zakat (charity) and other Gifts and some of the Islamic States got very few people who are able to pay Zakat to poor people thus creating a obstacle to establish exploited free society and with a sound and strong economy.

In the past there was no period without a Caliphate stronger or weaker like our present one when we abolished our Caliphate System but Islamic Caliphate was never abolished the way we abolished even there was a time when there were three Caliphate, one in Baghdad under Abased, one in Egypt under Great Fatimyt, and one in Spain under Ummayad and origin of those three sect were originated from present day Hejaj/Holy Mecca now part of Saudi Arabia which proof that in Islam there is no place of regionalism or nationalism.

The interested reader may purchase many religious books published by Sh. Muhammad Ashraf, many of which is in English mainly "An Interpretation of the Holy Quran" which we have computerized. Some other famous book is "The Holy Qur-an"; Arabic text with English Translation, Commentary and Notes by the same writer Abdullah Yusuf Ali; Sahih Muslim by M. Abdul Hamid Siddiqi; Miskat al-Masabih - al-Hadith by Dr. James Robson and many other several religious Books.

. An image of an Arab Muslim hero was now needed and Sa'd bin Abi Waqqass was chosen. He was a warrior who led the Mohammedan Arab troops to defeat the Persian army in the Al-Qadissiyah battle in AD 633, in which the armies of Islam defeated the forces of Zoroastrian Persia and opened the way for Islam eastward.

Nebuchadnezzar II, king of Babylonian from 604 to 562 BC., Shortly before his accession, he led the Babylonian army at the battle of Carchemish in central Palestine. The Egyptian army was defeated and Nebuchadnezzar brought Palestine and Syria into his empire. When the Egyptians assisted the Hebrew inhabitants of Judah to rebel in 596 BC and again in 587 - 586 BC, Nebuchadnezzar marched to capture Jerusalem and took large numbers of Israelites into captivity. They were among the slaves who built the Hanging Gardens. They were kept prisoners for half a century `by the waters of Babylon', an ambitious irrigation scheme in the marshlands of the Shatt al-Arab.

But why Saddam Hossain became so powerful that entire world with all the big powers had to fight him to drive him out from Kuwait.

The reason was that Arab leaders was afraid of Iranian leader Khomeni though Khomeni established a sort of democratic State keeping with him only religious power to protect islamic interest. According to the book published by Arab leaders paid Saddam around 40 billion dollar to fight with Khomeni,

So when Saddam thought that he could not defeat Iranian Khomeni he had to use large arms and instead he turned to KUWAIT to recover from financial problem.

Though Saddam talked about jihad earlier he always mentioned about Arab cause instead of Islam,

So what money paid to Saddam and again to joint forces to expel Saddam from Kuwait must be 100 billion-dollar. Can those Arabic leader give a account of how much thy have paid to poor Muslim or even non-Muslim countries during same period and which will prove that since the abolition of khelafat the Arabs has spoilt huge money and wealth and human life for the so many differences among themselves. Even for the division there was many wars among themselves and on many occasion they have used the term "Arab cause" which has no relation with cause of Allah, Prophet Muhammad (sm) or any Islamic cause.

The difference among the Muslim countries only created destruction without contribution to any Islamic cause.

I should again quote some other verses form Holy Quran in support of my idea and thought which will follow later part of this chapter. I am quoting Sura Number instead of Sura Name as The Holy Quran itself is vast Computer from which one can learn science, history of mankind and everything and 1400 years ago it came to us a Computer with number as reference as such it was not difficult for me to Computerize it as It is itself Computerized System with Ayat Number and Sura Number as code from which one can have any knowledge one needs.

Sura Number=2
Ayat Number=32
They said: "Glory to Thee of knowledge we have none, save what Thou hast taught us; in truth it is Thou who art perfect in knowledge and wisdom."

Sura Number=1
Ayat Number=6
Show us the straight way,

Sura Number=7
Ayat Number=62

I but fulfil towards you the duties of my Lord's mission, Sincere is my advice to you And I know from Allah something that ye know not.

Sura Number=64
Ayat Number=12
So obey Allah, and obey his Apostle but if Ye turn back, the duty of our Apostle is but to proclaim (the message) clearly and openly.

Sura Number=43
Ayat Number=3
We have made it a Qur-an in Arabic, that Ye may be able to understand (and learn wisdom).

Sura Number=14
Ayat Number=4
We sent an Apostle except (to teach) in the language of his (own) people, in order to make (things) clear to them, Now Allah leaves straying those whom He pleases and He guides whom He pleases and He is exalted in power, full of wisdom.

Sura Number=3
Ayat Number=7
He it is who has sent down to thee the book: in it are verses basic or fundamental (of established meaning) they are the foundation of the Book: others are allegorical. But those in whose hearts is perversity follow the part thereof that is allegorical, seeking discord, and searching for its hidden meaning, but no one knows its hidden meanings except Allah and

those who are firmly grounded in knowledge say: "we believe in the Book the whole of it is from our Lord"; and none will grasp the message except men of understanding.
Sura Number=11
Ayat Number=1
A. L. R. (this is) a book, with verses basic or fundamental (of established meaning), further explained in detail, - from one who is wise and well - acquainted (with all things):
Sura Number=17
Ayat Number=71
One day we shall call Together all Human Beings with their (Respective) Imams, those who are given their record in their right hand will read it (with pleasure), and they will not be dealt with unjustly in the least.

Sura Number=2
Ayat Number=20
The Lightning all but snatches away their light every time the light (helps) them, they walk therein, and when the darkness grows on them they stand still. And if Allah willed, He could take away their faculty of hearing and seeing for Allah hath power over all things.

Sura Number=2
Ayat Number=215
They ask thee what they should spend (in charity) say: whatever ye spend that is good, is for parents and kindred and orphans and for wayfarers. And whatever ye do that is good,- Allah knoweth it well.

Sura Number=2
Ayat Number=213
Mankind was one single nation, and Allah sent messengers with glad tidings and warnings and with them he sent the Book in truth, to judge between People in matters wherein they differed, but the people of the book, after the clear signs came to them, did not differ among themselves, except through selfish contumacy, Allah by his grace guided the believers to the truth, concerning that wherein they differed. For Allah guides whom He will to a path that is straight.
Sura Number=65
Ayat Number=8
How many populations that insolently opposed the command of their Lord and of his Apostles, did we not then call to account; - to sever account? and we imposed on them an exemplary punishment.
Sura Number=70
Ayat Number=28
For their Lord's displeasure is the opposite of Peace and Tranquillity;-
Sura Number=3
Ayat Number=102
O Ye who believe! fear Allah as He should be feared, and die not except in a state of Islam.

Ayat Number=103
And hold fast, all together, by the rope which Allah (stretches out for you), and be not divided among yourselves and remember with gratitude Allah's favor on you for ye were enemies and He joined your hearts in love, so that by his grace Ye became brethren and ye were on the brink of the pit of fire, and He saved you from it. Thus doth Allah make his signs clear to you, that ye may be guided.

Ayat Number=104
Let there arise out of you a band of people inviting to all that is good, enjoining what is right, and forbidding what is wrong:- they are the ones to attain felicity.

Ayat Number=105
But not like those who are divided amongst themselves and fall into deputations after receiving clear signs: for them is a dreadful penalty,-

Ayat Number=106
On the day when some faces will be (lit up with) white, and some faces will be (in the gloom of) black: to those whose faces will be black (will be said) "did ye reject faith after accepting it? Taste then the penalty for rejecting faith."

Ayat Number=107
But those whose faces will be (lit with) white,- they will be in (the light of) Allah's mercy: therein to dwell (for ever).

Ayat Number=108
These are the signs of Allah: We rehearse them to thee in truth: and Allah means no injustice to any of his creatures.

Ayat Number=109
To Allah belongs all that is in the Heavens and on earth: to Him do all questions go back (for decision).

Ayat Number=110
Ye are the best of peoples, evolved for mankind, enjoining what is right, forbidding what is wrong, and believing in Allah. If only people of Book had faith, it were best for them among them are some who have faith, but most of them are perverted transgressors.

Ayat Number=112
They will do you no harm, barring a trifling annoyance if they come out to fight you, they will show you their backs, and no help shall they get.

Ayat Number=134
Those who spend (freely), whether in prosperity, or in adversity who restrain anger, and pardon (all) men - for Allah loves those who do good.

Ayat Number=135
And those who, having done something to be ashamed of, or wronged their own souls, earnestly bring Allah to mind, and ask for forgiveness for their sins,- and who can forgive sins except Allah?- and are never obstinate in persisting knowingly in (the wrong) they have done.

Ayat Number=148
And Allah gave them a reward in this world, and the excellent reward of the Hereafter. For Allah loveth those who do good.

Ayat Number=149
O ye believe! if ye obey the unbelievers, they will drive you back on your heels, and ye will turn back (from faith) to your own loss.

Ayat Number=150
Nay, Allah is your protector, and He is the best of helpers.

Sura Number=5
Ayat Number=23
"O my people! enter the Holy land which Allah hath assigned unto you and turn not back ignominiously, for then will Ye be overthrown, to your own ruin." They said! "O Moses! in this land are a people of exceeding strength, never shall we enter it until they leave it, If (once) they leave, then shall we enter".

Ayat Number=28
He said: "O my Lord! I have power only over myself and my brother, so separate us from this rebellious people!."

Ayat Number=29
Allah said: "therefore will the land be out of their reach for forty years in distraction will they Wander through the land: But sorrow thou not over these rebellious people".

Sura Number=3
Ayat Number=7
He it is who has sent down to thee the Book: in it are verses basic or fundamental (of established meaning) they are the foundation of the Book: others are allegorical. But those in whose hearts is perversity follow the part thereof that is allegorical, seeking discord, and searching for its hidden meanings, but no one knows its hidden meanings except Allah and those who are firmly grounded in knowledge say : "we believe in the Book the whole of it is from our Lord"; and none will grasp the message except men of understanding.

Sura Number=11
Ayat Number=1
A. L. R. (this is) a Book, with verses basic or fundamental (of established meaning), further explained in detail, - from one who is wise and well - acquainted (with all things):

Sura Number=65
Ayat Number=8
How many populations that insolently opposed the command of their Lord and of his Apostles, did we not then call to account; - to severe account? and we imposed on them an exemplary punishment.

Sura Number=70
Ayat Number=28
For their Lord's displeasure is the opposite of Peace and Tranquillity;-

Sura Number=2
Ayat Number=177
It is not righteousness that ye turn your faces towards east or west; but it is righteousness-to believe in Allah and the last day and the Angels, and Book, and the Messengers; to spend of your substance, out of love for him, for your kin, for orphans, for the needy, for the wayfarer, for those who ask, and for the ransom of slaves to be steadfast in prayer, and practice regular charity to fulfil the contracts which ye have made; and to be firm and patient, in pain (or suffering) and adversity, and throughout all periods of panic. Such are the people of truth, the God-fearing.
Ayat Number=195
And spend of your substance in the cause of Allah, and make not your own hands contribute to (your destruction); but do good; for Allah loveth those who do good.
Sura Number=2
Ayat Number=215

They ask thee what they should spend (in charity) say; whatever ye spend that is good, is for parents and kindred and orphans and for wayfarers. And whatever ye do that is good,- Allah knoweth it well.

AL-QURAN

One can understand my motive from the Heading itself. My real idea is that we the Muslim know Holy Quran, we have a copy of our Holy Quran in our residence in Arabic or in translated form but we never tried to introduce it fully after Glorious period of Kholafae Rashedin (truthful Caliphate) and after greatest Tragedy of known history of mankind in Karbala and period of Omar the Second. Though non-Muslim countries of Western world took many good things of Islam like democracy, freedom, free Medical care, Human dignity, unemployment allowances (charity) and so many but we the Muslim World are now divided into about 47 pieces instead of one unified Khelafat and a strong nation, each of us is a weak nation unable to defend ourselves and all these are because we do not follow Allah's (God's) saying or Holy Quran and also Sunna.

If USA can be one strong nation/state with 50 different States and even in any single state there is no particular nation, race or culture. In each state of USA different people with different culture, race and even religion from around the world are united and 50 such different States created a State, a State with freedom, democracy, human dignity, human right, equal Law for each citizen which is called United States of America. The Constitution of USA ensures equal Law/Justice for the people of USA and as such there is no complain of any people of a particular state for any kind of exploitation against any state or the central Government.

I should quote the famous address of President Abraham Lincoln which is called Gettysburg Address some of which are as follows:

"But in a larger sense, we cannot dedicate-we cannot consecrate- we cannot hallow-this ground. The brave men, living and dead, who struggled here, have consecrated it, for above our poor power to add or detract. The world will little note, nor long remember what we say here, but it can never forget what they did here. It is for us the living; rather to be dedicated here to the unfinished work which they who fought here have thus far so nobly advanced. It is rather for us to be here dedicated to the great task remaining before us-that from these honored dead we take increased devotion to that cause for which they gave the last full measure of devotion-that we here highly resolve that these dead shall not have died in vain-that this nation, under God, shall have a new birth of freedom-and that government of the people, by the people, for the people, shall not perish from the earth. But 1st Democratic country with freedom and equal justice came 1400 years ago when our Holy Prophet (A. S.) came in this world. The great American people have been fulfilling the above wishes of their great president by upholding his wishes and the wishes of dead people who fought and united North and South into one great Nation.

But what we the Muslim people did; we divided the Khelafat (Caliphate) and the greatest Democratic nation in a Islamic way, first in world History founded by the greatest and last Prophet of Islam our Holy Prophet (Peace be upon him), into north and south, into east and west numbering around 52 states (including 5 states of former USSR). Even the land which consisted during Kholafae Rashedin (four truthful Caliphs after the Prophet(sm)) now divided into around 12 or 15 states thus we dishonored the last wishes of our holy Prophet (peace be upon Him) which he declared during his last Hajj Address "that each one of the Islamic Ummah or nation be he is a black or white or he be Arab or Non-Arab is equal to Law and be united". But we forgot the teaching of our Holy Prophet we forgot the sacrifices made by Hazrat Imam Hussain (peace be upon him) and other members of Ahle Bayet (peace be upon them) and other great Sahabis (R. A.) to uphold the originality of Islam for freedom, democracy for equal Law and overall Islamic principal.

Now how we can honor them, we can only honor them by upholding their great ideology of original Islam preached and established by our Great Prophet (peace be upon Him) and followed by 4 great Khalifas during the period of Kholafae Rashedin.

So in Computer age like this we can sit together and we can establish a unified Quranic Law in life, state administration in each corner of Muslim world which will be more powerful than any country of this world and which can dictate the whole world and without dictating by others (other countries/power).

The Jews are searching their all original tribes of 12 and even they have collected them from Ethiopia, during last few years they have been allowing Jews from former USSR, they are united around the world. In the present day world all nations with different ideology or religion are united say for greater sense United Nation, smaller sense USA, former USSR, China, Israel, India and even under the banner of NATO, WARSAW, EEC and so on. And in present day consent we are watching about Maastricht Treaty or present European Union, for which in the past there was no existence of a United Europe, they were always divided though were always united for Crusade war, not for equal benefit, economic justice among the European people, but in the Islamic Caliphate politically for long 1300 years Muslim were united, and though for some period they were divided **into three Caliphate, one in Baghdad, one in Cairo, and one in Spain, that was due to power struggle, not as separate entity and each of them wanted to include the other part under them and in such way Egypt or the area under Fatumyte Caliphate came under Abbaside of Baghdad, again entire area under Abbaside came under Turkish Osmani Caliphate. So at present** the Whole Europe are going under a process of election for the Maastricht Treaty (now European Union), lastly election was held in France and other European countries. The Muslim countries are conspiring against each other with the advice of Western countries, without any kind true democracy or equal life for all the people of their countries which was followed by Hadrat Abu Bakr, Hadrat Umar, Hadrat Ali (God be pleased with them). Those four Caliphs took very low quality food even less than their house holds servant, the same for their cloth and other necessity. Hadrat Umar was sleeping under a tree when Wasik was sent to kill him by Roman king Constantine, Hadrat Ali was offering and leading the early morning prayers in the Mosque of Kufa, now Iraq, when his assassinator attacked with his poisonous knife, even fifth Caliph handed over power for son of Abu Sufian and Hinda for the sake of a united Caliphate i.e. to Mawia, even second grandson of The Holy Prophet (Sm) did not asked the Muslims of Medina, Mecca or Yemen to revolt against Mawia's son Yazid, he just accepted an invitation from the people of Kufa and went there and faced the saddest event of Karbala, and in the evening of 9th of Muharram (lunar month), night before the 10th of Muharram, asked his follower that to stay with him means to accept the martyrdom so as they may feel sigh he put off light and asked to leave him, so it is all the historical fact that the family members and the descendant of the Holy Prophet did not encourage anything which may effect the division of the Islamic Umma instead they sacrificed their life and power for the only interest of keeping unity among the Islamic Umma. **And when the descendent of the holy Prophet were tortured and killed they went far and far, even to Hindu majority Ajmir in India and became the spiritual King of India, the name still to-day he is known in India, the other members of the Holy family also spread around the world and spread the Islam around the world. But to-day you will not find any Arab Muslim to go to any where of this world for that mission. The Arab Muslim used to go around the world with the mission of enjoying their life and used to stay in big hotels. All these are the main reasons for the downfall of the Muslim, politically and spiritually. The reasons are that many of us lost the Memory of the past and particularly, some of us lost due great love for The Great Lord God and his Prophet(sm). So we the Muslims are separated from each other, we are divided to fight ourselves among our Muslim brother. The result is since 1924 and since from the diplomacy of coastal diplomacy number of Muslims killed by** the fellow Muslims are many times more then number of Muslims killed by non-Muslims, for example the fellow Muslims were killed during revolt by the Arab Muslims against the Osmani Caliphate, again by the Turkish Government after 1924 for so called secular policy against the Mollas (orthodox muslims), during Iraq-Iran war, after invading of the Communist Russia into Afghanistan and fighting among the Muslim of Afghanistan and pro-Communist and freedom fighter, even after the fall of Communist in Afghanistan the killing among them is continuing, during the liberation movement of Bangladesh between majority Bengali population of present Bangladesh and former Pakistani Army, millions gave their life, even though ir Calcutta which is also capital of West Bengal, and previously capital of undivided Bengal and first capital of British India; the Bengalis and non-Bengalis from each part of India are leaving in peace and harmony except some Hindu-Muslim riot which present Chief Minister stopped since he came to power in West Bengal; again after the occupation of Kuwait by Iraq, and subsequent war for which Iraqi army was compelled to leave Kuwait. and again for the boycott of UN the Iraqi children have been dying, the Palestinian Muslim became victim in Kuwait for the policy of PLO leaders. So always the fellow Muslim kills the Muslims when the so-called leader of Muslim Umma kept them complete silent as if they know nothing. Where Mahatma Gandhi perhaps gave his life before a assassinator as he protested against the massacre of Muslims in Delhi, even Gandhi observed fast in protest of the killing of Muslims, but you will not find any Muslim leader to go for fast when the Muslims are killed in Arab, in Turkey, in Afghanistan. In Bangladesh (during liberation war with Pakistan) or during Iraq-Iran war. Still you he they and I claim to be the followers of Islam. But look to the Indian Muslims, before 1947 for the Pakistani movement they brought big procession in Calcutta, in Delhi, in Patna, Bombay or any where in India, though they knew that future Pakistan are unable to give them shelter as it was not possible, yet they gave blood without, without their blood no Pakistan, not only blood but everything. In an article in the daily news paper 'THE TELEGRAPH' date 06/10/1992 mentioned "Independence from Britain in 1947 brought disappointment. Independent Pakistan was dominated by immigrants from India (Muhajirs means Refugee) who were based in West Pakistan and were insensitive either to democratic elections or to the interests of the East Pakistanis. The language movement (to make Bengali a second national language alongside Urdu), beginning in 1948...' We got two problems, one is economic which was controlled by the immigrant Muslims from India, because almost all 22 Industrial family came from India leaving the Indian Muslims poor to poorer or poorer to poorest For example if only one Pakistani Bank namely Habib Bank Ltd. was not shifted from India till-today it was not hard to have 10,000 branches throughout India easily and easily in an average of 10 staffs for each Branch at least 1,00,-000 employment could be created and of majority of those could easily be Muslims, as we know with even proper education it is in fact impossible for a Muslim in India to get a job, and due to frustration of unemployment among the Muslims of India they are everyday becoming poor to poorer and education among them are declining due to poverty. So if for one Bank there could be employment of atleast 1,00,000 Muslims then think about those 22 family who migrated to Pakistan and moved their capital to Pakistan but deprived million of poor Muslims of India from Employment, education and created more sorrow and poverty among the Indian Muslims We must speak the truth for the luxurious politicians in Muslim World who are only power hungry but not honest politicians and their only aim is to go to power even in exchange of million's , in exchange of ,million of Muslims. Again for Pakistani cases we can think about language. Like the people of India present day Pakistanis accepted their state or national language 'Urdu' which was not language of Panzab because their language is Panzabi, so for Sindh it is Sindhi, for North Western Frontier it is Pastu, it is Beluchi for Beluchistan, so the fact Urdu is not the language of Pakistani people except the immigrant Muslims from India, again according to PCGLOBE software urdu is the laguage of only 8% population of Pakstan; where as Panzabi is the language of 48% Sindhi 12%, Pastu 8% and Beluchi 3% of the Pakistani population and even of the Ethnic group Iranian is 9% of the Pakistani population. So imagine 66% Punzabi, 13% Sindhi 9%

Iranian, Urdu 8% and Baluchi 3%, so as far ethnic group Urdu or Indian are less than the Iranian of 9% according to PCGLOBE Software though only 8% of the total Pakistani population's ethnic group's laguage is the State language of Pakistan because of only one reason which is to keep Pakistan in one State. So from Pakistan's instance or experiance we the Muslims of the world can get a great lesson of one single Brotherhood or Umma and the main topic of Caliphate because to the champion of Nation State on the basis of so narrow minded regional Politicians of the Muslim world who want to grab power creating so many Nation States on the basis of language or very artificial State like Turkey and 13 States in the Arab world which was only part of one Caliphate with only one language Arabic for long 1300 years is a logical reply for their so many pretext of the abolition of Caliphate is nothing but simple lie and act of Satan, the very act of the enemy of Islam and the one Allah (God) the Prophet(Sm) whose followers they claim to be; and their all kind of pretext is an example for powerful United States of America in the non-Muslim cases and modern new Pakistan for the Muslim case for the simple example that there is no language problem in present day Pakistan though it is greatness of the Pakistani people that they accepted a language which originated in Uttar Prodesh (U. P.) or particularly Delhi during Mogul period when this new language was developed by the Muslims which is also perhaps world record, and even the 200 years period British Government in India continued the Persian language as state language until 1860's when the British introduced English instead of Persian language, then still the British accepted Persian language for 100 years to maintain the unity of India. So as a language Persian kept British India united for 100 years, Hindi has helped present India to be united, so even Urdu helped Pakistan to be United. Though there are around 20 principal language in India the Indians are United, though there are at least 5 language in Pakistan, the Pakistanis are united. So why with only one language Arabic the Arab world are divided into around 13 states? If the Indian and Pakistanis can be united with so many language and the beauty of India lies in its unity not division for so many languages and culture and the same thing applies to Pakistan though not in term of India which is more bigger one in size and culture. So again if there is only one Caliphate from Morocco to Indonesia/Malaysia there will be far less language then in India or proposed but new, not like 1300 oldest Caliphate, Maastricht , (now European Union) Treaty because in India there are around 10-20 and in Europe at least around 10 languages. In the 1400 years (though lost during last 72 years) old Caliphate the major languages are Arab, Turkish, Persian, Pastu, Urdu, Bengali, Indonesian, and Malay, major 8 languages instead of 20 Indian or 10 European languages.

 But we the Muslims are separated into so many pieces since 1924 when Khelafat was abolished and when seeds of a Jews State was originated after thousands of year and we are now about to recognize that state after 40 years of it's creation. (kindly read Sura Number =5, Ayat Number=29 and think). Jews are united with one Government but we are divided though we claim Allah's (God's) Khalifa in this world and in fact we are.

(An unified Khelafat (Caliphate) under Constitution based on only Holy Quran and Sunna is Fundamental; as that System was established by our Holy Prophet (A. S.). Please Note that our Prophet (A. S.) did not nominate any Khalifa (Ruler) but Khalifa was elected by Muslims, and before Islamic period there was no such System where a Ruler was elected anywhere in this world and in known history, and even in Britain the people were ruled by Kings until King John during which first Magna Charta System was introduced, and before our Prophet came there was only might was right, no freedom, no democracy and justice).

I think we will get a positive answer of the question or we can have our mandate for the Islamic System established by Quran and Sunna. Quran is a complete code of life, for individual, for family life and for the State. Quran is not only for Muslims but it is for entire

Mankind who can understand it and in fact the teaching of Quran is followed indirectly by entire Mankind, Quran is for Islam and Islam was originated when Hazrat Adam (peace be upon him) came in this world. Quran is not only for dead Muslims which we nowadays practice for the blessing dead Muslims even though that dead Muslim never believed the word of Holy Quran or That dead man did not try to know or follow the teaching of Holy Quern during his life time and Quran came for the living one and to follow during life time and not for only blessing of dead Muslims.

We the Muslim countries are keeping Billion of Dollars (particular the well rich countries) in western world without any benefit of Muslim countries for aid but if we can utilize our wealth for the benefits of Muslims we can help not only Muslim countries but all non-Muslim poor coutries of Asia and Africa.

So why we only 43 to 47 Islamic States less than 50 states of USA can not be united under a single Khelafat under a common Constitution as per our Holy Quran and which is our part of faith too. Due to division of so many states some of the Islamic States do not have own people to accept Zakat and other Gifts and some of the Islamic States got very few people who are able to pay Zakat to poor people thus creating a obstacle to establish exploited free society and with a sound and strong economy.

Instead of following Holy Quranic Law we are following Law introduced by non-Muslims say British Law though we talking about Islamic Law in seminars and in various meetings or we should say we are introducing our own imposed Law inherited from British and other alien power thus British panel code became Indian, Pakistani and Bangladesh panel code and the same is followed by other countries too and these are just to rule our people depriving our people their right of proper food and day to day need thus though few people are benefited temporarily in this world we are destroying our moral trough corrupt practice/Law, we are destroying our society, our Islamic System and Islamic interest and in the long run we are defeated by alien powers and lost many lands like Albania, which has become Communist country and parts of Europe, Uzbakistan, Kazakistan some other parts of Russia and recently Afghanistan where Muslims are shedding their blood every day fighting each other.
So we must leave our personal interest and we must introduce a Law based on Holy Quran and Sunna and we should do it if necessary immediately and without any delay.

We have already crossed more than 1300 years so we should not wait for tomorrow but we should introduce it to-day. Each of us should ask our soul what we want, we want our self interest or the interest of Allah then we can avoid deceiving our soul because when we do something wrong we do it knowingly, we make plan for it knowingly and we introduce it knowingly but History is witness what we did during past 1300 years.

We claim to be Muslim but we never asked our soul whether we are deceiving our soul or not. We never tried to introduce Islamic System/Law in its true sense and thus we deceived ourselves, our nations. We are divided into 47 pieces because each of us want to be a Ruler, a President, a Prime Minister, a King and without thinking about Islamic interest.

In the past there was no period without a Khelafat stronger or weaker like our present one when we abolished our Khelafat System in 1924 but Islamic Khelafat was never abolished the way we abolished; even there was a time when there were three Khelafat, one in Baghdad under Abbaside, one in Egypt under Great Fatimide, and one in Spain under Umayyad and origin of those three sect were originated from present day Hejaj/Holy Mecca now part of Saudi Arabia which proves that in past there was no place of regionalism or nationalism within Muslim Umma.

Even the Umayyad was overthrown in 749 by Iranian General Abu Muslim Khorasani and
the Abbasyd took the advantage and grabbed the khelafat and even killed Iranian General
Abu Muslim.

One Abbasyd Khalifa Mamun tortured and killed Islamic scholars who protested against the
Motazila idea of "Khalqe Quran" Mamun's chief Justice Bishir Ibne Oalid and Ibrahim
Ibne Mehedi saved themselves when Mamun wanted and ordered to kill them if they
opposed his idea of "Khalqe Quran". Mamun forbade for any kind of discussion in any
mosque and particularly in Zame Roshafa the then greatest mosque in Baghdad except for
Bishir Mishir and Mohammed Ibne Zaham who were leader of Motazila. There was none in
Baghdad to protest this order . In such a situation Sheikh Abdul Aziz Ibne Yeahea Kenani
from Holy Mecca came to Baghdad and protested and finally he won the debate on "Khlaqe
Quran" and Mamun appointed him as Nadeem of "Elmi Majlish" and was allowed to preach
real Islam or teaching of Holy Quran.

Though at present we can not do that for various reasons but at least we can start with a
Confederation of Islamic States with Defense, Foreign policy, Finance, Science and
Technology with the center. Through Defense planning; we can create a vast army with
several million Muslims, a strong Air Force, navy through which we can mobilize our
forces quickly any where in the world where we will face a situation like Afghanistan,
Palestine or Iran-Iraq war, we can defend ourselves without any fear or favor from any
quarter or power Big or Small. The following verses of the Holy Quran (translation)
Is enough for the truth seekers.

2: 88 They say, "Our hearts Are the wrappings (which preserve Allah's
2: 88 Word: we need no more)." Nay, Allah's curse is on them For their
2: 88 blasphemy; Little is it they believe.
2:102 They followed what the evil ones Gave out (falsely) Against the
2:102 power Of solomon: the blasphemers Were, not Solomon, but The evil
2:102 ones, teaching men Magic, and such things As came down at Babylon
2:102 To the angels Harut and Marut. But neither of these taught any one
2:102 (Such things) without saying: "We are only for trial; So do not
2:102 blaspheme." They learned from them The means to sow discord Betweens
2:102 man and wife. But they could not thus Harm any one except By
2:102 Allah's permission. And they learned what harmed them, Not what
2:102 profited them. And they knew that the buyers Of (magic) would have
2:102 No share in the happiness Of the Hereafter. And vile Was the price
2:102 of which They did sell their souls, If they but knew!
3: 55 Behold! Allah said: "O Jesus! I will take thee And raise thee to
3: 55 Myself and clear thee (of the falsehood) Of those who blaspheme;
3: 55 I will make those Who follow thee superior To those who reject
3: 55 faith, To the Day of Resurrection: Then shall ye all Return unto Me
3: 55 And I will judge Between you of the matters Wherein ye dispute.
4:155 (They have incurred divine Displeasure): in that they Broke their
4:155 Covenant: That they rejected the Signs Of Allah; that they slew The
4:155 Messengers in defiance Of right; that they said, "Our hearts are
4:155 the wrappings (Which preserve Allah's Word; We need no more)";- nay
4:155 Allah hath set the seal on their hearts For their blasphemy, And
4:155 little is it they believe:-
5: 19 In blasphemy indeed Are those that say That Allah is Christ The son
5: 19 of Mary. Say: "Who then Hath the least power Against Allah, if His
5: 19 Will Were to destroy Christ The son of Mary, his mother, And all-
5: 19 everyone That is on the earth? For to Allah belongeth The dominion
5: 19 of the heavens And the earth, and all That is between. He createth

5: 19 What He pleaseth. For Allah Hath power over all things."
5: 67 The Jews say:" Allah's hand Is tied up. Be their hands Tied up
5: 67 and be they accursed For the (blasphemy) they utter. Nay, both His
5: 67 hands Are widely outstretched: He giveth and spendeth (Of His-
5: 67 bounty) as He pleaseth But the revelation that Cometh to thee from
5: 67 Allah Increaseth in most of them Their obstinate rebellion And
5: 67 blasphemy. Amongst them We have placed enmity And hatred till the
5: 67 Day Of Judgment. Every time They kindle the fire of war, Allah doth
5: 67 extinguish it; But they (ever) strive To do mischief on earth.
5: 67 And Allah loveth not Those who do mischief.
5: 71 Say: "O People of the Book! Ye have no ground To stand upon unless
5: 71 Ye stand fast by the Law, The Gospel, and all the revelation That
5: 71 has come to you from Your Lord." It is the revelation That cometh
5: 71 to thee from Thy Lord, that increaseth in most Of them their
5: 71 obstinate Rebellion and blasphemy. But sorrow thou not Over (these)
5: 71 people without faith .
5: 75 They do blaspheme who say: "Allah is Christ the son Of Mary." But
5: 75 said Christ: "O Children of Israel! Worship Allah, my Lord And your
5: 75 Lord." Whoever Joins other gods with Allah,- Allah will forbid him
5: 75 The Garden, and the Fire Will be his abode. There will For the
5: 75 wrong-doers Be no one to help.
5: 76 They do blaspheme who say: Allah is one of three In a Trinity:
5: 76 for there is No god except One Allah. If they desist not From
5: 76 their word (of blasphemy), Verily a grievous penalty Will befall
5: 76 the blasphemers Among them.
5:106 but most Of them lack wisdom.
6: 19 Say: "What thing is most Weighty in evidence?" Say: "Allah is
6: 19 witness Between me and you: This Qur-an hath been Revealed to me
6: 19 by inspiration That I may warn you And all whom it reaches. Can ye

29: 40 By a (mighty) Blast; some We caused the earth To swallow up; and

Mankind was one single nation, And Allah sent Messengers With glad tidings and warnings And with them He sent The Book in truth, To judge between people In matters wherein They differed, But the People of the Book, After the Clear Signs Came to them, did not differ Among themselves, Except through selfish contumacy. Allah by His Grace Guided the Believers To the Truth, Concerning that Wherein they differed, For Allah guides Whom He will To a path That is straight.

2:213

And hold fast, all together, by the Rope Which Allah (stretches out For you), and be not divided Among yourselves And remember with gratitude Allah's favor on you; For ye were enemies And He joined your hearts In love, so that by His Grace Ye become brethren; And ye were on the brink Of the Pit of Fire, And He saved you from it. Thus doth Allah make His Signs clear to you; That ye may be guided.

3:103

It is not righteousness That ye turn your faces Towards East or West; But it is righteousness- To believe in Allah and the Last Day, And the Angels, and the Book, and the Messengers; to spend of your substance, out of love for him, for your kin, for orphans, for the needy, for the wayfarer, for those who ask, And for the ransom of slaves; to be steadfast in prayer, and practice regular charity; to fulfil the contracts Which ye have made; And to be firm and patient, In pain (or suffering) and adversity, And throughout all periods of panic. Such are the people of truth, the God-fearing

2:177

And spend of your substance In the cause of Allah, And make not your own hands Contribute to (your destruction); But do good; for Allah loveth those Who do good.

2:195

They ask thee What they should spend (in charity). Say; Whatever Ye spend that is good, Is for parents and kindred And orphans And those in want and for wayfarers. And whatever ye do that is good,- Allah knoweth it well.

2:215

They ask thee Concerning wine gambling, Say: "In them is great sin, And some profit, for men; But the sin is grater Than the profit." They ask thee how much They are to spend (In charity); Say: "What is beyond Your needs." Thus doth Allah Make clear to you His Signs: in order that Ye may consider-
2:219

AL-QURAN

And our Holy Prophet Muhammad (Allah bless him) told during his Last Hajj Address from the top of the Jabal ul-Arafat (7th March, 632) " Ye people! Listen to my words and understand the same. Know that all Muslims are brothers unto one another. Ye are one brotherhood. Nothing which belongs to another is lawful unto his brother, unless freely given out of good-will. Guard yourselves from committing injustice."
"Neither any Arab is superior to any Non-Arab nor any Non-Arab is superior to any Arab; (Similarly) neither any black man is preferable to any white man nor a white man is preferable to any black man, and of course the only standard for ones superiority and nobleness is God fearing."
"Let him that is present tell it unto him that is absent. Haply he that shall be told may remember better than he who hath heard it."

Recent events in Communist countries like Eastern Europe and even USSR itself prove that only one political system namely Freedom and Democracy under a kind of Capitalist system may survive.

And if we go back to past history of Mankind we will find there was no chance of freedom or democracy and there was various kind of dictatorship either military or hereditary Kingship with only exception of the period when last Prophet of Islam Hazrat Muhammad (Allah bless him) came in this world 1400 years ago. He even had to leave his birth place Holy Mecca and the people of Holy Medina gladly accepted him where he established First democratic country in the world History with the support of it's majority people. Though the majority people of the Holy Mecca made conspiracy against him ultimately the Truth won against the all evil, but he took no revenge and instead he pardoned the people of Holy Mecca, his nation The Nation of God spread around the world within very short time to Asia, Africa and even to Europe, during his life time his Companions were sent around the world to preach Islam the religion Of Peace which started from original father Prophet Adam (may peace be him). Even when the spirit of the great Prophet (Allah bless him) took flight to the "blessed companionship on high" he left a Democratic process and a Law from God for which first 4 Caliphs (Leader of the Muslim State) or God's Representative in this world were elected by an Electorate of leaders of all sects/tribes and as such his son-in-law Hazard Ali (Allah be pleased with him) became the fourth to become the Caliph that is also at a very critical time of Islamic history. But Hazard Ali (Allah be pleased with him) was shortly after assassinated whilst engaged in prayer in a mosque at Chuff. And as Syed Amir Ali mentioned in his famous book "THE SPIRIT OF ISLAM" (page 299) which is as follows:

The star of Hind's son was now in the ascendant, and Abu Sufian's ambition to become the king of Mecca was fulfilled on a grander scale by Muawiyah" "With the rise of Muawiyah the oligarchical rule of the heathen times displaced the democratic rule of Islam."

Even Hazrat Imam Hassan (Allah be pleased with him) eldest son of Ali (Allah be pleased with him) was poisoned though he made peace with Muawiyah with the condition that after Muawiyah dies The Caliphate be handed over to truthful leader like Hadrat Imam Hussain, but Muawiyah did not fulfil that condition instead he nominated the Caliphate to his son Yazid and in this process Hazrat Imam Hussain (Allah be pleased with him) second grandson of Holy Prophet (Allah bless him) and second son of Hazrat Ali (Allah be pleased with him) did not take the oath to Yazid as it was against the principal of Democratic process which was maintained until now. So Hazrat Imam Hussain (Allah be pleased with him) with most of his family members had to accept martyrdom before a dictator and a force of evil and Hazrat Imam Hussain (Allah be pleased with him) became the first in this world who gave His life and life of his dear ones for the Democracy and divine Law and equal justice for all which we nowadays talk most around this world and that of freedom, the freedom limited with certain limit which was prescribed in the Holy Quran by Almighty God, and also Sunna (whatever our Prophet (Allah bless him) as messenger of God told was law) not a kind of freedom which violate ones' moral, ones' individual right or abuse a great man.

Many a time, Abu Huraira (Allah be pleased with him) reports, had the Prophet (Allah bless him) to go without a meal. Dates and water frequently formed his only nourishment. Often, for months together, no fire could be lighted in his house from scantiness of means. God, say the Moslem historians, had indeed put before him the key to the treasures of this world, but he refused it!

How much property was left by our Holy Prophet (Allah bless him) who was also the founder and first Head of a first united Islamic State and the Leader of Arab and non-Arab like Hadrat Salman Farsi (RA); and non-slave and slave like Hadrat Belal(RA) and particular irony is when our holy Prophet (SM) was the first who arranged to free many slaves and from when slave was banned, slave were given equal place in society, though after around 1000 years of our holy Prophet and after the fall of the Spain from Muslim; the so called civilized western people started the slave business in the American continent. Our Holy Prophet (Allah bless him) used to say "poverty is his proud". So we the Muslims also should be proud to be poor if we want to be companion of our Holy Prophet (Allah bless him) in the next world.

We are sorry to mention that in a local English daily news paper we saw a report that the richest man in this world is a ruler of a Muslim country with his wealth of 25 billion US dollars; another Muslim leader with 18 billion US dollars and another with 4.5 billion US dollars and a total of the wealth in possession of these three Muslim ruler is 47.5 billion US dollars. So imagine if the report is true (Though the names of the rulers were mentioned in that news paper none of them challenged this statement) then only with this 47.5 billion US dollars we can create a vast fund with which we can establish many production oriented in-dustry which will eliminate poverty not only in the Islamic world but from the entire world; probably with such fund we can establish several organization like Co-operative American Relief Everywhere these are US based organization founded after the World War. These organization have been giving various aid to the poor of about 40 countries, for example Title II of PL 480 of USA.

So instead of giving all responsibilities and burden to developed countries we the Islamic countries should share our vast resources to eliminate poverty from this world. We can take the help of Computer to calculate, to plan and distribute all our resources which may be food, technology, industry, manpower and any other resources.

Present day Information or Computer System can help to detect the reason of setback of Muslim World and point out various remedy through various research with the help of Computer.

For instance we have calculated average per capita Income of the major Islamic Countries and we have detected that average per capita Income of the Islamic countries is around US $ 800 and which will be even more probably around US $1000 to US $1200 if we can get the per capita Income of Iraq and Iran. My calculation is based on World Bank report of "World Development Report 1989".

We can abolish poverty not only from Islamic Countries but from entire world if we are compelled to re-establish and can re-establish real Islamic System/teaching. If you can go through World Bank Report you will see per capita Income of India and China is only $300 where as if we can establish one Caliphate (United States of Islamic country) our per capita Income will be between $1000 to $1200 and our differences among Islamic Countries is such that highest per capita Income are Brunei with $15390, Qatar with $ 12430, U.A.E. $ 15830 and Kuwait with $14610 where as the lowest is Bangladesh with $160, Guinea - Bissau with $160,Mali with $210. Even the World Bank remarked about Islamic Banking with the comments "Nevertheless, Islamic banking can be made to work quite well and provides an interesting contrast to commercial banking practices elsewhere. In countries such as Pakistan the introduction of Islamic banking has improved the functioning of the financial system in some respects for example, by making returns to financial instruments more market-driven".

Per capita income of some Islamic countries are given below:

COUNTRY (in million)	Population	PER.CAPITA INCOME	$	Popul. CAPITA INCOME	GNP	AVERAGE PER
Iraq						
Lebanon						
Afghanistan						
Iran						
Bangladesh	106.1	160		106100000		16976-000000
Guinea-Bissau	0.922	160		922000	147520000	
Mali	7.8		210	7800000	1638000000	
Zambia		7.2	250	7200000	1800000000	
Somalia	5.7	290	5700000	1653000000		
Maldives	0.2	300	200000	60000000		

296

Country	Population (million)	Per Capita Income US$	Popul.	GNP	Average
Sierra Leone	3.8	300	3800000	1140000000	
Guinea	0	0	0	0	
Sudan	23.1	330	23100000	7623000000	
Pakistan	102.5	350	102500000	35875000000	
Nigeria	106.6	370	106600000	39442000000	
Yemen(S)	2.3	420	2300000	966000000	
Mauritania	1.9	440	1900000	836000000	
Indonesia	171.4	450	171400000	77130000000	
Segal	7	520	7000000	3640000000	
Yemen(N)	8.5	590	8500000	5015000000	
Morocco	23.3	610	23300000	14213000000	
Egypt	50.1	680	50100000	34068000000	
Tunisia	7.6	1180	7600000	8968000000	
Turkey	52.6	1210	52600000	63640000000	
Jordan	3.8	1560	3800000	5928000000	
Syria	11.2	1640	11200000	18368000000	
Malaysia	16.5	1810	16500000	29865000000	
Algeria	23.1	2680	23100000	61908000000	
Libya	4.1	5460	4100000	22386000000	
Oman	1.3	5810	1300000	7553000000	
Saudi Arabia	12.6	6200	12600000	78120000000	
Bahrain	Bahrain	0	0	0	0
Kuwait	1.9	14610	1900000	27759000000	
U.A.E.	1.5	15830	1500000	23745000000	
Qatar	0.332	12430	332000	4126760000	
Brunei	0.235	15390	235000	3616650000	
Total	765.189		765189000	598211930000	781.78

Average Per Cap. Income= $781.78

We will get a positive answer of the question or we can have our mandate for the Islamic System as established by Holy Quran and Sunna. Quran is a complete code of life, for individual, for family life and for the State. Quran is not only for Muslims but it is for entire Mankind who can understand it and in fact it is followed by entire Mankind, Quran is for Islam and Islam originated when Hazrat Adam (peace be upon him) came to this world.

Per capita income of some Islamic countries are given below:

COUNTRY (in million)	Population INCOME US $	PER.CAPITA INCOME US$	PER CAPITA INCOME	Popul.	GNP	AVERAGE
Iraq	17.1	*2172	17100000	37141200000		
Lebanon						
Afghanistan						
Iran	*49.4	*4241	49400000	209505400000		
Bangladesh	106.1		160		106100000	16976000000
Guinea-Bissau	0.922		160		922000	147520000
Mali		7.8		210	7800000	1638000000
Somalia	5.7	290	5700000	1653000000		
Maldives	0.2	300	200000	60000000		

297

Sierra Leone	3.8	300		3800000	1140000000	Guinea
Bahrain	0	0		0	0	
Sudan	23.1	330	23100000	7623000000		
Pakistan	102.5	350	102500000	35875000000		
Nigeria	106.6	370	106600000	39442000000		
Yemen(S)	2.3	420	2300000	966000000		
Mauritania	1.9	440	1900000	836000000		
Indonesia	171.4	450	171400000	77130000000		
Senegal	7	520	7000000	3640000000		
Yemen(N)	8.5	590	8500000	5015000000		
Morocco	23.3	610	23300000	14213000000		
Egypt	50.1	680	50100000	34068000000		
Tunisia	7.6	1180	7600000	8968000000		
Turkey	52.6	1210	52600000	63646000000		
Jordan	3.8	1560	3800000	5928000000		
Syria	11.2	1640	11200000	18368000000		
Malaysia	16.5	1810	16500000	29865000000		
Algeria	23.1	2680	23100000	61908000000		
Libya	4.1	5460	4100000	22386000000		
Oman	1.3	5810	1300000	7553000000		
Saudi Arabia	12.6	6200	12600000	78120000000		
Bahrain	0	0	0	0		
Kuwait	1.9	14610	1900000	27759000000		
U.A.E.	1.5	15830	1500000	23745000000		
Qatar	0.332	12430	332000	4126760000		
Brunei	0.235	15390	235000	3616650000		
Total	824.489	98403	824489000	843058530000	1022.52	

Average Per Capita Income of Islamic Countries = $1022.5225

*This figure was taken from ICTVTR news bulletin(August 89)
From the World Development Report 1990 we came to know that the United States is the largest donor in terms of total volume; it provided $10.1 billion in aid in 1988. But the United States is near the bottom among DAC donors when aid is calculated as a proportion of GNP_ the figure is only 0.21 percent. Aid from Arab countries in 1988 totaled $2.3 billion, of which $2.1 billion was from Saudi Arabia and $108 million from Kuwait. Saudi Arabia's ratio of aid to GNP was 2.70, the highest for any donor (page 129 of World Development Report 1990).

We are sorry to mention that in a local English daily news paper we saw a report that the richest man in this world is a ruler of a Muslim country with his wealth of 25 billion US dollars; another Muslim leader with 18 billion US dollars and another with 4.5 billion US dollars and a total of the wealth in possession of these three Muslim ruler is 47.5 billion US dollars. So imagine if the report is true (Though the names of the rulers were mentioned in that news paper none of them challenged this statement) then only with this 47.5 billion US dollars we can create a vast fund with which we can establish many production oriented industry which will eliminate poverty not only in the Islamic world but from the entire world; probably with such fund we can establish several organization like Co-operative American Relief Everywhere these are US based organization founded after the World War. These organization have been giving various aid to the poor of about 40 countries, for example Title II of PL 480 of USA.

So instead of giving all responsibilities and burden to developed countries we the Islamic countries should share our vast resources to eliminate poverty from this world. We can take the help of Computer to calculate, to plan and distribute all our resources which may be food, technology, industry, manpower and any other resources.

If we submit a questionnaire like the following to all the Head of the present day Muslim countries, what will be their response? Even we held a referendum for re-establishment the 1300 years old Caliphate, what will be the response. I think it will be passed by the 90% person Muslims all over the world. So there is no alternate, but to elect a Caliph through election because when to save a Amir or king like Kuwait, when it was taken by Saddam, who talked about Arabism during his fight with Iran, and started talking about Jihad and Islam after taking Kuwait, it is nothing but madness because to save a Dictator like Saddam The Arab Leaders paid Saddam billion of Dollars, and again to save Amir of Kuwait who a Dictator of maximum 20,00,000 Muslims including some foreign workers and also to save some other Dictator in the Gulf, those so called Muslim Leaders spent Billion of Dollars for the war against Saddam, where as more Muslims live in Bombay in India alone, where at least 800 Muslims were called by the Indian Hindu Police, but here the whole world with so called leaders are silent, no action against India was taken, though around 200 million Muslims several time more than the Muslims of entire Arab world live in present India. This is the world and this is the leaders of the free World.

2. Religion:
3. Sect   :
4. Do you believe in all the word of the Holy Quran: Yes/No.
   (if the answer is No then you can not claim to be a Muslim)

5. Do you want to establish original Caliphate, an unified   Caliphate:Yes/No.

We think we will get a positive answer of the question or we can have our mandate for the Islamic System as established by Holy Quran and Sunna. Quran is a complete code of life, for individual, for family life and for the State. Quran is not only for Muslims but it is for entire Mankind who can understand it and in fact it is followed by entire Mankind, Quran is for Islam and Islam originated when Hazrat Adam (peace be upon him) came to this world.

So why we only 47 to 54 Islamic States equal to 50 states of USA but bigger in size and resources than USA; can not be united under a single Caliphate under a common Constitution as described in the Holy Quran and which is our part of faith too. Due to division of so many states some of the Islamic States do not have their own people to accept Zakat (charity) and other Gifts and some of the Islamic States got very few people who are able to pay Zakat to poor people thus creating a obstacle to establish exploited free society and with a sound and strong economy.

In the past there was no period without a Caliphate stronger or weaker like our present one when we abolished our Caliphate System but Islamic Caliphate was never abolished the way we abolished even there was a time when there were three Caliphate, one in Baghdad under Abased, one in Egypt under Great Fatimyt, and one in Spain under Ummayad and origin of those three sect who were all direct descendent Prophet Ismael and Prophet Ibrahim (A. S.), whose ancestor came from Holy Mecca and Holy Medina after last Prophet of Islam introduced last part of Islam according to The Holy Quran and his Sunna, originated from present day Hejaj/Holy Mecca and now Holy Medina now part of Saudi Arabia which proof that in Islam there is no place of regionalism or present day fake nation State, which is the creation of western countries for their control over all Muslim countries. Since 1924 no Muslim Leader from Morocco to Indonesia raise the re-establishment of 1300 year old **lost Caliphate or for the election of a Caliph** through election as first 4 truthful Caliphs were elected 1400 years ago in any forum, even not in meeting of Organization of so called Islamic Conference(OIC). Even most of do not know the following as mentioned in page 706 of Pandit Nehru's Glimpses of World History which are as follows:

A joint letter was sent to Kemal Pasha from London by the Aga Khan and an Indian ex-Judge, Ameer Ali. They claimed to speak on behalf of the millions of Indian Muslims, and they protested against the treatment given to the Caliph, and requested that his dignity should be respected and better treatment given. They sent a copy of the letter to some Istanbul papers, and it was actually published there before the original reached Angora(Ankara). There was nothing offensive in the letter, but Kemal Pasha seized hold of it and raised a tremendous outcry. He had got his chance at last, and he wanted to make the most of it. So it was announced that all this was another English intrigue to divide the Turks. The Aga Khan, it was said, was the special agent of the English; he lived in England, was chiefly interested in English horse-racing, and was always hobnobbing with English politicians. He was not even an orthodox Muslim, as he was the head of a special sect. It was further pointed out that during the World War the English had used him as a kind of counterpoise to the Sultan-Caliph in the East, and had increased his prestige by propaganda and otherwise and tried to make him the leader of the Indian Muslims, so that they might be kept in hand. If the Aga Khan was so solicitous about the Caliph, why had he not supported the Caliph in war time when a jihad or holy war had been declared against the English? He had sided with the English then and against the Caliph. In this way Kemal Pasha created quite a little tempest over the joint letter which its authors, all unaware of its consequences, had sent from London, and he made the Aga Khan appear in a far from favorable light. The poor Istanbul editors who had printed the letter were dubbed traitors and agents of England, and even were punished severely.
A short while before, India had been greatly agitated over the Caliphate when this was threatened by the British after the war. "Khilafat Committees" sprang up all over the country, and large numbers of Hindus joined the Muslims in this agitation, feeling that the British Government was doing an injury to Islam. Now the Turks (and Muslim) themselves had deliberately ended the Caliphate; Islam stood without a Caliph. Kemal Pasha was firmly of opinion that Turkey must have no religious entanglements with the Arabic countries or with India. He wanted no leadership of Islam for his country or for himself. He ha refused to become Caliph himself when asked to do so by some people from India and Egypt.

You can understand my motive from the Heading itself. My idea is if USA can be one strong nation/state with 55 different States and even in any single state there is no particular nation, race or culture. In each state of USA different people with different culture, race and even religion are united and 50 such different States created a State, a State with freedom, democracy, human dignity, human right equal Law for each citizen which is called United States of America.

So why we only 43 to 47 Islamic States less than 50 states of USA can not be united under a single Khelafat under a common Constitution as per our Holy Quran and which is our part of faith too.

Though at present we can not do that for various reasons at least we can start with a Confederation of Islamic States with Defense, Foreign policy, Finance and Science and Technology with the center. Through Defense planning, we can create a vast army with several million Muslims, a strong Air Force, navy through which we can mobilize our forces quickly any where in the world where we will face a situation like Maldives or Iran-Iraq war, we can defend ourselves without any fear or favor from any quarter or power Big or Small.

The Holy Quran is not for only Muslims but for all mankind and such during our glorious period various country and nation was benefited by the universal System of Islam. A modern poet of Spain says "their glorious periods was that of Islamic period and so is for India, India was divided into so many small states except some period and it is Muslim who first conquered Sind with the same pretext as India sent its Armed forces to Srilanka and Maldives and one should appreciate that Indian Armed forces maintained peace in Maldives. But why we can not develop such a Force which defend us and as well maintain world peace like UN forces around the world and if necessary with help from other nations for world peace and maintaining our glorious dignity without surrendering our interest and prestige.

And our Holy Prophet Muhammad (may peace be upon him) told during his Last Hajj Address from the top of the Jabal ul-Arafat (7th March, 632) " Ye people! Listen to my words and understand the same. Know that all Muslims are brothers unto one another. Ye are one brotherhood. Nothing which belongs to another is lawful unto his brother, unless freely given out of good-will. Guard yourselves from committing injustice."
"Neither any Arab is superior to any Non-Arab nor any Non-Arab is superior to any Arab; (Similarly) neither any black man is preferable to any white man nor a white man is preferable to any black man, and of course the only standard for ones superiority and noble-ness is God fearing."
"Let him that is present tell it unto him that is absent. Haply he that shall be told may remember better than he who hath heard it."

And indeed the first Democratic country with freedom and equal justice was established 1400 years ago by our Holy Prophet (peace be upon him). The great American people have been fulfilling the above wishes of their great President by upholding his wishes and the wishes of their dead people who fought and united North and South into one great Nation.

What did the Muslims do to honor our great prophet (may peace be upon him)? We divided the Caliphate and the greatest Democratic nation, first in world History founded by the greatest and the last Prophet of Islam our Holy Prophet (may Peace be upon him), into north and south, into east and west giving birth to 47 Muslim states. Even the land which constituted during Caliphate Rashedin is now divided into 12 15 states. Thus we did not act according to the last wishes of our holy Prophet (may peace be upon Him) which He declared during his last Hajj Address from the top of the Jabal ul-Arafat (7th March, 632); which was mentioned earlier in this preface.
But we forgot the teaching of our Holy Prophet (may peace be upon him). We for got the sacrifices made by Hazrat Imam Hussain (Allah be pleased with him) and other members of Ahle Bayet (Allah be pleased with them) and other great Sahabis (Allah be pleased with them) who made supreme sacrifice to uphold the principles and tenets of Islam for freedom, democracy for equal Law and overall Islamic principles.

Now how can we honor them? We can only honor them by upholding their great ideology of original Islam preached and established by our Great Prophet (peace be upon Him) and followed by 4 great Caliphs during the period of Caliphate Rasheda (truthful Caliphate).

The people of this world want to live together in peace and harmony as members of a single family. Towards the attainment of that goal, the United Nations and other regional bodies like NATO, EEC WARSAW, Common Wealth Countries and big states like USA, USSR, China, India have been established.

But we the Muslims are separated into so many pieces since 1924 when Caliphate was formally abolished after a long conspiracy.

Though we have some relation under the banner of Organization of Islamic Conference (OIC) we are unable to take any firm action in the fields of economy, politics or defense.

But recent events in Communist countries like Eastern Europe and even USSR itself prove that only one political system namely Freedom and Democracy under a kind of Capitalist system may survive.

And if we go back to past history of Mankind we will find there was no chance of freedom or democracy and there was various kind of dictatorship either military or hereditary Kingship with only exception of the period when last Prophet of Islam Hazrat Muhammad (may Peace be upon him) came in this world 1400 years ago. He even had to leave his birth place Holy Mecca and the people of Holy Medina gladly accepted him where he established First democratic country in the world History with the support of it's majority people. Though the majority people of the Holy Mecca made conspiracy against him ultimately the Truth won against the all evil, but he took no revenge and instead he pardoned the people of Holy Mecca, his nation The Nation of God spread around the world within very short time to Asia, Africa and even to Europe, during his life time his Companions were sent around the world to preach Islam the religion Of Peace which started from original father Prophet Adam (may peace be upon him). Even when the spirit of the great Prophet (may peace be upon him) took flight to the "blessed companionship on high" he left a Democratic process and a Law from God for which first 4 Caliphs (Leader of the Muslim State) or God's Repre-sentative in this world were elected by an Electorate of leaders of all sects/tribes and as such his son-in-law Hazart Ali (Allah be pleased with him) became the fourth to become the Caliph that is also at a very critical time of Islamic history. But Hazrat Ali (Allah be pleased with him) was shortly after assassinated whilst engaged in prayer in a mosque at Kufa. Even Hazrat Imam Hassan (Allah be pleased with him) eldest son of Ali (Allah be pleased with him) was poisoned though he made peace with Muawiyah with the condition that after Muawiyah dies The Caliphate be handed over to elected one and real Leader but Muawiyah did not fulfil that condition instead he nominated the Caliphate to his son Yazid and in this process Hazrat Imam Hussain (Allah be pleased with him) second grandson of Holy Prophet (may peace be upon him) and second son of Hazrat Ali (Allah be pleased with him) did not take the oath to yazid as it was against the principal of Democratize process which was maintained until now. So Hazrat Imam Hussain (Allah be pleased with him) with most of his family members had to accept martyrdom before a dictator and a force of evil and Hazrat Imam Hussain (Allah be pleased with him) became the first in this world who gave His life and life of his dear ones for the Democracy and divine Law and equal justice for all which we
nowadays talk most around this world and that of freedom, the freedom limited with certain limit which was prescribed in the Holy Quran by Almighty God, and also Sunna (whatever our Prophet (may peace be upon him) as messenger of God told was law) not a kind of freedom which violate ones' moral, ones' individual right or abuse a great man.

In the present day world where all the countries are dependent on each other and are willing to cooperate with each other we the Muslims can reestablish a exploitation free society and real Islamic System as per teaching of Holy Quran and our Holy Prophet (may peace be upon him).

Present day Information or Computer System can help to detect the reason of setback of Muslim World and point out various remedy through various research with the help of Computer.

Many a time, Abu Huraira (Allah be pleased with him) reports, had the Prophet (may Peace be upon him) to go without a meal. Dates and water frequently formed his only nourishment. Often, for months together, no fire could be lighted in his house from scantiness of means. God, say the Moslem historians, had indeed put before him the key to the treasures of this world, but he refused it!

How much property was left by our Holy Prophet (peace be upon him) who was also the first Head of a Islamic State. Our Holy Prophet (may peace be upon him) used to say "poverty is his proud". So we the Muslims also should be proud to be poor if we want to be companion of our Holy Prophet (may peace be upon him) in the next world.
We claim to be Muslim, but in fact we are not the follower of true Islam as we forgot the life style of our dearest Prophet (sm), his descendent, and his true and truthful companions. I am quoting followings from a book, Hadrat Umar Faruq' by Prof. Masud-Ul-Hasan.(pg. 231):

It is related that once while riding a camel the whip of Hadrat dropped. Many persons who saw the whip fall rushed to pick up the whip to hand it over to the Caliph. Hadrat Umar asked them to mind their own business and not to bother about his whip. Hadrat Umar dismounted and picked up his whip himself. Iqbal has dramatized the episode in his classic poem 'The Secret of Self', Iqbal exherts 'Like Umar, come down from the camel',
               Beware of incurring obligations, beware.
From this episode, Iqbal deduces a code of conduct, the highlights whereof are:
Do not incur the obligation of any person
Do not deceive yourself by receiving benefit.
Once Hadrat Umar asked his daughter Hadrat Hafsa (R.A.), who was Prophet's wife that 'what was the least of food that the Holy Prophet took'. She said that The holy Prophet's food was simple barley bread, then again he asked what was the bedding that the Prophet used, she said 'it was a piece of thick cloth, she also that it was a pair of cloth of red color which the Holy Prophet wore on Friday prayer or when foreign envoy came to meet him.
Once Hadrat Umar sought the advice of Hadrat Ali (R. A.) as to the amount of the allowances he should accept, Hadrat Ali suggested that he should take as much amount as might moderately suffice for an average Arab neither too much, nor too little. Hadrat Umar accepted that suggestion.
Hadrat Umar wept when he saw vast riches that were brought after the defeat of Sasanide Iran.
Hadrat Umar sought the advice of companions as to what should be done with the Carpet who advice him to take it then he asked for the opinions of Hadrat Ali. Hadrat Ali said "What they say is right, but if you set this precedent to-day, to-morrow there will be those who will claim such trophy and deserving them. 'Ali' you are right, verily you have given sound advice. The carpet was cut into small average pieces and distributed to others.
Heraclius gave Wasiq huge money for the killing of Hadrat Umar. Wasiq came to Medina from Constantinople for the mission as he was also an Arab, when he came to Medina he posed as Muslim and he saw Caliph Hadrat Umar sleeping under a tree as a ordinary citizen and was alone, but when he was about t kill Hadrat Umar his sword fall when Hadrat umar looked at him, Wasiq fell at the feet of the Caliph. Caliph Umar forgave him and he embraced Islam.

Reasons of Economic backwardness of Muslims also abolition of Caliphate and creation of so many Muslim nation State

We are quoting the following paragraphs from "REALMS OF PEACE" by Dr. Sheikh Mohammad Iqbal, published by IDARAH-I ADABIYAT-I, 2009, Qasimjan Street, Delhi-6 (India), pp. 214-216, 218-219, to prove that how a new type slavery of certain Arab Leaders did not serve any true economic development of Islamic and poor third world countries but those countries who installed them in power through various agreement which ultimately abolished the Caliphate in 1924. Instead poor countries had to pay million of dollar as extra money to import oil. Those poor countries could be benefited if those oil producing countries could come to invest their money their own country and some to the poor countries, instead of depositing their surplus oil money in the western developed countries. And with those surplus oil money deposited in the western Bank, the west earned more money which compensated them more then they use to spend for increase price of the oil. Thus price of food and the manufactured goods were increased, which the poor countries are bound to purchase for their minimum need along with extra money of increased oil price. Thus richer became richest in the developed world, the poorer became poorest in under developing countries. So if there was any Caliphate with vast land of the Middle East with their vast oil money the economy condition of poor countries could be better then what is now.

The West has completely failed in satisfying the oil exporters. They do nothing towards improving the situation. Again, it is the Arab States and not the developed consumer countries that "are taking the lead in stabilizing prices by the same means of relating the cost of petroleum to that of their imports from the West". The Emirates' representative at the United Nations was justified when he told the General Assembly that the price of the oil and the articles imported by the producers of oil should be taken together. He had stated: "It is not logical to deal with the price of oil in isolation from the price of manufactured goods and other commodities.[246] ....

The other problem is that the revenues from oil grow at a speed with which the exporters' capability to spend cannot keep pace. These are, however, simultaneously and increasingly being invested in major industrial projects in the Gulf, in the Arab world as a whole, and in the developing countries of Asia and Africa. But even then the money situation is still uncontrollable. The device of depositing it with the Western banks was once intensively used. But that too has been making the condition insecure. Entrusting of the surplus of Arab wealth to sterling has already proved adverse in effect. The devaluation of sterling was each time arbitrary. Massive sums were transferred to the domain of dollar but it also proved hazardous.[247] It is therefore evident that there is no use of depositing the wealth with the

---

[246] The representative at the time was Ahmad Khalifa Al-Suwaidi.

[247] Tomkinsons M., n. 1, p. 85. The exchange reserves of the Arab oil exporters including UAE are said to be immense. The foreign currency holdings of Saudi Arabia and Kuwait were $4000 and 3000 million respectively. The Arab Leage authorities predicted that by 1980, the total revenue of all Arab products would reach $100 billion. And according to an estimate of U.S. State Department "Arab holdings will equalise more than fifty per cent of the world's reserve" by the middle of 1980s.

Western banks. The reason is that the Arabs get no important benefit from the money kept in those banks. The Arab economists have surprised the world by revealing "that the $3000 million invested in the Middle East by the oil companies bring them an annual return of between 65 per cent and 114 per cent, while the Arab deposits in the West of some $10,000 million earn an average six per cent". Hence the suggestion that oil should be left unexploited for some years. This will give Western economics twice fatal blow: "the loss of petrol, their industrial life-blood, and the loss of Arab investment funds on which they are coming to spend.[248] It is really unfortunate that both the sterling and the dollar should, time again, be losing their value while the Arab depositors should be put to great loss. ... It has been sometimes felt that a few consumer countries, which are advanced industrially are attempting to create a wedge between OPEC members. This would be possible if the internal conflicts of the oil exporters were having their roots. At the meetings of the OPEC at various places, it has been seen, that good sense prevails usually. It has been stated that in spite of the differences in their economic and constitutional patterns, the members share four major objectives while framing their policies. These are:

1. Assuring stability of supply of oil and its products to the world market;

2. Setting crude oil export prices at a level fair to both producers and   consumers, based on its real economic value;

3. Using the proceeds from oil exports to develop and diversify their   economic resources; and,

4. Sharing their wealth with other countries in the region and the developing   countries in general by extending assistance in the form of grants,   concessaionry loans, and balance of payments support.[249]

Following the decision of the OPEC regarding freezing of petroleum prices, Dr. Manna Saeed Al-Utaiba, the Emirates Petroleum Minister spoke on February 6, 1978, at a television interview about the responsibilities of the organization.

It is no more a secret that petroleum is not an absolute commodity and can be compared to a two-faced coin: one economic and the other political. Therefore OPEC should practice their role with the utmost degree of awareness and alert as inspired by their important responsibilities towards Third World countries, and have their resolutions entirely based on consultation and co-ordination in the light of the current international circumstances and development. The OPEC has always proved that it is aware of its role in being careful not to harm world economy. The industrialized countries, on their part, should take necessary measures to improve international finance.

Fighting international stagnation and economic depression and coming out to a stage of development require concerted efforts and co-operation among the petroleum producing countries and the Third World States.[250]

Alfred Marshall's final version of 1920 (reprinted many times since then) provides his evolved definition of economics in these words: "Political Economy or economics is a study of mankind in the ordinary business of life; it examines that part of individual and social action which is most closely connected with the attainment and with the use of the material requisite of well being.

---

[248] Ibid, p. 85.

[249] The Arab News, New Delhi, Dec. 1976 p. 34.

[250] Emirate News, February 7, 1978.

I am also quoting an eminent Economist, Prof. Raihan Sharif, from his book
'Islamic Economics: Principles and Applications', some of which are as follows:

Points of Economic Philosophy

(1) "But seek, with the (wealth)
     Which God has bestowed on thee
     The Home of the Hereafter,
     Not forget the portion in this
     World : but do thou good
     As God has been good
     To thee, and seek not,
     Mischief in the land.
          (Sura Qisas: 77)

(2)   "Eat of the good
          Things We have provided
          For your sustenance but
          Commit no excess therein,
          Lest My wrath should justly
          Descend on you."
               (Sura Taha : 81)

(3)   "Verily the Lord doth provide
          Sustenance in abundance
          For whom He pleaseth, and He
          Provideth in a just measure.
          For He doth know
          And regard all His servants."
               (Sura Bani Israel : 30)

(4)   "And those in whose wealth
          There is a recognized right
          For the needy who ask
          And the destitute."
               (Sura Marej : 25)

(I) "Not person believes till I am dearer to him than the members of his household, his
wealth and the whole of mankind."
(Muslim : 70)

(ii) "None amongst you believes (truly) till one likes for his brother or for his neighbor that
which he loves for himself" (Muslim : 72)

(iii) "I swear by god that it is not poverty I fear for you but I fear that worldly goods may be
given to you lavishly as they were (given) to your predecessors that you may vie with one
another in desiring them as they did, and that they may destroy you as they destroyed
them." (Bukhari and Muslim : Mishkat, p 1072)

(iv)"Rivalry has engrossed you, and son of Adam says, My property, my property.' Have
you son of Adam, anything but what you eat and use up, or wear and make it threadbare, or
give assadaqa and make perpetual ?" (Muslim; Mishkat, p. 1073)

306

(5)"Economics, studied in complete abstraction from all human values, would be an insubstantial discipline, for economics is pivotally concerned with values. And even though an economist restricts himself to the values of market place as distinguished from the more fundamental ethical values of the philosopher, these values of the market place usually reflect these more fundamental values, inspite of frequent cases where the market values stand conspicuously at odds with ethical values... Whether he consciously admits it or not, the economist who goes for towards using his discipline as a means of recommendations, or who even steps beyond the stage of abstract logical structures in a vacuum, must develop some scheme of ultimate values as a criterion for his judgements."

From that point of view, it is necessary to provide a more socially desirable definition of economics as a discipline of social science. In 1890 , Alfred Marshall, the distinguished neoclassicist, provided a good basis of defining the nature of economics and the task of the economist, in the following words:

Again what happened in Somalia with the population of 100% Muslim, western neighbor of oil rich Saudi Arabia, and also of Yemen, Jordan and southern neighbor of Sudan and Egypt. But those Muslim countries closed their eyes and did nothing to feed those neighboring hungry and dying Muslims of Somalia. Result was President Bush had to come with food to feed those Muslims, with 20,000 army and in person what should have been done by an Ameer-ul-Muminin, (leader of the Muslims), if there was a Caliphate, at least for the Somalian Muslims, at least for the Orphanage Muslim children where he personally visited during his last month of office as USA President, where as, neighboring leaders of the Muslims of the Holy Land ignored them, ignored the hungry and dyeing Muslims of a land, or surrounding land, which is known to almost all Muslims of the world as Abyssinia, where Muslims went for asylum during life time of the last Prophet of Islam(Sm) and when the ruler of Abyssinia was a Christian. This is the face of modern so called leaders of the Muslim worlds. Where as some of those Muslim leaders are spoiling billions of Dollar in western countries, even in Spain where all the Muslims 500 years ago, numbering 40,000,00 were killed after the fall of the Islamic rule there. Following reference is enough proof of their anti-Islamic activities, which was published in almost all the Newspapers:

With the Arab-backed Bank of Credit and Commerce International (BCCI) still awaiting a decent burial through a satisfactory settlement with thousands of depositors in different parts of the world, the Gulf region has been hit by another financial scandal. Although somewhat localized, its implications may well produce echoes right through the global monetary world, especially in the Middle East and parts of Europe.

   The scandal centers on the collapse of Kuwait's investments in **Spain resulting in the loss of more than $4 billion in public funds through alleged mismanagement, downright cheating and lack of accountability. An opposition newspaper in Kuwait, Al-Qabas has just termed the loss as 'The Theft of the Century" in a banner headline on the report.**

 It relates to the move made by Grupo Torras, the Spanish unit of the London-based Kuwait investment Office (KIO), filing for receivership to stop further losses. Since KIO is very much the financial arm of the Government of Kuwait, which manages worldwide investment portfolio for the country, the crisis in the Spanish operation raises several questions, which can be - indeed, must be - answered through a high-level Enquirer into the whole episode.

One such question refers to what is described as "undue secrecy" surrounding all investments by KIO which keeps the authorities concerned, not to mention the media, the parliament and the public at large, very much in the dark on how the funds are being managed. Being an investment company rather than a bank, KIO probably remains outside the purview of Kuwait's central banking control mechanism.

In this contest, one must note, with regret, that this cash-rich region of Middle East and the Gulf has failed to create its own financial center to take the place of conflict-ridden Beirut, which can be compared to either Hong Kong or Singapore. Similarly, it has also failed to set up a bank of international standard, with a global network of its own, which can operate alongside ten top western or Japanese institutions. This meant since the mid-seventies when the countries of the region started earning enormous revenue from their export of oil, they placed their massive deposits with European and US banks, thus helping these western financial institutions to reap maximum benefit out of the oil boom. Much of these deposits were invested in Europe and the United States to reduce the adverse effect of the staggering rise in oil prices. If it goes to the credit of BCCI for seeing the need of recycling part of the deposit back to countries in the Third World, it is a shame that this UAE-backed institution bungled its way into a collapse.

The collapse of BCCI leaves a vacuum, which is unlikely to be filled in the near future. Meanwhile, the scandal that has now hit KIO creates new doubts about any of the existing financial institutions in the Gulf region, including this once-respected Kuwait organization, earning public confidence and credibility at home and abroad. In this respect, even such a well-known institution as the Islamic Development Bank (IDB) is yet to make much impact on Muslim countries in Asia and Africa.

It is high time that the Gulf region undertook a careful review of its financial scene, with particular reference to the role played by its banks, investment companies and credit organizations. Such a review should focus on the level of management expertise available to these institutions, the accountability which is practiced by the heads of these bodies and last not the least, on the monitoring role played by central banks in different Gulf countries. The crisis in KIO provides a signal that such a review is long overdue if the Gulf region is to enter the next century with better control than it has shown in recent past over its own financial fortunes, with a role to play throughout the developing world.

Again what about the BCCI? The answer is This was only one International Bank, founded by yet another Muslim, a Muslim from United Province, India, where the Babri mosque existed during last five hundreds years and recently converted into a Hindu Temple, where again the history of Spain was repeated, the founder of the BCCI was Mr. Saleh Naqvi, an Indian Muslim, but for it's destruction many Muslims from U. A. E. whose ruler was the main financier, from Saudi Arabia and from Pakistan.

2.   Approach to Social Philosophy and Economics.

        Islamic thinkers along with building the relevant different civilization itself pursued Establishment of 'Synthesized knowledge'. That would not have been possible without developing a master model of social philosophy to contain all that vital structural elements of
Social equilibrium withstanding the effects of time.

This was the model emerging out of the process of systematic recording of the Quran and Hadith literature (including the process of testing the genuineness of each Hadith) organized by the Holy Prophet and his first four Caliphs (Khulafa-e-Rashedin),

Muslim philosophers and scientists had this unique advantage. They could conduct inquiry and research within the constraints and parameters already identified in view of social and human objectives. They could easily know the nature and dimension of the constants for building up the structures of knowledge and also guide their application as techniques, strategies and institutions.

The Quran is intended to guide man and society, not to teach natural sciences, or history or philosophy (as is understood by the modern man with sophisticated western knowledge). The basic ideas and principles relating to all such sciences and philosophies are, indeed, recorded now as revealed knowledge as a complete code of individual and social life for mankind free past. But life itself was the laboratory of testing the ideas and principles; and that unique testing was done by the Prophet of Allah (sm.). Within the community organized by him.

That is why the Quran and Sunnah constitute the master system of knowledge, and systematization of it took quite a long time. Muslim scientists end philosophers undertook Relevant to the master system, search, research and development of knowledge with the rationality of approach surprising the modern West.

Western writers of history found that Islamic religion did have "far less cramping effects on human thought than that of Christianity". Particularly, with the advent of the Abbasids, the assimilated and developed a tremendous wealth of knowledge. The liberated the traditional learning and science of Persian culture. Baghdad and Lundishapur were the centers of research and learning where translation of the main Greek works of science was under with financial support from Caliphs and notables.

So under Islamic economy no Muslim or region can hold unlimited wealth and it should be distributed through one Islamic State of Caliphate. If we close our eyes and imagine we are blind we can feel how much helpless we are. So we should help the helpless the needy even though we are to share, sacrifice our individual wealth.

Muslim economics is based on trust and on giving out. It is dynamic and free flowing. There is no need
for Keynesian control techniques. Kaffir or Dajjal or antichrist economics is based on exploitation
of others and retention. It is static and stagnant. It stinks. Given the dynamic nature of Muslim economics,
It comes as no surprise to learn that the value of money, in the time of the first Muslim community
of Medina al Munawara, was based not on how much gold or silver it could buy, but on how much
grain it could buy.[251]

Manama, Dec 14: Saudi Arabia's largest bank, National Commercial Bank, is reacting bitterly to a lawsuit by accounting firm Touche Ross accusing the bank of fraud and racketeering over the failed Bank of Credit and Commerce International, reports AP. The NCB, in abatement faxed to the Associated Press on Sunday, says it will countersue over the "cheap allegations."

In Washington on Wednesday, Touche Ross filled a lawsuit on behalf of creditors of BCCI seeing 10.5 billion dollar from NCB and its former chief operating officer, Khaled bin Mahfouz.
NCB, however, distinguishes between the private holdings of Mahfouz, whose family owns most of NCB, and the BCCI, of which Mahfouz was a director.

---

[251] page 113 Dajjal by Ahmad Thomson

CONCLUSION *AND NEED OF THE HOUR FOR THE TRUE FOLLOWERS OF ISLAM AROUND THIS WORLD*

What happened in Ayodha on Dec 6, 1992; the root is lack of a Unified
Caliphate and a elected Caliph; because the followers of all
religions are united, the Hindus in India numbering around 800
millions with around more than 20 languages are united with a
single language 'Hindi' as it's State language, the United
States, Britain, Canada, Australia and other countries are united
with the only language 'English' who are the dominating force in
this world, whose majority people are Christian, even the European are
going to be united with around 10 major languages under the
banner of Maastrict (now European Union) for which referendum was held in whole of
Europe, and European Christians are cleansing the Muslims in Muslim
Majority Bosnia, here though Serbs have taken the responsibilities of this cleansing of
Muslims, the other countries of Christian Europe are silent, the Jews are united and as such
there is no problem for the Jews to go to Israel, and they may be Russians or French or with
any race to go to their
holy land Israel and to see their united interest around the world.
So the followers of all religions, are united, and whatever they use to say i.e. just for the
sake of saying. They use to plan everything for their next
generation and that is why before his death perhaps long before
his death as late of the eighteenth century Lord Chesterfield observed in a letter to his son"
'There is one part of political knowledge which is only to be had by inquiry and
conversation; that is, the present state of every
power in Europe with regard to the three important points of
strength, revenue and commerce, the collaborative efforts of the
European states, in the Eastern sections of the continent, did
bear fruit in one highly consequential way, in procuring the
defeat of the last great threat of an external imperial formation
of a traditional type- the Ottoman Empire'. Thus the repulsion of
the Turks at the gates of Vienna in the late seventeenth century
was an event perhaps as important to the late ascendancy of the
West as - if Edward Meyer and Weber are right- the Greek victory
at the Marathon was a millennium and a half earlier. And again
thus with the progressive retreat of the Turks, 'the 'Eastern
question' began to be posed in something like a recognizably
modern form, (Ref from THE NATION-STATE AND VIOLENCE BY ANTHONY
GIDDENS PG. 88), and to fulfill the above direction and to abolish the unity of Muslims
and Caliphate as in Nehru's language which he has mentioned in
page 632 of GLIMPSES OF WORLD HISTORY' 'Britain attacked Turkey
in many weak places of her ramshackle empire: in Iraq and, later
in Palestine and Syria. In Arabia the national sentiment of the
Arabs was taken advantage of by the British, and an Arab revolt
against Turkey organized with the help of liberal bribes of money
and material. Colonel T. E. Lawrence, a British agent in Arabia
was largely responsible for this revolt, and later he developed a
reputation as a man of mystery, acting behind the scenes of many
movements in Asia. Jawaharlal Nehru also mentioned in the same
book in pg. 769-770, 'During the World War Arabia became a hotbed
of British intrigue, and British and India money (the India was
taken from Muslim rulers)was lavishly spent in subsidizing and
bribing the various Arab chiefs. All manner of promises were made

to them, and they were encouraged to revolt against Turkey.
Sometimes two rival chiefs, who were fighting each other, were
both receiving British subsidies! The British succeeded in
getting the Sherif Hussein of Mecca to raise Arab standards of
revolt. ... Hussein was promised by the British the kingdom of a
united Arabia. Ibn Saud was clever. He got himself recognized as
an independent sovereign by the British. accepted a tidy little
sum of & 5000 (Pound) per month from them, and promised to remain neutral. So, while
others were fighting, he consolidated his position and strengthened it to some extent with
the help of British gold. The Sherif Hussain
was becoming unpopular in Islamic countries, including India,
because of his rebellion against the Sultan of Turkey, who was
also then the Caliph. ..... The end of the war found England
dominating Arabia and trying to use both Hussein and Ibn Saud as
tools.' And yet in another recent book 'THE SECRET HISTORY OF
SADDAM'S WAR UNHOLY BABYLON BY ADEL DARWISH AND GREGORY
ALEXANDER' published by Victor Gollancz Ltd, London, it is
mentioned in pg. 3-4 that 'Britain had recognized Kuwait's
independence on 19th June 1961, abrogating an agreement signed in
1899 which had made the emirate a British protectorate-..... the
1899 Anglo-Kuwait agreement signed by the former Sheikh of Kuwait
for 15,000 Indian rupees from the British commissioner in
Abadan.., in pg. 6 it is mentioned 'Britain proceeded to
establish posts and naval bases along the trade route to India
via the Suez Canal, which was opened in 1866, and also signed
exclusive agreements with Arab rulers throughout the Gulf. The
first was with Bahrain in 1880, prohibiting the sheikdom from
making any treaties or agreements with any state other than
Britain or establishing diplomatic relations with other countries
without British consent. In the comment of the same book it is
mentioned 'The authors, who were researching the book before the
invasion(of Kuwait), demonstrate that the events of 2nd August
1990 were the logical conclusion to twenty years of diplomatic
duplicity, intelligence bungling, greed and corruption,
particularly on the part of Britain, the US, France and Germany.
The pursuit of short-sighted and relentlessly self-interested
foreign policies led them to arm (Saddam) Hussein with a
terrifying arsenal capable of mass destruction while overlooking
his deplorable record on human rights and the legitimate
interests of other states in the area. But who created those other
states in place of a united Caliphate, the reply in the same book
in pg. 7-8, it is mentioned that 'On the eve of the First World
War, Britain was conspiring to use the warlike Bedouin to protect
its interest in the Middle East, either under the leadership of
their sheikhs or under British officers - such as T. E. Lawrence
- rather than deploying its own soldiers in the desert. To secure
the support of Mubarak, Britain agreed to recognize Kuwait as
independent of the Ottoman Empire. In exchange, Mubarak was to
support Britain against Turkey in the coming war..... Cox had
arrived in what was to become Iraq in October 1920, replacing as
High Commissioner Sir Arnold Wilson, who had wanted to set up a
British protectorate. Wilson's plan had been ill-received in the
newly founded country, already in turmoil since General Maude had
captured Baghdad from the Turks in March 1917 at a cost to the

British of two and a half years of bitter fighting and 98, 000
casualties. Maude proceeded to put into effect the secret Sykes-
Picot agreement, drawn up in 1916 between Britain and France, in
which the two powers shared out the spoils of their coming
victory over Ottoman Empire (Still a united Caliphate).
Mesopotamia, comprising the two former Ottoman velayets
(provinces) of Basra and Baghdad, was given to Britain. The
northern velayet of Mosul was initially given to France, but was
the subject of a dispute which was settled in Britain's favor in
1919.

In short the so called most leaders of the Muslim Umma are
now divided into around 55 countries in this world, are responsible for the insult, for the
mass killing of Muslims, sometimes by fellow Muslims and always by non-Muslim, are
those Muslims whose descendent are still holding power in the part of the Muslims world
which was part of a unified
Caliphate, who with the bribe from Britain and some western power
abolished the Caliphate just to uphold the political and Monetary
interest of the Britain and other western World and to grab power. But almost all the
Muslims of the world will say 'no' to the Organization of Islamic Conference, 'no' to all the
leaders whose ancestors took money and even Indian money to defeat the Caliph, at that
period based in Turkey and thus weakened Muslim interest around the world, we have no
need like those general, who are guarding their ruler, not any Islamic interest, but we need
general like 'Okaba', who in Nehru's language in pg. 146, Glimpses of World History,
which describe 'In the west they marched on and on. It is said that their general
Okba went right across northern Africa till he reached the
Atlantic Ocean, on the western coast of what is now known as
Morocco. He was rather disappointed at this obstacle, and he rode
as far as he could into the sea and then expressed his sorrow to
the Almighty that there was no more land in that direction for
him to conquer in His name!' From Morocco and Africa, the Arabs
crossed the narrow sea into Spain and Europe- the Pillars of
Hercules, as these narrow straits were called by the old Greeks.
The Arab general who crossed into Europe landed at Gibraltar, and
this name itself is a reminder of him. His name was Tariq,
Gibraltar is really Jabal-ut-Tariq, the rock of Tariq. Spain was
conquered rapidly, and the Arabs then poured into southern
France. So, in about 1000 years from the death of Muhammad (Sm.),
the Arab Empire spread from the south of France and Spain right
across northern Africa to Suez, and across northern Africa to
Suez, and across Arabia and Persia and Central Asia to the
borders of Mongolia. India was out of it except for Sindh. Europe
was being attacked by the Arabs from two sides-directly at
Constantinople, and in France, via Africa. .... Nehru
mentioned in the same book in page 116 that ' It took some time
for Christianity to reach China. But Islam came more swiftly. It
came, indeed, a few years before the Nestorians and during the
lifetime of its Prophet(Sm). The Chinese Emperor received both
the embassies-Islamic and Nestorian-with courtesy and listened to
what they had to say. He appreciated their views and showed
favor impartially. The Arabs were permitted to build a mosque in
Canton. This mosque still exists, although it is 1300 years old,
and is one of the oldest mosque in the world, in page 149 of the
same book he has mentioned that 'The Arabs, especially at the

beginning of their awakening, were full of enthusiasm for their faith. Yet they were a tolerant people and there are numerous instances of this toleration in religion. In Jerusalem the Khalifa Omar made a point of it. In Spain there was a large Christian population which had the fullest liberty of conscience. In India the Arabs never ruled except in Sindh, but there were frequent contacts, and the relations were friendly. Indeed, the most noticeable thing about this period of history is the contrast between the toleration of the Muslim Arab and the intolerance of the Christian in Europe. Nehru also mentioned in pg. 233 that 'The coming of the Muslims to India as invaders introduced an element of compulsion in religion. The fight was really political one between conqueror and conquered, but it was colored by the religious element, and there was, at times, religious persecution. But it would be wrong to imagine that Islam stood for such persecution. There is an interesting report of a speech delivered by a Spanish Muslim when he was driven out of Spain, together with the remaining Arabs, in 1610. He protested against the Inquisition and said: 'Did our victorious ancestors ever once attempt to extirpate Christianity out of Spain, when it was in their power? Did they not suffer your forefathers to enjoy the free use of their rites at the same time as they wore their chains?... If there may have been some examples of forced conversions, they are so rare as scarce to deserve mentioning, and only attempted by men who had not the fear of God and the Prophet (Sm) before their eyes, and who in doing so, have acted directly and diametrically contrary to the holy precepts and ordinances of Islam, which cannot, without sacrilege, be violated by any who would be held worthy of the honorable epithet of Musalman (Muslims). ...... Nehru also mentioned in the same book in pg 150 on division of Muslims that "And Egypt did likewise, and indeed went so far to proclaim another Caliph. Egypt was near enough to be threatened and forced to submit, and this was done from time to time. But Africa was not interfered with, and as for Spain, it was much too far away for any action. So we see that the Arab Empire split up on the accession of the Abbasides. The Caliph was no longer the head of the whole Muslim world, he is not now the Commander of all the Faithful. Islam was no longer united, and the Arabs in Spain and the Abbasides disliked each other so much that each often welcomed the misfortunes of the other.

So at that time there were only three Caliph, 1. Abbaside in Baghdad, 2. Ummide in Spain and 3. Fatimide in Egypt, and now imagine there are around 55 so called Muslim States, and the root of all misfortunes of the Muslim around the world are the division among themselves, who instead of proclaiming Islam al over the world and over all religion they are working as agents of non-Muslims and are busy with the destruction of fellow Muslims in the name artificial race, languages and so on, thus those leaders are worse than Hajjaj Bin Yussuf, because of the following:

Nehru also mentioned in pg. 154 in the same book which are that 'The Arabs reached the borders of India soon enough, even while Harsha was alive. They stopped there for a while and then took

possession of Sindh. In 711 A. D. a young boy of seventeen,
Mohammad ibn Kasim, commanding an Arab army, conquered the Indus
valley up to Multan in western Panjab. This was the full extent
of the Arab conquest of India. Perhaps if they had tried hard
enough they might have gone farther. It should not have been
difficult as North India was weak. ...... Muslim Arabs came and
went and built mosques, and sometime preached their religion, and
sometimes even converted people. There seems to have been no
objection to this in those days, no trouble or friction between
Hinduism and Islam.'

Now the irony is that even Hajjaj Bin Yussuf sent Kasim to punish
the then Hindu ruler in Sind as he insulted few Muslims
and thus Sindh became the part of Islamic Caliphate, where as at
present so called Muslims who are holding power with so many
division are silent for every miseries of the Muslims in this
world and there is every doubt if they are at all Muslim, they
pretend to be Muslim but they are only agent of non-Muslims, thus when
70% land of the Muslim Bosnia have been acquired by Christian Serb, they gave more time
to take remaining 30% percent, which already started after
OIC gave one month more time to take action, but those leader were
quick to bring all the latest arms in that region, including a
million army just to save one single family of Kuwait, though they helped
Saddam with billions of Dollar to fund and to continue the long 8 eight
years war against Iran, though with those billion dollars of money
could be used to feed the Muslim of Somalia, for the hungry
people of the world, Muslims and non-Muslims, those so called Muslim Leaders are silent,
though 1400 years ago the poor Muslims went to the then Christian Abyssinia, now
Ethiopia and may be that the present Somalia was part of Abyssinia, but the Muslims of
Somalia could not come to Saudi Arabia or Egypt
or to any Muslim country, near or far; for food and shelter, though few in number went to
Yemen, few from Bosnia went to Malaysia, but not in abandon, if
all these country including Somalia was a part of one single
brotherhood or Caliphate then there was no need for Western help,
western food, western Army, and what happened in Bosnia and in India
could not happen, because there could be a general like Kasim
who conquered Sind when he came to punish the Hindu ruler in Sind, and the Muslim could
capture anyone in this world, from anywhere just like the USA took Noriaga from Panama.

And again in Nehru's language which he has mentioned in pg. 144-
145 of the Glimpses of World History 'Mohammad (Sm) died in 632
A. C., ten years after the Hijrat. He had succeeded in making a
nation out of many warring tribes of Arabia and in firing them
with enthusiasm for a cause. He was succeeded by Abu Bakr, ... as
Khalifa or Caliph or chief. This succession used to be by a kind
of informal election at a public meeting. Two years later Abu
Bakr died, and was succeeded by Omar, who was Khalifa for ten
years. Abu Bakr and Omar were great men who laid the foundation
of Arabian and Islamic greatness. As Khalifas they were both
religious heads and political chiefs- king and Pope in one. In
spite of their high position and the growing power of their
State, they stuck to the simplicity of their ways and refused to
countenance luxury and pomp. The Democracy of Islam was living
thing for them. But their own officers and emirs took to silks

314

and luxury soon enough, and many stories are told of Abu Bakr and Omar rebuking and punishing these officers, and even weeping at this extravagance. They felt that their strength lay in their simple and hard living, and that if they took to the luxury of the Persian or Constantinople Courts, the Arabs would be corrupted and would fall. Even in these short dozen years, during which Abu Bakr and Omar ruled, the Arabs defeated both the Eastern Roman Empire and the Sassanid King of Persia. Jerusalem, the holy city of the Jews and Christians, was occupied by the Arabs, and the whole of Syria and Iraq and Persia became part of the new Arabian Empire. .... Like the founders of some other religions, Mohammad (Sm) was a rebel against many of the existing social customs. The religion he preached, by its simplicity and directness and its flavor of Democracy and equality, appealed to the masses in the neighboring countries who had been ground down long enough by autocratic king and equally autocratic and domineering priests.... But it (Islam) did lessen this exploitation so far as the Muslims are concerned, and made them feel that they belonged to one great brotherhood. So the Arabs marched from conquest to conquest. Often enough they won without fighting. Within twenty-five years of the death of their Prophet (Sm), the Arabs conquered the whole of Persia and Syria and Armenia and a bit of Central Asia on the one side; and Egypt and a bit of northern Africa on the west.....The Arabs went on advancing both in the east and the west In the east, Herat and Kabul and Balkh fell, and they reached the Indus river and Sindh.

So to the non-Muslim leaders Islamic political system is Democratic and it gave this world a Democratic System, first in World history, the State which within 50 years became far greater than Greece and at that time there was no existence of modern Britain or the city like London though during last 100 years the so called leaders in Arabic world have been working as agent of Britain and protecting the interest of non-Muslim western States and guarding their own personal interest keeping the Muslims in darkness depriving the human right and democracy and resulting the humiliation of the Muslims around world. But again the leaders in previous history of Islam was not such, they were great and brave in Nehru's language in pg. 194 "Saladin was also a great fighter, and famous for his chivalry. Even the Crusaders who fought Saladin came to appreciate this chivalry of his. There is a story that once Richard was very ill and was suffering from the heat. Saladin, hearing of this arranged to send him fresh snow and ice from the mountains. Ice could not made artificially then by freezing water, as we do now. So natural snow and ice from the mountain had to be taken by swift messengers'. In pg 142 of the same book Nehru mentioned that 'It is strange that this Arab race, which for long ages had lived a sleepy existence, apparently cut off from what was happening elsewhere, should suddenly wake up and show such tremendous energy as to startle and upset the world. The story of the Arabs, and how they spread rapidly over Asia, Europe and Africa, and of the high culture and civilization which they developed, is one of the wonders of history.

So where is that wonder of history when India is Democratic who
by its democracy, and it is keeping united a nation of now around 1000
million, the majority are Hindus, though they claim to be
secular, Muslims can not get any job or minimum human right, and
the Muslims are becoming poorer to poorer day by day, lastly even
a historical mosque in the name of someone, whom the Indian historian
described a pious one, as once he prayed for the recovery of his
son Humayun from his illness and in exchange he prayed to Almighty to take his (Babar)
life; for such a person some Hindus like BJP claim that there
was a Hindu Temple, where Nehru mentioned in the same book that
Hazrat Omar (R. A.) even did not offer prayer in the Church of
Jerusalem as he thought that in future the Muslims may convert the Church into a mosque.

I have quoted authors of two books who are non-Muslims Late Nehru
and Mr. Adel Darwish and Mr Gregory Alexander, from whom we knew
how the so called Muslim leaders became agent of non-Muslim
Western world and worked to abolish Caliphate which was formally
abolished in 1924 by late Kamal Ataturk due to division into two,
Arabs and Turkey and then around 13 Arabs states and 55 Muslims
States. We also knew from Nehru that in initial history of Islam
there was democracy and there was no existence of present day
Western World. We also know how the non-Muslims in India, in USA
and in Europe they are united for all the major decisions they
need, but we the Muslims are, everywhere, divided and fighting
among ourselves and thus giving chance to serve the non-Muslim
interest.

So to overcome all these problems we the Muslims of the Islamic
world must elect a Caliph or Khalifa for the single Muslim
brotherhood, Khelafat on the model of United States of America
with the same type of election system, which elected the First Caliph
1400 years ago, and even Hazrat Abu Bakr (R. A.) did not take any
major decision until he got allegation of Yemeni Muslims and the
present around 55 States will remain as the 50 states of USA
without any further delay because in almost each day we see some misery of the Muslims in
this or that way throughout the world some of the recent are as follows:

Medina (Saudi Arabia), Dec., 21: King Fahd of Saudi Arabia has warned his country's
religious leaders against using their mosques to attack the government, the Saudi press
agency reported today, reports AFP.
 "The pulpits are reserved for very specific business and should not be exploited by some to
harm others," the King said Saturday in the western Holy City of Medina in a speech to
religious leaders.
 "Our doors are open to all those who wish to criticize", the government's policy, he says,
but added that he was surprised that clerics had resorted to cassettes and publications to
express their criticism.
 "Have we reached the point of being carried away by foreign influences alien to our
nation? He asked.
 The King urged his subjects to come and see the government and express their opinions
orally, or better still, in writing.

His warning came following a report December 13 in the British Sunday Times newspaper about a conflict between the rulers and religious institutions in Saudi Arabia.

The paper said the retirement of seven clerics, attributed to old age and failing health, was a result of the conflict.

Riyadh categorically dismissed the allegations and denied the existence of such a conflict. King Fahd on Saturday alluded to the newspaper article, saying "you have learned or read what is being said currently overseas about our country."

In October, a Saudi opposition source said in a confidential document made available to AFP in Paris that significant numbers of the Saudi religious hierarchy had called for major reforms.

The document called for a strong indictment of the country's political, economic and social conditions and recommended radical changes in various areas.

In September, the Saudi Council of Grand Ulema - the highest religious authority in the Kingdom - denied that its leader, Sheikh Abdel Aziz Ibn Baz, was involved in an appeal for reform addressed to King Fahd by Koranic teachers and students.

On March 1, King Fahd announced the creation of a 60 member consultative council of appointees - promised during the Gulf crisis - but only its president has been chosen.

At the end of the Gulf war in February 1991 diplomats said religious leaders had protested the presence of "infidels" on Saudi territory, in reference to the multinational forces that ousted Iraqi troops from Kuwait.

We should change our Constitution of all the Muslim countries and accept the a Constitution based completely on The Holy Quran and Sunna and abolish all the facility of the existing rulers like Malaysian changed their constitutional amendment as bellow: At the end following verses of The Holy Quran may help all to accept the wishes of the Almighty Allah (God).

2   2 This is the Book; In it is guidance, sure, without doubt, To those
2   2 Who fear Allah (God);

2 24 But if ye cannot- And of a surety ye cannot- Then fear the Fire
2 24 Whose fuel is Men and Stones,- Which is prepared for those Who
2 24 reject Faith.

2 66 So We made it an example To their own time. And to their posterity,
2 66 And a lesson To those who fear Allah.

2 74 Thenceforth were your hearts Hardened: they became Like a rock and
2 74 even worse In hardness. For among rocks There are some from which
2 74 Rivers gush forth; others There are which when split Asunder send
2 74 forth water; And others which sink For fear of Allah. And Allah is
2 74 Not unmindful of what ye do.

2 112 Nay,-whoever submits His whole self to Allah And is a doer of good,
2 112 He will get his reward With his Lord; on such shall be no fear, Nor
2 112 shall they grieve.

2 114 And who is more unjust Than he who forbids That in places for the
2 114 worship Of Allah, Allah's name should be Celebrated?- whose zeal is
2 114 (in fact) to ruin them? It was not fitting that such should
2 114 themselves enter them Except in fear. For them There is nothing but

2 114 disgrace In this world, and in the world To come, an exceeding
2 114 torment.

2 150 So from whencesoever Thou startest forth, turn Thy face in the
2 150 direction Of the Sacred Mosque; Among wheresoever ye are Turn your
2 150 face thither: That there be no ground Of dispute against you Among
2 150 the people Except those of them that are Bent of wickedness; so
2 150 fear Them not, but fear Me; And that I may complete My favors on
2 150 you, and ye May (consent to) be guided;

2 155 Be sure We shall test you With something of fear And hunger, some
2 155 loss In goods or lives or the fruits (off your toil) but give Glad
2 155 tidings to those Who patiently persevere,-

2 177 It is not righteousness That ye turn your faces Towards East or
2 177 West; But it is righteousness- To believe in Allah And the Last Day
2 177 And the Angels, And the Book, And the Messengers; To spend of your
2 177 substance, Out of love for Him, For your kin, For orphans, For the
2 177 needy, For the wayfarer, For those who ask, And for the ransom of
2 177 slaves; To be steadfast in prayer, And practice regular charity; To
2 177 fulfil the contracts Which ye have made; And to be firm and
2 177 patient, In pain (or suffering) And adversity, And throughout All
2 177 periods of panic. Such are the people Of truth, the God-fearing.

2 180 It is prescribed, When death approaches Any of you, if he leave Any
2 180 goods, that he make bequest To parents and next of kin, According
2 180 to reasonable usage; This is due From the God-fearing.
2 182 But if any one fears Partiality or wrong-doing On the part of the
2 182 testator, And makes peace between (The parties concerned). There is
2 182 no wrong in him: For Allah is Oft-Forgiving, Most Merciful.

Why life of Muslims became so cheap?:

BANJA KOVILJACA (Yugoslavia) Mar 13, 1993: A large number of civilians were killed
and wounded in a Serb onslaught against a UN convoy held up by desperate Muslims in
eastern Bosnia, members of the convoy said here today, reports AFP. The convoy,
including eight British troops and three UN military observers, left the village of Konjevic
Polje to cross back into Serbia after Serb artillery gunners opened fire on Friday. Their
mini-convoy had been held up since Thursday in the village by Muslims fearing Serb
reprisals after their departure. Convoy leaders Alan Abraham said the UN troops pulled out
of Konjevic Polje after two hours of negotians with local Muslim leaders. Sources said the
Muslim enclave was on the point of falling to the Serbs and the front line was now running
through the middle of Konjevic Polje. "I saw about 20 casualties, mostly sharpnel from
shelling," doctor Simon Mardell told journalists here adding that he saw a lot of dead
civilians too. Mr Mardell, a doctor with the World Health Organisation, said it was "the
worst situation I've ever been in. The number of casualties overwhelmed me.".......
Conflicts-ASSAULT ON AZERBAIJAN

Armenian forces rout the Azeri army, grab territory and create a refugee crisis By LARA
MARLOWE BAKU wih reporting by James Wilde/Istanbul; published in 'TIME', April
19, 1993. pp. 24-25

318

Captain Azad Isazade started out his office window, unmoved by the cherry trees in full bloom below and the Caspian Sea beyond. It was a splendid spring afternoon in Baku, Azerbaijan's capital, but the Azeri Defense Ministry spokesman was too worried to notice. "Our army is young. We are no match for the Armenians, with all the help they are getting." Four maps on the office wall showed the progress of a two-week-old offensive by Armenian forces that had seized 4,000 sq km of Azerbaijan. Added to the contested Armenian enclave of Nagorno-Karabakh inside Azebaijan, the gains meant that 10% of Azerbaijan was under Armenian control. About 60,000 civilians had been driven from their homes, and fighting still flared on four fronts.

...... The Azeri Defense Ministry claimed last week that its forces had intercepted radio conversations between Russian officers fighting with the Armenians on the Kelbajar front. Wounded soldiers returning from both the Kelbajar and Fizuli battles told Time they had actually spotted Russians among the attacking Armenians. "It's easy to recognize them," said Muradov. "They are fair-haired, while the Armenians are dark, like us. The Armenians wear black uniforms; the Russians wear camouflage." The U.S., European nations and countries in the region are worried that Turkey, a member of NATO, might be drawn into the conflict on the side of fellow Muslims and ethnic Turks in Azerbaijan. Public sympathy for the Azeris runs high in Turkey, where the pro-Islamic Welfare Party has urged armed intervention. So far, Ankara has sent mixed signals. ...... Even if it has not reached the intensity of ethnic hatred that has bubbled up in the former Yugoslavia, the war in the Caucasus has claimed more than 3,000 lives so far and displaced half a million people on both sides. President Elchibey speaks of the suffering of Armenians as well as Azeris. "We got along fine until the war started," said Akif Ahkadov, a professorin Baku. "Some of my closest friends were Armenians. Some day they'll come back, but it will take a long time." Extremists on both sides are hardly so open-minded, but Western diplomats, on the basis of unofficial acceptance by the Azeri and Armenian governments that Nagorno-Karabakh should revert to autonomy within Azerbaijan, express optimism that a peaceful solution to the dispute can be found........

Manuel de la Torre, Uppasala, Sweden published in 'TIME', April 19, 1993. pg. 6
It is inconceivable that the UN had the idea to impose an embargo, which affected only the civilians (mostly Muslims) in Bosnia. It should have known that the Serbs from Bosnia would get their weapons (probably troops too) from nearby Serbia. Resolutions and actions in the UN and Security Council went smoothly and quickly when nations were concerned about punishing Iraq. Now, with Serbs doing whatever they want with civilians in Bosnia, everything is stuck. And the West has decided to remain a spectator while the carnage continues.

James L. Graff, Vienna reported in 'TIME', April 26, 1993, pg. 15:

"Bold tyrants and fearful minorities are watching to see whether 'ethnic cleansing' is a policy the world will tolerate. If we hope to promote the spread of freedom or if we hope to encourage the emergence of peaceful multiethnic democrats, our answer must be a resounding no."-U.S. Secretary of State Warren Christopher, announcing the Clinton Administration's initiatives on Bosnia, Feb. 10,1993.

BOLD TYRANTS TAKE HEART. FEARFUL Minorities take heed. As NATO jet fighters assigned to Operation Deny Flight screamed impotently across the skies of Bosnia last week, what resounded around the world was the thunderous crash of Serbian artillery, its canon and mortars trained on the Muslim town of Srebrenica, its shells primed for airbursts, which would cause maximum carnage. When one of those barrages lifted early last week, the shattered bodies of the dead, among them 15 children, lay in mute testimony to the world's age-old ability to turn its face away from the suffering and subjugation of others.

Even as fighting eased in Srebrenica under a cease-fire agreement brokered in Sarajevo late Saturday night, painful memories were being evoked half a continent away, in Polan, where preparations to mark the 50th anniversary of the Warsaw Ghetto uprising were under way. In 1943, 60,000 Jewish survivors of starvation and deportation roughly the same number as the people trapped in Srebrenica -confronted German troops in a final hopeless battle. Back then the outside knew little and could do less about what was afoot. But the horror of the last days of Srebrenica could not be ignored by a watching word kept abreast of every twist and turn in the bloody Bosnian conflict. **Despite a hardened stance forged in an emergency Security Council session on Saturday night, the guardians of the much touted new international order appeared at a loss to bring a definitive end to a war that has already claimed at least 134,000 dead and missing and created 2 million refugees.**

Fragmented accounts from Srebrenica painted a picture of final hours fraught with confusion and continued bloodletting. Efforts by Muslim commanders to bolster the morale of their outnumbered and battle-fatigued fighters had long since faltered as the soldiery forged for scarce food alongside starving civilians and Serb shells rained on the town. "In the name of God, do something!" cried one of Srebrenica's **ham radio operators on Friday. The next day began with an eerie silence that shattered when Serb gunners pounded the town with shells. There were reports of hand-to-hand fighting even as Bosnian Serb leader Radovan Karadzic issued another of his Orwellian statements. "We don't want to take** .

Social Equality and Economic Behavior

The principle of equality, preached and practiced by the Prophet(sm) and his four Caliphs, is common knowledge for the world as a whole. The application of this principle amounted to revolutionary changes in administration, attitude and behavior. The Qur'an lays down the fundamental principle of human equality with these words:

'O mankind; We created you from a male and a female and made you into nations and tribes that you may know each other. Verily the most honored before God is the most righteous of you; surely God is knowing and Aware'(49-13). The Prophet was also sent to establish the brotherhood of humanity- a brotherhood of faith, not of colour, race or geography. **Social equality is basic to the concept of one ummah for Muslims in the world. The nature of behavior and fellow-feeling expected from the concept can be understood from two indications in Hadith literature:**

(a) The Prophet (sm) stated: 'All Muslims in the world are one man; if he feels pain in the eye, his whole body feels the pain; if he has pain in head, his whole body suffers from the path'. (Muslim)

(b) The Prophet (sm) stated: 'I swear by Allah (God), one can not become fully Mumin (faithful) until he (or she) likes for others whatever he (or she) likes for himself (or herself).' (Bukhari and Muslim)

(c) The Prophet (sm) stated: 'A Muslim is the brother of another Muslim, he neither wrongs him, nor leaves him without help, nor humiliates him'. (Muslim)

In such a society, cooperation and mutual understanding can be the basis of both individual behavior and social and economic institutions. Naturally, social rights of the needy and the handicapped were not only recognized but enforced under Sharia. And in the social system, both rule of law and equality before law were maintained. Administration of law in the early period of Islam demonstrated this. Ensuring economic justice is also a vital objective of the Rule of Law. **The Qur'an urges: 'withold not things**

justly due to others (26:183), The Prophet (sm) warned: Beware of injustice; for injustice will be equivalent to darkness on the Day of Judgment' [Ahmed and Baihaqi).[252]

(a) Politically- Although Western writers have referred to the Abbasid period of history as one Islamic Empire, in analogy with the Roman Empire, it was a period social transformation under Islamic ideology. The process was guided politically by the chief Executive, designed as Amirul Mumurin (Leader of the Faithful), who guided with knowledge and norms drawn from the authority of the Quran and Sunna. This was possible over vast territories because of the nature of the ideology. People under jurisdiction were **overwhelmingly Muslim and Mumin [Faithful), imbued with the individual and social ethics of Islam. Their confidence and sworn allegiance make the chosen leader Amirul Muminin (Leader of the Faithful), known as Caliph who leads in significant political, social and other functions (from congregation prayers to fighting a war), When the Caliphate was established after wading through 'seas of blood', the declaration in the name of the first Caliph (Abu Abbas Abdullah called 'Saffah' was completed by his uncle on his behalf in the Mosque of Kufa (now part of Iraq) over the exhausted body of the Caliph' saying: "The sun has at last broken through the clouds, right is once more in power, through the family of your prophet which will hence forward show you mercy and love. How deeply we have suffered to see the oppression you have had to endure from Bani Umaiya. But we will rule you according to the command of God and His Holy Book.[253] The preceding Omaiyad period is thus condemnable and does not deserve the analysis in the light of the ideology based on the Qur'an and Sunnah. The Abbasid period was the culmination of the Abbasid Revolution at the cost of 'seas of blood towards' the end of 749 Ad. ... Mansoor ruled as Caliph, after Abdullah 'Saffah', between 754 and 775 A.D. R. A. Nicholson in his Literary History of the Arabs considered Mansoor to be 'perhaps the greatest ruler whom Abbasids produced',. He had to fight hard to put down the rebellion of the Ali'ites. Despite these emergencies, he could plan remarkable landmarks of economic development. In 762 A.D., he laid the foundations of his new capital, Baghdad. In the completion of this city, taking four years, he "employed about a hundred thousand architects, craftsmen and laborers, drawn from Syria, Mesopotamia and other parts" of the state. Historian Masoodi states: "The prudence of Mansoor, the correctness of his judgment and the wisdom of his policies are beyond description." On his death, it is said, he left in public treasury 600 billion dirhams and 14 million dinars. He was dedicated to the service of the people and worked early morning to night. His economic judgment and capacity of going deep into details are reflected in two instances: (i) He is known to have made an agreement with his cook that the cook would keep the heads, feet and skinsof the sheep slaughtered in the palace kitchens on conditions that he provided free firewood for cooking. (ii) A man , an old neighbor of Mansoor's pre-Caliphate days, approached him for financial assistance. After obtaining the details of the man's family members, Caliph Mansoor told him; "with four women spinning in your house, you are better off than most Arabs." Haroon al-Rashid ruled from 786 to 806 A.D.**

---

[252] ISLAMIC ECONOMY PRINCIPLES AND APPLICATIONS (BOOK I & II) BY PROF. M. RAIHAN SHARIF PUBLISHED BY ISLAMIC FOUNDATION, BANGLADESH PG. 68-69

[253] (John Bagot Glubb, op. cit (relevant chapters, especially pp. 53, 112, 321 and 333). Quotations used are also used by Glubb.; as mentioned in ISLAMIC ECONOMY PRINCIPLES AND APPLICATIONS (BOOK I & II) BY PROF. M. RAIHAN SHARIF PUBLISHED BY ISLAMIC FOUNDATION, BANGLADESH PG. 29-30

According to R. A. Nicholson, "Haroon's orthodoxy, his liberality, his victories over the Byzantine Emperor Nicephorous and.... the literary brilliance of his reign have raised him in popular estimation far above all the other Caliphs". His Caliphate of 23 years bore the stamp of his outstanding energy, decision and personality. Lover of music and poetry, He enjoyed the company of man of letters and of theologians. He hated hersy, and sought the advice of religious leaders in cases of doubt. E. G. Browne, in his literary History of Persia has quoted al Fakri's statement: "it was a dynasty abounding in good qualities, richly endowed with generous attributes, wherein the work of science found a ready sale, the merchandise of Culture was in great demand, the observances of Religion were respected, charitable bequests flowed freely, the world was prosperous, the Holy shrines were well cared for, and the frontiers were bravely kept".

(c) Development administration and economic management were facilitated by the 'unity of Islam' and territorial extension with decentralization. In the whole area; from Cardova to Bukhara, it was not one center like Rome of the Roman Empire. Not only the old cities like Alexandria, Antioch and Damascus obtained a new lease of life, but new cities of Cairo, Baghdad and Cardova. All these cities were in constant communication, their varied products supported expansion of trade and competitive improvement in technical efficiency.[254]

.... Meanwhile mercantile trade of the East poured gold into Baghdad, and supplemented the other enormous stream of money derived from the contribution of plunder and loot dispatched to the capital by the commanders of the victorious raiding forces which harried Asia Minor, India and Turkistan. The seemingly unending supply of Turkish slaves and Byzantine specie added to the richness of the revenues of Iraq and, combined with the vast commercial traffic of which Baghdad was the center, produced a large and powerful moneyed class composed of the sons of generals, officials, landed proprietors, royal favorites, merchants and the like, who encouraged the arts, literature, philosophy, and poetry as the mood took them, building palaces for themselves, vying with each other in the luxury entertainments, summoning poets to sound their praises, dabbling in philosophy, supporting various schools of thought, endowing charities and in fact, behaving as the wealthy have always behaved in all ages... The wealthier classes were rapidly losing all faith in the religion of the state; speculative philosophy and high living were taking the place of Quranic orthodoxy and Arabian simplicity. The solitary bond which could have held the empire together- the sternness and plainness of the Moslem faith, was completely neglected by both the Caliph and his advisers.[255]

If the above conditions of reality were real; and stand on historical evidence, the Abbasid economy cannot be treated as a successful reflection of Islamic economics. ... In reality, the conditions above support the hypothesis that the case of the Abbasid economy may have reversed the priorities of the Quranic objectives; instead of seeking the Home of the Hereafter as the principal objective and accepting a reasonable economic base for worldly life as a subsidiary objective, the Abbasid administration made the enjoyment of worldly

---

[254] J. D. Bernal, op. cit. p. 270; as mentioned in ISLAMIC ECONOMY PRINCIPLES AND APPLICATIONS (BOOK I & II) BY PROF. M. RAIHAN SHARIF PUBLISHED BY ISLAMIC FOUNDATION, BANGLADESH PG. 30-32

[255] Sir Mark Sykes, The Caliph's Last Heritage, quoted in H. G. wells, The Outline of History, Vol II, Doubleday, New York, 1961 pp. 498-99; as mentioned in ISLAMIC ECONOMY PRINCIPLES AND APPLICATIONS (BOOK I & II) BY PROF. M. RAIHAN SHARIF PUBLISHED BY ISLAMIC FOUNDATION, BANGLADESH PG. 41

life the principal objective and seeking the Home of the Hereafter as a nominal one. In those conditions, even the advisory role of the learned could not effectively correct the situation.

It is narrated in Imam Gazzali's Kimia-e-Sa'adat that Shaqiq Balkhi, a distinguished learned man, came to Caliph Haroon-al-Rashid s court and on the request by the Caliph offered several advises, finally adding:

"O Khalifa, remember, you are a fountain and the administrators and employees appointed by you in the various regions of the State are like the various large and small rivers. If the fountain itself is neat and clean, the impurities emitted by the rivers and canals will not do any harm. But if the fountain itself becomes impure and dirty, the impure and dirty water flowing out of it will spread into the whole river network and make the system impure." Again, Haroon al-Rashid took with him his dear companion Abbas and came to meet the learned man Fuzail Yaz. On reaching h s door, they heard him recite from the Qur'an: "What! do those seek after evil ways think that we shall hold them equal with those who believe and do righteous deeds, that equal will be their life and their death? Ill is the judgment they make."(Jathiya:21) There was no light in the house; in fact, the hour was dead of night. Abbas knocked the door and requested the honored Fuzail to open the door and meet Amirul Muminin (Leader of the Faithful). pg. 42   pg. -172-174

1. Antecedents

Al-Azhar

On the eastern side of Cairo, al-Azhar has stood for nearly a thousands years. It has been lofty beacon sending light in all directions and immortalizing the sciences of the Arabs and the civilization of Islam. Now here is the new university which will be built in this age on the western side of the city to spread the Arabic sciences together with Western learning. These twin brothers will cooperate henceforth in enlightening both banks of the blessed Nile, from the right and from the left, n the things which will restore the people of the valley to complete well-being and full glory.[256]

The Islamic madrasa had assumed its classic shape in the tenth and eleventh centuries to teach Sharia religious law as interpreted by one or more of the four Sunni schools. It combined the academic function of the mosque school with the residential khan or inn for out-of-towners, Charitable endowments supported the madrasa, as they did the medieval European college. The madrasa's (religious School) mission of training jurists was more specialized than that of the medieval European university, where the Arts faculty served as a preparatory school for the three higher faculties of Law, Medicine, and Theology. Founded in the tenth century by the Shite Fatimids and converted to Sunnism under the Ayyubids, al-Azhar eventually drew students from as far away as Morocco and Java, just as medieval European universities attracted Catholic students from Poland to Spain and from Scotland to Italy. Arabic, the language of the Quran and the early Islamic classics, was the main medium of Islamic learning just as Latin was for Western Christendom.[257]

---

[256] Ahmad Abd Allah Budayr, al-Amir Ahmad Fuad wa Nashat al-Famia al-Misriyya (Cairo, 1950), pp. 265-66[hereafter cited as Budayr]. qouted in Cairo University and the making of modern Egypt, BY Donald Malcolm Reid by CAMBRIFGE MIDDLE EAST LIBRARY:23 p. 11

[257] Cairo University and the making of modern Egypt, BY Donald Malcolm Reid by CAMBRIFGE MIDDLE EAST LIBRARY:23 pp. 11-12

An Islamic backlash against the secularism of the 1920s was gathering force. The Young Men's Muslim Association, founded in 1927, resembled its Christian analogue in providing sports, social, and service activities in a religious atmosphere. But the Muslim Brotherhood had a more dramatic future. Rashid Rida and the Salafiyya reform movement had influenced Hasan al-Banna, the Dar al-Ulum-trained teacher who founded the movement in 1928. Banna believed that the decadence of Muslims, the onslaught of the Christian West, and the aping of Western ways had brought Islamic society low. Secular nationalism was an alien import which only divided and weakened the **Umma. Banna called for a return to the Sharia and the pristine Islam of Muhammad(sm) and the Rashidun Caliphs. Uprooted young people fresh from the countryside found in the Brotherhood a charismatic leader, a vision of hope and righteousness, and a place to belong. After World War II, Hasan al-Banna and the Brotherhood would become major contenders for power in both student and national politics.**[258]

 The polarity between Cairo University and al-Azhar persists, though Cairo by no **means stands for unadulterated secularism nor al-Azhar for a purely religious world view. The two institutions have much in common; their dependence on - yet resentment of the interference of - the state, constituencies which can often frustrate changes pushed by state or university authorities, and a willingness to tolerate Islamists who stress personal piety and peaceful persuasion while coming down hard on revolutionary Islamists. As the noon call to prayer rang through Cairo University's central library in the spring of 1983, somewhat less than half of the women students were wearing Islamic dress. The dress itself, one suspects, concealed a wide variety of social and intellectual attitudes. A handful of male students left their books and went out to pray, but most continued reading or socializing. Seventy-five years after its founding, Cairo University still had no major mosque despite repeated statements of intention. A small mosque or two and makeshift places of prayer tucked into odd corners of existing buildings seemed grudging concessions to the Islamists. In the library, the prayer mats were wedged into a corner beneath a staircase. Cairo University is secular and it is Islamic, and after eighty years it is deeply rooted in Egyptian soil. It has outgrown the uncritical admiration for the West expressed by some of its founder. It is as authentically Egyptian as al-Azhar, and like al-Azhar** it will continue to play a vital role in Egypt's search for modern identity.[259]

Caliph, title of the successor of Muhammad as head of the Muslim community, an office initially both political and religious in its functions. After the murder of the caliph Othman in 656, the religious and moral basis of the caliphate was destroyed, leaving only the political, military and financial bonds. By the late 7th century, under the Omayad dynasty of caliphs, the center of gravity of the Muslim empire shifted from Arabia to Syria and evolved from an Islamic theocracy to an Arab secular state. After internecine feuding the Omayads were deposed in 750 in favour of the Abbasides, who moved the centre of power from Syria to Iraq, where they founded their new capital, Baghdad. Abbaside rule passed into the hands of the Turkish emir. The provinces rapidly became autonomous, retaining

---

[258] The standard work is Richard Mitchell, The Society of Muslim Brothers(London, 1969). See also Ramadan, Tatawwur, 1937-48, pp. 279-325; and Muhammad Zaki, al-Ikhwan al-Muslimin wa al-Mujtama al-Misri (2nd ed., Cairo, 1980) qouted from
Cairo University and the making of modern Egypt, BY Donald Malcolm Reid by CAMBRIFGE MIDDLE EAST LIBRARY:23 pp. 129

259

Cairo University and the making of modern Egypt, BY Donald Malcolm Reid by CAMBRIFGE MIDDLE EAST LIBRARY:23 p. 234

only nominal allegiance to Baghdad, and the authority of the caliph became moral rather than political. The caliphate proper came to an end in 1258 with the murder of the last Abbasside caliph, although a puppet caliphate continued in Egypt until its conquest by the Turks in 1516-17. From 1520 the title 'caliph' was borne by the Turkish sultans and was finally abolished in 1924 by the Turkish parliament.[260]

[260] The New Illustrated EVERYMAN'S ENCYCLOPAEDIA (A-Joachin), VOLUME ONE, P. 267

To Renew 1300 years old Caliphate

This work is for the judgement of all people of this. In the word of Jay Kinney the editor of "GNOSIS MAGAZINE: A journal of the western Inner Traditions. What is it about Islam that motivates such fervent enthusiasm among some adherents? Most media are primed to present Islam as a Problem; I've been curious about Islam as a solution.... Islam, which eschews monasticism, nevertheless instructs its followers to pray five times daily at prescribed times, a schedule of devotion paralleled in the West, these days, only at monasteries and convents. The average Westerner, witnessing the ordinary spectacle of a crowd on the street stopping on schedule to kneel and pray, is brought up short-- as if having wandered by mistakes into a convention of monks. The unselfconscious faith of the crowd contrasts with our own sophisticated faithlessness, making us ill at ease.
Muslim was spread and is still spreading through Spiritual Power. We mentioned very few lines in the "Spiritual Section" of this work. Many non-Muslim religious gentleman like Ram Krisna, Guru Nanak visited many Islamic holy sites and may be gathered knowledge of way to God. Many holy places in India like Ajmir in
Rajashtan, where BJP in power during last few years is one example. Khaja Mainuddin (God's mercy on him) entered India without any arms or Army and still still today he is called King of kings of India by
various Government media.

But still in West Muslims are described as a terrorist for the act of Western Terrorism.:

AS they did, Britain, in secret negotiation with France, was in the process of substantially diluting the promise her Resident in Egypt had made to the Arabs. If the Ottoman Empire (i.e. last Caliphate) was to be dismembered after World War I, the French insisted on their share of the spoils. A secret treaty known as the Sykes-Picot Agreement, for the two men who signed it Sir Mark Sykes for Britain and Charles Geeorge-Picot for France, without the Arabs' know or consent, a "sphere of influence" in much of the area in which Britain had promised to support an independent Arab state. .... It was not until 1925, eight years after the Balfour Declaration, that Chaim Weizmann warned: "Palestine is not Rhodesia and 600,000 Arabs live there who....have exactly the same rights to their homes as we have to our National Home."[261]
So the nation States in the holy lands of Prophets, peace be upon them, are divided
 into so many Nation States, violating The Political System of Islam i.e. Caliphate.
No Muslim can accept these nation States as these division is only contributing wastage of billion dollars of wealth which could be spent to abolish poverty. We, in the
West, talk loudly about Democracy and freedom. But when that democracy fails
in Algeria we are silent here. Why? Why we protect the Kings, Amirs, Bath
Party Chiefs and one parry dictator in the land of Caliphate? Why we supply
Army , fighter Planes to protect those Dictators? All these helped those
rulers to be more violent and more cruel to their own citizens, who can not
speak the truth, who can not express their grievances against the ruling
classes. This can not continue unchallenged. This must be changed, because
Muslims constitute one fifth of the World population. And The World can not
expect peace with antagonizing the World Muslim. The World owes to the Islam
for education , for University System and many good things. If Germany can be
united, if India and China can remain as a one State, even if Europe can be united
under European Union under one currency and even if United State can remain
with one great state with so many culture, language, race, so The 1300 years
olds Caliphate, which was abolished in 1924 after long conspiracy of British

---

[261] O JERUSALEM, DECISION AT FLUSHING MEADOW, PG 26.

Government and partly France, must be reestablished and the Western military powers should stop supporting their local Governor or Sub-contractors. and withraw support from those sub-contractors. Each Muslim has right to become a Lincoln in the Muslim world for the last Revolution of Caliphate.

The Khilafa is built upon eight pillars:
a. The Khalif.
b. The delegated assistance.
c. The executive assistants.
d. The Amir of Jihad (War)
e. The Judges.
f. The governors of the provinces (Wilayat).
   (Like Governor of Iraq, Egypt Syria, Turkey and other around 55 states)
g. An administrative system.
h. The consultative assembly (majlis ash-shura).

There are four opinions among Muslim scholars regarding the issue of choosing the Khalif.
a. By selection (bay'h).
b. By nomination.
c. By force.
d. By divine text.

It was shown that the bay'h is only legitimate method to appoint the Khalifah because Khilafah is contract of consent and selection. So the consent of the person who is given the bay'ah to hold the Khilafah and the consent of those who give the bay'ah are essential.
Thereupon, it is clear that nobody becomes a Khalif unless the Ummah (World Muslims)
appoints him in this post, and he cannot have the authority of Khilafah unless he is contracted to it.[262]

I hope that the Western media will stop making false propaganda against Islam and it's followers and instead allow world Muslims to place their true history before World Community, to express their important views and help to re-establish the Caliphate peacefully. Because Islamic Khalifah will act for Islam, the religion of peace and submission to God and not for any kind of ponder with God gifted wealth ; the way it is spent by Western military power like United State.

The International Institute for Strategic Studies calculates that the $262 billion US defense budget accounts for 37 percent of global military expenditure. Russia, Japan and China will spend $80 billion, $42 billion, and $7 billion. The six "rogue states"-- Cuba, Iran, Libya, Syria and North Korea -- have a combined annual military budget of $15 billion.. ....Muslim terrorist should not be major fear. Far more acts of terrorism and violent crime in US, according government statistics, are committed by non-Muslims than Muslims And if Muslims do pose a terrorist threat to the US, one hears little discussion of what it is that the terrorists really want. Perhaps, all they

---

[262] Website: http://www-personal.umich.edu/~luqman/Belief/Khilafah
For detail please see the Web page of 'sleeping Giant" under religion, Islam in www.yahoo.com
Please see other web page on Islam such as www.twf.org

want is for the West to stop interfering in their countries, in ways that we would never tolerate in the US.[263]

The King, Amir or military dictatorship including one party like Bath party dictatorship is
not allowed in Islam. Abu Ya'la Al-Fara' in the book Al-Mu'tamad fi Usul Al-Deen said: The way to choose the Khilafa is the choice of the people of Al-Hal Wa Al-'aqd and not the divine text. Al-Baqilani in the book of Al-Tamhid p 164 said:What refutes the Nass (opinion which says the Khilafah is appointed by divine text) is the evidences which proves that the Khilafah is by the choice of the people. There are many such references on election of Khilafah. And they all say it is Fard. Establishing the Khilafah (collective duty) upon Muslims, however all of them are in sin if they do not fulfil this duty. The Muslims members of the Majlis ash-Shura (who are the representative of the Ummah and are elected themselves by the Ummah) check and determine the number of the candidates to stand for election for the post of the Khilafah, these names are subsequently announced and the Muslims are asked to elect one person from this list of candidates. The results of the election is to be announced and the person who attained the majority of the votes is to be announced to the Muslims. The Muslims must hasten to give the bay'ah to the candidate-who has attained the majority of the votes- as the Khalifah to follow the Quran and the Sunnah of the messenger of Allah (pbuh). Thus all the nation states must come under that elected Khalifah and the Khalifah will appoint Governors for all the Provinces i.e. the present day nation states mostly created by western military power. Who can be candidate for Khalifah? The answer is who will follow or ready to follow Islamic Constitution of Quran and Sunna (Sayings of the last Prophet of Islam, peace be upon hom). So the candidates for Khilafah must have unquestionable knowledge and belief on Quran and Sunna.

Again what is The Caliphate and the Khilafat Movement?

The Caliph, successor to the Prophet ((Peace be upon him, sm.)), commander of the faithful, the shadow of God on earth- these exalted titles convey the symbolic importance of the Caliph to the community of Islam. Theoretically, he was both the spiritual and temporal leader of the Muslim community, insuring the defense and expansion of the rule of divine justice on earth, and in thus furthering God's purpose, helped assure eternal salvation for all Muslims. By the late nineteenth century, however, these theories of Caliphate power were about all that remained of the past glories of Islam. The Ottoman Empire was crumbling and Balkan nationalities and European powers alike coveted pieces of its territory. But Ottoman Turkey was still the bulwark of Islam against Christian aggression and the Sultan, Abdul Hamid II, was regarded with reverence by many Muslims in his capacity as Caliph, symbol of Islamic unity. Shrewdly, Abdul Hamid encouraged the pan-Islamic sentiments of Muslims everywhere in order to bolster his own power against European encroachments, and against political opposition at home. This pan-Islamic movement achieved few practical results in spite of the feelings it generated. Its chief propagandist, Jamal al-Din al-Afghani, died in obscurity, a prisoner of the Caliph he had served, albeit uneasily. The Young Turks deposed 'Abdul Hamid and installed a new Caliph. The Balkan wars wrested most of the remaining European territories from the Ottoman Empire, and when World I broke out and the Caliph

---

[263] Website:http://www.twf.org-- Press Contact:Enver Masud

declared holy war (jihad) against the Triple Entente, Indian Muslim
subjects of Britain nevertheless fought against the Turks, and the Arabs
declared their independence from the Ottomans. It was hardly an
inspiring record to encourage further Islamic appeals, and after the war,
the Turkish nationalists led by Mustafa Kemal, the secret Jew repudiated the idea of a
universal Islamic empire in favor of a regenerated Turkish homeland.

The victorious European powers, in seeking to carve up Ottoman
territories among themselves, encountered little opposition from the
Caliph, who was less concerned by the oss of Arab territories than he was by
the rising challenge of Turkish nationalism. Pan-Islam emanating from the
Caliph was a thing of the past. And yet, at the same time as the Arabs
were seeking to establish their independence from Turkey, and the Turks
themselves were drawing away from their.....

The 1300 years olds Caliphate, which was abolished in 1924 after the long conspiracy of
British Government and partly France, must be reestablished .
What Lincoln thought about the future if the division of United State
succeeded for Islamic World.

This republic was a fragile experiment in a world of Kings, emperors, tyrants,
and theories of aristocracy. If secession were allowed to succeed, it would destroy that
experiment. It would set a fatal precedent by which the minority stood for,
until the United States fragmented into a dozen pitfall, squabbling
countries, the laughing stock of the world. Now the United States was saved
from division, the Land of The Caliphate was divided into so many nation
States and thus contributing to the misery of the entire Muslim World. And
those nation States has become laughing stock of the World and particularly
to the Western Military power who divided that land by force and still they
are maintaining that division by force because they have powerful bomb or atomic and
and hydrogen bomb. This must be charged by any cost. To divide other's land by force is
not a
terrorist act? If you are a Judge what judgment you will pass from the
followings which I am quoting from "The Origins and Evolution of the
Arab-Zionist Conflict by Michael Cohen, published by University of California
Press; pg. 64:
"The new international agency, the League of Nations, was to allot
"mandates," or international trusteeships, under which the powers were to
prepare peoples liberated from the Turks for independence. .....
But once the United States abdicated any further role in the new European
order after the summer of 1919, it was left to Britain and France to divide
the Middle East between them. " Now What judgment you will pass against
those, who are responsible for the division of the land of Caliphate.

We should first quote from the Holy Bible; GENESIS 17, 18;
CHAPTER 17 WHICH IS:

**20 : And as for Ish-mael, I have heard the; Behold, I have
blessed him, and will make him fruitful,**

**and will multiply him exceedingly; twelve princes shall
be beget,? and I will make him a great nation.**

**24: And Abraham was ninety years old and nine, when he was
circumcise in the flesh of his foreskin.**

**25: And Ish'-ma-el his son was thirteen years old, when he
was circumcised in the flesh of his foreskin.**

26: In the selfsame day was Abraham circumcised, and

Ish'-ma-el his son.

We are also quoting from GENESIS 21; CHAPTER 2

14: And Abraham rose up early in the morning, and took bread, and a bottle of water, and gave it unto Ha'gar,
putting it on her shoulder, and the child, and sent her away; and she departed, and wandered in the
wilderness of Be'-er-sheba.
15: And the water was spent in the bottle, and she cast the child under one of the shrubs.
16: And she went, and sat her down over against him a good way off, as it were a bowshot; for she said, let me
not see the death of the child, And she sat over against him, and lift up her voice, and wept.
17: And God heard the voice of the lad; and the angel of God called to Ha'- gar out of heaven, and said unto her,
What aileth thee, Ha'-gar? fear not; for God hath heard the voice of the lad where he is.
18: Arise, lift up the lad, and hold him in thine hand; for I will make him a great nation.

How the followers of the above Holy scripture can conspire against the Caliphate and divide it for their worldly benefit.

Now how Muslims around the world can be silent when their Caliphate was abolished and The Caliphate was divided into so many nation state and most cases with one language and one religion violating the following verses of The Holy Quran:

21: 92 Verily, this Brotherhood Of yours is a single Brotherhood (Ummah) ,

21: 92 And I am your Lord And Cherisher: therefore Serve Me (and no
21: 92 other).
23: 52 And verily this Brotherhood Of yours is a single Brotherhood
23: 52 And I am your Lord And Cherisher: therefore Fear Me (and no other) .

As explained by The Presidency of Islamic Researches, IFTA, King Fahd Holy Qur-an Printing Complex which are: 2910 pg. 988 "The people who began to trade on the names of the prophets cut off that unity and made sects; and each sect rejoices in its own narrow doctrine, instead of taking the universal teaching of Unity from Allah. But this sectarian confusion is of man's making. It will last for a time, but the rays of Truth and Unity will finally dissipate it."

49: 10 The Believers are but A single Brotherhood: So make peace and
49: 10 Reconciliation between your Two (contending) brothers; And fear
49: 10 Allah, that ye May receive Mercy.

Here also the above book mentioned that :The enforcement of the Muslim Brotherhood is the greatest social ideal of Islam. On it was based the Prophet's Sermon at his last pilgrimage, and Islam cannot be completely realized until this ideal is achieved. (pg. 1591 note 4928.

And what last Prophet of Islam asked the Muslim for Caliphate? The followings are the quotation from SHAHIH MUSLIM, rendered into English by Abdul Hamid Siddiqi, volume three p 1032:

(4473) It has been narrated on the authority of Abu Huraira that the Messenger of Allah (may peace be upon him) said: People are subservient to the Quraish: the Muslims among them being subservient to the Muslims among them, and the disbelieves among the people being subservient to the disbelievers among them.

(4474) It has been narrated on the authority of Hammam b. Munabbih who said: This is one of the traditions narrated by Abu Huraira from the Messenger of Allah (may peace be upon him) who said: People are subservient to the Quraish: the Muslims among them being subservient to the Muslims among them, and the disbelievers among them being subservient to the disbelievers among them.

(4477) It has been narrated on the authority of Jabir b. Samura who said: I joined the company of the Holy Prophet (may peace be upon him) with my father and I heard him say: This Caliphate will not end until there have been twelve Caliphs among them. The narrator said Then he (the Holy Prophet) said something that I could not follow. I said to my father: What did said: All of them will be from the Quraish. (Who knows that what the Holy Prophet said, but could not be followed by the narrator is the event which we are facing on Caliphate).

(4568) It has been narrated on the authority of Abu Sa'id al-Khudri that the Messenger of Allah (may peace be upon him) said: When oath of allegiance has been taken for two caliphs, kill the one for whom the oath was taken later

I quote Prophet Muhammad's (Peace be upon him) Last Sermon on the Nineth day of Dhul Hijjah 10 A. H. *(7h March, 632).*

All Mankind is from Adam and Eve, an Arab has no superiority over a non-Arab nor a non-Arab has any superiority over an Arab, also a white has no superiority over black nor a black has any superiority over a white except by piety and good action.. Learn that every Muslim is a brother to every Muslim and that the Muslims constitute one brotherhood..... All those who listen to me shall pass on any words to others and those to others and may the last ones understand my words better than those who listen to me directly. Be my witness O Allah, that I have conveyed your message to your people. .... Allah has forbidden you to take usury (interest), therefore all interest obligation shall henceforth be waived. Your capital, hover, is yours to keep. You will neither inflict nor suffer inequity. Allah has judged that there shall be no interest and that all the interest due to Abbas ibn' Abu'al Muttalib shall henceforth be waived."

Why mankind divide this beautiful world into so many nation state?. What we can know from The Holy Quran is the following verse:

2:213
Mankind was one single nation, And Allah sent Messengers With glad tidings and warnings And with them He sent The Book in truth, To judge between people In matters wherein They differed, But the People of the Book, After the Clear

*Signs Came to them, did not differ Among themselves, Except through selfish
contumacy, Allah by His Grace Guided the Believers To the Truth, Concerning
that Wherein they differed, For Allah guides Whom He will To a path That is
straight.*

Can we divide the 1300 years old Caliphate into so many nation State. The
answer is no and The Holy Warn us with the following verse:

*And hold fast, all together, by the Rope Which Allah (stretches out For you),
and be not divided Among yourselves And remember with gratitude Allah's favor
on you; For ye were enemies And He joined your hearts In love, so that by His
As Grace Ye become brethren; And ye were on the brink Of the Pit of Fire, And He
saved you from it. Thus doth Allah make His Signs clear to you; That ye may
be guided.*
3:103

*As mentioned earlier, Saudi explanation of the above verse is given in page
171,as bellows :*

*"The simile is that of people struggling in deep water, to whom a benevolent
Providence stretches out a strong and unbreakable rope of rescue. If all hold
fast to it together, their mutual support adds to the chance of their safety.
Yathrib was torn with civil and tribal feuds and dissensions before the
Messenger of Allah set his feet on its soil. After that, it became the City
of the Prophet, Medinah, and unmatched brotherhood, and the pivot of Islam.
This poor quarrelsome world is a larger Yathrib: can we establish the sacred
feet on its soil, and make it a new and larger Madinah?"*

Nation States only divide the resources among people and contribute into more
poverty , conflict and misery among mankind. And even charity is not for a
fellow Muslim from Muslim but for all and the Holy Quran directs us in the
following way and even ask to give in charity which are beyond our needs so
that there is no poverty in this world.

*It is not righteousness That ye turn your faces Towards East or West; But it
is righteousness- To believe in Allah and the Last Day, And the Angels, and
the Book, and the Messengers; to spend of your substance, out of love for
him, for your kin, for orphans, for the needy, for the wayfarer, for those
who ask, And for the ransom of slaves; to be steadfast in prayer, and
practice regular charity; to fulfill the contracts Which ye have made; And to
be firm and patient, In pain (or suffering) and adversity, And throughout all
periods of panic. Such are the people of truth, the God-fearing
2:177*

And spend of your substance In the cause of Allah, And make not your own
hands Contribute to (your destruction); But do good; for Allah loveth those
Who do good.

2:195
 They ask thee What they should spend (in charity). Say; Whatever Ye spend
that is good, Is for parents and kindred And orphans And those in want and

for wayfarers.   And whatever ye do that is good,- Allah knoweth it well.
  2:215

They ask thee Concerning wine gambling, Say: "In them is great sin, And some
profit, for men; But the sin is grater Then the profit." They ask thee how
much They are to spend (In charity); Say: "What is beyond Your needs." Thus
doth Allah Make clear to you His Signs: in order that Ye may consider-
2:219

The land of The Caliphate was divided without approval of the Muslims around
the World. The result is such that the people of those countries can not utter
any word for re-establishing the 1300 years old Caliphate as they have no freedom as they
are under one party or one family rule or we can say under the Governor
appointed by Western Powers in the pretext of a United Arabia as promised by
the then British Government to their local agents.
So Muslims around the world can not accept and in fact never accepted this
division of the land of Caliphate by terrorist way, by force, by treachery
act.
So without re-establishing the 1300 old Caliphate the World can not expect
peace.
 Why so called Muslim leaders are silent about Caliphate?
Why Muslim Nation has been fighting among themselves? Why One Umma is divided
into so many Nation States? Why as a Muslim we have no place to speak the truth
about Islamic political System? Why Muslims can not speak the truth in their own
countries? Oil rich Muslim nation State leaders may not agree to surrender their vast
wealth to Caliphate. But how we the 50 States in the United States are united without
only looking self interest. For instance New York State give around 18 billion more
then what it get from rest of the country Then why rich Muslim
counties are reluctant to give to the Caliphate as New York State gives to
the rest of the United States?
. For instance in this country we can come from different part of the
world and can live without much difficulty and with equal opportunity and
right irrespective of race, language, religion or color. So we hope the whole
world should be like United State where all people can live in peace without
any war, any conflict and as one brotherhood of human race. For instance Muslims
from all Muslim countries live here where as in many of those Muslim countries we
see always some kind of civil war like Iraq-Iran War, Iraq-Gulf War
destroying billions of dollars worth of wealth and million of human life. The
Persian Gulf War alone cost US$676 billion for 1990 and 1991 excluding
ecological impact, the loss of jobs and income of thousands of foreign workers.
 (see Saudi Arabia, A Country Study by US Army, pg. xxviii) Iraq-Iran war
might have cost another $1000 billion dollar.

But as a Muslim our only political System is Caliphate or Khelafat (one
brotherhood) and no nation State is allowed according to The Holy Quran and
Sunna i.e. the saying of last Prophet of Islam (Peace be upon him). So these
nation States in the land of Caliphate is illegal or violation of Islamic
Law, which was created by British, France and other Western Government and
even by League of Nation, partitioning the land of 1300 years old Caliphate
without any public opinion or approval of those land in the Middle East.

So Muslims around the world can not accept and in fact never accepted this
division of the land of Caliphate by terrorist way, by force, by treachery
act.

So without re-establishing the 1300 old Caliphate the World can not expect peace in this world as Caliphate was abolished without the knowledge or wishes of the Muslims around the world and above all violating the principle of basic fundamental law of Islam.

If there was Caliphate, probably there could not be any war in the Muslim countries and we could use those wealth which was used for civil war among Muslim countries to abolish poverty from this world and in particular from some poor Asian and African countries.

And this is a only subject which is the main problem in the Muslim World in particular and the World in general. And what a irony of history that the terrorist war against Caliphate by the British and other Western Powers is still continuing under the pretext of United Nation resolution and this started when Abraham Lincoln defeated the southerners in United State and kept this great country of 50 States united where as the southerners in the Caliphate became the agent of Western Christian powers under the leadership of Britain. So it is a matter of right of each Muslims to become a Lincoln to defeat the few southerners who are still acting as Governors of those powers who installed their ancestors in power to look after the interest of the Western powers. And in fact this war is Third World war which started since First World war ended. So now is the time that the Western powers should stay away from the land of 1300 years old Caliphate and must stop the various pretext like United Nation/League of Nation resolution as Muslims are not bound to accept which was created by those for whom Caliphate was abolished and Nation States were established abolishing Islamic Universal brotherhood or one Umma in the name of western Government or League of Nation. And this is the only solution that we the civilized or rational people of the world can stop killing of Muslims in Bosnia, Chechenia or even in the land of Caliphate where million of Muslims were killed by the fellow Muslims as happened in Iraq-Iran war. And above all what happened in Muslim Spain 500 years ago i.e. cleansing of entire Muslims from that land after 700/800 years of Muslim (secular) rule is happening again in Europe like Bosnia in the name of religion though all the major religions of this world originated in Asia. And the question is that where western military power can protect few families in the name of national sovereignty in Kuwait, Saudi Arabia; they can not save poor Muslims of Bosnia.
Why this kind of double standard? Why this violation of democracy in Algeria, and in entire Gulf where few families are protected against the will of people who only want to establish Caliphate.

And there is no reasonable doubt that Lawrence of Arabia landed with British money,
arms , power and advice against the then 1300 years old Caliphate (Khalifat) and succeeded with local agent for which there is no reasonable doubt. And there is no reasonable doubt that France and Britain made secret
agreement for division of the land of Caliphate among themselves.. There is no reasonable doubt that League of
Nation, now know as United Nation also participated with this division which resulted
the division of so many Nation States.

Our Caliphate (Khilafat) Journey

When President Abraham Lincoln in USA resisted the division of the United State
defeating the southern separatists who revolted and tried to divide the United States;
almost during same time few so called Muslims in southern part of Islamic Caliphate
started conspiracy with non-Muslim British Government to defeat the northern i.e.
Turkish Caliphate. The aim of that conspiracy was to become rulers of small nation
States. They had no idea of their national boundary and some of them got the idea of a
United Arabia. Thus The British and France divided that land according to their strategy
mainly for oil and with the firm aim that never in future a United Caliphate can be re-
established.

The above conspiracy was never accepted by the common Muslims around the World,
which is the violation of democratic right of the World Muslims even though those division
was done under the umbrella of League of Nation/United Nation. So the war for Caliphate
did not end with the above north-south was conspiracy as the division of the Caliphate can
not be accepted by the Muslims and particularly which was imposed by the non-Muslim
Western military power in a terrorist way which only resulted
unnecessary bloodshed of Arabs, Kurd , Iranian, Iraqi, Afgan, Chechnya and other
Muslims. That division also created artificial hatred among the people of nation states.
It also created economic backwardness of all so called muslin nations. According to New
York Times which was published in 1994, Oil producing Muslim nation states invested
600 billion dollars in Europe alone. This figure did not include investment in America. If
you read various Country Study published by United Sates
Army on Saudi Arabia, Iraq, Iran and on other countries in the region you will understand
that around 1000 to 2000 billion in US dollar was spent on Gulf war and Desert Storm.
How much money they invested in the poor countries in general and Muslim countries in
particular.If they could invest only 100 billion dollars in India from Calcutta to Bombay,
from Delhi to Kerala/Madras then BJP could not come to power because not only Muslim
but also poor Hindus could be benefited with that investment. Part of that 600 billion dollar
could be invested in other Asian and African countries like Sudan, Somalia, Ethiopia,
Pakistan, Bangladesh, Egypt Turkey and poor counties.

I am quoting the followings which I got from internet:

THE ARTICLES OF THE BISHOP OF URAMIAH,
ON THE CREATOR, HOLY BOOKS AND PROPHETS
BY PROFESSOR DAVID BENJAMIN KELDANI, B.D.(died 1940c)
Former Roman Catholic Bishop of the Uniate Chaldean

Chapter 10
ISLAM IS THE KINGDOM OF GOD ON EARTH

In examination of that marvelous vision of the Prophet
Daniel (Chap. vii.) we saw how Prophet Muhammad was escorted
by the myriads of celestial beings and conducted to the
glorious presence of the Eternal; how he heard the words of
honor and affection which no creature had ever been favored with (2 Cor. xii.);
how he was crowned to the dignity of the Sultan of the Prophets and invested with power to
destroy the "Fourth Beast" and the "Blasphemous Horn." Further,
we saw how he was authorized to establish and proclaim the
Kingdom of God on earth; how all that human genius can
possibly imagine of the highest honors accorded by the Almighty

to a beloved worshiper and to His most worthy Messenger
could be ascribed to Prophet Muhammad alone. It should be remembered that among all the Prophets and Messengers of
Allah, Prophet Muhammad alone figures like a tower above all;
and the grand and noble work he accomplished stands a permanent monument of his honor
and greatness. One cannot appreciate the value and importance of Islam as the unique
bulwark against idolatry and polytheism unless the absolute Oneness of God is earnestly
admitted. When we fully realize that Allah is the same God whom Adam and Abraham
knew,
and whom Moses and Jesus worshipped, then we have no
difficulty in accepting Islam as the only true religion and
Prophet Muhammad as the Prince of all the Prophets and Worshipers
of God. We cannot magnify the greatness of Allah by con-
ceiving Him now as a "Father," now as a "Son," and now
as a "Holy Ghost," or to imagine Him as having three persons
that can address each other with the three singular personal
pronouns: I, thou, he. By so doing we lose all the true conception of the Absolute Being,
and cease to believe in the true God. In the same way, we cannot add a single iota to the
sanctity of the religion by the institution of some meaningless sacraments or mysteries;
nor can we derive any spiritual food for our spirits from feeding upon the corpse of a
prophet or an incarnate deity; for by so doing we lose all idea
of a true and real religion and cease to believe in the religion
altogether. Nor can we in the least promote the dignity of
Prophet Muhammad if we were to imagine him a son of God or an
incarnate deity; for by so doing we would entirely lose the
real and the historical Prophet of Mecca and fall unconsciously into the abyss of
polytheism. The greatness of Prophet Muhammad consists in his establishing such a
sound, plain, but true religion, and in the practical application of its precepts and principles
with such precision and resolution that it has never been possible for a true Muslim to
accept any other creed or faith than that which is professed in the formula: "I believe there
is no god except Allah, and that Muhammad is the Messenger of Allah." And this short
creed will continue to be the faith of every true believer in Allah to the Day of the
Resurrection.
The great destroyer of the "Eleventh Horn," that personified Constantine the Great and the
Trinitarian Church, was not a Bar Allaha ("Son of God"), but a Bar Nasha ("Son of Man")
and none other than Prophet Muhammad al-Mustapha who actually established the
Kingdom of God upon earth. It is this Kingdom of God that we are now to examine and
expound. It would be remembered that it was during the Divine audience of the Sultan of
the Prophets, as given in Daniel, that it was promised that:-

"The kingdom and the dominion and the greatness of the kingdom under all heaven shall be
given to the people of the Saints of the Most High; its (the people's) kingdom (shall be) a
kingdom for ever, and all dominions shall serve and obey it" (Dan. vii. 22 and 27).

The expressions in this prophetical passage that the Kingdom
of God shall consist of "the People of the Saints of the Most
High," and that all other dominions or powers shall serve
and obey that people, clearly indicate that in Islam the
Religion and State are one and the same body, and consequently
inseparable. Islam is not only the Religion of God, but also
His earthly empire or kingdom. In order to be able to form
a clear and true idea concerning the nature and the constitution of the
"Kingdom of God on earth" it is necessary to cast a glance upon the history

of the religion of Islam before it was perfected, completed, and formally established by God Himself under His Messenger Muhammad.

1. ISLAM BEFORE PROPHET MUHAMMAD WAS NOT THE KINGDOM OF GOD UPON EARTH, BUT ONLY GOD'S TRUE RELIGION

Those who believe that the true religion of Allah was revealed only to Abraham and preserved by the people of Israel alone, must be very ignorant students of the Old Testament literature, and must have a very erroneous notion of the nature of that religion. Abraham himself offered tithes to the King and Imam (1.) of Jerusalem and was blessed by him (Gen. xiv. 18). The father-in-law of Moses was also an Imam and a Prophet of Allah; Job, Balaam, Ad, Hud, Loqman, and many other prophets were not Jews. The various tribes and nations like the Ishmaelites, Moabites, Ammonites, Edomites, and others which descended from the sons of Abraham and Lot, knew God the Almighty though they too, like the Israelites, fell into idolatry and ignorance. But the light of Islam was never entirely extinguished or substituted by Idolatry. Idols or images, which were considered as "sacred" and as household gods by the Jews, as well as their kindred nationalities, and usually called "Traphim" (Gen. xxxi.) in the Hebrew, were, in my humble opinion of the same nature and character as the images and idols which the Orthodox and Catholic Christians keep and worship in their houses and temples. In those olden times of ignorance the idols were of the kind of "identity card" or of the nature of a passport. Is it not remarkable to find that Rachel (Rahil), the wife of Jacob and the daughter of Laban, should steal the "traphim" of her father? (Gen. xxxi). Yet Laban as well as her husband were Muslims, and on the same day raised the stone "Mispha" and dedicated it to God! [264]

2. THE NATURE AND CONSTITUTION OF THE KINGDOM OF GOD

There is a call to prayer repeated aloud five times a day from the minarets and the mosques in every part of the globe where the Muslims live. This anthem is followed by a most solemn worship of Allah by His faithful worshipers. This call to prayer is called Adhan (Azan). This is not all; every action, enterprise and business, however important or trifling it may be, is begun with the words Bismi 'l-Lah, which means "in the Name of Allah," and ends with an Al-Hamdu li'l-Lah, meaning "praise be to Allah!" The bond of faith which binds a Muslim to his Eternal King is so strong, and the nearness between the Sovereign and His worshiper is so close, that nothing, however powerful or seductive, can separate him from Allah. The Koran declares that Allah is nearer to one than the life-vain.

---

[264] (1) In Hebrew these old Imams are called Cohen,' and rendered by Christians as "Priest." A Jewish priest can never be identified with a Christian Sacramentarian priest.

Never was there a favorite courtier who, in his sentiments of affection, devotion, obedience, and respect for his beneficent monarch, could ever equal those which a Muslim entertains towards his Lord. Allah is the Owner of the Heavens, Earth and Universe, He is the King of kings and the Lord of lords. He is the King and the Lord of every Muslim in particular, for it is a Muslim alone who thanks and praises the Almighty King for all that happens and befalls him, be it prosperity or adversity.

It is evident, therefore, that the nature of Islam consists in its being the only real and truly Theocratic Kingdom on earth. Allah need no longer send Messengers or Prophets to convey His Messages to the Muslims as He used to do to Israel and other Hebrew peoples; for His will is fully revealed in the Holy Koran and imprinted on the minds of His faithful worshipers. As to the formation and the constitution of the Kingdom of God, inter alia, the following points should be noted: -

(a) All Muslims form one nation, one family, and one brotherhood. I need not detain my readers to study the various quotations from the Koran and the Hadith (Quotations of the Prophet) on these points. We must judge the Muslim society, not as it presents itself now, but as it was in the time of Prophet Muhammad and his immediate successors. Every member of this community is an honest worker, a brave soldier, and a fervent believer and devotee. All honest fruit of the toil belongs by right to him who earns it; nevertheless the law makes it impossible for a true Muslim to become excessively wealthy. One of the five foundations of Islam is the duty of almsgiving, which consists of sadaqa and zakat, or the voluntary and the obligatory alms. In the days of the Prophet and the first four Caliphs, no Muslim was known to be enormously rich. The national wealth went into the common treasury called "Baitu 'l-Mal," and no Muslim was left in need or want.[265]

The very name "Muslim" signifies literally "a maker of peace." You can never find another human being more docile, hospitable, inoffensive and peaceful a citizen than a good Muslim. But the moment his religion, honor, and property are attacked, the Muslim becomes a formidable foe. The Koran is very precise on this point: "Wa la ta'tadu" - "And you must not transgress" (or take the offensive). The Holy Jihad is not a war of offence, but of self-defense. Though the robbers, the predatory tribes, the semi-barbarous nomad Muslims, may have some religious notions and believe in the existence of Allah, it is the lack of knowledge and of religious training which is the root-cause of their vice and depravity. They are an exception. One can never become a good Muslim without the religious training and education.

---

[265] The Jihad or "Holy War" is also an obligatory practice of piety.

(b) According to the description of the Prophet
Daniel, the citizens of the Kingdom of God are "the People
of the Saints." In the original Chaldish or Aramaic text,
they are described as "A'mna d' qaddishid' I'lionin," an
epithet worthy only of the Prince of the Prophets and of his
noble army of the Muhajirm (Emigrants) and the Ansar
(Helpers), who uprooted idolatry from a great part of Asia
and Africa and destroyed the Roman Beast.

All the Muslims, who believe in Allah, in His angels,
Books, and Prophets; in the Day of the Resurrection and
Judgment; that the good and evil are from Allah; and perform their pious practices according to their ability and with
good will, are holy saints and blessed citizens of the Kingdom.
There is no grosser religious ignorance than the belief
that there is a person called the Holy Ghost who fills the
hearts of those who are baptized in the names of three gods,
each the third of the three, or the three of the third, and
thus sanctifies the believers in their absurdities. A Muslim
believes that there is not one Holy Spirit, but innumerable
holy spirits all created and ministers of the One Allah. The
Muslims are sanctified, not by baptisms or ablution, but their
spirits are purified and sanctified by the light of faith and by
the fire of zeal and courage to defend and fight for that faith.
John the Baptist, or rather Christ himself (according to the
Gospel of Barnabas), said: "I baptize you with water unto
repentance, but he who comes after me, he is stronger than I;
he will baptize you with fire and with the holy spirit." It
was this fire and this spirit with which Prophet Muhammad baptized
the semi-barbarian nomads, the heathen Gentiles, and converted them into an army of heroic saints, who transformed
the old waning synagogue and the decaying church into a
permanent and strong Kingcom of Allah in the promised
lands and elsewhere.

Reasons behind Our Caliphate Dream

As a Muslim our only political System is Caliphate or Khilafah (one brotherhood) and no nation State is allowed according to The Holy Quran and Sunna i.e. the saying of last Prophet of Islam (Peace be upon him). So these nation States in the land of Caliphate is illegal or violation of Islamic Law, which was created by British, France and other Western Government and even by League of Nation, partitioning the land of 1300 years old Caliphate without any public opinion or approval of those land in the Middle East. The result is such that the people of those countries can not utter any word for re-establishing the 1300 years old Caliphate as they have no freedom as they are under one party or one family rule or we can say under the Governor appointed by Western Powers in the pretext of a United Arabia as promised by the then British Government to Sheriff Hussain of Mecca, great grand father of King Hussain of Jordan and other sub-contactor with Ibn Saud of Nazd (now Saudi Arabia), Mubarak of Kuwait. And all this happened when Lawrence of Arabia a secret service agent arrived in Middle East. But France and Britain divided those land among themselves and a British ambassador Cox divided the land as Iraq, Kuwait etc. So Muslims around the world can not accept and in fact never accepted this division of the land of Caliphate by terrorist way, by force, by treachery act. So without re-establishing the 1300 old Caliphate the World can not expect peace.

Now who is responsible for this situation? The simple answer is the Muslims. Some Muslims will call some western Countries as Satan though they will compel the poor Muslim Countries to depend on the Western countries for everything, while they will be spoiling their vast God gifted wealth like oil with purchasing unnecessary arms which they will be using against the fellow Muslim countries violating the Islamic Law of the Holy Quran and Sunna and accepting the Jews and the Christians as their friend and advisor, not for the sake of Islam or The Lord Almighty Allah or His Prophet, but to grab power or to stay in power violating all the Democratic norm for which the Western World used to shop around the world, but the Western World overlooked when a dictator of any Muslim country takes power killing the democratically elected people for instances in Algeria, and if the western leader think that the democratically elected Government is the true follower of Islam, who intend to follow the life of a true Muslim Leader, want to enforce Quranic Law. Here Western shopping for Democracy failed. The power hungry and illegally occupied Leaders of so many Muslim Countries are not True Muslim but hypocrite as those Western leaders who talk about defending democracy and freedom around the world, who installed three members of a particular family, father and two sons in three divided and so called nation States which existed into a single state for long 1300 years. Yes I mean Hejaj where Sharif Hussein was in power and his two sons Abdullah and Faruque were installed in Iraq and Syria. How foolish were those Arab people that they were divided into so many states but power were give to few family like the Gulf States like Kuwait, Bahrain, Abu Dhabi and Saudi Arabia to the members of a single tribe called 'Utub', and Iraq, Syria, Jordan to another family i. e. the family of Sharif Hossain of Mecca, when ALEXANDER and published by VICTOR GOLLANCZ LTD, LONDON IN 1991, pp. 16.

It has been difficult for Western people to understand the violent Muslim reaction to Salman Rushdie's fictional portrait of Muhammad (Sm) in the Satanic verses. It seemed incredible that a novel inspire such murderous hatred, a reaction which was regarded as proof of the incurable into brain of Islam. It was particularly disturbing for people in Britain to learn that the Muslim communities in their own cities lived according to different, apparently alien values and were ready to defend them to death. But there were also uncomfortable reminders of the Western past in this tragic

affair. **When British people watched the Muslims of Bradford burning the novel, did they relate this to the** bonfires of books that had blazed in Christian Europe over the centuries? In 1242, for example, king Louis IX of France, a canonized saint of the Roman Catholic Church, condemned the Jewish Talmud as a vicious attack on the person of Christ. The book was banned and copies were publicly burned in the presence of the King. Louis had no interest in discussing his difference with the Jewish communities of France in a peaceful, rational way. He once claimed that the only way to debate with a Jew was to kill him 'with a good thrust in the belly as far as the sword will go.'[266]

In his best seller 'Journey from Paris to Jerusalem and from Jerusalem to Paris (1810-11), Chateaubriand applied his Crusading fantasy to the situation in Palestine. The Arabs, he wrote, 'have the air of soldiers without a leader, citizens without legislators, and family without a father'. They were an example of 'civilized man fallen again into a savage state'. (Ibid) Therefore they were crying out for the control of the West, because it was impossible for them to take charge of their own affairs. In the Quran there was 'neither a principle for civilization nor a mandate that can elevate character'. Unlike Christianity , 'Islam' preaches 'neither hatred of tyranny nor love liberty'. (Ibid., pg. 171) [267]

Even though Western scholars continued to attempt a more objective picture of the Arab and Muslim world, this colonial superiority made many people believe that 'Islam' was beneath serious attention.
certainly this offensive Western attitude has succeeded in alienating the Muslim world. Today anti-Western feeling seems rife in Islam, but that is an entirely new development. The West may have harbored fantasies of Muhammad as its enemy, but in fact most Muslims remained unaware of the West until just over 200 years ago. The Crusades were crucial in the history of Europe and had a formative influence on the Western identity, as I have argued elsewhere.(Holy War; The Crusades and Their Impact on Today's World(London, 1988). But, though they obviously deeply affected the lives of Muslims in the Near East, the Crusades had little impact on the rest of the Islamic world, where they were simply remote border incidents. The heartland of the Islamic empire in the Iraq and Iran remained entirely unaffected by this medieval Western assault. They had, therefore, no concept of the West as their enemy. When Muslims thought of the Christian world, they did not think of the West but of Byzantium; at that time Western Europe seemed a barbarous, pagan wilderness, which was indeed far behind the rest of the civilized world.
But Europe caught up and the Muslim world, which was occupied with its own concerns, failed to notice what was happening. Napoleon's expedition to Egypt was an eye-opener for many thoughtful people in the Near East, who were much impressed by the easy, confident bearing of the French soldiers in this post-revolutionary army. Muslims had always responded to the ideas of other cultures, and many were drawn to the radical, modernizing ideas of the West. At the turn of this century, nearly every leading intellectual in the Islamic world was a liberal and a Westerniser. These liberals may have hated Western imperialism, but they imagined that liberals in Europe would be on their side and would

---

[266] John of Joinville, The life of St. Louis, trans. Rene Hague and ed. Natalis de Wailly, London, 1955 pg. 36 which were quoted in **MUHAMMAD, A WESTERN ATTEMPT TO UNDERSTAND ISLAM BY KAREN ARMSTRONG published by VICTOR GOLLANCZ LTD., LONDON; PG. 21**

[267] **MUHAMMAD, A WESTERN ATTEMPT TO UNDERSTAND ISLAM BY KAREN ARMSTRONG PG. 38-39**

oppose people like Lord Cromer. They admired the quality of the Western way of life, which seemed to have enshrined many ideals that were central to the Islamic tradition. In the last fifty years, however, we have lost this goodwill. One reason for the alienation of the Muslim world has been its gradual discovery of the hostility and contempt for their Prophet and their religion which is so deeply embedded in Western culture and which they consider still affects its policy towards Muslim countries even in the post-colonial period. The Gulf War of 1991 showed that, whether we like it or not, we are deeply connected with the Muslim World. Despite temporary alliances, it is clear that the West has largely lost the confidence of people in the Islamic world. A breakdown in communications is never the fault of one party and if the West is to regain the sympathy and respect that it once enjoyed in the Muslim world it must examine its own role in the Middle East and consider its own difficulties vis-a-vis Islam. That is why the first chapter of this book traces the history of Western hatred for the Prophet of Islam (sm). But the picture is not entirely black. From the earliest days, some Europeans were able to achieve a more balanced view. They were always in a minority and they had their failing but this handful of people tried to correct the errors of their contemporaries and rise above received opinion. It is surely this more tolerant compassionate and courageous tradition that we should seek to encourage now.[268]

Rashidin, the Rightly Guided Caliphs, because they governed in accordance with Muhammad's principles. Ali in particular emphasized that a Muslim ruler must not be tyrannical. He was, under God, on a par with his subjects and must take care to lighten the burden of the poor and destitute. That is the only way for a regime to survive.
So if your subjects complain of burden, of blight, of the cutting of irrigation water, of lack of rain, or of the transformation of the earth through its being inundated by a flood or ruined by drought, lighten their burden to the extent you wish your affair to be rectified. And let not anything by which you have lightened their burden weigh heavily against you, for it is a store which they will return to you by bringing about prosperity in your land and establishing your rule. .... Truly the destruction of the earth only results from the destitution of its inhabitants, and its inhabitants become destitute only when rulers concern themselves with amassing wealth, when they have misgivings about the endurance of their own rule and when they protect little from warning example. (Instructions given by Ali to Malik al-Ashtar, when he was appointed governor of Egypt.[269]

After he had been elected, Abu Bakr addressed the community, laying down the principles that should henceforth apply to all Muslim rulers:

"**I have been given authority over you but I am not the best of you. If I do well, help me, and if I do ill, then put me right. Truth consists in** loyalty and falsehood in treachery. The weak among you shall be strong in my eyes until I secure his right if God will; and the strong among you shall be weak in my eyes until I wrest the right from him. If

---

[268] **INTRODUCTION IN MUHAMMAD, A WESTERN ATTEMPT TO UNDERSTAND ISLAM BY KAREN ARMSTRONG published by VICTOR GOLLANCZ LTD., LONDON; PG. 14-15**

[269] In William C. Chittick (trans and ed.) A shite Anthology (London 1980, p. 75) and as stated in MUHAMMAD, **A WESTERN ATTEMPT TO UNDERSTAND ISLAM BY KAREN ARMSTRONG published by VICTOR GOLLANCZ LTD., LONDON; PG. 24-25**

a people refrain from fighting in the way of God, God will smite them with disgrace. Wickedness is never widespread in a people but God brings calamity upon them all. Obey me as long as I obey God and His apostle, and if I disobey them - you owe me no obedience. Arise to prayer, God have mercy on you (Ibn Ishaq, Sira 1, 017, in Guillaume, trans. and ed., The Life of Muhammad p. 687.)[270]

We never saw any article in any Western Press or in the Middle Press on the main cause of Middle East
problem, which started on the arrival of the greatest International Terrorist Lawrence of Arabia at Jeddah, his supply of Bombs/arms and evil advice of separation and false deceptive promise of a united Arabia to Sharif Hussain and to other southern separatists and the abolition of the 1300 years old Caliphate by a secret Jew, Kamal Ataturk and division of the land of 1300 years old Caliphate by the Crusaders.
.

And history repeats itself. After the oppressive regime of some Ummyad Caliphate cross the limit of their torture towards the Muslims then Abu Muslim, one Iranian General mobilized all the Iranian people against the Ummayad, defeated them and at that stage the Abbaside took power instead of the direct descendants of the last
Prophet of Islam (Peace be upon him); for whom the Iranian fought.
Only Abdur Rahman of Ummayad fled to Span. Spain was then separated from Abbaside Caliphate in Baghdad. After the massacre of Abbaside at the hand of Halaqui Khan, there was no Caliphate for two years and Sultan Byber of Egypt re-established the Caliphate. Later Osmani took the leadership of the Caliphate. In short Arab or the direct descendants of Prophet Ismael (peace be upon him) ruled the Caliphate for around 700 years and the non-Arab Osmani around 600 years, which were abolished in 1924 by a secret Jew, whose ancestors were given shelter in Turkey after Spanish inquisition.

So the struggle for Caliphate was never ended in the past or at present.
It is a costly and madness war by the Western military powers against
1300 years old Caliphate starting before First World War till now, which only costs trillion of dollars of wealth.

So the only solution for all this war is to withdraw all the support from
present sub-contractors install in the land of Caliphate including their
military presence in Saudi, Bahrain, Kuwait and other places in the Gulf
and Mediterian. As I mentioned "history repeats itself", when Khomeni came to power in Iran; it was the repetition of the same history.
Now who are responsible for million of death in Iran-Iraq war and the so called Desert Storm and the destruction of trillion dollars of wealth?
So enough is enough and what those military powers can do is to
withdraw their forces in the land of Caliphate so that the people of that
can decide who will be their future Caliph as it is their internal affairs not
the internal affairs of the Western military powers who are responsible for the killing of million of people and destruction of trillion dollars of wealth. Look at Bahrain, how oppressive that Regimes is to it's own people, where there is Western military presence, and every day people are killed, where there is no freedom for Islamic Political System of Caliphate in Saudi Arabia and other countries including Iraq.

---

[270] (Ibn Ishaq, Sira 1, 017, in Guillaume, trans. and ed., The Life of Muhammad p. 687. and as stated in MUHAMMAD, A WESTERN ATTEMPT TO UNDERSTAND ISLAM BY KAREN ARMSTRONG published by VICTOR GOLLANCZ LTD., LONDON; PG. 258)

India was left as united single nation; but when those same Anglo Saxons left Arabia within short time, they divided that land into Saudi, Jordan, Egypt, Syria, Iraq and so many though with one language Arabic. Those same liars/Terrorists promised to Sharif Hussain, the great grandfather of another sub-contractor King Hussain that those Anglo Saxons will make a United Arabia, once Osmani Caliphate is defeated. But those Anglo Saxons made a secret treaty with France and divided that land among themselves. And what a irony that even two sons of Sharif Hussain; Abdullah and Faisal were installed in Jordan and Syria/Iraq. How sons of one individual can become Rulers of three states? There must be some limit of deception and lying.

So don't try to fool the World Muslims as you fooled few million Muslims in Spain, asking them to come to mosque and then burned those mosque and killed those Muslims inside those mosques, which is known in History as April fool. In this month of April don't fool us again. Red Indians were fooled as those Muslims who came in America long before Columbus were fooled. We know all the history. We will rewrite World map throwing that map drawn by Ambassador Cox, League of Nation/United Nation. We will go through our own constitution and faith. We will never interfere in other's land and we will never and never allow others to interfere in our internal affairs.

There must be the Caliphate if possible within few days, few months and in fact we don't bother about those illegal immigrants and it is future Caliph who can decide about them and not London, Paris, Moscow or Washington as World Muslims never intend to interfere about policies in those Capitals. And World Muslims threw into dustbin all the past United Resolutions or the map drawn by the then British Ambassador Cox for the land of 1300 years Caliphate. The following is from
"MANDATORY PROBLEMS, PG 64-65":

In April 1920, in the small Italian town of San Remo, Britain and France divided the Middle East into mandates while the American ambassador read his newspaper in the garden. Britain obtained Palestine, Tansjordon, and Iraq; the French acquired Syria Both countries had to crush rebellions against the mandatory system that summer- France in Syria, in the course of which the Hashemite regime was dismantled and Faysal sent packing; and Britain, a long and costly rebellion in Iraq. In Palestine,
Britain had to cope with Arab disturbances in March 1920 and May 1921 in protest against its "Zionist" policy.

So World Muslims never accepted the above acts of thieves and only International Terrorists of this World as quoted above. So Saudi Rulers or any Rulers installed by the above terrorists were never accepted by the World Muslims. The World Muslims will never accept al the above acts of International Terrorism and today Or tomorrow the above Terrorists must pay the price for their acts of true Terrorism. Good and lion hearted people of all countries must understand the true acts of International Terrorists and judge the future course of action of the World Muslims around the world. It is our land and only we the World Muslims will decide how that land is ruled and by who according to our faith. We will never and never compromise with any terrorists as quoted from the history above and all our acts are only defensive acts against the greatest Terrorists/Thieves of this World. Almost Every now and then the heads of Muslims in Cairo, Riyadh, Baghdad and other places of the land of Caliphate are beheaded. Thus no Muslim can dare to speak about Islam's only one Political System of Khilafat. Though the descendants of the Crusaders speak loudly about Democracy, they protect those killers in Cairo, Baghdad, Riyadh and other oldest Capitals of this World in the land of Caliphate. They even keep their powerful defense forces to protect those killers in the land of Caliphate. Even during annual Hajj,

Muslims can not speak their problem on Khilafat for the fear of their dear head as they saw many heades gone for ever. How long these injustices will continue and without any firm resistance. Is it not interference in the internal affairs of World Muslims? How we can get rid of the killers in the oldest Capital of this World in the land of Caliphate. How we can get rid of the protectors of those killer?

If we address all the mankind in the following language; what will be expected reply?

"O Mankind, can you please tell us, , where we the World Muslims will go during our life time? Who are ready to listen our cause, true Islamic cause of universal Brotherhood?"

Kindly go through the following question-answer session and know our situation in the World Stage, where once we were the creator of World history and World destiny on earth with God's mercy bestowed upon us; from Cordova to Baghdad and Cordova to Delhi and Yemen to wall of Vienna.

Q. Which country in the Middle East allow the Struggle for Islam and Islamic State of Caliphate/Khilafah

Answer: None as all the ruler's main job description is to stop Islam and Islamic State of Khilafah. There is no deference between sub-contractors and illegal immigrants.

Q. Who are behind the creation of illegal state of Israel and other Client States?

Answer: Shariff Hussain, his three sons, Ibne Saud and their masters British,, French and other Western military powers. (If Sharif Hussain, his sons could reject the advice of that Terrorist, known as Lawrence of Arabia then we could see another
World now, we could see a democratic elected Caliph other than Osmani Turk but Caliphate including the land of Turkey. Trillion of dollars were paid to the Western Powers for the Arms/bombs, running their military machinery's, and indirectly
helping illegal immigrants i.e. so called Israel.)

Q. What is the role of Organization of Islamic Organization?

Answer: To continue the existence of all client States and fool 1.5 billion World Muslims through their false speeches.

Q. Which country in the Middle East banned true Islam on one brotherhood and Internationalism

Answer: All But illegal immigrants allow Internationalism among Jews from all over the World but deny it to Muslims and Christians as per agreement with all other sub-contractors.

Q. Which sub-contractor of the Client States has no Muslim blood in his hand:?

345

Answer: None and there is no difference between illegal immigrants (so called Israel) and others.

Q. Which country in the Middle East, no follower of Islam and Khilafah are imprisoned for their faith?

Answer: None.

Q. Which religion allow to follow their religion secretly:
 Answer: Jews, and they are known as Secret Jews.

Last Question: Why we are facing such situation?

Answer: Because there is no True Islam and Islamic State of Khilafah."

One truth is better than 100 lies. One truth is Khilafah without which all the liars will be wining
their games through false propaganda and false history until Khilafah is re-established.
The fact is that the Khilafah was abolished through International Terrorism. The fact is that World Muslims are deprived from a single State. The fact is that all illegal nation/client States are simply a life of reservations where Muslims are denied their freedom of speech for Islam and Islamic State of Khilafah.

Lincoln is popular in United States as he kept the unity and defeated the
Southern separatist during the period when some southern separatists of
the Caliphate were
busy taking British money for the conspiracy against Khilafah/Caliphate.
Those thieves and criminal are now kings, Amirs, Bath party chiefs etc. of the illegal Nation States.
Gandhi is popular in India as he was able to get freedom for India with
around one billion population and with so many languages.
Even BJP in India is now popular as they mobilized their propaganda for a Hindu India.
 Even Netazi Subhash Chandra Bose is still popular in West Bengal, India as he
declared "Give me blood and I shall give you freedom". He went to German through
Afghanistan with a Muslim name from British captivity in Calcutta. From German
he went to Japan, formed Azad Hind Forces and fought the British Government in India.

But none of the above, from Lincoln to Subhash is called as terrorist.

```
When we call about Islam or Caliphate we are called
terrorist, fundamentalist,
militant and so many other adjective, new adjectives.

But how long we will be stopped with those adjectives. People
of this world
need food, cloth, basic education and Medicare and not the
technology of the
Anti-Christ or Dajjal(antichrist) System of cloning,
Internet, bombs and missiles.
And for that reason, we must and must re-establish
Khilafah/Caliphate
without further delay.
```

We want peace with honor and we don't want any war at this era of bomb and nuclear bomb as next War may destroy this World and entire mankind.

Kindly judge and give advice after going thorough some of the books like "The Secret Jews by Joachim Prinz", which is available in the Jewish Division of the New York Central Public Library at Manhattan between 5th annd 6th Avenue.

When question of beda i.e. new innovation comes, is it not beda in Islam to create illegal nation states like Saudi, Kuwait, Iraq, Egypt, Syria, Jordon, Turkey etc out of one Islamic State i.e. Khilafat? Thus illegal client/Nations Are the greatest beda or rejected one.

Lastly you all advocate Swiss Banks tc return the Jewish money and for the condemnation of holocaust.
Are Britain and other Western Power ready to return Kohinoor and other looted property by British from Muslim India? Are they ready to return trillion of dollars to us which you looted from oil money in the name Arms/Bombs sale? Are you ready to end your military presence in the land of Caliphate and allow us to decide our fate and destiny of Caliphate? Are you ready to compensate the World Muslims for the holocaust in Spain? Are you ready to return the America and Australia to it's original inhabitant There is no freedom in the birth place of Islam i.e. so called Saudi Arabia. Muslims have no right to proclaim 1300 years old Caliphate. Muslims have no right to ask how the money is spent. This is true for all the nation states in that area. For Muslims there is no difference between Saudi or Israel as in both places Muslims are unable to speak the truth. That is the problem. No dictatorship is allowed in Islam. In Islam all are equal and the Ruler is the servant of the people. The people must take oath of a legation to the Caliph..

Now at present day World, some people who worship money suffers from one decease, which is "Jihad or Islamic Holy War" To spread that decease they even refer to Holy Quran.
But they forgot that Islam was not spread by any Jihad. Islam grew in many region where it started from zero and became majority and without any jihad or army:
Such as south India, Ceylon, Mal islands, coasts of China, Philippines, Indonesia, Malay, central Africa, Senegal, Nigeria, Somaliland, Tanzania, Madagascar, Zanzibar etc.Mongols were converted to Islam even though they were conquerors and they prosecuted the Muslims but the defeated Muslims converted the conquerors and surely through spiritual power of Islam

But how Christianity was spread? Dr. Gustav Lebon in his book Civilization of Arabs says:

347

Egypt was made by force to believe in Christianity and the inhabitants there by degenerated to complete state of decay out of which they were picked up and delivered by the Arabs......(Civilization of the Arabs, p 336 chapter 4: The Arabs in Egypt).
In Denmark king Cnut spread Christianity in his regions or dominions by force and terrorism. Then he subjugated the defeated peoples to the Christianity....
In Russia the Christian missionary work was spread by a group of people called <<brethren of the sword>>and another known as Vladimier Duke of Kiev (985-1015, a descendant of Rurck (ref Fischer's History of Europe in Middle ages). I can give many detail. Such as Vasco da Gama who discovered the route to India was a missionary.

Dr. S. A. Ashur in his valuable book "The Crusade Movement" writes on p. 294, part 1:

"When some of the people of Caesarea took refuge in the town mosque the Crusaders persuade them there and slew them altogether men, women and children and the mosque was like a big pool of blood of Muslims"

The massacre of Jerusalem in 1099 was a stain of disgrace to the first Crusade campaign according to European Historian (Greusset's History des Croisaders 1 p. 161)

Having discussed the shameful doings of the Inquisition Courts in Spain, Dr. Lubon in his book Civilization of the Arabs pp. 270 and 271 says" The monk Bleeda was delighted when he slaughtered a hundred thousand emigrants out of a caravan of 140 thousand Muslims refugees on their way to Africa"

Then Lubon mentions the Muslims loss of three million victims slain, burnt and deported Then on page 272 he says: "We cannot help admitting that we did not find among beastly savage Spanish conquerors anyone to censure for committing deeds of murder similar to those committed against Muslims"

One day we will produce hundreds of volume from great non-Muslim sources. So all liars must stop history of lies against Islam. What happened in Philippine Muslims from 1899 to 1914. (Read country study of Philippine published by US Army page 27, read it, I hate to mention.

Do you know that Ramakrishna, a great Indian Hindu practiced Islam under a Sufi for some time? Do you know that Vivekananda stated once that he believed that the Koran was one of the few books unaltered through time since it was authored?

We know Swiss banks are returning gold to Jew; but what about wealth looted by British Government from India and other part of Islamic World?The museums of Britain are overflowing with the treasures that Britain looted from the Muslims and in fact the Kohinoor diamond which was looted from the people of India is part of the Crown Jewels. Can we get back all our vast wealth from the looters including 1300 years old Caliphate peacefully?

The followings are from Philippine, country study, published by US Army pp. 5, 27 and 99:
The first recorded sighting of the Philippines by European was on March 16, 1521, during Ferdinand Magellan's circumnavigation of the Globe. Megellan landed on Cebu, claimed the land for Charles I of Spain (it is a irony that only civilized part of Europe, Islamic Spain of 800 years; where Muslims were cleansed),
and was killed one month later by a local chief...... Permanent Spanish settlement was finally established in 1565 when Miguel Lopez de Legazpi, the first royal governor, arrived

in Cebu from New Spain (Mexico). Six years later, after defeating a local Muslim ruler, he established his capital at Manila........

United States rule, even more than that of Spanish, was seen as a Challenge to Islam..... More province remained under United States military rule until 1914, by which time the major Muslim groups had been subjugated.

When Legazpi embarked on his conversion efforts, most Filipinos were still practicing a form of polytheism, ALTHOUGH SOME AS FAR NORTH AS MANILA HAD CONVERTED TO ISLAM.

Thus Islam was spread in Philippines without any army or Jihad but by Islam's spiritual power and in return Islam was destroyed my military powers of the European as elsewhere.

Long live Caliphate to protect Islam and poor peoples of the World from domination of the Worshippers of money.
Any one can go THE TREATY OF MEDINA
51 CLAUSES letters of The Holy Prophet by Sultan Ahmed Qureshi published by Noor Publishing House, Farash Khana, Delhi-110006, pp. 31 37. This is again borne out by the plaque at Licoln's Inn, in which the name of the Holy Prophet (S.A.W.) appears at the top.

We must bring all the people of this World under the banner of one state of Khilafah from without Khilafah at 74:

And listen greatest Jihad is to fight with one's own self of evil desire of power, money etc.

And what about the following Jihad(Crusade)?

Our war with the ENEMIES OF KHILAFAH is not exactly a walk-over. Our enemies are well versed in the art of spinning historical lies and inaccuracies. It is well versed in the art of brainwashing and the make-believe techniques.

Here is some fact again from "ARAB REACH" BY Hoag Lavins, pp 49.

In his memoirs President Nixon recounted that "I was stunned by the failure of Israeli intelligence....

....Golda closed the door behind him and wept openly

....Dayan wants to talk about the condition for surrender, she sobbed, brushing away her talks.

The Prime Minister at that time indicated to her aides that she would commit suicide rather than surrender.

She ordered that Israel prepare for a nuclear Masada - an atomic holocaust which would consume Israel as well as the surrounding Islamic capitals and oil fields.

Time magazine reported, "Israel's 13 [atomic] bombs were hastily assembled at a secret underground tunnel during a 78-hour period at the start of the war. .....

Why West is silent about those bombs
Introduced in the holly land and make
All kind of hue cry for Indian Sub-continent? We are fooled
and deceived. And we are stateless/leaderless people in Earth

It is our fault to trust each of internal and external enemies; and instead of getting our guidance from The Holy Quran and Sunna we heve been running to London, Paris, Moscow and Washington for guidance, from Lawrence's arrival in Jeddah to last veto in the so called Security Council i.e. The Council for making pieces from One Piece of Brotherhood/Ummah/Khilafat.

What is The Way to Islam? Only prayer, charity, Hajj etc. are
not The Way to Islam Present illegal Nation States is not The
Way to Islam.
In the language of a non-Muslim, BERNARD LEWIS; which he
mentioned in his book, "The Arab in History, pg. 144:
"Islam-the offspring of Arabia and the Arabian Prophet-was
not only a system of belief and cult. It was also a system of
state, society, law, thought, and art-a civilization with
religion as its unifying, eventually dominating factor. From
the Hizra onwards Islam meant submission not only to the new
faith,
but to the community-in practice, to the suzerainty of Medina
and the Prophet, later of the Empire and Caliph. .....
.... According to the Sharia, the head of the community is
the Caliph, the chosen vicegerent of God with supreme power
in all military, civil, and religious matters and with the
duty of maintaining intact the spiritual and material legacy
of the Prophet"

Thus even a non-Muslim Scholar like above knows the true way
of Islam.
So where is Khalifah/Caliph?
Let me quote from "The Secret Jews" by Joachim Prinz, pp 20,
21 55:

"While thousands of Jews suffered in the rest of Europe,
while the crusaders murdered them in the Rhineland and
wherever they carried the cross toward Palestine in their
holy war, Spanish Jewry celebrated its Golden Era...
But the financial backing essential to the battle had come,
as we know, from Abravanel, the Jew, who was now in exile.
Not a single believing Jew was left in all of Spain or in the
Baleric Islands. The Muslims were defeated. Spain was a
purely Catholic country. And on August 3, 1492 another
glorious triumph was beginning. Christopher Columbus sailed
his three ships towards an unknown world on a voyage which
was to fulfill two of the great goals of Spain, gold and
honor"

But why Abravanel, the Jew, helped Spain to defeat Muslim
Ruler? Is it the same present day game against Khilafah?

And so called Israel was created after Sultan Abdul Hamid
Khan refused that state in Palestine. And the result was that

one Islamic State of Khilafah was destroyed during First
World war and in fact Third World War was started since 1916;
when Khilafah was destroyed and illegal nation/client States
were created.

So let the World Muslims elect a Caliph out of so many
illegal sub-contractors of client States.
What is United Nation? Who founded it and under what
circumstances?

If I say it was founded to divide the Islamic State of
Caliphate/Khilafah comprising three continent of Africa, Asia
and Europe. This is my observation. Go through the history
book and know the detail. From Yemen to Albania and Egypt to
Iraq/Kuwait; it was one State of Caliphate. How that State
was divided into illegal Client States?
In the past, people of Middle East or World Muslims decided
their own destiny and let them decide their destiny. Indian
people or Chinese people decide their destiny. So why foreign
powers will interfere in the internal affairs of Middle East?

Let us erase the map drawn by the red pencil of British
Ambassador Cox or United Nation and re-draw the original map
of Khilafah.

That is the only solution as enough is enough, as trillion
dollars of wealth were destroyed since the destruction of
Caliphate. Why West is afraid of Khilafah and Islam and not
BJP in India where 200 million Muslims live?
The followings are from "THINK AND GROW RICH" WRITTEN BY A
non-Muslim:

The rise of Islam began. Out of the desert came a flame which
would not be extinguished- a democratic army fighting as a
unit and prepared to die without wincing. Mohammad had
invited the Jews and Christians to join him; for he was not
building a new religion. He was calling all who believed in
one God to join in a single faith. If the Jews and hristians
had accepted his invitation Islam would have conquered the
world. They didn't. They would not even accept Mohammad's
innovation of humane warfare. When the armies of the prophet
entered Jerusalem not a single person was killed because of
his faith. When the crusaders entered the city, centuries
later, not a Moslem man, women, or child was spared. But
the Christian did accept one Moslem idea-the place of
learning, the university."

So we must re-establish Khilafah without any further delay.
If Germany can be reunited, if India, China can remain as a
State with more than one billion population each, if European
can be united under European Union, then World Muslims also
can be united under Caliphate.
If you read a newspaper any day and any where in this World
you will read some news on the

killing of Muslims. It may be in Algeria, in Palestine, in
Bosnia, in Central Asia, in India/Pakistan or in China. And
you will observe that in average out of 10 people killed 8
are Muslims. And it is not new. There is none to propagate
the holocaust of Muslims in this World. There is none in this
world to kill any United State citizen or resident as the
killers will be hunted and will be brought to justice for his
crime. Even Ummayad Caliphs were far better than any present
day sub-contractors as it was during that period ; when Hindu
King Dahir imprisoned some Muslims or Muslim sailors and only
for this reason Sindh (present Pakistan)was invaded and
became part of Khilafah   1300 years ago.
But now the blood of Muslim become very cheap when Muslims
are divided and when Muslims defy Allah's/God's order and the
order of the Prophet (Peace be upon him).

This happened 500 years ago in Spain as Spain was separated
from mainland Khilafah, when six million Muslims were killed
in Spain and   when several million Muslims and   Indians
were killed in America..

This happened at the hand of Stalin/Lenin in Central Asia
under Communist rule and during Afghan war when   several
million Muslims were   killed. If central Asian Muslim
Provinces could be united under communist rule then why they
are divided now?

This happened during long 9 years Iraq-Iran war, when several
million Muslims were killed.

People of Asia, Africa and Europe was united under Khilafah
for long 1300 years till last European (so called World)
Wars. So why it is not possible now and at the time when
people are so closed through modern communication?

Caliphate is a reality and it is better to re-establish it
now. And when question of fundamentalist comes;
Why it is only related to Islam and not any other religion.
What about BJP in India, which formed Government. Though
those leaders of BJP are Aryans and not Indian or non-Aryans.
I am to mention that if Muslims in India are outsiders then
the Brahmins or other upper cast Hindus are also outsiders as
they invaded India and treated the majority Indians as lower
casts, though Muslim Rulers in India did not create any cast
System. Under Islam all human are equal.
Khilafah.

We do not like to see any more Catastrophe, war and
bloodshed.

Let me end my never ending resarch work on only one problem
to be solved in this
World i.e. re-establishment of Islamic Caliphate/Khilafah
quoting from:

A Painful Peace By Mr. Noam Chomsky

Power and Propaganda

The phrase "Day of Awe" is not out of place. The U.S. has carried out a very impressive power play. The events are a remarkable testimony to the rule of force in international affairs and the power of doctrinal management in a sociocultural setting in which successful marketing is the highest value and the intellectual culture is obedient and unquestioning. The victory is not only apparent in the terms of Oslo I and II and the facts on the ground, but also in the demolition of unacceptable history, the easy acceptance of the most transparent falsehoods, and the state of international opinion, now so submissive on this issue that commentators and analysts have literally forgotten the positions they and their governments advocated only a few years ago, and can even see that "Israel agrees to quit West Bank" when they know perfectly well that nothing of the sort is true. That is really impressive, and instructive.

In case after case, that is just what we find. Open discussion is a fine thing, as great as democracy itself, if only it is kept within the bounds that support power and privilege. It's about as close to a true historical generalization as one can find that respectability is won by adhering to these fundamental principles, and that rending these chains is a first step towards freedom and justice."

353

BIBLIOGRAPHY

An Interpretation of the Holy Quran" which we have computerized. Some other famous book is "The Holy Qur-an"; Arabic text with English Translation, Commentary and Notes by the same writer Abdullah Yusuf Ali; Sahih Muslim by M. Abdul Hamid Siddiqi; Miskat al-Masabih - al-Hadith by Dr. James Robson and many other several religious Books Including many in English of published by Sh. Muhammad Ashraf,
Lahore, Pakistan
As explained by The Presidency of Islamic Researches, IFTA, King Fahd Holy Qur-an Printing Complex
MUSLIM, BEING TRADITIONS OF THE SAYINGS AND DOINGS OF THE PROPHET MUHAMMAD AS NARRATED BY HIS COMPANIONS AND COMPLIED UNDER THE TITLE AL-JAMI-US-SAHIH BY IMAM MUSLIM, Rendered into English by ABDUL HAMID SIDDIQI VOLUME THREE, With Explanatory Notes, AND Brief Biographical Sketches of Major Narrators,
PUBLISHED BY Nusrat Ali Nasri for KITAB BHAVAN, 1214, Kalan Mahal, Darya Ganj, NEW DELHI-110002
AN-NAWAWI'S FORTY HADITH
TRANSLATED BY EZZEDDIN INRAHIM AND DENYS JOHNSON-DAVIES (ABDUL WADOUD);
(HAS BEEN PRINTED AT THE EXPENSE OF HIS HIGNESS SHEIKH ZAYED BIN SULTAN AL-NAHAYNAN FOR FREE DISTRIBUTION., HADITH 38, printed in the United States by R. R. Donnelley & Sons Company
SUFI THOUGHT BY S. R. SHARDA M. A., Ph. D. pp. 11, 35.
The Life of Muhammad, A Translation of Ishaq's SIRAT RASUL ALLAH, PUBLISHED BY OXFORD UNIVERSITY PRESS
MOHAMMAD IN WORLD SCRIPTURES BY ABDUL HAQUE VIDYARTHI, DEEP & DEEP PUBLICATIONS, D-1/24 Rajouri Garden, New Delhi-110.
William Muir, The life of Muhammad, Preface Vol, I.
SIRAT-UN-NABI (THE LIFE OF THE PROPHET) BY SHIBLI NU'MANI
Deuteronomy, 21:17
Ibid.
The Life of Muhammad, a translation of Ishaq's SIRAT RASUL ALLAH THE QURANIC SUFISM" BY DR. MIR VALIUDDIN M. A.; Ph. D. (London), Bar-at-law, Formerly Prof and Head of the Department of Philosophy,
Osmania University, by MOTILAL BANARSIDASS Delhi; Vanarasi : Patna,
The Theology of Unity, by Muhammad Abduh, Translated from the Arabic by Ishaq Musa'ad and Kenneth Cragg, published by BOOKS FOR LIBRARIES, A DIVISION OF ARNO PRESS NEW YORK, 1980,INTRODUCTION
The Life of Muhammad, a translation of Ishaq's SIRAT RASUL ALLAH
THE QURANIC SUFISM" BY DR. MIR VALIUDDIN M. A.; Ph. D. (London), Bar-at-law, Formerly Prof and Head of the Department of Philosophy,
Osmania University, by MOTILAL BANARSIDASS Delhi; Vanarasi : Patna. India

EDITOR'S NOTE on The Mystics of Islam by *REYNOLD A. NICHOLSON,* Published by ROUTLEDGE AND KEGAN PAUL, LONDON,BOSTON AND HENLEY, Printed in Great Britain by Lawe & Brydone Printers Ltd., Thetford, Norfolk p. 28.
MOHAMMED AND THE RISE OF ISLAM BY D.S.MARGOLIOUTH Published VOICE OF INDIA, 2/18, ANSARI ROAD, NEW DELHI-110002, P.458.
MUHAMMAD, A WESTERN ATTEMPT TO UNDERSTAND ISLAM BY KAREN ARMSTRONG published by VICTOR GOLLANCZ LTD.,

My Huzur by Abdul Gaffar, Calcutta
GULISTAN-E-QADERI by Justice Syed Mahbub Murshed(A barrister from London), and
Ex Chief Justice of East Pakistan (now Bangladesh) High court
FUTUH AL-GHAIB, [THE REVELATION OF THE UNSEEN], BY HAZRAT SHAIKH
MUHYUDDIN ABDUL QADIR GILANI, Translated by Maulvi AFTAB-UD-DIN
AHMAD, Formerly Imam, The Mosque, Waking Associate Editor, Islamic Review
published by KITAB BHAVAN, NEW DELHI-110002, Introduction,pp-xix-xx, 1.12
"BEFORE COLUMBUS, LINKS BETWEEN THE OLD WORLD AND ANCIENT
AMERICA" by CYRUS H. GORDON. PUBLISHED BY Crown Publishers, Inc., New
York..
THE OTHER JEW, The Sephardim Today by DANIEL J. ELAZAR published by Basic
Books, Inc, New York and know millions of Jews lived under Islamic Rule and from
Morocco to India.
The Letters and Papers of Chain Weizman
Anthony Giddens : THE NATION-STATE AND VIOLANCE
Various Country Study of Middle East published by US Army
From an article is a paraphrased transcript of a series of four lectures delivered by Gharam
Allah Al-Ghamdy to the Muslim Student Association at the University of Southern
California between November 1991 and January 1992.
[1] The Literary Digest, October 14, 1922.
The Secret Jews, Joachim Prinz, Randon House, 1973
Dajjal, The King who has no clothes by AHMAD THOMSON, Published by TA-HA
PUBLISHERS LTD., 1 Wynne Road, London SW9 0BD
img align=center src="http://www-personal.umich.edu/~luqman/graphics/bis.gif">
tmur@tnc.airtouch.com
Syed Yusuf
http://www.uidaho.edu/~yusuf
From: yusuf921@goshawk.csrv.uidahc.edu (Syed Yusuf)
Newsgroups: soc.religion.islam
Subject: Bani Isra'il punishment and Muslims' punishment identical
Date: 29 Jan 1996 08:36:57 -0800
Organization: On-and-On-Anon
Lines: 446
Sender: ariel@shellx.best.com
Approved: ariel@best.com
Message-ID: <4eit39$fuk@shellx.best.com>
NNTP-Posting-Host: shellx best.com
Status: RO Moderator: ariel@best.com (Catherine Hampton)
HISTORY OF THE SARACENS BY SYED AMIR ALI
THE SPIRIT OF ISLAM BY AMEER (AMIR) ALI, PUBLISHED BY B.I.
PUBLICATIONS, BOMBAY,CALCUTTA,DELHI,MADRAS, BY ARRRANGEMENT
WITH CHATTO & WINDUS, LONDON, PP. 279-281.

**Glimpses of World History, by JAWAHARLAL NEHRU, PUBLISHED BY
JAWAHARLAL NEHRU MEMORIAL FUND, OXFORD UNIVERSITY PRESS,
NEW DELHI**
Discovery of India by JAWAHARLAL NEHRU
India wins freedom by Moulana Abul Kalam Azad
    [1] **A STUDY OF ISLAMIC HISTORY BY PROF. K. ALI PP. 179-181.**
**THE 100, A RANKING OF THE MOST INFLUENTIAL PERSONS IN HISTORY
BY Michael H. Hart, published by MEERAA PUBLLICATION, Madras 600 040,
India;(51 'UMAR IBN AL-KHATTAB), (WILLIAM THE CONQUEROR) (9 CHRIS-
TOPHER COLUMBUS), pp. 275, 361, 77, 281-282, 35,213.**
    [1] **TIME, MAY 24, 1993 No. 21, p. 11.**

355

[1] TIME, MAY 24, 1993, No. 21, by JAMES L. GRAFF, ZAGREB, PP. 22-26.
Shahristani
The`Uyun-ul-Masail (Dieterici's ed. p. 52)
The Tarikh-ul-Hukama.
Why I accepted Islam by ABUL HUSSAIN BHATTACHARJEE
The Theology of Unity, by Muhammad Abduh, Translated from the Arabic by Ishaq
Musa'ad and Kenneth Cragg, published by BOOKS FOR LIBRARIES, A DIVISION OF
ARNO PRESS NEW YORK, 1980,INTRODUCTION,
INSIDE THE MIDDLE EAST BY DILIP HIRO, PUBLISHED BY ROUTLEDGE &
KEGAN PAUL, 39 STORE STREET, LONDON WCIEE7DD AND BROADWAY
HOUSE, NEWTON ROAD,HENLEY-on-Thames, Oxon RG91EN.
The Palestine issue and The Muslim World by Mr. A. M. M. Abdul Jalil, M. A. L.L.B, Sr.
Advocate of Bangladesh Supreme Court
**A HISTORY OF ISLAMIC SOCIETIES by Ira M. Lapidus, Cambridge University
press Cambridge ,New York Port Chester,Melbourne, Sydney. pp. 134-135, 170,182,
184-186, 189, 351-355, 358, 441, 557.**

[1] **THE MOHAMMADAN DYNASTIES,** CHRONOLOGICAL AND
GENEALOGICAL
  TABLES WITH HISTORICAL INTRODUCTIONS by STANLEY LANE-
POOLE,FIRST EDITION 1893, REPRINT 1977; PUBLISHED BY MOHAMMAD
AHMAD FOR IDARAH-I, ADBIYAT-I DELHI, 2009, QASIMJAN ST., DELHI-6 AND
PRINTED AT JAYYED PRESS, BALLIMARAN, DELHI-6, P. 3.
THE POLITICAL ECONOMY OF THE ISLAMIC STATE, A COMPARATIVE STUDY'
BY Ausaf Ali (1934), A Dissertation Presented to the FACULTY OF THE GRADUATE
SCHOOL UNIVERSITY OF SOUTHERN CALIFORNIA In partial Fulfillment of the
requirements for the degree, DOCTOR OF PHILOSOPHY (Economics)

**The Theology of Unity, by Muhammad Abduh, Translated from the Arabic by Ishaq
Musa'ad and Kenneth Cragg, published by BOOKS FOR LIBRARIES, A DIVISION
OF ARNO PRESS NEW YORK
 INSIDE THE MIDDLE EAST (on ARAB MONARCHES) BY DILIP HIRO,
PUBLISHED BY ROUTLEDGE & KEGAN PAUL, 39 STORE STREET, LONDON
WCIEE7DD AND BROADWAY HOUSE, NEWTON ROAD,HENLEY-on-Thames,
The Challenge of Islam edited by Altaf Gauhar, Foreword by Salem Azzam, Islamic
Council of Europe, Islamic Information Services Limited, Radnor House, 93/97
Regent Street, London**
UNHOLY BABYLON, THE SECRET HISTORY OF SADDAM'S WAR" by ADEL
DARWISH AND GREGORY ALEXANDER and published by VICTOR GOLLANCZ
LTD., LONDON IN 1991:
A HISTORY OF ISLAMIC SOCIETIES by Ira M. Lapidus, Cambridge University press
Cambridge ,New York Port Chester,Melbourne, Sydney
Article in TIME by Mr. James Walsh
The history of Albania, Routledge of Kegan Paul, London, Boston and Henly,
 History of Islamic civilization by JURJI ZAYDAN, Translated by D. S. MAR-
GOLIOUTH, D. Lit, Prof. of Arabia in the University of Oxford
Cambridge Middle East Library: by Donald Malcolm Reid; Cairo University and the
making of modern Egypt
THE NATION-STATE AND VIOLENCE Volume two, A contemporary Critique of His-
torical Matter, Alerson Anthony
THINK AND GROW RICH" WRITTEN BY A non-Muslim
THE CAMBRIDGE HISTORY OF ISLAM, IB,
Greusset's History des Croisaders
A STUDY OF ISLAMIC HISTORY BY PROF. K. ALI

THE 100, A RANKING OF THE MOST INFLUENTIAL PERSONS IN HISTORY BY
Michael H. Hart, published by MEERAA PUBLLICATION, Madras 600 040, India
TIME, MAY 24, 1993, No. 21, by JAMES L. GRAFF, ZAGREB
http://www.lbbs.org/zmag/articles/jan96chomsky.htm
Dan Stewart Gilliland (1972)
Gilliland, Dean Stewart, 1928-
African Traditional Religion in Transition; The influence of Islam on African
Traditional Religion in North Nigeria
The Hartford Seminar Foundation, Ph. D. 1971
Religion, Watt, Islam and Society, chap. ii
THE CRESCENT AND THE RISING SUN
INDONESIAN ISLAM UNDER THE JAPANESE OCCUPATION OF JAVA 1942-45
A Thesis presented to the Faculty of the Graduate School of Cornell University for the
Degree of Doctor of Philosophy
Civilization of Arabs byDr. Gustav Lebon
This is an authorized facsimile and was produced by microfilm-xerography in 1981 by
UNIVERSITY MICROFILMS INTERNATIONAL, Ann Arbor, Michigan, U. S. A.,
London, England, THE CRESCENT AND THE RISING SUN
INDONESIAN ISLAM UNDER THE JAPANESE OCCUPATION OF JAVA 1942-45
A Thesis presented to the Faculty of the Graduate School of Cornell University for the
Degree of Doctor of Philosophy, by Harry Jindrich Benda, M. A. june,
Ansab al-ashraf, al-Baladhuri, vol. 5 pp.33-35; al-Aghani, Abu'l-Faraj al-Isfahani, vol.5
pp.91-92; at-Tabari, vol.1, pp.2843-2850; Ibn al-Athir, vol.3, Ibn Abi'l-Hadid, vol.17
Letters of The Holy Prophet (Sm) by Sultan Ahmed, Noor Publishing, Qureshi House,
Farash Khana, Delhi.
TIME Magazine dated August 24, 1992
NEWSWEEK (PG. 25) in the last paragraph, Mr. David H. Hackwort
Newsweek issue of January 11, 1993.
TIME magagine dated December 21, 1992
Time magazine dated June 15, 1992 issue under the caption "THE SWORD OF ISLAM" by
JAMES WALSH
"THE CONSEQUENCES OF POWER" by MICHAEL S. SERRILL
World Development Report 1989".
ICTVTR news bulletin(August 89), Dhaka, Bangladesh
The World Development Report 1990
Hadrat Umar Faruq' by Prof. Masud-Ul-Hasan.
REALMS OF PEACE" by Dr. Sheikh Mohammad Iqbal, published by IDARAH-I
ADABIYAT-I, 2009, Qasinjan Street, Delhi-6 (india), pp. 214-216, 218-219, t
Islamic Economics: Principles and Applications by Prof. Raihan Sharif
Bukhari and Muslim : Mishkat, p 1072)
THE NATION-STATE AND VIOLENCE BY ANTHONY GIDDENS
A report of December 13 in the British Sunday Times
Ahmad Abd Allah Budayr, al-Amir Ahmad Fuad wa Nashat al-Famia al-Misriyya (Cairo,
1950), pp. 265-66[hereafter cited as Budayr]. qouted in Cairo University and the making of
modern Egypt, BY Donald Malcolm Reid by CAMBRIFGE MIDDLE EAST LIBRAR-
Y:23 p. 11
Cairo University and the making of modern Egypt, BY Donald Malcolm Reid by
CAMBRIFGE MIDDLE EAST LIBRARY:23 pp. 11-12
The New Illustrated EVERYMAN'S ENCYCLOPAEDIA (A-Joachin), VOLUME ONE,
The standard work is Richard Mitchell. The Society of Muslim Brothers(London, 1969).
See also Ramadan, Tatawwur, 1937-48, pp. 279-325; and Muhammad Zaki, al-Ikhwan al-
Muslimin wa al-Mujtama al-Misri (2nd ed., Cairo, 1980) qouted from Cairo University and
the making of modern Egypt, BY Donald Malcolm Reid by CAMBRIFGE MIDDLE
EAST LIBRARY:

The Literary Digest, October 14, 1922, p. 50

Ataturk, The Rebirth of a Nation Lord Kinross, 1965, p. 437

TIME February 20, 1933 p. 18

TIME January 9, 1933 p. 64

TIME February 15, 1926 pp. 15-16

Turkey Emil Lengyel 1941, p. 134

Cairo University and the making of modern Egypt, BY Donald Malcolm Reid by CAMBRIFGE MIDDLE EAST LIBRARY:

Encyclopedia of the Third World Third Edition Volume II (Guinea-Bissau to Peru) by George Thomas Kurian, PRINTED IN

Website: http://www-personal.umich.edu/~luqman/Belief/Khilafah

detail please see the Web page of "sleeping Giant" under religion, Islam in www.yahoo.com

Please see other web page on Islam such as www.twf.org

http://www.compsoc.man.ac.uk/~moawalla/dbhp/gallery1.htm

http://www-personal.umich.edu/~luqman

http://www.unn.ac.uk/societies/islamic/about/caliph/choose1.htm

http://cwis.usc.edu:80/dept/MSA/fundamentals/hadithsunnah/muslim/040.smt.html

http://www.twf.org

http://www.hizb-ut-tahrir.org/

http://www.mena.net/panarab/

The hypocrisy of it all from: By Noam Chomsky

http://web.ahram.org.eg/weekly/1998/388/in3.htm

Printed in the United States
19907LVS00002B/4-9

9 781581 128772